SOCIAL PROBLEMS 84/85

LeRoy Barnes, *Editor*
Middlesex Community College

Cover Credit: Tom Goddard, artist.

ANNUAL EDITIONS

The Dushkin Publishing Group, Inc. Sluice Dock, Guilford, Ct. 06437

Volumes in the Annual Editions Series

- Abnormal Psychology
- Africa
- Aging
- American Government
- American History, Pre-Civil War
- American History, Post-Civil War
- Anthropology
- Biology
- Business
- China
- Comparative Politics
- Criminal Justice
- Death and Dying
- Deviance
- Early Childhood Education
- Economics
- Educating Exceptional Children
- Education
- Educational Psychology
- Energy
- Environment
- Ethnic Studies
- Foreign Policy
- Geography

- Health
- Human Development
- Human Sexuality
- Latin America
- Macroeconomics
- Management
- Marketing
- Marriage and Family
- Microeconomics
- Personal Growth and Behavior
- Philosophy
- Political Science
- Psychology
- Religion
- Social Problems
- Social Psychology
- Sociology
- State and Local Government
- Twentieth Century American History
- Urban Society
- Western Civilization, Pre-Reformation
- Western Civilization, Post-Reformation
- World History
- World Politics

● Indicates currently available

©1984 by the Dushkin Publishing Group, Inc. Annual Editions is a Trade Mark of the Dushkin Publishing Group, Inc.

Copyright ©1984 by the Dushkin Publishing Group, Inc., Guilford, Connecticut 06437

All rights reserved. No part of this book may be reproduced, stored, or transmitted by any means—mechanical, electronic or otherwise—without written permission from the publisher.

Twelfth Edition

Manufactured by George Banta Company, Menasha, Wisconsin 54952

Library of Congress Cataloging in Publication Data
Main entry under title: Annual editions: social problems.
    1. United States—Social conditions—1960.—Periodicals.
I. Title. Social problems.
HN51.A78   309.1'73'092   84-78577
ISBN 0-87967-512-8

CONTENTS

1

Perspectives

2

Politics

3
Economy and Employment

4
Inequality

5

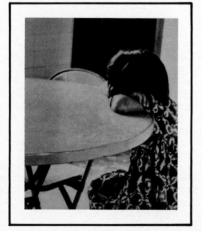

Victims

Future

TOPIC GUIDE

This topic guide can be used to correlate each of the articles in *Social Problems 84/85* to one or more of the topics normally covered by social problems books. Each article corresponds to a given topic area according to whether it deals with the subject in a primary or secondary fashion. These correlations are intended for use as a general study guide and do not necessarily define the total coverage of any given article.

TOPIC AREA	TREATED AS A PRIMARY ISSUE IN:	TREATED AS A SECONDARY ISSUE IN:
American Dream	1. What Has Happened to the American Dream? 2. An America in Need of Repair 3. Utopia or Disaster 4. In Search of American Optimism	34. How Drugs Sap the Nation's Strength 43. When the Economy Rebounds Will "Smoke Stack America"? 48. A Generation at Risk
Aging	25. The Social Security Fix 48. A Generation at Risk	18. New Faces of Poverty 19. Economic Cold Spell Freezes "Outsiders"
Children	26. Kids as Consumers and Commodities	20. Carla
Crime	27. Why Crime's Rapid Rise May Be Over 28. Crime and Punishment 29. Some Causes of Crime 30. Coping with Justice 31. Are Boston's Fires an Omen for All Cities	32. Families and Crime
Drug Abuse	34. How Drugs Sap the Nation's Strength	
Economy	11. America's Real Farm Problem 12. Big Oil vs. Cheap Gas 13. Rescuing the Banking System 14. The Potential Impacts of Robotics 15. The End of the "Labor Society"	19. Economic Cold Spell Freezes "Outsiders" 46. Economic Strategies for a Narcissistic Society 47. Japan
Energy	44. Untying the Energy Knot 45. Photovoltaics	12. Big Oil vs. Cheap Gas

TOPIC AREA	TREATED AS A PRIMARY ISSUE IN:	TREATED AS A SECONDARY ISSUE IN:
Environment	40. Beyond Dumping 41. The Navy's "Hot" New Plan	38. Inheriting the Earth 43. When the Economy Rebounds Will "Smoke Stack America"?
Family	32. Families and Crime 33. 19 Million Singles	26. Kids as Consumers and Commodities
Foreign Policy	49. Foreign Policy 50. A New Look at the Population Problem	12. Rescuing the Banking System
Future	38. Inheriting the Earth 39. The Information Society	45. Photovoltaics 48. A Generation at Risk
Gays	36. The Real Epidemic	35. Hunting for Hidden Killers
Government	5. Bureaucrats 2, Presidents 0 6. How Lawmakers Misuse Your Campaign Donations 7. PAC's Americana 8. Off the Books	16. Richer Than All Their Tribe 17. The Secret History of the Deficit
Health	34. How Drugs Sap the Nation's Strength 35. Hunting for Hidden Killers	36. The Real Epidemic

TOPIC AREA	TREATED AS A PRIMARY ISSUE IN:	TREATED AS A SECONDARY ISSUE IN:
Labor	14. The Potential Impacts of Robotics 15. The End of the "Labor Society"	39. The Information Society
Law	30. Coping with Justice	
Mental Health	37. A Key to Unlock the Asylum?	
Minorities	21. The State of Education for Black Americans 22. Hyphenated Americans 23. How Long Till Equality 24. Coming into Your Own in a Man's World	18. New Faces of Poverty 19. Economic Cold Spell Freezes "Outsiders" 35. Hunting for Hidden Killers 36. The Real Epidemic
Nuclear Issues	9. Bureaucracy and the Bomb	41. Radioactivity for the Oceans
Pollution	38. Inheriting the Earth 40. Beyond Dumping 41. Radioactivity for the Oceans	10. At N.R.C. It's Safety Last 42. When the Economy Rebounds Will "Smoke Stack America"?
Population	50. A New Look at the Population Problem	48. A Generation at Risk

TOPIC AREA	TREATED AS A PRIMARY ISSUE IN:	TREATED AS A SECONDARY ISSUE IN:
Sexism	23. How Long Till Equality 24. Coming into Your Own in a Man's World	
Social Change	15. The End of the "Labor Society" 18. New Faces of Poverty 33. 19 Million Singles	23. How Long Till Equality 26. Kids as Consumers and Commodities 37. A Key to Unlock the Asylum? 39. The Information Society
Technology	14. The Potential Impacts of Robotics 45. Photovoltaics	
Unemployment	19. Economic Cold Spell Freezes "Outsiders" 20. Carla	18. New Faces of Poverty
Violence	31. Are Boston's Fires an Omen for All Cities	
War	9. Bureaucracy and the Bomb	
Welfare	20. Carla	22. Hyphenated Americans

PREFACE

Is society moving toward stability or chaos? Judging from recent studies, we, as members of society, seem certain to face a continuing series of problems—problems such as inflation, unemployment, inequality, and crime—which develop as part of the human condition.

As students of social problems we must consider two points. First, it is important to recognize that a social problem is similar to a personal tragedy. Long-range solutions aren't comfort enough to the millions of people affected by social problems.

Second, social problems are not caused by people out to destroy the world. Social problems occur because people can't always foresee the consequences of change. For instance, no one predicted the energy crisis when creating the automobile a generation ago.

Behind all this is the need to be informed and think clearly. This twelfth edition of *Annual Editions: Social Problems 84/85* will assist you in these tasks. A course on social problems provides a challenging introduction to the nature of American society and to sociology as a scientific discipline for studying society. This collection of articles is designed for such a course. Each article combines social theory with a common sense approach to real problems. The articles are culled from a multitude of leading periodicals.

Article selection was based on providing balance within the anthology. Often an article was included because it complemented or created an effective contrast to another article. Many topics parallel those most often included in social problems texts. Special attention was given to "data background" articles, particularly in economics, minorities, and the changing family. You are urged to use the Topic Guide as a tool in your reading selection.

No collection of articles can meet the needs of every instructor or student. That's why this and future editions depend on input from readers. Please fill out the article rating form at the back of the book. We welcome your comments.

LeRoy Barnes
Editor

Perspectives

To begin your study of social problems you should become aware of the needs of society. Those needs include improved living conditions, education, and greater human rights—all of which can be regarded as the American dream.

During the 1960s, members of society believed the United States was headed toward an age of prosperity and justice. Do people today still hold those same outlooks for the future? None of the authors in the first section seem too optimistic about the present or the future.

Sociology—the study of society—succeeds through detailed self-examination. Hard thinking, whether it be negative or positive, provides the best means for arriving at a better future. The readings in this section assess the current predicament of American society. The authors share similar concerns, but analyze the basic problem differently and offer different solutions. The authors of the first two articles raise the basic question: What has happened to the American dream? Both sense the disillusionment among members of society that plans are not taking shape as once hoped. One author justifies the right to be disappointed and disgruntled, but finds promise in the fact that our society has been able to overcome periods of national pessimism in the past. The other questions whether the system itself has become flawed. In the third article, famous psychologist B.F. Skinner, renowned for his work on human behavior in *Walden Two,* discusses his outlook for the future. He ponders whether the world has gone beyond a point from which it can learn to control its own behavior. Finally, an article from the British perspective considers the questions: Do Americans understand themselves and their society? Do they realize where they are headed? Can they analyze themselves well enough to articulate their needs?

Each article in this section focuses on signs that our social system is decaying. Certainly our nation has changed over the years. Change is normal and expected, but does it inevitably lead to deterioration? Your task when reading the articles is to understand how the authors define and analyze the problems of American society, and how they differ in the extent to which they assign blame for the problems. Do more than condemn. Determine whether social needs can be fulfilled by repairing or improving our social organization.

Looking Ahead: Challenge Questions

What was the American Dream? Was it realistic, or did it place a burden on the future—namely on our generation?

What signs exist visibly that America is in need of repair? Do unrepaired roads necessarily mean that the system itself needs fixing?

How has Skinner's view of human behavior altered over his lifetime? Does he think his principles can be applied today?

Do you agree that Americans have a problem understanding where they are headed? What implications may such a fact have on the future?

What Has Happened to the

AMERICAN DREAM?

". . . Until very recently, the American dream, and most people's perception of it, was realizable—e.g., owning a home, getting a college education, obtaining a job, prudential saving, and old-age security."

Charles W. Kegley

Dr. Kegley, Associate American Thought Editor of USA Today, *is chairman of the Department of Philosophy and Religious Studies, California State College at Bakersfield.*

HAS a nation ever been born which so deliberately and wholeheartedly dedicated itself to the realization of a dream as the U.S.? Probably not. "Conceived in liberty," it was organized in such a way that *all* of its citizens—regardless of race, color, or religion—could have the opportunity to try to achieve the "good life." Originating with educated leadership, unparalleled resources, and a sense of God-guided destiny, two centuries have been devoted to the realization of that dream.

What are some of the main features of that dream? Why is it that increasing numbers of our citizens are disillusioned, believing that it is going wrong? Is the present pessimism merely one more in the many stages in American history and so not to be taken seriously?

Dreams notoriously may be vague and amorphous, but the American dream has a remarkable specificity—economic, political, social, ethical-religious. That very clarity and specificity, however,

makes the disappointments the more painful.

We must distinguish between the American dream and the reality in American history. Thus, it would be a falsely optimistic interpretation to hold that the dream was in all major respects and in high degree realized. This is not so, of course. However, until very recently, the American dream, and most people's perception of it, was realizable—*e.g.,* owning a home, getting a college education, obtaining a job, prudential saving, and old-age security.

Consider the economic dream, both in its general, national, and international features, and in specific hopes and desires. As for the former, what nation in history has enjoyed the natural resources, size, and will-to-work of this nation? For two centuries, it has not only housed, fed, and serviced itself, but has given and "loaned" billions in war relief, in aid to underdeveloped nations, in unmatched support of the UN and similar world organizations. The wildest dreams of the Founding Fathers did not envision such growth and productivity. Why, then, has dismay and pessimism replaced pride and optimism?—because, for almost 50 years, the U.S. government has spent more money than it has taken in. By the turn of the century, the total expenditure of the

Federal government was $525,000,000—about $6.90 for every American. Today, the budget is over $700,000,000,000. Divide that by 220,000,000 citizens and you get $3,200 for every American, or $12,800 for a family of four. How dreamy is the future when the average income of an American family is scarcely above $12,800? The dream has become an economic nightmare—a national debt of one trillion dollars. Don't even talk of paying off the principal; if Congress began doing that at $1,000,000,000 a year, it would take 1,000 years to pay off the debt.

It is what these and related facts mean to John and Mary Doe and to their family that sours the dream. To be specific, they dream of purchasing a home; an affordable, safe, decent place to live has been at the heart of the American dream. Now, however, inflation and interest rates make that impossible in most cases. Between 1970 and 1980, the cost of a modest home increased 156%. The wealthy can manage it, but the American dream held that the middle and lower classes should have the same opportunities. Clearly, they not only do not have an equal share in that dream, but, even worse, two large groups are effectively eliminated—the young family and "senior" citizens. What young family can afford a house or condominium when

Reprinted from *USA Today*, March 1983. Copyright 1983 by Society for the Advancement of Education.

the *average* cost of a modest-size house is over $66,000 and interest rates are not the traditional six to eight per cent, but 18-20 + %? As for the elderly, in eastern metropolitan areas alone, it is estimated that 65,000 are "streetpeople" who not only have no home, but sleep in doorways, flop-houses, or single-room-occupancy hotels. If they rent their houses, they are squeezed by skyrocketing utility and rental costs and threatened with eviction. No dreams, just nightmares.

If someone objects that I have gotten carried away, that "nightmares" is too strong a term, I reply: there is no more suitable word to describe the desperation of hundreds of thousands of the elderly. Consider hunger. It is not in Calcutta, India, but in the American city of Detroit that one sees old people ordering a cup of tea and then sitting at uncleared tables so they can unobtrusively eat the leftovers from other customers. It is here that one sees these people open and eat from packages of cold cuts on the supermarket shelves while pretending to shop. It is here that such citizens have the forced choice—a can of tuna fish or an economy pack of toilet paper. The testimony of William T. Cunningham before the Senate Special Committee on Aging, Feb. 25, 1982, should be required reading not only for lawmakers, but for all citizens. Ponder the following:

Hunger in Detroit is illness, another trip to the hospital because an egg in the morning, tea and toast at noon and hot dogs at night were not enough.

Hunger in Detroit is guilt. It is old people who won't tell you their children's names, because they don't want to be a burden. It is the guilt of sons and daughters who have to abandon their parents because, in today's economy, they can hardly feed their own children.

And hunger in Detroit is anger. It is old people saying, "They treat us like an old horse, only they don't shoot us, they just starve us inch by inch. They've got the food, but they just won't give it to us." The anger of old people is quiet despair, knowledge that the refusal of food is a final rejection, that one's fate is a lingering and lonely and fearful and disregarded wait for death.

Every lasting human society has held the aged in reverence.

The details of America's decline as an industrial nation have been documented by Magaziner and Reich.[1] In per capita GNP, the U.S. is now tied for *tenth* place among industrial nations, trailing Switzerland, Denmark, Sweden, Germany, Iceland, Norway, Belgium, Luxembourg, and the Netherlands. The French equal us, but Japan is moving up rapidly. Few citizens realize that we rank eighteenth in infant mortality. Our air pollution exceeds that of other countries and our homicide rate is eight to nine times that of other industrial nations. What most citizens can scarcely escape seeing is that American industry conspicuously loses in competition in the production of steel and automobiles, TV sets, and so on and on.

A litany of failure

We pride ourselves in giving the world the Model T Ford, but American automobile manufacturers seem incapable of competing with foreign made cars in durability and economy and their annual losses run into the millions. We have made and fly the planes of the world, but not only did Braniff, a major international airline, go bankrupt, every other major air line is threatened with bankruptcy. We "conquered the continent" with the iron horse, but only the German, French, and Japanese have high-speed trains—we are left with freight trains.

A separate article could be written on the losses being recorded in the socio-ethical realm. We assume that we celebrate Thanksgiving as families gathered around the table, but now we are disillusioned by the fact that an incredible 50% of American marriages end in divorce. The family unit of working father, homemaking mother, and supervised children is rapidly becoming a curiosity in American history. One state after another sponsors special bond issues to vastly increase jail capacity because of soaring crime rates. Even tolerant sociologists become alarmed by the fact that 23,000,000 Americans are regular users of marijuana.

Ponder another specific threat to the American dream. The expectation of the average family that their children can have a college education is generally dashed by realization of the cruel reality that its costs have become prohibitive for most youth, at least so far as private institutions go, and even state institutions see enrollments drop because of Federal and state budget cuts—both to the institutions and to students in terms and loans and aids. The cost of a college education has increased 193% in the 1980's alone, and the worst is yet to come.

The cloud spreads. Harsher still is the frightening fact that, for the first time in our history, hundreds of thousands of what we never dreamed of calling the poor or underclass have no predictable way of escaping from their plight. When the government and its citizens become reconciled to this apparent fact, a lethal kind of disillusionment occurs. This is not the time to give Horatio Alger stories to unemployed youth. Even post-high school youth find it difficult to understand how a Pentagon budget of $258,000,000,000 can be too sacred to be criticized and made subject to over-cost controls, while social programs that help the poor and needy, that educate for self-improvement, and that relieve the sick and dying are severely cut or abolished. The sense of frustration bordering on despair is especially keen among minorities. In spite of almost a quarter of a century of emphasis on "equal opportunity," the unemployed rate among black youth climbs with every quarterly report until, in many parts of the country, it is over 40%.

The political dream does not survive much more easily. Inherited from Plato and inspired by Judeo-Christian ideals, it maintained that an office-holder, however lowly or exalted, is a public *servant,* chosen on the basis of intelligence and character. Plato expressed it perfectly in describing the ruler as looking upon the state as if it were his own person or family. Far from being dreamy idealism, those qualities characterized Lincoln, Jefferson, Wilson, and thousands of public officials. The dismay of the middle-age American and the cynicism of our youth is based in part on the tragedy of a president and his associates forced out of office; here a Senator, there a governor forced to resign. The sheer amount of money spent by candidates for major state and national offices eliminates many a worthy candidate and raises deep suspicions on the part of the average citizen that the candidate's ambitions are other and much less lofty and honorable than service.

If space permitted, the destruction of the American dream could easily be documented in the case of judges. Always looked upon as symbols of objectivity, fairness, and intelligence, we have descended to the point at which Senators Dennis DeConcini (D.-Ariz.), Birch Bayh (D.-Ind.), and Edward Kennedy (D.-Mass.) offered a bill, the Judicial Conduct and Disability Act, which would empower the Judicial Councils of the 11 Federal circuit courts to investigate and rule on complaints against judges. In one state, California, when such a law was adopted in 1960, 71 judges resigned or retired; since that time, six others have been censured by the California Supreme Court and at least five more have been removed from office. When Federal judges are influenced if not controlled by major corporations and special interests, when others have been convicted of arbitrariness and partiality, the American image is severely damaged.

The disillusionment of the public with other professions could easily be documented. Norman Rockwell's picture of the family physician, as concerned and helpful as the good samaritan, at the

---

[1]Ira G. Magaziner and Robert B. Reich, *Minding America's Business: The Decline and Rise of the American Economy* (New York: Harcourt Brace Jovanovich, 1982).

home bedside of the child, has given way to the view of doctors as more concerned with money than with relief of illness, and more ready to cover up another's deadly errors than to police their profession. The American dream surely never aimed at the demoting of a profession—medicine, teaching, law—to the level of a trade or a business.

There are two additional issues which demand attention in answering our second main question. One concerns the fact that Americans feel, and non-Americans increasingly perceive, the U.S. as having moved from a mighty nation to be a battered and bewildered one. The other area, closely related to this, is the question of our role in the nuclear decades ahead.

The American dream, nourished by our two centuries-plus of growing influence, is emphatically an ambitious and morally demanding one. We have been and continue to be a leader—some would say *the* leader—in the 20th-century effort to achieve order, justice, and the spread of democracy and respect for human rights throughout the world. Our leadership in two world wars and our "big brother" assistance appear to document the dream symbolized in the Statue of Liberty, but one does not need to read Arnold Toynbee's 10 volumes or Oswald Spengler's *Decline of the West* to realize that nations and empires rise, thrive, and then decline. Not a single one, it is worth recording, was ever reborn. The disturbing, nay frightening, thought is that we appear to have lost our capacity for leadership, our ability to determine the outcome. Americans are almost always good sports on the tennis courts and the football, baseball, and basketball arena, but we are used to winning all the points in the field of international relations. Has our self-image been shattered by the Bay of Pigs, the Vietnam war, our helpless and flawed efforts in Iran, the fiasco in El Salvador, Alexander Haig's recent recklessness in trying to arbitrate the Falklands, and a score of other crises in which we appear to be confused failures? Accustomed to being the winner of wars for justice, of arguing from strength, of "speaking softly, but carrying a big stick," must we wake up to the reality that we speak loudly, but lose diplomatic battles and ground wars? The point is not merely that the U.S. is challenged militarily, politically, and commercially as never before in our history; this is a bald fact. The point is that the American dream which envisions us as invincibly strong and self-sufficient is not held by the majority of educated citizens, probably for the first time in recent history.

The nuclear threat

A closely related source of dismay and disillusionment is the realization that,

for the first time in world history, we face the threat of total destruction by various forms of radiation. It is probably safe to say that Americans, deeply convinced that our scientists and our technology are the finest in the world, never thus far have seriously entertained the thought that we could not only survive a nuclear war, but would win in any nuclear encounter. Indeed, with our sense of fair play and reverence for life, we did not really believe that, in this enlightened age, any nation would be so wicked and barbaric as to use poison gas, massive nuclear bombing, and the like. That dream and assumption was shattered as a result of World War II and the Vietnam experience. As Fritz Haber, the so-called father of chemical warfare, put it, "In no future war will the military be able to ignore poison gas. It is a higher form of killing."[2] The fact is, it *was* used on April 22, 1915; by the end of the attack upon the Allies, 500 men lay dead. In the Vietnam War, Vietnamese aircraft dropped gas bombs which caused dramatic and horrifying death to combatants and civilians alike. Far more terrifying is the readiness, for the first time in history, with which national leaders, armed with nuclear weapons, seriously utter absurd statements about a "limited" nuclear war and a first strike. *No* such use of nuclear weapons is possible which would avoid terrifying lethal effects on people, animals, and crops all over the globe. If ever dreams must give way to nightmares, this is the time.

Here again, lest I be accused of exaggeration, I quote the statements of Hans Bethe who, of all living scientists, is probably the wisest and most trusted voice on these issues. Asked to speak to one justification of the arms race—*i.e.,* that the Soviets are aiming at gaining the capability to win a nuclear war—he responded:

I quite believe that we could win an arms race. But it is, of course, absolutely crazy to think of winning a nuclear war. You cannot win a nuclear war, neither they nor we, even if some fraction of the population might survive.

. . . if you talk about an all-out nuclear war, with attacks on industry and attacks on cities and so on, then I would think that, while there will be survivors, the United States as a functioning society would not survive. Such an attack, it has been estimated by the Defense Department, could mean 100,000,000 casualties, but that doesn't fully describe it. The important thing is the after effect.

. . . I was very much afraid in 1946. My wife and I discussed this matter and concluded that probably within 10 years there would be nuclear war. That has not happened and it is a ray of hope. It has not happened because the statesmen, both in this country and in the Soviet Union, have clearly recognized that

nuclear war is unthinkable. It is impossible, it would make such destruction that we have to use every means to avoid it.

This realization (that nuclear war "is unthinkable. It is impossible.") seems to have escaped the present government. I think the real danger lies in this loss of understanding. Until the end of the Carter Administration, whether the President was Republican or Democrat, it was a generally recognized principle: Nuclear war must be avoided by all means. We are now told that this is not so. So here is a psychological difference. I think it is traditional, and therefore perfectly legitimate, if you want to win an election, to play up the relative armaments of the United States and the Soviet Union; that is good election propaganda. But once you are the government, you must not make this primitive approach the basis of your military and foreign policy. That is very dangerous.[3]

One aspect of America's dream of its role in international affairs deserves more careful analysis than can be undertaken here. This is the accusation, voiced most forcefully and recently by Noam Chomsky in *Towards a New Cold War: Essays on the Current Crisis and How We Got There,* that our behavior in foreign affairs no longer embodies the idealism of Woodrow Wilson or the isolationist stance of the past, but is now determined by the narrow aggressive interests of the industrial military complex. The consequence is a moral schizophrenia, a double standard which assumes that we are good and, if only strong enough, will *do* the good; yet, in fact, we are selfish and bad. Worse, the American people, this view holds, rarely sees our role in foreign affairs in its harsh reality because the government, the corporations, and the media systematically control and distort public opinion. This voices a disgust with the U.S. and its actions in this century. I suggest that two things are needed: documentation of the claim that we have behaved and now behave so badly that the American character in international affairs deserves condemnation, and a candid recognition of Reinhold Niebuhr's emphasis on the ambiguous character of moral judgments in national affairs. We live in a world of imperfection and evil—in motives and acts—and our "dream" must be "realistic"; if *they* are bad, *we* are not necessarily "good"—*e.g.,* in our Vietnam actions, our absurd praising of Marcos' dictatorship in the Philippines as a democracy, and so on and on.

Can we overcome pessimism?

The third main question asks whether the present pessimism concerning the loss or betrayal of the American dream is merely one more of many periods of pessimism which we have endured, but are

---

[2]Jeremy Paxman, "Forget About A-Bombs, 'Yellow Rain' Just May Get You First," *Los Angeles Times,* March 28, 1982.

[3]*Los Angeles Times,* April 11, 1982.

destined to overcome. The answer calls for careful discrimination.

First, considerable weight must be given to the many outstanding historians who claim that we have constantly experienced major changes which were, at the time, identified as signifying the end of the American dream, but the judgment was incorrect. This is the good news. Even the New England colonists preached and wrote of the "falling away" from our aims and practices. If now we cite the Nixon tragedy, soaring unemployment, the drug culture, and the like, we must not forget, we are warned, that Americans are equally alarmed, for example, by the deplorable leadership of Presidents Franklin Pierce and James Buchanan, and that pessimism swept the nation between 1890 and World War I. In 1893-97, the economy of the nation was viewed as in its death throes and demographic changes frightened the nation; over 1,000,000 immigrants a year were seeking jobs—how could these people participate in realizing the dream? Henry Adams predicted the imminent depletion of natural resources and of energy. We had reached the frontier, expansion was over; the dream of ever-new opportunities was just a dream, we were told, not a vision calling for realization. All this we now recognize as unwarranted pessimism.

What needs to be determined is whether the differences between the present and past crises are more significant than the parallels, and we must assess the totally new factors. If David Riesman is correct, the scarcity of natural resources, the role of labor unions, the competitive world economy, and the threat of nuclear war are only four of a larger number of new and different threats to the American dream. These and related considerations cited in answering our second question constitute the bad news. Crime waves, Mafia influences, and the power claims of labor unions—these America has tolerated moderately well. Indeed, to consider only the last named, there is solid evidence that labor unions may be growing up psychologically and learning from their European counterparts that cooperation, rather than confrontation, is the hope of survival. However, other elements pose unquestionable threats. What is the likelihood of a modern nation surviving widespread drug abuse? What evidence is there that the unquestionably high level of intelligence and leadership ability will be dedicated, as Plato correctly claimed it must be, to the service of this nation? What evidence is there that, with the capacity for total nuclear destruction, the alleged wisdom and goodwill of the traditional American are equal to the present crises?

Americans basically hold to their dream, almost pathetically. It remains to be seen whether their faith can be sustained.

An America in Need of Repair

Harvey C. Bunke, Editor

Ask anyone of my generation where they were when they heard about Pearl Harbor, V.J. Day, or John F. Kennedy's assassination and you can bet you will get a detailed report. For me and my boyhood friends who enjoyed the lazy, cool Wisconsin days of September 1938, there is a day that ranks right alongside those historic events: It was the day, when all seemed lost for the Chicago Cubs, that Gabby Hartnett hit the legendary home run that beat the Pittsburg Pirates and enabled the Cubs to go on to win the national league pennant. Back then the Chicago Cubs was still a major league ball club and such players as Gabby Hartnett, Billy Herman, Stan Hack, Phil Cavaretta, and Charles Root were saints who made those desperate depression years more bearable for kids and adults alike.

There is, as always in looking at the past, a tendency to romanticize the decade of the 30s. Such efforts are misplaced, for the 30s was a time of suffering, despair, and bewilderment when America seemed to have lost its way and for a time lost much of the hope that is so characteristic of the American spirit. But those of us who were very young couldn't know just how bad things really were. In our childhood and early adolescence we enjoyed the luxury of a sheltered innocence permitted few children of today. When school let out in June our world centered on such things as swimming and sailing, catching perch, crappie and bluegill, going to ice cream socials on Sunday nights, engaging in harmless rubber gun wars, playing rounders—a form of workup baseball—and, of course, being glued to the radio breathlessly following every pitch in the Cubs baseball game. Going to Wrigley Field to see a Cub's baseball game—especially a double header—was planned for months in advance.

There was only one thing I looked forward to more than going to Chicago to see the Cubs play, and that was "going up north" to visit my Great Uncle Henry on his farm just outside the tiny hamlet of Tilleda, Wisconsin. Summers during those bitter depression years were sweetened by the trip up north. "Up north" was where I learned the rudimentary skills of milking a cow; "up north" I learned to hunt the gray squirrel, which often turned up as part of the large, delicious farm breakfast served by my Aunt Rose. "Up north" I learned to love the north woods, with its birch, maple, spruce, and pine, and "up north" at the local pond I learned to catch big, fat, ugly bullheads without cutting myself on their punishing spines. "Up north" was where I met Sport and Lady, two enormous and powerful but very gentle work horses, and gave my undying affection to three pretty ladies who showered me with sarsaparilla and ice cream, and who ran the local bar in the hotel that looked every bit like ones that we saw in the western movies on Saturday afternoons.

Time "up north" passed so quickly that it always seemed to me that we barely got there before we had to think about going home. When it came time to say farewell to all the relatives, our car was filled with squash, pumpkins, turnips, melons, cucumbers, homemade sausage, and heavy cans filled with the sweet maple syrup drawn from the woods I so came to love. As we pulled out of the driveway, our sorrow at leaving was mixed with the dread of the drive home. It was only some 70 miles, but we knew it would take a minimum of three hours. The first part was the worst. Between Tilleda and Caroline, a tiny hamlet without even a creamery, was a punishing dirt road with bumps and holes that threatened life and limb of both car and passengers. Speeds in excess of 10 m.p.h. were risky and bone-rattling. Between Caroline and Marion the road wasn't much better. From Marion to New London the road improved enough to be merely washboardy. Once we got to New London everyone breathed a sigh of relief; from there on the road was paved.

In the early 1970s I had occasion to go back up north to the annual pancake fry celebrating the completion of the maple syrup cook-off. Things were not quite as I remembered them. Cows were now milked by machine, and in place of the great and powerful work horses that had attracted and frightened me stood a stark, cold, John Deere tractor. The old hotel, although crying out for paint, still seemed unchanged, but the three color-fully dressed ladies I liked so much had long ago left, though not before, I was told, bilking several widowed and lonely farmers out of their life savings. Having lost the innocence of my childhood, these things surprised me less than the ease and rapidity of my trip. What in my youth had been a three-hour ordeal over a rough, dangerous, and winding road, now took barely an hour over a new, shorter, well engineered asphalt road.

As I drove back from my brief visit I could not help but reflect how, in my lifetime, a steady improvement in what I later learned to call the "infrastructure" had made America a better place to live. The road I was driving on was only one example; the Chicago subway was another. But towering above all improvements in public facilities was the interstate highway system, which exemplified the American spirit of energy and confidence and endowed ordinary citizens with the kind of mobility known only in America. In addition to giving vitality and economic health to thousands of communities across the land, the system was a major factor in the growth of the automobile, travel, and tourist industries. Without these highways there would be no Disney Land, no chain of Holiday Inns, no Florida real estate boom—at least not on today's scale. I knew these accomplishments didn't come without cost. Building roads, subways, and sewage systems were forms of public investment. And investments, be they private or public, are not to be had unless a society is willing to forego consumption so that resources may be diverted into investments. Workers building roads or subways are not available to make shoes, wagons, or steel. The bricks and cement used to build highways and county buildings cannot be used for homes or driveways. But even as I speculated on our remarkable infrastructure in the early 70s, forces unknown to me were at work which threatened the very public facilities and services which we Americans see as part of our birthright. Even in 1970 as I was congratulating America on her accomplishments, our bridges, our sewage and water systems, and our mass transit systems were losing ground as a growing population imposed even larger loads on an aging and decaying infrastructure. The decline has been a quiet but steady one at all levels. In recent years voters wanted more policemen, more teachers, and more social workers. They also wanted ceilings on transit fares and on sewage and water rates. Politicians readily responded, and when money was available our political leaders capitalized on the knowledge that a picture of a ribbon cutting ceremony would surely produce more votes than replacing a sewage line. But as voters turned down tax increases and politicians got reelected, the infrastructure slowly, quietly, crumbled.

The problem is both pervasive and awesome. Every region of the country and every aspect of economic life is affected by our failure to build new public facilities and to maintain what we already have.

Item: An estimated 25 percent of the country's 300 metropolitan transit systems will cease to operate by the year 1985. New York City alone will need over $100 billion in the next decade for the rehabilitation of its rail and bus system, not to mention funds it needs to resurface 6,000 miles of street, 2,400 miles of an antiquated water system, and 6,100 miles of a decaying sewer system.

Item: The 756 urban areas with populations of over 50,000 will require between $75 billion and $110 billion to maintain their water systems over the next twenty years.

Cleveland needs $250 to $500 million to renovate its water system.

Dallas must raise almost $700 million for water and sewage treatment systems over the next nine years.

The vast underground water table tapped since World War II to irrigate the Texas and Oklahoma panhandles and surrounding farmland (10 million acres which produce 40 percent of the nation's processed beef and much of its wheat and other crops) will be depleted by the year 2000 at current levels of usage.

Most of the West and Southwest needs to develop water resources and systems to keep up with the population growth and agricultural requirements.

Item: There are no estimates of the amount required to renovate the railroads of the Northeast and the Midwest. Modernizing the railroads is critical for the efficient shipment of coal and for the reduction in the cost of energy required for shipping goods.

Item: Two out of every five bridges in the U.S. currently need reconstruction or rehabilitation. Estimated cost: $41.1 billion. In fiscal year 1981, $1.3 billion was allocated to repair bridges.

Item: Nearly 26,000 miles of interstate, arterial, and collector highways need resurfacing or reconstruction each year to preserve pavement conditions as they were in 1975. Capital improvements and maintenance for these major U.S. highway systems would cost $11.2 billion annually in constant 1975 dollars. On strips of our proud interstate highways system traffic crawls at 30 miles per hour because of crumbling pavement and potholes.

Item: It will cost an estimated $75 billion to complete the final 1,500 miles planned for the interstate system. (The original cost estimate in 1956 for the entire interstate highway system was $27 billion.)

Item: The costs of rehabilitation and new construction necessary to maintain *existing* levels of service on non-urban highways will exceed $700 billion during the 1980s, an amount greater than *all* public works investments made by all units of government in the 1970s.

1. PERSPECTIVES

How is it that America has let its public facilities fall into such disrepair? How is it that we have squandered a legacy of public facilities that provided the base for our unprecedented wealth? How is it that in days past when the GNP, per capita income, and family median income all were much lower than today, we as a nation could build, improve, and maintain America's infrastructure, while in recent years as we enjoyed rising prosperity and affluence beyond all expectations, we as a nation have stood by as our infrastructure slowly but steadily deteriorated? In 1960, when we were in the early stages of constructing the interstate highway system, the GNP in constant dollars was barely half of what it was in 1981, while per capita income and family median income after adjusting for inflation since 1960 was only about 65 percent of the 1980 figure. How, with considerably less, did we do more? Clearly there has been a change in our priorities. In 1960 the federal tax on gasoline was 4 cents per gallon, the same as it is today. A gasoline tax of 4 cents per gallon in 1960 when gas cost 31 cents a gallon would be comparable to 16 cents per gallon now. Yet while our system of roads deteriorates, calls by Drew Lewis, Secretary of Transportation, for doubling the federal gas tax to 8 cents per gallon go unheeded.

Loss of momentum is not limited to our federal level. States are equally reluctant to spend money on public facilities. The state of affairs in Indiana illustrates the point. In 1957 when gasoline sold for 31 cents per gallon, the state tax was 6 cents. Raised to 8 cents in 1969, the tax remained at that level until 1980 when the legislature enacted a price-index fuel tax which translated into 8.5 cents in 1980, 10.5 cents in 1981 and 11.1 cents in 1982. At the same time gasoline prices at the service stations fluctuated wildly from a high of $1.50 to a low of $1.00 per gallon. Under pressure of a temporary "oil glut," they declined in early 1982, but with the coming of the summer prices jumped some 12 cents per gallon between Memorial Day and July 4th. Given these wide price fluctuations at the pump, one might assume that a 5 cent or even 10 cent increase in gas taxes would hardly be noticed by the average motorist. But the Indiana legislature, sensitive to the nation's anti-tax mood, slowly increased the gasoline tax by only 2.6 cents even as the price of gas at the pumps jumped some 50 cents.

Indiana is not alone Indeed the Indiana gas tax is one of the higher ones levied by a state. Texas imposes a levy of 5 cents per gallon, California and Missouri 7 cents, and in Alaska, Kansas, Louisiana, and New Jersey the gasoline tax is 8 cents. Leading the way in taxes are Iowa at 13.5 cents and Nebraska at 13.7 cents per gallon. Even at the 13 cents plus per gallon we cannot expect to maintain and improve our present system of roads.

It is not that our political system is incapable of generating funds. Indeed, between 1960 and 1981 federal outlays jumped from some $92 billion to over $650 billion, while during the same period state and local governmental expenditures rocketed from $50 to $390 billion. But as governmental revenues multiplied, the nation's priorities changed. Just as in the private sector, where the emphasis has shifted from producer to the consumer ethic, so too in the public sector we are reluctant to defer the satisfaction of our immediate wants to build and maintain facilities that will make a better world tomorrow. Deferring consumption so that we may build and maintain public facilities requires political leadership and courage that will foster national maturity and discipline. In recent years America has not been blessed with such leadership. Some say that, given the rise of single issue politics and the decline of our political parties, we can no longer expect such leadership.

What is to be done? We can continue along our course and watch our infrastructure gradually fall apart, or we can take action. Ultimately what is to be done will, of course, be determined in the political area. Even seemingly simple steps—such as raising the federal gas tax—will take political leadership and, even more importantly, political courage. With a general decline in confidence in government at all levels, there are signs of tax resistance everywhere. Proposition 13 in California and Proposition 2 1/2 in Massachusetts are merely dramatic illustrations of a general resistance to taxes. Moreover, with interest rates, even for tax exempt securities, at 12 percent and more, the cost of borrowing money for projects seems prohibitive, at least for the political leaders, who must think of the next election.

In the booming postwar years, the U.S. came to believe that our resources and powers were infinite. On the global scale this view led to the disaster of Vietnam. On the domestic scene it brought us inflation that undermined traditional behaviors by encouraging the human instinct for irresponsible and destructive gambling and by discouraging prudence and diligence—the essential ingredients of which economic growth and prosperity are made. A casualty of this mentality of infinite power and resources which has been less obvious until recently is our decaying infrastructure. Gradually America is joining the rest of the world in the recognition that it too has limits. Today in straining to respond to calls for increased defense expenditure and social programs, we ignore the decline of roads, sewers, and water systems. For the fiscal year 1983 Congress approved a budget of $769.8 billion, with a projected deficit of $103.9 billion.

Yet from every side there are cries for more—from the elderly Americans, some of whom enjoy Social Security checks in excess of the wages they earned as workers, from dialysis patients who quite legitimately fear for their lives, from dairy product farmers who, under present federally financed support prices, are filling American caves with mountains of cheese, butter, and dried milk, from sponsors of school lunches, which for the most part are consumed by children of middle class families, from students who claim the right to a government-financed college education. Less widely supported organizations also line up for federal help. Federal grants have been made to help the staff of the Los Angeles Gay and Lesbian Community Center and to promote the "Feminist Press." Also the taxpayers' monies have been used to help finance such organizations as the Sierra Club, The United States Student Association, the Women's Equality Action League, and even the well-heeled League of Women Voters. By financing these and many other organizations, the government helps to support and promote parochial and often partisan political or social objectives. Whatever the wisdom of such expenditures, they are a political reality which must be re-examined if we are to alter government priorities at all levels.

Changing the priorities is not likely to be easy.

Neither conservatives nor liberals are, of course, oblivious to our needs for public investment. Both favor increased investments in public facilities, and both agree that further investments in public facilities are not possible without cutting expenditures in other areas. But while the liberals argue for slashing defense expenditures and the conservatives push for cutting social programs, the infrastructure continues to deteriorate. Should we continue our course, should our priorities remain unchanged, America will have no choice but to watch the erosion of the very base on which our industrial civilization rests and adapt to a steady decline in its standard of living and quality of life—something quite alien to the nation's historic driving force: the American Dream.

INTERVIEW: B.F. SKINNER

UTOPIA OR DISASTER

Once in a while, a scientist becomes so committed to his theories that they color every aspect of his life. B.F. Skinner, the prominent Harvard psychologist, now 78, lives behaviorism, the controversial school of psychology he developed.

The essence of behaviorism is simple: the sum of our past experiences determines our present behavior. A behavior that is rewarded is more likely to be repeated. Skinner's original work involved laboratory animals. A rat in a cage would be rewarded with food each time it pressed a bar. After a short time, the rat learned to press the bar when it was hungry. A new behavior had been formed. Those rewards or punishments that follow an action he referred to as "contingencies of reinforcement," and this process of behavior formation has been called "operant conditioning."

In the 1940s, he attracted national attention by raising his daughter Deborah, now an artist, in a mechanical baby tender called an air crib (later dubbed the "baby box"). In 1962, with the publication of his fictional Walden Two, *he became something of a cult figure. The book described a utopian community in which ideal behavior is molded by the contingencies that the society has established. In* Beyond Freedom and Dignity *(1971), his message became more urgent and provocative: society, he said, must use its new knowledge of behavior not to create utopia but to avert disaster.*

Assistant editor Libby Rosenthal's meetings with Professor Skinner took place in his office, decorated with his daughter's artwork, at Harvard University.

Science Digest: Professor Skinner, in your writing you have stressed how operant conditioning could be used to create a utopia—at least a better world. Yours is a big vision, one that requires major overhauls in our society.
B.F. Skinner: I'm afraid it is that, and I just wish I could see how it could be done. But at the moment, I don't. The world

now has four and a half billion people and is on its way to having five. We really are running out of essential things: water, air, crucial energy and materials. We are polluting the environment and facing the real danger of a nuclear holocaust.

These things, I think, could be corrected by active resolve and a change. Operant conditioning allows you to change governments and religions, to redesign cultural practices. But the question I now raise is not whether we have the means to make these changes—I'm sure we have—but whether there will ever be a reason to make them.
SD: Can contingencies really affect a society's behavior? We all know about Hiroshima and the dire consequences of nuclear war, and yet the arms buildup continues.
BFS: I think it's beginning to be clear that those who have really been exposed to war are likely to be against it. We've suffered the loss of fifty thousand in Vietnam, a hundred thousand in World War I and four hundred thousand in World War II, but people in America don't know what war is like. The Japanese who lived in bombed cities—they know. And I suspect the French and Germans do too.

The real trouble is that human behavior is only affected by immediate consequences. And in a war, consequences happen much later than the events that precipitate them.
SD: So an order for invasion decreed in Washington is not mentally connected with the death five thousand miles away.
BFS: Right. In *Science and Human Behavior,* I reported a little trick that used to be done on sailing ships in the old days, when people would get bored. The crew would take four or five cabin boys and fasten their left hands to a ring around the mast. Then they gave each one a stick. All each boy had to do was to hit the boy ahead of him when he was hit from behind. It is in everyone's interest to hit lightly. But the hit you feel is always a little harder (it seems) than the one you

give, and in no time at all, quite predictably, the boys would be lashing at each other violently.

Now, we do this in a war. Our threats to others do not seem at all as strong as their threats to us. So we threaten harder, and they threaten harder. It builds up, and a war comes. So the immediate behavior is not influenced by the devastating contingencies of war but by the little events leading up to war.
SD: That's a bit worrying, isn't it? If you have to experience consequences close up, we have to bomb ourselves off the Earth before we learn not to go to war.
BFS: Well that is it, you see. And that is why, I think, we are going to do just that. We may never have the chance to make the mistake, then try something else.
SD: Professor Skinner, earlier you said you were sure we had the means to discourage practices such as excessive fuel consumption. But if you have lots of fuel you can drive fast cars, you can fly all over the world. How could you design contingencies to counterbalance these natural reinforcers?
BFS: In a way, it's the same problem. It's very difficult for your behavior to be changed by something that happens years from now—like running out of fuel. That's the way the organism evolved.

But some institutions—government, religion, industry—have already learned how to construct immediate reinforcers which get people to work for the future. Industries pay workers to aggrandize the company. And governments and religions have always used operant conditioning to get people to die for them. Let's say there is a place with some wolves, and somebody goes out and kills one. That's great; he gets a medal. And next time, he kills an even more dangerous animal. That's great too—another medal. Finally, he tries to kill the dragon. But he doesn't kill the dragon, the dragon kills him.

Unfortunately, the future of government, religion or an industry doesn't jibe with the future of the species. I can say,

First appeared in SCIENCE DIGEST, January 1983. © by The Hearst Corporation.

well, we've got to do something about population. But industrial leaders don't care; zero growth would be very bad for the market. Governments don't care; after all, the size of the army depends on the number of young people. I can't get to the four and a half billion to get them to practice birth control. Only those organizations can do it. But religions and governments and industries have other fish to fry. The government is not going to take action for a hundred years from now. Elected officials are only thinking of the next election.

SD: In an ideal situation, where you did have power, what kinds of contingencies would you create to achieve your goals? What sort of contingencies would you create to prevent crime?

BFS: First of all, in an ideal world, I would be philosopher-king of the republic. Of course, I would make guns as rare in America as they are in England. Then . . . there was something in the paper this morning about someone who was strangling a person and then stopped when he thought of the electric chair. I don't know, I wouldn't be strongly against the death penalty on the grounds of someone dying.

A government *could* insist upon sterilization, contraception, abortions and so on to keep the population down. It could forbid free sale of sugar and alcohol—we'd all be much healthier. It could arrange contingencies so that people would not produce too much and not pollute.

SD: The very mention of forced sterilization gets people's hackles up. Would you support this kind of thing?

BFS: No, I wouldn't support that at all. And I'm not saying it's a solution. But I suspect—and this is the worst thing possible—that if I were to predict the state of the world a hundred years from now, I would say that there would be one single ruthless government dictating what people can and can't do. By that time, such a system will be necessary to cut population and stop pollution. I hate to think of it. It will be like the Roman Empire, which was actually a pretty good political system—but it was very ruthless. The Holy Roman Empire influenced its citizens in the same manner, through religious sanctions. Hitler tried it too: the glorification of the Aryan race and so on.

SD: In all these models of control you mention, there's nothing very exemplary—no philosopher-kings. Think of the Soviet Union where people *are* told how many cars to have, how to work . . .

BFS: Yes, I've been to Russia and I never want to go back. These are not models that one wants to follow at all. But what are you going to do if you're thinking of the future of the species? Personally, I'd like to see education take over and do a decent job.

SD: It worries me that the outcome of behaviorist conditioning seems to depend so much on the moral framework of the person who is forming the contingencies.

BFS: Well, I don't feel that's an explanation of anything. Some systems are concerned with the behavior of the individual and some are concerned with the welfare of mankind. I'm quite sure that I could raise children in a Walden Two who would enjoy life more than the average person does today, while consuming almost nothing and being productive.

SD: Isn't that, perhaps, because you would set up the right contingencies? What I'm saying is: in all these systems *someone* has to set up the contingencies.

BFS: In the past, they've come about by accident. But now, if we're going to design an entire culture, we set them up.

SD: Who is *we?* That's my question.

BFS: Yes, well, those who know how . . . scholars, writers. I think someone could get the money and a good cross section of people and construct a Walden Two. The first generation would have all kinds of problems, because it would come from a very bad culture. But with the proper educational systems, the second generation, I think, would live in a relatively happy, productive and creative world. People would flock to it.

SD: So you're convinced that, if operant conditioning is done well, the individual doesn't feel controlled?

BFS: That is the point. After the publication of *Beyond Freedom and Dignity,* there was a cover story in *Time:* "Skinner says we can't afford freedom." I didn't mean that at all. I want people to feel as free as possible. And to feel as worthy as possible. That can be done by turning to positive reinforcement rather than negative punishment. I want people to behave because of positive reinforcement, and to feel as if they were doing it themselves.

Nobody's passing out M&Ms at Walden Two. Those who start such societies won't control. They will create a world that just naturally reinforces the very behavior that should keep it going.

SD: You have a utopian vision. Most people think of operant conditioning as a sterile, manipulative process.

BFS: You *are* a physical system. You have responded to reinforcements, and that has built what I now see as one personality. You ask: "Can I do anything about it?" Yes, you can. But not because you can initiate anything. Not because you can simply say: "I don't like this, I'm going to change." But because you belong to a culture which has taught you to arrange for a world that will reinforce the behavior you desire.

SD: Can operant conditioning maintain something like creativity?

BFS: When people start talking about creativity, I know they're lost. It means

nothing. Where does it come from? I delivered a paper once at the Guggenheim Museum on creating a creative artist in which I said that you encourage artistic behavior by reinforcing the individual artist. You look at a picture. If it's a beautiful picture, you reinforce looking at it. These paintings in my office are my daughter's, by the way. They're done by the baby-box baby.

SD: So she's turned out well.

BFS: Someone called me and asked, "Did you put your child in a cage?" No. Many of these air cribs are still in use. It's just an ideal environment for the baby . . . and it does save an awful lot of work. My daughter Deborah is very happily married. There were rumors that she committed suicide, that she became insane. The latest one is that she is suing me. She's very active, and galleries show her work. I'm pleased to say that we have a very affectionate relationship.

SD: A few times now you've referred to the power of education in changing society. If you could design a school system, what would it be like?

BFS: You bring up a very touchy point. I've just seen a volume published by the American Academy of Arts and Sciences on the American school. There's not a thing in there about teaching. Programmed instruction is a terribly effective way of teaching. The student takes very small steps and can answer almost every question he is asked because of the way in which the steps are set up. So he's constantly reinforced. But you won't find programmed teaching in the school. You'll find it in industry, where they know a good thing when they see it.

I hope that what's-his-name—who is now president?—Ronald Reagan will get rid of the Department of Education, because it's doing all the wrong things. And I would also say, throw out the schools of education. Throw the rascals out. They spend no time on how to teach better.

In 1960, in the Roanoke School, an eighth-grade class covered all of the ninth-grade algebra in one term on programmed-teaching machines, and their grades were right on the ninth-grade norm. Retention a year later was better than normal. But it's been forgotten.

SD: Programmed instruction seems very efficient, but do you think it's lacking in a human element?

BFS: Well, what is the human element in mathematics? I mean, do you have to be cozy with your mathematics teacher? There's nothing personal in mathematics, you know. Mathematicians are a lonely people.

SD: I think statements like this have led some to the accusation that B.F. Skinner views both men and women as if they were pigeons or rats.

1. PERSPECTIVES

BFS: It has been abundantly demonstrated that all the reinforcement schedules seen in rats and pigeons can also be seen in the behavior of humans.

All gambling systems are based on what we call a variable-ratio schedule for reinforcement. If you go to Atlantic City, you see acres of people pulling slot-machine levers. In the long run all these people lose, but once in a while, they may go home happy—so they keep coming back.

But, you know, the same schedule can have better effects. Science pays off on a variable-ratio schedule. You can't predict the next success, but if you continue to have an occasional success you go on being a scientist. A dedicated scientist is simply one who's had a good schedule of payoff.

SD: Is that why you set out to become a psychologist?

BFS: Well, in college, I was going to be a writer. I got a lot of encouragement, including a letter from Robert Frost. So after college, I tried for a year to write— and I failed miserably. A depression came about when the only repertoire of behavior I had which was appropriate to a career didn't work. So what could I do? I had to acquire a different repertoire, one that worked better.

SD: I'm struck by the degree to which behaviorism dictates your vision. Is there anything that could convince you that behaviorism is wrong?

BFS: Well, I suppose experimental data that didn't fit. I don't see any. I might give it up for the wrong reasons: if I felt we had to believe in ourselves as creative individuals in order to survive. I'd go along with that the same way that an intellectual Catholic goes along with the Church, knowing perfectly well that it's not true.

SD: One last question then: I like to think that I'm free to do whatever I want in my life. Do you feel the same way?

BFS: I'm doing what I want, because I've arranged a world in which I'm positively reinforced by everything that surrounds me. Certainly I feel free to go on or stop—in the sense that I've had a long history and either one of these types of behavior could easily be explained. But I don't really have a choice. I will do one or the other.

But fifty-three years after I went to Harvard to study psychology, I can certainly say this: if, at that time, someone had shown me my present position, I would have settled for that. I would have said, "I'll take that as a career."

BOOKS BY SKINNER

About Behaviorism. New York: Random House, 1976.

Beyond Freedom and Dignity. New York: Bantam, 1972.

The Shaping of a Behaviorist. New York: Knopf, 1979.

Science and Human Behavior. New York: Free Press, 1965.

Technology of Teaching. Englewood Cliffs, NJ: Prentice-Hall, 1968.

Walden Two. New York: Macmillan, 1976.

In Search of American Optimism

A visitor ponders a legacy of disillusionment

W. L. WEBB

W. L. Webb is literary editor of the liberal "Guardian" of London, from which this report is excerpted.

Strange things have been happening in the richest country in the world. People who have lost their livelihood have been selling what was left to sell, loading up their families, and setting out cross-country to look for work. Finding none, they settle in makeshift camps on the edge of unwelcoming Southern towns. It is just like *The Grapes of Wrath*, except that these modern Okies have been fleeing not from the dustbowl of Oklahoma but from the very powerhouse of the old American economy ("the rust bowl," they call it) — from the dying steel industry and crippled car factories of the American North.

In New York City the most immediate evidence that hard times, not happy days, are here again has been the rising tide of homeless people, sleeping in the streets, stretched out by the stairs or along the walls of Penn Station, being stirred none too gently by police. Many of the newcomers to this rough scene aren't washed-up drunks or junkies but young job-hunters out of funds. Polite Manhattan has become famously expert at averting its gaze, knowing to the very block the limits of the nighttime no-visit areas, and even by day mostly preferring not to face the Apocalypse Now of its subway system — the rats that scamper in the corridors, the junkies and cripples with their begging bowls, and the incredible

assault of the wall-to-wall calligraphy that covers the cars, inside and out, like a psychotic parody of the painted agit-prop trains of revolutionary Russia.

But it's not just the extent of human misery and dislocation involved in the recession, nor even the always dramatic local scale of the too-familiar "insoluble problems of the inner city" that many decent people seem reluctant to face or able to ignore. What launched me on a tour of the U.S. was my wish to understand the present American political and social consciousness. Having read piecemeal accounts of the 1980 National Census, I wanted to know more about what had happened to America in a decade.

The census discloses the reality behind phrases that have already become clichés — the "white flight" from the cities; "the tilt to the sunbelt" of industry, wealth, and political power. It reveals population movements and social dislocation on a scale previously caused only by wars or epidemics.

Have Americans, accustomed to mobility and the private affluence-public squalor syndrome, been able to comprehend the scale of what has been happening? My impression is that many have barely begun to do so. They may not even have grasped what historian Theodore H. White records in his latest book, *America in Search of Itself.* By the time the 1980 census was concluded, he writes, "Baltimore was no longer a city of white majority; nor was Detroit; nor Washington; nor Atlanta; nor Chicago; nor San Antonio; nor New Orleans; nor half a dozen smaller cities."

As usual, de Tocqueville, contemplating *Democracy in America* a century and a half ago, had words for it: "Placed in the middle of an always-moving scene, himself driven by the irresistible torrent which drives all around him, the American has no time to tie himself to anything; he grows accustomed only to change, and ends by regarding it as the natural state of man." But what if the rush and volume of the torrent has swollen to such an extent that the ground beneath your feet begins to shift? And what if this coincides with a time when the bright miracles are fading, or bloom for shorter and shorter seasons?

I had been struck with the fear and anger at the condition of American cities that Saul Bellow expresses in his latest novel, *The Dean's December.* There also are hints at what may be their future: the abandonment of a largely black "underclass" that would contain or destroy itself in a darkness of poverty, drugs, and crime. Homicide is now "the leading cause of death among young black men," the National Urban League reported last year.

Both in the novel and in conversation in Chicago, where he lives, Bellow acknowledges that his view of blacks is not a conventional liberal one. Unlike the European migrants to the melting-pot, he says, American blacks brought with them to the cities "almost nothing." They had come "out of a desolation in which they were stripped of everything — no trades, no skills, no experiences that fitted them for an advanced life." He sees their chaos and violence as threatening. and their

1. PERSPECTIVES

potential political power as dangerous.

In the vast plateau of the Texas Panhandle, far away from nearly everywhere except Amarillo and a little town called Goodnight, I drove down long dirt roads under immense gunmetal skies. I had come to look at the place where for a quarter of a century people at the Pantex assembly plant have been fitting together the tens of thousands of editions of the Big Bang that are deemed necessary to preserve the American way of life. These now include the warheads for cruise missiles destined for Britain and the Pershings ordered for Holland and Germany.

In 1977 three workers were killed in part of the plant where conventional explosives are manufactured. Recently there have been moral detonations as well. The new Catholic Bishop of Amarillo, Bishop Leroy Matthiesen, made a statement following hearings about locating the MX missile in the western Panhandle and the Reagan administration's announcement that it was going ahead with the manufacture of the neutron bomb. He said, "We urge individuals involved in the production and stockpiling of nuclear bombs to consider what they are doing, to resign from such activities, and to seek employment in peaceful pursuits."

The Southern Baptists, whose red brick temples blush with prosperity in Amarillo, are solidly anti-Matthiesen and for the bomb. The Southwest Baptist Church went so far as to hold a Pantex Appreciation Day to which 180 people turned up to be told by the Rev. Alan Ford, "You do not have to feel guilty working at Pantex."

The vagaries of acquaintanceship have thrown me into contact with a very rich man in Texas who parlayed one year's salary into a fortune. He now controls a powerful company that international oil concerns watch carefully. He has his own view of the predicament of the great cities.

"The politicians sold out," he says. "They bought votes. [They] took taxpayers' money and, in different ways, passed it out to people. And what that did was weaken a lot of people who would have been willing to work."

My friend continued: "Close to 50 [per cent of the population is] getting some sort of check from the government .... And at some point you are

going to find, whether Democrat or Republican, [the populace will divide according] to who works and wants to work, and who does not."

The house we drove back to was substantial, and monitored with cameras by security men downtown at the plant. "It would not shock me for us to be sitting here right now and see three guys come through that gate and head for the house," said my host. "I would hate to do it but I could shoot all three."

In Houston, Dallas, and San Diego millions of white Americans have turned their backs on the cities of the East and Midwest. But things are going wrong. The oilman told me that his industry has cut exploration 50 per cent in the past year, and it is the lawyers who are now making money — on litigation by incensed investors against collapsing oil-prospecting companies.

"One of the longest journeys in the world is from Brooklyn to Manhattan," wrote Norman Podhoretz, who famously "made it" from the Brownsville section of Brooklyn — then a Jewish neighborhood — to Columbia University, Cambridge University in England, and back to the U.S. and editorship of *Commentary* magazine. He now belongs to the far Right as a sort of intellectual fundraiser for the President.

Today it is an even farther cry from the topless towers of mid-Manhattan to the shellshocked black ghetto of Brownsville or even to the charred blocks of Harlem beside the northern rim of Central Park. It would be hard to exaggerate the dereliction of these areas of New York. A black Democratic Congressman, Rep. Ronald V. Dellums of California, is not straining rhetoric when he speaks of Reagan's increase in arms spending and reduction in social spending as "bombing our own cities."

It seemed to me during this journey that the old liberal America had grown tired, perhaps depressed almost to the point of withdrawal. When I suggested this to the novelist E. L. Doctorow he said, "There seems to have been a terrible loss of energy .... If you could apply a mass encephalograph test to the head of America, you would find that the brainwaves had gone flat."

I looked for an antidote to this feeling at a symposium on the 50th anniversary of the New Deal, which reconvened administrators and legislators

associated with Franklin D. Roosevelt's great program, in the Lyndon Baines Johnson Memorial Library at Austin, Tex. It was an extraordinary occasion — the summoning of a political court in exile — but there was little cheer.

Leon Keyserling, the economist who was a principal draftsman in the 1930s of the National Industrial Recovery Act and the National Housing Act, declared, "Our great America now is in a terrible condition." Some 60 million people are suffering from the injustice and misery of unemployment, "and we are threatened with a tiny recovery that will merely be an abortive prelude to successive periods of more stagnation and recession."

What one must learn from the New Deal, he added, is not "academic generalizations about how glorious it was, but what do we do — about inflation and public spending, about taking care of the unemployed?" Keyserling believes, "The New Deal can provide a precise example of what we should be doing now."

Economist John Kenneth Galbraith was even more forthright. Cut the military budget, he said, and reverse monetarism — which only creates unemployment. He also wants the government to come strongly to the rescue of the cities.

"At a time when this should be the focus of all our national energies, we have an administration with a policy of determined inaction, not to mention a cutback of the form of income these people depend on. And the danger of a loss of social tranquility is very great." That was becoming a cheerless refrain.

"Come out to Vermont and cheer yourself up," said writer Grace Paley, a veteran of good American causes. "You should see a Vermont town meeting." If places like Amarillo or Dallas raise doubts about the American way, Thetford, Vt., is the place to come for reassurance. Following an authentic town supper in the school hall was the vigorous exercise of a three-centuries-old tradition of direct democracy.

When it ended Thetford had beaten off a conservative attack on the school budget, and passed two resolutions of wider concern. It had instructed its officers from selectmen to dogcatcher to refuse to take part in civil defense plans to receive 5,000 evacuees from a town in Connecticut in case of nuclear war. Then Thetford became the first town in Vermont (others followed) to pass an ordinance restricting shipments of high-level nuclear waste on a nearby interstate highway.

Thetford has an impressive public record; this was the first place in America to pass a resolution demanding the impeachment of Richard Nixon. The townspeople know that in some ways they live in "a privileged democracy" in Vermont. But they see what was accomplished at their town meeting as part of a shift in American politics, part of a new coalition that is gathering across the country.

One strong thrust toward coalition comes from the nuclear freeze movement. John Kenneth Galbraith, one of the people who got the freeze on the ballot at the 1980 Democratic convention, says, with the conviction of a man who has seen many tides in American politics, "This is one of the strongest movements of our time. The underlying anxiety is enormously powerful."

This is a strange moment in America. Part of the received wisdom about the Reagan phenomenon is that middle America is tired of "being good," of putting up money for welfare programs and being rewarded, it was perceived, only by inflation and cities that grew ever more frightfully alien. As for the young, fewer than 30 per cent of those between eighteen and twenty-one bothered to vote in 1980.

David Bennett, a historian at Syracuse, told me that students inviting him to a symposium on the future recently wrote, "Please give us something cheerful." "They get only negative messages," he said. "They're the first U.S. generation to have that."

The political problems and opportunities presented by the needs of the cities, and the wider one to repair the neglected infrastructure of the nation — estimated by Walt Rostow at the New Deal symposium to cost some $2.5 trillion — cannot be postponed much longer. "Even for a $3-trillion economy, if spread out over ten or fifteen years," he said, "this is a formidable increment of required investment, with large implications for employment prospects over a wide range of skills."

In one way or another it looks as if America is going to have some new kind of New Deal. Those who are beginning to fight for it will need to keep up their courage. Franklin D. Roosevelt said it when he paraphrased Henry David Thoreau's "Nothing is so much to be feared as fear."
(Apr. 4-8)

Politics

The twentieth century has been an era of increasing government responsibility for social problems. At the turn of the century, the demand for government assistance was at the town and country level; by the 1930s it moved to the state level; and today it is at the federal level. Government is the social institution which organizes the population by mobilizing finances and human efforts. Whether the task is building pyramids or inventing the atom bomb, government supplies monumental power. Why not, then, use government to create a great society?

The federal government has become large and bureaucratic. It is often dominated by special interest groups and is not coping effectively with a variety of problems. Consequently, many of the articles in this edition question the practicability of using government—particularly federal government—to shape our future. Many sociologists berate government regulations and bureaucratic mismanagement and complain that government is insensitive, corrupt, and malicious. Our biggest social problem today, according to some, is a need to remodel government so that it can continue to be our foremost arbitrator of social problems.

The lead article in this section presents the attempts made by presidents Carter and Reagan to control the inefficiency in government. Carter didn't succeed, and President Reagan hasn't accomplished the task yet either. Other articles suggest that government bureaus, organized to aid our society, are often indifferent to the public needs which created them. The message they convey is that government has changed very little in the last decade. Attempts to organize political groups to bring the people's voice to our democratic leaders have become levers for the moneyed and powerful.

The articles in this section consider the role of government in matters of peace, war, radiation, and the safety of future generations. In order to understand the causes of societal problems, we must first look at the way society is organized and the way it runs.

Looking Ahead: Challenge Questions

Why do people turn to government for help with social problems?

What unique powers does government have that other parts of society such as family, schools, and businesses lack?

Is our national government inefficient, or are we going through troubled economic times and looking for someone or something to blame?

BUREAUCRATS 2, PRESIDENTS 0

Leonard Reed

Leonard Reed worked in the civil and foreign services for twenty-four years, mainly at the Voice of America. He is currently a contributing editor of the Washington Monthly.

EDITORIAL writers casting about for kind words to say about Jimmy Carter, after his humiliation in November 1980, found one apparent bright spot in the departing president's otherwise dismal record of domestic accomplishment: his efforts to reform the government. *The New York Times*, in a representative pronouncement entitled ONE IMPORTANT PROMISE KEPT, credited Carter with "the first overhaul of the Federal bureaucracy in almost a century."

Carter's reforms, it was said, had gone a long way toward eliminating three of the most annoying defects of government enterprise. Was it once virtually impossible to fire an incompetent civil servant? "Thanks to the 1978 Civil Service Reform Act," the *Times* reported, "it has become easier to rid the Federal bureaucracy of duds." Were employees who exposed corruption and malfeasance in their agencies typically punished rather than rewarded? Not to worry. "A special counsel has been provided to protect whistleblowers who risk their jobs to report wrongdoing." Did top government managers lack flexibility, as well as adequate incentive to perform well? Carter had "established a Senior Executive Corps of 6,000 highly skilled managers who may now transfer among government agencies without loss of rank, and are therefore less likely to abandon public service."

It all sounded very impressive—but did it ultimately make much difference to the performance of the clanking, wheezing federal machine? A look at the evidence four years after Carter's reforms were enacted suggests not.

LET'S start with the problem of incompetence. In the prereform year of 1976, out of 2.5 million federal workers, only 3,500 tenured civil servants were dismissed for poor performance. That's a discharge rate of one seventh of one percent. Of that one seventh of one percent, a substantial number were reinstated after appeals to the courts.

And now that the reforms are in place? The government hasn't retrieved the most recent data from its computers, but in 1980, two years after reform, the number of civil servants fired for poor performance (throwing in for good measure those who resigned under fire) had reached a grand total of . . . um . . . 2,632. That is about one tenth of one percent, a lower percentage than the 1976 prereform figure. At this rate, a firm in the private sector with 1,000 employees would fire only one person a year. Or, putting it another way, a company that had maintained an even payroll of fifty employees since the Declaration of Independence would have dropped only ten for incompetence and other inadequacies in more than two centuries.

In the battle between Jimmy Carter and the bureaucracy's "duds," the duds seem to have triumphed. This is nothing new. They have been gaining ground since 1883, when, following the assassination of President James Garfield by Charles Guiteau, a frustrated office-seeker, the Pendleton Act established a tenured career civil service based on the principle of merit hiring. The Pendleton Act was designed to eliminate the mass political firings that accompanied elections under the spoils system, not to hinder the dismissal of individual incompetents. But in the name of merit principles, further restrictions on firing civil servants were legislated in 1912. The Civil Service Commission, delegated with sole responsibility for amending the firing procedures, generated a plethora of such amendments, almost all of which resulted in greater protection for government employees.

Then the judges got into the act. Starting in the late 1950s, they began to allow dismissed federal workers to sue in court to get their jobs back, after their executive branch appeals were exhausted. In 1974 the Supreme Court bought an odd theory popularized by law professor Charles Reich (who also gave us *The Greening of America*), and declared that under the Constitution government employees had a "property right" in their jobs of which they couldn't be deprived without "due process of law." Due process came to mean that every civil servant was entitled to a full-dress trial before an administrative tribunal, followed by an excursion through various layers of federal courts.

These protections were prompted by a laudable concern for fairness to individual workers. But in practice, all this fairness meant that firing a civil servant who really deserved it was a task that only the brave or brash would undertake— and rarely successfully. A highly paid manager might expect to spend 25 to 50 percent of his working days for the better part of two years constructing and defending the paper record required to discharge a single goof-off clerk. In the process, the manager ran the risk of having the clerk file a "grievance" against him, of having to defend himself against the charge, of having *his* superior view *him* as a troublemaker or a bad manager who had a "personality conflict" with his employees.

Small wonder, then, that government bosses learned to handle the problem differently. They palmed off incompetents on unsuspecting fellow managers, who in time did likewise. If an incompetent was of relatively high rank, he might be shipped off to one of the yearlong training courses or study projects known in-house as "turkey farms." In general, managers learned to tolerate unproductive employees, working around them rather than trying to fire them.

THE 1978 reforms were hardly enough to cause a sane supervisor to change these tactics. The Carter changes did eliminate some superfluous stages in the firing process—lawsuits, for example, now go directly to an appeals court without having to pass through the trial-level court first. But Carter didn't come close to testing the limits of the Supreme Court's requirement of "due process." So the supervisor who contemplates firing a federal employee can still anticipate a veritable festival of paperwork and multilevel appeals.

To sack someone in the new, reformed civil service, an agency must first advise the alleged incompetent of his failings, and give him thirty days' notice of its intention to dismiss him. The employee can then take his case to the regional branch of the newly established Merit Systems Protection Board (a four-month process); if the regional branch upholds the firing, the employee can appeal to the MSPB's headquarters in Washington (now thoroughly clogged with about 10,000 appeals from the fired air traffic controllers). If *that* decision goes against him, he can still take

his case to a federal appeals court before throwing in the towel.

Not only are the new procedures scant improvement on the old, but in order to get the Carter reforms past the federal unions, concessions had to be made. Federal unions are a peculiar breed. Unable to bargain over "bread and butter" (since federal salaries are set by Congress), they can attract and hold membership only by their aggressive activity on behalf of each employee's "job security." Nor is this zeal tempered —as it often is with private-sector unions—by any fear that their employer might go bankrupt if inefficient work practices are maintained.

What the unions got out of the 1978 reforms was the right to bargain over virtually any change in working conditions. The Department of Transportation in Denver soon discovered that it had no authority to remove a TV set from a "break" room (although there was no contractual obligation to provide one) without consulting the union. The Portsmouth Naval Shipyard learned that it could not require mobile crane operators to keep a lubrication log without negotiating the matter with the union. And the management of a military installation, when making temporary out-of-town assignments, now has to choose the person assigned on the basis of seniority. Even the rearrangement of desks—that central activity of bureaucratic life—can now be the subject of union-management bickering.

IF THE Carter reforms were supposed to make it easier to fire incompetents, they were supposed to make it harder to fire other civil servants—namely, the "whistleblowers" who expose various forms of hanky-panky in their agencies. While compared with European bureaucracies the American civil service is a hotbed of rampant integrity, it has its share of hidden scandals and—more important— scandalously misguided practices that deserve some embarrassing publicity. The archetypal whistleblower is the almost legendary A. Ernest Fitzgerald, the Pentagon offi-

cial who in 1968 exposed the $2 billion cost overrun on the Lockheed C-5A cargo plane. Fitzgerald's enhanced standing in the eyes of a grateful government was best expressed by that master of nuance, Richard Nixon, whose response was "Get rid of the son of a bitch!"

Government agencies, for reasons familiar to every student of bureaucracy, do not look kindly on employees who, like Fitzgerald, "commit truth." To protect—even encourage—government employees who speak out, the 1978 reform law set up an independent Office of Special Counsel, endowed with impressive powers. The Special Counsel was to investigate allegations of reprisals against whistleblowers, and then—if the allegations checked out —take the victim's case to the Merit Systems Protection Board.

Unfortunately, the new Special Counsel's office has pursued this mission with a zeal that makes Nixon's "personal investigation" of Watergate look like a triumph of dogged prosecution. Since June 1981, the Special Counsel has sought stays of agency action against whistleblowers in a grand total of four cases (in one of which it withdrew its request). It pursued only four allegations of wrongdoing with government agencies, and not once did it use its statutory authority to question the adequacy of an agency's internal investigation of its treatment of a whistleblower. The performance of the office has been so poor that one of its original proponents, Rep. Patricia Schroeder, has introduced legislation to abolish it.

Within the fraternity of whistleblowers and their supporters, in fact, the Office of Special Counsel is regarded as more foe than friend. Veterans like Fitzgerald argue that the office lures bureaucratic dissenters (who might otherwise choose to leak anonymously to the press) into the open with false promises of protection, the better to expose them to their superiors. Fitzgerald characterizes the office as "a sting operation whose purpose is to identify and deal with troublemakers. The whole process is a sham."

In one of its few concrete actions,

the Special Counsel's office recently produced a 123-page manual on how to deal with whistleblowers that seems to bear out Fitzgerald's claim. "On the surface the manual's 'guidance' looks innocent enough," says Michael Spekter, a trial attorney with the Office of Special Counsel until he quit in disgust early this year, "but for the sophisticated manager it's a blueprint for getting rid of a whistleblower and making it stick."

The manual suggests several questions (and for each one gives references to court decisions) for a vengeful manager to be guided by. One question, for example, asks, "Was [punitive] action taken close in time to the whistleblowing?" Says Spekter, "To the smart manager that translates: make sure you don't take any reprisal too soon after the whistleblowing; see court decision for how much time should elapse." Another question is "Was there disparate treatment of the whistleblower?" English translation: if you want to pack the whistleblower off to a job where he has no access to information, cloak it with a reorganization that affects several people. The manual also contains samples of letters of dismissal, memos to be put in the file, and pointedly structured performance ratings. Says Spekter, "It's as if the FBI put out instructions telling bank robbers how to avoid tripping the alarm system."

N O ASPECT of the 1978 civil-service reform received more publicity than the creation of the Senior Executive Service. The SES, as it is known, was designed as an elite corps of about 6,000 government managers drawn primarily from the top grades of the permanent civil service. On joining the SES, proponents of this reform implied, government executives would be giving up their secure tenured positions for what President Carter called "the risks and rewards of competitive life." Executives with moxie would be rewarded with sizable bonuses; for those who didn't measure up, it would be the sack.

Beyond rewarding the stars and weeding out the clods, the new system was supposed to give the government a flexibility it never had before—the ability to move executive talent from one agency to another as the need arose. As if to assure skeptics that the new system would indeed frighten off the faint of heart, the head of the program predicted that only 60 percent of those eligible would sign on. The dangers of joining the "high-risk, high-reward" SES were much discussed in the Washington press as the Carter plan worked its way through Congress.

In fact, when the time came, fully 98.8 percent of those eligible signed on. Most of the other 1.2 percent had reached retirement age. This stampede was not the product of a sudden devil-take-the-hindmost spirit infecting the bureaucracy. It simply reflected a hidden truth about SES: while its rewards are quite substantial, its risks are practically nonexistent.

The Senior Executive Service, to be blunt about it, was not the brainchild of Jimmy Carter but a fond hope of the senior executives, who for decades had nurtured plans for being anointed an "elite corps" as a way of acquiring elite salaries. Periodically, the senior elements of the permanent bureaucracy had suggested this "reform" to the task forces or blue-ribbon commissions appointed to study the causes of government inefficiency. It surfaced in the 1949 Hoover Commission as a proposed corps of "Career Business Managers," and six years later—in the Second Hoover Commission—as a "Senior Civil Service," and once again during the Nixon administration as a "Federal Executive Service." It was dusted off, shined up, and sold to Carter as the Senior Executive Service.

The joy of SES, for the executives, is clear in dollar terms. Although currently held down by an annual $58,500 ceiling, the schedule of SES salaries ranges from $56,945 to $67,200. But the real goodies come in the form of the bonuses. The 1978 reform law provided that bonuses of up to 20 percent could be added to the salaries of senior executives, as

long as not more than half the executives got bonuses in a given year. This might mean that almost every executive could expect a whopping bonus every other year. In 1979, however, after the executives at NASA, the very first agency to award bonuses, indiscreetly distributed checks to 46 percent of their fellow SES men, an embarrassed Congress set a 25 percent limit, later lowered to 20 percent. Beyond these bonuses, the 1978 law allows one percent of career executives to receive $20,000 awards, and another 5 percent to receive $10,000 add-ons.

Do federal executives need this shower of financial rewards? That is certainly the impression assiduously cultivated by federal executives, who argue that underpaid managers are leaving the government in droves every year. But while federal salaries don't soar to the level of top executive salaries in large corporations, many middle-level and senior government managers would be hard-put to match their salaries and benefits outside government. In government they enjoy a job security that many a corporate executive would give his pet ulcer for. They also enjoy a pension system with few parallels in the private sector. A federal executive who retired at fifty-five as recently as seven or eight years ago, after thirty years of service, would now have a pension higher than his salary at the time he left—and in the course of his expectable life will collect more than a million dollars in pension money.

In a poll taken in February 1981, 3,128 SES members said they planned to leave government within two years. Fifteen months later, only 352 SESers had left, not counting retirees. Apparently the vision of higher private-sector salaries failed to materialize.

What of the risks of SES that supposedly go with its substantial rewards? In particular, can an incompetent SES manager be fired? Well . . . sort of. He can be dropped out of the SES—but only back into the regular civil service. Even if that should happen, the statutory fine print provides that he shall be "guaranteed a suitable position *at his most recent SES salary or above*." This is not what most people would call a risk. But even this possibility is largely academic: in more than three years of operation, out of the 6,200 career members of SES, exactly one has been dropped for poor performance. Risk?

CONTRARY to the assumption underlying the SES idea, the main problem in government is not lazy executives who must be motivated by the promise of higher pay. In my experience, at least, senior government executives are as smart and energetic as their private-industry counterparts. The problem is the way they expend their energy, which is largely on bureaucratic dynamics —turf battles and lobbying for higher budgets—rather than in serving the broader public.

This is why one of the most sensible ideas included in the original SES plan would have allowed executives to be shifted to jobs outside their agencies, a reform that would have broken the link that ties an executive's own prosperity to his agency's expansion. He could even abolish his agency, if required, and look forward to another assignment when the job was done. Unfortunately, the career executives prevailed on Congress to drop this provision from the 1978 law. Today, no member of SES may be involuntarily transferred out of his own agency.

Instead, the SES often reinforces the worst sort of bureaucratic self-interest. A good example comes from the Department of Housing and Urban Development, where two of the three "critical elements" established for judging whether an executive deserves a bonus read as follows: "Decisions rarely, if ever, questioned by client groups"; "Decisions consistently praised by affected groups." "Client groups," of course, are interest groups that benefit from one or more of an agency's programs. They have their members to look after, but the public servant's task is not necessarily to make their job easier. But HUD and other government agencies get valuable support from these lobbies, and from the congressional committees that are also responsive to them. So the HUD official who bucks the construction lobby instead of cultivating it is not likely to be the one who finds a bonus in his stocking.

RONALD Reagan's contribution to reform of the bureaucracy has been the "RIF"—Washington jargon for "reduction in force." The size of the Reagan RIF has been in no way proportionate to the publicity it has received, or to the panic and indignation it has caused in the ranks. Some 9,600 people have so far been dropped—approximately one of every 260 civil servants. That is hardly on a scale that would strike the citizens of, say, Flint, Michigan, as catastrophic. But in a city like Washington, where the government is sometimes considered to exist for the purpose of providing jobs for civil servants, the outcry was horrendous.

The real tragedy of the Reagan RIF, however, was that it missed a rare opportunity to weed out the least productive members of the federal force. RIF procedures practically guarantee that any attempt to lay off bureaucrats will further decrease government efficiency— something Carter's reforms did nothing to change. In a RIF, seniority is everything; competence hardly enters into the equation. Somebody whose job is eliminated may "bump" a less senior fellow worker in the same or lower grade out of *his* job; the bumpee, in turn, may bump someone else, etc., until eventually the last bumpee is slid out the door. For every worker eventually laid off, three or four are displaced in this process.

The results are sometimes startling. At the Railroad Retirement Board in Chicago, a doctor whose job was abolished wound up accepting a job as a clerk. At the Office of Personnel Management, a former GS-14 psychologist is, as of this writing, working as a GS-3 in the mailroom. Several public health analysts (GS-14) at the U.S. Public Health Service ended up as secretaries (GS-5), jobs they can probably be expected to louse up thoroughly. For at least two years all of these downwardly mobile professionals will retain their original salaries (at or close to $50,000 a year), thus assuring the government of a prestige clerical force.

The Reagan administration, currently contemplating further RIFs, has toyed with the idea of changing the rules to make performance on the job the primary criterion for the retention of workers. But faced with the opposition of the federal unions, which are devoted to seniority systems, the effort has already been abandoned, at least for this year. James R. Rosa, the general counsel of the American Federation of Government Employees, says that if the administration ever does try to change the rules without getting Congress to pass a new law, the union will take it to court. If the administration tries for a new law, the union will bring its muscle to bear in Congress, as it did against Jimmy Carter.

IT IS possible to reform the bureaucracy. There is nothing inherent in government that prevents the performance of those who run it from being judged, that precludes breaking the career ties between senior executives and their agencies, or that requires whistleblowers to be punished. Nor is it clear why the federal civil servant must be afforded extravagant protections against being erroneously fired that his counterparts in the private sector do not enjoy. Even the decisions of the Supreme Court on government employees' "property" rights are vague enough to be challenged by a determined president. But on the unglamorous issue of civil-service reform, Jimmy Carter was about as determined a president as we are likely to get for a long time. If he didn't change much —and he didn't—who will?

How Lawmakers Misuse Your Campaign Donations

Clothes, parties, household expenses, travel—the sky's the limit when political funds are paying the bills.

Official reports now coming to light are providing an instructive glimpse into how some lawmakers spend campaign money—and fueling demand for tighter controls over such funds.

According to the latest disclosure statements filed with the Federal Election Commission, senators and House members last year dipped into campaign kitties—often totaling hundreds of thousands of dollars—to pay for an endless array of purchases, from cars to foreign trips. For example:

■ Representative Robert Badham (R-Calif.) spent $3,380 of his funds for his wife to accompany him overseas, and $1,369 for dresses for her.

■ Representative Gillis Long (D-La.), who was unopposed in last fall's election, spent $11,405 for a new campaign car and $928 for football tickets.

■ Former Representative Ken Holland (D-S.C.), who recently retired, paid $5,735 for a campaign car, which he is keeping.

■ Representative Joseph Addabbo (D-N.Y.) uses campaign money to pay for the Cadillac limousine that he leases for $661 a month—a total of $7,932 in 1982.

Those are only a sampling of the ways lawmakers spend campaign cash. Reports to the FEC for the 97th Congress reveal that some members are tapping political accounts to pay for gifts, loans, staff parties, household expenses, legal fees—almost anything that they cannot or dare not charge to the taxpayers.

Prudent users. Most members, to be sure, are careful in handling political funds. Many find such money too scarce to waste. Even among those who wind up with surplus campaign cash, effort often is made to return it to contributors, donate it to charity or give it to other candidates.

Still, abuses are common enough to infuriate some campaign contributors. Robert Busha of the National Asphalt Pavement Association says his group is disbanding its political-action committee, which last year gave $60,000 to House and Senate candidates.

Busha explains: "After the November elections, we felt the practices of members of Congress had simply gotten out of hand. When members wind up using the money in little kitties to buy lunches, plane tickets, gifts and so on, that smacks of personal use and is simply beyond the realm of what's needed to get elected. We are one little voice, but we did what we felt was right. We're not going out there and raise any more money."

Comments Senator William Proxmire (D-Wis.): "I anticipate some serious scandals someday. Apparently some members of Congress feel they can spend campaign funds on anything they want."

House and Senate rules and, at least in some cases, federal law prohibit members from diverting campaign funds to personal use. Yet, critics charge, violations are routinely ignored by both Congress's ethics committees and the Federal Election Commission, which regulates campaign financing.

The problem, the FEC contends, stems from ambiguity in the federal election act that Congress revised in 1979. For instance, lawmakers elected after Jan. 8, 1980—but not those in office before—are forbidden to make personal use of leftover campaign funds when they retire.

As for personal expenditures during a campaign, "federal law says almost nothing other than requiring that they be fully disclosed," says Fred Eiland, an FEC spokesman. Although Capitol Hill experts deny any intent to legalize personal spending, the FEC has interpreted the law's silence as an endorsement of wide latitude in spending.

"When asked, we say that House and Senate candidates have broad discretion on spending funds during a campaign," says Eiland.

Congress's own rules have long held personal use of campaign funds to be a violation of ethical standards. Senate Rule 38, for instance, says, "No contribution . . . shall be converted to the personal use of any member." Similarly, House members are forbidden to write off any purchase "not attributable to bona fide campaign purposes."

Side step. Enforcement is another matter. Historically, members have avoided questioning one another's spending. Critics cite huge loopholes such as House phrasing that allows each member to decide personally whether a particular expense is for political or official purposes.

The distinction is important because campaign funds spent on personal use are considered income—which the Internal Revenue Service says is taxable. Even so, according to experts, the IRS rarely checks on such spending.

The FEC originally was authorized to make random audits of campaign expenditures, but Congress removed that power in 1979, a move that Senator Charles Mathias (R-Md.) calls "an act of self-protection and self-interest which did a disservice to the election laws."

Mathias is among only a handful of lawmakers willing to publicly discuss campaign-spending practices. Even Representative Louis Stokes (D-Ohio), chairman of the House Committee on Standards of Official Conduct, refuses to talk about ethics as it relates to political expenditures.

Bound by so few constraints, members are constantly coming up with new uses for campaign money.

Several lawmakers used such funds to pay rent last year. Representative Phillip Burton (D-Calif.) spent more than $11,000 for lodging at San Francisco's Sir Francis Drake Hotel. Burton notes that he could have charged his hometown lodging to the taxpayers but says that he considered it fairer to pay such bills out of campaign funds.

Storage. A campaign committee for Representative Lawrence Coughlin (R-Pa.) paid $2,566 for part of the rent and utilities for his residence where, an aide says, Coughlin stores campaign records.

Some members used campaign funds for legal fees. Representative John Paul Hammerschmidt (R-Ark.) paid $20,000 to an Arkansas firm. His campaign manager's only comment: "They were bona fide political expenses."

The report of Representative John Murtha (D-Pa.) lists $26,000 in legal fees involving the so-called Abscam cases. His press aide said the expenses were approved by the House committee that Stokes heads. Murtha was mentioned but accused of no wrongdoing in the cases, in which seven lawmakers were indicted on bribery and other charges. He testified in one of the trials.

Under an antinepotism law, members may not have close relatives on their official payroll. But relatives are permitted on a campaign payroll.

Says former Representative Holland, whose wife was a paid worker in his campaign: "By profession, she's a bookkeeper, and she kept my campaign books for half the price I would have had to pay on the market."

Five of the six children of Senator Frank Murkowski (R-Alaska) received a total of $17,750 for working in their father's campaign office.

Paula Hawkins (R-Fla.) paid her son Kevin $11,850 for his services as a certified public accountant during and after her 1980 race for the Senate.

Thousands of campaign dollars were spent on travel for members' spouses. The campaign manager for Representative Henry Hyde (R-Ill.) explains the $1,036 in airline tickets purchased for Mrs. Hyde: "She's his most valuable campaign asset, and anytime I want her in the district, we reimburse her expenses."

Some lawmakers paid for their spouses' travel overseas. Representative Badham spent $3,380 for his wife to go with him to Germany, where he attended a North Atlantic Assembly meeting.

The expenses were paid from campaign funds, said a Badham aide, because they enhanced Badham's political image. The dresses for Mrs. Badham, he said, "were worn to events at the White House and the inauguration. People in his district expect them to look and áct like members of Congress."

Other members used campaign money to pay moving costs. Senator Jeremiah Denton, Jr. (R-Ala.) spent $3,808; Representative Kent Hance (D-Tex.) paid $11,813 to move two of his staffers.

Representative Mervyn Dymally (D-Calif.) makes loans to staffers out of campaign money. He loaned $2,000, $500 and $700 to staff members in 1981, and $500 to another in 1982. The loans are being repaid bit by bit, Dymally says.

Those who tapped their campaign treasuries for parties included Representative Dan Rostenkowski (D-Ill.), chairman of the House Ways and Means Committee, who threw a $2,309 Christmas party for the committee and staff.

Disclosure reports also list several cases in which campaign funds were tapped for decorating congressional offices. Representative Doug Barnard (D-Ga.) paid $5,370 for draperies and decorator's fees for his Georgia office. From her campaign money, Senator Hawkins spent $760 for draperies and $439 for refrigerators in her offices. Senator Spark Matsunaga (D-Hawaii) purchased a $365 microwave oven for his local office.

Among other expenditures: Representative Cecil Heftel (D-Hawaii) paid $2,186 for macadamia nuts and candy that he gave to House colleagues. Senator Christopher Dodd (D-Conn.) spent $650 to reimburse a campaign staffer for four suits that had been stolen while on the campaign trail. Representative Gus Yatron (D-Pa.), who stores campaign records at home, outfitted his residence with a security system costing $3,058.

Senator John Tower (R-Tex.) used campaign funds to pay $2,000 each in honorariums to Senators Denton, Strom Thurmond (R-S.C.) and Pete Domenici (R-N.M.) for their appearances at Tower's 20th-anniversary dinner in 1982.

Call for tighter controls. No one knows precisely how much was spent in all the races for Congress in 1982, but when all the bills are added up, experts believe the figure could top 300 million dollars.

With spending almost certain to soar even higher in 1984, some members of Congress are stressing the need for tighter controls and urging their colleagues to face up to campaign-finance abuses before it is too late. Said Senator Proxmire to *U.S. News & World Report:* "At some time in the future, some reporter is going to get on top of it all, and all hell is going to break loose."

Mathias, Representative Bill Frenzel (R-Minn.) and others want Congress to reinstate the FEC's authority to conduct random audits of political expenditures. Others believe that clearer campaign-spending rules and penalties would solve the problem.

But, so far, no groundswell has developed in Congress for a hard look at campaign spending. Although dear to their hearts, the subject remains a Pandora's box that most lawmakers prefer not to open.

KATHRYN JOHNSON

PAC's AMERICANA:
THE THREAT OF POLITICAL ACTION COMMITTEES

"A government of the people, by the people, and for the people can not be a government where influence is purchasable through substantial campaign contributions."

Jim Leach

Rep. Leach (R.-Iowa), a member of the House Banking, Finance, and Urban Affairs Committee, makes a point of not accepting PAC contributions.

IN recent months, the public limelight has revealed a number of troublesome shortcomings in the Congressional decision-making process. Americans with varied political philosophies have become alarmed by the perception of a Congress influenced less by the need for fair and open debate than by the legislative agendas of power elites.

Our Founding Fathers labored to create a representative democracy accountable to the common concerns of individual citizens. They protested, for instance, not just high levels of taxation, but taxation *without representation*. This political tradition was perhaps best expressed by theologian Reinhold Niebuhr when he noted that "the temper and the integrity with which the political fight is waged is more important for the health of our society than any particular policy."

Against this cultural backdrop, it is therefore difficult for Americans not to be disheartened by the revelations that an estimated $80,000,000 of special-interest funds were distributed to candidates in the last Congressional election. The magnitude of special-interest giving stretches thin the fabric of American democracy. At issue in the largest sense is how the democratic process works. At issue in a more immediate sense is the ability of Congress to make public policy decisions in the public interest.

Moneyed interests have always played a role in the political process. However, what distinguishes the conflict-of-interest problem today from that faced by legislators in the first two centuries of our country's existence is the increased cost of campaigns and the concomitant dependence by candidates on those who provide the capacity to purchase radio, television, and newspaper advertising and the kaleidoscope of campaign paraphernalia so characteristic of modern politics.

Special-interest campaign contributions are distributed today largely through legal entities known as political action committees or PAC's. While not an unprecedented phenomenon in American political history, PAC's through sheer size have taken on a new dimension in the last decade. Now one of America's largest growth industries, PAC's have grown sixfold in number and tenfold in dollar contributions since 1972.

Virtually all labor unions and several thousand business and professional groups sponsor PAC's, as do many liberal and conservative causes. The vast majority represent only a narrow fraction of the public viewpoint. The wide-ranging economic, social, and foreign policy concerns of the common citizen are seldom the *raison d'etre* of any PAC. The totality of PAC giving reflects a spectrum of special interests which not infrequently are at variance one from another, but PAC's make no pretense of representing a full spectrum of societal concerns. Unmoneyed interests simply aren't represented by moneyed PAC's.

Several of the largest PAC's—those associated with the American Medical Association, the National Association of Realtors, the National Conservative Political Action Committee (NCPAC), and the United Auto Workers—contributed several million dollars each in the 1982 election. Oil and gas PAC's contributed more money to candidates than did the Democratic National Committee. Still, it is a myth to assume the Republican Party is the primary beneficiary of PAC giving. Actually, the primary beneficiaries are one definable group—incumbents. Whereas labor is partisanly oriented, funding Democrats by a 20-to-one margin, business interests are more power-oriented and generally split their contributions about evenly between the parties. The largest recipients are invariably the most powerful members of Congress—who, for most of the past 30 years, have been Democrats.

In the last two elections, business and professional PAC's have become somewhat more Republican-oriented, but only by a narrow margin. While there was a concerted effort in the 1980 election to target incumbents considered particularly liberal and particularly vulnerable, business and professional PAC's in last November's races pulled in their horns and concentrated on protecting their favorite incumbents. The ideological PAC's, notably on the Right, kept a heavy emphasis, in most cases unsuccessfully, on defeating incumbents, but the vast majority of PAC money went to well-known incumbents or candidates in races where no incumbent challenged for the seat.

It may be debatable how nefarious or constructive PAC participation has been in recent campaigns, but, if the growing role of PAC's is a guide to the future, it would appear that both labor and business are girding for future Armageddons—political campaigns that in quantum magnitudes are likely to be more expensive than Americans have ever experienced.

If this trend toward more expensive races and thus heavier financial obligations for candidates is not curbed, individuals elected to Congress will increasingly become indebted to either big business or big labor. Congress will become a legislative body where the small businessman, the farmer, the worker, and the ordinary citizen are only secondarily represented. In fact, it is no accident today that the middle class frequently bears a heavier tax burden than the rich; that small companies lack the tax advantages of the integrated oil companies; that discussions in Congress of tax cuts all too often lack reference to tax equity; and that inflation is the economic issue of the day.

Promises and obligations

The last point should be stressed —inflation is not unrelated to campaign financing abuses. The roots of inflation begin in Federal spending and Federal spending begins in promises and obligations, and all this begins with politicians.

It begins in the way campaigns are run, in politics as usual—in commitments to large contributors, no matter who they are.

In America today, the most effective way for a candidate to achieve support in a bid for legislative office is to isolate every identifiable group—especially moneyed groups—and announce support for the group's vested interest. However, going along with the most powerful interest groups inevitably leads either to the proliferation of Federal programs or the weakening of the tax structure. Fiscal balance and equitability are impossible to maintain after lawmakers—that is, the successful candidates—have committed themselves in advance to support specific tax advantages or government programs favoring those having made generous campaign contributions. America may be a society of individuals, but power groupings—not individuals—are represented in legislative bodies where money is the key determinant of election outcome.

A government of the people, by the people, and for the people can not be a government where influence is purchasable through substantial campaign contributions. The subordination of individual rights to indiscriminate moneyed influence is the subordination of representative democracy to institutional oligarchy.

It is simply a fact of life that, when big money in the form of group contributions enters the political arena, big obligations are entertained. Groups seldom reflect the same collective judgment as all their members. This is particularly true in labor unions today where labor PAC funds go almost exclusively to candidates of one political party, but where, in many instances, almost half the actual membership vote goes to candidates of the other. This problem is not exclusively one of labor leadership being out of step with membership. It is also true in many farm and corporate organizations where individual farmers and corporate executives often oppose the very candidates who the managers of their PAC's support.

This membership-leadership divergence of judgment is natural and largely irreconcilable since uniformity of views regarding political parties and candidates is not a hallmark of any part of the American free enterprise system as we know it today. If PAC funding battles go unchecked, it is quite conceivable that American political parties could increasingly become copies of European parties, and that group self-interest, rather than individual views, will be fought out in the electoral process.

Decisions for most organizations occur at the top, rather than the bottom, of the leadership ladder and, whether it be a corporate or union PAC, there is implicit peer or advancement pressure to con-

tribute. In the case of larger corporations and unions, abdication of local control over funds leads to the aggrandizement of power for a very few within organizations and thus within any government channel where the organizations' impact is felt. Individuals who control other people's money become power-brokers in an elitist society. Their views, not those of the small contributors to their association, become the views that carry influence.

More unfortunately, the perspective of power-brokers who control PAC funds is frequently that of out-of-state interests which have little to do with the concerns of individual constituents. The giving of a significant policy voice to people who have no ties with the state or area from which a member of Congress is elected is one of the most striking ingredients of modern politics. It weakens constituent ties to a Representative once elected; it also undercuts the desire of constituents either to contribute campaign funds in modest amounts or participate enthusiastically in volunteer activity.

This out-of-state giving problem is more than theoretical fancy. It is forcefully relevant to the nuts-and-bolts politics of rural America today. In my home state of Iowa, for instance, it is impressive how often in the last decade candidates for office from both principal political parties have found a determinative portion of their financial support coming from corporate or union groupings with few ties to the agriculture and small business that is Iowa's heritage.

Our forefathers designed a representative democracy for America—a democracy where the particular views of every state and Congressional district would be reflected in the legislative process. As today's candidates become increasingly dependent on special-interest contributions, however, constituencies become gerrymandered along interest-group lines. In nationalizing funding sources, PAC's have the effect of nationalizing electoral input. In smaller states particularly, Senate races have been disproportionately nationalized by interest groups in recent elections. Those who control PAC's understand, for instance, that a South Dakota Senator's vote carries as much weight as a California Senator's. Thus, rural states like South Dakota have found more money spent per voter than larger urban states, and frequently this money reflects interest groups' concerns alien to the state itself. The citizens of smaller states thus run the risk of becoming disenfranchised as their candidates develop effective indebtedness to out-of-state concerns.

Two recent Congressional issues underline the PAC giving problem. During the summer of 1981, Congress debated a variety of tax cut proposals which were sincerely offered to provide real tax relief to individual taxpayers and businesses. Looking beyond the smokescreen of political rhetoric, both political parties recognized that a strong public consensus existed in favor of efforts to stimulate savings and investment, improve our lagging rates of productivity, and generally provide financial incentives for healthier economic performance.

While public attention focused on debate relating to whether the tax cuts would be implemented over two years or three, an army of well-financed lobbyists prodded members of the Congressional tax-writing committees to include a number of technical, though expensive, amendments in tax legislation. The lobbyists were reinforced by political action committees which had donated hundreds of thousands of dollars during the 1980 elections. Their interest in the political process was rewarded with a series of special-interest amendments resulting in tens of billions of dollars in tax relief for the interest groups involved. Interestingly, while the Republican-supported tax bill prevailed, the Democratic alternative contained just about as many special-interest provisions, though packaged in somewhat different form. A substantial tax cut was in order, but the final legislation approved by Congress contained a series of egregious provisions that neither had been proposed by the White House nor considered by the American public.

An even more glaring example of special-interest pressure on Congress can be found in the legislation passed a year ago to authorize the pre-billing of consumers for the costs of the $50,000,000,000 Alaskan natural gas pipeline—regardless of whether the pipeline ever becomes operational or the high-priced gas becomes competitively marketable.

The oil and pipeline companies involved hired everyone from former Vice Pres. Walter Mondale and former Democratic Chairman Robert Strauss to some very prominent Republican lobbying firms to press their case. Bill Moyers, the CBS journalist who pointed out some of the conflicts of interest involved, told me that he had three signed affidavits indicating that, if enough members of one political party supported the pipeline project, that party's Congressional campaign treasury would be well-rewarded in the 1982 elections. Motives are always difficult to ascribe in any endeavor, but it would appear no accident that many so-called consumer activists cast silent votes in favor of legislation which represents what one member described as the biggest consumer rip-off in history.

Ideological PAC's

Attempts to influence the outcome of governmental decisions through the distribution of money is not new to American democracy. What appears to be new is the use, particularly by ideological PAC's, of political issues for profit. The ideological PAC's have in recent years used mass mail techniques to raise impressive sums of money, the preponderance of which goes to pay overhead, rather than to advance the causes espoused.

Some New Right fundraisers, for instance, appeal to fundamentalist values in their solicitations, but appear in their use of funds to stand less for the politics of morality than the politics of profit. New Left fundraisers, on the other hand, are using New Right scare tactics to invoke a countervailing fear on the Left, with the result being a break-down in responsible dialogue on such extraordinarily consequential issues as Social Security and oil and gas leasing.

This reliance on sensationalist and divisive rhetoric is the most pernicious aspect of the tactics of the ideological PAC's. There are, and always will be, a multiplicity of issues in American politics on which reasonable people may differ, but what distinguishes the ideological PAC's from business- and labor-oriented ones is the manner in which issues are joined and used for personal gain. Appealing to the lowest, rather than the highest, instinct in the American psyche, they have inundated the country with fundraising appeals that tear apart the ethic of tolerance which binds our society together.

Reinforcing fear and exaggerating biases in mail solicitations has become a new art form. The implications of the millions of pieces of hate literature sent out each year has yet to be adequately analyzed, but it bodes poorly for a pluralistic political system built on the premise of respect for minority views.

No legislative process can ever be perfect nor can decisions always be wise, but the public interest today demands that restraint be placed on the capacity, through hefty campaign contributions, of a few large interests to influence political decision-making.

What is needed is legislation capping—or, preferably, eliminating entirely—special-interest group giving in campaigns. The current fundraising system should be replaced with a public financing approach, perhaps involving a formula whereby public funds are used to match private in-state contributions to candidates. This type of domestic SALT agreement between big business and big labor is likely to be disliked by each, but it should work to the stark advantage of the individual citizen and taxpayer.

What is also needed is increased public attention to be focused on the tactics of the ideological PAC's. The spotlight of decency and tolerance should be turned on those who attempt to pick the pocket of concerned citizens by accentuating the negative.

America has always stood as a land of hope and opportunity. Those who play on the fears, rather than the aspirations, of citizens should not be rewarded in the political process. In politics, as in sports, it does matter how you play the game.

OFF THE BOOKS: Uncle Sam's Creative Accounting

James T. Bennett and Thomas J. DiLorenzo

JAMES T. BENNETT is professor of political economy and public policy, and THOMAS J. DILORENZO is assistant professor of economics, at George Mason University.

AS GOVERNMENTS at all levels have increased taxes, ever more restricting the ability of Americans to accumulate wealth, taxpayers have been moving hundreds of billions of dollars beyond the reach of the tax collector. This growth in the so-called underground economy—economic activities not reported in official statistics because of their illegality or the simple desire to avoid taxes—is perhaps the ultimate stage of the tax revolt of the 1970s and '80s. The first stage of the revolt was characterized by numerous statutory and constitutional limitations on state and local government taxing and spending powers, such as Proposition 13 in California, and the campaign to add a balanced-budget or tax-limitation amendment to the federal Constitution.

But the response of government to this tax revolt has received much less attention. The politicians are every bit as calculating as ordinary citizens, and evade constraints placed on their ability to accumulate wealth and power. For nearly a century, state and local governments have responded to taxpayer revolts, and the consequent limitations on taxing, spending, and borrowing, by giving lip service to fiscal responsibility while simultaneously creating scores of "off-budget enterprises" (OBEs) to conduct business as usual. Taxpayer demands for fiscal responsibility have also spawned increased "off-budget" activities by the federal government. In short, just as tax-imposed constraints on individual incomes have provided an impetus for the growth of the underground private economy, taxpayer-induced constraints on the politician's "income" have generated a growth of the "underground government."

Federal spending is hidden and kept off the budget in three different ways. First, numerous agencies have simply not been listed in the official budget. Second, government has guaranteed loans made to specially privileged individuals, businesses, and governments. Third, government has sponsored and controlled privately owned enterprises, such as the Federal National Mortgage Association, that are also off-the-books borrowers. (Federal politicians have also increasingly recognized that almost anything that can be accomplished through taxing and spending can also be accomplished by regulation.)

Placing agencies off-budget is the most obvious subterfuge for hiding spending. The Congressional Budget and Impoundment Control Act of 1974 has been widely praised as "a revolutionary budget reform intended to give Congress a tighter grip on the nation's purse strings." The act was passed because the budgetary process was biased toward overspending and budget deficits: The total amount of federal spending had no explicit limit, for it was the product of many individual appropriations decisions.

The Budget Act made total taxing, spending, and deficit levels explicit and held Congress accountable for them. It did nothing to curb spending, but even its mild budgetary discipline elicited a great amount of "back-door" federal spending, as numerous agencies have been and continue to be placed off-budget and beyond the purview of the appropriations process. With antics that would earn the envy of Houdini, Congress has preached fiscal responsibility while practicing fiscal profligacy. By 1981, off-budget spending hit $21 billion (see table), though it fell in 1982 for the first time since 1975. Off-budget spending grew by 35,000 percent between 1973 and 1981. Most recently, the Strategic Petroleum Reserve was placed off-budget.

The penchant for back-door spending is nonpartisan: Both the Democratic-controlled House and the Republican-controlled Senate, at the insistence of the

Reagan administration, voted to place the Strategic Petroleum Reserve off the books. There have even been bipartisan proposals for placing the entire social security program, which accounts for nearly one-fourth of the federal budget, off-budget.

The Federal Financing Bank (FFB) is the most active off-budget agency serving as an intermediary to place federal spending off-budget. The FFB, a part of the Treasury Department, does business with both on- and off-budget agencies. Its predominant activity is to purchase agency debt using funds borrowed directly from the Treasury. FFB borrowing is not included as part of the Treasury's budget outlays; interest payments from the FFB to the Treasury are, nevertheless, counted as deductions from Treasury outlays. Consequently, FFB borrowing results in a *reduction* in outlays reported by the Treasury Department.

The FFB also purchases agency loans or loan assets. When a federal agency sells a loan to a private entity, the loan is considered repaid by the budget. The same happens when the FFB is the purchaser: Proceeds from the sale are counted as loan repayments rather than as a means of financing. Thus an agency's on-budget loan can be converted to an off-budget loan by selling it to the FFB, as about 85 percent of all federal agency loans and loan asset sales were in 1982. Or an agency can sometimes pool its loans and issue securities backed by the pooled loans. These securities, called "Certificates of Beneficial Ownership," are then purchased by the FFB; this simple process places them off-budget. The agency has more cash to loan, and can repeat the process as many times as it chooses, which allows it to make loans to privileged customers with virtually no budgetary limit.

Finally, the FFB can grant off-budget loans to guaranteed borrowers. Typically, a federal agency guarantees a loan between a private lender and a private borrower. The borrower gets an interest subsidy at no *explicit* cost to the Treasury unless a borrower defaults. Frequently, however, an agency will ask the FFB to act as the private lender by purchasing the borrower's note. The loan guarantee becomes, in effect, a direct loan from the government that is not reflected in the budget. In 1982 such FFB purchases of loan guarantees amounted to $13.6 billion.

THESE various activities of the FFB give federal politicians a virtual blank check, with no *direct* budgetary consequences, with which to subsidize favored interest groups. The political costs of this federal largesse from taxpayers' retaliation are significantly reduced because the pork-barreling is hidden from public view.

The FFB also provides greater opportunities for nonelected government bureaucrats to build empires at taxpayer expense. One example is the $2 billion in off-budget loans recently extended to the Tennessee Valley Authority (TVA), itself a federally sponsored off-budget enterprise.

In 1979 the TVA decided its nuclear-fuel inventory had become excessive due to nuclear power-plant construction delays. To eliminate this burden from its books, the TVA created a wholly owned subsidiary—the Seven States Energy Corporation—to purchase TVA's nuclear-fuel inventory and then lease it back to the TVA as needed. To finance the arrangement, the TVA originally approached a private investment banking firm, which suggested a $1 billion line of credit. Before the agreement was completed, however, the Treasury Department suggested that the FFB provide the loan, and increase it to $2 billion. Thus the TVA essentially extended a $2 billion line of credit to itself without even congressional review. The implications of this with respect to the federal government's role in allocating credit—a role that it has consistently mishandled with regard to both equity and efficiency—is far-reaching. According to the act creating the FFB, *any* entity wholly owned by the federal government has this access to

OFF-BUDGET OUTLAYS BY AGENCY
(billions of dollars)

	1973	1974	1975	1976	TQ†	1977	1978	1979	1980	1981	1982
Federal Financing Bank (1974)	—	.1	6.4	5.9	2.6	8.2	10.6	13.2	14.5	21.0	14.1
Rural Electrification and Telephone Revolving Fund (1973)	.1	.5	.5	.2	−.1	.4	.1	−*	−*	*	*
Rural Telephone Bank (1973)	*	.1	.1	.1	*	.1	.1	.1	.2	.1	.1
United States Postal Service Fund (1974)	—	.8	1.1	1.1	−.7	−.2	−.5	−.9	−.4	.1	−.6
United States Railway Association (1973)	—	—	*	.1	*	.2	.1	.1	*	−.3	−*
Strategic Petroleum Reserve (1982)	—	—	—	—	—	—	—	—	—	—	3.7
Total Off-Budget Outlays	.1	1.5	8.1	7.4	1.8	8.7	10.4	12.5	14.3	20.9	17.3

*less than $50 million

†TQ refers to the "Transitional Quarter" that occurred when the federal government shifted from a July–June fiscal year to an October–September fiscal year.

SOURCE: Office of Management and Budget, *Federal Government Finances, 1984 Budget Data,* February 1983.

off-budget federal financing. At least twenty such entities already exist and have the legal authority to order the FFB to lend money to anyone, provided that they guarantee the loan.

In addition to the functions of the FFB there are more than 150 loan-guarantee programs, administered by federal agencies, that comprise yet another category of off-budget operations. Loan guarantees to individuals, businesses, state and local governments, and foreign governments are only reflected in the budget if the borrower defaults to a private bank, in which case the federal government is liable for part or all of the principal and interest on the loan. Loan guarantees serve the same purpose as direct government expenditures: They provide transfer payments to select groups at the expense of the general public. The major difference, of course, between the two types of subsidies is that loan guarantees are far less visible and do not arouse as much taxpayer resistance.

Guaranteed loans are often (mistakenly) not considered to be subsidies. The partial or full guarantee of such loans, however, permits the favored borrowers to borrow at reduced interest rates. Because of the hidden nature of these interest subsidies, loan guarantees have become the largest component of federal credit activity, accounting for almost two-thirds of it—$118.3 billion in 1982, compared to $27.5 billion in direct off-budget loans, and $40.1 billion in on-budget loans. They are also the fastest-growing type of federal credit activity, having increased by 360 percent since 1974.

The costs of federal loan-guarantee programs, like the benefits, are indirect. But as with most government spending programs, the benefits of loan guarantees accrue to well-organized interest groups, while the costs are widely dispersed among the general public. The indirect cost of federal loan guarantees is borne primarily by less-favored borrowers who are crowded out of the credit market or who must pay higher interest rates on the loans that they obtain. Loan guarantees tend to increase the overall demand for credit while reducing the supply of credit available to nonguaranteed borrowers. The rates charged to nonguaranteed borrowers increase to levels higher than they would otherwise be, which crowds out much private borrowing by businesses and individuals.

Instances of private businesses and investments crowded out by government-sponsored investments are many. In 1980, for example, when a 20 percent prime rate and 16 percent consumer-loan rate contributed to the bankruptcy of thousands of small businesses such as auto dealerships and grocery stores, the Rural Electrification Administration started a new program to provide thirty-five-year loans at 5 percent interest to finance rural cable-TV systems. Rural home mortgages were available at 3.3 percent, and insured student loans went for 7 percent.

The loan-guarantee process seriously distorts the market process, which would leave borrowers free to compete without political advantages and which would allocate credit to its most highly valued uses, enhancing economic growth. This is so because credit markets evaluate the riskiness of alternative projects, and (to meet consumer demand) charge higher borrowing costs to those with higher probabilities of failure. In this way, the credit markets provide consumers and producers with invaluable information regarding the most productive uses of resources. Loan guarantees, by socializing risk, make it impossible for consumers and producers to accurately calculate real costs, and resources are put to lower-valued uses. At times when high interest rates force private firms to invest in only the most productive projects promising very high yields, federally assisted borrowers may continue to invest in projects that yield only a fraction of what the nonguaranteed investments yield. Thus the federal government is actively subsidizing inefficient investments, reducing the productivity of the nation's capital stock, and consequently lowering the rate of economic growth. The slower rate of economic growth is, of course, accompanied by higher inflation and higher unemployment.

I T IS difficult, if not impossible, to gauge the amount of crowding out caused by federal loan guarantees, but some esti-

mates have been made. Economist Herbert M. Kaufman of the University of Arizona studied federal loan guarantees and figured that for every $1 billion in loan guarantees, between $736 million and $1.32 billion in private investment is crowded out. These are rough estimates, but they nevertheless indicate that loan guarantees, which are being extended at a rate of over $100 billion per year, have a profound negative impact on economic growth, employment, and inflation.

Federal loan guarantees, once extended, are often used to influence the behavior of the recipients of the subsidies. Once a firm or an industry is dependent upon government financial assistance, the dependence is often used as a lever to impose additional regulatory controls that may be totally unrelated to the government's potential financial liability. For example, the Federal Housing Administration, which administers the largest loan-guarantee program, attempts to implement various social policies by vetoing a loan application if a builder does not comply with the FHA's regulations on marketing to minority groups, environmental-impact statements, architectural review, minimum wages, and so on. Because the responsibility for enforcing these objectives is divided, considerable confusion and delay usually arise, which increase housing construction costs. Efforts to deregulate the private sector are sure to be confounded by these sorts of regulations, which accompany the rapidly growing volume of loan guarantees.

Government-sponsored "off-budget enterprises" are yet another form of federal off-budget operations. The principal types of federal OBEs engage in credit activity; they include the Federal National Mortgage Association, the Farm Credit Administration, the Federal Home Loan Banks, the Federal Home Loan Mortgage Corporation, and the Student Loan Marketing Association. These agencies once were on-budget, but their large and rapidly expanding borrowings began to embarrass Congress, which then voted to take the agencies out of the budget in 1968.

Though privately owned, these agencies were originally chartered by the federal government, are subjected to government supervision, and by law must consult the Treasury Department in planning the marketing of their debt. In addition, many of their board members are presidential appointees, and various decisions must be cleared by other government agencies as well as the Treasury. (For example, many of the Federal National Mortgage Association's actions must be approved by the secretary of HUD.) These agencies are also granted special preferences and certain tax exemptions, which allow them to borrow funds for governmentally authorized purposes at rates only slightly above the Treasury's own rates, and then lend the money to favored groups. Thus federal OBEs are private in name only, and are yet another way in which the federal government directly allocates billions of dollars of credit without being subject to the budget-review process. By 1984 the estimated volume of borrowing by federal OBEs will be about $56.2 billion, with more than $337.3 billion in debt outstanding.

The underground federal government has ominous implications for those attempting to constrain the growth of government with constitutional restrictions. In fact, such constraints, among others, have been in effect at the state and local level for nearly 100 years, but have been routinely evaded by the simple expedient of redefining the budget—in particular by creating OBEs owned by one or more political jurisdictions (often referred to as authorities, districts, commissions, agencies, boards, and so on). There are thousands of OBEs at the local level, including more than 2400 in Pennsylvania alone. Their activities include the entire spectrum of "governmental" functions, from airports to zoo maintenance, and are financed by issuing nonguaranteed (and not voter-approved) revenue bonds. Such bonds are backed not by taxes, but by user fees from the services provided. Although OBEs are, in theory, "financially independent," they are typically heavily subsidized by other units of government. The managers of OBEs are usually patronage appointees who enjoy far greater discretion than do managers of regular governmental departments. In most cases, OBEs are exempt from compliance with civil-service restrictions, pay no taxes or license fees (as private firms do), are not regulated by public utility commissions, are exempt from compliance with many federal regulations, and may have

powers of eminent domain that extend beyond the boundaries of the political entity that created them. Moreover, the expenditures, borrowing, and employment of OBEs are not reported in the official statistics of the political jurisdictions that form them.

The principal reason OBEs are created is to subvert taxpayer demands for fiscal restraint. An example of how this device has been used is provided by Nelson Rockefeller, who, as governor of New York, became the nation's foremost architect of OBE schemes.

New York States does have a constitutionally imposed referendum requirement for all state borrowing, but it has had little impact. In the late 1950s voters rejected a $100 million housing bond issue for the third time; Governor Rockefeller created the off-budget Housing Finance Authority, which issued massive amounts of nonguaranteed debt, at one point in excess of the entire guaranteed (voter-approved) debt of New York State. In 1961 voters rejected a $500 million higher-education bond issue for the fourth time; the governor created the off-budget State University Construction Fund. In 1965 voters rejected, for the fifth time, a housing bond issue; Rockefeller created the Urban Development Corporation. By 1975, 81 percent of the total outstanding debt was the nonguaranteed debt of OBEs. Such debts contributed substantially to the state's new bankruptcy in 1974.

ROCKEFELLER was somewhat more brazen than most politicians, but his political instincts are common. Others have followed his example and created thousands of OBEs. Indeed, the off-budget state and local public sector rivals in size the on-budget sector: Of $43.5 billion in new issues of state and local government securities in

1979, $31.3 billion, or 71 percent, was nonguaranteed revenue bonds issued by OBEs. This compares to only $6.1 billion in nonguaranteed debt issued in 1970, about 34 percent of total security sales. State and local governments, though regarded by many as the "most responsive" to taxpayers, are also largely beyond the control and scrutiny of the electorate.

For decades American taxpayers have attempted to reduce the burden of government by limiting taxes, spending, and borrowing. To placate voters (and pacify lenders) state politicians have enacted both constitutional and statutory constraints on the fiscal powers of government. However, such limitations have had little impact on the expansion of public-sector activities, for off-budget enterprises not subject to direct voter control have been established on an enormous scale nationwide.

At the federal level, pressures have been building for fiscal restraint: More than thirty state legislatures have called for a constitutional convention to adopt a balanced-budget amendment, and public-opinion surveys reveal that a strong majority of America's taxpayers favor such an amendment. But the balanced-budget amendment is unlikely to be a truly effective constraint on federal spending so long as politicians are permitted to engage in the budgetary magic of off-budget spending. Politicians will continue to subvert the wishes of taxpaying citizens, because such fiscal limitations restrict their ability to accumulate power and wealth.

Unfortunately, the process of government involves an inherent conflict between the objectives of politicians and the taxpaying citizens whom they govern. Only when people recognize this fact about government are we likely to see truly effective constraints placed on its size and growth, and on the perpetual plundering of the taxpayer's purse. In the meantime, politicians should be held fully accountable for *all* spending and borrowing, both on- and off-budget. The point is, if these activities are "legitimate" functions of government, then why are they so well hidden from their supposed beneficiaries, namely, the American taxpayers?

Bureaucracy and The Bomb:

THE HIDDEN FACTOR BEHIND NUCLEAR MADNESS

Fred Kaplan

Fred Kaplan writes on defense for the Boston Globe. *This article is an excerpt from his book,* The Wizards of Armageddon

For all the recent talk about a nuclear freeze and halting the arms race, too little attention has been paid to explaining just how we got into our current predicament. Notions that rightfully strike most of us as absurd—shuttling MX missiles around on an underground racetrack, digging foxholes to protect against a nuclear blast—have not been the products of Dr. Strangelovian scientists, but of quite ordinary government officials, adhering to some very common rules of bureaucratic behavior.

One of those rules is quite familiar to the readers this magazine—the propensity of individual military services to protect and expand their own turf. The Army wants its short-range nuclear missiles for Europe, the Navy wants more nuclear submarines, and the Air Force wants both the B-1 bomber and the MX. But inter-service rivalries have done more than influence decisions on deploying specific weapons; they have also shaped the most basic tenets of the nation's nuclear strategy. The article that follows describes the origins of the most important of these rivalries— the one between the Air Force and Navy—and illustrates how bureaucratic jealousies have been a major force behind the irrational proliferation of nuclear weapons.

The inter-service rivalry over nuclear strategy between the Air Force and the Navy first broke out in 1949. In reaction to severe budget cuts, the top echelon of naval officers broke all traditions of subordination and publicly testified against the official emphasis being placed on the atom bomb, on the Strategic Air Command, and on the Air Force's B-36 bombers—at the expense of more traditional modes and weapons of combat, as represented by the Army and the Navy.

The chief Navy testimony came from Rear Admiral Ralph Ofstie. Ofstie had served on the U.S. Strategic Bombing Survey shortly after World War II and had been among those who concluded that the Army Air Force's strategic bombing had accomplished little for all the resources and lives that the effort had cost. In public congressional hearings in 1949, Ofstie condemned Air Force plans for strategic nuclear bombing as "ruthless and barbaric. . . random mass slaughter of men, women and children. . . militarily unsound. . .

morally wrong. . . contrary to our fundamental ideals. . . ."

The Navy's arguments were to no avail; support for SAC Air Power within Congress was too strong to be crumbled. So in 1951 the Navy started to assemble its own atomic arsenal. Suddenly the atomic bomb was no longer so "barbaric." Some naval officers even began to argue, along Air Force lines, that atomic bombs should be used at the outset of a conflict. Admiral Arthur Radford, as Eisenhower's Joint Chiefs of Staff chairman, later became the most vociferous proponent of John Foster Dulles's "massive retaliation" policy, the doctrine that called for the U.S. to unleash its entire nuclear arsenal against Soviet population centers upon even a small provocation.

In the mid-1950s the Navy began work on a project that would prove truly threatening to the Air Force—the nuclear-powered Polaris submarine. Each Polaris would hold 16 nuclear missiles; by continuously moving underwater these subs would be virtually impossible to detect or track. With a growing number of studies showing the vulnerability of SAC bases to a surprise Russian attack, the Polaris suddenly looked like a superior weapon for purposes of "massive retaliation." As one Navy captain told an Air Force friend, Colonel Richard Yudkin, assistant director of Air Force plans, "We've got something that's going to put you guys out of business."

In 1958, Admiral Arleigh Burke, chief of naval operations and the driving force behind the Polaris program, approved a study by the Naval Warfare Analysis Group (NAVWAG), "National Policy Implications of Atomic Parity." The study asserted that SAC's strategy—increasing the number of bombers and missiles as the Soviet buildup made them more vulnerable—could only be seen as a "prescription for an arms race, and an invitation to the enemy for preventive-war adventurism." NAVWAG's way to "get off the arms race treadmill" was to secure the strategic force through "mobility and concealment" in submarines rather than in the "hardening and active defense" of bombers, missiles, and anti-missile missiles. And, to avoid "the provocative over-inflation of our strategic forces, their size should be set by an objective of generous *adequacy for deterrence alone* (i.e., for an ability to destroy major urban areas), not by the false goal of adequacy for 'winning.'"

The Navy, in its new official line, had come full circle: from an abhorrence of city destruction in 1949 to its doctrinal glorification in 1958. The one consistent element in this 180-degree shift was opposition to whatever the Air Force happened to be plugging at the time. Since submarine-launched missiles would lack the accuracy to hit anything but enemy cities, the Navy urged that the necessary number of strategic weapons be kept to a minimum, restricting targets to major enemy cities (of which there were only a couple of hundred), and thereby making a strong case for putting all the strategic weapons underwater.

The NAVWAG study also pointed out that with the money saved from not having to build an "excessive" number of nuclear weapons, the U.S. conventional force could be built up so that in the age of "atomic parity" Soviet aggression at "lower levels of conflict" would not result in the free world's getting "nibbled to death." It was this sort of argument that frightened Air Force officers to distraction. There was a genuine logic to the Navy case and it was just the sort of thing that could do the Air Force in.

The Navy promulgated the message of NAVWAG through all available channels. Admiral Burke delivered speeches on the virtues of a mobile deterrent geared to the threat to destroy enemy cities ("mutual deterrence") and the dangers of relying on the current vulnerable land-based force. An unclassified version of the study was sent out in a letter to all retired naval officers with instructions to speak out on these issues in public as much as they could. General

Tommy Power, commander of SAC, obtained a copy of this letter and sent it to General Tommy White, Air Force chief, adding that "we would be well advised to match this action in concept and to exceed it in distribution." As the director of Air Force plans and policy, General Hewitt Wheless, wrote to his SAC counterpart, General Charles "Westy" Westover, in May 1959, "There is an all-out battle going on right now."

Bureaucratic Fallout

More disturbing to officials like White was that the Air Force, especially SAC, in the construction of its own targeting plans and philosophy, was setting itself up for this Navy onslaught. The Air Force war plan involved destroying an "optimal mix" of urban and military targets. The report of an April 1959 "Coordination Conference" between SAC and Britain's Bomber Command referred to city destruction as the "Primary Undertaking" and destruction of military targets as the "Alternative Undertaking."

Tommy White conveyed his concern to Tommy Power: "This would lead to the conclusions. . . that attacking 'cities' constitutes the most important segment of the strategic effort. This conclusion would not only be used as further justification of Polaris but. . . also be used as a strong position (which is already emerging) to eliminate virtually any strategic requirement other than Polaris, i.e., SAC."

Under siege, the Air Force sought aid from a familiar ally: the RAND Corporation, a think-tank in Santa Monica, California. At Rand a new strategic concept was emerging—one that seemed ideal for the current battle with the Navy—called "counterforce/no-cities targeting." This strategy had been developed over the previous decade by an analyst named William Kaufmann and his colleagues as an alternative to the doctrine of massive retaliation. The obvious drawback of massive retaliation was that it called for an all-out nuclear attack even if the Soviet Union lobbed only one bomb on, or moved one brigade against, West Germany. This struck many as foolish over-reaction now that the Soviets had the H-bomb, too; NATO allies also understandably wondered if the United States would really risk nuclear holocaust on their behalf. As General De Gaulle put it, would America really be willing to sacrifice New York to save Paris?

Kaufmann's counterforce doctrine sought to avoid that dilemma by proposing that Soviet aggression initially be met with a nuclear attack that included only military targets. The Soviets would realize that a retaliatory strike against our cities with their few remaining bombs would cause us to obliterate their cities. Thus, the Soviets would restrict their retaliation to military targets, too—or perhaps not retaliate at all and surrender. This idea that a nuclear war could be limited and perhaps even "won" was central to Kaufmann's counterforce doctrine—and could even be seen as "liberal" and "humane" in comparison with John Foster Dulles's policy of massive retaliation. Most important, Polaris could play only a limited rôle in such a strategy; as Kaufmann observed in a February 1, 1960, memo entitled "The Puzzle of Polaris," the Navy's missiles lacked the explosive yield and accuracy to allow the U.S. "to pursue meaningful counterforce and damage-limiting strategies."

In June 1960 Kaufmann got a call from George Tanham, RAND's liaison with the Air Force Staff, asking him to come to Washington. Tanham had been talking with an Air Force general named Noel Parrish, who was worried that the Air Force was about to take a beating from the Navy. Tanham had told Parrish that Kaufmann had some reassuring ideas.

Parrish, who had been involved in some of the earlier disputes over the worth of aircraft carriers versus land-based bombers, hated the Navy. But he was no SAC lackey. As early as 1950 he wrote speeches for Air Force Chiefs of Staff Hoyt Vandenberg and Nathan Twining that entertained the notion of using the bomb against military targets only. So it was only logical that in June 1960, when Kaufmann told Parrish that his solution to the "Polaris Puzzle" was to alter SAC's strategy to attacking military targets only, avoiding destruction of enemy cities as long as the enemy avoids destruction of our cities, Parrish's eyes lit up.

Parrish was now assistant deputy for coordination under the director of Air Force plans. He had just put together a briefing, a compilation of all Air Force statements over the past year on targeting and strategy, to show just how inconsistent they were and to show that the Air Force really didn't have a strategy strong enough to beat the Polaris. When he gave the briefing to General Curtis LeMay, the vice chief of staff, LeMay had been dismissive of counterforce, saying that SAC studies showed that no matter what our targeting or Russian targeting might be, the number of people killed on both sides remained about the same. LeMay, though for completely different reasons, shared the belief of many modern critics of nuclear policy that a "limited nuclear war" was nonsense.

To help sway LeMay, Parrish arranged for Kaufmann to do a study on counterforce with particular concentration on comparing casualties under the different targeting plans. During the early summer of 1960, Kaufmann and two young RAND analysts—David McGarvey and Frank Trinkl—slaved away on a mathematical model they had developed for this purpose, working through the numbers and taking them through dozens of permutations.

The team's initial findings were as dramatic as Parrish hoped. One scenario, corresponding to the Navy's city-destruction strategy, had the Soviets launch a surprise attack against our SAC and submarine bases. The United States orders a full-scale retaliatory strike against Soviet urban-industrial targets with the small number of Atlas and Titan ICBMs, Polaris missiles, and alert B-52 bombers that have survived. The Soviets react by destroying our cities. The results: Three-quarters of the American population, 150 million people, dead; 60 percent of U.S. industrial capacity destroyed. By comparison, 40 million Russians, less than 20 percent of their population, are dead; about 40 percent of their industries are ruined.

In the second scenario, corresponding to SAC's Optimum Mix strategy, the Red Army attacks Western Europe. Conventional NATO forces cannot contain them, so SAC launches a full-scale attack against Soviet cities, airfields, missile sites, rail centers, shipyards, factories—all the targets. Several Soviet missiles and bombers escape the attack and rain destruction on as many American cities as they can. The result: Half the industrial base of both countries is destroyed; 75 million Russians are dead, 110 million Americans.

The third scenario, the counterforce/no-cities strategy, produces entirely different results. The Soviets attack Western Europe. Conventional forces cannot hold them; the U.S. launches a nuclear attack against the U.S.S.R. but restricts the targets to bomber fields, missile pads, submarine pens, and control centers associated with the Soviet Strategic Rocket Forces. The Soviets retaliate but, seeing that we have avoided their cities, find it in their interest to avoid ours as well, and likewise confine their attack to SAC striking forces. We "mop up" their remaining air defense and strategic forces, holding some of our weapons in a reserve force. We then send a message to the Russians, telling them to stop or else we will start picking off their cities one by one. The Soviets, clearly out-gunned, surrender. The war is over. Only three million Americans have died, and only five million Russians.

Parrish was thrilled. Kaufmann headed off to Washington to deliver a summary of the study to a larger, broader, and higher-level group of Air Force officers. Some of the officers had problems with Kaufmann's conception of counterforce. What if the Russians don't fight according to the counterforce rules? What if the "loser" uses his remaining weapons to destroy the "winner's" cities? Won't counterforce weaken the bedrock of nuclear deterrence and stimulate an arms race, resulting in heightened suspicion on both sides and higher danger of war by accident, miscalculation, or preemption?

Kaufmann was the first to admit to a whole series of uncertainties over how the war would actually proceed or end. But he was convinced that the threat of blowing up Soviet cities was inappropriate and not very credible now that the Soviets also had the power to blow up American cities. And in that context counterforce appeared to be the best hope in an awful situation.

Debate within the Air Force Staff came to a halt when General Tommy White, Air Force chief, embraced Kaufmann's briefing wholeheartedly.

As late as June 1958 White had told an audience of national-security specialists that he was "disturbed" by the recent tendency among some analysts "to consider seriously self-restraints in nuclear weapons planning in the face of sure knowledge that no such restraints will be applied by the enemy. Our preoccupation with niceties in nuclear warfare. . . would, I am sure, delight the Kremlin." Now, only two years later, White endorsed without reservation a strategy that imposed just such "self-restraints" and elevated to high wisdom the "preoccupation with niceties in nuclear warfare." The key difference between the summer of 1958 and the summer of 1960 was that the Polaris had evolved into a much more serious threat to the Air Force.

Convincing White was one thing; convincing SAC was something else entirely. On paper, SAC was merely one of several commands under the Air Force Staff's wings; in truth, it was a fiefdom, not easily challenged, much less defeated. And the commander of SAC in 1960, General Tommy Power, abhorred any departure from the strategic-bombing traditions of World War II.

Power was a brutal, easily angered man who struck Air Force Staff officers outside SAC as dim-witted and insensitive to the dilemmas that the bomb raised. Once, when Herman Kahn was briefing Power on the long-term genetic effects of nuclear weapons, Power suddenly chuckled, leaned forward in his chair, and said, "You know, it's not yet been proved to me that two heads aren't better than one." Even Kahn was outraged, and sternly lectured to Power that he should not discuss human life so cavalierly.

At Tommy White's repeated urgings, General Power finally agreed to hear Kaufmann's counterforce briefing. It took place at SAC headquarters in Omaha on December 12, 1960. Not two minutes into the lecture, Power interrupted with a long, angry tirade against everything that Kaufmann was saying.

"Why do you want us to restrain ourselves?" Power bellowed. "Restraint! Why are you so concerned with saving *their* lives? The whole idea is to *kill* the bastards!" After several minutes of this, he finally said, "Look. At the end of the war, if there are two Americans and one Russian, we win!"

Kaufmann—his patience exhausted—snapped back, "Well, you'd better make sure that they're a man and a woman." At that point, Power stalked out of the room. The briefing was over.

SIOPted

However much SAC abhorred the notion of limited nuclear war, it had no intention of letting the Navy gain the upper hand in nuclear strategy. It had other plans for maintaining its supremacy, and they revolved around something known as the Single Integrated Operational Plan.

The SIOP was ostensibly the creation of Thomas S. Gates Jr., secretary of defense in the last year of the Eisenhower administration. By mid-1960 it was becoming all too clear that nuclear weapons were multiplying out of control. Each Air Force Command had control over the detailed war planning of its own nuclear arsenal, as did the Navy fleets and the Army units with their battlefield weapons. As things stood, many targets in the Soviet Union would be struck by American weapons twice, three times, or more. All strategic nuclear weapons, Gates thought, should be integrated under a single planning command and targeted according to that command's direction.

By 1960, faced with the prospect of having to live with the Navy's Polaris, the Air Force turned to the SIOP as a way to co-opt the submarine by taking all nuclear targeting out of the hands of the Navy. The Air Force Staff's original position, ardently advocated by White, was to create a unified "Strategic Command," putting SAC in charge of all the strategic weapons of all the Air Force commands *and* of the Navy fleets, including the new Polaris missiles. When resistance from the Army and the Navy in the working committees of the Joint Chiefs of Staff proved too adamant, White adopted what he had previously planned as a "fallback position" for the Air Force: creating a Joint Strategic Target Planning Agency, which would maintain the separate services but integrate the targeting of all their weapons and designate the commander-in-chief of SAC as the director of Strategic Targeting.

By early August Admiral Burke, still chief of naval operations, got wind of what the Air Force was up to. One of his aides happened to be over at the Weapons Systems Evaluation Group—a JCS think-tank—to transmit some technical data, at the group's request. Two Air Force officers also happened to be there, and they started to tease him. "At last," one of them said, "we've got control of the Polaris."

"What are you talking about?" Burke's man asked.

"We've got it in the bag. The decision's been made," the Air Force rep snickered. "All you have to do is find out about it."

When it came to threats from the other services, Burke was even more sensitive, protective, and paranoid than his Air Force counterpart, Tommy White. The Polaris was Burke's conception: he had pushed it through an unwilling Navy bureaucracy; he had calculated the technical requirements; he had helped devise the doctrine that justified it strategically; he had led the assault on the Air Force, using the Polaris as the opening wedge of the attack. Burke knew he was in a bureaucratic shooting war, and he wasn't about to let the Air Force get hold of his Polaris.

Arleigh Burke counted a few Air Force officers among his friends, but he hated the Air Force as an organization. "This is just like Communism being here in the country," he said, after catching on to the Air Force's SIOP ambitions. To Burke's mind, the Air Force was doing to national security what Castro had done in Cuba. "They're smart and they're ruthless," he warned Navy Secretary William Franke. "It's the same way as the Communists. It's exactly the same techniques."

The effort by Gates and Eisenhower to integrate the services' nuclear war plans was long overdue. But Burke understood—and knew that White and Power also understood—the politics underlying war plans in a way that Gates and Eisenhower apparently did not. Burke knew that whichever service controlled the target list, made the rules, and defined the criteria of what degree of damage must be inflicted on what targets and with what probability would in effect be the service that decided how those weapons would be used, how many weapons of what type the nation should buy, and how much money should be spent on each service's nuclear weapons.

Burke feared that if SAC were allowed to invent the definitions and criteria, it would invent "damage-expectancy" numbers that would require SAC to build a lot more bombers. He also feared that SAC would give the Polaris missiles such tasks as destroying Soviet air-defense sites, "paving the way for the B-52s," or hitting highly blast-resistant targets, which the inaccurate Polaris missiles could not destroy, thus proving "that it takes 67 of them to knock out this target."

Burke's predictions and fears came close to the truth. Everywhere SAC Intelligence looked it found targets, thus justifying the need for more weapons. SAC assumed the Soviets would have 700 ICBMs by 1962, while the Navy thought there would be only 200. The Air Force won the battle, to the extent that there was one, and the result was 500 extra targets, requiring more than 500 extra weapons. (The actual number of Soviet ICBMs in 1962, revealed later by satellite reconnaissance photos, was four.) Similarly, SAC listed 1,115 airfields that should be targeted; the Navy analysts found only 770. SAC also assumed that a fairly high percentage of its bombers would be destroyed on the ground or shot down by Soviet missiles and interceptors. If, subsequently, the resulting operational force were only one-third the size of the total force, that would mean the total SAC bomber force would have to be tripled. Meanwhile, as Burke anticipated, most Polaris missiles were shunted off to hit surface-to-air missile sites or wasted on targets they had scant chance of destroying alone.

The initial guidance for the SIOP also specified that there be at least a 75 percent chance of destroying certain targets. Power and his staff pounced on those magic words "at least." They initially specified that the 202 most important targets be destroyed with 97 percent probability, the next 400 targets with 93 percent. Eventually, this was modified, but in the final result of the first SIOP, seven targets had to be destroyed with 97 percent assurance, 213 with 95 percent assurance, 592 with at least 90 percent, and 715 with at least 80

percent. This meant, just as Burke had predicted, that a lot of targets would be hit with a lot of weapons. For example, nine weapons were to be "laid down" on four targets in Leningrad, 23 weapons on six target complexes in Moscow, 18 on seven target areas in Kaliningrad.

On November 3, George Kistiakowsky, chairman of Eisenhower's Science Advisory Committee, traveled to SAC headquarters for three days, at the request of the president, to be briefed on the status of the SIOP. Arleigh Burke had planted suspicions about SAC's manipulations through Eisenhower's naval aide, E. P. Aurand, prompting Eisenhower to have Kistiakowsky check out the rumors. "Kisty" brought along one of his aides, a weapons scientist named George Rathjens, who looked through SAC's atlas of Soviet cities, searching for the town that most closely resembled Hiroshima in size and industrial concentration. When he found one that roughly matched, he asked how many bombs the SIOP "laid down" on that city. The reply: one 4.5 *megaton* bomb and three more 1.1 *megaton* weapons in case the big bomb was a dud. The explosive yield of the atomic bomb that destroyed one-third of Hiroshima on August 6, 1945, was a relatively puny 12.5 *kilotons*.

SAC—or its SIOP incarnation, the Joint Strategic Target Planning Staff, the JSTPS—finished the SIOP on December 14, 1960, just as Eisenhower had ordered. It was labeled SIOP-62, meaning that it was to go into effect in fiscal year 1962, which would begin June 1961. In the event of a war, it called for shooting off, as quickly as possible, the entire portion of the U.S. strategic nuclear force that was on alert. That meant 1,459 nuclear bombs, ranging from ten kilotons to 23 megatons, totaling 2,164 megatons in all, against 654 military and urban-industrial targets in the U.S.S.R., Red China, and Eastern Europe. China was targeted because it was part of the Sino-Soviet bloc, Eastern Europe because it hosted hundreds of Soviet air-defense radar and missile sites that had to be "taken out" so SAC bombers could fly safely to the Russian heartland. JSTPS calculated that the U.S alert force alone would kill 175 million Russians and Chinese.

In mid-December, Secretary of Defense Tom Gates, along with several Pentagon officials and the Joint Chiefs, listened to one of Tommy Power's aides run down all the facts and figures of SIOP-62 in a lengthy briefing. They heard it two days in a row—the first by themselves, the second with a slightly broader audience including the service secretaries. After the second presentation, Gates asked the chiefs what they thought. Tommy White of the Air Force naturally thought it was splendid. The Army and Navy chiefs, George Decker and Arleigh Burke, privately thought it excessive, but they knew when they were outgunned, and Burke had by now decided that his best strategy was to take over the SIOP when the new Kennedy administration came into office. They too expressed general approval.

Then General David Shoup, commandant of the Marine Corps, spoke up. The Marines had virtually no involvement in the nuclear game, so Shoup could take a position close to that of an outsider. The day before, during the first briefing, Shoup had been bothered by a graph that showed tens of millions of Chinese being killed by the U.S. attack. He had asked General Power what would happen if the Chinese were not in the war. "Do we have any options so that we don't have to hit China?" he inquired.

"Well, yeh, we *could* do that," Power reluctantly replied, squirming in his front-row seat, "but I hope nobody thinks of it because it would really screw up the plan."

As the nation's military leaders endorsed SIOP-62 before the secretary of defense, David Shoup stood and said, "Sir, any plan that kills millions of Chinese when it isn't even their war is not a good plan. This is not the American way."

Early in the Kennedy administration, Robert McNamara's "Whiz Kids"—several of whom had been RAND analysts—convinced the defense secretary of the merits of counterforce/no cities. McNamara revised the SIOP to allow for this limited nuclear-war option, only to see both the Navy and the Air Force exploit the change to their advantage. The Navy's Burke convinced McNamara to designate the Polaris a "reserve force" under this strategy—a rationale that prompted the massive buildup of the nuclear submarine fleet in the 1960s. The Air Force used McNamara's endorsement of counterforce as the justification for 1,000 extra Minuteman missiles, the B-70 bomber (later cancelled), cruise missiles, and a host of other weapons that McNamara didn't want to buy.

Largely to suppress the Air Force's appetite for more weapons, McNamara eventually renounced counterforce and reverted to a form of massive retaliation that later became dubbed "mutual assured destruction," or MAD. But the actual targeting plan—the SIOP—remained fundamentally the same.

In ever-more refined form, the RAND strategy survives today. And—as displayed in such debates as the MX (Air Force) versus the Trident II (Navy) missiles—so does the bitter inter-service rivalry that helps sustain the arms race.

At N.R.C. It's Safety Last

ROBERT POLLARD

Robert Pollard is a nuclear safety engineer at the Union of Concerned Scientists. Additional research was provided by John Tirman.

Wheeler Lake winds along the northern plain of Alabama, a slither of water that was the Tennessee River until the Tennessee Valley Authority built the dams that changed the river and the region alike. On the lake's southern shore, near Decatur, stands a more modern emblem of the T.V.A.: the Brown's Ferry nuclear power plant. On a lazy March afternoon in 1975, a workman holding a lighted candle while checking for air leaks in the plant's electrical cable room started a fire. The power and safety systems connected by the cables were promptly disabled, and the nuclear reactor, running at full tilt, had to be shut down. The fire raged for hours, destroying electrical systems and confusing plant operators. A lone water pump that kept the reactor cool prevented a disaster.

Four years later and 700 miles away, in another tranquil river valley, similar failures of technology and training triggered a near meltdown at the Three Mile Island Unit 2 nuclear reactor near Harrisburg, Pennsylvania. Maintenance oversights, stuck valves, a poorly designed control panel and faulty safety systems caused the worst accident in the history of the nuclear power industry.

The reactor at Three Mile Island came within thirty to sixty minutes of a total meltdown, replacing the Brown's Ferry fire as the industry's most serious "nuclear event." Yet according to the Nuclear Regulatory Commission's calculations, neither accident should have been possible. The Alabama fire attracted little notice and was soon forgotten, but the accident at T.M.I. shook the industry. Several investigations were initiated to determine its causes and to evaluate the performance of the N.R.C.

Though their findings differed in many particulars, the various probes—including several in Congress, two internal N.R.C. inquiries and the Presidential commission headed by John Kemeny, then president of Dartmouth College—were unanimously scathing in their criticisms of the nation's nuclear chaperone. "To prevent nuclear accidents as serious as Three Mile Island," said the Kemeny Commission's report, "fundamental changes will be necessary in [the N.R.C.'s] organization, procedures, and practices—and above all else—attitudes." The Special Inquiry Group led by Washington attorney Mitchell Rogovin found that the N.R.C. "is not focused, organized, or managed to meet today's needs." And the General Accounting Office, in its 1980 review of the commission, concluded that its "regulatory performance can be characterized best as slow, indecisive, and cautious—in a word, complacent." Indeed, it appeared that if the N.R.C. didn't clean up its act, its very existence—and the future of nuclear power itself—would be in jeopardy.

Four years later, it is clear that the commission's act has changed very little. The lessons of T.M.I. have been ignored, and although the problems of nuclear safety have become increasingly apparent, the N.R.C. has responded with indifference and delay. Worse, the White House fully supports the agency's inaction.

"We all know the political winds have shifted," N.R.C. Commissioner Victor Gilinsky told an industry audience last May. "The N.R.C. staff certainly senses a different mood: some of the very same senior N.R.C. officials who were outdoing each other three years ago in proposing new safety requirements are now competing to eliminate such requirements." Former N.R.C. Commissioner Peter Bradford is more blunt: "The Reagan Administration is the first in my knowledge to put political patronage into nuclear safety. There are purely political reasons for much of what is going on."

The T.M.I. Action Plan was supposed to contain the commission's comprehensive, long-term recommendations for improving reactor safety. With Roger Mattson, now a top N.R.C. expert on reactors, at its helm, a working group convened in late November 1979, and after seven months and four drafts the plan was completed and approved by all five commissioners. The document, which is nearly 600 pages long and contains 347 recommendations, seems to deal with every conceivable weakness in reactor safety. But it was undermined by the kind of enforcement laxity in response to industry pressure that has characterized nuclear regulation for three decades.

While the plan was still in embryo, three industry lobbies acted to influence the N.R.C. working group. The most determined of the interveners was the Atomic Industrial Forum, which formed a task force to meet regularly with Mattson and his group. By late February, the A.I.F. had prepared a critique of the working group's fifty-one most important recommendations for reform and an estimate of the cost to industry of implementing the plan. Its efforts were not wasted: in the final draft of the Action Plan, thirty-six of those top-priority items had been modified or their implementation postponed. For example, in response to an industry request, the N.R.C. toned down the strict qualifications for plant operators proposed in earlier drafts.

The Action Plan committee heard no testimony from consumer groups. Indeed, no public comment of any kind was sought until July 1980—some two months after the Action Plan was completed. And instead of publishing the plan as a regulation—or "substantive rule"—the N.R.C. decided to issue it as a "general statement of policy," and decreed that the public could not challenge its sufficiency even though industry groups had been permitted to question the necessity of its requirements. Two commissioners dissented from that decision. Gilinsky called it a "manifestly unfair and unwise policy," and Bradford said that "the action embodies precisely the complacency that the Kemeny Commission, among others, suggested as a strong contributing factor to the accident at Three Mile Island."

In September 1980, more than seventeen months after the T.M.I. accident—and after the public comment period had passed—the agency *invited* licensees to petition for relief from the technical changes and the implementation schedules outlined in the plan. The utilities wasted no time seizing this opportunity: licensees made 202 requests for delays or "technical deviations" on the twenty-four items slated for implementation between July and December 1981. The commission has been equally dilatory. Of the 347 items in the Action Plan, more than 40 percent are still being "studied" or "developed" or are receiving no attention at all.

But putting important issues on the back burner is an N.R.C. tradition. A longstanding practice in hearings on license applications for new plants is to label any pervasive safety flaw—one that is found in more than just the plant under review—"generic." As the Kemeny Commission noted, "Once an issue is labeled 'generic,' the individual plant being licensed is not responsible for resolving the issue prior to licensing. That, in itself, would be acceptable, if there were a strict procedure within NRC to assure the timely resolution of generic problems. . . . However, the evidence indicates that labeling the problem 'generic' may provide a convenient way of postponing decision on a difficult question."

The N.R.C.—and the Atomic Energy Commission before it—has always thought that a partial meltdown, or "degraded core," such as occurred at T.M.I., would be an "incredible event." Therefore, the commission has not required plants to have equipment that could respond to a meltdown emergency. That was true at Three Mile Island, and it was also true at the Enrico Fermi II reactor near Detroit, where a partial meltdown occurred in 1966. The hazard is enormous: the radioactive material released from an overheated reactor core affects safety systems in unpredictable ways. But the commission continues to believe that the likelihood of such events is too remote to justify forcing utilities to take the necessary safety measures.

Both the Kemeny Commission's and the Rogovin group's reports spotlighted the problem of inadequately trained operators. They called for additional training and for the stationing of a nuclear engineer in the control room at all times, which would insure that someone with scientific background would be on hand to deal with emergencies operators are not trained to handle. But that recommendation has thus far been resisted by the industry, despite the fact that the near meltdown at T.M.I. showed that it can take hours, even days, to find the cause of an accident.

There are other human factors in the safety equation—the operators' almost total dependence on the control panel for information about malfunctions, for example. The bewildering array of thousands of lights and levers virtually defeats crisis management. At T.M.I., some vital displays were located on the back of the panel, out of view of the operators. There seems to be little rhyme or reason to panel design. During an accident involving loss of coolant water, for instance, more than 500 warning lights may flash the first minute, another 800 the next. The Action Plan does little to encourage corrective action.

The plan also postpones requiring utilities to take measures that would prevent interruptions in the flow of coolant water. The emergency cooling systems now in use are supposed to rush water to reactor vessels if the normal cooling systems fail. But steam or hydrogen gas bubbles can form within the pipes of these systems and inside the core itself, making it impossible for coolant water to reach the core in sufficient quantity to stop it from melting. That happened at T.M.I. There have been several gas-bubble incidents at nuclear plants since then, including the January 1982 accident at the Ginna nuclear plant near Rochester, New York.

The investigations of the T.M.I. accident did address the bubble problem. "We believe," the Rogovin report concluded, "that the capability to remotely vent the high points in the [coolant systems] . . . is an important feature that should be provided." In fact, vents that can readily discharge trapped gas are built into the pipes, but they cannot be worked by remote control, and once an accident occurs, no one can enter the containment building to open them. The N.R.C. called on all plants to install remotely operable vents by January 1981, then moved the date to July 1982. The actual deadline remains in doubt. N.R.C. spokesmen have testified in Congress that while the vents are "necessary," the installation schedule is "not feasible."

The shortcomings of the Action Plan are symptomatic of the N.R.C.'s regulatory failures in other areas. It has not addressed such issues as the reliability of electrical safety equipment during an emergency; the capacity of the "embrittled" carbon steel walls of many older reactors to withstand the stress of an accident; and the corrosion of the tubing and piping of many plant systems. All of those problems—which were known before the accident at T.M.I. and which are still unresolved—reveal the inadequacy of the nation's present system of nuclear oversight. And the N.R.C.'s lackadaisical attitude toward tightening and expediting safety standards finds favor in the Reagan Administration. White House energy adviser John Marcum says that tube ruptures (the cause of the Ginna accident) and reactor embrittlement "are not N.R.C.'s responsibility. It is the responsibility of the industry. It's an economic issue, not a safety issue."

There is disturbing evidence that speeding up the pace of licensing nuclear plants has become the Administration's number-one priority. . "The N.R.C. budget is skewed toward things like safety," says Marcum. "Only a small fraction is carrying out the N.R.C. mission, which is licensing. It's becoming a big R & D bureaucracy." That description of "the N.R.C. mission" is debatable, but Marcum's message is clear: licensing *new* plants comes first; making *existing* plants safe is of secondary importance. "The real problem with the Action Plan implementation," says former N.R.C. Commissioner Bradford, "is Ronald Reagan. In combination with the Bevill Committee in Congress, the Administration has eroded the positive changes in N.R.C. attitudes following T.M.I." (The House Appropriations Subcommittee on Energy and Water Development, which controls the N.R.C.'s purse strings, is chaired by Tom Bevill and is widely regarded as strongly pro-industry.)

"My intent is to not only sustain but increase this [licensing] momentum," said N.R.C. chairman Nunzio Palladino in an industry speech. "We will increase overtime if needed. We will make whatever use we can of technical assistance from the National Laboratories, and we will continue to explore additional changes to our rules where a significant payoff is evident. For the immediate future there will be no slowing down."

The industry claims that since the accident at T.M.I., the N.R.C. has not acted promptly on license applications, but Bradford calls the charge "utterly bogus." The issue was investigated in 1981 by a House energy subcommittee, which was sharply critical of the N.R.C.'s policy of speeding up licensing at the expense of safety. It concluded "that the NRC and the utilities' commitment to learn from the [T.M.I.] accident has waned as the memory of the accident fades. That tendency has been exacerbated by the excessive and unfounded diversion of NRC attention and energy to the question of licensing delay." The subcommittee noted that it is "ill-timed to devote resources to rushing more plants on line at a time when basic safety programs and the inspection of reactors already operating are not being fully implemented."

The Nuclear Regulatory Commission is undoubtedly more attentive to safety concerns than was the rough-and-ready Atomic Energy Commission. As N.R.C. Commissioner Gilinsky puts it, "We are getting closer to the equipment and people we're regulating, and that's good." But the progress that has been made is now coming under great political pressures, with the result that the agency is de-emphasizing safety issues and focusing instead on ways to speed up licensing and minimize the utilities' costs. As licensees come to see that delays will be tolerated, tight schedules for compliance will become meaningless.

That attitude convinced me to resign my job as an N.R.C. project manager in 1976. The government has licensed more than seventy nuclear power plants; each has major safety deficiencies in design and hardware, and each does not have stringent enough personnel qualifications. There have been serious accidents, yet few senior N.R.C. officials even consider forcing the industry to take the steps needed to make plants safe. If there are not enough skilled workers, the answer is *not* to "stretch out" compliance schedules but to close plants or reduce their power levels until all problems are remedied. The N.R.C.'s own regulations indicate that such a course is essential.

And so the agency—with the White House's encouragement—permits the industry to take risks with Americans' health and safety in order to protect the utilities' financial health. When people say, "You can't completely tear down and rebuild a plant," what they're really saying is that it costs too much to do so. But there is a cost in not rebuilding the plant—an increased risk to the public. That cost is borne by the people affected because they do not have a voice in the design, construction and operation of nuclear power plants.

As the Reagan Administration seeks more reactors, it is sobering to consider America's twenty-nine-year record with the first generation of nuclear technology. The troubling lesson learned from Three Mile Island and Brown's Ferry is that even near catastrophies have not moved the government to act decisively on behalf of the public's safety and economic well-being.

Economy and Employment

3

Many social problems are influenced by the economy and employment. If the economy runs well people will have jobs, income, and material needs for a decent life. In a troubled economy, workers are often faced with lay-offs; training funds dry-ups; construction lags behind population growth—in short, society lacks the resources needed to bring the economically deprived into the mainstream. There is a direct connection between the economy and monies available for social agencies. Since taxes depend on people's earnings, any downswing in the economy means fewer resources for special programs.

The authors of the first three articles in this section agree that the economy is in trouble. They examine the effects of government policy on farmers, oil companies, and bankers, and try to determine what changes in economic policy might mean for the poor, aged, women, and ethnic minorities.

The fourth and fifth articles in this section move beyond immediate economic and financial dilemmas to survey the impact of technological change in the world of work. What does the coming of robots suggest for industrial workers? Will our society, which has, for a century, been based on labor, be transformed into a new non-laboring people?

The problems of the economy and problems in the workplace are interrelated. A troubled economy is not just an economic problem; it is a social problem that affects every individual in our society.

Looking Ahead: Challenge Questions

What is the connection between economic prosperity and progress in social problems?

Explain how government policies toward farmers, energy, and banking have or have not changed in the past decade.

What is the relationship between United States financial institutions and the world economy? Must the United States help to solve the world social needs in order to have the economic strength to confront our social problems at home?

How might the use of robots affect the future of industrial workers in the United States? Will there be a day when America will cease to be a laboring nation?

If moving from prosperity to recession can have an impact on social problems, what might permanent changes in the economy, such as the loss of our laboring workers, mean to society?

America's Real Farm Problem:

It can be solved

Rep. Bryan Dorgan

Representative Byron Dorgan is a congressman from North Dakota.

Recent scenes from America's farm belt seem like a grainy film clip from the thirties. Young families putting their home and farm machinery on the auction block. Men, choked with emotion, breaking down in tears as they describe their plight. Angry farmers organizing, getting madder and madder.

It's not as bad as the thirties yet; no governor has called out the National Guard to stop the foreclosures, the way North Dakota's William "Wild Bill" Langer did in 1933. But the pain is running deep. Losing a farm is not like having a new Chevrolet or a color TV repossessed. In many cases, what's lost is land that's been in the family for generations—and a way of life that for many is the only one they've ever known or wanted.

It's not that other victims of the recession deserve less sympathy. But there's an important difference between the plight of the farmer and that of other producers. What's happening in the farm belt is a far cry from what's happening in Pittsburgh and Detroit. Nobody is berating our farmers for falling behind the foreign competition and losing their edge, like the auto and steel industries. Nobody is shoving books on Japanese management into their faces. To the contrary, American farmers are our all-star economic performers. When other countries want to find out how to improve agriculture, they don't send their delegations to Tokyo. They send them to Iowa and Kansas and the Dakotas.

And the farmers' reward? Most North Dakota wheat farmers are getting $4 for a bushel of wheat that costs them $5.50 to grow. Farmers are making less in real income today than they did in 1934. Creditors are foreclosing in record numbers; the Farmers Home Administration alone reports that at least 4,000 of its borrowers were forced out of business in 1982.

Rural Myths

Agriculture is a $140 billion-a-year industry, our nation's largest, far bigger than steel, automobiles, or any other manufacturing enterprise. Farming and food-related businesses generate one out of five jobs in private industry and account for 20 percent of our GNP. Sooner or later the problems on the farm catch up with the rest of us, as the laid-off employees of International Harvester already know too well. Students of the Depression will also recall that it was long *before* the 1929 crash—while the market was still revving up—that farm income began falling. The troubles on the farm were a large part of the weight that ultimately dragged the entire economy down into the Depression.

If you read the editorial columns of *The Wall Street Journal*, you know that some people have a simple explanation for the farmers' plight. Too much production is the problem, they say, and if government would only stop subsidizing overproduction by keeping prices artificially high, the free market would work its will and weed out the inefficient producers. What's more, many conservatives and liberals alike believe farmers are only getting their just deserts, having grown fat and happy on government price supports and double-digit inflation. You've seen the caricatures on "60 Minutes"—farmers driving big Cadillacs, spending their winters in Boca Raton—and still complaining that the government doesn't pay them enough not to grow certain crops.

Those aren't the farmers I know. But with less than four percent of all Americans now living on farms, it's little surprise people have so many misconceptions about our farm program. Start with the "overproduction" argument. There are children and older people in this country who still don't have enough to eat, and roughly 450 million people in the world who go hungry most of the time. That people talk about "overproduction" rather than "underdistribution" is rather telling in itself. But more to the present point: almost from the time the early settlers planted their first row, American farmers have been growing more food than the nation could consume. The tendency toward producing surpluses is a perennial problem. It hardly explains the extraordinary difficulties our farmers now face.

As for the "60 Minutes" caricatures, they are just that—caricatures. Last year the federal government paid farmers $1.5 billion in direct subsidies (it loaned another $11.4 billion that farmers must repay). Money from these federal programs came to about two percent of total receipts in 1982 for the average farmer, whose farm netted just $8,000. Add in what he and his family earned away from the farm, and his household still made less than a GS-11 civil servant and about half as much as a young lawyer on Wall Street. That's for working from morning to night and doing what many Americans no longer do—produce something the rest of us need.

But this is no blanket apology for the nation's farm policies—far from it. There are some farmers who get more than they deserve from the government, and nobody gets madder about that than the vast majority of farmers who bear no resemblance to them. Egregious abuses do exist, and it's time that representatives from the farm states (of which I'm one) begin to eliminate them. If we ignore such problems or dismiss them as inevitable, they will continue to act as lightning rods for attacks on all farm programs. Representatives of farm states must clean their own house for if they don't, I'm afraid, someone else will do it—hurting farmer and non-farmer alike.

The nation needs a federal farm program; to think otherwise in today's highly competitive international economy is self-defeating and naive. But we need the right kind of farm program, one that not only meets the test of fairness, but that promises to keep American agriculture second to none.

Unfortunately, that's not the kind of farm program we now have. Approaches that were fine in the thirties are no longer doing the job. In fact, what began as survival programs for family farmers are becoming the domain of extra-large producers who often elbow aside the very family farmers for whom these programs were originally intended. Congress must bear much of the blame for this. We continue to target most farm assistance not according to the circumstances of the individual farmer but largely according to the volume of the commodity he grows. While these federal programs have all been done in the name of the family farmer, the interests of the various commodity groups have not always been identical to those of the nation's family farmers.

This is not to criticize these groups, for everyone is entitled to his say. But it is to suggest that we in Congress have talked too much about programs for feed grains and wheat and corn and assorted "market prices" and "loan rates"—and not enough about the kind of agriculture that's best for the country. And we've done more than waste money in the process. For if our agricultural policy continues largely unchanged, I'm concerned the criticisms that now so tragically apply to the nation's automakers—that they became too big, too inflexible, and too inefficient to compete—may one day be appropriate for America's agriculture.

Farm Economics

To understand the failings of existing farm programs, it's important to understand the roots of the current farm crisis. At the heart of the problem is money—how much there is and how much it costs to borrow.

A farmer is a debtor almost by definition. In my own state, it's not unusual for a wheat farmer with 1,000 acres to owe several hundred thousand dollars for land and machinery. In addition to making payments on these loans, it's common for such a farmer to borrow about $40,000 each spring to cover fertilizer, diesel fuel, seed, and other operating expenses. The months before the harvest will be anxious ones as the farmer contemplates all the things that could bring financial hardship: bad weather, crop disease, insects, falling commodity prices. If he has a good year, the farmer can repay his loans and retain some profit; in a bad one, he can lose his whole farm.

Money thus becomes one of the farmer's biggest expenses. Most consumers can find some refuge from high interest rates by postponing large purchases like houses or cars. Farmers have no choice. In 1979, for example, farmers paid $12 billion in interest costs while earning $32 billion; last year they paid $22 billion in interest costs, while earning only $20 billion. In a business in which profit margins are small, $4,000 more in interest can mean the difference between profit and loss. Since 1975, 100,000 family farms have disappeared, and while interest rates have fallen recently, they still imperil the nation's farmers.

This is why the most basic part of our nation's farm policy is its money and credit policy—which is set by Paul Volcker and the Federal Reserve Board. The Federal Reserve Board's responsibility for nearly ruining our economy is well-known. What's often overlooked is how the board's policies have taken an especially devastating toll on farmers. While high interest rates have increased farm expenses, they've also undermined the export market farmers have traditionally relied on. High interest rates, by stalling our economic engines, have been a drag on the entire world's economy. Developing and third-world nations have been particularly hard hit; struggling just to meet interest payments on their loans from multinational banks, they have had little cash left over to buy our farm products.

Even those countries that could still afford our farm products abandoned us for other producers. Our interest rates were so high they attracted multinational bankers, corporations, and other who speculate on currencies of different countries. These speculators were willing to pay more for dollars in terms of pesos, yen, or marks because those rates guaranteed them such a substantial return.

The news commentators called the result a "strong dollar," which gave us a rush of pride. But what did this strong dollar really mean to the farmer? It meant people in other countries found themselves suddenly poorer when they went to buy something made or grown in America. In 1981, for example, West Germans paid 21 percent more for American soybeans, even though our farmers were getting 11 percent *less* for those very same soybeans than they had the previous year. Overall, our "strong dollar" has been jacking up the price of American farm exports by a full 25 percent, biting our potential foreign customers with a 25 percent surcharge the moment they start thinking of buying American. No wonder these exports have dropped for the first time in 12 years. This isn't a strong dollar, it's a big banker's dollar—and with a central bank like the Federal Reserve Board, who needs soil erosion, grasshoppers, or drought?

To be fair, interest rates aren't solely responsible for undercutting our farmers' export markets. President Carter's grain embargo did more than close the Russian market; it also drove away other foreign customers who wondered how dependable we were. Reagan has lifted the embargo, but to little avail, since he still refuses to sign a long-term grain contract with the Soviet Union. Meanwhile, our foreign competitors have quickly stepped into the breach, supporting their farmers with generous subsidies that make ours look miserly by comparison. Last September, for example, wheat from the U.S. and the Common Market countries was selling for almost the same price on the international market. But while the U.S. farmer was getting about $3.40 a bushel, his Common Market counterpart received $5.37.

Both the Federal Reserve Board's market-skewing policies and the hefty subsidies that foreign agriculture receives illustrate an important point. Those who say America should go back to a "free market" in agriculture are asking our farmers to go back to something that no longer exists. In today's world there's no free market in agriculture, just as there is none in steel, automobiles, or other major industries.

We learned during the Depression that agriculture, by its very nature, requires a moderating hand to smooth out the violent cycles that otherwise could destroy even the best farmers. No other producers have to confront the sudden price shifts with which farmers regularly contend. Automakers, for example, don't have to worry that prices for their product may drop 50 percent, as wheat prices did from 1974 to 1977. This is why even that bastion of free-market orthodoxy, the Heritage Foundation, concedes the need for a government role in agriculture.

Home-Grown Depression

For the nation's first 150 years, there was no farm program as such. The Department of Agriculture wasn't created until 1862, and when President Lincoln proposed it to Congress he could applaud the nation's farmers as a "great interest so independent in its nature as to not have demanded and extorted more from government." For the next 70 years the department limited itself largely to statistics and research. Farmers received little in the way of subsidies; like all other consumers, they helped subsidize manufacturers through the tariffs they paid on imported goods.

Contrary to popular belief, the Depression hit our farms long before the Okies started their desperate treks across the dust bowl in their sputtering Model T's. During World War I Europe bought our food like it was going out of style. Prices rose to record heights; farmers expanded their operations and borrowed heavily to do so.

Then the war ended. Export markets quickly dried up as European countries started to rebuild their own agriculture. American farmers watched helplessly as prices plummeted, leaving many with huge debts to repay and no income with which to pay them. A rash of foreclosures followed, rehearsing a cycle that bears an eerie similarity to the current one. By 1932 farm income was less than one-third of what it had been in 1919. During this period, more than 1.5 million Americans left the farm. (The exodus was reversed during the Depression, when many returned to the farm in order to survive.)

Then, as now, the conventional economists and their camp followers in Congress and the press found little alarming in this hardship. The "invisible hand," they said, would force farmers to produce less until prices returned to normal levels. The "weak" and the "inefficient" might be cut down in the process, but that was the way the free market was supposed to work. It didn't.

Unfortunately, someone forgot to tell the nation's farmers about the economic etiquette that professors and journalists expected of them. As prices continued to fall, the farmers didn't produce less—they produced more. It's not hard to understand why. Farmers have certain set costs—such as debt—whether or not they plant a single seed. When prices dropped, many tried to produce more to make up the difference. Besides, to farm is to hope. The market may be terrible one year, but who knows what will happen next? Will there be drought in Europe? Blight in Russia? When you have to decide how much to plant in the spring, you have little idea what the market will really be in the fall. The worse things look, the more you pin your hopes on a sudden surge in prices. So you plant.

Those who put all the blame on government for today's excess production and low prices are long on theory and short on history. We produced "too much" throughout the twenties, when there was no farm program to speak of. And it wasn't the weak and the inefficient who tumbled then. It was just about everybody.

Blind Generosity

The New Dealers recognized that when it comes to agriculture, the invisible hand can end up shooting farmers in the foot. Their solution was straightforward—and effective. Remedies like the Agricultural Adjustment Act were begun to prop up the prices of certain commodities so that the farmers who grew them could count on at least a minimal return. The main approach was to link government assistance to the farmers' agreement to cut production, thus forcing prices to rise according to the laws of supply and demand.

These relief programs were not geared to the circumstances of individual farmers. They were aimed at regulating the supply and price of certain commodities. Still, the commodity approach amounted to a relief program for the family farm because there just weren't many other kinds of farms around. In 1932 one of four Americans lived on a farm, and for that reason the commodity programs were a major part of the whole New Deal relief effort.

Over the last half century, this commodity approach has remained relatively unchanged, while American agriculture has changed radically. The number of farms today is one-third what it was during the Depression, and just seven percent of these control over half the farmland and account for over half the sales. Yet while farming has become more concentrated, the government still dispenses federal aid with a blindfold on, treating a multi-thousand-acre agrifactory giant as if it were a bedraggled Okie with a hand-crank tractor and a cow. As a result, 29 percent of all federal farm benefits go to the top one percent of our farmers.

The government distributes this largess in a variety of ways. Some programs amount to government-guaranteed prices. For a few crops—

tobacco and peanuts, for example—the government sanctions an allotment system by which the marketing of these is strictly controlled. The government also provides crop insurance, disaster relief, and subsidized loans for such things as purchasing more farmland and meeting operating expenses.

The traditional mainstay of the farm program is the "commodity loan." Each year the government establishes a loan rate for major crops, including wheat, corn, barley, sorghum, and soybeans. The rate for wheat, for example, was $3.55 per bushel in 1982. Early in the year, a farmer must decide whether he is going to sign up for the program; if he does, he may have to agree to cut back his production to help keep surpluses down. If the eventual market price goes above the loan-rate level, the farmer simply repays the loan, takes back his wheat, and sells it on the open market. But if the market price is below the loan rate, the farmer may take the money and leave the wheat with the government. In addition to the commodity loan, there is a "deficiency payment" that supposedly helps bridge the gap between what the farmer earns in the market and what his crop costs to produce.

It's important to understand two things about this price-support program. First, a guaranteed price is not a guaranteed profit. The loan rates and deficiency payments do not necessarily return the farmer's cost of production, and in recent years they haven't. In 1982, for example, the target price for wheat was more than a dollar less than the farmer's cost of production.

More important, the way these programs work, the more you have, the more the government gives you. A wheat farmer with 250 acres producing 30 bushels per acre gets a support loan of $26,625. A farmer with 2,500 acres of similarly productive land gets approximately ten times that much. The deficiency payments work in pretty much the same way.

For deficiency payments there is a nominal $50,000 cap that in practice does not have much effect. For support loans, there is no limitation at all. Thus, while smaller farmers get a little help, the largest farms walk off with a bundle. In a recent editorial attacking all farm subsidies, *The Wall Street Journal* fumed about a midwestern wheat grower who received $68,760 last year from the government yet "rides around his 4,000-acre farm on a huge four-wheel-drive tractor with air conditioning and a radio."

I'll bet the editorial writers of *The Wall Street Journal* have air conditioning, radios, and a whole lot more in their offices; still, they do have a point. As Don Paarlburg, a conservative agricultural economist who toiled in the last three Republican administrations, has put it, the result of the present federal farm program is that "average farm income is increased by adding many dollars to those already well-off and adding little or nothing to those at the low end of the income scale."

This bias toward bigness runs through most of the federal government's farm program. One of the best illustrations is the Farmers Home Administration, a case study of how a federal program that began to help only those in need became a safety net for just about everybody else.

The FmHA was created in the depths of the Depression as a lender of last resort for small and beginning farmers who had a reasonable chance to survive. For most of its life, the agency did serve family farmers struggling to get their operation on its feet and unable to obtain credit elsewhere. But in the 1970s, Congress tacked on something called the Economic Emergency Loan program. To qualify for this new program you didn't have to be small, needy, or even a family farmer. You just had to be in economic trouble. Soon the "economic-emergency" loans were pushing aside the kinds of loans the FmHA was orginally intended to provide. By 1980 FmHA was lending *four times* as much in such "emergency" assistance as it was in the so-called "limited-resource" loans for needy farmers who were now receiving less than ten percent of the agency's total. Ninety percent of these emergency loans went to bigger, more established farms, many of which were unlikely candidates for public philanthropy. One politician and judge with a net worth of $435,000 and a non-farm income of $70,000 a year received $266,000 in such low-interest "emergency" loans.

After "60 Minutes" exposed a $17 million emergency loan to a California agrifactory, an embarrassed Congress imposed a $400,000 limit on the program. Though this was an improvement, the still-generous limit enables the larger farms to eat up the bulk of FmHA's loan resources.

Showing nicely its concept of the "truly needy," the Reagan administration tried to abolish completely the limited-resource loan program that was targeted to the smaller farmers the agency was established to help in the first place. Congress wouldn't let it, so the Reaganites discovered the value of bureaucracy and gave it the red-tape treatment. Nationwide, the FmHA in 1982 managed to lend only about half the money Congress had approved for these loans—this during the worst year for farmers in half a century.

In fairness, the administration has also stopped making economic-emergency loans. But that misses the point. Those loans should be made, but only to family farmers who need them. The FmHA's recent crackdown on delinquent borrowers, moreover, has fallen most heavily upon the smaller farmers. It's a cruel irony: having lavished so much money on the largest farmers, at least some of whom could have gotten credit elsewhere, the government now has too little left for smaller farmers who have nowhere else to turn. Not surprisingly, many are going under.

Meanwhile, the Reagan administration has introduced a Payment-In-Kind program that gives farmers government surplus commodities they in turn can sell, if they agree to take acreage out of production. PIK is thus a variation on traditional New Deal programs. But while the PIK program offers many beleaguered farmers some genuine help, it also embodies the same most-for-the-biggest approach.

Agricultural Bloat

Of course, some will argue there's nothing wrong with a farm policy that encourages bigger and bigger farms. This will only make them more efficient, so the argument goes, and past gains in agricultural productivity will continue indefinitely as farms get bigger.

To such people, a concern for the family-size farm seems a mushy and misplaced Jeffersonian nostalgia. In fact, it is anything but. Family farming is practical economics. Anyone who's looked recently at our automobile and steel industries knows that economies of scale stop beyond a certain point. When Thomas Peters and Robert Waterman examined successful American businesses for their book *In Search of Excellence*, what were the qualities they found? Small work units. Lean staffs. A minimum of management bureaucracy. Managers who get their hands into what they manage. Enterprises that stick to their knitting instead of using their assets to flit from one business to another.

It sounds like a profile of the American family farm. It's also a description of what we *lose* when we allow factory-in-the-field agglomerations to gobble up individual family farmers.

There's growing evidence to suggest that in agriculture, as in other endeavors, the old "bigger is better" saying is a myth. A decade ago the Department of Agriculture was telling Congress the optimum size for a California vegetable farm was 400 acres, though 73 percent of the state's vegetables were already produced on farms much larger than that. A 1979 USDA study found that the average U.S. farm reaches 90 percent of maximum efficiency at just 314 acres; to attain 100 percent efficiency, the average size has to quadruple to 1,157 acres. Beyond that, farms don't get any better—they just get bigger. They may even become more bureaucratic and less efficient.

Consider, for example, the matter of debt. The very largest farms are twice as debt-prone as smaller family farms. This is of little consequence when times are flush. But when trouble hits, as it has with Mr. Volcker's interest-rate policies, it's like sending a fleet of large sailing ships heading into a gale with twice the sail they normally carry.

Just as a rope of many strands is more flexible and resilient than a single strand, a diverse agriculture of many relatively small units can adjust and change. Unlike the very largest operations, family farmers don't have so much capital tied up in what they did yesterday to keep them from doing what needs to be done tomorrow. Small farmers don't have to push paper through tedious chains of command. If they see a way of doing something better, they can do it right away. This kind of flexibility is important if sudden shifts in market conditions warrant different crops or production techniques.

There's also the question of rural communities. I grew up in Regent, North Dakota, a farming community of 400 people. Family farms were and are the economic bloodstream of that town. When such farms are eaten up by larger ones, towns like Regent wither, and the government finds itself with a tax-consuming social problem instead of a healthy and tax-providing community.

In short, there is a link between the *way* we have farmed—in traditional family-size units—and the extraordinary productivity of our agriculture as a whole. Yet our farm policies are pushing us towards a top-heavy agriculture that threatens to mimic the same problems we are facing in other areas of our economy. The high interest rates of the last two years have made the problem even worse: whether family farmers go bankrupt or simply decide to sell out, the trend toward concentration is hastened.

Even worse, this trend feeds on itself. The alteration of the FmHA is instructive. Having helped create large farms, the government felt compelled to keep them from failing. When a small family farmer bites the dust there may be a few condolences but nobody worries much. When a multi-thousand-acre agrifactory totters, its bankers and creditors get the jitters over the millions of dollars at stake. It's a prairie twist on the maxim familiar to international bankers: "Make a small loan and you create a debtor. Make a big loan and you create a partner."

Are we encouraging farms so big that we can't afford to let them fail? I fear we are and I think it's an ominous prescription for slowly but inevitably undermining the very things that have made agriculture one of the few American industries still competitive in international markets. Despite high interest rates, agriculture still contributed more than $40 billion in export sales last year, helping defray the costs of our unhappy dependence on imported oil and automobiles.

Help for the Family Farmer

What does all this mean for our farm policies? Mr. Paarlburg recommends that we eliminate the current "tilt in favor of big farms" in our federal programs, and at least keep the playing field level. I agree with that, but would go a step further. For the reasons I've discussed, I think we should retarget the current programs toward family-size units. For example, we should put a cap on the commodity price-support loans to eliminate the exorbitant amounts going to the very largest farmers, thus freeing up more for those who need it more. In 1981, for example, I proposed capping these loans at $150,000, which would have affected less than ten percent of all farmers but

would have enabled us to increase the support price by about 35 cents per bushel for the rest. (This new level, incidentally, would have still been below production costs.) Farmers could become as large as they wanted—the federal government just wouldn't pay them for doing so.

We should alter the FmHA loan program in similar fashion, restoring this agency to its original purpose of providing economic opportunity to beginning and smaller farmers. In the present crisis, the money saved should be used to extend loan deferrals to family farmers who have fallen behind on their FmHA loans because of economic circumstances beyond their control. At the same time, we should alter other federal policies, such as tax laws that invite lawyers and doctors to invest in farms as tax shelters, driving up land prices to the detriment of the beginning farmer.

Of course, it would not be fair to pull the plug suddenly on these larger farm operations. Many are essentially family farmers who overextended themselves during the 1970s, with a good deal of encouragement (including subsidized loans) from the government. Some of these farms may need emergency loans; the question is the direction in which our farm program goes from here.

These are the broad outlines of a farm program that I think would dispense agricultural benefits more fairly while promoting the right kind of agriculture. But the high interest rates of the last two years should serve as a stark reminder that the best farm program in the world will not do a great deal when a Federal Reserve Board accountable to no one can unleash an interest-rate tornado that levels the economic landscape. The best thing the government can do for the nation's farmer is not to subsidize him, but to promote the kind of monetary policies that make credit available at a fair price.

Interest rates must continue to fall as they have begun to do. Rates are still too high for the average farmer, however, and powerful pressures are building to increase them again. As I write these words, on March 8, 1983, the front page of *The Washington Post* business section reports that a group of prominent economists called the Shadow Open Market Committee "today called for the Federal Reserve to slow sharply the recent rapid growth in the nation's money supply even though that might risk another recession sometime in 1984."

More than a century ago, President Abraham Lincoln warned us that "the money power of this country will endeavor to prolong its reign until all wealth is aggregated in a few hands and the Republic is destroyed." While its policies have moderated somewhat in recent months, the board has taken us in precisely this direction. Money and credit should serve production, not the other way around. Regaining control over them is of utmost importance not only to the family farmer, but to all independent businessmen as well—not to mention the rest of us.

Rescuing the Banking System

First aid gives world bankers a chance to consider permanent reforms. Wanted: Better information, a source of funds and an economic upturn.

DAVID FAIRLAMB
WITH HENRIETTE SENDER

For five months—ever since Mexico declared last August that it could not pay its foreign debts—the world's banking system teetered on the brink of collapse. Then, thanks to unprecedented cooperation among public and private banking groups, just as the old year was ending the system was pulled back from the brink. Confidence, an indispensable quality in any banking operation, is growing once more, so much so that many bankers say not only that the crisis is over, but that it was vastly exaggerated to begin with.

They are wrong. The actions taken so far are no more than first aid, designed to prevent the situation from getting very much worse very much faster. Now the hunt is on for a permanent cure. Meanwhile, both the face of international banking and the fate of nations are changing.

Most observers trace the system's present sickness back to the oil embargo of 1973–74. The huge price increases that the oil cartel shoved through at that time, and again in 1979–80, created massive currency surpluses for many of the cartel members. Many of these billions were deposited in banks in the industrialized countries, which in turn lent them out to underdeveloped nations.

Initially, this recycling of petrodollars was a great service. The loans enabled many less-developed countries to pay for essential imports of expensive oil and to continue with some semblance of their economic development programs. Almost inevi-

Recycling petrodollars

tably, however, the situation got out of hand, threatening everyone involved with disaster.

International lending became a good way to grow, and as glamorous bankers roamed the world looking for customers, loans to non-oil-producing LDCs soared 25%-to-30% a year. Competition grew as new lenders entered the market—U.S. regional banks, for instance, and Japanese institutions. This heightened competition reduced the spreads between what banks paid for their funds and what they charged for loans. "The spreads were too low," complains Governor Henry Wallich of the Fed-

eral Reserve Bank. "Had they had better pricing, not as much would have been borrowed, and the banks would have put on fat to provide for losses."

By the end of last year, the developing world was burdened with a crushing $625 billion in foreign debt. About 60% of that was owed to banks, an amount equal to the combined capital and reserves of all the commercial banks in the industrialized world.

These high levels of lending left both sides vulnerable, notes William Cline of the Institute for International Economics: banks, because an imprudently high proportion of their capital was exposed to one major borrower or to a small group; debtors, because they became vulnerable to any decrease in bank lending.

This vulnerability was turned into painful reality by a number of developments that came along practically at the same time. World trade has stagnated during the past two years and commodity prices have slumped sharply—by 14% in 1982 alone. This has had a brutal impact on the trade balances of the borrowing countries, making it just about impossible for them to earn enough from exports to make their huge interest and principal payments.

Then there was the Polish economic and political crisis of 1980–81. When Poland could not pay the interest and principal due on $29 billion in foreign loans and fears rose that it might default, Western bankers had to "reschedule" them—a euphemism for postponing payment—and to throw in new funds, to boot.

Jolted by the experience, the bankers accelerated their shift to short-term lending, which is supposedly more secure for the banks and cheaper for the borrower. Thus, for the developing nations, 50% of new syndicated Eurocredits (large scale international loans put together by groups of banks) granted by mid-1982 matured in a year or less versus 16% in 1978, while the average life-span of longer-term credits fell from eight-and-a-half years to seven-and-a-half. As a result, countries that had to refinance their debts quickly built up short-term loans to unwieldy and dangerous proportions. An estimated 30% of Brazil's $90 billion foreign debt now matures in one year or less; for Mexico, $85 billion in hock, it is reportedly more than half.

On top of this, the tight, inflation-fighting monetary policies of the industrialized countries sent interest rates soaring beyond the borrowers' ability to pay. In recent years, the international syndicated loan market has been almost entirely converted from fixed to floating rates. At the same time, a growing portion of new Eurocredits has been linked to the U.S. prime rate. Thus, when U.S. interest rates skyrocketed, the developing countries were immediately hurt. Between 1977 and 1982, bankers estimate, the effective interest charged on a typical international bank loan more than doubled, from 8% to 17.5%. And, say the experts, each one point rise in interest rates adds as much as $2 billion to the borrowers' annual debt service.

Already reeling from all this—and from almost $50 billion in rescheduling applications from East European and smaller developing countries—many world bankers were totally unprepared when Mexico said it might have to repudiate its $85 billion debt. Nor did they anticipate that Brazil, the world's biggest borrower, or heavily indebted ($39 billion) Argentina would follow suit. The specter of repudiation followed by major bank failures and a worldwide depression seemed not so wild a dream anymore.

Overnight, confidence evaporated as banks rushed to pull out of syndicated Eurocredits. New lending crashed to an annual rate of only $15 billion in the fourth quarter compared to $134 billion in 1981. Spreads widened as bankers rushed to limit their exposure to anything Latin American. Developing countries that had been paying three-quarters of a point over London interbank rates (LIBOR) for loans before the crisis found themselves paying 1.5 points more.

The Latin American problems shook American bankers, in particular, in a way they hadn't been shaken by the Polish affair. Many who believed in the old theory that countries can't go bankrupt now wondered and worried that such might indeed happen in Mexico. But with default seemingly imminent, the Washington-based International Monetary Fund and the Basel-based Bank for International Settlements speedily got to work with government agencies to patch together a quilt of financial support to see the three troubled borrowers through their immediate liquidity crisis.

First, the BIS put up a $1.85 billion bridging loan for Mexico until terms of a $3.9 billion IMF credit could be hammered out. Then similar arrangements were made for Brazil (with $1.2 billion from BIS and $6 billion from the IMF), while negotiations began in earnest to bail out Argentina.

At the same time, both the international agencies and domestic regulatory authorities persuaded, and in some cases bullied, reluctant commercial banks to chip in new money —$5 billion for Mexico and $4.4 billion for Brazil. (The bullying tactic: If the banks didn't go along, the international agencies wouldn't put up any money, and everyone would lose.) To make the job easier, supervisory standards governing the treatment of problem loans, among other things, would be temporarily relaxed. "When new loans facilitate the adjustment process and enable a country to strengthen its international debt in an orderly manner, new credits should not be subject to supervisory criticism," explained Federal Reserve Chairman Paul Volker.

The financial Band-Aid in place, world bankers had more time to reflect on why the situation had gotten so precarious and what would be done to prevent a replay. Predictably, much of the blame was laid at the doors of bank supervisory authorities, both national and international. "A history of partly profligate lending succeeded by record high interest rates reflects a

Poor supervision

history of lax banking supervision," huffed one London banker. There were calls for an improved monitoring system and tighter controls on banks.

Bankers and banking authorities have already addressed some of the problems, but others are not so easy to resolve. The inadequate supervision that allowed so many banks to engage in reckless lending was remedied in part by the 1975 Basel Concordat (box, left). Likewise, the activities of offshore bank branches and offices in the Bahamas, the Cayman Islands and elsewhere permitted many banking activities to escape official review. But the requirement, in the U.S. and elsewhere, that banks file consolidated financial statements has brought many of these subsidiaries to heel. Thus, says Peter Cooke, head of the Bank of England's supervisory team, "There are no rogue herds of unregulated bankers tramping through international markets."

Different countries also have different supervisory standards, and this can create competitive advantages or disadvantages and contribute to reckless lending, says John Heimann, former U.S. Comptroller of Currency and now co-chairman of Warburg Paribas Becker. French and German banks do not have to maintain as high a ratio of capital to loans as do banks in, for example, the U.S. and the U.K., so they can extend more loans per dollar of capital. Competitors trying to keep up with the French thus run the risk of over extending themselves.

Heimann would like to see the various national standards brought more

Impractical standards

in line with one another, but most banking supervisors oppose the idea. Leonhard Gleske, a director of Deutsche Bundesbank, the West German central bank, believes standardization is impractical because different

countries often have different definitions (of assets and liabilities, for instance), measure financial data differently and operate in different domestic environments.

Although the situation has improved somewhat, commercial bankers say they could avoid the kind of crisis that did develop if they knew who was lending how much to whom. Without information on how much, say, Chile had already borrowed on world markets, a bank being approached for a loan wouldn't know whether it was prudent to grant the additional credits. More and more of this kind of informa-

tion is becoming available—from the Ditchley Institute, a clearing house for 35 competing banks that was set up last month, for example, and the monitoring operation set up by leading Japanese banks. But bankers say that these are not enough.

The IMF and BIS have a wealth of information, gathered when they extend credits to countries around the world. But this is available to commercial banks only on an informal and patchy basis, and the banks would like better access.

But the international agencies get the information on a confidential basis

---

Creating a Last Resort for the Troubled Banking World

If confidence in the international banking system is in danger of collapsing—as it often appears to be these days—then the most important function of the banking authorities is to provide reassurance. And the ultimate reassurance is a commitment to provide liquidity by acting as the lender of last resort. "You have to have emergency funding mechanisms and a clear lender of last resort for the confidence effect," says Richard Dale, a fellow at the Brookings Institution who specializes in international banking regulation. This is easier said than done.

Nobody advocates bailing out commercial bankers who have overextended their operations or failed to sufficiently diversify their exposure. "Every bank would like to think it has a guardian angel who will save it. But there are no fairy godmothers," says Governor Henry Wallich of the Federal Reserve Board. "What needs to be protected is the system, not individual bank managements or their shareholders."

The trouble is, current arrangements for protecting the system are, in Dale's words, "extremely murky." Generally, central banks act as lenders of last resort for their countries' commercial banks; if the

central banks have problems, they may turn to the Bank for International Settlements, but only for short-term aid; the International Monetary Fund lends money to governments. But the arrangements are for the most part informal, variable and ambiguous. Otherwise—if banks knew under what conditions they could get help—they might assume they had been given a blank check to bail them out of imprudent loans.

"You have to have a deliberate guessing game," agrees Dale. "But there are problems when people guess wrong. If, for example, there is no lender of last resort, it is better that everyone knows it, so nobody is operating under false assumptions."

A lot of bankers were laboring under false assumptions when

Ambrosiano's collapse

Banco Ambrosiano Holdings, a Luxembourg subsidiary of Italy's Banco Ambrosiano, collapsed last year. They had expected the Italian central bank to act as a lender of last resort so that the holding company could meet its $450 million in obligations to other banks. But the central bank refused on the technically correct grounds that the Lux-

embourg subsidiary was not a bank.

Such false assumptions arise in part from a misunderstanding of the Basel Concordat of 1975. That document was drawn up by the central bankers of the Group of Ten after the world banking system was rocked by the failures of the Herstatt Bank in Germany and the Franklin National Bank in New York, and it is intended to indicate who has primary responsibility for supervising the liquidity and solvency of banks —an important step, because a central bank that does not supervise an institution is not likely to accept lender of last resort responsibilities. But these rules of supervision are not very explicit, and more than that, notes John Heimann, co-chairman of Warburg, Paribas, Becker and former U.S. Comptroller of the Currency: "Few people understand that the concordat deals *only* with supervision; lender of last resort has never been formalized at all."

Moreover, the ambiguity surrounding these questions is not all deliberate. In part, it reflects the lack of agreement among Group of Ten nations about what the guidelines should be. "It is a very sensitive area. Each country operates in a different environment and is anx-

and fear their client countries and central banks would not be so candid if they knew the information were going to be made available to others. So there's a problem. Besides, says an official of one of the international agencies, referring to the go-go spirit that pervaded much of the banking world in the Seventies: "The banks knew what they were doing. The outcome would have been no different if we had shared our information."

Crises have a way of springing up, even when rules are strict, supervision first-rate and information readily available. So growing numbers of bankers now say that, if all else fails, there should be an international lender of last resort to bail out collapsing financial institutions (page 48).

Whatever the fate of these proposed adjustments and reforms, there is no question that the glamour days of go-go international banking are gone for as far ahead as anyone can see. Regardless of what the authorities decide to do, the fact is that commercial bankers have been so badly burned and shaken that they are not about to be adventurous. Their profits have declined and their stocks have slumped in all major markets except Tokyo. While the situation is painful, regulators hope that it will persuade the banks to reassess their low-margin, profit-crunching international business, widen their spreads and improve the overall quality of their loan portfolios.

That certainly seems to be happening. And from now on, observers say, loans will be tied much more closely to trade or to financing specific projects. "The day of the jumbo, all-purpose loan is passing," says one international banker. "We are at the end of overlending on a broad scale."

Ironically, the most crucial problem right now is not to rein in the banks but to keep them lending so that the liquidity problems of the big Latin American borrowers do not deteriorate into a vicious circle of economic dislocation. If the developing countries can't borrow, say economists, their demand for goods from the industrialized countries will crumble, possibly turning the European-American recession into a full-blooded depression. A World Bank source calculates that if financial help for the developing countries dries up and their exports remain at 1982 levels, they would have to cut their imports by $50 billion in order to maintain the debt-service ratios dictated by their loan agreements. This would mean a 6% cut in the real income of middle-income countries, zero growth in the lower-income states and the loss of hundreds of thousands of jobs in the industrialized nations.

There has never been any real doubt that the 85-to-100 major international banks, which account for about 80% of the international lending of commercial banks, would stay in the market to see their clients through their current difficulties. As Gleske points out, they have no choice. They would court disaster, for themselves as well as their customers, if they were to stand by and watch Mexico, Argentina or Brazil default.

For the smaller banks, the dilemma is sharper, especially for the small and regional U.S. Johnny-come-latelies that are finding the heat in the financial kitchen difficult to stand. Managing director Stan Yassukovitch of the European Banking Co., a London consor-

---

ious to preserve its sovereignty." says Heimann. "The great need is to harmonize national divergences, but that will take time."

Another worry is that even if a central bank is willing to be the lender of last resort, it may not have the funds. Most international loans are denominated in dollars. And while Governor Wallich notes that the Federal Reserve has "swap" arrangements with most countries that would make U.S. currency available, some critics say that it is not inconceivable for some central banks to run out of dollars. Swaps with the Fed are not automatic. Moreover, "there may be limits to a central bank's ability to lend, and there may be a reluctance to depress the local currency to obtain dollars," says William Cline, a senior fellow at the Institute for International Economics. "I am not satisfied that this is a non-problem." Indeed, aside from the question of finding an adequate source of funds, Cline wonders whether there is enough liquidity in the entire international banking system.

Proposed remedies for all these problems run from the modest (clear up some of the ambiguity about who is responsible for what) to the radical (create an entirely new international lender of last resort). In between these two extremes are suggestions for extending the authority of the BIS (so that it makes long-term as well as short-term loans) and beefing up the IMF (by providing it with more money to lend).

Johannes Witteveen, former managing director of the IMF, advocates "an effective IMF safety net to contain liquidity problems at the country rather than the bank level." Wallich supports the idea of an international lender of last resort "as long as you stress 'last.' It should not be a lender of *first* resort. You want to keep your powder dry as long as possible." He is also studying the possibility of some sort of insurance for bank portfolios, despite the difficulties in funding such a plan.

In his most recent statements, Treasury Secretary Donald Regan has called for increasing international liquidity, but only on a transitional basis. The IMF, he says, "must have, and must be seen to have, the means to deal with the extraordinary financing demands that do arise."

But before a well-thought-out system can be put into place, the immediate situation has to be resolved. "All the reforms being proposed are well intended," says Governor Wallich. "But they come at the least convenient time. It is an expensive way to learn a lesson."
—H.S.

tium bank, comments: "There is a view, which I believe proper, that in the last analysis their first responsibility is to their depositors and not their shareholders, customers or whatever."

Regulators disagree. Says one: "Every banker knows that there are situations where, in order to work out a difficult situation with a customer, the balance of arguments tend towards some further extension of support, even though a decision to do so may be not without some risk." Other central bankers say they appreciate the conditions that currently make the small banks reluctant to increase their exposure—and they are glad that the banks have learned a lesson—but they stress the need to consider carefully the wider picture and the broader interests of the financial system as a whole. "To lend extra money now allows the system collectively to make the sensible adjustment over a reasonable time scale," says one regulator.

And they *are* lending extra money, whether they like it or not. Under pressure from national authorities and international agencies such as the IMF, both big and small banks increased their lending to Mexico and Brazil by 7%. There is little doubt that the banks will be similarly persuaded to bail out other troubled countries, if called upon. "There is no way they can get out," says one regulator. "They have to stay in." Small wonder, then, that Richard Dale, international banking expert at the Brookings Institution, remarks on the radical change that has taken place in the business: "There is no longer a free market in banking. You now have a regimented quota system."

Just how long quota banking will have to prevail is unclear, but most bankers queried by DUN'S BUSINESS MONTH talked gloomily of twelve months or more, at least until the IMF can get more money to lend. To speed that day, Otmar Emminger, former

president of Deutsche Bundesbank, suggests that the IMF borrow in international markets and then relend the funds to the big troubled countries.

But conservative IMF officials— including Sir Geoffrey Howe, British Chancellor of the Exchequer who is also chairman of the Fund's policy-making interim committee—are anxious to avoid this unprecedented step. Instead, they want to push ahead quickly with a proposal to increase the Fund's quota (or members' subscriptions) by as much as 50%, to $90 billion, a plan that was approved by the U.S., France, Great Britain, Germany and Japan at a conference in Kronberg, West Germany, in December. This would take more time than the borrowing route, because a legislative OK is needed in the U.S. and some of the other countries.

However quickly the higher quotas are approved, the Fund isn't likely to have any extra money to lend until mid-1984, at the earliest—opening a yawning gap in the resources of the world's chief financial policeman at the most critical time in its history. In an effort to fill in that gap, Howe and IMF managing director Jacques de Larosière recently journeyed to Riyadh to persuade Saudi Arabia to extend and increase its special $12 billion IMF contribution, which expires in March. And the $6.5 billion General Arrangement to Borrow among the industrialized Group of Ten nations, which is currently restricted to making loans only to its members, is being increased to $19 billion and its franchise broadened so that it can extend aid to other nations.

Of course, the IMF insists on "conditionality" when it grants a loan —a set of economic targets that usually spell austerity for the borrower and that are always politically unpopular. In fact, rather than go that route in order to obtain IMF aid, both Mexico and Brazil last year threatened to repudiate their debts. But repudiation is a no-win game, and both countries even-

tually agreed to IMF conditions, including cuts in public spending and a commitment to cut their payments deficits. Inevitably, these measures change the growth potential of the countries involved.

Today, the IMF reports sterling progress in both countries toward meeting their targets. Both have scrapped overambitious or unrealistic targets and tightened their belts— witness the recent curtailment of the nuclear programs of Mexico and Brazil. The belt-tightening is beginning to pay off. Mexico, for instance, showed a $5.4 billion trade surplus last year compared with $3.5 billion in 1981.

Mexico and all the other troubled borrowers are being helped even more by the sharp drop in U.S. interest rates since mid-1982. The five-point decline is already saving the developing countries an estimated $10 billion a year in interest payments, and the savings will grow if rates go still lower. This, in turn, would cut their borrowing needs and ease the pressure on banks and the IMF.

Ultimately, however, the world financial system can't recover fully unless there is a full-scale economic recovery. Says Peter Kenen of the prestigious Group of Thirty: "All the technical arrangements tend to divert

---

Need for economic recovery

---

attention from the fact that nobody will get out of this if the international economy continues to stagnate." Only then will the small banks be able to extricate themselves from Eurobanking and the larger banks feel comfortable about increasing their loans.

And until then, the likelihood is that the debtor nations won't be able to meet their balance-of-payment and fiscal targets and will need continual new financing. "It's a Perils of Pauline situation," comments Kenen. "You can't rule out reschedulings, annually, for several years."

BIG OIL
VS. CHEAP GAS
By Alfred J. Watkins

Photo: American Gas Association

Alfred J. Watkins is the Washington correspondent for the Texas Observer.

There is an old political maxim: If it ain't broke, don't fix it. The Natural Gas Policy Act of 1978 ain't broke. By almost any yardstick it is working better than expected. Working so well, in fact, that a lot of people—from Exxon to the National Audubon Society—want it repealed.

What are some of the complaints against the NGPA? It is disturbing the free market by providing too many incentives to find and develop new gas reserves. By encouraging drilling in the geological strata where large natural gas strikes are most likely, it is prolonging the life of easy-to-deplete, known reserves. By flooding the once shortage-plagued interstate market with gas, it is reducing demand for other fuels such as coal, uranium, OPEC oil—and even solar energy.

If these criticisms strike you as slightly surrealistic, welcome to the topsy-turvy world of natural gas regulation, where many people tout success as failure and the only good natural gas reserve often is one that stays undiscovered. It is a world where the NGPA is considered the worst kind of energy policy—even though it offers the United States' best hope for delivering the knockout blow to OPEC.

This last point gets to the real motive behind a growing campaign in Congress to gut the NGPA. Ask yourself a simple question: What could possibly send tremors of fear through such diversified energy corporations as Mobil and Exxon? Another OPEC price hike? A new windfall profits tax? Don't be silly. Try something really scary—like a cheap, clean, and abundant substitute for petroleum.

Natural gas is all these things. Though its price has been rising in recent years for reasons that have little to do with NGPA (see sidebar), it is still a bargain; it can heat homes and factories at approximately half the cost of fuel oil. As for cleanliness, natural gas is composed almost entirely of methane, a very simple molecule that when burned breaks down into carbon dioxide and water—not the sulphur, nitrous oxides, and assorted toxics that result from the combustion of gasoline and coal.

The abundance claim may be hard to believe, particularly if you remember all the talk five years ago that natural gas was fast going the way of the humpback whale. In 1978, the Carter administration estimated all the nation's natural gas would be gone in 10 years, a prospect that so panicked Congress it mandated that utilities and certain factories switch *from* natural gas *to* coal or even imported oil.

Then a funny thing happened. By partially decontrolling prices, the NGPA did exactly what any Economics 101 freshman might have predicted: it increased natural gas supply. In fact, in large part because of NGPA, we're now rolling in the stuff, the result of a natural gas rush that even the most die-hard free marketeers never imagined. Since the act's passage, drillers have been discovering natural gas almost everywhere they've looked—and in staggering quantities. In the Anadarko Basin of western Oklahoma alone, 70 new superwells, each capable of producing the energy equivalent of one million barrels of oil a year, had been discovered by late 1981. In a single deposit in Louisiana called the Tuscaloosa Trend, geologists have estimated gas resources of up to 24,000 trillion cubic feet—more than a thousand years' supply. According to estimates by the generally cautious Potential Gas Committee of the Colorado School of Mines, the United States could double its current consumption of about 20 trillion cubic feet a year and still never worry about shortages.

What's so great about a natural gas glut, you ask? As Gregg Easterbrook pointed out in these pages ("Why Not the Cheapest?" October 1980), natural gas is our ticket to destroying OPEC. Though U.S. oil imports have fallen to around five million barrels a day, and there are signs OPEC is weakening, oil prices are still an exorbitant $34 a barrel—10 times higher than they were a decade ago. And as the Iranian oil shortage of 1979 demonstrated, the sheiks and the Seven Sisters are adept at manipulating small supply disruptions into full-fledged crises in order to find a new pretense to continue their price gouging. Nothing less than a full-fledged effort to reduce oil consumption will topple OPEC—and this is where natural gas comes in. Though natural gas can't easily replace gasoline, less than half our daily consumption of 15 million barrels of oil goes for transportation. About nine million barrels a day go to fueling utilities and factories, and heating homes and businesses. Converting these uses to natural gas is fairly simple, sometimes involving little more than adjusting a few boiler valves. At an estimated one-time cost of about $20 billion, the nation could convert more than half these existing oil uses to natural gas. If that seems expensive, consider this: the Pentagon has spent far more for a Rapid Deployment Force whose major purpose is . . . protecting foreign oil sources.

Gassy Debate

It's not that this scenario is too good to be true—it just happens to be too true to be good for everyone. Owners of coal wouldn't be happy with an aggressive conversion process that takes full advantage of our abundant natural gas supplies—they have completely different notions of achieving energy independence. The nuclear industry has enough troubles without adding natural gas to its list. Independent fuel oil dealers also fear for their livelihood; dealers in New York have even launched an aggressive advertising campaign to keep their residential customers from switching to natural gas.

But natural gas poses the most risk to the nation's large oil companies—which, not coincidentally, also happen to own the majority of the nation's coal and uranium. Because they also produce half the nation's natural gas, these companies are not against using natural gas and some are actively developing new resources. Most are, however, opposed to an all-out effort to promote natural gas *at the expense of other energy sources*. A dramatic increase in natural gas use might cause oil prices to collapse as demand drops precipitously. To big oil companies, natural gas poses far more peril than even the most aggressive FTC lawsuit.

This explains why the major lobbying arms of the oil industry such as the American Petroleum Institute and the Natural Gas Supply Association (a consortium primarily of oil companies that also produce gas) have made the evisceration of the NGPA their top legislative priority in the next Congress. The oil industry would replace the NGPA's complicated system of price controls and incentives with total decontrol of all gas prices. This would have two salutary effects as far as the oil giants are concerned: First, it would vastly increase the revenues they would receive for their own gas, most of which is now subject to strict price controls. Second, by effectively tying all gas prices to oil prices, decontrol would ruin the best chance we have to break free of the OPEC stranglehold that has so debilitated our economy.

Big Oil's Gas Pains

To understand how the NGPA poses such a threat to the oil companies—and why its continued life is the most sensible energy policy for the rest of us—it's necessary to consider the act's benighted origins. It took Congress 19 months to come up with the NGPA, which it completed in 1978, and the process was living proof that sometimes the ideal recipe for good policy is two false premises, a flurry of special interest lobbying, and a compromise that both sides consider a rip-off.

One of those false premises belonged to James Schlesinger, who belonged to the "Chicken Little" school of energy analysis. Because we were running out of both oil and natural gas, he asserted, we should either force lower use through higher prices or simply give up altogether. He took the first course with oil, arguing for decontrol in conjunction with a windfall profits tax that would help balance Carter's budget. He took the latter course with natural gas, proposing that existing gas price controls be maintained while only very limited incentives be given for finding new gas. After all, Schlesinger argued, if there really wasn't much natural gas left, why bother to encourage anyone to look for it?

Schlesinger believed so strongly in the "vanishing gas" scenario that the last thing he was going to do was let the facts stand in his way. In preparing estimates of U.S. energy reserves, a research team headed by geologist Charles Knudsen of the Department of Energy concluded that natural gas reserves would last at least 40 years, not ten. Knudsen was promptly demoted. When the head of the U.S. Geological Survey, Dr. Vincent Mc-Kelvey, began making estimates that natural gas resources were "ten times the energy value of all [previously discovered] oil, gas, and coal reserves in the U.S. combined," he earned a different fate. He was fired. Schlesinger ordered the numbers redone to reflect his pessimistic scenario; one participant recalled: "Schlesinger said he didn't care where the numbers came from, as long as they were bad."

Carter's opponents erred in an opposite direction by trying to remove almost all price controls on natural gas. Led by the oil companies and dominant gas producers, they wanted to let the market determine prices on all "new gas"—that is, any gas discovered and sold in interstate commerce after January 1, 1977. (Though these producers favored the removal of controls on existing "old gas" as well, they did not press their case because they realized that was then politically impossible.) Decontrol enthusiasts argued that letting all gas prices rise was the best way to encourage more exploration and production, thereby relieving the widespread gas shortages then plaguing the interstate market.

Decontrol advocates were right in saying higher prices would lead to the discovery and development of large new gas supplies. But they were wrong in urging decontrol for all new gas. To understand why, think of natural gas as Coca-Cola. If you are thirsty, you can either plunk a second straw into your friend's bottle or you can go out and try to find a new case of soda. The decontrol proponents never distinguished between these two approaches. Instead, they wanted to set the same price for gas from new reservoirs (finding a new case of soda) and gas from additional wells in old reservoirs (adding a second straw).

Gas producers may be born gamblers, but they are not fools. If you offer them the same reward for betting on a long shot (exploring for new gas) and betting on a sure thing (drilling in existing fields), they will naturally prefer the latter. Unfortunately, in the case of natural gas the consequences of this are altogether self-defeating. Letting gas producers reap a bonanza simply for increasing production from known fields would have increased consumer costs by more than $60 billion (thereby fueling more inflation), while doing little to identify new supplies.

After months of acrimonious debate, all-night sessions, and a spirited filibuster led by senators Howard Metzenbaum and James Abourezk, Congress worked out a compromise that few liked and even fewer understood. The NGPA managed to come up with 23 legal varieties of a molecularly identical substance. There were categories for old gas, new gas, interstate gas, intrastate gas, onshore gas, offshore gas, shallow gas, deep gas—not to mention a category for gas that didn't fit any of the other categories. The diagrams showing which natural gas falls into what category looked like a post-modernist painting of a plate of spaghetti.

Yet for all the byzantine complexities, a certain logic lay behind the NGPA, a "supply-side theory" of energy as it were. Where higher prices would make little difference in production, as in the case of gas already being pumped from existing fields, price controls were left intact. These prices ranged from $.18 to $1.45 per thousand cubic feet, depending on the date the gas was first sold in interstate markets, and were allowed to rise with inflation. To relieve immediate supply problems and encourage more drilling in already discovered fields, such "new" gas was priced at $1.75 per thousand cubic feet ($1.75/mcf in the gas industry's cryptic shorthand) and also allowed to rise with inflation. Gas from most newly found fields also was priced at $1.75 but allowed to increase *faster* than inflation. And where producers risked the most capital looking for new gas, the incentives were greatest. The biggest went for "deep gas," found below 15,000 feet; for it, the NGPA imposed no price controls at all.

The Gasmen Cometh

The gas bonanza of the last five years is the story of deep gas—which in turn is largely the story of a man named Robert Hefner. The head of a natural gas drilling firm called the GHK Company, Hefner for the past 20 years has devoted his time, energy, and money drilling exclusively for deep gas. He has sung the praises of deep gas throughout this time, explaining to anyone who would listen that the United States was a "world-scale frontier as a natural gas province," entering the "new age of methane." To friends and business partners, Hefner was a visionary; to most people in the oil and gas industry, he was an eccentric, if not a raving lunatic.

Not that there weren't good reasons to suspect Hefner's sanity. Historically, finding oil has been two to three times more lucrative than finding gas. Wildcat drillers who inadvertently found gas in their search for oil weren't loathe to market it, but they didn't see much sense in specifically looking for it. Moreover, because oil is seldom found below 10,000 feet, drilling deeper seemed downright silly. Deep wells can take up to two years to complete and cost up to ten times as much as the average shallow well, and even if gas was discovered under price controls it was likely to fetch less than it cost to produce. A well Hefner drilled in 1969 produced large quantities of gas at 24,000 feet, but it was a financial flop with prices at only $0.17/mcf.

After widespread natural gas shortages occurred in the winter of 1976-77, Congress finally realized something had to be done to guarantee future supplies. So Hefner did what many self-respecting businessmen do when they want the government to help make them millionaires: he began to lobby. Success came rather easily, and not only because of his movie-star good looks and charm. When Jimmy Carter finally decided to compromise on the natural gas issue after the House had passed his version of the bill but the Senate had endorsed decontrol, Hefner called him to suggest that those hardy entrepreneurs looking for deep gas deserved an incentive. When Carter embraced the notion, many liberals accused him of caving in to special interests who stood to profit handsomely from NGPA—which was true. Hefner, for example, recently was listed by *Forbes* as one of the 400 wealthiest people in America.

It would be easy to dismiss the NGPA as special-interest lobbying at its worst were it not for one thing: what was good for Hefner also happened to be good for the rest of us. As a result of the incentive for deep gas, the number of new wells mushroomed. In the Anadarko Basin alone, for example, deep wells soared in number from 160 at the end of 1978 to 750 by December 1981. In the oil industry, a 15-percent success rate is considered exceptional: the success rate for deep-gas wells so far has been 57 percent in Texas, 63 percent in Wyoming, and 64 percent in Oklahoma.

Though it's plentiful, deep gas is also expensive to produce. In fact, the average price of $3/mcf that pipeline companies are now paying for gas is too low to cover costs of all but the most productive deep-gas wells. So why have deep-gas producers like Hefner been so willing to explore for new reserves? The answer lies in something called "rolled-in pricing," which is the reason for NGPA's success so far—and the real object of the oil companies' enmity.

Oily Reaction

Rolled-in pricing works like this: Let's say a pipeline company pays $1/mcf for half its natural gas. It buys the remainder from other suppliers at prices ranging from $1 to $7/mcf. By averaging costs, the pipeline company can sell its gas for $3/mcf, which keeps it less costly than the price of its main competitor—oil. Yet the pipeline company can still afford to buy high-priced deep gas because old, price-controlled gas provides a cushion.

As opposed to government tax breaks or depletion allowances, rolled-in pricing stimulates new exploration by subsidizing it with existing supplies of gas. As existing reserves of price-controlled gas are exhausted, prices will rise, but not in disruptive leaps, as has been the case with oil. Rolled-in pricing thus offers the best of both worlds: tremendous incentives to find new gas while sheltering consumers from the full brunt of its costs. And by encouraging exploration *now* rather than when existing supplies are on the verge of disappearing, rolled-in pricing has given the nation the rare good fortune of identifying in advance how to end dependence on imported oil.

And herein lies the problem: Not everyone is keen on seeing the energy crisis go the way of 29-cents-a-gallon gasoline. And it's no small irony that those most anxious to destroy the old-gas price cushion—the oil companies—also happen to own most of the nation's natural gas.

Why the oil companies dislike the NGPA so much becomes clear when one realizes what kind of gas they own. A study based on government figures by the Consumer Federation of America shows that the nation's major oil companies own 72 percent of the nation's old gas—that is, gas subject to the NGPA's indefinite price controls.

This is in stark contrast to deep gas. Though many large oil companies are exploring for deep gas, most producers are the epitome of that much-vaunted species, the relatively small, independent businessman. Such entrepreneurs own 80 percent of the deep gas discovered so far—and many continue to gamble their savings to explore for more.

What would happen if all gas prices were decontrolled? Owners of old gas—namely, the major oil companies—would, according to the CFA, gain up to $70 billion in windfall profits through higher prices. Gas prices to the consumer would probably stay just as high—though the incentives for looking for new gas would be reduced substantially.

This is what the oil companies want: immediate decontrol of all gas, old and new. As a fallback position, they say they are ready to accept "accelerated decontrol" of all gas. However, since NGPA controls on non-deep new gas (remember, there were 23 varieties) will expire January 1, 1985, this is nothing more than a code word for gutting the controls on old gas that otherwise would remain in effect. This is gas that was profitable to produce before 1977 at prices of less than $1.45/mcf; more than half the nation's production falls into this category.

The industry is doing more than just talking

Soaring Gas Prices: Don't Blame the N.G.P.A.

If you happen to use natural gas to heat your home, all this talk about the glorious age of methane no doubt leaves you somewhat perplexed. So much new gas has been discovered since 1978 that a natural gas glut has developed. Yet in the past year gas prices have skyrocketed. According to the American Gas Association consumers will pay an average of 25 percent more for gas this year than last; in some parts of the country increases will exceed 50 percent.

If you think this defies everything you ever learned about supply and demand, you're absolutely right. Under normal circumstances these surpluses should force prices down, but in the perverse world of natural gas a vicious circle has developed. Bigger surpluses mean higher prices, which in turn mean lower demand and even bigger surpluses.

The reason for this lies in what are known as "take-or-pay provisions." In the mid- and late 1970s, pipeline companies signed contracts (mostly with producers of expensive, recently discovered gas) that amounted to little more than legalized larceny. The provisions obligated pipelines to pay for up to 95 percent of a producer's output regardless of whether it could be sold. Pipelines would either take the gas and pay for it, or not take it and still pay for it.

The pipeline companies (which in turn pass their costs on to consumers) blundered into these contracts for two major reasons. First, they assumed that natural gas was disappearing so fast they had no choice but to sign such long-term contracts to guarantee supplies. At the same time, they assumed oil prices would continue to soar, thereby increasing demand for natural gas.

The pipelines were wrong all around. Discoveries of new gas far exceeded most predictions. An oil glut developed and the recession that began in 1979 reduced demand for all energy. And though homeowners began converting from heating oil to natural gas at a clip of 400,000 a year, per capita use dropped sharply as customers practiced conservation. In 1977, the U.S. consumed 19.9 trillion cubic feet of natural gas; in 1981, when the supply outlook was as rosy as it was gloomy four years earlier, consumption had dropped to 19.8 trillion.

But under the take-or-pay provisions, pipelines have had to refuse delivery of much cheaper gas. The Northern Natural Gas Pipeline Company of Duluth, for example, is now refusing gas at 90 cents per thousand cubic feet in favor of Canadian gas at $6. According to the *Kansas City Star*, consumers in 14 midwestern states will pay $545 million extra this year because pipeline companies are drastically reducing purchases of gas at 27 to 50 cents to buy gas as high as

$9, some of it liquefied gas from Algeria. Columbia Gas System Inc., which supplies customers in seven eastern states, signed contracts that promised not only to take 90 percent of a producer's expensive gas, but to let prices automatically increase with inflation plus three percent. Some industrial users, paying double what they were two years ago, are switching to cheaper residual fuel oil.

Take-or-pay contracts aren't the only reason for escalating gas prices. According to a detailed investigation by the Consumer Federation of America, the nation's largest gas producers appear to be making $500 million a year in illegal profits by selling natural gas at prices far in excess of levels mandated by the Natural Gas Policy Act of 1978 (see sidebar on page 30). Another device for artificially raising gas prices is something known as "self-dealing," whereby pipeline companies buy gas from their own subsidiaries at inflated prices, sometimes in lieu of much cheaper gas from other sources. For example, Columbia's West Virginia branch recorded a "loss" last year because it bought expensive "company gas" while passing up much cheaper gas from independent West Virginia drillers. Take-or-pay contracts notwithstanding, such sleight-of-hand helped Columbia generate record high profits in 1981.

All this has prompted a hunt for villains, and NGPA's price controls head many people's list. Yet this ignores the fact that pipelines would have signed these contracts even if Congress had removed all price controls on natural gas in 1978. The impetus for entering into these agreements was the fear of a shortage—which actually might have occurred had Congress taken the decontrol route. But by maintaining price controls on already discovered old gas while removing those for difficult-to-develop new gas, the act was directly responsible for the new discoveries that now make it possible to use natural gas as a means of crushing OPEC (see main story).

The call for decontrol also ignores the best and most obvious solution. Congress simply can require pipelines and producers to renegotiate certain take-or-pay clauses, forcing gas prices to respond to supply and demand.

Unfortunately, for many powerful interests the most obvious solution isn't the best one. Some producers would lose their money with renegotiation. But more important, this approach would eliminate any pretext for decontrolling all natural gas prices, particularly those in effect on already discovered old gas. The top 20 oil companies own 72 percent of this gas—and stand to reap up to $70 billion extra if all controls are lifted.

about decontrol. Political action committees representing oil and gas companies, as well as industry executives and investors, spent more than $7 million on the 1982 congressional elections. The biggest recipient was Texas Senator Lloyd Bentsen, a staunch decontrol supporter who got $143,000. President Reagan pledged his support for decontrol—without any windfall profits tax—in the 1980 election. This November he reiterated his desire for decontrol legislation in the next Congress.

The most superficially plausible argument for decontrol comes by way of analogy. When Reagan decontrolled oil prices over a year ago, infuriated liberals predicted gasoline soon would hit $2 a gallon. But in the last year, domestic oil exploration has increased while gasoline prices actually have declined slightly; those same congressmen are now paying an average of seven cents less per gallon when they send their interns out to fill up their tanks. Decontrol enthusiasts say the same thing will happen with natural gas.

A closer look reveals the apples/oranges analogy. Controls on domestic oil were self-defeating because they discouraged domestic exploration and, by creating a cushion of cheap domestic oil, made the importation of OPEC oil seem less painful than it really was. Decontrol stimulated domestic exploration, removed that cushion and reduced imports. This in turn put pressure on OPEC to moderate its prices.

The immediate decontrol of natural gas will have entirely different results. Removing price controls on domestic oil could increase our domestic oil resources; removing controls on old gas, by definition, can do *nothing* to increase old-gas supplies. The amount of gas classified as "old" under NGPA is finite, and letting its price suddenly rise would only encourage its faster depletion by producers in search of windfall profits. Finally, while drillers would still look for new gas, decontrol would dampen their enthusiasm since it destroys the current cushion of cheap old gas that now offers an extra incentive. In our efforts to substitute natural gas for OPEC oil, it's only sensible that we use old gas to help with the transition.

But there's a far more telling objection to immediately decontrolling all natural gas prices. Instead of real decontrol, the result would be just another kind of price fixing. Except in this case, it wouldn't be the government that determined the price of natural gas: the major oil companies would call the tune.

This particular scam has the kind of devious elegance that's easy to miss when looking into the

The Old Gas Shuffle

There are many obscure reasons your natural gas bill will be a lot higher this winter. But one reason is quite simple: the nation's pipeline companies appear to be breaking the law.

One of the main provisions of the Natural Gas Policy Act of 1978 was its continuation of federal price controls for "old gas"—that is, gas discovered before the law's enactment. Under the law, pre-1973 gas carries a maximum legal price of $1.07 per thousand cubic feet. Yet according to the Consumer Federation of America, the nation's 15 major pipeline companies are purchasing about 23 percent of their pre-1973 gas at prices substantially higher than the legal ceiling. The Natural Gas Pipeline Company of America is paying an average of $2.27 per thousand cubic feet; Columbia Gas Transmission Corp. is paying $2.04; Panhandle Eastern is paying $2.22. According to CFA director Ann Lower, whose findings are based on information the pipelines regularly supply to the Federal Energy Regulatory Commission, these apparent overcharges exceed $500 million a year.

Pipeline company officials offer two explanations, both of them dubious. The first is that the NGPA permits minor price hikes for natural gas that has a higher-than-average energy content. However, natural gas experts generally agree this so-called "BTU adjustment" rarely amounts to more than a few cents. The pipelines also claim that some of this gas comes from contracts signed with gas producers *before* 1973 but on which they did not make good until after 1978, when natural gas prices had roughly tripled. The pipelines' questionable business acumen in this matter notwithstanding, such an explanation begs a more obvious

question: If this really is "new gas," why are the pipeline companies reporting it as old gas, risking some unpleasant questions by nosy FERC auditors?

The answer is that they have little to worry about, if FERC's response to Lower's study is any indication. Last August, Lower asked for a formal response from FERC. She has yet to receive one. Rochelle Patterson, a spokesperson for FERC, now claims that "the people in the enforcement division concluded that there was nothing in Lower's data that indicated any violation [of the law]." But no one in enforcement ever told Lower that; despite repeated requests, FERC officials still refuse to meet with her. Assistant General Counsel Gary Lloyd has a copy of the report, but apparently hasn't read it. Asked to explain why pipeline companies might be reporting extra-legal prices for gas, Lloyd claimed that it was "unclear" they were even misreporting. Pressed on how he had reached that conclusion, Lloyd admitted he had not discussed the matter with the pipeline companies themselves or even asked officials in his own agency who monitor the pipeline filings.

This behavior is most curious—particularly when FERC officials, after initially indicating Lower's criticisms had no merit, admitted several days later that an investigation of old-gas pricing had been going on for nearly a year. But Lloyd refuses to say if FERC has cause to believe the law is being broken. "They're investigating this but they're doing it their way" says Patterson.

And how quickly can consumers expect results? That's hard to say, though it is worth noting that last month the agency announced a $57 million settlement in another natural gas case. The violations occurred nearly ten years ago.

—A.W.

natural gas controversy. According to a 1981 survey of gas contracts conducted by the American Gas Association, something known as indefinite price escalators exist in 67 percent of the current gas contracts between producers and pipeline companies and in virtually all contracts written since the mid-1970s. Some of these clauses stipulate that upon the deregulation of natural gas, prices will rise to 110 percent of the price of number 2 fuel oil, natural gas's major competitor in industrial and home-heating markets. But in most cases the tie with oil is far more subtle: prices will rise to the same level as the highest price received by other gas producers in the vicinity.

This sounds innocent enough—until you realize that if even a few gas contracts in an area are tied to the price of number 2 fuel oil, they can touch off a chain reaction that will eventually pull up *all* gas. Officials of the American Gas Association, which represents pipeline companies, warn that a "critical mass" of contracts with the 110-percent clauses now exists to do just that.

So much for the free market. In effect, these contract provisions guarantee that the decontrolled price of natural gas will be forever higher than the price of oil—natural gas's *major competitor*! This is a little like ordering Chrysler to forever keep its prices above GM's. That would be good for GM, but far less desirable for struggling Chrysler—and disastrous for consumers.

Decontrol Delusions

If you're still skeptical about keeping the NGPA, consider the conclusions of Reagan's own Department of Energy. Earlier this year it conducted a study that wholeheartedly endorsed the immediate decontrol of natural gas prices. But when one examines the supposed "effects" of decontrol as outlined in the study, one gets the impression that DOE has been hiring some of its consultants out of Riyadh. Among the predicted results of the deregulation:

—"Consumer well-being declines by $79 billion because higher gas prices occur sooner."

—"Production from unconventional sources of gas is likely to be lower. In addition . . . overall production is somewhat lower in the late 1980s and 1990s compared to the NGPA."

—"Because of the more rapid depletion of current reserves. . . . oil imports are reduced in the early years of decontrol but increased in the later years."

With arguments like these from supporters of decontrol, one wonders how the oil industry's lobbyists ever expect to find a sympathetic ear in Congress. But in addition to the usual crew of free-market worshipers, the industry is getting assistance from some unusual quarters.

Among the oil companies' unlikely allies are the Conservation Foundation and the National Audubon Society—who favor decontrolling natural gas prices on the theory that it will discourage consumption, preserve a scarce resource, and stimulate the development of alternative sources such as solar energy. What they overlook is that natural gas is the best energy source to rely on in the transition to renewable fuels; the nation should be encouraging its production and consumption rather than doing the opposite.

The NGPA faces another danger: talk is beginning among some liberals in Congress to freeze all gas prices. But this approach runs the risk of ignoring the grim lessons of the 1970s, when stiff price controls on gas so discouraged exploration and production that widespread shortages developed, particularly in the winter of 1976-77.

Carter was right about one thing: America does need an energy policy. And as unexpected as its beneficial effects may have been, the NGPA offers an energy plan unlike most of the energy plans we've heard about in the past decade: one that works. It's a plan that involves not reams of computer printouts or a 20,000-employee department of energy, but a national commitment to match the cheapest and best-suited energy sources to our actual needs.

NGPA offers just that. Other than making a few minor adjustments, Congress should do what it seems to do so well with other matters of national importance: nothing at all. Of course, taking full advantage of natural gas's promise won't be quick or easy. The conversion to this abundant fuel will require an aggressive national effort and the removal of obstacles such as the 1978 law, passed during the throes of panic, that still prohibits some uses of gas. But the effort is more than worthwhile; not to make it would be to squander the only real chance we have to return to those pre-1973 days when inflation was low, energy was plentiful, and we could devote our money and resources to things far more important.

The Potential Impacts of Robotics

Welding on an automobile assembly line, a hot, dirty, and uncomfortable job performed by humans can be taken over by robots (left). Robots are already replacing some human workers in mass-production industries such as car manufacturing. Substitution effects, such as unemployment, are the first wave of impacts that occur when a new technology is introduced. Other impacts occur when industries adjust to take advantage of the new technology and when they discover new opportunities the technology makes possible, says author Coates.

FORD

Vary T. Coates

Vary T. Coates, vice president of J.F. Coates, Inc. (3738 Kanawha Street, N.W., Washington, D.C. 20015), has investigated policy issues and technology assessment for industry and government.

J.F. Coates, Inc., is a futures research and policy analysis group directed at assisting decision-making in public and private organizations. The group conducts projects and studies dealing with such issues as the future of machine tools and robots, computers, the environment, water, genetic engineering, population, energy, appropriate technology, and many other vital areas.

Industrial robots are machines that can be reprogrammed to do a variety of simple repetitive tasks that are usually done by human workers in a factory. Robots can weld, spray paint, cut cloth with lasers, and load and unload materials for other machines.

Like human workers, robots can be moved from one job to another and can be taught to do new tasks, in some cases after merely being led through a task once. But unlike human workers, they can work two

or even three shifts, six or seven days a week, without coffee breaks, vacations, sick leave, or disputes with management. Unlike human workers, they work tirelessly and with great precision and low error rates. Unlike human workers, they are insensitive to toxic chemicals, radioactivity, and dust.

Most of today's robots are both blind and stupid. They can attach one part to another, but only if both parts are presented in an exact, predetermined location and a pre-

From The Futurist, February 1983, published by the World Future Society, 4916 St. Elmo Avenue, Washington, D.C. 20014.

cise orientation. But the next generation of robots, now approaching commercialization, will have "sight" and other sensory capabilities. Furthermore, while humans come in a very limited range of sizes and shapes, robots could be shaped to meet the requirements of their work in ways that are impossible for humans.

Unlike human workers, industrial robots do not buy houses, automobiles, or food; they do not pay taxes or draw Social Security checks.

If they are to play a large part in the future of American industry, it behooves us to think seriously about the possible consequences. Here we can mention only a few, and we must not forget that we are talking only about industrial robots, which constitute only a very small part of a new era of automation based on the microprocessor, which will affect nearly every aspect of work and the economy throughout the world.

A useful technique for thinking about the potential impacts of technological innovation is a simple conceptual model that my colleagues and I have developed. It's called the Technology Diffusion or User-Institution Model. According to this model, the first wave of impacts comes from *substitution* (users substitute the new technology for older systems because it can fulfill their functions more efficiently or effectively than the older technology). The second wave is from *accommodation* (industries make internal changes to make better use of the new technology) and the third wave is from *innovation* (new uses for the technology are discovered).

Mass-production industries, especially automobile manufacturers, are now adopting industrial robots to replace human workers in such tasks as spot welding and spray painting. The first impacts to be considered, therefore, are those on employment.

The Effects on Employment

There are now only about 5,000 industrial robots in use in the United States, the number having increased by about 30% in 1981 alone. That would represent about 15,000 jobs, but most of those workers have probably been shifted or upgraded, and the number is certainly well

GI Robots

The speed, precision, and cost-effectiveness that make robots attractive to private manufacturing are also making them attractive to the military.

Robots enhanced with sensors and with artificial intelligence—computer programming that enables them to "think"—would be able to take over many routine or dangerous jobs of soldiers, or even to do things soldiers cannot do, says a report by Dennis V. Crumley of the Futures/Long-Range Planning Group of the U.S. Army War College's Strategic Studies Institute. Some tasks that smart robots may be able to perform on the twenty-first century battlefield are:

• Identify aircraft, control air traffic, and transmit deceptive noises to confuse the enemy.

• Identify and track targets and select the highest-priority target from among several on the battlefield.

• Handle materials that have been contaminated during nuclear, chemical, or biological warfare.

• Load weapons, set fuses, and transfer rounds of ammunition from storage areas to guns.

• Collect, correlate, and transmit information about the enemy to command posts.

• Detect enemy minefields and implant "smart" mines capable of recognizing enemy movements.

• Dig ditches, make craters, or build obstacles based on the robot's programmed knowledge of the enemy, reducing the need for soldiers to perform these routine tasks.

The greatest near- to mid-term potential applications for robots in the military, however, will probably be off the battlefield, the report notes. For example, physical examinations could be automated—an expansion on the coin-operated blood-pressure machines found in shopping centers today. Robots with artificial intelligence could conduct aptitude tests, process payrolls, issue uniforms or equipment, and perform other administrative chores. Another application could be computer-assisted training in weaponry, with robot targets, automatic scoring, and voice-supported critiques of trainees' performances.

Other military uses of robots could include space exploration, underwater search for enemy mines and submarines, and situation assessment during or after a nuclear strike when people may be under too much stress to make rational judgments.

The report emphasizes that research and development of robotic technology have not yet been aggressively pursued in the United States, and, for the Army to take full advantage of robot potential, "an effort on the scale of the Manhattan Project would likely be required." Since such an effort is unrealistic at present, Crumley concludes that to make best use of robots, the Army should establish priorities; the most important potential applications should then be pursued with further research and development.

For more information, see "Concepts for Army Use of Robotic-Artificial Intelligence in the 21st Century" by Dennis V. Crumley. U.S. Army War College, Strategic Studies Institute, Futures/Long-Range Planning Group, Carlisle Barracks, Pennsylvania 17013. 1982. 27 pages.

within normal attrition rates. The potential market, right now, with currently available robots, is probably between 100,000 and 200,000 sales. Even conservative market projections call for about 50,000 to 70,000 robots in use in the U.S. by 1990. But these low estimates are based on a number of constraints that appear to be inhibiting the market (for example, the recession). Several large manufacturers are

The Technology Diffusion Model
How an Institution Responds to a New Technology

EXAMPLE
Possible Impacts of Robots on an Automobile Company and Its Market

STEP 1

INNOVATIVE TECHNOLOGY

Institution adopts technology to carry out existing functions more efficiently

ROBOTS

Automobile company buys robots to perform welding, painting, and other chores on the assembly line, finding them more cost efficient than human workers.

Technology may be modified to suit needs of users better

STEP 2

Institution changes internally to take better advantage of new efficiencies

Robots are modified to perform new tasks designed by users.

Company creates a department to manage the purchase, installation, and repair of robots. Workers displaced by robots are shifted to other jobs in factory. Some workers welcome the change but others may not like their new assignments. Executive named to head the robot department becomes a new power in company politics.

STEP 3

Other institutions may be created, or old ones changed, to utilize new technology

Institution develops new functions and activities made possible by additional capabilities of the technology

New firms are started, specializing in:
• Recruiting robot specialists
• Soothing workers' feelings as robots are introduced
• Repairing robots
• Providing accessories such as heavy rubber coats to protect workers dealing with robots.

The robot department discovers that the robots can be used in the company cafeteria to dispense food efficiently. Market research indicates big potential for robots in food service, and the robot department sets up a task force to develop robots specifically for the food-service industry.

Competition between institutions

Competition develops among robot manufacturers, repair shops, etc.

STEP 4

Institution may become obsolete, be replaced, or be radically transformed

Large profits from food-service robots contrast with declining profits from automobiles. Company decides to switch from making autos to making robots. At the same time, it expands robot production to include robots for household use (cleaning rugs, washing windows, washing dishes, etc.).

Impact of technology innovation on user institutions (after Joseph Coates, *Telecommunications Policy,* 1:196-206, 1977)

poised to enter the market, and several giants are signaling that they will greatly increase their use of robotics, so some analysts offer far higher projections for both sales and robots in use. It is entirely possible that within two to three decades we could see a million or more robots filling up to three million of today's jobs.

To put this into context, U.S. industry now employs about eight million "operatives" (blue-collar workers). As a percentage of total employment, the operatives' jobs have been declining for decades. All manufacturing jobs represented 37% of total employment in 1950 and 24% in 1980. Within manufacturing, production jobs—those on the work floor—constituted 82% in 1950 and less than 70% today. More and more Americans are in white-collar jobs.

If fewer and fewer operator jobs are available for those entering the work force in 1990 and afterward, it may be no great loss—provided better jobs are available, and provided the entering workers are qualified for these jobs. Automation, and innovation in general, has over the long range created more jobs than it has destroyed, although not always in the same industries and often only after some period of dislocation and transition.

How important the effects of a much smaller number of operatives' jobs for those entering the work force in 1990 and later will be depends on whether the economy is growing, what kinds of new jobs have been created, and especially what effects the new automation has had on alternative occupations. By 1990, the number of people entering the work force each year will be smaller, and they will be better educated. New industries such as biotechnology may be growing rapidly, and robotics itself may directly create many jobs. But we must also remember that lower-level white-collar jobs, which could be alternatives to blue-collar work, may have been sharply reduced by office automation. Other service occupations may also have radically changed: for example, post office jobs will be changed by the growth of electronic mail.

At present, 41% of all operatives' jobs are filled by women. Many of these women have had little opportunity for formal education; they have entered the work force after raising children or between childbearing stints, or their job mobility is sharply curtailed because of family responsibilities. About 16% of operatives' jobs are filled by non-whites. Unskilled and semiskilled jobs have, in the past, been an important socializing institution or channel for upward mobility for immigrants and for internal migrants from depressed or less-developed regions of the United States. Hence the loss of operatives' jobs to industrial robots could have a much greater impact on women and nonwhites than on the work force as a whole, since they may have much less opportunity to fill alternative, or upgraded, jobs.

These two groups—women and nonwhites—together account for about 3.5 million blue-collar jobs. We have already noted estimates that industrial robots could displace just about that many workers in about two decades. Since women and nonwhites are less likely than other workers to be represented by unions, and since as already noted they may also have poorer qualifications, less locational mobility, and less job experience than others, they will almost surely suffer the greatest direct impacts of increased movement toward industrial robotics.

About half of all operatives' jobs in manufacturing are in metal-working industries, and about half of these are concentrated in the four Great Lakes states (Illinois, Indiana, Michigan, Ohio), New York, and California. With the exception of California, these states have already been losing jobs and are threatened with loss of population. The economic impacts of industrial robots could therefore be sharply concentrated in a few states.

Industrial robots, at the present, are usually adopted to cut labor costs; to cut error rates, improve quality, or solve particular production problems; or to perform tasks that are hazardous for human workers because of toxic materials, heat, fumes, radioactivity, or a high potential for accidents. Because of the ris-

ing costs of compliance with occupational health and safety regulations, the last motivation may well be the strongest. One consequence of greater use of robots, therefore, may be fewer work-related injuries and illnesses.

However, there is a darker side to this possibility. The threat of job displacement may constrain workers, and their unions, from complaining about unsafe or unhealthy conditions, and may further reduce political support for improvement of the work environment.

Increased Productivity

We have so far looked chiefly at potential negative effects of industrial robots. But it is still possible that these might be far outweighed by the effects of increased productivity. In the mass-production industries (such as automobiles and appliances, for example), better quality and lower labor and regulatory costs might improve the competitive position of the United States *vis-a-vis* Europe and Japan and thereby prevent jobs from migrating overseas.

Far more important, potentially, are the possible benefits for batch manufacturing (the production of 50 or fewer identical items per order), which constitutes the larger part of American manufacturing and has so far benefited far less from hard automation (nonreprogrammable machines performing fixed tasks) than has mass production. Industrial robots can be easily, quickly, and cheaply reprogrammed for new tasks, and, combined with computer-assisted design (CAD), computer-assisted manufacturing (CAM), and flexible manufacturing systems (FMS), can bring to batch manufacturing the efficiencies gained for mass production by hard automation.

Future markets probably will stress wide diversification in consumer products, with more frequent model changes. If the unit cost of 10 copies of a hundred models could be as low as the unit cost of a thousand copies of one model, the effects throughout the world economy are almost inconceivable. Even before this point is reached, a significant drop in the costs of producing consumer goods would have economic effects that could far outweigh the direct labor displacement.

Accommodating the Robot

The Technology Diffusion Model tells us that the second wave of impacts comes when industries, having adopted a new technology, make internal adjustments and accommodations in order to use it more efficiently.

At present, industrial robots are being introduced only into existing assembly lines. But since robots have neither the flexibilities nor the restrictions of humans, a work environment organized for human labor is not necessarily the environment that is best for robots. A multi-task robot, for example, may be surrounded by the various tools and supplies of materials with which it interfaces to create a work cell.

To use robots most efficiently, the flow of work and the factory floor may have to be completely redesigned. The resulting work environment may be inefficient, unsafe, and inhospitable for human workers, thus encouraging manufacturers to speed up their move to total robotization.

An equally pervasive (but less visible) accommodation to robots will be organizational, including changes in the work force to reflect new skill requirements and retraining of both managers and workers.

New Functions

Our model shows that institutions that adopt robots will develop new activities and functions to make still better use of the new technology. Adopted to perform existing tasks more efficiently, robots will also offer new capabilities that industry will seek to use productively.

For example, since robots are impervious to conditions that are hostile to humans, they can be used to increase exploration and development in outer space, underground, and in the oceans. The potential hazards of nuclear power and chemical industries could be minimized by using robots to handle all toxic materials. Robots also can be made in new shapes and sizes to perform specific tasks that humans cannot do, such as to inspect pipelines from the inside or to carry out safety inspections inside structural components of operating aircraft.

Thus, robotics can enormously extend our ability to use, to change, and to protect our physical environment. They can help us avoid the consequences of human error and fallibility.

The Technology Diffusion Model suggests that robots will bring enormous changes in institutions and society. Institutions that adopt robots may be radically transformed, and those that fail to do so may become obsolete. A nation may improve its position in world markets by making use of this technology— or lose its markets to foreign industries that adopt it more efficiently. Will society intervene to control, reduce, and avoid social dislocations that may result during the transition? Will government and industry work cooperatively to help society reap the technology's latent benefits?

There are many dangers and problems inherent in robotics technology. Most of them are transitional problems, but they can inflict pain and grief on individuals, families, communities, and regions if they are not managed with foresight and judgment.

The benefits of the new robotics technology arise from improved quality, scale, and control. Combined with other emerging technologies, robotics can contribute to a transformation of society—both in the United States and throughout the world—that is as all-encompassing a change as the Industrial Revolution.

The End of the 'Labor Society'

The counterproductivity of policies for 'full employment'

RALF DAHRENDORF

Ralf Dahrendorf is Director of the London School of Economics. This is excerpted from the liberal weekly "Die Zeit" of Hamburg.

Everyone talks about unemployment. It is something we can all grasp. Back in the mid-1970s the unemployment rate in the European Economic Community (EEC) was 3 to 4 per cent. Today it is 10 per cent, and in the U.S. it is even higher.

Who is concerned about unemployment, and what is the nature of their concern? Labor unions and the Socialist parties linked to them in some countries say they detest unemployment, and there is no reason to disbelieve them, but their action invariably leads to increased unemployment. Only where unions are represented in management — at Chrysler in Detroit, for example — are they willing to consider wage reductions as a means of preserving jobs. The ultimate goal of unions and Socialist parties is to eliminate the labor society, and that implies the elimination of work itself.

Conservative parties are particularly concerned about rising unemployment. So are the people who have not lost their jobs — especially those whose jobs are threatened. Work is an instrument of control; where there are no jobs the rulers of a labor society lose their base of control and society's structure is called into question.

It is not surprising that two proposed remedies for unemployment both envision a return to a labor society. Both of them, however, are worthless.

One embraces supply-side economics: The recession can be cured by means of tax cuts, reduction in government spending, and the deregulation of business. If at the same time inflation can be checked by controlling the money supply, the argument runs, then renewed economic growth will allow unemployment to correct itself.

But neither the British nor the American experience of the past few years has proved the effectiveness of supply-side economics. Even where there has been economic growth it has not led to any significant increase in jobs. For nations as a whole it is doubtful whether an annual growth in the gross national product of 1 or 2 per cent would, in the foreseeable future, lead to more jobs.

If supply-side theories have nothing to offer, what about the traditional methods of repairing the labor society? Government stimulation of demand coupled with a policy of creating jobs with state funds is the alternative response to unemployment. Here, too, the results are questionable. The policy of stimulating demand has been no more effective than to encourage business leaders and investors, and government programs to create jobs have had only a modest impact on unemployment.

Does all this mean that unemployment has become inevitable? No. What it means is that the current proposals have not gone far enough. Certainly some special measures, like those to stem youth unemployment, divide up jobs, or offer early retirement, make sense for the labor society. But they do not get to the heart of the problem. They do not deal with the obvious paradox that much work needs to be done, yet unemployment increases.

Today the distribution of wealth makes it impossible for the public sector to be rich. Because wages have risen to such a high level we can no longer afford labor-intensive public services, so our railroads, prisons, hospitals, and schools fall apart. The contradiction between things that need doing and jobless workers is clear.

The stabilization of wage levels — often called "wage and price control" — might halt the rising level of unemployment (if such a policy functioned, which is doubtful). But it would not create jobs.

Today's wage levels are the result of a long process of upgrading workers' rights. This is especially true if we consider such protective measures as job security and worker safety as part of real income. They make labor more expensive, and unemployment is affected by the price of labor. The growing strength of the employee is the driving force behind the labor society — and the force that will lead to its demise.

It often is said that unemployment is due to technological progress, but that does not go deeply enough. Technology is the result of social developments. Without rising wages much new technology would have remained theory. Technical innovations are introduced because they are cheaper in the long run than human labor.

This so-called structural or technological unemployment is actually unemployment due to the changing costs of labor versus technology in the final price of goods. It is not just that the technology is getting cheaper, but that labor also is getting more expensive. The price of labor has climbed so high that certain jobs just can no longer be done, while others are done only by machine. The inherent dynamic of the labor society itself leads to the elimination of labor.

There is no cure for today's unemployment. What the statistics now show as joblessness is an almost accidental downpour in the midst of a major storm. Labor is disappearing from the labor society, and that would be true even in the unlikely event that unemployment were to fall to "normal."

There are three main causes of this phenomenon. First, people spend less and less time at work. In Western Europe, it is estimated that over the past hundred years work time has been halved, perhaps even has fallen to a third of former levels. The forty-hour week is just a part of this. There is also longer training, earlier retirement, longer vacations, and more holidays.

Second, the amount of voluntary joblessness has risen rapidly in the past few decades. This is not true just for women who do not register as out of work. In certain respects students, too, are voluntarily unemployed; although they are of working age, they are not part of the statistics.

The third factor is the true scourge of the labor society — underemployment, typically in government job programs that "occupy" people uselessly. Such degrading underemployment is the best possible proof that labor is disappearing from the labor society.

Unemployment is merely the visible expression of the much more widespread reduction in labor in modern society. It has, however, led to a public discussion that has shown that the old remedies no longer work. The route back to the labor society is closed.

The idea that we live in a labor society from which the labor could disappear originated with Hannah Arendt. Even in her book *Vita Activa* she spoke of "the prospect of a labor society from which labor had been eliminated, thus destroying the only activity that the society understood." For Aristotle, the "active life" was nothing worth striving for, and for Hannah Arendt, too, the imminent disappearance of the labor society was no cause for regret. For her, work — by which she meant activity — was preferable to labor. "Work" could mean the building of society, the construction of institutions.

For Aristotle the difference between the "active life" and the "contemplative life" was a class difference. One class had to devote itself to practical matters so that the other could enjoy the esthetic side of life. This difference between those who had to work and those who could choose their activity was for many centuries the basis for the class structure of society.

Today the important question is to what extent work can become activity. If, for Aristotle, activity and labor were the marks of different classes, for Marx they were the characteristics of different levels of life and social structure — but in such a way that every society remained in degree a labor society.

Labor at the center of society means that every aspect of life must accommodate it — education, vacations, and retirement. In the labor society education conforms to the discipline and demands of work. Vacations serve as recovery periods, time to renew energies in order to return to work refreshed. For progressive labor societies, at least, retirement is "a well-earned rest after a lifetime of hard work."

The four compartments of life in a labor society — education, work, vacations, and retirement — are not static entities. The last century has seen changes in which all the other compartments grew at the cost of work. In spite of all the warnings by labor societies' representatives, education has become more and more an independent activity. The mere fact that in many developed nations more than a tenth of the adult population is engaged in either teaching or learning fulltime marks a change.

The "education" class has taken over

political parties or founded new ones. At the other end of the labor society's dwindling life are the Gray Panthers, the aware group of aging retired people whose impact is growing.

Then there is the world of free time. The leisure industry has assumed a life of its own, but what is more significant is that free time represents an enormous vacuum that must be filled.

At the instant when it ceased to be the essence of human existence, the struggle between those who had to work and those who did not have to work lost its absolute character because it was now possible to work less. The Marxist pronouncement that "the shorter workday is the basic requirement" now makes only limited sense in some occupations. Where it does make sense, the fight for the shorter work week continues.

For a long time this fight was a positive-sum game. Increases in productivity due to technical progress and economic growth permitted higher real wages for the same number of workers. But like all the contradictions of modernity, a point was reached at which what had been compatible no longer was, and the labor society began to capsize. All concerned realized that while those still working got high real wages, the realms of education, free time, and retirement had drained almost all the work out of a system that once had been defined by work.

The struggle between those who had to work and those who did not has led to total success: those who once did not have to work have become those who should work, while those who once had to work can often no longer do so. The class struggle has undergone a complete change of fronts.

The labor society concealed many troubling questions: How will human life be organized when the discipline of work is gone? How will the basic necessities be guaranteed if they are no longer apportioned in exchange for labor? How will the state carry out its basic functions if its major source of income dries up? How will people define their identities if they can no longer describe themselves by profession?

What are some alternative roads? There is the hope that work will increasingly be replaced by activity, or at least that work will be imbued with the characteristics of activity. The decisive questions for tomorrow's society are not issues to be dealt with by governments or parties; they are much more questions about what human beings actually do.

What will people do in a society in which labor has been eliminated? "The humanization of work" has become a cliché, but that does not minimize its value. The power of the term "work activity" rests in the fact that it reflects the Marxist dichotomy between free time and necessity. "Labor in the realm of necessity" can be rational; it also can be filled with activity.

Many have proposed the workgroups in Volvo factories as an example to be followed, and these do provide an example of just how much autonomy workers can attain. The same is true for many other institutions. From the elimination of time clocks to the introduction of quality control circles, there are many ways in which work can be transformed by filling it with activity.

Some experts suggest that social services be complemented or even replaced by friendly "social nets." Improving the condition of cities, protecting the environment, encouraging creative talent, and even maintaining law and order — these are all activities for people in groups. They are not jobs for civil servants even if they require some public funding.

Alternative forms of life and work also generate new small businesses. Unfortunately, some people self-employed in such alternative businesses complain that they are able to succeed only through "self-exploitation." They have not been able to escape the vocabulary of the labor society. Actually there is nothing more satisfying than self-exploitation when it means turning one's energies to one's personal goals — to the point, if necessary, of exhaustion. That is what human activity is all about — liberty.

There are many signs that the society

of activity we have been talking about will not materialize. The long recession is changing not just attitudes but real conditions. For example, it encourages protectionism, which will mean new poverty. Then appeals — self-evidently absurd — to work harder will be plausible. But they will mean only that those who have work should take even more jobs from others.

Whether a change occurs depends on a phenomenon that is a key to the future — "black labor." Black labor — "black-market" labor, "labor off the books" — understandably is not much liked in the official world of the labor society. But it is proof of the unquenchable human desire to do something meaningful, regardless of what unions and the tax authorities say.

Black labor begins at home. All housewives work on the black market. And anyone who helps a neighbor fix a car or paint a house or who gives advice on how to turn free time into activity is showing the way to a better future.

Inequalities

Our society has a long history of inequality. Social and economic inequality not only affect the poor, but also many other groups. The articles in this section consider several minorities: the poor, black, hyphenated Americans, women, elderly, and children. These groups have not shared fully in the opportunities and equality for which our country is famous. Working with an unequal system, therefore, challenges social thinkers. How can a non-earning child or retired person attain the same power as a working forty-year-old?

Current economic doldrums leave a smaller piece of the American dream to go around. The squabble over the remaining portion pits groups against one another, making national commitment hard to unify. Lay-offs intensify the dilemma for those who lack job skills. When the government receives less revenue because out-of-work citizens can't pay taxes, it is difficult to locate the monies to help the unemployed. It is equally difficult for one to progress in an unequal land in hard times. The articles in this section provide insight into the tools by which we can tell whether or not we are gaining ground. Many of the articles concentrate on the use of demographics—the statistical study of where people are within our society—to determine who is entering minority status and who is leaving.

The key words for studying minorities are jobs, education, and housing. Analyze the statistics available concerning minorities to discover what within the system can be changed to benefit them. The gulf between various economic and political classes is a problem that is not likely to be resolved soon. Nevertheless, it remains the goal of many in our society to alleviate the degree of inequality as much as possible.

Looking Ahead: Challenge Questions

Describe some differences between the rich and poor. Explain how the social system favors the rich.

How should our system change in order to aid the disadvantaged?

Who is entering the "poor" status? Is anyone leaving that category?

Why does an economic cold spell hurt the poor more than others?

Are blacks moving into "artificial" middle class positions created by social reforms?

How have women progressed in the past decade? How does the progress of women compare with the progress of blacks? Do black women suffer more discrimination for being black or for being women?

Does the fact that the elderly and children do not work for a living explain their traditionally lower status within society?

RICHER THAN ALL THEIR TRIBE

BY MARK GREEN

Mark Green is the president of a new progressive research institute, the Democracy Project, and the author of the forthcoming book, *Winning Back America: Alternatives to Reaganism* (Bantam).

At his confirmation hearings, Alexander Haig disclosed that his salary as Secretary of State, $64,630, would be less than one-tenth of his salary as president of United Technologies, $738,000.

Last April, Braniff International increased the salaries of 864 management-level employees by 11.4 percent, just when the firm was imploring 11,500 employees covered by union contracts to accept a 10 percent salary cut to keep the airline flying.

Two months before Conoco was acquired by Du-Pont, its board of directors awarded nine top executives lucrative contracts in case they quit or were fired after a takeover. Chairman Ralph Bailey was assured at least $637,716 a year until 1989, even if he should leave his job tomorrow.

As chairman of ITT, Harold Geneen earned $934,564 in salary and bonus in 1976. When questioned about this Croesean figure, an unrepentant Geneen said, "I still feel underpaid. Maybe I'm worth $5 million a year!" *Fortune* magazine added, "Perhaps he is right."

The chairman of Nissan Motors makes $140,000 annually, and the top ten officers at Renault earn, on the average, $100,000 a year, with no one's salary exceeding $150,000. The chairmen of GM and Ford earn $942,000 and $892,000 respectively.

SUPPLY-SIDE THEOLOGIANS tell us that we should increase the after-tax income of the rich to inspire them to greater levels of work and investment. This is the goal of President Reagan's tax cuts, and there is even talk in business circles about getting rid of capital gains taxes entirely. But just how much are these beneficiaries of Reagan's largesse already earning, and what evidence is there that they will use their additional income to help stimulate a sluggish economy? Business executives, for example, seemed to be doing very well indeed even in the "confiscatory" pre-Reagan era. The rewards listed above are not aberrations. They are as commonplace as coffee-fetching secretaries in the upper reaches of American business.

Back in 1902 Bethlehem Steel instituted the first bonus plan for its managers. By the late 1920s, 64 percent of all manufacturing companies had them, and Alfred Sloan, the Citizen Kane of General Motors, attributed his company's phenomenal success to the practice. A few years later, a headline in the *Literary Digest* over an article describing the one-year take of Eugene Grace, the president of Bethlehem Steel, told the whole story: "SALARY $12,000, BONUS $1,623,753."

The economic upheaval of the 1930s predictably subjected regal managerial rewards to attack and investigation. A 1934 article in the *Nation*, "Pay or Plunder?," asked "just what Mr. Grace does for his million and more a year that could not be equally done by any one of a number of persons for a fourth or a tenth of that sum." That same year the Federal Trade Commission released a controversial study on business income, and the Securities and Exchange Commission began requiring high corporate officials to disclose their pay.

In the following decades, the form of executive compensation varied with external events. As stocks plummeted in the Depression, there was a shift away from stock options and toward higher fixed salaries. Extraordinary tax rates on earned income in the 1940s and 1950s, which reached 91 percent, encouraged deferred and "unearned" compensation (stocks and bonds). A dipping stock market and a cut in the maximum personal income tax in 1969 led companies to emphasize salary and perquisites. Yet throughout these decades, large corporations have been able to absorb all changes and intrusions without seriously altering the practice of offering very high rewards to high managers.

These rewards come in two ways—indirectly as perks, and directly as pay. Perquisites can be defined technically as noncash fringe benefits, or, more popularly, as the good life that accompanies high executive living—the company cars, clubs, planes, boats, apartments, insurance, and credit cards. These indirect rewards—known in the trade as "golden handcuffs"—are seen as benefiting the company as well as the individual manager. "Dollars are too expensive," explains a vice president at General Tire. "You have to make it up to the man with the incentive gimmicks, bonuses, stock options, or fringe goodies."

Executives have come to take the everyday amenities for granted. Robert R. Dockson, the president of the California Savings and Loan Association in Los Angeles, can see no reason why his country club dues should not be paid by his firm, since "I'm always working when I play golf." Chessie Railroad requires its top executives to spend three days a year at the Greenbrier Hotel in White Sulphur Springs, West Virginia, at company expense. They spend mornings taking medical tests at Greenbrier's clinic and afternoons golfing, running, and swimming. A company manager explains: "It's a benefit to Chessie to make its executives aware of their health problems."

COMPANIES ROUTINELY provide their top executives with cars (two years ago Hartz Mountain Corporation leased cars to 21 managers at a cost of $51,000); country club dues (for which Eastern Airlines paid $38,000 in 1977); special deals on their own products (Goodyear Tire gives 40 of its top people free tires), free lawyers, free financial and legal advice, and better medical benefits than other employees get. Marc & Company, a Pittsburgh advertising firm, has a pleasant villa on the east coast of Spain for its top executives, and Pepsico and Owen-Illinois have jointly leased a salmon stream in Iceland. Perks, large and small, add up. A Philadelphia management consulting firm, Hay and Associates, found in a survey of 468 companies that the average $100,000-a-year executive gets $30,000 in fringe benefits.

Beyond the champagne of perks are the staples of direct pay:

Bonuses can be such a substantial addition to base salary that men like Richard Bressler—not Tony Dorsett or Larry Bird—should be considered the real "bonus babies." When Burlington Northern lured Richard M. Bressler away from Atlantic Richfield in 1980 to be its chief executive officer, they sold him 25,000 shares of Burlington stock for 10 cents a share. Its real value was $40.69 a share. The difference is $1 million. This is what businesspeople call a "front-end bonus." B. F. Skinner would appreciate the theory: by giving an executive a stake in the performance of the company, you motivate him to do well. The theory is frequently borne out in practice. A director at Arthur Young & Company tells of one CEO who urged his board to declare a large company-wide bonus one year because of good profits. It did, and the CEO then promptly arranged to take it all himself, arguing that it was he who had hired such good vice presidents.

Stock options are a favorite gimmick of capitalists who preach Adam Smith but practice profit without risk. Since a stock option allows an executive to gain the entire appreciation of a stock above the low market price, and since it is taxed at lower rates than income, there are often huge windfalls for its beneficiaries. In 1975 the chairman of General Dynamics bought $4.2 million worth of stock for $2.1 million, for a profit five times his salary and bonus.

Stock appreciation rights and *performance shares*—executive-suite versions of a guaranteed income—are the latest vogue in managerial compensation. SARs and performance shares allot a number of shares to managers without requiring them to purchase stock. Many large firms make use of this approach, since managers don't need to take out personal loans to purchase the stock, and the firm can control the profits on the books (as they can't with the stock market), making it hard for shareholders to decipher just how much of the company stock is in the hands of managers. As stock specialist Graef Crystal said of this approach, "DuPont has found a simply fantastic way to bury executive compensation."

Finally, there is the old favorite of *deferred compensation*. According to the *Harvard Business Review*, "Deferred pay arrangements ordinarily provide the greatest compensation benefit per dollar of employer cost . . . by giving the employee the advantage of the lower tax rates that normally occur after retirement." A Conference Board poll of 1,100 large companies in 1976 found the median annual pension of the three top executives would be $38,400, or three times as much in retirement as the median blue-collar worker makes. One-fifth of all the companies had an executive on a pension of at least $80,000 a year.

THE CUMULATIVE result of all these benefits is, predictably, staggering. In 1977 five business executives earned over $1 million a year. Last year the salaries of at least 35 executives exceeded $1 million, and 12 CEOs earned over $2 million. Eleven of the leading 25 were from energy firms; number one was Robert Charpie, the president of Cabot Corporation, at $3.3 million. According to SEC proxy filings, at least 101 executives in 1978 earned over half a million a year, not including stock options or perks. A study by Arthur Young & Company of 400 large manufacturing firms found that the average chief executive officer was taking home $325,700 in salary and bonus. The tobacco industry paid its top executives the most handsomely, an average $448,500 annually. A survey by the Financial Executives Institute of companies with over $5 billion in sales found their chief executives earned an average salary and bonus of $528,000 annually. In 1975 the Corporate Accountability Research Group found that the average salary, bonus, dividend income, and pension income "earned" that year by the top officer at the 50 largest industrial corporations (not counting seven companies whose CEOs had inherited a "founder's share") was over $700,000 per year. Today that number would easily exceed $1 million.

Comparisons here are useful. The average worker in the U.S. earns $12,621 annually; the average UAW assembly-line worker, $24,273; a top civil servant in the federal government, a GS 18, $57,500; a U.S. member of Congress, about $60,000; the average doctor, $76,720; a Supreme Court Justice, $93,000; the CEO of most industrial firms abroad, between $100,000 and $200,000. A statement of economist Paul Samuelson illustrates the disparity between the compensation of businesspeople and the majority of Americans: "If we made an income pyramid out of a child's blocks, with each layer portraying $1,000 of income, the peak would be far higher than the Eiffel Tower, but almost all of us would be within a yard of the ground."

BUSINESSMEN, of course, are quick to justify their high remuneration. Back in 1936 the presiden: of U.S. Steel explained that "the matter of compensation is minor, for the whole capital of the company is in their hands, and their responsibilities are commensurate with the size of their enterprise." A spokesman at GM says that such compensation is essential to encourage upward mobility in a huge company. Malcolm Salter, a professor at Harvard Business School, gave a more homespun rationale in the July 9 *U.S. News and World Report*: "A lot of money goes to taxes, other money to charity. The chief executive officer lives in a big house—he's got to. He sees his children almost never. He is always traveling. He would like to eat breakfast at home but he can't." Beyond the explanation that excessive pay compensates chief executive officers for the sacrifices they make for their jobs, it is said that no one is really hurt when the high compensation is spread among all the thousands of a firm's shareholders. Indeed, William F. Buckley Jr. said at a recent conference of business executives in New York City that the cost of such compensation is trivial. He cited Lee Iacocca's $400,000 income at the Ford Motor Company in the early 1970s as "only 16 cents per car sold." (Once you get the hang of this "free lunch" analysis, anything seems to cost nothing: the top executive at Exxon earns "only" .00003¢ per gallon sold; tobacco subsidies cost about a buck per citizen per year or, better yet, 1/3¢ per day.)

Finally, there is the businessman's coup de grace, the star analogy: if Dave Winfield and Dan Rather each earns over a million dollars annually, why not big businessmen, who have similarly limited years at top salaries? These rationales are fetching but flawed. There is obviously a function for pay differentials in hierarchies, private and public. Even John Rawls in his 1971 *Theory of Justice* justified inequality when the results benefit all, as an efficient and profitable corporation presumably does. But does this mean a differential of 300 to 1? Is it reasonable for an executive to earn as much in one day as some of his workers do all year? As Salter concedes, rewarding top executives does have its price. "Extensive use of options can seriously dilute a stockholder's equity in a company and eventually increase its cost of capital." If an executive acquires 1,000 shares at an option price of $20 a share when the actual price is $30, the $10,000 paper profit is paid for through an increase in the number of shares issued, which in turn dilutes shareholders' equity and puts pressure on earnings per share. Worse, unlike the payment of a bonus, these costs cannot be deducted from taxable income, so there is a dollar-for-dollar loss. And this is no hypothetical problem for companies like General Dynamics, which recently had as much as 15 percent of its equity under option.

Are such rewards essential to retain and motivate managers? Would the heads of major businesses be slothful at a $500,000 income and work hell-bent only at $800,000? John Maynard Keynes, no egalitarian, said in his 1936 book, *General Theory of Employment, Interest, and Money*, "Executives are certainly so fond of their craft that their labor can be obtained much cheaper than at present." Though a chief executive officer may feel entitled to a share in his company's profits, as Irving Kristol said in the *Wall Street Journal* a few years ago, "he is an employee of the firm, not a partner of it, and his compensation is to be judged by managerial rather than entrepreneurial standards." So, when a Land of Polaroid, a Carlson of Xerox, or a Disney of Disney takes out a healthy chunk of the firm's profits as compensation, that may be a fair reward for entrepreneurial invention and risk. But today's managers are more technicians than pioneers.

Should big-business executives be financially rewarded like big athletes and media stars? Unlike the latter, whose salaries are set by management after arms-length negotiations, the CEO "himself is the one who decides what compensation he shall receive," says Clarence Randall, the former head of Inland Steel. "This is a very tough spot for a man to be in." Even Kristol has observed that "too many corporations have compensation committees that are under the thumb of management." Given how corporations govern themselves—even beyond the stacked compensation committees, shareholder resolutions can never overcome management's control of the proxy machinery—there is no free market of supply and demand setting the compensation level of top corporate officials.

SO HOW DOES one judge a manager's performance in order to justify a very high reward? An athlete's or star's performance is glaringly visible to the millions of fans watching his performance or the thousands of families that comprise the Nielsen ratings. Yet in business it is not infrequent for a manager's compensation to go up even when profits don't. At Bethlehem Steel, which had a mammoth $448-million net loss in 1977 and had to lay off 7,300 workers, chairman Lewis Foy arranged for his earnings to rise 17 percent. Two years ago the president of Dow Chemical got a 51 percent raise while his company's profits fell 9 percent; the chairman and president of Union Carbide enjoyed increases of 27 percent and 39 percent, though the company's earnings dropped 13 percent. In 1980, counting only companies whose profits declined, *Business Week* found that although profits plunged an average of 24 percent, total compensation for their executives *rose* 6.5 percent.

Indeed, William Albrecht and Philip Jhin of Brigham Young University concluded in 1978, after surveying 146 high-salaried officials, that a top executive's salary has very little to do with his level of performance and responsibility." Albrecht and Jhin observed that once executives rise to the top, "they continue to use their toughness, imagination, and political know-how to find ways to justify their huge salaries." And when they systematically matched chief executive officers' salaries with their companies' performance, they found "absolutely no relationship (either positive or negative) between stockholder return and executive pay." Such conflicts of interest and rewards unrelated to performance led Kristol to remark that "the issue of compensation, as regards both amount and form, is a far more sensitive issue than most executives realize."

Although stockholders are starting to look askance at executive pay, and some executives are beginning to feel defensive about their high incomes and comfortable lifestyles, for the moment they should not be unduly worried. The Securities and Exchange Commission does require some reporting of perks (for example, the cost to the firm of maintaining leisure facilities for executive use); but even Republican Senator John Chaffee of Rhode Island thinks existing rules "fall short [because they] require little more than reporting the aggregate remuneration received by certain company officers and directors, both individually and as a group." (Chaffee went on to say, "It's little wonder that the public feels that management has feathered a nice nest for itself at the stockholder's, and the taxpayer's, expense.") And a 1976 Harris survey asked people to say whether they wanted the "federal government to try to make a fairer distribution of the wealth of the country"; 47 percent said no and 38 percent yes. A nation that spends its evenings watching "Dallas" and "Flamingo Road" may or may not feel compassion for the poor, but it is not likely to feel resentment even of the undeserving rich.

N OR HAS THE history of efforts to tax excessive corporate pay and perks been an unalloyed success. President Kennedy's proposal that business meals, first-class airfare, and some other "personal" benefits be considered nondeductible luxuries never went anywhere. At the end of the Ford Administration, Treasury Secretary William Simon ordered the IRS to abandon 11 draft rulings that would have explicitly taxed perks after airline groups, and others protested. When President Carter asked Congress to cut back the deductible three-martini lunch, Congress instead cut capital gains taxes. As part of an anti-inflation campaign, Carter's Treasury Secretary, Michael Blumenthal, wrote 200 large companies to ask that they voluntarily hold executive pay hikes to under five percent. A few (Uniroyal, GM, Allied Chemical, Merck, AT&T) agreed, but most never even responded.

Ironically, it may be an Administration explicitly supportive of big business that will provoke the kind of genuine change of high executive pay that earlier generations of Democratic reformers never accomplished. What will happen when it becomes clear that allowing executives to depreciate their Jaguars more rapidly doesn't unleash new investments, and when public services shrivel because, in part, the very rich are paying taxes at a rate not far different from the $30,000-a-year middle-American? There may well be a citizen backlash, with people demanding that something be done about excessive executive compensation.

I T IS VERY unlikely that Congress would get into the business of setting executive compensation at more reasonable levels—although it was Peter Drucker, in the *Wall Street Journal*, who suggested that a top corporate official make no more than a fixed multiple of the lowest-paid employee, up to 25 to 1. Still, there are at least three public policy alternatives to continued toleration of executive self-enrichment. First, Congress could increase the tax on such extraordinary levels of compensation, rather than decrease it as the Reagan tax cut did. According to the Treasury Department, the *effective* tax rate on income over $200,000 annually is between a high 20 percent and mid-30 percent. This is what the average taxpayer pays. Instead of a flat tax rate on average- and upper-income taxpayers, there should be a progressive rate, which was the theory, though not the practice, before the Reagan Administration.

Second, Congress could impose stricter standards on the deductibility of business entertainment expenses. In Margaret Thatcher's Britain, the government has disallowed deductions for all business lunches, except with foreign clients. And in François Mitterrand's France, the government imposed a 10 percent tax on the value of meals, receptions, gifts, limousines, and apartments that a company provides its ten highest-paid executives. If it is possible for Thatcher and Mitterrand to adopt comparable approaches to a common problem, then reform should be possible in post-Reagan America as well. Senator Gary Hart, Democrat of Colorado, has already introduced a measure to reduce the deductibility of business meals and entertainment by 30 percent, which would produce exactly the amount of revenue necessary to rescind recent cuts in the school lunch program.

Third, state incorporation laws should require that only a compensation committee comprised entirely of "independent directors" (those not handpicked by management) could approve the pay and perks of managment.

Until such changes occur, the ethic of Andrew Undershaft, the businessman in George Bernard Shaw's *Major Barbara*, will prevail throughout the executive suites of America. When Major Barbara asked him his religion, he replied, "Why, I'm a millionaire."

The Secret History of the Deficit

John McDermott

John McDermott, a professor of labor studies and the coordinator of the labor studies program at the College of Old Westbury, is the author of The Crisis in the Working Class *(South End Press).*

After drawing up a 1983 budget with a deficit of considerably more than $100 billion, President Reagan exhorted Congress to pass a constitutional amendment requiring a balanced Federal budget. That was a bit like W.C. Fields calling for Prohibition.

Everybody in Washington deplores deficits, but nobody can agree on what causes them. Some blame the growing national debt on excessive spending for social programs. Others pinpoint Pentagon waste. Still others blame the recession, with its concomitant high interest rates and rising unemployment. Liberals and conservatives, hawks and doves, Keynesians and supply-siders all have different theories.

But these explanations fail to consider an obvious cause: Federal tax policy. A cursory look at the nation's tax history since World War II (see graph) shows that tax policy has been consistent in one area. The tax burden on big business has been systematically eased by shifting it— or at least part of it—to individual taxpayers. The resulting shortfall in revenues has been made up by borrowing.

Let me illustrate. In 1946, individual taxpayers paid 50.1 percent of all the taxes Washington took in; 45.9 percent of this amount was paid in income taxes and 4.2 percent in payroll assessments. Corporate taxes made up 30.7 percent of the total, with virtually the entire amount coming from taxes on profits. For every $5 in Federal revenues paid by individuals, corporations paid $3.

By 1976, the picture had altered dramatically. Personal income taxes made up 52.6 percent of Washington's take, and payroll taxes (which are notoriously regressive) had climbed to 24.5 percent. Big business's share of the tax load, meanwhile, had fallen to 15.5 percent. In other words, the Internal Revenue Service was drawing 77 percent of its collections from personal income taxes. For every $5 in Federal revenues paid by individuals, big business paid $1. By 1980, the corporations' share was 13.9 percent, and this should drop another percentage point or two once all the tax breaks written into the Reagan Administration's "economic recovery program" have taken hold.

The massive transfer of the tax burden from business to individual taxpayers has been a steady process throughout the postwar years, occurring under Democratic and Republican administrations alike. Some years, major tax breaks were handed to business, but minor "reforms" were enacted nearly every year. There has been nothing secret about the write-offs made available to corporations. The important ones—generous depreciation allowances, credits for taxes paid to foreign governments, deferrals of taxes on overseas profits and the like—are vaguely familiar to most people. Taken together, however, they have had an important and little-understood effect. They have made it relatively easy for businesses to write off their capital assets— plants, land, machinery—and convert them into liquid assets in the form of tax refunds. Tax write-offs also shield a portion of a company's profits from those who would normally have a claim on them—the I.R.S., workers, suppliers and shareholders. Management is free to dispose of these retained profits more or less as it wishes. Multinational corporations, for instance, can shift the money to overseas branches. As a result, nearly half of all U.S. corporate profits never find their way onto the balance sheet.

The retention of huge sums in unencumbered liquid assets, mainly by U.S.-based multinationals, has contributed to the "decapitalization" of American industry— that is, the failure to maintain current industrial assets and the refusal to improve or replace them. It has also triggered the wave of corporate acquisitions, the outbreaks of currency and commodity speculation and the rapid expansion in the Third World that have marked the past decade. The recent proliferation of corporate political action committees, which will .spend an estimated $80 million in the next Presidential election, must also be attributed in part to the cash that is swelling corporate coffers.

To be sure, the great tax giveaway to business has been carried out for an ostensibly sound economic reason: it is supposed to "encourage investment." But even a few economists, a generally conservative breed, have questioned the assumption that business will recycle untaxed profits into new plants and equipment. In a 1976 Brookings Institution study, for example, it was argued that the investment tax credit in the manufacturing sector alone cost the U.S. treasury $13.7 billion in uncollected revenues from 1954 through 1966. Yet the credit generated only $4.8 billion in new investment during those years.

Tax breaks for corporations have not only failed to produce the investment flow they were supposed to; they have also had the unforeseen effect of causing a rightward shift in American politics. Beginning in the 1970s, the perception among many Americans that they were being forced to bear a heavier tax burden has been translated into a backlash against government spending.

Imagine two people pushing a car up a hill. One of them isn't pushing very hard, so the other has to make more of an effort. To him, the hill seems to be getting steeper, the load heavier. At some point, the harder pusher (read "taxpayer") is bound to say, "This is too much for me. I've got to figure out another way." Enter Ronald Reagan, offering to lighten his burden by slashing wasteful and unnecessary spending.

The chronic hard times of the 1970s, which increased the Federal deficit, have thrown liberals on the defensive. The debate on the causes of the deficit focused on Federal spending, and the supply-siders in the White House and in Congress rammed through their tax cuts. The questions in the debate were framed in terms favorable to the right. First, should we have bigger deficits or cuts in spending? Answer: cuts in spending. Second, should the reductions be in social programs or in the defense budget? Answer: social programs.

The best way to alter the terms of the debate is to calculate the long-range effect of tax policies on the national debt. In the 1970s, U.S. corporations paid a total of $470.2 billion in taxes, or 16 percent of Federal tax collected. In the 1960s, they paid roughly 22 percent of Federal tax collected. Had corporations paid the same share of Federal receipts in the 1970s as they did in the previous decade, the government would have collected an additional $171.3 billion and would have saved an estimated $64.9 billion in interest payments on the money it borrowed to make up the difference. Thus the effect of tax changes during the 1970s was to divert $171.3 billion from the Federal treasury into the coffers of private corporations and to shift an additional $64.9 billion to big banks. And the national debt grew by just over $500 billion.

Since the 1960s were prosperous years for big business, the 22 percent burden was apparently not harmful. The 1950s were also banner years for big business—indeed, just about the best ever. During that decade business paid about 28 percent of all Federal taxes collected. Had it continued to pay the same share throughout the 1960s and 1970s, the Federal treasury would have gained $424.5 billion more than it did and there would have been a further savings on interest of an estimated $215 billion. Thus, changes in Federal tax policy from 1960 to 1980 deflected $639.5 billion from the U.S. treasury.

In 1980, the total Federal debt stood at $907.7 billion, having grown by $616.8 billion in the previous two decades. The significance of that shift of $639.5 billion to big business becomes apparent. We can account for the entire rise in the Federal debt in terms of tax reductions that benefited big business and big banks.

This analysis of the causes of the huge Federal deficit and of the Federal debt itself is admittedly unorthodox. Orthodox liberals single out expenditures for defense and for related space and foreign military-aid programs as the culprits. Yet during the 1970s, when the Federal debt grew rapidly, defense expenditures as a percentage of the gross national product even fell a bit. Perhaps more to the point is the fact that much, if not most, of the money turned back to big corporations and big banks finds its way overseas. There, the immense new flow of funds to international corporations pays for their aggressive expansion in the Third World. And that expansion is dependent on a U.S. foreign policy that is forever finding points of conflict: unceasingly with the Soviet Union and Cuba; yesterday with Vietnam, Chile and Iran; today with El Salvador, Nicaragua and even

CORPORATE INCOME TAX AS A PERCENTAGE OF IRS TAX COLLECTIONS 1944-1979

Note: Pre-1944, the percentage hovers near 50%.

4. INEQUALITY

Grenada; tomorrow with some new threat to the subsidizing of private economic power.

Orthodox conservatives prefer to blame the deficit on excessive spending on social programs. But in recent years the United States has spent only about 12 percent of its G.N.P. on social programs, compared with those paragons of fiscal rectitude, Japan, which allocates almost 20 percent to such programs, and West Germany, which spends 30 percent.

Progressives must no longer allow the issue to be framed in terms of spending policies, and they must no longer take part in the search for the magic number that would denote the "right" proportion of the G.N.P. to be spent on the poor and the needy. For those who oppose the dismantling of the welfare state at home and the intensification of conflict with the Soviet Union abroad, the problem is political. In the past, liberals made a tacit deal with business, the terms of which could be summarized as follows: "If you'll let us expand the welfare state, you needn't worry that we'll make you pay for it with your taxes." Business was excused from bearing its fair share of the cost on the theory that it would create an ever-expanding economic pie that would enable real wages to rise along with revenues.

The shift of the tax burden from corporations to individual taxpayers, and the consequences of that shift, should become a political issue for progressives. It gives them a compelling argument against conservative preachments that profligate social spending is the root of the deficit evil. Once this argument is met, the way will be clear to restore social programs to the national agenda. When voters realize that business has not been pulling its weight, they will likely reject its claim that profits are falling and that deeper cuts in corporate taxes and in workers' wages and benefits are needed to stimulate investment. When business says it has no money to invest and writes off important industrial assets (along with jobs) at the same time as it engages in an orgy of mergers and takeovers, commodity and currency speculation, and expansion overseas into low-wage areas, the conservatives' arguments for low corporate taxes simply don't wash. The real issue is democratic control over private economic power. A fair tax policy would allow social programs and moderate tax cuts to individuals to go hand in hand.

To sum up: government cannot be counted on to improve living conditions, solve social problems or even maintain the minimal public services that are necessary to a decent life for all Americans if the wealthiest sector of the economy is allowed to evade its share of the tax burden. Second, the arms race and an aggressive, interventionist foreign policy are inevitable so long as corporate expansion overseas is subsidized by U.S. tax dollars. Corporate dollars spent abroad must ever be guarded by Pentagon dollars. Finally, progressives must abandon their tacit alliance with big business, which allows business to devolve its share of taxes upon the rest of us; to continue this unholy alliance is to acquiesce in their own political suicide.

New Faces of Poverty

Beth B. Hess

Beth B. Hess is professor of sociology at County College of Morris, Randolph, New Jersey.

When poverty became a national issue in the early 1960s, the image of America's poor still bore a resemblance to portraits of the Great Depression: grim-faced farmers, prematurely old women surrounded by children, elderly white folk, perhaps a dignified black or two.

It was not difficult to evoke public concern over the plight of impoverished rural Yankees in the midst of unprecedented affluence in the nation as a whole. To a large extent the image of the poor was rooted in reality. In 1960 poverty was endemic among farm families, Appalachian whites, and both white and black rural Southerners. Close to one-third of the elderly fell below the poverty threshold, as did almost one-half of families with seven or more members.

The programs initiated under Lyndon Johnson's War on Poverty had widespread public support, especially when targeted to Appalachia and to the elderly. It is the accepted wisdom today, however, that these programs have failed. Yet there has been a marked decline in the proportions of

both families and individuals below the poverty level: from 19 percent in 1959 to 11 percent today of all families in the U.S., and from 22 percent to 14 percent of the nation's total population. We also can see a consistent downward trend for the decade 1965–74, reaching a floor for the remainder of the 1970s, and turning gradually upward with the recession.*

But such omnibus statistics obscure the changing face of poverty in the United States. Between 1959 and 1981 the incidence of poverty was greatly reduced among certain groups: the elderly, Southerners, farm families, and residents of Appalachia. Less dramatic declines occurred for whites in general and for large families.

Not all of this decline can be attributed to public programs. Much of the reduction of poverty in the South is due to the relocation of industry from the Northeast. But it is unlikely that the sharp drop of the mid-1960s

*Major data sources for this article are the Statistical Abstract of the United States, 1981; Current Population Reports, Series P-60, No. 133 (Characteristics of the Population Below the Poverty Level, 1980) and No. 134 (Money Income and Poverty Status of Families and Persons in the United States: 1981, Advance Data from the March 1982 CPS); and various other government publications and selected social science reports.

would have occurred without federal intervention.

Most notable were the amendments to the Social Security Act in 1965, including liberalization of the benefit formula, and the introduction of medicare, relieving the elderly of the full burden of health care expenses. As a consequence, poverty among the elderly has been more than halved—from over 35 percent in 1959 to 15 percent today.

The New Poor

Despite these achievements, almost 32 million Americans still fall below the poverty threshold—and an additional 8 million are the "near poor" (below 125 percent of the index). In comparison to the poverty population of 1959, today's poor are somewhat more likely to be black—29 percent black in 1981 versus 25 percent in 1959—and to live in central cities in the Northeast.

The proportion of children in poverty has greatly declined—from almost 27 percent of children under 18 in 1959 to 16 percent in 1979. This is due to the decrease in large families in general and the lowering of the average number of children in poor families from 3.2 in 1959 to 2.3 in 1980.

There also has been a change in

the age distribution of poor house-holders, with higher percentages at younger ages. That is, family house-holders in poverty today are more likely than in the past to be between the ages of 15 and 44 (64 percent versus 47 percent in 1959), and less likely to be 45 to 64 (22 percent versus 30 percent), or 65 and older (14 versus 22 percent). This shift re-flects the dramatic reduction of pov-erty among the elderly, as well as the presence of the large baby-boom gen-eration in the young-adult ages.

Declines in old-age poverty, how-ever, have been considerably less marked for blacks than for whites, while the increase in young-adult poverty for blacks has been at twice the rate of their white counterparts. For example, in 1980, half of black family householders aged 15 to 24 had incomes below the poverty threshold compared to 18 percent for whites in this age group.

In fact, poverty among young black family householders is actually high-er than it was a decade ago, and the chief reason is an increase in female-headed family households. This change in the composition of the poor fuels debates over the causes of pov-erty in America today.

Women are almost twice as likely as men to fall below the poverty lev-el. Among the 32 million American poor today, 39 percent are women and only 22 percent are men. And though the proportion of children in poverty has diminished during the past two decades, approximately 39 percent of Americans in poverty are children under 18.

These percentages are not so dif-ferent from the past; in 1959, for example, adult men accounted for one-fifth of the poor, and women for about one-third. The real change has been that poor women in the past were likely to be the wives of impov-erished men. Today, however, they are much more likely to be the head of their own household or part of a non-family household.

In 1959 about two-thirds of the poor—black as well as white—lived in families headed by men. In 1981,

however, this proportion was only about 49 percent for whites and 28 percent for blacks. Today people who live alone or with nonrelatives rep-resent 25 percent of all white poor and 15 percent of all black poor. Twenty-six percent of white poor and fully 57 percent of black poor live in families headed by women.

The Female Face of Poverty

Who are these poor women? A small fraction are unwed teenage mothers. Contrary to popular belief, teenage pregnancy rates have not risen but have steadily declined since 1959, as have fertility rates in general. What has changed is that pregnant teen-agers today are only half as likely to marry as in the past.

In 1960 about 15 of every 1,000 unmarried women aged 15 to 19 were unwed mothers, compared to 28 in 1980—a rise entirely accounted for by white teenagers (black rates hav-ing declined in this period). There were approximately one million nev-er-married mothers in 1976: one-third between ages 15 and 19, and the remainder aged 20 to 44. Over two-thirds of these mothers were black. Approximately 60 percent had incomes below the poverty level, and three-fourths of those aged 15 to 19 were receiving Aid to Families with Dependent Children (AFDC).

A recent study of black, urban mothers suggests that teenage unwed motherhood is associated with sus-tained "mother aloneness"—remain-ing the only adult in the household for a decade or more after the child's birth. Historically, too, women who begin childbearing at young ages are likely to have more children than do women who postpone childbearing, but this difference is gradually dimin-ishing, as are differences in the fer-tility of black and white women.

Another category of the female poor are "displaced homemakers"—divorced, deserted, or widowed women whose children are over age 18, thus making them ineligible for AFDC, but who are too young to qualify for Social Security benefits. These women typically have few

marketable skills and few resources of any kind.

When they reach age 62, most will be eligible only for minimal Social Security benefits. In general, wid-ows' benefits are contingent upon the earnings level of their deceased or ex-spouse, giving them a monthly in-come higher than they would be en-titled to on the basis of their own employment history, if they have worked at all. The average monthly full Social Security benefit for wom-en in 1980 was approximately $350, compared to $420 for men, but only 31 percent of women receive full benefits, in contrast to 44 percent of male beneficiaries.

Women aged 65 and over account for half of the 4.2 million impover-ished unrelated women, while pov-erty for unrelated men is most com-mon among those aged 25 to 34. The great majority of elderly poor outside of institutions are widows over age 75. Particularly at risk are black and Hispanic unrelated women 65 and over, with poverty rates of 67 percent and 64 percent respectively. Being female, old, and nonwhite is a pre-scription for poverty.

Most attention, however, has cen-tered on the 9 percent of the poor who are female family household-ers—women without husbands but with children under age 18 in the household—typically one or two (but not the four or five so often assumed).

In half of these families, at least one child is below the age of six, limiting the mother's labor force prospects. Given the many disincen-tives to employment (low wages, travel time, lack of jobs, inadequate child care, and so forth), most of these women are entirely dependent upon AFDC payments, averaging $280 per month in 1980.

Also contrary to popular belief, over half of AFDC families have been on the welfare rolls for under three years, and only 7 percent have been recipients for ten years or more. Nor are these families necessarily receiv-ing all the benefits to which they are legally entitled. For example, fewer than 60 percent of all poor households in 1981 were enrolled in non-cash benefit programs: medicaid stood at 39 percent, food stamps at 41 percent, school lunches at 63 percent, and subsidized housing at 39 percent.

The Floating Poor

None of these data lend support to the popular thesis that there is a large permanent core of families, characterized by a "culture of poverty" transmitted from parent to child, who learn to manipulate the welfare system by cheating or bearing illegitimate offspring. To the contrary, it appears that there is continual movement across the poverty threshold, with a sizeable number of "floating poor," or families and individuals who remain suspended somewhere slightly above the poverty level until illness, rent increases, unemployment, additional children, or family dissolution plunges them into the ranks of the legally defined poor.

There is mounting evidence that changes in household composition predict change in economic status better than any of the variables usually thought to determine success or failure, such as intelligence, level of aspiration, achievement motivation, education, future orientation, and the like. Rather, decisions regarding marriage, divorce, number of children, or whether or not to share a household have immediate impact on the resources available to family members. These factors tend to have greater effect on the economic status of women than of men, who are more directly influenced by labor force conditions.*

The single most important predictor of economic well-being for women is marriage (or a stable attachment to a wage earner). When the relationship ends because of death, desertion, or divorce, the effect on a woman's income is instant—and typically negative. Conversely, divorce and separation often enhance the economic status of men because they

*For example, see "Who Gets Ahead? And Who Gets Left Behind?" by Greg J. Duncan, American Demographics, July/August 1982, p. 38.

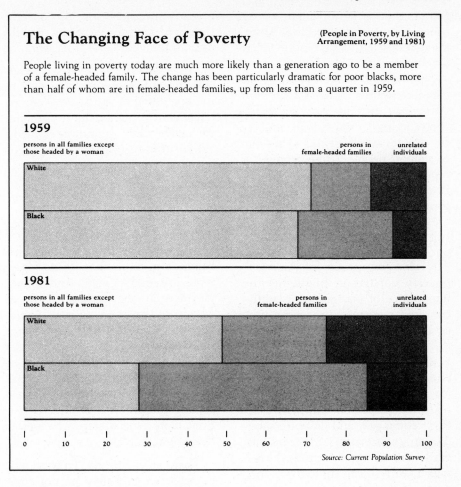

The Changing Face of Poverty

(People in Poverty, by Living Arrangement, 1959 and 1981)

People living in poverty today are much more likely than a generation ago to be a member of a female-headed family. The change has been particularly dramatic for poor blacks, more than half of whom are in female-headed families, up from less than a quarter in 1959.

1959

persons in all families except those headed by a woman · persons in female-headed families · unrelated individuals

White

Black

1981

persons in all families except those headed by a woman · persons in female-headed families · unrelated individuals

White

Black

| | | | | | | | | | | |
|0|10|20|30|40|50|60|70|80|90|100|

Source: Current Population Survey

then have fewer people to support.

This is so because not all mothers are awarded child support (about 60 percent in 1978, but only 40 percent of those in poverty), and only half of those received full payment—with 28 percent receiving none of their award. The average amount received was under $2,000 and represented only 20 percent of the mother's total income. As for alimony, only 14 percent of all ever-divorced or separated women had an agreement for income maintenance, of whom 40 percent received the full amount, while 30 percent received nothing.

As a consequence, remarriage leads to greater income gains for women than for men. Since the great majority of divorced women, especially in the young adult ages, do remarry, their tenure in poverty is usually temporary. If there is a hardcore poverty population, therefore, it is composed primarily of elderly widows and women who became unwed mothers in their teens. The one characteristic

that sets today's poor women apart from those of the past is the high probability of their being unmarried.

Their Own Fault

Poverty no longer arouses the passions it did two decades ago. One reason is the changing face of poverty. People distinguish between the "deserving" and the "undeserving" poor. Since marriage is so critical a factor in whether a woman is poor or not, Americans are likely to believe that unmarried women have brought about their own fate, and they therefore have less claim on the public conscience.

The "Protestant work ethic" still informs our attitudes, so that those who succeed are considered virtuous, while those who fail are flawed. Above all, people still believe that it is the individual who is responsible for his or her own condition. If poverty can be attributed to irresponsible sexual behavior, poor work habits, or an inability to keep a marriage together, then is it not unfair to ask other people—hardworking, abstemious, conscientious spouses—to pay for these mistakes?

Survey data, as well as the 1980 election returns, suggest that most Americans attribute poverty to the shortcomings of individuals, and see themselves as unfairly taxed in order to support people whose behavior is repugnant. Sinners must be punished—by being unable to enjoy that for which others work so hard.

What to Do About It?

The changing profile of America's poverty population highlights the importance of marriage and family-centered decisions in determining economic status. A solution offered by the New Right is to discourage divorce by making wives more dependent upon their husbands (thus reinforcing men's attachment to the labor force). In this view, affirmative action, equal pay, and day-care subsidies only exacerbate family tensions, while providing dissatisfied homemakers with the means to live alone.

At the same time, advocates of free enterprise may not be determined to eliminate altogether the vast reserve of low-skill, low-pay labor provided by female heads of households and displaced homemakers. Indeed, providing poor women jobs may not reduce poverty, unless they can earn over the minimum wage. A woman with two children, working 40 hours a week for 52 weeks a year, at minimum wage, would have a yearly income below the poverty threshold, plus the expenses of child care and travel to and from work.

The reduction of poverty through employment, therefore, will require the upgrading of skills, day-care arrangements, higher-than-minimum pay scales, and a guarantee of medical insurance (which many poor women lose when they earn only slightly over the poverty level). All of this raises labor costs to employers.

It is doubtful that market forces will solve the problems of poverty among women without working husbands, any more than these forces have lessened poverty and unemployment among working-class men who have remained married. A sudden and dramatic drop in divorce rates is also unlikely, as it is that older women will cease to outlive their husbands. Recognizing the facts of modern life is one crucial step toward solving the problem of poverty. An even more crucial step, however, is deciding to act.

There are solutions. They are not inexpensive, and they are not comforting to those who believe that sinners must be punished. But take into account the hidden social costs of poverty in wasted lives, violence, abuse, illness, and urban degradation, and perhaps the price for its reduction will not appear too high. Certainly, women with dependent children can be provided safe housing, adequate nutrition, clothing, and health care. Those who wish to enter the labor force could be provided with schooling, training, and child-care assistance.

Old women should not have to choose between semi-starvation and losing their hard-won independence by joining the household of a family member or entering an institution. Surely the United States ought not to be the last modern nation to meet the housing, social service, and health needs of its elderly.

But nothing will change until the general public once again perceives that poverty is largely brought about by forces beyond the control of individuals—the shift from labor-intensive to capital-intensive industries, segmented labor markets, the flight of the middle class from urban centers, banking and real estate practices, extended life expectancy, and changes in the ideals of family life from relationships of obligation to those of personal choice and fulfillment. These are all trends that have greatly benefited the educated elites and most members of the middle class.

There is today no strong constituency behind a new war on poverty; most people are having a difficult enough time maintaining their accustomed level of consumption. It will be only when enough "deserving" individuals and families approach the poverty threshold that a general reconsideration of the issue will become possible. Until then we must live with anecdotes about "welfare queens" and a vision of today's poor as victims of their own worst impulses.

Economic cold spell freezes 'outsiders'

By Kathleen Fisher
Staff Writer

The white male has been the sole concern of most respected studies that have explored the psychological repercussions of losing a job.

There was a valid reason for that emphasis: In rosier economic times, when the only opportunities for large-scale studies were occasioned by the shutdown of large manufacturing plants, other populations were a small proportion of the work force.

With evidence mounting of the correlation between long-term unemployment and debilitating psychological problems, however, some social scientists are becoming concerned about the additional stress placed on the worker who remains unemployed because of discrimination, or because he or she is not plugged into the traditional job-finding networks. That group includes the elderly, racial and ethnic minorities, women and the young.

One slim silver lining in the current recessionary climate is the number of studies which address that concern. Some research is only now beginning, while other studies are at the stage of data analysis or final printing.

MINORITIES

One of the more ambitious of recent studies was conducted by Terry Buss of the Center for Urban Studies at Youngstown (Ohio) State University and F. Stevens Redburn of the Department of Housing and Urban Development, who interviewed 273 steelworkers and 55 managers one and two years after the shutdown of a steel mill there. They also interviewed a subsample of minorities, which included blacks and European ethnic group members, as long as four years after the shutdown.

"In every U.S. economic downturn, blacks suffer more economic hardship than others, and are more likely to exhaust their personal and family financial resources," Buss said. When the average American's economic status declines, theirs declines more.

Because affirmative action efforts have been so recent, blacks and women may be victims of the "last-hired, first-fired" phenomenon, he observes. In addition, blacks have been concentrated in low-skill positions and have less education to qualify them for new jobs, and in their job search, they are thwarted not only by direct discrimination but institutional barriers such as housing patterns.

The most pervasive psychological symptom Buss and Redburn found among minorities, compared with whites, was a sense of victimization which worsened over the four-year period. On that measure, as well as feelings of weakness, helplessness and depression, they were higher than their white co-workers through the second year. Blacks reported more somatic problems than did the other two racial groups.

By the second year, minorities felt more anxious and distrustful, increasingly immobile and were drinking more alcohol, but were having less somatic symptoms. Their family relationships seemed even better, but had deteriorated by the third year when most other symptoms had abated. Buss suggests that the families may have pulled together originally, but that ties had been strained over the long-run.

In summary, they concluded that all of those whose initial coping efforts were less successful experienced the greatest psychological

stress, and that minority workers were more likely than others to be in that category. Buss cautions that the results can't necessarily be used to make assumptions about more pathology among minorities, since different racial and ethnic groups score differently on personality tests under normal circumstances.

In fact, some social scientists claim that minorities may cope better than white workers with unemployment because they have experienced such erratic employment that they have developed other social supports. And among blacks, suicide appears to be a less acceptable response to economic and other setbacks.

Anthropologist Elliot Liebow, chief of the National Center for Work and Mental Health at the National Institutes of Health, said that the minority "underclass" suffers as much as those who are unemployed for the first time. Theirs is simply a chronic, as opposed to an acute, anguish, he suggests.

Brandeis University sociologist Paula Rayman and Boston College economist Barry Bluestone, in their study of aircraft workers in Hartford, Conn., have suggested that among minorities, as among women, racial groups continue to serve as an important source of support following a plant closing.

Liebow, in his well-known "Tally's Corner" of the mid-1960s, described a support group that formed on the streets of Washington, D.C., among urban blacks who were chronically un- or underemployed. "Each man comes to the job with a long history of being unable to support himself and his family. Each man carries this knowledge, born of his experiences, with him. He comes to the job flat and stale, wearied by the sameness of it all, convinced of his own incompetence, terrified of the responsibility . . . of being tested still again and found wanting.

" . . . low self-esteem generates a fear of being tested and prevents him from accepting a job with responsibilities." When he does, Liebow added, he knows he will fail and proceeds to do so.

He said that a manuscript he reviewed recently noted that today's black middle-class is a much threatened group, because their gains have been due to political, rather than economic, pressures. They have moved up faster, and in greater numbers, in government jobs which are in greater jeopardy than most private positions.

However, recent contacts with about half of the 20 principal characters in that book indicate that their children are not the blacks who benefitted from civil rights legislation, he said. The future of most appears to be a mirror of their parents, although two men have used the armed services as a ladder to hope. But now, as in Tally's time, many urban blacks get a sense of their future from looking at those standing idle on the street corner with them.

YOUTH

Frank Dearden has the same fear for the youngsters he works with as director of "A Place for Us" in Baltimore. "A Place" is a group home for 12 delinquent boys, ages 13 to 15. "At this point, we're trying to keep them in school. But it (high unemployment) has an impact on the community."

Dearden said the young people feel keenly the disheartening atmosphere. "The hardest thing is that they have no sense of hope, no sense of the future. If you have a low self-image, and no real hope, you act accordingly." Of more immediate concern, he said, is that the older, jobless teenagers push the younger ones into drugs, burglaries and other illegal activities.

These youngsters must fight a class discrimination in hiring that seems to hinder low income whites as well as blacks, he continued. But it is a stumbling block that is not new to them. "They've been going through 30 to 40 percent unemployment for a long time. Now the rest of the country is getting a big, fat taste of it."

In a study of youths aged 14 to 21 in four communities, William Kornblum, a professor of sociology in the graduate program at the City University of New York, likewise found an increase in illegal activity as unemployment increased. That relationship held true for teenagers in Meridian, Miss., as well as in a New York City ghetto.

Among young women, he and his colleagues found a "virtual epidemic" of pregnancies among those who could find neither jobs nor job training programs to offer an alternative future.

Both races showed increased negative self-expression: black teenagers by calling themselves "nigger" and white teenagers through increased use of drugs and alcohol in various combinations. "Although the white youngsters are suffering, too, they have a greater possibility of coming out all right because they live closer to where the [legal] jobs are," Kornblum said.

There are few examples of such research focusing on the young, although Brenner has addressed them in his work, finding more automobile deaths, mental hospital admissions and arrests among those aged 15 to 24 and higher mortality among all unemployed youths.

Jeanne Spurlock, a Washington, D.C. psychiatrist, told those attending last fall's annual meeting of the American Academy of Child Psychiatry that she found only two entries on the subject in the index of the American Handbook of Child Psychiatry, and those referred to brief paragraphs in one text.

The teen unemployment ranks may be unrealistically swollen by such factors as the increased number in school who want to work only evenings or weekends, she suggested. In interviewing young unemployed blacks, she found just what many larger and more systematic studies have concluded: some adolescents, as some adults, persist in remaining hopeful in spite of negative experiences, and others exhibit despair that is only accentuated, but not caused, by unemployment.

Kornblum agreed that research in this area is quite scant. "When there is a severe recession, people in the press call us and we quickly correlate what we have," he said. But, even more at a time when so many adults are out of work, "young people are hardly considered legitimate entrants in the job market."

THE ELDERLY

Unlike other special populations, America's older workers do not fall victim to the "last-hired, first-fired" phenomenon. But their seniority works against them in a paradoxical way when unemployment reaches its current levels: They find that when they are eventually laid off, younger workers have already filled the jobs that match their skills.

At a recent congressional hearing by the Select Committee on Aging of the U.S. House of Representatives, information obtained through the Bureau of Labor Statistics indicated that, since January, unemployment among those aged 55 to 64 had jumped 24 percent, compared with 11 percent for youth and 16 percent for the total work force.

The elderly worker is unemployed 23 percent longer than other workers, and can expect a salary cut — averaging $500 per year for each year of age — on finally being rehired. Those over 60 are three times as likely to become "discouraged" and retire prematurely — with no access to their pensions and a loss of medical benefits when they need them most. They are more likely to be bread winners with children in college, yet are likely to have less in the way of formal education or broad skills that would carry over into a new job. They find that potential employers are unwilling to train them for only a few years of productivity.

Rayman said that, in previous recessions, older workers were afforded some protection from job loss through seniority and recall rights, but the depth of the present economic decline has stripped away these shields. She told of interviewing one 63-year-old man who was laid off and recalled only two weeks after his seniority rights were lost, then laid off again.

Thomas J. Lucas, 61, a former advertising executive from Wilmette, Ill., told the special committee that the older worker is also less able and willing to relocate. Their houses are probably paid for, and they are tied to their communities because their children are in school, or their older children and grandchildren live nearby.

In small towns the grown children often are unemployed as well. Genevieve Carthew, 61, an out-of-work waitress from Johnstown, Pa., told the committee that both her son and son-in-law had lost their jobs.

M. Harvey Brenner, a sociologist at Johns Hopkins University, noted that the elderly suffer from being left behind when it is the younger family members who must relocate to find a new job. "The problem of social isolation is particularly important to problems of ill health in the elderly who, because they are usually not employed, may lose a vital source of social contact and family assistance when their children or other relatives must emigrate," Brenner told the House committee. .

Lucas said his first reaction to the loss of his job was "mute shock. Depression set in. My sense of self-worth was damaged, almost destroyed." He said potential employers will sometimes say bluntly that hiring older workers will destroy their pension or insurance program by drawing on those benefits more than their share. Other times, the excuse will be euphemistic, such as "you're overqualified."

Despite a long-term trend of decline in labor force participation among men aged 55 to 64 and men and women 65 and over, in the late 1970s 20 percent of men and 8 percent of women age 65 and older remained in the labor force, Brenner said. His statistical analyses indicate that unemployment among older workers increases mortality and morbidity, especially among males, and also seems to be connected with a higher death rate even among the traditionally retired ages 65 to 75.

Unemployment seems to be a blow for the elderly for the same reasons it is demoralizing to the middle-aged, Brenner continued. "Since most of their age peers are not in the labor force, however, we would hypothesize that for older participants in the labor force work plays an especially critical role as a source of income and/or a source of social contact, individual identity and self-esteem."

The elderly are out of work an average of 19 weeks, 23 percent longer than the labor force as a whole. Robert Dorang, 61, a Chestertown, Md., production manager, has been seeking a new job for almost six years.

"After the unemployment checks ran out . . . after going through our savings . . . I was so depressed that I even considered suicide." Through his church, he heared of a position funded by a Title V Older Americans Act program, Green Thumb, which has paid him $128 every two weeks to do maintenance work at an activity center for mentally retarded. He had been earning $35,000. "Green Thumb may have saved my life," Dorang said.

WOMEN

At a time when women were just beginning to move into many traditionally male crafts and skilled blue-collar jobs, they are among the hardest hit of the "last-hired, first-fired" aspect of this recession.

Just as with minorities, it is impossible to generalize about how women workers are hurt by this recession. Barbara Gutek, an associate professor of psychology at Claremont (Calif.) College, said although the working class has been very hard hit in depressed areas such as Michigan, managerial and clerical workers are also suffering because there are no new openings, and teaching positions, for instance, are being reduced through attrition. Women aged 30 to 50, re-entering the job market after raising a family or completing a degree, find they are unneeded.

Overall, women seem to have a harder time finding comparable jobs, or any jobs, once they lose those they have.

In the Hartford study, Rayman and Bluestone found that female aircraft workers who held blue-collar jobs were much more likely than their male counterparts to be thrust out of the primary sector and into more marginal, unskilled jobs that meant lower pay and fewer benefits.

Rayman said in an interview that women in lower-paid service jobs are less likely to lose them because there aren't men to displace them. Those in the primary sector occupations — unionized, higher paying, with better benefits — take what they assume will be "make do" positions as nurses aides or waitresses or at smaller, non-union plants, and hit a skidding pattern from which they never recover.

Men, because they hold greater seniority, may wait for recall. Because of women's conception of themselves, Rayman said, they may not consider it so demeaning to take such jobs. Women define themselves in a more comprehensive way, identifying themselves as members of their communities and homemakers as well as workers, she and other researchers agree.

Women not only kept up friendships outside work, such as those made through their children, but were also much less embarrassed about seeing former co-workers and even went job hunting together, Rayman said. Men, on the other hand, retained little social support outside their families, and might never again see someone they had worked with for 12 years.

Rayman said that past research has indicated very little about how unemployment affects women. Even those studies in which women workers have been interviewed, correlation with somatic symptoms has not been measured accurately because women's symptoms such as gynecological problems have not been included on check lists. Rayman's study, in which she sent out questionnaires to 206 workers and interviewed 80, including 11 women, did indicate a link between unemployment and sex-related ailments, she said. Women had more psychosomatic problems such as headaches, while men turned to alcohol.

It would be easy to assume that women who are not heads of households might feel less stress about losing their jobs. But Ellen Rosen, in a study for the Social Welfare Research Institute in Boston, found significantly more stress after job loss whether women were married or not. Children seemed to be the significant stressing factor, Rosen said.

She was looking at more than 400 women in traditionally female jobs — electronics, garments, and other non-durable goods.

"These women believed their responsibilities as mothers included working" for the relatively high wages they could get in these factories, Rosen said, and they indicated no intention of dropping out of the job market.

What they missed was the paycheck, she said, rather than any job satisfaction or the camaraderie of co-workers. Older women were an exception to that rule, she added, especially widows who found "the girls in the shop" an important source of social support.

These blue-collar women are additionally stressed because they are less likely than professional women to get help from their husbands with domestic chores, although there was a great deal of cooperation in child care. Nor did they get any psychological support at home. "They would say, 'He misses the money, but he likes having me at home making meals.' " Only one woman suffered a psychological breakdown in the six months of this study.

When it is the husband who loses his job, women must bear the brunt of the reversal — not only those who are already working at what is invariably a lower-paying job, but those are forced into the job market. "Women can only find low-paying jobs, but men can't find any," Rosen noted.

She said that in some of these

occupations, women compete against minorities to see who is more willing to work. "One women told me, 'I'm willing to leave my kids for $8.50 an hour, but not for $4.' Yet they ask 'What should I do?' and not whether they should work."

A study at the Institute for Social Reseach at the University of Michigan found that men and women want the same things from their jobs. An equal percentage of each·sex said it was very important that their work be interesting and that they have an opportunity to develop their special abilities. The social aspects of the job were also of comparable importance.

An atttempt to find a correlation between women's work and suicide is made difficult because women's occupations are less likely to be entered on death certificates. John F. Newman of the Uiuversity of Chica-go and two colleagues, however, have found some correlation between work force participation and suicide in white, middle-class neighborhoods.

They suggest that these women are more apt than black women to feel pressure from role conflict. A previous study indicated that failure in one significant area of life is not usually linked with suicide, they note. Thus today, when women are increasingly expected to succeed as breadwinners, there is a high chance of double failure among such women, and thus a higher probability of suicide.

Sharon Harlan, a research associate at the Center for Research on Women at Wellesley College, found that women who need jobs even face discrimination from federal job training programs, because of eligibility requirements which tend to exclude women and because they are enrolled more often in classroom training programs than in subsidized training programs. Research during the 1975-76 recession in New York and Pennsylvania found that, as the unemployment rate got higher, the number of positions declined for women and increased for men in a CETA programs.

These programs, she said, "reflect the cultural bias against the service-providing work that women traditionally do and the devaluation of its social contribution." In current proposals for public works programs, she noted, "congressmen are talking about paying for hundreds of thousands of construction jobs to rebuild highways, and not about teachers, social workers, public health workers or child care attendants to meet human needs."

Carla: 'It's Very Hard to Say I'm Poor'

Maxine Kumin

Maxine Kumin makes poetry of recognizable life: splitting wood in the cold, watching Casablanca, *bumping hips with her daughter when they cook together. She has won a Pulitzer Prize, been a poetry consultant to the Library of Congress, taught at major universities and published four novels, several collections of stories and essays, and many books of poetry. She writes from Warner, New Hampshire.*

In the converted attic of the old clapboard house where 39-year-old Carla Sanderson (not her real name) rents a second-floor apartment for one half of her $718 monthly take-home pay, her little boy keeps a white rat with boudoir-pink eyes in a cage. Its bedding of pine shavings is fresh, the water dish is clean, there are food pellets in the miniature bowl. The rat's name is Lester and he is tame enough to handle, a fact that 10-year-old Paul demonstrates by taking him out and encouraging him to crawl up his shirt.

Julie, the daughter, has a kitten which is at that rangy stage when the legs look too long for the body. Carla is worried that the kitten may be pregnant, having recently got loose two days in a row. Feeding three children, one kitten and one rat on food stamps and a stringently budgeted salary may be possible, if not highly plausible, but a litter of kittens, or the bill for neutering the cat, would create still another financial crisis in a life peppered with them.

The baby of the family, a blond 3-year-old juggernaut named Nicholas, tugs his one-armed highchair across the kitchen floor to use as a stepladder. In seconds he's up on the counter, reaching for a bottle of soap-bubble liquid.

The family's three chairs are all in the kitchen. This makes an awkward situation on the evening of my visit. As Carla and I attempt to have a conversation, the two older children vie for the remaining seat. Supper, it turns out, hasn't been served. Gradually the reason becomes apparent. There's nothing in the house to eat except a package of frozen waffles. The November food stamps didn't arrive in the mail, although this is the sixth day of the month. Grudgingly the kids settle down to eat what they scornfully label breakfast food. The main course is toasted waffles and tap water. For dessert, some applesauce I brought, along with a batch of homemade cookies. I hadn't thought to pack the pot of soup now simmering on my stove, twenty miles away. Rather, I *had* thought of it, but I hadn't wanted to come on like Lady Bountiful, with all that might imply about Carla's inability to provide for the family she is so fiercely and agilely bringing up alone.

I muse a minute on frozen waffles, something I classify with fast foods in general as tasteless, uneconomical and minimally nutritious. On the other hand, where is the spare half-hour in this mother's hectic schedule to devise the wholesome, upper-middle-class batter with wheat germ stirred in for extra protein?

The terrible irony of holding a household together on little better than the minimum wage is that Carla can never amass any savings to buy items on sale. She can't afford to order a case of frozen orange juice to take advantage of the bulk price. No half a side of beef for the freezer, at a bargain rate. No bargains. The poor are at the mercy of gougers. The only grocery stores that will extend credit until the next paycheck are corner shops that have to charge much more than the chains in order to make a profit. So it's a vicious circle; it's frozen waffles and water for Friday night supper instead of roast chicken and cranberry sauce.

Of course, one reason for Carla's financial problems is that she spends too much on housing. But she is determined to stay on this quiet street. Her apartment in this blue-collar neighborhood is far better than the ramshackle, unheatable place she started out in. There, she had to contend with transients and drifters. Here, people plant petunias in their front yards and obediently put out their trash barrels on pickup days. The district's elementary school is considered one of the best in the

"Carla: 'It's Very Hard to Say I'm Poor'," Mazine Kumin, *The Nation,* May 7, 1983. Reprinted by permission.

city. It's worth the struggle to make ends meet—not that they ever do—to be able to stay here.

Poverty American-style doesn't announce itself in rags and tatters. The first time I met Carla she was wearing a plaid skirt, a white blouse, a tan vest and the comfortable People's Republic of China cotton shoes that have become the preferred footwear of a generation of young American women. The variety of relatively inexpensive, mass-produced ready-to-wear clothes, and the ease with which the middle class discards and replaces its garments, make Outgrown Shops and One-More-Time boutiques meccas for people like Carla Sanderson. Good used items for kids are not so easy to come by. For one thing, outgrown clothing gets handed on, even in affluent families. For another, kids are notoriously hard on their clothes. Nothing about Carla's attire hints that she is below the official poverty level—the single parent of three children, willing to enter into hand-to-hand combat with the bureaucracy to insure them a decent upbringing.

Carla has a secretarial job with a municipal agency in this New England town. Although I call it a town, with its comfortable, three-buckboards-abreast Main Street crisscrossed by seven or eight side streets, and farmland around the edges, it's actually a city. Much of what Carla does from 8:30 to 5 involves meeting the public, providing information about city and state agencies, and channeling complaints and requests to the proper doorway of City Hall. She impressed me that first day as a calm, efficient, attractive daughter of the middle class, a picture hard to reconcile with her impassioned letter to a women's group, printed in a newsletter that had crossed my desk a few weeks earlier.

My own daughter is a single parent in Switzerland, juggling a year-old child and a sensitive job involving political refugees with the exigencies of her private life. Although Swiss social service agencies provide exceptional day care, and her problems are not compounded by financial difficulties, she too suffers from single-parent burnout. She too endures the frequent frustration and often bone-chilling loneliness of the life she has chosen. Through her I've become more aware of the desperate problems confronting young women who are going it alone, particularly those in this country who, like Carla, are under the knife of Reaganomics.

But let Carla tell it: "Have you ever been there?" she demanded in her letter. "Have you ever wondered how many more days you can let your child go to school in stormy weather with shoes that are torn apart and you simply do not have the money to buy new ones? Have you ever used your food stamp change to buy toilet paper, or get one load of wash done? [Such purchases are illegal under the food stamp program.] Well, I have—and much more.

"Do you know what it's like to face the coming winter months on $700 a month when your apartment rent and utilities total $365, and you have no winter clothing for your children, and they need shoes, never mind boots?

And the administration says, 'tighten your belts more, please'—more cuts are coming, probably in food stamps, child nutrition, medical benefits, heating assistance."

Carla has been trapped in one double bind after another. In flight from an alcoholic, abusive spouse in California, she returned to New England with her children a little more than a year ago, when, as she puts it, "I decided it was time to take control of my life again. I sold my possessions, forwarded twenty-seven cartons to relatives, packed two foam mattresses and three children into my station wagon and headed home. I was really feeling adventurous—sort of a reverse pioneer—heading East in *my* wagon. I had never camped out, had never done any long-distance driving. Twelve weary days later we arrived."

Within two weeks she found a job and an apartment, but soon discovered that on a salary of $4.46 an hour she could not quite do it all on her own. Although eligible for day care, she had to choose from a list of sitters approved by the state. But her sitter needed to be paid each week, and the state would not reimburse Carla until after at least three, and possibly as many as twelve, weeks. When Carla remonstrated, she was told, "Maybe you can't *afford* a job right now, honey. Maybe you'll just have to go on welfare."

Nevertheless, she persevered. She found a summer camp program at the Y and a bus service that would take the two older children directly from school to the day-care center once classes began in September. Her precarious schedule worked. She was almost elated at her new-found ability to cope.

Then, on October 1, 1982, the Reagan budget cuts abolished the bus service and eliminated the $60 a month she received through Aid to Families with Dependent Children. Further Reagan pruning decreed that she was no longer eligible for Medicaid because she earned more than $521 per month. That loss was a disaster for Carla. Since she had been hired as a temporary employee, she did not qualify for the medical insurance her employer provided. And with three dependents, coverage was essential. The welfare caseworker was right. She couldn't afford the luxury of a job.

Now that she is a permanent employee, Carla manages without the A.F.D.C. supplement, but she still avails herself of food stamps and day care assistance. Recently she received a 2 percent raise, but since benefits are calculated on the basis of gross earnings, she faces a 5 percent reduction in food stamps—even though her take-home pay will be reduced 4 percent because of mandatory deductions for a retirement program. No redress for this kind of paradox exists in the system.

A statewide food stamp heist, meanwhile, is depriving Carla and all other recipients of two weeks' worth of stamps: the date of issue is being pushed back, three days at a time, from the first of the month to the fifteenth, meaning that each month's allocation must last an extra three days. The stamps are not being prorated, and it appears that everyone is expected to stretch her benefits for the next five months while the Administration makes up for what looks suspiciously like a shortfall in funding for the program. That is hard enough for Carla to do—but what about a family with seven or eight children? What about infants and the elderly? How do you tell *them* not to eat?

"Who has the luxury of intellectualizing about the Reagan Administration?" Carla asks. "When we do stop to think about it, we realize that the government has morally turned its back on single-parenting women and their families; further, it seems to be shoving our problems under the rug because somehow *we're* immoral. We should be home with our families and not out in the working world. The message seems to be that if the programs are taken away, women will have no choice but to 'stay in their place,' even if the place is a violent battleground.

"During a legislative budget hearing, a state representative who is a Reagan enthusiast said in an aside that he had heard that people facing cuts would be forced back onto, or into, the [welfare] system, and he felt that if they wanted to be *spiteful,* let them. Spiteful! Would it be spite to give up a low-paying position with no medical benefits in order to gain Medicaid for a chronically ill baby? If you cannot get children to after-school day care, can you as a mother keep from wondering what's the sense of working in a dead-end job? Is letting a 6-year-old come home from school alone and afraid to an empty house a 'viable alternative'? Our children need and deserve a lot better.

"I'm still from that middle-class upbringing that makes it very hard for me to say that I'm poor," Carla says, as we talk across the battered kitchen table. "To accept the truth, I am *poor.* The last week in August we ate oatmeal three times a day because that's what was left in the cupboard; can you believe that?"

If it hadn't been for the WIC vouchers, there might not have been cereal during that critical period in August between the end of summer camp and the start of Carla's new job. Yet WIC—a food-supplement program for women, infants and children up to age 5 with proven nutritional deficiencies—injects another irony into Carla's life. The program is a direct outgrowth of the Vietnam War. So many recruits were rejected by the armed services because they were physically unfit that a Federal program was devised to improve the diets of nutritionally substandard families. As much as one quarter of the population in the rural South is malnourished; the figure is easily that high in some pockets of chronic, severe unemployment elsewhere.

Although Carla would have to be pregnant to be eligible for the program herself, it provides orange juice, certain cereals and eggs for her youngest child. But the vouchers have only another two months to run, and Nickie, who is the picture of robust good health, will then be deprived of these high-protein treats. Carla may reapply for the grant in six months. If Nickie is deemed

malnourished at that time, the coupons will be reinstated for another six months. Another paradox in a nation with a mountain of surplus butter slowly going rancid, with warehouses chock-full of dried milk solids and cheese aging to the point of no return.

Still, Carla is quick to point out that she is luckier than most women in her situation. She has some job skills; she has a start on a college education—two years of credits. She has ambitions to complete a degree in human services at a local college. At the moment, this is unthinkable. Even if she received a Pell grant, which is not considered income, she would also need a student loan, which is, and which would put her over the maximum level at which she would qualify for day care and food stamps. Once again, she can't *afford* the luxury, this time the luxury of a loan that would enable her to improve her skills and move up the economic ladder far from these pitiful entitlements.

Entitlements—benefits people qualify for on grounds of age, occupation or income—are not synonymous with welfare, although programs like A.F.D.C., WIC, food stamps and so on fall within the entitlements budget. But only about 17 percent of that budget is spent on so-called "means-tested" allotments—or aid to the poor. The total outlay for A.F.D.C., the program the new conservatives are most likely to attack as subject to the most fraud and abuse, constitutes about one third of the money paid out for civil service pensions. Military retirement pay costs the Federal government 1.3 times as much as its total outlay for the food stamp program. (See James Fallows's November 1982 article in *The Atlantic* for chapter and verse.)

Carla is outraged by the bureaucracy's unwillingness or inability to pursue delinquent fathers. "It is against the law *not* to support your children, but 80 percent of the divorced fathers are breaking the law," she declares. Many men who owe child support claim to be unemployed while holding jobs that pay them under the table. Carla feels that a substantial number of them see this as a kind of vengeance. "But women are somehow made to feel guilty" for the failure of their former husbands to provide even minimal monthly payments.

"I don't know what else will happen this winter," Carla says. "I don't know what else *can* happen. Last year we managed to stay warm, thanks to the Federal heating assistance grant. This year there are going to be more cuts—maybe I won't be eligible. Right now, I don't want to know. It takes all my energy juggling this—" she gestures at the three jack-o'-lanterns she carved out of pumpkins a local farmer gave her for the children the day before Halloween. "I couldn't justify buying them, and he had a field full he said he had no use for."

The sweep of her arm takes in Lester the rat and Nicely the kitten. The gesture encompasses Nickie's day-care finger paintings taped to the refrigerator; the letter Julie received from the United Way thanking her for her $1 contribution, which the child proudly brought out for my inspection; the snapshots of all three children neatly framed and hanging on the wall; the philodendron plants hanging in Carla's bedroom; the surplus Army cots arranged as an L-shaped couch and covered with a floral-patterned spread in the living room.

Carla is hanging on, barely, in a system that is stacked against her. There is little room in her life for recreation or socializing. Weekends are given over to marking time in the laundromat, attending Paul's soccer games, getting everyone off to church and Sunday school.

Would she like to meet a good man, fall in love, remarry? Right now, Carla says, "It's doubtful. I feel that for eight years I stayed in abusive situations out of feelings of powerlessness. I thought I deserved what I got, that I wasn't good enough, that wanting anything for myself was selfish. Now I'm independent; I'm making a life for my kids. So my singlehood—or celibacy, if you want to be accurate—is a trade-off."

She says she is frequently scared, angry and depressed, but she's a scrapper. She will battle the bureaucracy for her missing food stamps, she will wear out shoe leather campaigning for sympathetic candidates for public office. She is articulate, creative and passionately maternal.

"What do I want for my kids? How do you answer *that* in twenty-five words or less! I want them to have a chance, to explore doing the things they're good at—Paul, his flair for acting; Julie, her gymnastics." She pauses, shaking her head. "But those are only the externals. I want them to be kind and aware, to add something to the world as they grow up."

I balance Carla's staunch optimism against the ukases of Reaganomics: less and less for more and more people. As the little they receive is taken from them, it will be harder for Carla's kids to add something. And the more harshly society treats its Carla Sandersons, the deeper each one of us is driven into a spiritual wilderness.

The State of Education for
BLACK AMERICANS

"Much remains to be done to finish the uncompleted task of guaranteeing all children in this nation an equal chance at a quality education."

Beverly P. Cole

Dr. Cole is Director of Education Programs, National Association for the Advancement of Colored People, New York City.

THE struggle to obtain equal access to quality education for black Americans has been long and arduous. Before the Civil War, every slave state had laws against blacks being educated. When the education of blacks was finally permitted, it was established on a separate and decidedly unequal basis. Not until 1954 (*Brown v. Board of Education*) did the Supreme Court hand down its historic decision that, in the field of education, the doctrine of separate but equal had no place. The court further declared that "It is doubtful that any child may reasonably be expected to succeed in life if he is denied the opportunity of education. Such an opportunity is a right which must be made available to all on equal turns."

In the 1980's, this right is being greatly undermined at the Federal level by anti-busing legislation, severe budget cuts in education and student assistance, proposals for tuition tax credit, the granting of tax-exempt status to schools that blatantly discriminate, the exemption of certain schools from civil rights regulations, the revision of affirmative action requirements, and the abdication to the states of the Federal government's role of monitoring and enforcing equal access to quality education.

On the local level, the right to a quality education is being denied by indifferent and insensitive teachers and administrators, by the lack of school accountability, low expectations of students' potential, pushing-out due to discriminatory disciplinary practices, inadequate equipment, poor curricular and career counseling, racially isolated schools, labeling, tracking, and discriminatory school financing policies.

In spite of these obstacles, blacks have made some progress educationally. There has been a significant increase in school enrollment, with 51% of blacks aged 25 or older graduating from high school. Today, more blacks stay in school longer and go on to college than they did a quarter of a century ago.

On the other hand, this progress has been inadequate to close the gap between black and white educational attainments and, indeed, is miniscule when compared to the overwhelming educational needs of blacks. In many ways, the progress can be described as one step forward and two steps backwards.

In evaluating the educational attainments of blacks, one must not only look at enrollment rates, but also at completion rates, as well as the quality of the educational experience.

● The dropout rate for blacks in high school is 28%, as compared to 17% for whites. Although blacks comprise 10% of the college population, whites are still twice as likely as blacks to be college graduates. Many attribute these statistics to an unresponsive school system.

● In most inner-city schools, where approximately 75% of black students are in attendance, achievement levels are usually two or more years behind the national norm.

● Studies have shown that black children tend to drop below grade level in elementary school and fall further behind as they get older, until, at age 16, at least 35% are below their modal grade.

Many theories have been offered to explain this disgrace; most built upon the notion of "blaming the victim." "Cultural deprivation," "the culture of poverty," the deficit model, "the disadvantaged"—all explained why the low socioeconomic student could not overcome the problems of poverty and social pathology and be expected to learn.

Nevertheless, the results of the "effective schools" research clearly demonstrate that children can be educated successfully, regardless of their family background. However, one of the main prerequisites is a belief and expectation on the part of the teacher and principal that this feat can be accomplished. Schools must demonstrate respect for the dignity of all students and be committed to the principle that all students are educable, regardless of their race or economic background.

Educators know what practices make schools effective, but in many cases are unwilling to implement them. We must hold schools accountable and stop entertaining excuses. As parents and interested citizens, we must also accept our fair share of the responsibility for motivating students, supporting them, and serving as advocates to insure that they receive a quality education.

Improving the quality of education

NAACP branches across the nation are

attempting to improve the deteriorating quality of education received by blacks by insisting upon:

● Equal access to quality integrated education at all levels from pre-school to professional schools.

● High expectations on the part of teachers in terms of achievement and behavior.

● Basis academic skills being taught and mastered at an early age (reading, mathematics, written and oral communications).

● A curriculum that develops skills of logic, analysis, problem-solving, and test-taking.

● Multi-cultural textbooks and materials.

● Teachers trained in multi-ethnic education/relations with more inner-city student teaching experiences.

● The utilization of a multi-method approach to evaluation and assessment.

● The elimination of tracking or homogeneous grouping.

● More teacher accountability.

● Counseling programs that encourage and advise students concerning varied career opportunities, the required courses, financial assistance, and other resources needed to pursue post-secondary education or other experiences consistent with their career goals and potential.

● Policies and procedures which insure racial fairness in classrooms and schools such as fair grading and evaluations, fair involvement in student activities, and fair discipline.

● Participation of parents and community leaders in the school process.

● Affirmative action in the hiring and promotion of black teachers and administrators to ensure that black students have appropriate role models.

These goals and objectives were chosen because of various reasons. Black children continue to be confined to separate and unequal schools; over 70% of black students are in predominantly minority schools. When desegregation occurs, research such as the seven-year study on The Effectiveness of School Desegregation produced by Vanderbilt University has shown that the achievement scores of minority students increase significantly and the achievement gains are likely to be maximized when desegregation is begun in the early grades. These findings notwithstanding, "neighborhood school proponents or anti-busing foes are accusing mandatory pupil assignments—for purposes of desegregation—of destroying public education and blighting entire communities across the country with its divisive impact." This is a myth and a gross exaggeration. Approximately 50% of schoolchildren are bused to school and, of this number, only three per cent are bused for purposes of desegregation. It is obvious that busing is not the real issue.

The real issue is avoidance of quality integrated education.

Busing is not the goal, but only a means or technique for accomplishing the goal. If the purpose of education were only to teach selected academic subjects, then perhaps there would be no need for the desegregation of schools. All that would be needed is the enhancement of the present racially isolated schools. However, since the education institution is one of society's primary means of socialization, then it needs to teach our children to associate with different races and economic groups in order to exist compatably in this pluralistic country and the world. Integration is an essential component of a quality education for everyone—black, white, brown, yellow, and red. The anti-busing amendment recently passed by the Senate as well as local initiatives are threatening to prevent this ideal from ever becoming a reality.

As was alluded to earlier, teacher expectation is one of the most crucial determinants of student effort, motivation, and achievement. Rosenthal's famous Pygmalion experiment demonstrated how teacher expectation creates the self-fulfilling prophecy. If teachers expect that some children will fail, more than likely the children will fail. This occurs because the varied expectations, based often on race and income, are translated into different behavior. This treatment communicates to the students what behavior and achievement the teacher expects from them and affects their self-concepts, achievement motivation, and levels of aspiration.

The curriculum is another major source of concern. Students must be offered competent instruction in reading, writing, mathematics, and the process of logical thought. Beyond the minimum basic skills, the curriculum should be challenging in order to stimulate students to develop skills of logic, analysis, problem-solving, and test-taking—all of which they will need in this highly technological society. Stressing minimum basic skills is good only if the minimum does not become the maximum offered.

Secondly, our society is a pluralistic one, and the textbooks and materials must reflect this. Black children need to know about the contributions that their race has made to America. They can not learn to be proud of their heritage if all they encounter in school are the achievements of whites. In an effort to enhance the self-image and sense of worth of minority students, as well as to inform white youth, school officials should replace all biased and stereotyped schoolbooks and curriculum aids with materials which accurately reflect in text and illustrations the history and participation of blacks and other minorities.

In order for teachers to be responsive to the needs of minority children, they need more training in multi-cultural/multi-ethnic education and they need more inner-city student teaching experiences. Most teachers have very little knowledge of the poor's urban experiences. For this reason, teachers and administrators should be required to attend in-service training programs geared toward helping them come to terms with their own behavior and attitudes toward students from different cultural, ethnic, racial, and social backgrounds.

In addition, we must press for affirmative action in the hiring of black teachers and administrators to insure that black students have appropriate role models. In order to achieve this, educational systems must set goals and timetables in order to measure the effectiveness of recruitment, retention, and promotion efforts.

In terms of teacher accountability, administrators should expect more and demand more. New procedures need to be instituted for relieving the school system of those teachers who are indifferent, ineffective, and unwilling or unable to improve.

The I.Q. tests, the standardized aptitude tests, and the recent competency tests have been greatly misused in relation to black students and have caused great harm in terms of damaging self-images and life chances. Tests have been used for channeling black students into "slow tracks" and mentally retarded classes and for screening them out of higher education and jobs. For blacks, tests have meant exclusion, rather than inclusion into America's mainstream, and thus have been used to further stratify the society.

It is obvious that some type of assessment is needed, and testing for purposes of evaluation or diagnosis, when used in order to improve skills of the student, is both meaningful and desirable. A good assessment program utilizes a multi-method approach for evaluation. No one sole criterion should be used for such critical determinations as graduation, promotion, certification, college entrance, and hiring. Yet, the reality is that it is much easier to accept a standardized test score than to analyze systematically the strengths and weaknesses of students by multiple means. Therefore, accuracy has been sacrificed for expediency.

Culturally biased I.Q. tests are infamous for causing a disproportionate number of blacks to be placed into "special education" and mentally retarded classes. It would amaze you to know the number of outstanding black professionals who at one time in their early life were labeled in this manner.

Competency testing, which is being used by some 38 states, tends to place the burden of accountability solely on the students. This form of testing should be done at a stage where remedial action can be taken, and teachers as well as students should be held accountable in terms of which skills have been introduced and which skills have been mastered. In those school systems which use competency tests for purposes of promotion, students should be assigned to non-graded classes where they can advance according to their individual achievement and where the stigma of repeating a grade would be avoided.

"Tracking" or homogeneous grouping is synonymous with "trapping" at a very early age. This procedure can cause a child to view himself as being incompetent and consequently establish the self-fulfilling prophecy. Based on test scores, students are often placed into a "slow group" and kept there in the less rigorous dead-end curricula all the way through school, which often creates segregation within a desegregated school. No child is slow in everything. In a heterogeneous environment, there is opportunity for the strong to help and inspire the weak.

Another area that requires careful monitoring is guidance and counseling. The counseling is very limited in inner-city schools; often, a student will not see a counselor unless he is in trouble. It is important that when advice is given it is not based on false assumptions about presumed abilities and aspirations because of the student's racial or class identification. Counseling programs must be provided that will encourage and advise students concerning the required courses and available financial aid to attend college, post-secondary education, or other experiences consistent with their career goals and potential.

In terms of administrative practices, there is a need for the elimination of dehumanizing and exploitative practices for all students. Policies and procedures must be designed to insure racial fairness in classrooms and schools such as fair grading and evaluations, fair involvement in student activities, and fair discipline and suspension. It has been shown that, at the high school level, blacks are suspended three times as often as whites. While minority students are about 25% of the school population, they constitute about 40% of all suspended and expelled students. Furthermore, black students are suspended for longer periods of time. All schools need to examine carefully those conditions at the school which precipitate pushouts and dropouts.

Parental and community involvement are essential ingredients for quality education. Confidence in the school and support for its endeavors occur when parents believe that they have access to school personnel and have some influence over what happens to their children. The family and community must support school efforts and the school must serve the community. Lack of parental involvement in the educational system to a large extent has been primarily because parents feel intimidated and unwelcomed, and lack the skills and information to impact upon the school system. Therefore, many black parents become disenchanted and withdrawn from the educational process. Yet, they still hold high hopes for their children's education, for they know that education is the means to employment, upward social mobility, recognition, and esteem.

Another factor that explains the difference in the scope, content, and quality of the education that blacks receive is the inequitable distribution of revenues and resources to inner-city schools. Despite the overwhelming need, our society spends less money educating inner-city children than children of the suburbs. This is due largely to the declining city tax base and increasing competition from municipal needs (e.g., police, welfare, fire) for the tax dollar. The suburbs, where these demands are less, allocate twice the proportion of their total budgets to education as do the cities. Several judicial decisions have attempted to make school spending independent of property values in order to reduce the gap in per-pupil expenditures between wealthy and low-income school districts.

Researchers have also studied the relationship between students' socioeconomic status and the amount of school resources made available to them and have found that school districts allocate substantially fewer dollars to schools in poor and black neighborhoods. The intra-district disparities are often just as great as the inter-district ones. Other formulas and methods for financing need to be devised.

The budget squeeze

The Reagan Administration has taken steps that will widen the gap between black and white educational attainment. The budget requested for education for 1983 is $10,300,000,000, as compared to $13,000,000,000 proposed to be spent on education in the fiscal year 1982. These proposed budget cuts adversely affect minority education programs the most and represent a big step backward in educational opportunities for the disadvantaged.

The Council of Great City Schools is an organization that represents the nation's 28 largest urban school districts, serving 5,000,000 students, of which 75% are minorities. This council stated that the proposed cuts in education would be especially severe in their areas where 16% of big-city school revenues come from Washington, as compared to the national average of eight per cent.

These school systems estimate a loss of $300,000,000, which will have the cumulative effect of jeopardizing 12,000 jobs and curtailing or eliminating services to about 235,000 inner-city youngsters. The bulk of the cuts would occur in Title I funding, a program designed for low-achieving students in low-income areas. Some 78% of U.S. school districts receive Title I aid and approximately 50% of the children served are from minority groups—29% being black.

Several research studies have shown that the Title I program has been very successful in improving achievement, especially for minority students. The National Assessment of Educational Progress indicated improvement in the relative performance of black youth at ages nine and 13 in five learning areas. It is believed that this may be attributed to Federal programs designed to foster equal educational opportunity, especially Title I.

In spite of Title I's success, the President is proposing to cut its funds by 40% from the 1981-82 funding level. If Congress approves the proposed budget cuts, it would eliminate nearly 2,500,000 children from the program, leaving only 27% of the nation's children who need the services actually receiving them.

Another move which would restrict access to higher education—and consequently to the mainstream of society—is the drastic reduction in student financial assistance. Proposed for 1983 is a 44% reduction in the over-all student assistance program, which will impact approximately 2,000,000 needy students. Since over 80% of all black students enrolled in post-secondary institutions receive some form of Federal assistance either through a loan or a grant or both, black progress in higher education stands to be severely impeded.

The Pell Grant program, the largest of the Education Department's major aid programs for needy students, has been cut by 36% for 1983, requiring parents to contribute more for their children's education. Changes in the eligibility criteria for Pell Grants would eliminate about 1,000,000 students by 1983. Three programs—Supplemental Grants, State Incentive Grants, and National Direct Student Loans—would not receive any funds for 1983. The proposed reduction of college workstudy funding would eliminate 250,000 needy students from the program. The trio program specifically designed for the disadvantaged would be reduced by 47%. The budget would kill three of the five trio programs. The pre-college counseling programs—Talent Search and Equal Opportunity Centers—would vanish under the proposal. Graduate and professional opportunity fellowships as well as assistance to needy students in the law school Cleo program would be eliminated.

Graduate students would be eliminated from the Guaranteed Student Loan program under the new proposal. Six hundred thousand students, more than half the current graduate school enrollment, depend on guaranteed student loans, and the majority of them probably will not be able to stay in school if the Administration's proposal to withdraw graduate aid entirely is approved by Congress. In addition, the Social Security Administration is planning to phase out payments to children of deceased, retired, or disabled parents at the rate of 25% each year until the program ends in 1985—with no checks being issued for the summer months. Any student not enrolled in college full-time by May, 1982, would not be eligible for Social Security aid. It is estimated that over 150,000 high school seniors will become ineligible for Social Security assistance for college.

The cumulative effect of such cuts, at a time of rising college costs (15% to 20%) and reductions in other programs, can tip the balance between the student's looking to education to better his employment possibilities or giving up. For blacks, attrition in higher education to a great extent is affected by financial aid policies. The dropout rate for blacks who do not receive any aid is 46%, as compared to 29% for whites.

Costs to society

The costs to our society of not educating one person in terms of crime, welfare expenditures, and foregone productivity are far higher than the expense of a quality education from birth. When considering the cost effectiveness of programs like Title I, we should remember that it costs $26,000 a year to keep a man in prison.

The black community is quite concerned about Congress placing educational categorical programs such as the Teacher Corps and the Emergency School Aid Act—a program designed to assist school districts struggling with problems of racial isolation and desegregation—into block grants. It is feared that the objectives of these programs will be lost, and that the special needs of the poor and minorities

will be left to the discretion of thousands of state and local officials, whose decisions about the allocation of funds will be based upon the political pressure in their jurisdictions. Past experiences have shown that states have not provided sufficient funds for the disadvantaged and minorities, and their funding formulas have been discriminatory.

Increased Federal legislation had to be developed in order to address the needs of the poor and minorities. If more control is relinquished to the local school systems, then the Federal government in turn must ensure that minority and disadvantaged students will receive adequate and appropriate resources.

With the proposed dismantling of the Department of Education and replacing it with the Foundation for Education Assistance, the Administration has decided to redefine the Federal role from one of promoting and ensuring equal access to quality integrated education to one of data collection and analysis, administration of block grants, and student financial assistance. The Foundation's civil rights role is limited to providing counsel, advice, and technical assistance concerning civil rights compliance upon request to recipients of Federal aid. Civil rights enforcement, however, would be turned over to the Justice Department.

Regardless of what happens to the Office of Civil Rights in the Department of Education, the Administration has made it clear that the role of the Federal government is one of advancing civil rights, not enforcing it, using cooperation rather than threatened sanctions to achieve its objectives.

The laws and regulations that took decades to achieve are being dismantled in a matter of months. The new affirmative action regulations would require fewer employees to file affirmative action plans and subject them to fewer reviews. Approximately 80% of the colleges and universities which previously were investigated and ordered to draw up detailed affirmative action plans to hire and promote women and minorities will be exempt. This poses a serious problem not only in terms of employment for minority professionals, but decreases appropriate role models for minority youth as well.

In addition, the Reagan Administration has decided to exempt from anti-

discrimination laws those colleges at which guaranteed student loans are the only form of Federal aid. The new rules would significantly limit the number of colleges and universities that must comply with civil rights laws. This shift in policy and reinterpretation of what constitutes Federal assistance is designed to have the same effect as the decision to grant tax-exempt status to schools which racially discriminate.

Finally, the President has introduced tuition tax credit legislation. When you begin to analyze the implications of these actions, you can not help but conclude that access to the mainstream is being deliberately restricted by those who have a stake in their privileged position. When you see being proposed at both the local and national levels legislation that would provide tuition tax credits for parents of children enrolled in private schools, you realize that these tax credits are not designed to provide all parents with a choice concerning the education of their children, for it would not help the 8,600,000 blacks below the poverty level. It was designed to provide relief for the tax-burdened middle class and to encourage escape from the urban public schools with their growing enrollment of poor and minority youngsters. If enacted, these measures would increase social class and racial isolation by establishing a two-tiered educational system in this country—the private schools for the white and middle class and the public schools for the poor and minority. Private education should not be enhanced at the expense of public education, which is the cornerstone of our democracy.

Much remains to be done to finish the uncompleted task of guaranteeing all children in this nation an equal chance at a quality education. The issues of the 1980's are difficult, but not impossible. More concerted effort is needed on the part of all to ensure that black children will receive the kind of training that will equip them to thrive in the pluralistic technological society of which they are a part. We can no longer afford to point the finger and pass the blame. We should all heed the words of Thomas Carlyle: "That there should be one man [to] die ignorant who had the capacity for knowledge, this I call a tragedy."

Hyphenated Americans—Economic Aspects

Martin Bronfenbrenner

W.R. Kenan, Jr. Professor of Economics, Duke University.

According to the 1970 Census of Population, nearly 10 million persons living in the United States were born in a foreign country, and either one or both parents of another 24 million are foreign born. The foreign stock (the foreign-born and the native-born with foreign-born parents) are therefore 17 percent of the population, making them one of the largest "minority" groups in the country.[1]

There is absolutely no question that relative earnings of black Americans increased during the decade (1960s). There are, however, real questions about root causes of this change. . . . [A]lthough by historical standards the gain of the sixties is truly prodigious, the absolute magnitude of the change is not overwhelming. In 1959, the average earnings of employed black men came to 57 percent of the amount earned by employed white men. This percentage had increased to 64 by 1969—i.e., about 16 percent of the wage differential was bridged during the decade.[2]

I. Introduction

This paper is an income-distribution theorist's attempt to discuss for noneconomists certain primarily economic problems of the hyphenated American in American society. This general discussion includes evidence relative to two embarrassing questions:

(1) How seriously has the notorious American "racial prejudice" or "racism" handicapped the eventual economic assimilation of American minority members? ("Economic assimilation" here means the attainment of parity in income, if not in wealth.)

This is a revised version of a paper presented at the Hokkaido University (Sapporo, Japan) American Seminar (August, 1980) on "Hyphenated Americans." A Japanese language condensation of the original paper has appeared in Haifunzuki Amerikanizumu *(J. Suzuki & K. Ogawa 1981).*

(2) Marxian writers see "the economics of racism" as the effort by employers with monopsony (buyers' monopoly) power individually or as a group to keep "their" labor forces disunited on racial, linguistic, or religious lines, and therefore to keep them economically weak. Conservative and antiunion writers see "racism" as arising more commonly from unexplained exogenous and possibly genetic "tastes for discrimination" and/or from "cartel" activities of trade unions to bar newcomers and outsiders from the privileges of membership. What is the relative importance of each of these theories?

These questions interest me both as an economist and as a multiply-hyphenated American. (My father was born in Russia, my mother in Austria, both in mixed Jewish-Gentile families. I myself belong to the first American-born generation in my family. My wife was born in Japan, and is therefore an immigrant, i.e. a first-generation hyphenated American.)

II. Hyphenated Americans

A. Who Are "Hyphenated" Americans?

A hyphenated American may be an immigrant or a descendant of recent immigrants. His political allegiance to the United States may become questionable when the United States and the "Old Country" find themselves on opposite sides of international controversy. Or he may try in some organized way to embroil the United States in the Old Country's controversies with some third country, or at the very least, to maintain and strengthen linguistic and other cultural ties with the Old Country.[3] The term "hyphenated American" arose to describe Irish Catholic immigrants who sought to use the United States as a staging area for rebellion against English Protestant rule in Ireland, and also to describe

German and Scandinavian immigrants who sought to keep America neutral during World War I. America has thus far been spared actual hyphenated American separatism,[4] except in Puerto Rico. (Our northern neighbor has been less fortunate as regards the French-Canadians of Quebec.)

I should consider our black population as hyphenated, whether or not their ancestors emigrated recently from Africa or from the West Indies, and whether or not they are concerned with the particular Africa or West Indian land from which their ancestors came. Alex Haley, author of the best-seller *Roots,* is a black American rather than a Ghanaian-American, even though search for his family's roots led him to present-day Ghana. He is "hyphenated" insofar as his ancestry makes him especially hostile to the Republic of South Africa. I also consider the American Indians hyphenated Americans, even though their ancestors inhabited the country for centuries before any white people arrived.

B. Two Confusing Terms

Much of our data are published in terms of two weasel words, "nonwhite" and "Spanish-speaking." Both require further discussion.

"Nonwhite" does not mean "black," although blacks dominate the category numerically. "Nonwhites" include both Asians, who have fared better than the blacks in economic terms, and American Indians, who have fared worse. Black leaders are probably correct when they maintain that the average "nonwhite" is better off than the average black, so that our usage tends to understate the severity of the blacks' problems.

"Spanish-speaking" or "Hispanic" is an even more mixed bag. The representative Hispanic has Spanish or Portuguese as a native language, or has a name generally identified as Spanish or Portuguese. He is racially mixed: sometimes pure white (from Spain), more commonly a mixture of white and Indian (from Latin America), sometimes Asian (Filipino), pure Indian, or largely black (Puerto Rican). European immigrants coming directly from the Iberian peninsula constitute only a small minority of America's Hispanic population. Spanish-surnamed people in the Southwest are classified as Mexican-Americans (Chicanos), even though they may have emigrated from other Spanish-speaking countries, may have taken their Spanish names only by marriage, or may be members of families which have lived in Texas or California for hundreds of years without ever visiting present-day Mexico.

C. The Moron and the Crook

American racial prejudice is not simple, but manifold. The racists' denunciations of Immigrant Group A would lead a man from Mars to expect these same racists to welcome Group B, which they decidedly do not. Indeed, anti-A and anti-B racists are often the same people. I am reminded of the tale about a storekeeper who put a sign in his window, "This Store is 100 Percent American" because he hated Catholics, Jews, blacks, and Asians. A competitor then put up a sign "This Store is 200 Percent American" because *he* hated *everybody!*

American prejudices against the various hyphenated groups can be divided into two types, which I like to call "the moron" and "the crook." The moron stereotype reads: The typical A has a low I.Q. and is allergic to soap and water. He is academically subnormal; he is too "dumb" and lazy to learn proper English; he is incapable of anything but unskilled labor; he is given to violent crime and alcoholism; he is afflicted with a dangerously quick temper. The "crook," or "chiseler," on the other hand has a high I.Q. and may even be physically clean. He is academically gifted; he considers himself too good for manual labor; he is dishonest and unreliable; he is given to the "white-collar" legal and economic crimes of embezzlement, bribery, fraud, tax evasion, industrial espionage, price cutting, etc. Any new immigrant group may be shunted by common consent into the moron category until it, or its children, learns English, and then may be shifted into the crook category—"too clever by half," as the British put it. For examples of such shifts, consider the Eastern European Jews, Lebanese, Armenians, Greeks, Chinese, and Japanese.

Both these stereotypes, the moron and the crook, are still with us. We can see them operating in the cases of Koreans, Indo-Chinese, Cubans, and Central Americans. First we call them morons because their English is poor, and then we call them crooks or chiselers when they cut corners in their haste to get ahead.

My thesis is that Prejudice I, against "moron" immigrants, can and does inflict permanent economic damage upon any hyphenated American group which can be recognized readily, and which cannot break loose from a set of concentrated ghettos. But Prejudice II, against "crooks" or "chiselers," has yet to damage any hyphenated-American group economically. (Immigration restrictions have even insulated the early arrivals against the further competition of later ones. The concentration camps of World War II accelerated the Japanese-American breakout from "Little Tokyo.") It is important that the "moron" stereotype be disproved, outgrown, or both; there is no faster means than by learning English well.

We can see the attitudes and activities of recent immigrants as directed primarily at overcoming Prejudice I, while letting Prejudice II take care of itself later. Even the black community is following a similar course. Its problem has become largely one of "two-stage" integration, first to "bourgeois" or middle class status within the immigrant community and from there to full integration. The first stage now seems both longer and more difficult than the second.[5] A more general example is the widespread immigrant acceptance of the public school "melting pot" assimilation of their children, despite its often crude and sometimes racist accompaniments, and despite the cleavages "Americanization" often creates between their children and themselves.

I should like to expand on the "often crude and sometimes racist" aspects of the educational melting pot as they affected me personally as a child in Massachusetts and New York in the 1920's. I experienced neither overt discrimination from teachers nor group conflicts along racial or national lines among my schoolmates; to this extent I seem to have been more fortunate than many others. I did experience Protestant Christian daily prayers in some school classes, and some linguistic teasing—not because of defects in my English but because I also spoke a foreign language. I had lived in France, picked up French, and was called "Frenchy." Speaking a foreign language, I think, implied that one's family could not speak English and was therefore inferior—the "moron" prejudice. (Not needing French to communicate at home, I may have lost my fluency in French earlier and more completely as a result of this teasing than I might otherwise have done.)[6]

D. The Boss or the Union

By mentioning the key question, whether "the boss" or "the union" has been the prime mover in economic prejudice against hyphenated Americans, or by some hyphenated Americans against the rest,[7] I have doubtless suggested that I have examined evidence on the points at issue, and have thereby drawn a conclusion. But this is not the case. I have no answer to this key question. In fact, I have no clear idea about what sorts of evidence would be directly relevant to answering it.

Historically speaking, organized labor—which includes earlier immigrants—has long been a leader in anti-immigration and similar agitation. Early examples were bloody Irish-led, anti-Negro "draft riots" in New York in 1863 and anti-Chinese riots in San Francisco in 1869. The obvious economic purposes of such agitation were to reduce labor supplies and to maintain or increase wage rates, but the great majority of the rioters could not have been union members. As unions grew in strength, however, they developed natural interests in safeguarding whatever degrees of skill and other monopoly they were able to secure.

After World War I and the Russian Revolution, however, organized labor was joined by members of the middle class, if not necessarily "the bosses," who desired to quarantine the American masses against dangerous thoughts from central and eastern Europe, and who were also infected with a mild eugenic strain of the Nordic-supremacy disease which later culminated in Nazism. Given the continuing weaknesses of organized labor, it is doubtful that numerical restrictions on immigration, including the absolute ban on Asian

immigration in 1924, could have been imposed by labor's political influence alone. (I myself recall being told by middle class teachers in both public and private schools that non-Nordics were somehow less assimilable into American society and its institutions, at least in large numbers, than were Nordics. I do not recall resenting such remarks. Probably, I did not realize that my family did not qualify as Nordic, or that "non-assimilable" was a code word for "inferior.")

However exclusive and antiforeign—or at least anti-"new immigrant"—American craft unions may have become by the first third of this century,[8] the new industrial unions after 1933 ostensibly welcomed hyphenated Americans to full membership and often to positions as union officials. I say "ostensibly" because, at times, separate, industrial-union locals for skilled workers were established within the steel, auto, electrical, or other industries. These locals patterned themselves on craft union practice, remaining closed to certain hyphenated Americans, particularly to blacks.

E. Who Does What?

Visitors to America are often surprised by what one might call the "fine structure" of hyphenated American economic assimilation. Why are groups (a,b) disproportionally concentrated in occupations (x,y)? And why are occupations (x,y) disproportionally attractive to groups (a,b)? I doubt if anyone, even a professional historian of American immigration, can answer all the questions that come to mind. (Why, for instance, do Iroquois Indians do so much of the lucrative and dangerous structural-iron work in skyscraper construction? How do we explain the affinity between Greek-Americans and the confectionary industry? Why are the best bakeries German in one city, Scandinavian in another city, Jewish in a third city?) A few generalizations, however, may be helpful:

(1) If an immigrant group has concentrated in certain occupations in its Old Country, it is apt to continue this specialization in the New World, other factors being equal. Thus, we find Jewish-Americans in the liberal professions, in banking and jewelry, in tailoring and the garment trades; Armenian-Americans and Lebanese-Americans are prevalent in the rug and carpet business and, more generally, in importing from the Middle East; while Welsh and Silesians (German, Polish, and Slovak) are found in the mines.

(2) When a country becomes known internationally for certain specialties, it is natural for immigrants from that country to bring those specialties to America. The international repute of French, Italian, and Chinese cuisine, for example, gives rise to numerous restaurants in America owned and managed by immigrants from these countries, or by their descendants. A smaller and localized example of the same phenomenon is a concentration of dairying and cheese making in a "little

Switzerland" near the small city of Monroe in southern Wisconsin.

(3) The temporal order of immigration has been important. When German and Scandinavian peasants were immigrating in large numbers during the generation following the Civil War, good farmland was still abundant and cheap, and those immigrants turned naturally to agriculture. When waves of Italian and Slavic peasants arrived a generation later, the good land had already been acquired and the immigrants went into the mines, mills, and factories, often after apprenticeship in unskilled pick-and-shovel construction work. Had the order of immigration been reversed, the Swedish farmer of southern Minnesota and the Polish steelworker of western Pennsylvania might have traded places.

Similarly, the rise of closed unionism among Yankee, Irish, and Scandinavian building tradesmen operated to bar "new immigrant" (and later black and Hispanic) workers from the higher reaches of the skilled building trades. Perhaps because of skills they brought with them in stonework and masonry, however, Italians have been much more successful than other new immigrants in overcoming barriers against them..

(4) Prior knowledge of English has made a difference too, particularly in the case of the Irish-Americans. Why did the Irish so naturally assume, and retain for so long, political leadership among the hyphenated Americans? They arrived early and their English was fluent, though accented, while both their extreme poverty[9] and their Roman Catholic religion aroused Yankee prejudice against them.

(5) As an example of historical accident approaching pure chance, consider Chinese laundries. These are products of the great California gold rush, which began in 1849 and lasted for most of the subsequent decade. Laundry facilities for the prospectors' and miners' clothing were almost entirely lacking. Chinese immigrants, not only in California, but as far away as Hawaii, found ready employment and income in the laundry business.

As an upshot of such considerations as these, we have retained such folk humor as the saying about New York City: "The Italians built it, the Irish run it, and the Jews own it."

III. Economic Analysis

A. The Whites and the Asians

We come at length to the technical economic analysis of the economic positions of the hyphenated Americans, which has become a special province of labor and manpower economists. The economic adjustments of white and Asian immigrants have become the particular interest of Professor Barry R. Chiswick of the University of Illinois (Chicago Circle). Interest in the economic problems of the blacks has been more widespread because they are still America's largest minority. (They

may soon be displaced from this questionable honor by the Hispanics.) In descriptive economics my principal debts are to the work of two economists who happen to be black: Professors Thomas Sowell (Hoover Institute, Stanford University) and Walter Williams (George Mason University). For quantitative analysis, however, my three principal authorities are white: Professors Richard B. Freeman (Harvard University), James P. Smith (Pennsylvania State University), and Finis R. Welch (University of California, Los Angeles).

We deal first with the whites and Asians, and therefore with the work of Chiswick. A readable summary of his principal results is available for the layman under the title *The Earnings of Immigrants and Their Sons*,[10] but at the other (scholarly) extreme of analysis, one is struck by his thoroughness in investigating even the minutiae of the subject.[11]

The following sample of Chiswick's results tends to contradict standard views about discrimination in the American economy. He has found that, as for the immigrants themselves, the major determinants of their economic progress are (1) the transferability to America of whatever skills the immigrants acquired in their former country, and (2) their personal characteristics and motivations.

When male immigrants first arrive, they receive lower earnings than both native-born persons in general and native-born persons of similar ancestry,[12] age, sex, education, and other demographic characteristics. This is because their skills are often nontransferable.[13] But ten to fiteen years after immigration—Chiswick estimates the cross-over point at thirteen years for Europeans—the economic immigrants (other than political refugees) overcome this initial handicap and earn, on the average, two to five percent *more* than the same comparison group.

Political refugees, however, are less fortunate economically. "Although with the passage of time their earnings approach those of the native-born, the catch-up never occurs or requires several decades."[14]

Chiswick ascribes the superior economic performance of the nonrefugee immigrant to self-selection for both general ability and economic motivation. The differential between economic immigrants and political refugees supports this theory. So does the frequent Old Country complaint of ports being thronged with "the sturdiest of their peasantry" headed for the New World. "The most poor and ignorant remain (at home) involved in growing misery. Those who leave are those who have the physical energy and mental capacity to remake their destinies."[15]

The pattern for women is significantly different from that for men.

Other things the same, foreign-born white women earned 6.7 percent more per hour in 1969 than their native-born counterparts. Although among white men, the foreign-born have lower weekly earnings during the first decade in the U.S., this is not true among white women. Foreign-born women have hourly earnings two percent greater than the native born when evaluated at arrival, five percent higher earnings at ten years since migration, and seven percent higher earnings at 20 years.[16]

At least in a New York sample, Japanese, Chinese, and black female immigrants initially have lower earnings than the native born, but catching-up occurs within five years. Among Mexican and Filipino immigrants, earnings do not seem related to the number of years since migration; also, these two groups are peculiar in that the foreign born have consistently lower earnings than the native born.[17]

Molière had no use for the medical profession; we recall Le Médecin Malgré Lui and Le Malade Imaginaire. Molière lets his doctors boast of the sun's shining on their successes, but only to prepare for the rebuttal that the earth covers their failures. A similar difficulty is hard to avoid in statistical investigations like Chiswick's. His samples cover only immigrants on whom the American sun was shining in 1969 or 1970, and who were to that limited extent "successes." But what of the disappointed failures—whom the American tourist in Europe may often encounter—both those covered by the earth and those retired from the American sun to the more congenial shade of the old country? The Chiswick samples could not include them, and we cannot estimate the seriousness of the resulting bias in his results.

Passing from the immigrants themselves to their sons—from my parents' generation to my own—Chiswick's conclusions ring yet more optimistically. Comparing only males with zero, one, or two foreign-born parents, he finds 5% to 10% differentials in favor of the sons of immigrants with at least one foreign-born parent, the variation depending on the birthplace of the immigrant parent or parents. The differential is largest when the father is an immigrant and the mother native American without a foreign-born parent, smallest when the parental origins are opposite to these, and intermediate when, as in my case, both parents are foreign born. The results hold in varying degrees for all eleven countries studied. (The Mexican-Americans are to some extent special; we shall deal with them separately below.) On the average, there seems to be no economic *advantage* to being the son of a nonpolitical refugee immigrant parent.

B. The Black American

American blacks, Negroes, or Afro-Americans are unusual in several ways. Persons classified as black—including many who are less than half black, genetically speaking—are a full ninth, possibly an eighth, of the American population. The proportion is increasing, since black families are generally larger than other American families.[18] Their color makes them both more identifiable—and, given American prejudices, less assimilable—than any white immigrant group, even after many generations and even though a certain number of light-skinned blacks "pass for white" every year.

Nearly all black Americans are of West African descent. Nearly all of their ancestors were captured or purchased by slave traders and were thus involuntary immigrants. These ancestors were a selected group only in the sense of surviving the abominations of the "windward passage" from West African to American or West Indian ports, followed by a variable number of generations in slavery, usually as field hands on corn fields, tobacco farms, or cotton plantations.[19]

Concern for blacks and for their future antedates the Civil War by more than a generation. Its initial manifestations were abolitionism and colonization. Abolitionism aimed to free all slaves without compensating their owners, while colonization aimed to found colonies of freed slaves in an area which later became the Republic of Liberia in West Africa.[20] Northern victory in the Civil War led to three constitutional amendments (the 13th, 14th, and 15th), which not only abolished slavery but also purported to guarantee the civil rights and electoral suffrage of blacks. The 14th and 15th amendments, however, were widely ignored in the Southern States, where the bulk of the black population continued to reside.[21]

For nearly a half-century after *Plessy v. Ferguson,*[22] most white Americans were content to sweep the Negro problem under the rug of "separate [decidedly] but equal [seldom]" and leave southern states free to perpetuate their "peculiar institutions" of race relations. In many circles, "nigger-lovers" were suspected of communism, since worldwide Communist propaganda laid great stress on black oppression in the American South.

Paradoxically, we can date much renewed interest and renewed sympathy for the black American from revulsion against the racist excesses of Nazi Germany, particularly after the United States entered World War II.[23] The Swedish social economist Gunnar Myrdal led a Carnegie Corporation team which published the influential *American Dilemma* in 1944.[24] Following the "G.I. Bill" and mass demobilization in 1946, a series of higher education court cases permitted black students to attend an increasing number of graduate facilities in southern white universities when black families in the applicants' home states were either nonexistent or flagrantly inferior. Finally, the landmark United States Supreme Court decision of *Brown v. Board of Education*[25] directly overruled *Plessy v. Ferguson* to begin a civil rights revolution. The Civil Rights Acts of 1956, 1960, and 1964 extended the *Brown* doctrine to other public facilities, and a Voting Rights Act (1965) revived the fifteenth amendment, which had lain moribund in much of the South. Boycotts against segregation in private transportation facilities began in Birmingham, Alabama in 1955 and made Martin Luther King a national figure. A movement for sit-ins in "white only" private facilities began in North Carolina in 1960. Both movements spread through the South. Gains in the South were offset by increasing hostility in other sections of the country, to which blacks had been migrating rapidly for economic as well a social reasons since 1940, and where the black vote was becoming crucial in the urban areas. A series of race riots followed, beginning in the Watts area of Los Angeles in 1965 and culminating in a nationwide "long, hot spring and summer" following Dr. King's assassination in 1968.[26]

A further development of the 1970's, resulting from earlier legislation, has been the rise of affirmative action. Under this principle, minority members and women[27] can, under some circumstances, be granted a preference in hiring, training, and promotion if they meet minimum standards for skilled occupations, even though white male candidates appear more promising, until their proportions in these occupations have been approximately equalized.[28] Furthermore, formal tests and examinations having the statistical effect of excluding minorities or women have been ruled illegal unless they can be related directly to entry-level competence in the jobs or professions concerned.[29]

Economists are professionally less interested in these historical and legal developments than in their consequences for the position of the black worker in the American economy. The black worker has been the most acutely and the most prolongedly victimized by what I have called Prejudice I, against alleged morons. To what extent have his political and legal victories permitted the black to overcome this prejudice, or to rise economically despite the survival of this prejudice?

Economists have concentrated upon comparisons of the black male worker's condition, relative to the white male worker, as evidenced numerically (and therefore incompletely) by the 1960 and 1970 Censuses, between which the bulk of recent black economic gains have supposedly occurred. After the collection and tabulation of 1980 Census results, much of the work will surely be replicated, and the results confirmed or modified.

Attention has been concentrated upon the black *male* worker for two related reasons: (1) male-female sex differentials in earnings have historically been lower in the black than in the larger American community, even after allowance for the greater prevalence of full-time employment among black women and particularly among *married* black women; and (2) black-white earning differentials have historically been higher for males than for females or for families.

The quotation about black workers at the beginning of this piece, which was taken from a Rand Corporation report to the U.S. Department of Labor, shows that the historical black-white male earnings differential fell nearly one-sixth in a single decade—aided, the authors admit, by a decrease in measured unemployment from 5.5% to 3.5% of the measured labor force.[30] The

authors, Professors Smith and Welch, also indicate the multiplicity of the explanations, none mutually exclusive, which may be combined to account for the changes.[31] Their principal candidates are five:

(1) Blacks and whites have become more alike in their income-producing characteristics and attributes, particularly in their formal education.

(2) They have also become more alike in the *quality* of these attributes;[32] again, particular emphasis is placed on education.

(3) Black workers have continued to migrate from historically low-wage areas (South and Southwest) to higher-wage areas (North, Middle West, Pacific Coast).

(4) Government policies of affirmative action and breaking down labor-market discrimination have become important only since 1960.

(5) A number of business-cycle variations operated favorably in the 1960–1970 decade.[33]

Among these five explanations, Smith and Welch follow the "human capital" hypothesis, associated with Chicago and Columbia economists, in placing their primary emphasis upon the first factor, particularly its educational component.

[S]uccessive cohorts of blacks and whites are simply becoming more alike in those attributes producing higher wages. In 1930, the typical black male began a work career with 3.7 fewer years of formal schooling than his white counterpart. . . . By 1970, [only] 1.2 years of schooling separated black and white males at the time of their initial labor force experience.[34]

However supported it may be by statistical regression analysis, this result runs counter to the conventional wisdom of the period immediately preceding, which had found much lower rates of return (as measured by income) for black and poor Americans than for the American population as a whole, and which had therefore attributed the black-white differential primarily to discrimination.[35] Why the difference?

Smith and Welch find this difference in their second explanation, namely educational *quality,* so that education accounts in all for 46% of "the relative growth in black male wages due to greater characteristics similarity."[36] They summarize their case on quality in the following passage:

Data on schooling quality reinforce the story conveyed by nominal years of schooling. The data of nominal characteristics of schools clearly show the improving relative quality of black schools. In 1920, black youths attended school only two-thirds as many days as white students, but by 1954 there were no real black-white differences. Similarly, in 1920 teachers of black students had one and three-fourths times as many pupils as the average teacher in the country. By 1954, this difference had been substantially reduced. The extraordinarily high ratio of first- to second-graders suggests that on average a black student took about two years to complete the first grade in the 1930s. Retention rates that average 100 percent indicate low-quality education coupled with inflexible standards. Between 1940 and 1954, implicit retention rates in southern Negro schools moved toward the national norm. It is difficult to link attributes of schools to educational achievement. Indeed, some of the measures offered may have had little effect on achievement, but the consistent picture of simultaneous convergence in all these dimensions makes the case for improving quality of black schools plausible.[37]

Migration is also an earnings-related characteristic, since a person is more likely to earn a high income if he lives where higher wages prevail. Contrary to many people's a priori beliefs, however, black migration from the South to the North and West has had only a marginal effect on the reduction of the black-white earnings differential. This result is apparently explained by the substantially greater degree of earnings equalization in the South itself, as compared particularly with the Northeast and West in which the racial differential was higher in 1974 than in 1956. (See table 1.) The South's pattern, however, remained most unfavorable to the blacks.

ance; it does not explain the trend itself. It suggests that a fall (rise) of 0.04 points in the earnings ratio will result from every 1% rise (fall) in the unemployment rate.[40] This regression confirms conventional wisdom regarding its sign, but it suggests to me that cyclical oscillation is somewhat less important than seems to be implied by the "last hired, first fired" proverb.

These results, of course, fall significantly short of any full explanation of the results for even the 1960's. The results for the 1970's, not to mention the 1980's, may involve quite different statistical patterns, and perhaps also different choices of explanatory variables.

Conforming generally with the Smith-Welch hypothesis, the gains in the relative economic position of black Americans in the 1960's appear concentrated in the younger age cohorts and also in the more highly educated. Both of these groups have been in the best positions to gain from the improved relative quantity and quality of black education. Table 2 provides results for both annual and weekly earnings; the annual figures are influenced more strongly by differences in employment and unemployment. The pattern indicated by the table would surely be clearer had 1960 data for recent graduates been available.[41]

TABLE 1

Changes in Nonwhite-White Earnings Differentials

Region	Nonwhite-White Earnings Differential Ratio			
	1956	1974	Change	Percent Change
South	.423	.634	.123	29.1
Northeast	.730	.719	−.011	−1.5
North Central	.768	.811	.043	5.6
West	.764	.744	−.020	−2.6
Entire U.S.	.523	.634	.111	21.2

Source: J. Smith and F. Welch, *Race Differences in Earnings: A Survey and New Evidence 5,* Table 2 (1978).

Turning to affirmative action, Smith and Welch doubt its effectiveness in the 1960's. (If one may generalize from the academic world, this result would be substantially different in the 1970's.[38])

If affirmative action has an effect, it should be strongest on the employment and wage trends in industries that are most susceptible to the government's influence. However, the rise in black-white wage ratios has not occurred primarily in those industries, and the popular notion that government pressures have driven these changes has little empirical support.[39]

As for cyclical influences, Smith and Welch have regressed the black-white earnings ratio on four variables: (1) the measured unemployment rate of the economy, (2) a time trend, (3) the square of (2), and (4) the cross-product of (1) and (3). This statistical regression accounts for some 86% of the 1948–1974 vari-

It is easy but inaccurate to ascribe these results to some conscious or semiconscious gesture, splitting and side-tracking the "black liberation" movement by co-opting much of its potential leadership, the "talented tenth" on which W.E.B. DuBois laid such stress. The reason for rejecting any such conspiratorial interpretation is historical. The black income distribution has *traditionally* been less equal than the white; black-white income ratios have *traditionally* been greatest at the low ends of the income distributions, and increased as one moves up, except at the very top. The most that can be said against the gains achieved in the last generation is that the traditional patterns have not changed greatly in any egalitarian direction, so that the elite position of the black elite has not been eroded. Tables 3 and 4 reveal these points.

We have not even sampled from the vast quantity of available statistical information showing convergence

4. INEQUALITY

between the educational, occupational, and demographic patterns of the black and white populations. More meaningful, it seems to me, are the data of table 5, dealing with the poverty-stricken, which show opposite results. Although the incidence of measured black poverty has decreased along with the incidence of measured white poverty, the ratio between the two incidence figures shows no sign of decreasing, and the proportion of blacks in poverty remains between three and three and one-half times the proportion of whites.

TABLE 2

Black-White Earnings Ratios for Cohorts, 1960 and 1970

Years Out of School	Average Annual Earnings Ratio			Average Weekly Earnings Ratio		
	1960	1970	Difference	1960	1970	Difference
I. Elementary School Graduates (8 years)						
1 - 5	—	.835	—	—	.865	—
6 - 10	—	.779	—	—	.802	—
11 - 15	.673	.708	.035	.703	.737	.034
16 - 20	.688	.710	.022	.713	.717	.004
21 - 30	.671	.749	.078	.708	.763	.055
31 - 40	.719	.721	.002	.741	.740	.001
II. High School Graduates (12 years)						
1 - 5	—	.775	—	—	.806	—
6 - 10	—	.769	—	—	.791	—
11 - 15	.654	.729	.075	.714	.749	.035
16 - 20	.676	.731	.055	.714	.750	.036
21 - 30	.655	.678	.023	.685	.698	.013
31 - 40	.623	.675	.052	.648	.690	.042
III. College Graduates (16 years)						
1 - 5	—	.716	—	—	.775	—
6 - 10	—	.647	—	—	.692	—
11 - 15	.618	.662	.048	.655	.688	.033
16 - 20	.559	.654	.105	.582	.675	.093
21 - 30	.446	.519	.073	.470	.557	.087
31 - 40	.389	.504	.115	.421	.522	.101

Source: J. Smith and F. Welch, *Black/White Male Earnings and Employment: 1960-70* at 3, Table 1 (1975).

TABLE 3

Nonwhite and White Money Income Distributions, Families and Unrelated Individuals, U.S., Selected Years, 1947-1977: Percent of Total Money Income in Each Fifth and Top 5 Percent

	Nonwhite						White						Quintile Ratios (Top/Bottom)	
Year	Bottom	2d	Middle	4th	Top	Top 5%	Bottom	2d	Middle	4th	Top	Top 5%	Nonwhite	White
1947	3.3	9.5	15.8	23.9	47.4	17.8	3.8	11.1	16.9	23.4	44.9	18.6	14.4	11.8
1952	3.7	10.3	17.1	24.7	44.1	16.8	3.6	11.4	17.5	23.9	43.6	18.2	11.9	12.1
1957	3.0	8.6	16.4	26.2	45.8	15.8	3.7	11.5	18.1	24.4	42.2	16.3	15.3	11.4
1962	3.3	8.8	15.8	25.1	47.0	17.5	3.7	11.0	17.7	24.6	43.1	16.5	14.2	11.6
1967	3.4	9.2	16.0	25.0	46.4	17.0	3.8	11.1	17.7	24.6	42.8	16.3	13.6	11.3
1972	3.4	8.7	15.4	24.9	47.6	17.6	3.9	10.4	17.1	24.5	44.2	17.1	14.0	11.3
1977	3.6	8.6	14.9	24.7	48.3	17.9	4.0	10.0	16.7	24.7	44.5	17.1	13.4	11.1

Source: U.S. Census, Current Population Reports, Ser. P60/118, *Money Income in 1977 of Families and Persons in the U.S.* 44f, Table 13 (1979).

TABLE 4

Non-White/White Income Ratios at Selected Positions on Money
Income Distributions, Selected Years, 1947-1974

| Year | Income Percentile | | | | |
	20	40	60	80	95
1947	0.43	0.49	0.53	0.58	0.64
1953	0.44	0.53	0.59	0.65	0.68
1959	0.40	0.45	0.57	0.62	0.67
1964	0.52	0.53	0.59	0.67	0.71
1969	0.55	0.60	0.66	0.73	0.74
1974	0.53	0.58	0.67	0.76	0.74

Source: U.S. Census, Current Population Reports, Ser. P23/80 *The Social and Economic Status of the Black Population in the U.S.: An Historical View, 1790-1978* 25, Table 18 (1979).

TABLE 5

Percentage of Persons with Money Incomes Below Poverty
Lines, U.S., Selected Years, 1959-1976

Year	Nonwhite	Black	White	Black/White Ratio
1959	53.3	55.1	18.1	3.04
1964	49.6	—	14.9	3.33*
1969	31.0	32.2	9.5	3.39
1974 (revised)	29.5	30.3	8.6	3.52
1976	—	31.1	9.1	3.42

*Nonwhite/White ratio

Source: U.S. Census, Current Population Reports, Ser. P23/80, *The Social and Economic Status of the Black Population in the U.S.: An Historical View, 1790-1978* 41, 202, Tables 33, 147 (1979).

C. The Mexican-American

The immigrant group of Mexican-Americans is a hyphenated American minority on its way to becoming the largest of such groups. It is positioned economically midway between the ordinary immigrant from Europe or Asia and the native-born black American. Without the special handicaps of slavery, the "Chicano"[42] has as yet outgrown neither his moron image nor his widespread relegation to low-paid unskilled labor, particularly in agriculture.

About three-fourths of all Mexican-American adult males are American born; half of them have no foreign-born parents. Concentrated in urban or rural ghettos in a half dozen southwestern states, where they have long been the principal minority element, Chicanos have been victims of both racial and religious prejudice. Their social and economic position is roughly comparable to that of the black minority in other sections of the country. Chicanos have also been outstandingly resistant to the melting-pot version of "Americanization"; 98% of even the native born with native-born parents were raised in Spanish-speaking homes which often were not bilingual.[43] They have a low level of schooling, much of it of low quality, particularly when filtered through a language handicap.

This mixed picture presents us with mixed results. As Chiswick writes:

The significantly lower earnings of immigrants from Mexico appears to be a Mexican ethnic-group effect. Other things the same, the earnings of first, second, and higher-order generation Mexicans are lower than the earnings of other white men of the same immigrant status. The ethnic-group differential does not appear to narrow with the greater the number of generations in the United States. Otherwise, the patterns observed among men of Mexican origin are similar to the patterns observed among white men in general. For example, when the earnings of Mexican immigrants are compared with those of native-born men of Mexican origin, other things the same, the immigrants initially have substantially lower earnings, their earnings rise with time in the United States, and equal those of the native born after about 15 years, after which the immigrants have higher earnings.[44]

The economic experience of Mexican-Americans confirms, or at least does not disconfirm, two hypotheses derived from comparisons between the immigrant European or Asian and the native-born black experiences.

The first hypothesis: The significant American prejudice against particular hyphenated groups is that they are considered morons, fit only for unskilled labor. Once this prejudice is overcome, it makes no economic difference whether or not it is succeeded by some other prejudice against the groups as crooks, or even as "rugged individualists—with accents." The Chicanos' resistance to learning English and acquiring effective English education has accentuated their difficulties.

The second hypothesis: Immigrants, or at least economic immigrants, are self-selected as potentially superior economic men. This explains why, after a relatively short period, they fare better economically than their native-born compatriots of similar ancestry, and why, after a longer period, their children fare better economically than native-born Americans without foreign parents.[45] In this view, the Chicano problem is precisely that so few Chicanos are immigrants, since the recent immigrants quickly outperform the native-born Mexican-Americans, while Mexican-Americans alone, of all the immigrant groups studied by Chiswick, fail to overtake native Americans without foreign parentage.

IV. A Few Conclusions

(1) Prejudice and discrimination against recent immigrants and other hyphenated Americans is of two types. Prejudice I calls them morons and Prejudice II calls them crooks or chiselers.

(2) Most immigrant groups proceed from being considered moronic, through being considered less than honest, to being almost accepted. The principal obstacles to this evolutionary process have been dark skins, concentration in ghettos, and resistance to learning proper English. These three weaknesses are not mutually independent.

(3) The Chiswick studies suggest that neither immigrants nor their children suffer long-term economic damage, measured by income, from the prejudice against them. The exceptions to this generalization have been black Americans and Mexican-Americans, the two largest hyphenated American groups.

(4) One reason for these important exceptions may be the lesser importance of self-selection of the original immigrants on any economic basis.

(5) Both organized labor and exploitative employers have at times delayed the economic progress of hyphenated Americans. Organized labor has reduced access to apprenticeship and skilled training. By setting one group of workers against another, employers have improved their bargaining positions and increased their monopsony power. We have reached no conclusion about the relative importance of these obstacles.

(6) In the special case of black Americans, the main gains from the civil rights revolution have thus far gone to middle-class blacks who have already escaped from the ghetto and the moron label.

(7) The most recent immigrants do not seem to be exceptions to our historical generalizations, although statistical evidence is not yet available. Asians (principally Koreans and Indo-Chinese) and Cubans are doing well. Black Haitians are doing badly. About non-Mexican Central Americans we know little; if the theories in this essay are correct, these immigrants should fare better than the Mexican-Americans because they are self-selected for economic reasons. On the other hand, many, if not most, are "illegal immigrants," hiding in and among Spanish-speaking Mexicans and Puerto Ricans in ghettos and barrios, and may not avoid the barrio culture.

Footnotes

1. Chiswick, "The Earnings of Immigrants and Their Sons," *Challenge*, May-June 1978, at 55.

2. J. Smith & F. Welch, *Black/White Male Earnings and Employment: 1960-70 v (1975).*

3. Americans see it as a sign of "hyphenation" when a linguistic minority insists upon public school instruction in the Old Country language for children (other than children who are themselves recent immigrants), but not when the minority community supplies such instruction at its own expense on a voluntary basis as a supplement to the public schools.

4. In the 1930's, the American Communist Party considered the advocacy of an autonomous black republic composed primarily of those southern counties with black majorities in their populations, but this proposal was shelved. Most of the counties in question became white by 1950 as the result of black migration during and after World War II, but some black nationalists continue to campaign for a "Republic of New Africa."

5. *See* R. Freeman, *Black Elite* (1976).

6. Perhaps for the same reason, I never learned enough Russian to communicate with Russian relatives who *were* living with my family. I recall expecting my grandmother and uncle to speak English if they wanted to talk to *me!*

7. The subject of interminority relations fascinates sociologists. On the one hand, many hyphenated American groups have as common enemies such racist organizations as the Ku Klux Klan and American Nazis, and therefore join forces against them. But each minority group, in its search for acceptance and assimilation, is tempted to take over the majority's prejudices against one or more other minorities.

The checkered history of Negro-Jewish relations is currently (1983) of special interest from this point of view. An earlier example involves Japanese-Americans. Confined in camps during World War II, Pacific Coast Japanese particularly resented the "inferior" Jews among the camp staff members, whom they scornfully called *kuichis*. (In Japanese, 9 (*ku*) + 1 (*ichi*) = 10 (*ju*).)

8. The "closed" union or union local was often an exemplar of nepotism rather than racism, despite racist statements in some union constitutions and charters. The right to union membership became a form of human capital, analogous to a share of stock. It was handed down from father to son, uncle to nephew, older to younger brother, and not uncommonly sold to friends and neighbors. Membership in an "Irish" local, then, was not in fact open to all Irish-American applicants. Why then, it was argued, should it be open to non-Irishmen, not to mention non-Catholics, non-Christians, or even nonwhites?

9. The earliest concentration of Irish immigration came to the New England and Middle Atlantic states following the Irish potato famine or "great hunger" of 1845-1849, which was to directly or indirectly reduce the population of Ireland from nearly 9,000,000 in 1845 to 6,500,000 in 1851. *See* C. Woodham-Smith, *The Great Hunger* (1962).

10. Chiswick, "The Earnings of Immigrants and Their Sons," *Challenge*, May-June 1978, at 55 (largely based on Chiswick, "Sons of

Immigrants: Are They at an Earnings Disadvantage?" *American Economic Review,* Feb. 1977, at 376). A later semipopular summary for lay readers is Chiswick, "The Economic Progress of Immigrants: Some Apparently Universal Patterns," in *Contemporary Economic Problems* 357 (W. Fellner ed. 1979).

11. An example: The previously married, foreign-born wives of native-born Americans generally report only marginally lower hourly earnings in the United States for 1970 when their previous marriage came prior to immigration than when it did not. The exception is Japanese born women, for whom the difference is highly significant. Apparently this difference is due to special characteristics of the wives of former U.S. servicemen. (Any Japanese-born woman whose first marriage was prior to immigration, was in 1945 or later, and whose current household head is either white or black, is assumed to be the wife of a former U.S. serviceman.)

Since Mrs. Bronfenbrenner is Japanese-born, Professor Chiswick included me in a sample of persons to whom he has inquired about this anomaly. Is it related primarily to something in Japanese society, or something in a special "serviceman's marriage market?" I do not know, and neither does my wife.

12. Thus, Japanese immigrants would be compared in Chiswick's studies not to native Americans generally, but to *Nisei* and *Sansei* of the same age, sex, and education.

13. "The disadvantage is greatest for refugees from countries with a different language and economy (for example, Cuban and Chinese refugees) and least for economic migrants . . . from English-speaking countries." Chiswick, "The Economic Progress of Immigrants: Some Apparently Universal Patterns," *supra* note 10, at 358.

14. *Id.* at 359.

15. Dadodag, "Source Regions and Composition of Illegal Mexican Immigration to California," 9 *International Migration Review* 499, 510 (1975).

16. B. Chiswick, *Analysis of the Economic Progress and Impact of Immigrants* (1979) (unpublished manuscript).

17. *Id.* at 9-32.

18. The black percentage was 11.12% of U.S. population in 1970, up from 10.52% in 1960. *Statistical History of the United States* 9 (B. Wattenberg 1976).

19. The conditions of the field hand were harsher than those of the domestic servant or "house nigger" minority. To this day, "cotton-pickin" is used in black English as a derogatory adjective, as in "keep your cotton-pickin hands off me!" At the same time, the extremes of brutality made even less economic sense for slaves than for cattle or draft animals; this is not to deny their existence or even prevalence. *See generally* R. Fogel and S. Engerman, *Time on the Cross* 144-57 (1974).

20. The black historian, Lerone Bennett, Jr., dates abolitionism from the activities of a free Negro, David Walker, who published the pamphlet *Walker's Appeal* (Boston 1828). The first freed slaves were landed in the present Liberia even earlier (1822), but colonization under white auspices never had significant black support and was regarded as basically anti-Negro. L. Bennett, *Before the Mayflower: A History of the Negro in America* 131 (1964). President Lincoln, incidentally, not only freed the slaves but seems to have favored the deportation of free Negroes back to Africa. L. Bennett, *Confrontation: Black and White* 62 (1965).

21. In the *Civil Rights Cases,* decided in 1883, the Supreme Court of the land said that the 14th amendment forbade states, not individuals, from discriminating. Finally, in 1896, the Court formulated the doctrine of separate but equal, holding in *Plessy v. Ferguson* that laws requiring segregation were a reasonable use of the police power of the state. L. Bennett, *Confrontation: Black and White, supra* note 20, at 78.

22. 136 U.S. 537 (1896).

23. Japanese antiwhite propaganda directed to American blacks was not of great importance, although it had been feared widely in the period immediately following Pearl Harbor.

24. The original two-volume publication comprised 1024 pages of text and 526 pages of introductions, footnotes, appendices, and bibliography, divided into 45 chapters. A single-volume, 19-chapter, 324-page, authorized condensation is A. Rose, *The Negro in America* (1944).

25. 347 U.S. 454 (1954).

26. American race riots directed *against* blacks are not new. These riots of the late 1960's were directed *by* blacks against whites. For equivalents, one must apparently go back to the occasional slave revolts of pre-Civil War days, some of which may have been only mass escapes from slavery. On these see L. Bennett, *Before the Mayflower: A History of the Negro in America, supra* note 20, at 97-126, and H. Aptheker, "Negro Slave Revolts in the U.S., 1526-1860," in *Essays in the History of the American Negro* 1-70 (1945).

27. The term "minorities" in this connection includes not only blacks but the Spanish-speaking and American Indians. The term does not include Asians or "poor whites."

28. Questions both of constitutionality and statutory interpretation in this field are in a state of flux, following the Supreme Court's decisions in University of California v. Bakke, 438 U.S. 265 (1978), and Weber v. Kaiser Aluminum, 444 U.S. 889 (1979). Further statutory enactments are, of course, possible.

29. The leading Supreme Court case on this point is Griggs v. Duke Power Co., 401 U.S. 424 (1971).

30. The black worker has traditionally been last hired in a recovery and first fired in a recession.

31. J. Smith and F. Welch, *Race Differences in Earnings: A Survey and New Evidence* v *passim* (1978). *See also* Smith and Welch, "Black-White Male Wage Ratios: 1960-1970," *American Economic Review,* June 1977, at 323.

32. Equalization may result both from the improvement of facilities open to blacks and from the deterioration of facilities open to whites (or to all Americans).

33. *See supra* note 30.

34. J. Smith and F. Welch, *Race Differences in Earnings, supra* note 31, at vi.

35. T. Ribich, *Education and Poverty* (1968) uses this position to argue that the economic benefits of the educational components of the Kennedy-Johnson "war on poverty" would not be worth their costs; B. Harrison, *Education, Training, and the Urban Ghetto* 1-40 (1972) makes the case explicitly; L. Thurow, *Generating Inequality* 51-74 (1975) has perhaps become the standard statement of the anti-"human capital" position, building on L. Thurow, *Poverty and Discrimination* (1969). A more radical position is presented in S. Bowles and H. Gintis. *Schooling in Capitalist America* 98-124 (1976). An early attempt at balanced weighting is M. Blaug, *An Introduction to the Economics of Education* 169-234 (1970).

36. J. Smith and F. Welch, *Race Differences in Earnings, supra* note 31, at vii.

37. *Id.* at vi. *See also supra* note 35.

38. Smith and Welch also admit this possibility. J. Smith and F. Welch, *Race Differences in Earnings, supra* note 31, at 24.

39. *Id.* at viii. Professor Freeman, however, takes a more positive view of affirmative action, with special references to the highly educated. R. Freeman, *supra* note 5, at 119–49.

40. J. Smith and F. Welch, *Race Differences in Earnings, supra* note 31, at 25.

41. Professor Freeman includes data for a single occupation, college teaching. After adjusting for quality differences, he finds that male, black faculty members earn 6.6% more than white, or about $1000 per year at the 1973 salary level. R. Freeman, *supra* note 5, at 195-213. There will, of course, be disagreements about the quality-adjustment factor. In Freeman's regression, an institution-quality factor has a high rating, and he ascribes his results largely to affirmative action by prestigious and high-quality institutions to hire black faculty members.

42. "Chicano" is an abbreviation of "Mechicano," which is itself a dialect pronunciation of the Spanish "Mexicano."

43. The statistics in this paragraph are from Chiswick, "The Economic Progress of Immigrants: Some Apparently Universal Patterns," *supra* note 10, at 379.

44. Chiswick, "The Effect of Americanization on the Earnings of Foreign-Born Men," 86 *J. Pol. Econ.* 897, 914 (1978) (footnotes omitted).

45. We need not decide here whether the advantage of the immigrant's *son* is genetic or environmental. Chiswick puts the issue this way:

The higher level of ability or work motivation of the foreign-born may be passed on through genetic inheritance or environment to their native-born children, although presumably from one generation to the next there is a regression toward the mean. On the other hand, native-born men with foreign-born parents may be at a disadvantage if they were raised in a home less familiar with the institutions of the United States. This could occur because these factors affect productivity or because of discrimination against the children of immigrants. Apparently, however, the factors favorable to the earnings of the men with foreign-born parents tend to dominate.

Chiswick, *supra* note 1, at 60.

How Long Till Equality?

And yet.

All the gain is on the near side of that first simple word, all the distance lies right beyond the second. There are more women working now than ever before, more women in politics, more teaching, more learning. And yet.

Most of the women hold down-scale jobs and draw salaries smaller than a man's for the same work; many live below the poverty line. The majority of American college students now are women, and yet the faculties instructing them are still mostly male. There are, all together, more women in state legislatures, more in the House and Senate than at any time in history. And yet. Neither these increasing numbers of women politicians, nor their male colleagues could manage to get women something that once looked elementary, something that should have been so simple: a constitutional guarantee of equal rights under the law.

There are also the numbers, statistics like measured mile markers, flashing along a dawn drive toward a still distant reckoning. There were 301 women state legislators in 1969, 908 in 1981; 5,765 female elected officials in 1975, 14,225 just four years later. And yet, those 908 legislators are only 12% of the members of state legislative bodies. Only 19 of the 435 members of the U.S. House of Representatives are women, only two of the 100 Senators.

The numbers mark distance traveled and distance yet to go. Eighty percent of all women who work hold down "pink-collar jobs" and get paid about 66¢ of a man's dollar. Seventy percent of all classroom teachers are women, yet for the same job, they make an average of $3,000 a year less than their male colleagues. More than a third of all candidates for M.B.A. degrees are women: the numbers encourage. Only 5% of the executives in the top 50 American companies are women: the numbers numb. Where once, even recently, there was nothing, all those statistics and all their corollaries now show there has been something: some progress forged for women over the past decade of challenge and confusion. Perhaps those numbers are really a crude scale for a new geography, exploring the wide gulf between something and satisfaction.

But when I began to consider the subject . . . I soon saw that it had one fatal drawback. I should never be able to . . . come to a conclusion. I should never be able to . . . hand you after an hour's discourse a nugget of pure truth to wrap up between the pages of your notebooks and keep on the mantelpiece for ever. All I could do was to offer you an opinion upon one minor point—a woman must have money and a room of her own.

Virginia Woolf published *A Room of One's Own* in 1929. It remains the best book about the situation of women, which says much for the perpetual pertinence of art, and little for the mutability of men and social politics. "There is no mark on the wall," she wrote, "to measure the precise height of women," and, in the absolute sense, she is still right. The deepest impact of the women's movement is intangible. Some of feminism's greatest advances are revealed in the everyday auguries of the family, home and job; some of its greatest power has come in altering the cadences and the promises of a woman's daily life. In 1972 women wondered hard about the possibility of having a family and a career, and being able to manage both. In 1982 more women—including some of the daughters of the past generation—take all this as a birthright.

Realistically, now, it will have to stand as a birthright deferred. Feminists of both genders attached a strong symbolic importance to the passing of the ERA and find in its final and formal defeat last week intimations of national malaise. "It is an appalling obscenity not to pass the ERA, when everyone knows women have to work and society wants them to work," says Novelist-Critic Elizabeth Hardwick. "There is an illiberal and I think tyrannical minority imposing its will on obvious needs for social change," remarks Novelist John Irving, who wrestled questions of feminism and family into contemporary myth, *The World According to Garp.* "Feminism is simply one of many human rights. The whole thing is very depressing."

Feminists took things somewhat less hard than the writers. Eleanor Smeal, president of the National Organization for Women, and other leaders vowed to concentrate women's new consciousness and resources (NOW has reported recent monthly political contributions of $1 million) on building legislative strength to win eventual passage of a resubmitted ERA. *Ms.* magazine Co-Founder Gloria Steinem has already drafted marching orders for the '80s (reproductive freedom, democratization of families, more respect for work done in the home and comparable pay for the work done outside it).

"I'm very disappointed that the ERA didn't pass," admits Donna Shalala, 40, president of New York City's Hunter College, who does not hesitate to add that "most of the critical breaks in my career would not have happened if it wasn't for the women's movement." Says Shalala: "It's going to be tough. The problems of the future are going to be more sophisticated. But I rarely meet a young woman who isn't more militant about control over her own future, as well as her own body. I'm just very positive about the future, and I think we all ought to be positive too."

The possibility—and, perhaps, the urgency—of positive feeling is in itself a product of progress. For a time, at the beginning, there seemed to be only occasions of rage.

I: MAKING ROOM

I thought how unpleasant it is to be locked out; and I thought how it is worse perhaps to be locked in.

Feminism was the last focus of the civil rights movement and the more general social activism of the late 1960s. Its potential constituency was the broadest and the deepest, but so were the problems it addressed: too wide, too varied, rooted too deep in sexuality and self-image, even in language. Ms.? An abbreviation for manuscript; an affectation otherwise, a pretense. Abortion? A moral question, never a biological one. Right to work? Something the unions settled during the Depression.

After the batterings of Selma and Viet Nam, several assassinations and summers of psychedelic overload, the country needed a warm bath and a bit of soothing. What it got instead was a fresh, hard needlepoint shower from the ranks—indeed, from the home. It was a little too much. Doors slammed, windows rattled shut. The national circuits had temporarily shorted out, and, in the prevailing gloom, the feminist torches looked less like beacons than sputtering pilot lights from the stoves the women were threatening to abandon.

Women's lib it was called then, short for liberation, of course, but unconsciously, closer to women's lip, with all attendant condescending connotations ("Ah shut up, I've had enough of your . . ."). It was tough to be called a libber, even if you took pride in the politics, and those at first were mean. They were the politics of long frustration and new anger, and it was men who took the heat: as repressive husbands, lackadaisical fathers, selfish sex partners, exclusionary businessmen, blind-sided artists and perpetrators of a patriarchy that had to be overthrown. Even Shakespeare was a sexist for a little while.

4. INEQUALITY

The press cut in on the dark carnival atmosphere, and in some measure contributed to it. On the occasion of a Miss America pageant, a marginal faction of young women threw their underwear into an Atlantic City, N.J., garbage can, attempting some clumsy metaphorical gesture, and grabbed headlines, air time and a disproportionate share of posterity. If "libbers" were the dreary drones of the movement, "bra burners" were the lacy lunatic fringe. (A note: no bras were actually burned that day. Not a single flame was lighted, not in any sense.) "Bra burners" was a convenient, slightly comic way of dismissing demands and resisting confrontations that had been deferred too long. Those women were a curiosity and thus a comfort to the opposition.

Unfortunately, part of the opposition belonged in the feminist constituency. The fierce, early rhetoric of the women's movement boggled many of the same women it should have enlightened. Instead of challenging women who had made lives of substance and happiness with husbands and children, it put them on the defensive, made them think they had betrayed not only their womanhood but their selfhood as well. There was a self-righteousness among feminists that kept all kinds of potential recruits away. Emily Anne Smith, the second female designer-builder in Atlanta's history, recalls, "When the women's movement came along, I was involved in what I wanted for me. Then, when I did meet with NOW, I was put down. They told me I was selfish." Her friend Flo Bruns, who helped found Atlanta's high-powered Women Business Owners club (because "I didn't want to talk business to a man. My experience is he is going to patronize me") had a similar experience. "I walked into a NOW meeting wearing a business suit and ready to volunteer. I was treated like an outcast by all these young women in jeans. Power comes from money, honey, but they didn't recognize that." They did not recognize Raquel Welch either, who reasoned, "Maybe it might help the movement to be associated with someone less abrasive, more feminine. They weren't interested."

Maybe Welch should reapply. There has been much talk lately among feminists about community and consensus, and building a broader base, just as, outside the movement, there is a growing awareness of how much feminism and the battle for the ERA has meant to most American women. Bruns says, "Our acceptance in the general business community has a lot to do with what the ERA people started." Renae Scott, who got herself some college education and worked herself off welfare to an administrative job with the Haymarket People's Fund of Boston, says, "No one, and I mean no one, got here by herself. Women in the past have paid a heavy price for the women of today. What affirmative action programs we have, what salaries—no matter how small—were made possible with help from another person."

Scott, who is black, is a solid refutation of the widely held notion that feminism is strictly a white, middle-class issue. That remains a common enough criticism, as if the whole movement could be bundled up in a Volvo station wagon and sent off for a spin into irrelevancy. In fact, minority women may still be more concerned with problems of employment and discrimination than with the comparatively rarefied legalities of a constitutional amendment. But even their priority issues, in the words of former NOW President Aileen Hernandez, "flow out of the ERA." Adds Ruth Mandel, director of the Center for the American Woman and Politics at Rutgers University: "I'd be willing to bet that there is only a small minority of families in the U.S. that has not had to deal over the past ten years with the fact, or the consequences, of the women's movement."

Some families may have dealt with the consequences so extensively that for the younger members, the problem has just about blown away. "Equality is not as big an issue for us as it is for grownups," says Demetrius Toney, 17, of White Plains, N.Y. Maybe the reason is that, for Demetrius, it has long been a part of his second nature. His mother is a day worker, cleaning other people's houses, "so I do everything in our house. I sweep, I wash dishes. This week my brother is doing the laundry." At U.C.L.A., Director of the Women's Resource Center Tina Oakland says, "Most college women think the movement has worked. Girls

don't think they need a women's movement. They think society is fair." Lori Harrington, 21, of Yonkers, N.Y., is not quite so sure. "I haven't lived long enough to know exactly what I'd be giving up for equality, but I do know what I'd be giving up if we went back to the '50s," she says. "I wouldn't be in school. There'd be no reason for me to be in school. I could forget becoming a journalist, unless I wanted to write a cooking column some place."

If Harrington is serious about a column, she might consider one about women and the law. Along with other benefits, it could shake up some of her peers. She might explain the immediate practical need for the ERA ("We are probably not going to see many more gains without some major legal change such as the ERA": Donna Lenhoff of Washington's Women's Legal Defense Fund. "I think we have gone as far as we can under the 14th Amendment": Gail Harmon, president of the fund). She might point out that the Supreme Court, lacking any clear standard for sex discrimination cases, has ruled both that the Martin Marietta Corp. was guilty of sex discrimination by not hiring women with children and that a California state disability plan was not discriminatory, even though it excluded pregnancy as a disability. If Harrington wants to stir things up a little more, she might speculate on whether the country's first woman Justice, Sandra Day O'Connor, was more a jurist or a feminist. Her deciding vote in a case establishing that seniority systems are immune to suits under Title VII of the 1964 Civil Rights Act will probably not guarantee a Women's Legal Defense Fund testimonial. But her majority decision, handed down last Thursday, that an all-woman nursing school in Mississippi was guilty of sex discrimination is sure to rekindle a few low-burning fires in the feminist camp. O'Connor even added a kind of bonus in her written decision, when she pointed out that such segregation by sex only succeeds in reinforcing the stereotype of nursing as a woman's profession.

For all the sense of debts owed and steps taken, there is a simultaneous impression of reluctance, on the part of many women, to be drawn even into the fringes of the movement. Some of this may be attributable to residual resentment of old rhetorical putdowns, and some of it may have to do with resistance to being commandeered as unenlisted political foot soldiers or being spoken for by proxy. "A lot of the failures of the movement are built into the people who are speaking for women," says Novelist Anne Tyler. "Basically I agree with everything they say, but I find myself wanting to disagree because of the way they say it. If people like me, who are pro-women, are put off by it, imagine other people." Or imagine a sympathetic parent, particularly a father, leafing through the beginning of a feminist guide to child rearing and banging a shin on the following parenthesis: "(See Chapter 24 for a full discussion of language as an exclusionary tool of male supremacy)." Imagine getting to Chapter 24; imagine turning the page.

It does not do, though, to be so easily put off. Movements all have their excesses. They come with the territory, even if they sometimes seem to cover it, like drifting snow over new paths. Indeed, should the father have persevered, he might have found some first-rate advice about children in that very same book. He would also have found a kind of zip-lock naiveté that insulates Author Letty Cottin Pogrebin inside a cocoon of ideology. How else could a writer suggest, never mind believe, that children might be encouraged to forsake the music of the Rolling Stones (sexist, of course) for the uplifting ballads of Gay Feminist Holly Near. Ideology infringes on reality; one suspects it can also skew the sense of rhythm. It may not interfere with a woman's getting a job, however. And it may be able to show her why she cannot get a better one, or get paid in full for the very one she is doing now.

II: LEAVING ROOM

I had made my living by cadging odd jobs from newspapers, by reporting a donkey show here or a wedding there; I had earned a few pounds by addressing envelopes, reading to old ladies, making artificial flowers, teaching the alphabet to small children in a kindergarten . . . I need not, I am afraid, describe in any detail the hardness of the work, for you know perhaps women who have done it; nor the difficulty of living on the money when it was earned, for you may have tried. But what still remains with me as a worse infliction than either was the poison of fear and bitterness which those days bred in me.

When Woolf wrote those words, some women might work, and a woman alone had to work. Now, more and more, women must work. During the early 1970s, work was often a matter of finding pride and alternatives. There was much discussion of "self-realization" and "growth potential." The idea that a woman might also grow and realize herself through her children got short shrift; the notion that a man might experience the same satisfaction was either radical or sentimental and rated no attention. Fatherhood as fulfillment and as a responsibility, full-time, is a concept that may be more popular in the '80s, when American families struggle to play catch-up with an inflationary economy and an increasingly competitive consumer society. For a woman, fulfillment may or may not remain a priority. Work has become a necessity.

Says Congresswoman Patricia Schroeder: "The primary reason women are entering the labor force in such unprecedented numbers is to maintain their family's standard of living." Statistics are the arithmetic of social revolution: from 1960 to 1980, one-earner households have declined from 49.6% to 22.4%, a staggering change. The percentage of married women in the work force during the same period has risen from 32% to 51%. The number of children with mothers who work (31.8 million) has become, for the first time, larger than the number of children with mothers at home (26.3 million).

"Even though a woman's paycheck is less than a man's, it keeps many an American family alive," says Betty Friedan. "Given the realities of human, family and national survival, there can't be any serious consideration that women will go home again." Elizabeth Hardwick puts it this way: "I certainly don't think the clock will be turned back, not because of any kindness on the part of society, but because it does not suit society for women to be in the home. It is not economically possible, it is not convenient, and it's not practical. The wife economy is as obsolete as the slave economy." At the very least, Hardwick's "wife economy" has mutated—out of the kitchen, into the office, onto the assembly line—even as the wages paid for the new-woman's work range significantly below the male median.

Traditionally, jobs are the tools of success. In America they have become something more. "We have learned that jobs do not simply earn money, they also create people," says Barry Stein, president of Goodmeasure, a Cambridge, Mass., business consultancy. Jobs, we have on good authority from the forefathers, confer respect, status and community well-being. The foremothers were apparently not consulted on the subject. It is difficult for a woman to find status in a pay envelope that is substantively thinner than a male co-worker's.

Not only has the current Administration made little effort to redress the wage imbalance, in the eyes of many feminists it has set out to blunt the victories of the past ten years. Around the Women's Legal Defense Fund, President Reagan's popularity rating is about as high as the heels on a California rancher's boots. Among the grievances: Administration suspension of stronger affirmative-action regulations for businesses receiving Government contracts; withdrawal of wage-discrimination and sex-segregation guidelines for federal contractors; elimination of the $500 million set aside for child care in the federal budget.

Whether intended to do so or not, this has sent a clear message to feminists and working women alike. When Republican Congresswoman Margaret Roukema of New Jersey spoke at a Cape Cod, Mass., conference of women state legislators to plead for recognition of "reality" according to Reaganomics, she faced considerable heat from the floor. "I have the feeling you people want to shoot the messenger," she objected. State Representative Arie Taylor from Denver shouted back: "We don't want to shoot, but we don't have any jobs in Colorado, and we can't take care of our children! You take that message back to him!"

The President has never been noticeably receptive to messages of that tone or type. It is even unclear whether he is all that keen on sending women out to work at all. Last April, at a luncheon with editors and broadcasters, he said that part of the reason for high unemployment "is not as much recession as it is the great increase in the people going into the job market, and ladies, I'm not picking on anyone, but [it is] because of the increase in women who are working today and two-worker families." Rosalind Barnett, a psychologist at Wellesley College's Center for Research on Women, has little patience with such an analysis. "Once you see work as crucial to both men's *and* women's sense of who they are," she says, "that kind of statement is abhorrent." Barnett and a colleague, Grace Baruch, completed a study demonstrating that, for women between the ages of 35 and 55, a paying job is the overriding factor that enhances a sense of worth.

Kinds of jobs, however, and ranges of salary remain a significant stumbling block—indeed, in some cases, a barrier. "Pay for full-time women clerical workers is extremely low," says Karen Nussbaum, executive director of 9 to 5, the National Association of Working Women. "It averages just over $11,000 a year for women, as compared with male clericals, who earn over $17,000. We feel if we could just get equal pay within our job classification we would be doing well." To date, 9 to 5 has initiated legal action that won over $3 million in back pay for women in publishing and banking, in addition to major pay raises for female employees in banking, insurance and engineering, including a sizable $1.34 million settlement from Bechtel.

Nonetheless, equal pay lies beyond the grasp of many women workers. Pamela Yore, 28, earns just over $10,000 a year in a small Boston hospital. (Males performing similar or the same duties get more.) She has to take care of a five-year-old son and an ailing husband and would certainly be helped by more equitable pay. However, she says, "You learn not to make too many waves in the workplace. If you do, there will be ten people there waiting for your job, and probably half of them have more education than you. You see women and men sitting side by side in the same office, doing the same job and making different salaries, and you have to tell yourself it is more a social attitude than a personal one directed at you. But it is hard when you are not making as much as you could or should."

The situation is not a lot brighter on the management level. In 1980 the median salary for women managers and administrators was $12,936, *vs.* $23,558 for their male counterparts. A 1981 study by Wellesley researchers demonstrates that once she reaches middle management, a woman is likely to be marooned there. As Management Consultant Carol Weiss, who collaborated on the Wellesley study, points out: "If these women have got this far, you know they've had to be crackerjacks to get there. Men look around and they feel threatened."

Some of the greatest progress has been made in admissions to law and medical schools. A third of the graduating class of Harvard Medical is made up of women. Law has had to practice what it has preached and legislated. When Justice O'Connor graduated from law school in 1952, the only job she was offered by major West Coast law firms was that of legal secretary. Now, if a firm wants the top of the law school class, it has to skim women along with men in the cream of the crop; 30.2% of 1981's graduates were women.

Over the past ten years, women have made significant progress in professional education. Women who left the campus with engineering degrees, for example, rose from .8% in 1971 to 10.4% last year.

But lawyers, doctors and women in what might be called high-profile jobs (journalism, publishing, broadcasting, fashion) take an outsize portion of public attention, partly because they are attractive exemplars of what is possible. But it is at the nether

4. INEQUALITY

end of the economic scale that the hardest battles are being fought, and it is there that the statistics begin to take on the proportions of a body count.

Poverty is a longstanding social problem that hits American women with particular force. "Female heads of households are the disproportionate group of people in poverty," says Columbia University Economist Eli Ginzberg. "The feminization of poverty" is Sociologist Diana Pearce's blunt phrase for it. A Census Bureau report covering 1980 just goes by the numbers: "About one-half of all families below the poverty level in 1980 were maintained by women with no husband present. The poverty rate for such families was 32.7%, compared with 6.2% for married-couple families, and 11% for families with a male householder, no wife present." The report indicates that 50.8% of the female-headed families with related children under age 18 were poor. Seventy-five percent of absent fathers contribute no child support at all. The Aid to Families with Dependent Children program, which spent $6.8 billion in fiscal 1981, will be spending only $5.4 billion in fiscal '83.

Work must be done, but work cannot always be had. When government services are curtailed, it is not only a small, fixed income that is lost, but jobs as well. The people dealing out federal funds are often one step away from poverty themselves, and as Cornell University's Barbara Wertheimer points out, "when you cut out services to the poor, you're also cutting the jobs that are held by women—child-care attendants, home health aides and the like. It's a double whammy." The disproportionate share of the reduction in federal programs is inexorably borne by the black working woman. "For me," adds M.I.T.'s Phyllis Wallace, "the shocking thing is that most families with black women as heads are impoverished, and nearly half of all black children are in these families. The problem is how to improve the chance for these women to get jobs in the private sector." Women in black families almost always had to work; the need may be more acute now, but the situation is not new. "Even the most highly educated black women had no choice," says Wallace. "If they wanted their children educated, or if they wanted to buy a home, or just have a middle-class standard of living, they had to work. Young black women had working mothers, and they knew that would be their fate. This is new for white families."

Federal programs that would train women of any color for jobs have been cut back. Recession has hit the heavy industries, and experienced male workers are competing for jobs with women just entering the field. "It is not only that women and men doing the same work don't get paid the same," says Barbara Wertheimer. "It's that women are segregated into certain jobs where they are paid less. What we have to do is look at the value of the work to the society and determine pay based on that." What once was a cry for "equal pay for equal work" will, accordingly, become a demand for "equal pay for comparable work." How this will be measured and worked out is still a mystery—how does an hour at the computer keyboard prorate against the same time spent in the typing pool?

If the work equations are ever resolved, they may even help answer a question some men now ask only with amusement: "Have women's rights done anything for me?" It may have seemed funny and a little silly when feminists started talking about men sharing housework and wives began insisting to husbands that homemaking was a tough job all its own. But the joke may seem strained indeed to whoever is left in the kitchen. And, guaranteed, there will be more diapers and dishes in Dad's future.

III: LIVING ROOM

First there are nine months before the baby is born. Then the baby is born. Then there are three or four months spent in feeding the baby. After the baby is fed there are certainly five years spent in playing with the baby. You cannot, it seems, let children run about the streets. People who have seen them running wild in Russia say the sight is not a pleasant one.

So many of the issues of the women's movement, from housework to abortion, were so basic to so much received wisdom that they seemed, by prospect or in perspective, either trivial or threatening. "Attention was finally being paid," Joan Didion wrote in a 1972 essay, "yet that attention was mired in the trivial. Even the brightest movement women found themselves engaged in sullen public colloquies about the inequities of dishwashing and the intolerable humiliations of being observed by construction workers on Sixth Avenue. . . . It was a long way from Simone de Beauvoir's grave and awesome recognition of woman's role as 'the Other.'" Those examples can be trivial issues only to women who, in suburban smugness, no longer have to endure them. Their metaphorical weight—as symbols of the wife economy, and of victimization—should have been difficult to miss. Difficult, apparently, but by no means impossible. "Well, I wrote that in 1972 and I haven't really thought about it since then," Didion remarked recently. "I'm sorry. I've been thinking about other things."

For many other women, without Didion's intellectual range and without her literary privilege, it is still hard to think about much else. Assaultive language masquerading as sidewalk compliments can remind any woman of her vulnerability. Rape is still a waking nightmare, but at least a little daylight has been let in. The physical wounding and emotional trauma are now discussed openly. America is being educated; more stringent laws and penalties are now in effect and reflect a greater understanding of the crime. But feminism, in its widest application, is still a home-front revolution, and it is in the apartment, the tract house and the split-level that its greatest impact has been felt.

This is a fact that was more quickly grasped and used by Phyllis Schlafly and her resistance camp than by the feminist insurgents, who were, at first, so busy recruiting for the barricades that they left the main base vulnerable. Schlafly, however, was a good deal more cunning than anyone first thought. She has potentially a strong feminist background: a daughter of the Depression, she worked in a munitions plant to put herself through Washington University in St. Louis. Feminists might initially have mistaken her for a kind of grandstanding Betty Crocker, but Schlafly and her supporters marshaled all the fear and uncertainty that trails every social revolution, trimmed it and turned it against the opposition. ERA would encourage everything from rampant homosexuality to unisex bathrooms, from women draftees in combat to women victims of some squalid unisex millennium. Cheap and scary, sure, but as they say about such quibbles in Hollywood, "Hey, it worked."

No one took much notice that Schlafly's insistence upon strength through inequality could have been based on a fear and contempt for men at least as deep as, say, Radical Feminist Ti-Grace Atkinson's. What emerged instead was the image of Phyllis Schlafly as defender of the traditional values, defender of the home. No matter that all the sociologists and all the statisticians and all the activists said Ozzie and Harriet were gone for good, that the conventional nuclear family, with Dad bringing home the bacon and Mom cooking it for him and the kids, survived in only 28% of American homes. The divorce rate almost doubled in the past decade, and the percentage of people living alone rose from 5.3% to 8.3%. Still, that family with the bacon is for many Americans not just the ideal family, but the American dream itself. Schlafly not only defended the home, she defended the dream, and her constituency has triumphed, for the moment, because dreams die hard.

But the lasting strength of families is not in tradition, it is in the capacity for change. Few novelists in years have written as well about the ferocious fragility of family love and family life as John Irving. *The World According to Garp* has a protagonist—no, a hero—who breaks conventional roles as if they were a half-hearted hammer lock, who not only tends the kids while his wife works and keeps the house in order, but actually takes joy in his tasks. Pride. Fulfillment. The book was more than a smash. It was a true literary phenomenon, and there are surely very few admirers of Garp who think, as the boys in the barroom still say, that he got his balls busted.

Nitpickers will be quick to raise a point: T.S. Garp was a writer, and writers work at home. What of the millions of other men who have to work away? What happens to the children with both mother and father off on the job? They cannot, as Virginia Woolf observed, "run about the streets." The options are limited, and so far imperfect. These days, what Woolf called "that deep-seated [male role] desire, not so much that *she* shall be inferior as that *he* shall be superior" may have moderated into an awareness that a different equation is wanted. Finding and holding the balance, however, requires some acrobatic skill. It also demands flexibility and a good deal of resilience.

ABC Newsman Ted Koppel took a year off from a steady job so his wife Grace Anne could finish school. He sustained no visible career damage—indeed his boss gave him a daily three-minute radio program to keep the bills paid—and after his wife graduated, he went on to his greatest success as host of ABC News *Nightline*. On the other hand, Don Demers, an industrial engineer in Dayton, took the kids while his wife finished med school, then found, after more than two years away, that he could not find another job. Commented Charles Arons, president of a Los Angeles employment firm: "There isn't a male I know of in an executive position who would accept raising kids as a legitimate excuse for not working for three years." Note the "not working": to Mr. Arons, a one-way ticket to the T.S. Garp Hit-the-Mat Seminar and Backyard Barbecue, held yearly on the grounds of the Hotel New Hampshire.

Aron's point, however, has a goodly amount of immediate, and unfortunate, practicality. There are not many executives who can appreciate or allow that the skill, say, of time management at home might be applied to office management, just as there are still very few corporations with personnel departments set up to accommodate the needs of the new work force and the flexible family. Other than enlisting the aid of family members, day care remains the most common way to manage the children during work hours. Centers all over the country have been damaged by budget cuts and by some strong conceptual questions. Edward Zigler, director of the Bush Center in Child Development and Social Policy at Yale University, estimates that 40% of the children of working mothers may be in "home day care" (that is, they are cared for either in their own home or in the sitter's), while fully another 40% are in "family day care," where a sitter outside the home cares for four to six children. "It is an open issue for children of every age," he says. Says Psychologist Michael Meyerhoff, who spent 13 years in the Harvard Pre-School Project: "If there is any element of choice, we've been trying to get people to be aware that the job they would be doing with their child is more important than any job outside the home. And you don't have to be a woman to be a good mother."

These doubts about day care can put a crimp in the family future, and a dent in the budget, but they do not, as Schlafly might have us believe, atomize the American nuclear family. The quality of the day care and its basing near the job may come a little closer to a workable solution. In Massachusetts both Wang Laboratories, Inc., and Stride Rite Corp. have inaugurated model projects with long waiting lists of applicants. Stride Rite's program also includes the options of dental care and psychotherapy. Adjustments made to work schedules, so-called flextime, are another component of the solution, as are extended maternity leaves for both parents.

There is still a long road to travel before such leaves become common in the U.S. and probably even a more tortuous route before men as well as women will want to press hard for them. Author Maxine Hong Kingston is right when she says that "in the feminist movement, there are advantages for both sexes. It's like liberation for both, and not one at the expense of the other." Getting the majority of men to see those advantages, never mind seize them, may take a while. Down in the juke joints, the boys are listening to Merle Haggard sing a tune called *Are the Good Times Really Over*, a litany of wistful memories from "back when the country was strong." The song yearns for a time "when a girl could still cook and still would." Those boys may not be able to get a hot meal on the table themselves, but they won't abandon without a fight their inalienable right to have it rustled up by the little woman.

It will be a losing fight, ultimately, and it will not take place exclusively in the roadhouses. There have already been skirmishes up in the loftier precincts, where a well-turned antique compliment (Dr. Johnson to Boswell: "Men know that women are an overmatch for them") now sounds more like a neat way of undercutting a woman with awe. James Thurber, invited to talk to the graduating class of Mount Holyoke College of 1949 ("The idea of addressing the flower of American womanhood would terrify me even if I could see"), declined by invoking a story about a World War I soldier who, peering down into a bottomless enemy trench, allowed that "I wouldn't go down there even if they was Fig Newtons down there."

The cookie does not crumble that way any more. The cookies, in fact, do not crumble at all. This does not mean charm is passe, or compliments are sexist, any more than it means that, contrary to all those shoo-fly Schlaflyisms, men and women will be less distinctive, or less sexual, if they work at the same jobs or compete at the same sports.

Biology is immutable. Basic physical differences will not change, but the law will. Absolute equality between men and women may be impossible—absolutes are—but it is approachable at least, and now just a little closer.

Equality does not eradicate differences in gender, it exalts them, which should be some comfort to cowering sexists still clinging to every advantage they have ever wangled or wrung out of women. Equality is only a threat if reality is. In the rubble of busted pedestals and shredded stereotypes are the pieces of a new perception: of the real, working, workable way of equality, of self-awareness, of mutual respect.

The women usually picked to symbolize change and re-evaluation are those like Gloria Steinem and Jane Fonda, who have achieved a popular success that has turned them into celebrities. Steinem therefore becomes an articulate and snazzy figurehead, Fonda a role model whose movie trajectory (from bimbo to feminist beacon) mirrors very neatly the way in which women are supposed to see themselves. Watching and listening to them, though, is not as striking by half as tuning in on a single studio audience of the *Phil Donahue Show*. Fifteen years ago, these same women might have been sitting in the same seats, whooping it up when the host gave them a pair of nylons, a month's supply of Palmolive and dinner for two at Casa Claude. Now, encouraged by a host who is a professed feminist, women wrangle with each other over issues like abortion and disarmament, and ask tough questions of guests ranging from Alan Alda and James Watson to transsexual twins and Henry Kissinger, who might have an easier time of it on *Meet the Press*. The Donahue show is one striking illustration of women, five times a week, finding a voice.

Even the defeat of the ERA means just another redrafting, a further extension of the debate. There is one point on which feminists and most of their foes can now agree: there is no going back. The only question is how to define the future and how to cope with the challenges that the changing role of women will present.

In certain subtle ways, it might be argued that women may have succeeded too well. Their hopes have been so frequently dramatized and debated that they have turned into clichés of fiction before they have become matters of fact. The abundance of persuasive reexamination and the wealth of fine writing that have come from this woman's decade—Anne Tyler and Gail Godwin, Maxine Hong Kingston and Joyce Eliason, Ann Beattie and Elizabeth Hardwick and, yes, Joan Didion—have created a consciousness that is both more aware and a little restless, a little reckless, even, about mistaking gains for guarantees. Critic Janet Maslin summed up the plot of a movie this way: "[The heroine]

4. INEQUALITY

confronts her new situation. She redefines her relationship with her children. She re-enters the work force and examines her anxieties about men, sex and love. She learns that she is as much of a person without a partner as she was with one—perhaps even *more* of a person." That breeziness may just be emblematic of a generally renewed spirit, but somehow one prefers the rejoinder to a persistent cigarette ad printed boldly on a T shirt: I HAVEN'T COME A LONG WAY, AND I'M NOT A BABY.

IV: A ROOM OF ONE'S OWN

Women have served all these centuries as looking glasses pos-sessing the magic and delicious power of reflecting the figure of man at twice its natural size.

These things are not measurable by surveys or shows of hands or random samplings. If they are knowable at all, it is through some almost incidental combination of art and intuition, force of feeling and shock of knowledge. Finally it all comes to this: that women, after years—after centuries—are stepping through Virginia Woolf's looking glass. The measure of all the change and growth of the past decade is that women, finally, are coming out the other side of the mirror. The limit is that they have not shattered the glass. Not yet.

And yet.   —*By Jay Cocks. Reported by Anne Constable/Atlanta, Ruth Mehrtens Galvin/Boston and Janice C. Simpson/New York*

Coming Into Your Own
In a Man's World

Elizabeth Janeway

Elizabeth Janeway, author, social historian, critic and lecturer, is one of America's most influential writers and speakers. Her first nonfiction work, Man's World, Woman's Place, *published in 1971, is an exploration of social change, taking woman's role as a field of study. This was followed by* Between Myth and Morning, Women Awakening, *in which she extended her exploration of the mythological basis for woman's self-image and the world's image of her.*

In Powers of the Weak, *published last year, she analyzes the power relationship from a new perspective: not from the traditional point of view of the strong, but from the experience of "the oldest, largest and most central group of human creatures in the wide category of the weak and the ruled"— women. In relating so-called women's issues to their roots in power and the misuse of power, Mrs. Janeway places women's lives within the context of major social change.*

F THERE'S ONE THING WOMEN WOULD AGREE ON ABOUT the facts of female life, it's surely that our roles and activities are subject to change, often without notice or much input from us. Traditionally, we've moved house as our husbands' jobs demanded, sometimes enthusiastically, sometimes with considerable anguish over the loss of our friends and our children's roots. We've been expected to implement or organize the volunteer work that communities have depended on for generations. We have fund-raised, car-pooled, undertaken Den Motherhood, steered the wheels with the meals that go to the elderly, helped to plan parenthood or else not, manned (or womanned) phones for myriad causes ranging from good to moderate, and we know well who's going to be asked to lick stamps and address envelopes, ferry voters or baby-sit on election day—you may add your own specialties to this list. We've grown used to becoming experts in model plane building, batting averages and horsepersonship as children's hobbies require. And now, of course, more and more frequently we go to work at that job outside the house for which we get paid, while still holding down the one we do at home for love.

Flexibility has been our middle name, and an honorable one too, as long as its purpose has been to support the activities of other people. But with the growing participation of women in the job market, appreciation of our capacity to do six things at once has become more problematic. As well it might. Working wives and working mothers know they are juggling an awful lot of break-

ables. But it isn't exactly our skill at juggling that seems to be in question. What causes concern is not our ability to adjust, but the uneasy feeling that our loyalties may shift. Will a woman with a paid job be as ready to move from Boston to Denver if her husband's company schedules a transfer? Who's going to ferry the young from one stimulating activity to another if the ex-head of ferry command is now newly fledged as the holder of a law degree? Will a devoted Frau Professor enjoy typing her husband's research notes if she's pushing to finish her own dissertation?

The return of married women to a labor market they left as brides has been going on for a long time, but for a couple of decades it was seen as pretty much an individual matter. Yes, so-and-so's wife was selling real estate or mutual funds. Mrs. this-and-that was after an M.A. in social work at the state university campus, while many a mother of schoolagers had refreshed her typing skills or dusted off a teaching certificate and headed back to work long before the phenomenon went public. In fact, more women were in the labor force in the mid-fifties than when Rosie the Riveter was a cover girl during World War II; and their number has grown steadily ever since. New entrants to the job market, the statistics tell us, are overwhelmingly female. Back in 1950, six married men were breadwinners for every married woman; now it's less than two. And these aren't short-term jobs to tide a family over difficult times. Women currently stay in the labor force for an average of more than twenty-five years.

Sooner or later, working women are going to be taken as normal, but that hasn't quite happened yet. On the one hand, the economic value of a two-income marriage rises along with the rate of inflation. On the other hand, there's still a felt need for married women to justify working for pay. Either money pressures require it (and plenty of husbands find that a painful admission to make), or the working wife should have more than just a job. Only a professional career is considered acceptable as a reason for moving out of the domestic sphere. If the best you can do is another routine job, you might as well carry on with the PTA.

This attitude says something about the ambiguity our society harbors about a woman's proper role. It also displays a good deal of ambiguity about our view of work. The double doubts feed each other. How positive do most people feel about their jobs? There's been a fair amount of negative testimony on this point, going back at least as far as Thoreau's famous observation, "Most men lead lives of quiet desperation." The conversations Studs

4. INEQUALITY

Terkel reports in his book, *Working*, indicate respect for work honestly done, resentment toward the pressures that often surround it and toward the hype that can falsify its purpose. A number of studies have been made of "job satisfaction." But satisfaction obviously depends on what one expects from a job. Is it "meaning, purpose, intrinsic enjoyment and self-development" that professional people expect from their work? If so, they can be more easily disappointed than blue-collar workers assigned to routine, mechanical tasks. Most of us assume that professional work is indeed more satisfying, but a number of recent studies cast doubt on the rewards it brings, pointing to the incidence of "mid-life crisis" and depression. Job alienation, it appears, can show up where it's least expected.

If man-the-breadwinner is dubious about the rewards for his activity in the workplace, why should woman-the-homemaker be fleeing the haven of family and feeling in so determined a fashion?

Primary is the inarguable need to earn. Widows, women responsible for themselves and, even more necessitous, women who are also responsible for children are primary breadwinners in exactly the same sense as any male head-of-household. They are not, however, the only women aware of money pressure. And why should they be? The idea that one pair of busy hands, one working adult, can support a family may contribute to masculine pride (or shall we call it the macho mystique?), but it's a very recent artifact. Women have worked throughout history—worked hard and long, using remarkable skills and great creative talent.

Still, though history may make the idea of women at work legitimate, it doesn't necessarily make it desirable. The fact that our ancestors did things one way while we do them another doesn't imply that we should, for example, trade in our automobiles and get a horse. The record of women as competent workers should have something more to say if it's going to persuade us that work's good in itself. Does it? I think it does—something important. Women's ability to do well the same things that men take pride in doing well points to the wide overlap of human feeling, capability and experience that both sexes share. It underlines our common interests. Too many stereotyped images picture men and women as different kinds of creatures with different missions in life, so different that we are taken to be unable to share work and purpose. The sturdy, laborious lives of our ancestors, forefathers and foremothers too, reveal an enduring capacity for both to learn new ways of living and managing.

This doesn't mean that men are going to turn into women, or women into men! Human beings provide a rich diversity of potential for change. If women begin to do some of the things that men alone have undertaken in the recent past, and we can see them doing so; if young fathers take a hand in the daily care of their children, and we can see that as well; then both sexes are evidencing a profoundly significant capacity for growth.

But, though the psychology of men and women may be adaptable to different lifestyles, aren't there real physiological differences that direct women away from some kinds of work? We certainly hear more about sex differences than about similarities. Yet when the U.S. Employ-

ment Service tested sex differences in the seven areas important to success in the skilled trades, where women are regarded as most disadvantaged, they turned up only one area—spatial reasoning—in which women tested lower than men. In two—numerical reasoning and manual dexterity—no difference was apparent; and in four, women were superior—form perception, clerical perception, motor coordination and finger dexterity.

Most jobs today don't call for appreciable physical strength or more dexterity than is needed to use a typewriter or word-processor. If we can accept the idea that it's psychology rather than physiology that dictates our notions of sex differences in the workplace, we'll be better able to deal with the problems those notions present.

Our biggest problem is adjustment to change in the world around us and in intimate relationships. It's a problem that's complicated by our tendency to carry images of each other that are appropriate to one place but not to another. Men may assume that they can adjust their behavior from public arena to private sphere, but doubt that women (so emotional) can do the same. When changing roles force us to improvise new ways of dealing with each other, we can do it best if we hold to a sense of the similarities between the sexes, instead of scaring ourselves with the notion that men and women, like east and west, are a twain fated never to meet. We do meet, often, and our feelings frequently run the same course. If women feel shy about moving into new settings, men are still worried about being turned down when they ask a woman for a first date. It seems that we're all sensitive to making a wrong move and being rejected.

Or take that well-known study on women's fear of success. Before we jump to the conclusion that women are nonachievers, we ought to ask about the kind of achievement that did not attract the young women who took this test some fifteen years ago. It was "leading her class at medical school," that female students at a Midwestern college shied away from, while men did not. At the time, however, going to medical school was a daring venture for a young woman. They expected, and got, fairly tough handling from their male comrades and their male professors too. Anyone who aspired to lead her class in medical school would need quite exceptional motivation, plus a thick skin. Today, of course, women in medical school are much more numerous and a good deal more welcome; and today several attempts to duplicate the earlier study have failed. We have to ask whether it really indicated fear of success, or a prudent realization that pioneering in a field where you're unwelcome is a tough job, better not taken on without great self-confidence and dedication. Heckling and ostracism act as real social and psychological deterrents for those who would otherwise want to enter new fields. Once the pioneers have broken the barriers (as they also have in law school and are doing in engineering school), others follow promptly.

Of course deterrents remain. Today they operate most strongly with mature women, even those whose daughters have eagerly embraced nontypical careers. Some are home-grown. The reactions of husbands and family are seldom totally positive when a woman in middle-life first speaks up about career ambitions. She herself may be doubtful of her own drive and potential. Women returning to college to finish undergraduate work or to get a higher degree typically express "fear of success." And then they go on to place in the top tenth of their classes, and often lead them. A little counseling helps at the start, and it's most useful when it comes from returning women who've been there a little longer and have found that courage can be learned just as well as fear. We see here the factor of normality, the strengthening sense that plenty of others are doing the same thing.

This isn't always easy to communicate back home. Helen Yglesias, who herself embarked on a new career as author at the age of fifty-four, followed a couple of successful novels with a book, *Starting: Early, Anew, Over and Late*, investigating just this subject of people of nontypical ages taking up new activities or trying to—for, of course, it doesn't always work. One comfortably-off husband responded to his wife's desire to take a job quite simply. "I said no, I need you at home." She gave in and, he reported, "has been perfectly happy with volunteer work." But don't her obligations there, Yglesias asked, keep her as busy as if she had a full-time job? "Yes," was the reply, "but she's not committed to that work. She can refuse to take on a particular task when I need her at home." Interestingly, this gentleman went on to praise the women in his company for "native brilliance, dash, intuitive business sense" and support of each other. His wife's comments, however, are not included.

Here again is ambiguity surrounding the proper role of women—paid work is all right for others, but not for "my wife." Perhaps less evident is the valuation of work that comes through. Volunteer work is all right because it can be put aside when family obligations arise. Work for pay cannot. What does that say about the work that women do at home? It isn't paid for. Is it, therefore, worth less than the labors of the breadwinner? Breadwinners often say no, that it's simply "different." If that's all, why isn't it as suitable for men? Why is working for money specifically male, working for love specifically female?

We are back to the old doctrine of innate male/female differences that outweigh our similarities in importance. And one of the differences is cash value. Women can work, yes; but they must put family first. Of course, if what a wife earns is essential for the family, then it's okay for her to take a job. Even so, it should be an undemanding job so that she can still fulfill her family duties. In such a job, of course, she'll never earn what a man does. Which goes to prove that breadwinning is really man's work. Excuse me—that's *proof*? It looks rather more like a deck that's been stacked to give a woman a primary mission that has to be done before, or while, she works for pay. The lower pay that she naturally receives from routine and undemanding work is then taken to show her inability to manage jobs that pay well (and are demanding of time and energy). Those jobs may bring more satisfaction, meaning, challenge, opportunities for self-development, but they ask too much of homemakers, says the stereotypical image of women. And they do. Which seems to mean that the greatest deterrent to success in the world of work isn't a woman's fear of achievement, but the fear felt by others in her life that ambition, normal to men, has to be turned off in her case. She can take a job, *if* she refrains from acting in a way that will

get her anywhere. The proper attitude of women toward work is summed up in the description of volunteer work: you can opt out when you want to.

I don't think that view has much to do with the psychology of women, but it has a lot to do with the psychology of men. It turns up in the workplace as well as at home; not everywhere, but in many settings still. Male bosses, too, expect that working wives and mothers respond to family demands, and that this is a "proper" way for a woman to behave. As a result, though entry-level jobs have certainly been made more available to women (with pressure from Affirmative Action directives a factor), promotion beyond them is harder to come by. Higher-level jobs require long hours; frequent travel; independent, swift decisions. And (the stereotype repeats) women are family oriented, putting others first. Male executives can be sent off to San Francisco on short notice or transferred from Omaha to Daytona Beach, but the boss who considers doing that to a woman is very likely to ask himself first, "How will her family react? Will her husband put up with it?" If the answer carries the overtone, "I wouldn't like it if she were my wife," another element may enter the picture: the image of an ambitious, hard-driving boss lady whose femininity is very questionable indeed. It is difficult, one must conclude, to be both a normal woman and a normal human being.

According to masculine psychology, that is; but women are very sensitive indeed to male thinking. We needn't attribute that to a special kind of female intuition. It's due to the fact that men are the holders and wielders of power. A woman whose work is confined to the home is dependent on the male breadwinner both for her status in society and for plain old cash. A woman in the workplace knows that top bosses are male and expects the commonplaces of male feeling and thinking to be guidelines to behavior—theirs and hers. Women moving into new activities carry with them an old image of woman-as-man-expects-her-to-be, "normal" woman geared to her "proper" role of nurturing, caring, responding to demands and guiding personal relationships. That role doesn't fit the workplace. Consequently, women at work feel themselves under the shadow of contradictory expectations that don't originate with them, but that have to be taken into account in public and in private too. Female flexibility is put to a particularly grueling test when it's asked to satisfy such ambiguous assumptions.

Certainly many men are getting over that double vision as more perfectly normal females turn out to be admirably competent at their professional vocations. But the confusion is still widespread enough for women to be wary about it. And, if it's there, dealing with it is usually up to women themselves, for even companies that proclaim themselves "Equal Opportunity Employers" seldom feel it their duty to try to change the inside of executive heads. Reducing male sexism is taken to be a female task; which is like saying that racism is solely the problem of blacks or other minority members.

In *Men and Women of the Corporation*, her study of how a major American company operates at the human level, Rosabeth Moss Kanter discusses the management problems that result from this sense of *difference* from women, and from minorities. Uncertainty, she observes, plagues all bureaucracies. It is "the fundamental problem for complex organizations, and coping with uncertainty [is] the essence of the administrative process." Uncertainty is countered, she goes on, only when those charged with making decisions know and trust each other. But how is this trust established? By forming "homogeneous groups" whose "mutual understanding [is] based on the sharing of values." There is no room here for difference.

Input from strangers is unwelcome, whoever the strangers may be: it's taken well over a year of a disastrous economic squeeze for American auto companies to begin investigating the remarkable success of their Japanese rivals. Women are seen as at least as different; Simone de Beauvoir put it succinctly when she used the word *other* for the male description of women. One wonders whether the free-floating dissatisfaction with work, noted earlier, may not be connected to this "uncertainty" at large in major companies. People who aren't sure about the effects of their policies are bound to be uncomfortable about making plans for the future; but that, of course, is what male executives are supposed to be so good at. These doubts, I believe, should be seen as the result of pressure from the limitations of the *masculine* role. By devaluing the experience of others, it serves to keep what used to be called "the white man's burden" weighing heavily on the same male shoulders.

So we come round again to the question of women's ambitions. If decision-making is uncertain, if job satisfaction means settling for little, if those who have traditionally sought meaningful work are experiencing depression and opting for shifts in their careers, why do women want to get out of the house and into the office?

One unpleasant answer rears its head promptly: work at home is so isolating, so unrewarding, that anything is preferable. I'm reminded of George Bernard Shaw's reply to the reporter who asked whether he was happy to have attained the age of ninety. "Only when I consider the alternative," said Shaw. But the truth, as well as the prevalence, of such a reply simply can't be estimated. For one thing, it's extremely personal, depending (like job satisfaction) on expectations. For another, its implications are very upsetting, not easy to face even if true. "And so they were married and lived happily ever after," say the fairy tales, and we hate to give them up. Instead, women tend to assume that unhappiness is a sign of personal failure: dissatisfaction with the job done for love at home brings on a case of the guilts more readily than does dissatisfaction with work for pay. Homemaking is still very deeply felt as our primary job. Expecting little reward from marriage is much harder than expecting little satisfaction from a paid job, where we all tend to be reasonably skeptical rather than romantic.

One problem is that we fail to see that many elements that operated in the past to keep marriages together have diminished or vanished entirely—the profitable work done at home, the active companionship between husband and wife who were managing a farm or a business in tandem, the longer time spent raising larger families in which fathers at home took a greater part, closer ties with kin and the neighborliness of small-town life that provided affectionate friendships. All these contributed support to the central male/female relationship, and supplemented it if difficulties arose within it.

Let us remember, too, that we all live longer nowadays. *The New York Times* recently quoted Dr. Holger Stub of Temple University, a specialist in the study of aging. "Longevity," said Dr. Stub, ". . .exposes marriage to a phenomenal increase in disruptive influences and culminates in high divorce and separation rates." In response to this increased life span, the good news is that "almost all women can plan for a second career of twenty to thirty years." But the good news of active golden years is mixed with the bad. "Increased longevity allows men and women virtually to bargain for two marriages, one for the young family years and another for the post-parental period." Dr. Stub makes no judgment of this new sort of ambiguity, he simply states that it's "not merely a possibility but is actually taking place." If Dr. Stub is right and the fairy tales wrong, it seems that older wives have two choices: either to stay home and pray that their husbands will too, or go after that second career that can provide a suddenly necessary paycheck.

Dr. Stub declares his data to be realistic, however amoral or cynical they may sound "to romantics or the religiously oriented." I must confess that they sound a bit exaggerated to me, even though I'm neither of the above. But if they are increasingly a fact of life, even if not a major one, they add other reasons for women to think seriously about that second career. In any case, modern science and medicine have given us many more years of healthy life. If, with children grown and gone, we find ourselves severely unemployed at the old job of homemaker, those years will be more rewarding if they are filled with self-directed activities that build competence and self-esteem. Volunteer work can serve this purpose—but only if it's taken seriously; when it's perceived as something that can be put aside at will, it is being trivialized. I am sorry for that. Volunteer work is at least as valuable and as needed as it ever has been, but in a society that reckons the worth of labor by how much it brings in, we can't be surprised by finding work done for free dropping lower on the scale of values. At present, women who have been involved for years as volunteers know that top posts often go to professionals—that is, to workers who are paid and who will therefore not take off when demands from private life pull women away from their responsibilities in this area of public service.

We humans are social creatures. We all need some part in the web of community, some involvement in the networks that bind us together and serve common purposes, whether the work we do is paid for or not. Each of us aspires to be more than a helpmeet to someone else. We have a psychological need, as well as a right, to aspire to success without fear, success that is more than vicarious, even though it will often be shared with others. A true community is made up of individuals with ideas and resources that are both personal and accessible for use by society. I believe that such authentic individuality grows out of continuity in action, engagement in ongoing processes of effective work. One way to think of it is by the rather clumsy name of a "career identity"—the sense of a repeatedly competent, activating self, trustworthy not simply by living-to-rule but as an individual capable of judging, acting, learning, persisting, gaining in knowledge and skills; a person willing and able to engage directly with events and analyze them on the basis of her own experience, female experience that is part of human experience; a person moved by unsuppressed ambition toward achievement that can be enjoyed *realistically*— neither doubted, nor overvalued.

The development of such an identity brings a confidence that enlarges the familiar image of female flexibility. It assures us that we can learn new skills even if they lead us into unfamiliar territory. It points to the common humanity of men and women. Married couples who have shared their lives long past the period expected by Dr. Stub often arrive at this sense of mutual understanding by another road that embodies the real meaning of living happily ever after. But that private road doesn't diminish the value of public evidence testifying to human mutuality, visible along with the differences that male or female experience engenders. An awareness of human similarity speaks to the growth of trust, the decrease of uncertainty and anxiety, and an increasing conviction that neither sex should function as "other" in private or public.

The entrance of women into the workplace is not going to cure the ills that have accumulated through the proliferation of repetitious, routine jobs, timed to machines and hard to call "meaningful" by any standard except that they provide the wherewithal to live by one's own efforts. The knowledge that you can do that is not to be sneezed at, but if we're ever going to make work more satisfying, we need to see "earning a living" as a part of living, not necessarily a burdensome process to groan our way through. I believe we got ourselves into that fix because we have split the human race in two by gender, and have assigned the task of earning a living to one half and maintaining important personal relationships to the other. Both segments lose value and significance as they diverge. The rising concern with "quality of life" may well be a consequence of our unfortunate estimate that work for pay has to be a "rat race." When we assume that competition and confrontation are needed for success on the job and that these are strictly male qualities, and add the corollary idea that women don't and can't employ these useful qualities but are uniquely fitted to express the warmth and affection all humans require to thrive, then we are dividing not only society, but our own feeling, reasoning, active and responsive selves. We are denying the essential mutuality of male and female members of the species *Homo sapiens*.

If we downplay the simple gender difference set up by the stereotypes of masculinity and femininity, we open the door to a richness of individual differences instead of scaring ourselves with a polarized view of the world. When each sex is ignorant of the life-experience of the other, attraction is shadowed by fear of the inner mysteries of your closest companion. I don't think the fear is necessary to the attraction! Indeed, people who understand the pressures and pleasures of each other's lives are surely able to establish better and more permanent relationships than those who haven't a clue about what's going on with their nearest and dearest.

The work-roles of women are here to stay. The psychological problems they raise don't have to be. They can best be solved if we trust ourselves—and each other— enough to share them.

THE SOCIAL SECURITY FIX

A. Haeworth Robertson

A. Haeworth Robertson, formerly Chief Actuary of the Social Security Administration, is a managing director of William M. Mercer, Inc., the employee benefit and compensation consulting firm. He is one of the nation's leading actuaries and social insurance experts and is the author of The Coming Revolution in Social Security *(Reston, 1982).*

Last January 20, the National Commission on Social Security Reform issued its long-awaited report on Social Security's deeply troubled finances and some proposals for "realistic, long-term reforms to put Social Security back on a sound financial footing." These recommendations (summarized on page 37) represent as closely as possible a consensus of the conflicting views of leaders in Congress, the White House, and the diverse interest groups represented on the Commission—in short, a compromise that might well be enacted by Congress. It is notable that President Reagan and Thomas P. (Tip) O'Neill, Jr., the Speaker of the House of Representatives (where Social Security legislation must originate), have publicly stated their support of the report.

Congress will attempt to pass legislation by May 7, since that is the latest date—for administrative reasons—that the cost-of-living adjustment for the June 1983 benefit can be delayed (one suggestion by the Commission). At least *some* legislation must be passed by June 30, 1983; otherwise the old age trust fund will be inadequate to continue benefit payments beyond June.

To me, the work of the National Commission on Social Security Reform, though politically realistic, was extremely disappointing. Not because it failed to resolve all of Social Security's financial and design difficulties—that would be asking too much—but because it failed to identify and report forcefully the full extent of the system's weaknesses so that the Congress and the public would know that such frightening weaknesses do exist. This failure to be honest with the public will, if not corrected, result in the continued erosion of public confidence not only in Social Security but in the government itself.

During its meeting November 11–13, 1982, the Commission adopted a Background Book of actuarial cost estimates that defined the size and scope of Social Security's financial problems this way:

Old-age, Survivors, and Disability Insurance (OASDI)

☐ During the period 1983–1989, provisions must be made to increase income or decrease benefits, or some combination of both, by $150 billion to $200 billion (i.e., 9 to 12 percent of projected expenditures).

☐ During the next 75 years, 1982–2056, average annual expenditures of 14.09 percent of taxable payroll and average annual tax income of 12.27 percent of taxable payroll are predicted. Result: an average annual deficit of 1.82 percent of taxable payroll.

Hospital Insurance (HI)—Part A of Medicare

☐ During the period 1983–1989, scheduled taxes will be barely adequate to pay benefits; increased taxes or decreased benefits must be adopted not later than 1990. Under less optimistic assumptions, this remedial action must be taken in the mid-1980s.

☐ During the next 75 years, 1982–2056, average annual expenditures of 8.10 percent of taxable payroll and average annual tax income of 2.89 percent of taxable payroll are assumed. Result: an average annual deficit of 5.21 percent of taxable payroll.

The Commission's recommendations attempt to assure the *near*-term solvency of the OASDI program by increasing projected net income during the period 1983–1989 by $169 billion (achieved by increasing income by $129 billion and decreasing projected benefit increases by $40 billion). This would satisfy the requirement stated above that net income be increased by $150 billion to $200 billion. Based on more recent economic projections, however, still further changes may be necessary in the mid-1980s to keep the system solvent.

In the long-range, the Commission's recommendations would decrease the average 75-year OASDI deficit of 1.82 percent of taxable payroll to 0.58 percent, thus eliminating only about two thirds of it. No agreement could be reached by the Commission on how to tackle this remaining deficit. Some members favor a higher retirement age, some prefer higher taxes, and some prefer reduced benefits.

The Commission's January report virtually ignored the Hospital Insurance deficit of 5.21 percent of taxable payroll, which is almost *three times* the OASDI deficit of 1.82 percent. It also completely ignored the Supplementary Medical Insurance (SMI) part of Medicare, 25 percent of which is financed by participant premiums and 75 percent of which is financed by general revenue. The total cost of SMI is now the equivalent of about 1.0 percent of taxable payroll and is projected to rise to some 5.0 percent of taxable payroll during the lifetime of today's youth.

There is nothing really mysterious about Medicare and there is no excuse for ignoring it. It is a life annuity, paid in kind rather than cash, primarily to Social Security beneficiaries aged 65 and over. Almost one fifth of the taxpayer's Social Security tax is now used to finance the Hospital Insurance portion of Medicare. Social Security *includes* Medicare and ignoring Medicare's deficits will not make them disappear.

Moreover, despite the Hospital Insurance program's imminent financial difficulties, the Commission recommended that the OASDI trust fund be authorized to continue borrowing from the HI trust fund during the period 1983–1987. A new study by the Congressional Budget Office projects ominously that the Medicare trust fund will be empty by 1987 or 1988.

Thus, the Commission's recommendations do not come close to resolving Social Security's financial problems—except those of the OASDI program for the next seven years. To pay the longer-range bill, the tax rate would have to rise considerably above its currently scheduled level of 7.65 percent in 1990:

☐ Under "intermediate" assumptions (adopted by the Commission) the tax rate would have to increase to about 14 percent early in the next century (within the working lifetime of today's young taxpayers). This is nearly twice the ultimate scheduled tax rate of 7.65 percent.

☐ Under less optimistic assumptions, the tax rate would have to increase to about 20 percent (a combined employer-employee tax rate of 40 percent). This is almost three times the ultimate scheduled tax rate of 7.65 percent.

All this is in addition to the cost of the SMI part of Medicare, projected to rise to some 5 percent of payroll and which is financed primarily from general revenue.

(This is not the place to provide a full-scale prescription for Medicare. It may be useful to point out, however, that Medicare's financial troubles could be ameliorated by increasing the age at which benefits become payable, to match the inevitable increased age for receipt of normal retirement benefits, and by increasing the "deductibles" and "co-insurance" so the beneficiary has a greater financial stake in the selection and provision of medical services. It is likely that a major restructuring of the medical-care delivery system will some day be required. The point is that no serious attempt can be made until we first admit the enormity of the challenge—something the Commission was reluctant to do.)

It is tempting to criticize the Commission for not recommending the "correct solution" to Social Security's problems; however, there is no such correct solution. The "proper design" for Social Security depends upon one's individual value judgments and is not something on which unanimous agreement should be expected among diverse interest groups. Nevertheless, the following limited commentary may be of value in assessing the recommendations offered by the Commission.

Broken promises

For 47 years, the public thought Social Security's benefits were inviolable. If the government promised a certain type and level of benefit, it would be paid. People were told that by paying "contributions" to Social Security, they were acquiring "earned rights" to certain benefits. In fact, there has been a steady expansion of benefits and people have generally received even *more* than promised. As recently as December 7, 1979, the Advisory Council on Social Security had the temerity to say: "After reviewing the evidence, the Council is unanimously convinced that all current and future Social Security beneficiaries can count on receiving all benefits to which they are entitled."

It should be evident that it is no longer true that benefits, once promised, will assuredly be paid. Witness the cuts in student benefits and minimum benefits that occurred in 1981. Witness the Commission's recommendation to defer the COLA benefit increase for six months, or the recommendation to decrease benefits currently being paid to persons with other income of $20,000 or more for a single taxpayer, or of $25,000 or more for joint return taxpayers. (This benefit reduction would be accomplished indirectly by taxing half of their Social Security benefits.)

One disturbing aspect of this selective benefit reduction by taxing benefits is the introduction of the philosophy that if a person saves successfully for his own retirement the reward will be a reduction in benefits that were presumably counted upon in making retirement plans. If this means-test philosophy is carried to its logical conclusion, the government will effectively discourage private saving and individual self-reliance, and it may even encourage recipients to conceal other income. Such a government-induced change in behavior would be extremely damaging to the character of our nation.

Furthermore, the breaking of these benefit promises will have a far-reaching effect on the public's perception of Social Security, as well as of the government itself, as a reliable institution. This will make it difficult to convince the younger taxpayers that Social Security will in fact make good on its promise to pay benefits to them some 30 to 50 years hence. And without this conviction, taxpayers will be very reluctant to pay the high taxes necessary to support the system in the years ahead.

Higher retirement ages

The Commission's recommendations make no mention of the inevitable increase in normal retirement age for persons now under age 35 or 40. This will be absolutely necessary to provide the nation an appropriate-sized work force, not just to resolve Social Security's financial problems. If today's youngsters retire at age 70 in the next century they will have more years left to live than those who retired in the past at age 65. A higher retirement age is *not* a benefit cut; it is a natural consequence of increased life spans and improved health. The only tenable way that today's youngsters can retire in their early 60s is to retain the same short life spans as their forebears—not a very attractive alternative.

Increased taxes

The Commission's proposals to increase net income to Social Security by $169 billion during the next seven years, 1983–1989, are comprised of both benefit decreases and revenue increases, with emphasis on the latter.

Unfortunately (as a result of waiting until the last possible moment to resolve the system's financial crisis), a substantial part of the recommended tax increase has to come from general revenue (at least for 1983 and 1984). Relying on general revenue to pay benefits, at a time of huge budget deficits, is tantamount to borrowing—not a very sound basis on which to operate a social insurance system. The extent of the Commission's proposed use of general revenue may not be obvious at first since it is done rather circuitously:

☐ The increase in the employee Social Security tax for 1984 (from 6.7 percent to 7.0 percent) would be returned to the employee as a tax credit or cash refund, thus reducing general revenue by the same amount as the tax increase.

☐ One half of the total increased self-employment Social Security tax would be deductible as a business expense, thus reducing general revenue by a substantial portion of the tax increase.

☐ A lump sum reimbursement to the old-age trust funds for military wage credits would be from general revenue. (This is the only source of additional revenue to Social Security in 1983.)

Although it is not widely known, general revenue is already used to finance three fourths of the cost of the SMI portion (Part B) of Medicare. In 1982, the total cost of SMI was about $17 billion, or the equivalent of about 1.0 percent of taxable payroll. With the total cost of SMI projected to rise to 5 percent of payroll, this means eventual general revenue financing equivalent to nearly 4 percent of payroll. This is twice the cost of the entire Social Security program (a combined employer-employee tax of 2 percent) when it was originally adopted.

Anyone who is worried about an increased use of general revenue to finance Social Security should start worrying harder.

Universal mandatory coverage

As desirable as universal participation in Social Security might be from several viewpoints, it seems grossly unfair to ban withdrawal from the system by state and local governmental employers. These employers (and their employees) voluntarily joined Social Security with the understanding that they could withdraw in the future. A unilateral change in this participation agreement seems highly questionable, if not illegal. At the least, state and local governments should have a grace period in which to make an irrevocable decision whether they withdraw from Social Security or continue to participate.

Mandatory coverage of newly hired Federal employees may be desirable in some respects but it is doubtful that it will really save the nation any money—as some advocates of mandatory coverage suggest. It is likely that new hires would receive the same *total benefits* from Social Security and a revised Civil Service Retirement System as they now receive from their present system. If so, the total cost of retirement benefits for Federal employees would not be reduced. It would simply be rearranged.

Mandatory universal coverage would be defensible if Social Security provided only a minimum floor of protection. It would then be reasonable to impose Social Security's benefits on all employees, including employees of the Federal government, nonprofit organizations, and state and local governments. But Social Security is not just the lowest floor of protection—it is much more. It provides an array of benefits far beyond those that everyone would agree is a socially desirable minimum. Accordingly, it does not seem reasonable to impose the existing Social Security program on everyone whether they need it or not. If Social Security were reformed to provide a reasonable level and array of benefits that most people could agree was socially desirable, then mandatory universal coverage would be in order.

In defining the size and scope of the Social Security challenge, the Commission gave practically no attention to the strong likelihood that the long-range answer lies primarily in a new *design*, not just *financial* fixing. The social and economic environment will be considerably different 30 to 50 years from now, when the children of the post-World War II baby boom approach retirement. Obviously, the role of women in society and the workplace has changed and will continue to evolve. At present about 80 percent of the nonretired population is under age 45. It is this huge group that is questioning whether Social Security will still be around when it retires. The system depends precisely on whether or not today's young people will support it, and that in turn depends on whether it suits their needs and whether they believe it to be fair. It is entirely reasonable, therefore, to give serious consideration to a completely new type of social insurance system for the relatively young segment of the population.

My own thoughts about a new type of social insurance system—thoughts that are not inscribed on a bronze tablet—were set out in an article drawn from my book, *The Coming Revolution in Social Security*, in the July/August 1981 issue of *across the board*. The title of the piece was "The Freedom Plan for old age." Here are the three essentials of that plan:

A mandatory Senior Citizen Benefit program. This would provide a genuine floor of protection against financial adversity in old age—whether caused by misfortune or poor planning. At age 70, a monthly benefit of a uniform amount would be payable to all resident citizens, men or women alike, regardless of whether they had worked in paid employment. An appropriate benefit level for 1983 would probably be in the neighborhood of $350 per month. In contrast, the present average Social Security benefit for a retired worker is $420. However, approximately one third of the retired workers are receiving *less* than $350. Therefore, the Senior Citizen Benefit program would provide *increased* monthly retirement benefits for approximately one third of the population—the segment with the lowest earnings. It would provide lower benefits for approximately two thirds of the population—the seg-

ment most capable of providing supplemental benefits for its own retirement. The benefit would be financed on a "current-cost" basis; that is, taxes would be collected each year in the amount estimated to be necessary to pay benefits for that year. The amount of the benefit would be adjusted for changes in the average wage index or other index to which it was originally related. The establishment of 70 as the age for the Senior Citizen Benefit does not imply that everyone should work until 70; and it does not imply that the elderly should live out their lives on that low benefit. Rather, it implies that no one has the right to demand support from one's fellow citizens except from age 70 onward and except at the subsistence level.

The Freedom Bond program. If we believe that it is healthful for individuals to take responsibility for themselves and save for their retirement, and if we believe that high inflation is a possibility, there seems to be no alternative to getting the government involved—not to pay, but to provide a mechanism by which the active working population can preserve the value of any savings for retirement. It is proposed that the government offer retirement savings bonds—designated Freedom Bonds—under the following general conditions:

The Bonds would be sold after July 4, 1984 to any resident citizen between ages 45 and 70 provided he or she was under age 45 on July 4, 1984. (July 4, 1984 is my arbitrary pick for a date; certainly, unfortunately, no new social insurance system will be created by then.)

The maximum amount of Bonds an individual could purchase in any year would be 10 percent of his taxable earnings in the prior year; but any eligible individual could purchase a specified minimum amount of Bonds regardless of earnings (approximately equal to 10 percent of average earnings of the nation's employees for the prior year).

Each year the value of Bonds purchased in a prior year would be adjusted to reflect changes in the relative purchasing power that had occurred between the purchase date and the current valuation date. No interest would be payable on the Bonds, however.

No Federal, state, or local taxes would be payable on the Bonds, including any increase in nominal value, when they are redeemed. The Bonds would have been purchased with funds that had already been subjected to tax.

The Bonds would be redeemed for their current value upon the individual's death. They would be redeemable, at the option of the individual, upon his bona fide disability or anytime after his attainment of age 60.

The Bonds could be redeemed in a lump sum or in a series of installments, at the option of the individual or his survivors. If taken in installments, the unredeemed Bonds would continue to be indexed to reflect

What the Commission said

Here are the major provisions of the compromise proposal to resolve Social Security's financial problems:

☐ The Social Security tax on employers and employees would be:

1983	6.70%
1984	7.00
1985	7.05
1986–87	7.15
1988–89	7.51
1990	7.65

In effect, this means higher taxes in 1984, 1988 and 1989 than those scheduled under present law. In 1984 only, the worker would be allowed a refundable tax credit equal to the entire increase (0.30 percent) in Social Security taxes.

☐ The Social Security (OASDI) tax on self-employed persons, now three fourths of the combined employer-employee rate, would be increased to the full employer-employee rate, but half of the total payment could be deducted from taxable income for income tax purposes (but not for purposes of determining OASDI-HI tax). Many self-employed would thus pay a higher net of Social Security and income taxes.

☐ The annual cost-of-living adjustment, now paid in July, would be postponed this year until next January, then paid each January. The change would affect all 36 million beneficiaries. A special provision would reduce the impact on low-income elderly and disabled persons also receiving welfare.

☐ Half of a person's Social Security benefits would be subject to Federal income tax, but only if he or she had adjusted gross income of $20,000 from sources excluding Social Security, or, in the case of a married couple filing jointly, $25,000. Proceeds of the income tax would be paid into the Social Security trust funds. Some 3 million persons, or about 10 percent of the OASDI beneficiaries, would pay added taxes under this provision.

☐ As of next January 1, mandatory Social Security coverage would be extended to all new Federal workers. It would also be extended to all employees of nonprofit organizations for whom participation is now optional. Federal workers covered by the Civil Service Retirement System would not be affected. It is anticipated that the government would establish a supplementary employer pension for new Federal employees, so they would end up receiving Social Security plus a supplementary pension, as is now the case with many private-sector workers.

☐ Local and state governments covered by Social Security would be barred from opting out of the system as of the date of enactment of the proposed plan unless the process of termination is completed by such date.

☐ The so-called windfall portion of Social Security benefits received by Federal, state and local government employees who qualify for Social Security on the basis of relatively short periods of employment in the private sector would be eliminated for those first eligible to retire after 1983. They would receive a benefit, but less than under current law.

☐ Beginning in 1988, the plan would seek to stabilize the Social Security trust funds by providing that whenever the combined OASDI trust funds drop to less than one fifth of a year's benefits, the annual cost-of-living adjustment would be equal to either the annual rise in prices or the annual rise in wages, whichever is less.

☐ For each year a person delays retirement beyond 65 and before 70, the plan would phase in, from 1990 to 2010, a larger bonus. That bonus would be equal to 8 percent a year instead of the current 3 percent.

☐ Benefits and eligibility would be improved for certain widows and widowers, divorced persons and survivors.

☐ In the case of salary-reduction plans qualifying under the Internal Revenue Code, any salary reduction thereunder would not be treated as a reduction in the wages subject to Social Security taxes.

—A.H.R.

changes in purchasing power until fully redeemed.

An individual who purchased Freedom Bonds worth 10 percent of his earnings every year from age 45 to age 70 would accumulate enough to provide a lifetime retirement benefit from age 70 onward of 20 to 30 percent of his average preretirement earnings (depending upon the individual's earnings pattern and sex).

The Bonds would be available to persons even though they were not in paid employment. This provision is intended primarily for spouses. Of course, a spouse not in paid employment would not normally have any funds to save except funds provided by the other spouse.

Cost-of-living supplement for private pension plans.

Ideally, the proposed Senior Citizen Benefit system and the Freedom Bond program would be the extent of government involvement in retirement planning. The majority of the nation's workers are covered by a retirement program sponsored by their employer or groups of employers. Once again, however, the specter of inflation rises to impede the smooth functioning of our financial institutions and suggests the need for some form of governmental intervention. As inflation erodes the purchasing power of private pensions, they are sometimes adjusted upward. It is unusual, however, for a private pension to be adjusted fully to reflect changes in the cost of living.

It is proposed that the government provide cost-of-living supplements for all private pension plans in accordance with the following general guidelines:

Private pension plans, including those of Federal, state, and local governments, would be covered provided they met Federal standards for approved plans (Internal Revenue Service requirements for "qualified" plans, for example).

Monthly pension benefits payable for life would be covered, but only with regard to benefits payable after age 70.

Every year, benefits payable to persons aged 70 or older would be supplemented by the amount necessary to sustain the purchasing power in the prior year in accordance with a cost-of-living index constructed especially for the elderly.

The cost of these supplemental benefits would be paid from general revenue, that is, primarily by the active working taxpayers.

It may be worthwhile to remind ourselves that these supplemental benefits do not represent a "government subsidy" since the government does not pay the cost of anything. The government is simply formulating a standard with which the majority of the population presumably would agree (namely, the protection of the elderly population against the ravages of inflation with respect to certain monthly retirement benefits) and then providing a mechanism by which the active working taxpayer can support that standard.

Although much of the Commission's work may be commendable in light of the circumstances, adoption of its recommendations will clearly not resolve a very large part of Social Security's financial problems. If Congress just adopts the Commission's limited recommendations, and then assures the public that all is well, the following scenario seems probable:

☐ In the mid-1980s the near-term Medicare financial problems will become as evident as the near-term OASDI problems are now. But, to reemphasize a point, the Medicare problems are about *three times* the magnitude of the OASDI problems.

☐ The short-range Medicare problems will be studied for the balance of the 1980s and finally "resolved" at the last possible minute—in about 1987. The public will again be assured that all is well with Social Security.

☐ Simultaneously, in the late 1980s, discontent with the relentlessly increasing taxes will be aggravated by the inappropriate design of Social Security. The social and economic environment will continue to change faster than Social Security is changed. By then people will have a full understanding that they are not buying and paying for their own benefits and that Social Security is a huge income transfer program, and they will be extremely restive.

☐ In the late 1980s or early 1990s, the long-range financial problems of both OASDI and Medicare will start becoming more believable as they become more crushing. It will be clear that people will have to remain in the work force beyond their early 60s—probably until age 70 or so. The first children of the post-World War II baby boom will be approaching age 50 and they will not take kindly to a suggestion that they work another five years or so beyond their planned retirement at age 65. "Why didn't you tell me sooner?" they will ask. They should be informed right now.

There may still be time to forestall much of the discord in this scenario. We must stop kidding ourselves. Realism may be painful but it is not nearly so disastrous as unjustified optimism.

Kids as Consumers and Commodities

**Barbara Ehrenreich and
David Nasaw**

Barbara Ehrenreich is the author of The Hearts of Men
(Doubleday/Anchor Press). David Nasaw is the author of
Schooled to Order *(Oxford) and the forthcoming* On Their
Own: Children of the Street *(Doubleday).*

While Nancy Reagan was publishing her second book, *To
Love a Child,* a tearful ("I weep easily," she has said,
"which can be embarrassing sometimes") tribute to the joys
of intergenerational affection, her husband's Administration
was pocketing the lunch money of 3 million American
children and depriving millions more of subsidized snacks,
dinners and breakfasts. Confronted by these conflicting
signals from the nation's First Family, a sensitive foreign
observer like E.T. might conclude that there is an unacknow-
ledged tension in American's attitudes toward children.

Within the middle-class family, parental love appears to
be far from spontaneous. Parents do not expect to love their
offspring at first sight; they must first undergo the uncertain
process of "bonding." In the suburbs, bumper stickers confront drivers with the unsettling question, "Have You
Hugged Your Child Today?" Returning to update his classic 1919 history of the family, Arthur Calhoun would find
that children had slipped from the center of the American
family to the status of live-in guests who are finally beginning to wear out their welcome.

The Reagan Administration's war on children—most directly in cuts in the social welfare programs that so many
children depend on for shelter and sustenance—builds on a
deeper American ambivalence toward the young. In a culture dominated by laissez-faire ideology, children's status
can only be precarious; to put it bluntly, children do not pay
their own way. The New Right, for all its rhetorical devo-
tion to children and family, is quite clear on this point. In a
1982 interview, Connaught Marshner, chairman of the Pro-
Family Coalition, proposed to us that children make economic contributions to their families, adding that "the
humanistic reforms of the nineteenth century made children
into economic liabilities." From a hardheaded economic
perspective, she is right. Rejected by the labor market,
children subsist on the charitable contributions of their
parents or, failing that, make do on the meager offerings of
the state. Economically, they are on a par with other labor
market rejects, like welfare recipients and unemployed black
males, and prone to subconscious labeling as "bums" and
"idlers."

Roughly speaking, the status of children peaked during
the Progressive era, when middle-class optimism was running high. Social scientists designated the new century the
"century of the child," and predicted that the new genera-

tion would lead immigrant families to Americanization and the American economy to new productive heights. During the next few decades the reasons for optimism declined considerably, but children were still holding their own. In the post-World War II period, in fact, they became the indispensable proof of adult achievement, without which no man or woman could claim to be "adjusted," mature or even securely heterosexual. The first signs of America's disillusionment with its offspring can be traced to the launching of Sputnik in 1957, which occurred soon after the advent of rock-and-roll. Certainly "Ivan" had been doing his homework. Both phenomena raised troubling questions about how young people in this country were passing their time. If, in the 1950s, it appeared that American kids were too soft or too stupid to beat the enemy, in the 1960s they *were* the enemy. Beginning with *Rosemary's Baby* (which ends with the birth of a devil child), a series of films, including *The Exorcist* I and II, *Children of the Damned* and *The Omen* I and II, nurtured the adult suspicion that children, even babies, are potential demons, assistants to demons or matricidal maniacs. In the 1970s, psychologically hip adults often opted not to have children but to cultivate the "child in themselves," while the unhip organized to repress the libidos of the young by curbing sex education and the availability of contraceptives. Adult America was prepared, at some unconscious level, for an Administration that could seriously propose that fourth graders contribute to the fight against inflation by eating ketchup for lunch.

Like other economically nonproductive and socially suspect groups, children in this century have had to find ways to defend their right to subsistence and to maintain a modicum of self-respect. For children the key "strategy" has been consumerism. Ever since the first nickelodeons opened their doors almost eighty years ago, the young have done their part to keep the wheels of commerce turning. Neither recessions nor depressions nor declining fertility rates have slowed the growth of the kiddie markets. According to a survey by the Rand Youth Poll for the National Restaurant Association, while the teen-age population declined 6.6 percent between 1975 and 1980, teen spending rose more

---

THE CASUALTY LIST

Twelve million children—more than one fourth of the total—now live in poverty. . . . 7.9 million of these children receive A.F.D.C. or other public assistance; 4.1 million of them do not. . . . Since Ronald Reagan took office, 2 million children have entered the ranks of the poor. . . . More than half a million children are wards of the state. . . . 5.26 million children live in homes where one parent is unemployed. . . . Nearly 1 million children depend on single mothers for support.

---

than 50 percent. Trade journals—with little else to glow about in the depressed 1980s—report enthusiastically on the continuing growth of the kiddie markets, accelerated in the last few years by the volatile commerce in video games.

Children are the last of the big time spenders. Marketing experts predict that they will not only increase their purchases of toys, games, cosmetics, soft drinks and designer jeans, tops and sneakers, but will double their consumption of snacks and become major buyers of big-ticket items like audio and video equipment and home computers. In many households, children are replacing their mothers as chief decision makers on some purchases. As *Seventeen* magazine reported in a full-page ad in the January 17 *New York Times*, the child has become the "Speaker of the House." Children play a major, often *the* major, role in choosing their families' foods, appliances, diet sodas, breakfast cereals, toothpaste and soap. As *Seventeen*'s ad noted, "Last year they personally spent 37% of the family food budget, or $13 billion."

For children, the marketplace provides a kind of autonomous zone, which insensitive, interfering and pushy adults cannot easily enter. By choosing what, where, when and how to spend, children create their own subculture in opposition to the adult world. In the 1950s, they organized that subculture around comic books and *MAD* magazine (with its vicious satires of the adult-dominated consumer culture). In the early 1960s, preteen girls horrified adults with their frenzied worship of the Beatles and all things Beatle-related; for years rock remained a youth enclave almost impenetrable to adults. In the 1980s, children aggregate around video games and baffle large corporations by unpredictably switching their allegiance from Pac Man and Ms. Pac Man to Donkey Kong and Frogger. In the latest minifad, the Valley Girls and their imitators satirize consumerism even as they celebrate it—making the whole enterprise look pointless and affected. ("Like, gag me with a *spoon*!")

It is as consumers that children have been able to win a supportive constituency among wealthy and powerful adults. Manufacturers of retail goods (and not only those consumed solely by the young) have long promoted the idea that children are worthy of high levels of parental subsidy. Both through their advertising and the TV programs their advertising pays for, they reliably endorse the notion that children are fun to be around and that their needs—whether for Pampers or Pop Rocks—merit serious adult consideration. As Ellen Peck, author of *Pronatalism* and a leading advocate of nonparenthood, observed of some of the more cloying TV commercials, "Frankly, one wonders what is being sold: Pampers? Or babies? . . . Hershey bars or children's faces?" Thus, by becoming consumers, children came to be promoted as commodities—either indispensable adjuncts to adulthood, as in the fervently pronatalist ideology of the 1950s, or as interesting additions to a household, as they are more likely to be portrayed today.

But the consumerist strategy has its psychological costs. For one thing, it strains whatever affection parents spontaneously feel for their young. Kiddie market manufacturers spend $800 million a year on television ads urging children to wheedle, whine or harangue their way to new acquisitions. These ads find their way not only to the homes of the upper middle class but to the homes of the unemployed and the chronically hard pressed, where the expense of a single Smurf figure (from "the collectible world of Smurfs") could sabotage a family meal. For the poor as well as the merely thrifty, nothing undermines parental affection more decisively than a trip to the supermarket with a couple of TV-wise junior consumers. Any vestigial sentimentalization evaporates; the kids are revealed as "economic liabilities" or, worse, as the real-life counterparts of the filmic monsters who devour their parents and entire civilizations.

Children themselves pay an immediate psychological price for their dual role as dependent consumers and likable commodities. In the emotional economy of the American family, they are expected to be "cute"; that is what they learn from prime time programming and very often from the adults they encounter in real life. But from a child's vantage point, cuteness involves a performance in which dignity must constantly be sacrificed for attention—a parody of adulthood which exploits the handicaps (small stature, lack of motor coordination, defective pronunciation) of the performer. Diminutive television star Gary Coleman would not be cute, for all his wit, if he achieved his full growth; toddlers are cute not only because they walk but because they stumble. (And, of course, what is cute one moment, like a chocolate-smeared face, may be punishable the next.) For many children, the strain of being cute leads to a state of perpetual embarrassment, manifested either as a desperate silliness or a guarded withdrawal from adult contact.

Women, finding themselves in a similar role as financial dependents and displayers of obligatory cuteness, took immediate measures to change their situation. Betty Friedan advocated women's return to the work force because the housewives she surveyed for *The Feminine Mystique* seemed to be losing their sanity and self-respect. The worst she could say about them was that they had been "infantalized," and the best she could suggest was that they grow up and get out of the house. But for children there is no such clear-cut escape. All that remains is to burrow deeper into the consumer culture, while, of course, dipping deeper into their parents' pockets.

Consumerism, whether as acquiescence or escape, is always a limited and risky strategy. Moon Zappa (daughter of Frank and template for the Val Gals) may cruise the shopping malls with a full deck of credit cards, but other little girls must nag their parents or learn to shoplift. In poor neighborhoods, small children hustle pizza parlor patrons for quarters to play Frogger; some of them will soon be big enough to mug pedestrians for the wherewithal to buy "muscle-builder (radio/tape deck) boxes." Seventy-four years ago, Jane Addams reported from Chicago that much of the "petty pilfering" that went on was a result of the children's need for nickels for the nickelodeon. In the 1980s, the nickels have become $5 bills and some of the petty pilferers carry guns. So long as children are both financially dependent on their parents and exposed to a spectacle of consumer temptations, the disjunction between their "needs" and their families' incomes will regularly generate child outlaws. As the incidence and intensity of child crime increases, adult sympathy for children as a class declines.

The effect of the Reagan Administration's policies has been to destabilize what is already an economically precarious situation for children. No age group, of course, can be counted a winner in the mammoth shift from spending for social welfare to spending for the military, or the retreat from governmental responsibility for the environment. But for children there is an especially nasty twist to the combination of deregulation and cutbacks in social welfare programs. The slashes in Aid to Families with Dependent Children, food stamps and categorical nutrition programs pose a direct threat to the health of millions of children. In addition, the cuts are a clear signal to all adults, including those on the verge of poverty, that this Administration believes the sole responsibility for a child's welfare lies with his or her immediate kin. Lose your job or gain a mouth to feed and it is, more so than at any time since the advent of the New Deal, *your* problem. With hard times and a shrinking welfare state, children look more like economic liabilities and less like little blessings—a shift of perspective that no doubt contributes to the recent recession-associated rise in child abuse.

At the same time that the Administration is shedding financial responsibility for children, it is encouraging their exploitation as consumers. During the previous three Administrations there was a definite, if glacial, drift toward upgrading children's television. The Federal Trade Commission and the Federal Communications Commission at least considered proposals that would require the networks to offer a minimal amount of educational programming and clamp down on the more outrageous advertising claims (for example, that a breakfast consisting largely of sugar will endow the eater with the strength of a superhero). Although the sugar lobby and its allies in the toy industry blocked the F.T.C. from cracking down on commercials, the networks were sufficiently apprehensive about a crackdown on pap programming that they began to offer some more intelligent fare, like CBS's short-lived *Thirty Minutes*. Then came Reagan; and, according to Peggy Charren, the director of Action for Children's Television, "It was as if a signal went out through the industry." The networks dropped their quality programs, and the F.T.C. started shrugging off consumer complaints about commercials, including some that Charren believes are deceptive enough to be "clearly illegal." All that remained to protect children from even more frequent and mendacious commercials was the industry's own code, which was dropped after it became the target of an antitrust suit by the Justice Department. While many industrial nations regulate advertising for children and offer generous social welfare programs, the United States moves further into the anarchy of the marketplace, where it is every man for himself—and little boys and girls for themselves.

A truly pro-child public policy should be based on the recognition that in many ways the needs of children are like those of any subordinate social group: they need economic security, and they need dignity and respect. Since we do not, and should not, expect children to work for a living, we can guarantee their economic security only through a program of income support, and this should be pegged to a level high enough to sustain children through the vagaries of their family fortunes. An income-support program designed to help children (unlike our present welfare system, which is designed to discipline adults) would have a positive impact far beyond its immediate beneficiaries. If all children had a claim on public services and resources—day care, health services, etc.—no child could be regarded as an economic burden by the very adults he or she must look to for love.

Beyond that, children need some source of dignity other than consumerism. Some countries, like China and Cuba, build children's sense of dignity by enlisting them in a collective enterprise. We who would no doubt reject a U.S. equivalent of the Red Guards or Young Pioneers have left our children to find autonomy and purpose in the hands of Atari, Mattel and McDonald's. We seem to lack the confidence to treat children as fellow persons; we prefer to see them as cute rather than as competent; we would rather leave their fantasies to the kiddie market than engage them in our own. Our abdication of responsibility reflects our own condition in a society where, as Paul Goodman observed, there is very little work that is worth a man's (or woman's) time. If we cannot collectively give dignity and meaning to childhood, it is perhaps because we have not yet found these things in our adult lives.

Victims

The word *victim* can be used to define many members of our society. Whether they be addicts, arsonists, gays, or mentally ill—victims can be found within any social class or racial group. Those discriminated against because of class, age, and gender are also victims, but their behavior is considered to be socially acceptable, and society distinguishes between them and the socially unacceptable behavior of criminals, drug addicts, and gays. Because society tries to protect itself from unacceptable behavior it takes a firm stand when dealing with criminals, gays, drug addicts, and mentally ill. Each group included in this section has been outlawed at one time or other. However, criminal statutes have changed over the years and as a result gays and the mentally ill are no longer isolated or locked away.

This section begins with a look at crime and law enforcement. Although, technically, laws exist against all groups included in this section, the articles will focus on the "controversial" definition for crime—namely violent behavior.

The family is an area which seems to have many victims. Family related problems—especially crime within families—are on the increase. The family was once viewed as the foundation of our society, but the traditional family is changing and may not be able to serve as the rock on which to anchor our future.

Other articles consider victims of health related problems including those who suffer from disease and drug addiction. Drug abuse, a problem once associated only with youth, is now so widespread it affects every region, age group, and social class.

Looking Ahead: Challenge Questions

Should society protect itself even if it makes life worse for some of its members?

Does society have an obligation to protect the innocent from the actions of the few?

How can a society know when its criminal laws are just and when they need to be changed?

How can society protect itself from an epidemic such as AIDS without restricting the needs and rights of the individuals?

Has the United States become so permissive a society, that criminal law as a social protecting device is no longer viable?

Why Crime's Rapid Rise May Be Over

Streets are slowly becoming safer as muggers, rapists and other repeat offenders get longer terms behind bars.

It may be no accident that the first dip in U.S. crime totals in five years coincides with a nationwide crackdown on "career criminals."

The Federal Bureau of Investigation reported on April 19 that serious crime dropped by 4 percent in 1982, after rising more than 21 percent since 1977 and 254 percent since 1962.

Police, prosecutors and judges credit the turnaround in large part to a controversial, double-barreled drive that is dishing out—

■ For adult repeat violators: Longer prison sentences and harsher treatment all along the line.

■ For juveniles: Stiffer punishment combined with greater opportunities to lead a straight life.

More than 100 prosecutors' offices around the country have set up special teams to make sure that career criminals get the book thrown at them in court.

Of the first 19,000 suspects handled by federally financed career-criminal units, 88 percent were convicted of the most serious charge against them. The average sentence: 14 years in prison, which authorities say is far longer than could have been expected if the prosecutions had been handled routinely.

Because about 10 percent of criminals commit more than half of the serious violations, the judiciary also is giving special attention to the problem. Four Chicago judges comprise a "Repeat Offenders Court," for example,

that deals speedily with cases involving habitual lawbreakers. The conviction rate is higher because "evidence and witnesses are fresher," reports Judge Thomas Fitzgerald.

In Philadelphia, where three judges are assigned to hear charges against career criminals, the average case goes to court six weeks sooner than in the city's other 32 criminal courts.

Police, too, are deploying a growing share of their resources against hardened law violators. Minneapolis detectives recently started a "Target 8" drive to maintain close surveillance over the eight ex-convicts in the area considered most likely to commit additional offenses.

Colorado Springs, Colo., police keep tabs on 50 persons who score 20 or more points on a scale based on conviction records. California officials have allocated 2.5 million dollars to finance police habitual-offender units in 28 cities. The units seek to match reported crimes with the MO's—modes of operation—favored by previous known offenders.

Minimum prison terms required by new state laws, coupled with public pressure on judges to impose harsher penalties, have filled prisons to overflowing. The federal and state inmate population increased last year by 11.6 percent to more than 412,000—one of the highest growth rates ever recorded.

To spot habitual criminals, authorities increasingly use sociological profiles

that focus on the number of convictions a suspect has had, the time spent behind bars, his juvenile-crime record and any history of drug abuse and irregular employment. The more these elements are present in a person's background, the more likely he is to go on breaking the law, the theory goes.

"Selective incapacitation." Few experts dispute the practice of basing penalties partly on a defendant's conviction record, but the notion of linking punishment to a sociological theory of the likelihood of future violations is provoking sharp debate.

Among those promoting the concept is the Rand Corporation, a California-based think tank that believes judges should launch a "selective incapacitation" drive aimed at locking up the criminals deemed most inclined to commit new crimes. Giving "high-rate offenders" unsparing treatment while being more lenient with others "might result in significant reductions in crime without any overall increase in the level of imprisonment," asserts Rand's Peter Greenwood.

Critics, however, see this approach as badly flawed. They argue that career-criminal profiles tend to be based largely on data from interviews with inmates—and that such information is unreliable. "Crime prediction is very inexact, with a high rate of error," says criminologist Andrew von Hirsch of Rutgers University. He adds that "it

When Courts Go After Career Criminals

Robber-rapist Nathan Turner will never menace society again. A judge has put him away for 174 years.

Stick-up man Kirby Thompson won't be poking a pistol in anybody's face for at least 20 years—the earliest he could be paroled.

Likewise, two decades will pass, if not longer, before Eugene Grier gets another chance to add to the violence on America's streets.

What happened to these three hoodlums illustrates the growing crackdown on career criminals—

Down after 49 counts. Turner's time ran out after he was identified as the man who had robbed 19 San Diegans in their homes, raping many of the women victims. The 26-year-old began his crime career as a teenage burglar in North Carolina. In and out of custody for break-ins and a firearms offense during much of his youth, Turner ended up in 1981 on parole in a San Diego halfway house.

It was on the basis of this record that prosecutors decided to try him on as many robbery and assault charges as possible. He was convicted of 49 counts. Only commutation by the governor could free him from his 174-year term.

"Before the career-criminal program, we might have allowed him to plead guilty to a few charges just to get him in prison for 20 years," comments prosecutor Mike Carpenter. "Now, we make sure these offenders don't get out."

"Painter" with pistol. The arrest record of Thompson, 32, began when he was 14. After the New Yorker shuttled back and forth to prison twice as an adult for violent crimes, police viewed him as a habitual offender, scoffing at his claim that he was a self-employed painter.

Out on bond in 1981 while appealing a firearms conviction, Thompson was picked up for a robbery in which he forced three men to lie face down on the floor and threatened a hotel clerk by holding a pistol to his head.

Prosecutors invoked a New York State "persistent offender" law that mandated a prison term for Thompson of 18 years to life on top of his 2½-to-5-year sentence in the gun case. He will not be eligible for a parole hearing until he serves a minimum of 20 years. Without a career-criminal unit and a tough-sentencing statute, he might have received a 25-year term and been eligible for release in less than eight years with good behavior.

"We move quickly on these cases and use mandatory-sentencing laws if we can," says prosecutor Steven Gutstein. "We have quite a few cases like this—a lot more than we'd like to see."

Jinxed job. The justice system of Charlotte, N.C., first encountered Grier in 1966, when he was charged with rape but pleaded guilty to a lesser charge and received a two-year sentence. A cycle of conviction, imprisonment and release for breaking and entering and armed robbery followed over the next 10 years.

Last year, a man shot and wounded two employes of an architectural firm he was trying to rob. Grier was fingered as the gunman, but only one witness from the crime scene could identify him.

"In the past, we would have accepted a lesser plea to make sure he was convicted of something," says prosecutor Gentry Caudill. "But even though we had a weak case, we decided to take a chance and go to trial because of Grier's record."

A jury last November found Grier guilty on three charges, and he received a 40-year sentence. He will be 56 when he completes the minimum of 20 years he must serve in the penitentiary.

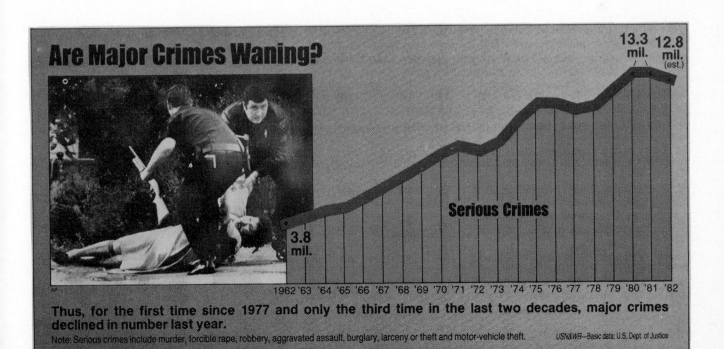

Are Major Crimes Waning?

13.3 mil. — 12.8 mil. (est.)

3.8 mil.

Serious Crimes

1962 '63 '64 '65 '66 '67 '68 '69 '70 '71 '72 '73 '74 '75 '76 '77 '78 '79 '80 '81 '82

Thus, for the first time since 1977 and only the third time in the last two decades, major crimes declined in number last year.

Note: Serious crimes include murder, forcible rape, robbery, aggravated assault, burglary, larceny or theft and motor-vehicle theft. USN&WR—Basic data: U.S. Dept. of Justice may be immoral to base a sentence partly on how long you held a job."

Similar objections are being raised against the idea of police officers' bearing down on those believed to be crime prone. "These people have paid their debt to society, but police are harassing them and invading their privacy," complains Bill Kennedy, public defender in Minneapolis.

The argument may have to be settled eventually by the U.S. Supreme Court.

Amid the demand for severity, rehabilitation efforts for adults are getting short shrift. Juvenile offenders face different prospects. Officials in many places are redoubling attempts to guide them away from a life of crime.

"Escape route." In one Florida program, youths convicted of violent offenses are put through a process that starts with imprisoning them in a wilderness area and ends with vocational training near their homes. Judge William Gladstone, who directs the program, says the idea is to punish youths first, then "give them an escape route from their hopeless neighborhood."

Another plan, being tried in Boston, Phoenix, Newark and Memphis, forces delinquents to sign "behavioral contracts" under which they advance from strict supervision to greater and greater freedom as they master certain job skills or levels of reading and writing.

Such programs are expensive, eating up as much as $20,000 a year for each participant. But proponents point out that it costs almost as much per year to keep a juvenile or adult locked up without attempts at rehabilitation.

Youths who commit especially hei-nous crimes still receive stiff penalties. More than a dozen states require sending juveniles with serious charges against them to adult courts. In one such case, an Alabama judge last year sentenced a 15-year-old boy to life in prison for killing his foster mother.

Some analysts maintain that, even without the stepped-up anticrime campaign, crime would continue to drop simply because persons between 18 and 25—who are responsible for a disproportionate amount of violence—will comprise a smaller share of the population in the years ahead.

Still, the 4 percent decline in serious crime in 1982 is only a tiny step down a long road. If the rate continued to fall by that same percentage, it would take 30 years to reduce crime in America to its level in 1962.

By TED GEST

Crime and Punishment

Robert Nisbet

Robert Nisbet is Albert Schweitzer Professor of the Humanities, Emeritus, Columbia University, and author of many books, including Prejudices: A Philosophical Dictionary, *from which this article is drawn.*

Of all changes in recent American history, the most macabre and chilling is the breakdown of one of mankind's oldest and most salutary communities of will and purpose: that of crime and punishment. Consider. A murder is committed in the village or town. The impact goes far beyond the victim; it goes to family and kindred, indeed to the entire village or town. Tensions compounded of fear, dread, pity, anger, desire for revenge mount quickly and steadily among the inhabitants. A life has been foully taken, a sacred value violated. The tensions become higher as the search takes place, still higher when the murderer is captured and found guilty. Only with his just punishment do the tensions within the locality subside. The stain upon the group has been washed away by the discovery and punishment of the villain. That drama, that pattern or community of elements, is one of the most ancient in the history of human society. It is also one of the most powerful in respect of the development of morality and the preservation of social order.

But this community of crime and punishment is being destroyed today. There are more than 25,000 murders a year in the United States. Each of several cities has an annual rate of murder in excess of that of any other nation in the world. But numbers are not the whole story. The entire ritual of crime and punishment is being lost, the recurrent, stabilizing, and reinforcing drama of crime followed by hue and cry, by search and capture, by trial, judgment of guilt, and then punishment. Once it was possible to find in most murders elements of Raskolnikov's murder in Dostoevski's *Crime and Punishment*: some kind of rejection of the life process, the triumph of materialistic passion over morality, the surrender to evil means in the accomplishment of some good, the agony of punishment, the presumption of remorse and of transfiguration through suffering. But Dostoevski would not recognize crime

A 38 caliber bullet moving at 1,000 ft./second is captured at the split second (10/1,000,000 second exposure time) it emerges from the muzzle of a pistol. The image was achieved by firing the pistol into a mirror and the use of an electronic micro flash. Photograph by William Hyzer, Janesville, Wisconsin.

and punishment as he understood them in the Walpurgis Night that has become the American scene in the late 20th century.

The community of moral and legal elements which once characterized crime and punishment has been fragmented, and in the process the individuality, the distinctiveness of crime, especially murder, has been lost to human contemplation. Memory could hardly persist in a country where 25,000 murders take place each year, a loss of human life greater than that of most wars in history. Not very far back in time, murders and other crimes possessed individuality. Memory is vivid of some of the more celebrated murders of the 1920s and 1930s, including the Judd-Gray murder and execution, the Hall-Mills case, the Hickman kidnap-murder, the Lindbergh kidnap-murder, and the Loeb-Leopold murder. It is no more difficult to recall celebrated murders and trials of earlier vintage—Lizzie Borden with her ax and 40 whacks, the Stanford White murder by Harry K. Thaw. These murders all fell into a pattern as old as mankind. They were one and all committed either in the surge of uncontrollable hatred or else with malice aforethought. Within the latter, *cherchez la femme* could be elaborated to include not only the woman but the will, the money, the jewelry, the accomplice. Murder for the most part had a raison d'être, however sordid and squalid the reason may have been. It was this that served as the efficient cause of the mobilization of the community of crime and punishment. Few hearing or reading about the murder could remain immune to the tantalizing, even preoccupying questions of motive, opportunity, time. Not only did such a murder, with all that followed, seem like a mystery-detective novel, but the mystery novel drew much of its appeal from its likeness to what could happen in any community in the land.

Fascination with the individu-ality of murder extended through trial to punishment, usually execution duly reported in full by the press. Many may remember the impact upon the country of the illicit newspaper photograph of the murderess Ruth Judd, taken in the electric chair after the current had hit her, straining cataclysmically against her bonds. Nor was the murder of Bobby Franks much out of the mind of the American people after the story burst from Chicago, its drama not diminished by the presence of Clarence Darrow arguing for clemency for the youthful Loeb and Leopold, clemency meaning life imprisonment instead of execution. The country was unequally divided over the true justice of the judge's decision, life imprisonment, with more people favoring execution than imprisonment, because murder was taken very seriously then, as it had been through the whole of human history. But at least no one could reasonably doubt that the judgment would be an unequivocal guilty, with punishment, not psychiatric care, the denouement.

Punishment was as stark and memorable to society as was the crime leading to it. Until recently in the West, especially America, it has always been this way. In the community of crime and punishment there was a functional reciprocity between the deed and the punishment; the first aroused the thrill of horror; the second the thrill of retribution. Payment was made. The community could become dormant once again—until some new murder, robbery, burglary, or other violation of the social contract took place.

Crime fiction followed life with extraordinary fidelity, containing indeed its own community. Typically the murder case—with its murderer-principal, victim, motive, method, trial, conviction, and punishment, just as in actual life—was the substance of the works of Doyle, Sayers, Christie, and the other front-runners in the fictional community of crime and punishment. There was, in novel as in life, little tergiversation about guilt and innocence. The essence of the community was that black and white were the dominant hues, with little if any gray. Often it was assumed that a single murder could, for purposes of the novel, rivet the attention of city and nation. The murders dealt with by Philo Vance in the Van Dine books of the 1920s invariably galvanized the entire city of New York. Nor was fiction much larger than truth. Single murders did rivet public attention until only recently.

The almost epiphenomenal relation that so long was peculiar to the classical murder mystery and to actual life is gone completely now. The ways most murders take place today in life, and the way the guilty party is likely to be treated, if ever captured at all and if ever found guilty of his committed murder, make for an enormous chasm between actuality and the classic mystery novel. No one indeed cares who killed Roger Ackroyd. Edmund Wilson's dismissal of mystery-detective literature many years ago, which outraged so many readers of the genre, has come to possess a significance he did not quite intend. For in the presence of the bizarre mass murders which now befoul the American landscape, no one can much care whether the murderer of one individual is ever found. To read about the sleuth sifting through clues ad nauseam merely to arrest, try, and punish some inheritance-grasping relative, while mass murders and atrocities are taking place all over the United States, is an experience in transient schizophrenia.

Howard Unruh is from all accounts a decent young fellow; it is merely that one day on a Camden, New Jersey, street he emptied two Lugers, in the process of which play 13 people were killed—without reason or motive in any ordinary sense of these words. James Ruppert of a small Ohio town, also a decent fellow by all accounts and "bright" in school, decided one Easter Sunday afternoon, following dinner, that things must change. Within 10 minutes he had killed his mother, brother, sister-in-law, and eight children. Gacy of Chicago captured, sodomized, tortured, killed, and then buried under his house some three dozen youths over a period of a year or two. He was preceded in this modus operandi by a Texan, with about the same number of scalps, but as that was almost a decade ago, no one can be expected to remember his name or, for that matter, whatever happened to him. Do not forget the "disturbed" student at the University of Texas who, from the top of a tower in the heart of the campus, fired away with high-powered rifles until a dozen or more students lay dead, others badly wounded. Or there is the amiable fat boy in Kansas a few years back, also a "bright student in school," who, suddenly inspired by the thought of leaving home to go to Chicago and become a hired killer, wandered into the living room and shot his father, mother, and sister.

It would be a grievous oversight to neglect two other patterns of murder most foul in the late 20th century in America. The perpetrator of the first type is epitomized by Russell Baker as "the Cleaver, the Slasher, the Machete Hacker and the Crazed Motorist." The enlarging number of these people simply dash into a subway car long enough to kill and mutilate with a cleaver, randomly slash throats in doorways, playfully apply machetes to any who may be available on the street, and suddenly turn the automobile on sidewalk pedestrians, accelerating furiously and usually getting a good bag. The second pattern is in many ways the most depressing. It is the murder, with or without loot, of the very elderly—in their houses, in their small rooms, or while shopping on the street.

The present world of murder and crime makes a community of crime and punishment no longer possible. This form of community has suffered the same demise that so many other forms have in the 20th century. No kind of reaction, after all, no kind of mobilization of emotion and mind, no kind of tension to be eventually relieved by outcome, is possible in such slaughters. It is no more possible to fit the elements of these crimes into a community that dissolves itself when the guilty has been punished than it is to fit the horrors of Dachau, the Gulag, and Cambodia into anything resembling the community of war.

The community of crime and punishment will be missed. It has been a building block of society. Émile Durkheim referred to crime as both necessary and, in proper degree, desirable. Only through an individual's flouting of a sacred value, such as the sanctity of life, can people remind themselves from time to time of the value itself and of its indispensability to the community at large. Crime is inevitable because of the high differentiation of human behavior. It is natural that, just as there are prophets and saints, so there are the villainous, both being deviants from the norm. But so long as crime remains within limits and occurs infrequently, it is salutary, because it reaffirms in the minds of members of the community the social bond. Punishment may be viewed in the same light. The guilty one, according to Durkheim, must be punished if the community is to recover its normal state, for the crime has been one against the community as well as against some discrete individual. And until a catharsis has been effected through trial, through the finding of guilt and then punishment, the community is anxious, fearful, apprehensive, and above all, contaminated.

This view of crime and punishment was once a reasonably apposite picture of the matter in American society, down through the 1930s. Perhaps it was the horrifying revelations from Nazi Germany and Stalinist Russia, especially during World War II, that changed the picture. But that still would not explain why things are so different in other countries, which also suffered the shock of those revelations. The American people are, on the historical record, as kind, generous, cooperative, gentle, and compassionate as any people ever known to history. Yet America is also the home at present of the largest number of crimes proportionately of any nation on earth, the largest number of murders, and the largest number of brutal or sadistic murders and mass murders. And everything suggests an increase, not decrease, in these numbers.

The reason is not far to seek. In no country of the world has the community of crime and punishment been so badly disintegrated. It is hardly putting too strong a light on the matter to say that America has lost the villain, the evil one, who has now become one of the sick, the disturbed, demanding therapy or at worst incarceration in an asylum, rather than prison or the death house. America also lost the victim, who is more likely to be denigrated for having gotten in the way of the disturbed one than to receive commiseration. America has lost the moral value of guilt, lost it to the sickroom. And finally, America has lost that most vital element, punishment. To punish anyone—child at home, pupil in school, rapist, murderer—embarrasses Americans today. When President Reagan was shot and wounded, even he almost immediately afterward spoke of a "disturbed youth" and commiserated with his parents—which youth, John Hinckley, many months following the indisputable fact of his shooting the bullets, itself the consummation of several weeks of preparation in which above-average acumen, skill, patience, and poise were required, was still undergoing careful examination and reexamination by psychiatrists in a hospital environment to determine whether he could be held responsi-

5. VICTIMS

ble and thus guilty. By contrast, in Italy, the would-be assasin of Pope John Paul II was in prison, guilty, serving a life sentence, a mere three months after the shooting.

It is no small thing in a social order to erode away the ethic of guilt and replace it by the ethic of nonresponsibility for one's acts in matters of crime. Responsibility lies on the other side of the coin of individual freedom. People are free if they hold themselves responsible for their actions. So thought the Founding Fathers and their European philosopher guides. To press instantly for a therapeutic context in which to examine criminals is to deny them their rights as free citizens.

Not strangely, the Soviet Union, its premise doubtless Marx's contempt for the doctrine of free will, increasingly uses the psychiatric asylum as its means of punishment or exile from society. To be sure, none of this came about in the Soviet Union until well after Stalin had, without any trial at all or with a contrived one at best, sentenced to execution millions of Russians between 1930 and 1941, sending many more to the horrors of the Gulag. They were guilty in Stalin's judgment, not sick and irresponsible as Marxian writ would have it. Were the Soviet Union not so ineradicably bound to its 60 years of horrors, one might find elements of humor in the spectacle furnished. In the beginning, elaborate extenuations were furnished for crimes of property and passion, for such

crimes could, by definition, exist only in countries based upon private property and individualism. Foreign visitors and pilgrims were invariably shown hospitals and asylums where the wayward were treated as sick rather than as violators of law. This was in its way a reflection of Samuel Butler's *Erewhon*, where those who committed crimes were hospitalized and those who caught pneumonia were given stiff prison sentences. But side by side with the Potemkin's villages that the Soviet leaders offered with respect to property crimes went a harshness for political "crimes," namely dissent or suspected dissent, which became steadily more murderous. Forgiveness or simple therapy for the burglar and murderer, but death, torture, and imprisonment to the ideological dissenter.

Something of this Soviet mentality is to be found in the mind of the Western liberal at the present time, with due allowance for scope and intensity. When it comes to muggings, rapes, burglaries, and murders, the liberal is characteristically so concerned by the injustices—as the liberal sees them—done by society to the wretches responsible that he finds himself poised between sympathy for the criminal and a certain animosity toward the criminal's victim, who the liberal sees as a personification of society-the-offender. It is hard for the liberal to see the mugger as guilty, as a violator of law and morality and therefore deserving of pu-

nishment, irrespective of the presumed state of his mental health. Thus the steady decline in the United States during the past half century of the mentality of crime and punishment and the steady rise and spread of the mentality of sickness and therapy.

But it must not be overlooked that the same liberals who weep for the killer instead of the slain can scarcely control their fury at mention of the "authoritarian" nations and their leaders. In such leaders there is no illness, sickness, or maladjustment—only hard and vicious criminality. Death to all apartheidists, Ku Klux Klanners, Watergate conspirators, makers of nuclear reactors, and their like on the earth; but mercy and therapy for radical terrorists, murderers, rapists, and other takers of life and property. Thus it is that in America at present it is possible for a man found guilty and sentenced to double life imprisonment for having dismembered two women to be given early release, only to murder savagely another woman within the first week of release.

There is little if any community of crime and punishment left in the United States, though the overwhelming majority of Americans, as polls reveal steadily, wish there were. In place of this community there is only the pseudocommunity of sickness, victimization by society, and therapy. How that scourge of Victorian society, Samuel Butler, must be laughing from the shades.

Some Causes of Crime: Crime, Bureaucracy, and Equality

Christie Davies

Professor Davies is reader in sociology at the University of Reading in England.

Crime is one of America's most serious social problems. Crime rates and particularly rates of serious crime, such as homicide, robbery, rape, and other crimes involving violence, have risen to high and unacceptable levels. The gravity of the problem is only underlined by the eagerness with which the small recent easing of crime rates due to the recession and the diminishing proportion of young people in the population has been greeted. Overall, however, American criminologists and crime policy-makers are pessimistic about the possibility of combating crime; their work abounds with dismal phrases such as "nothing works" or "society must learn to live with high crime rates." This pessimism stems from the fact that most policy-makers looking at the question of crime have concentrated their attention exclusively on what has happened in America itself. When American criminologists have looked at Europe, they have in general noted only that crime rates in Europe tend to be much lower than in America but are rising. And they have not been able to draw sensible conclusions from either of these facts. What is needed is a careful, comparative assessment of how crime rates differ between various European countries and how they vary over time. Such an assessment would give those concerned with making American policy new ways of thinking about the causes and cure of crime. Perhaps the best place to look is at Britain, the European country that most resembles America in its legal and political traditions.

During the last fifty years, Britain has changed from being a relatively crime-free society to one in which serious crimes of violence and dishonesty occur on such a scale as to constitute a significant social problem. The situation has been well summed up by Leon Radzinowicz and Joan King: "In 1900, the police of England and Wales recorded under a hundred thousand crimes, less than three for every thousand people. In 1974, it was almost four for every hundred people. That is, over thirteen times as many. And those are indictable offenses, not minor infractions. By the beginning of the 1980s, the number of serious offenses recorded by the police was even greater and was of the order of two and a half million offenses (i.e. about five for every hundred people). These figures give a very rough idea of a major and unpleasant social change that has overtaken Great Britain in the course of the twentieth century.

Some of the increase in recorded serious crime may of course be statistical rather than real. People may, for example, be more willing to report crimes to the police than they were in the past—possibly a result of increasingly easier access to telephones. Additionally, the police may have improved their procedures for recording such complaints. As more people take out insurance policies against burglary, so, too, they are more likely to report such crimes to the police because otherwise they cannot claim the insurance money. Explanations of this kind, cannot, however, account for more than a tiny fraction of the enormous increase in serious violent and acquisitive crimes known to the police. The recorded increase in personal violence, robbery, burglary, and other serious offenses reflects a very large real increase in the incidence of these crimes. In consequence, the ordinary British citizen is more likely to become the victim of violence or dishonesty than he or she was in the past.

If we are to seek effective policies to halt and reverse the increase in crime that has plagued modern Britain and which is an even greater problem in contemporary America, it will prove helpful and perhaps necessary to try and explain why the increase has taken place. A knowledge of the causes of crime may not, in itself, enable us to devise a policy for dealing with the problem, but it can demonstrate that certain popular leftist panacreas are irrelevant and unlikely to work, and it can provide a framework within which policies can be discussed and implemented. Any policy-maker, whether British or American, who fails to look at the historical and comparative evidence regarding the growth of crime is likely to come up with policy suggestions that are at best incomplete and unconvincing.

The Decline of Traditional "Causes" of Crime

The most striking lesson to be learned from Britain's qualitative lurch from a crime-free to a relatively crime-ridden society is that in modern societies criminal behavior, taken as a whole, is *not* rooted in poverty, in bad living conditions, or in social inequality. It is, of course, possible that these factors do act as causes in individual cases, but since they have all markedly declined in Britain during the twentieth century, it is difficult to see how they can be used to explain the steady rise in crime that has taken place. In 1900 or 1930, there was far more poverty, far more slums, far greater social inequality than there is in Britain today; *but there was also far less crime.* Swedish society has experienced an even greater transformation by affluence, welfare, and state enforced egalitarianism than Britain; but Swedish crime rates have also risen remarkably in recent years. Thus, in 1955 only 225,000 offenses against the Swedish penal code were known to the Swedish police, but by 1979, the corresponding figure was nearly 700,000. The implication of this is that policies that aim to reduce crime by improving welfare or living conditions or by promoting greater social and economic equality are unlikely to succeed in contemporary industrial societies. During the current period of economic difficulties that afflicts Britain, western Europe, and the United States alike, these traditional left-wing theories regarding the socio-economic causes of crime and, hence, the appropriate policies to be pursued, may well become fashionable again. But the evidence from Europe's affluent (and not so affluent) recent past is solidly against them.

Some different and more positive insights into the relationship between crime and society can be gained by looking at the trend of British crime before 1900 and at the historic changes in the incidence of noncriminal forms of misbehavior such as illegitimacy in Britain and other societies. British rates of recorded crime in the latter part of the nineteenth century *fell* almost as steeply as they have risen in the middle of the twentieth century. When we take into account the steady improvement in the efficiency of Britain's nineteenth-century police forces in recording and dealing with crime of all kinds, it seems probable that the real fall in the incidence of both minor and serious crimes was even more spectacular than that shown by the statistics. Britain in 1900 was not only a much less violent and dishonest society than it is today, but it was also a much less violent and dishonest country than it had been in the middle of the nineteenth century. Indeed, the overall rate of serious offenses recorded by the police in the 1890s was only about 60 percent of what it had been in the 1850s. The successful reduction of previously high levels of crime and violence and the creation of a secure, well-policed society was one of the great achievements of Victorian Britain. It is an achievement which later generations have carelessly thrown away; but, if we can achieve an understanding of the factors that underlay this achievement, there is no fundamental reason why it should not be repeated in Britain or in America.

Crime in Britain seems to have followed a rough U-curve over time with a period of steadily falling crime from 1850 to 1890; a period of relatively low, stable rates of crime from 1890 to about 1935; and since then, a period of rapidly increasing crime rates. A similar U-curve pattern exists, though with slightly different turning points, if we look at other forms of deviant behavior such illegitimacy or the misuse of narcotics or alcohol. Illegitimacy rates are in a sense an index of the level of female deviant behavior in a society, just as crime (a predominantly male activity) rates are a measure of male deviance. If we exclude the marked fluctuations in the rates of illegitimacy that occurred during the two world wars, the pattern of changes in the incidence of illegitimacy in Britain is rather similar to that of crime. During the latter part of the nineteenth century, illegitimacy rates fell; they then remained at a fairly low level in the early years of the twentieth century; but they rose again sharply in the mid-1950s, despite the widespread availability of reliable methods of contraception and in recent years of free socialized abortion. It is more difficult to trace out a coherent pattern of drug abuse, but in general, the same three states emerge. The nineteenth century saw much casual consumption of opiates (e.g. laudanum) and a great deal of hard drinking and public drunkenness. There then followed a period of greater private temperance and public sobriety in the last quarter of the century and in the early and middle years of the twentieth century. This was a period in which narcotic addiction was also an extremely rare phenomenon. In recent years, the abuse of alcohol has again become an increasing problem, and since about 1960 there has been a very rapid rise in the number of known addicts to heroin and related drugs.

British society appears to have a so-called U-curve incidence of deviant behavior during three distinct stages over the last one hundred and thirty years or so. We may term these three periods: Reforming Britain (the Victorian era); Respectable Britain (the end of the nineteenth century and the early years of the twentieth century); and Permissive Britain (the middle years of the twentieth century down to the present day).

Reforming Britain

Reforming Britain saw the mastering and reduction of various forms of criminal and deviant behavior. Respectable Britain was a period of orderly stability when the norms of good behavior that had been gradually established by the reformers were on the whole upheld and maintained, albeit with increasing difficulty towards the end of the period. Permissive Britain saw the breakdown of these hard-won norms of respectability, the growth of crimes of violence and dishonesty, and a rise in other forms of deviance such as illegitimacy and the abuse of drugs and alcohol.

This peculiar pattern of long-term changes in the levels of deviant behavior and of crime in particular in recent British social history cannot be easily explained in terms of the fundamental demographic, economic, technological, or political causal variables usually cited. Urbanization and industrialization; the mechanization and automation of work; improvements in longevity and in real living standards; the growth of government power; responsibility and expenditure were all relatively well advanced during the period I have termed Reforming Britain and continued to increase inexorably throughout all three periods. Changes in the age-structure of the population or in levels of economic activity and employment may be used to explain certain short-term fluctuations in crime rates, but they are not able to account for the broad long-run trends outlined. In order to find an explanation for the rise and fall of Respectable Britain, I examine the growth and, more important, the changing nature of bureaucracy in Britain—a social change which directly affected the moral outlook of the British elite and indirectly influenced the degree to which those individuals and groups most likely to commit serious crimes were morally restrained from doing so.

The early nineteenth century in Britain was a period of economic and moral turmoil. Urbanization, industrialization, and increased social and geographical mobility had broken down the traditional local social controls that had held antisocial behavior in check; the result was an increase in crime, illegitimacy, and other symptoms of social disorder. However, the Victorian elite tackled these problems successfully by gradually imbuing all classes with a morality that I have termed moralism. This morality, rooted as it was in British Protestant individualism and in the ideas natural to a society whose central institution was the free market, had as its central tenet the idea that each individual was morally responsible for his own behavior. The duty of the individual was to behave well, and social morality was a matter of deciding who was morally in the right and who was morally in the wrong, rewarding or protecting the innocent, and restraining or punishing the guilty. For those who believed in moralism, fairness was seen as the distribution of rights and penalties according to the moral worthiness of the parties.

These ideas were diffused throughout society by the operation of its religious and legal institutions and of the marketplace. The way in which the free market could operate so as to inculcate an ethic of personal responsibility, even in the humbler strata of society at this time, has been well described by Bryan Wilson:

> In a more complex social system where even for the least privileged there was a diversity of moral choices and moral stances, a man distinguished himself and marked himself out as a candidate for social mobility by being a moral man. In Britain, for example, it was quite normal in the late nineteenth and twentieth century for a workman—any sort of workman in the humbler walks of life—to rely not merely on, and perhaps not mainly on, any certification of his technical skills (that day was still to come) but on evidence of his moral worth. He often had, sometimes literally in an envelope in his breast pocket what he called "my character"—a testimonial from some employer that affirmed the man possessed those moral virtues so much prized among nineteenth century workers. Those virtues were, typically: honesty, willingness, industry, conscientiousness, punctuality, sobriety, and a sense of responsibility.

Religion played an equally important role in diffusing these ideas throughout society. "In Methodism and the subsequent Holiness movement and in the general inter-denominational revivalism of the period there was an attempt through evangelical religion to disseminate to new lower social classes a new morality associated certainly with the work ethic but by no means confined to the narrow sphere of work."

Efficient Police and Compulsory Schooling

The nineteenth century also saw a growth in the size and importance of government agencies in Britain notably with the "progressive introduction of police forces throughout the country as a result of the legislation of 1829, 1835, 1839 and 1856" and with the provision of universal compulsory education after 1870. In the long run, these changes may be viewed as part of a general growth in the size of the state bureaucratic apparatus that was eventually to undermine the moral achievements of the Victorians. During the nineteenth century, however, the establishment of increasingly efficient police forces and of compulsory schooling almost certainly helped to reduce crime rates. At the very least, the former acted as an effective deterrent to the criminal and the latter as a means of incapacitating potential juvenile delinquents. Both police and schools were probably even more important as moral agents in the society. Their effectiveness was a result of their peculiar combination of local organization and national ethos. The police were organized on a local basis, and the police officer knew his local community, but the responsibility of the police was to uphold a uniform national code of criminal law and not to make too many concessions to local moral eccentricities. Similarly, the new schools were the responsibility of the local authorities and were small enough to act as effective means of social control in the immediate neighborhood from which they drew their children, but the morality with which they sought to inculcate their pupils was the moralism of the wider society. Both schools and police acted as local agents of a national morality, and eventually this national morality prevailed over any local or subcultural excuses that particular groups might previously have advanced as their reason for not living up to it. In consequence, by the end of the nineteenth century, "The separate criminal districts had more or less disappeared though there remained streets with evil reputations. The great mass of juvenile criminals was no longer to be found and the remaining groups of professional criminals formed it seems a smaller proportion of the population."

All these changes which went into the creation of Respectable Britain were well summed up by Geoffrey Gorer in the early 1950s—ironically enough just as the society he described was about to go into rapid moral decline:

> During the nineteenth and the first half of the twentieth centuries, the strict conscience and self-control which had been a feature of a relatively small part of the English population became general throughout nearly the whole of the society, as the present study has indicated. The forces which led to his transformation in character [from "one of the most lawless populations in the world" to "one of the most law-abiding"] are difficult to establish; although religious belief is not nowadays typical of the prosperous working class it is possible that the evangelical missions of John Wesley . . . may have played a significant part in their time, particularly in the industrial Northern regions. So, too, may have done the gradual spread of universal education. On the basis of the evidence available to me, however, I should consider that the most significant factor in the development of a strict conscience and law abiding habits in the majority of urban English men and women was the invention and development of the institution of the modern English police force.

Professor Gorer, in 1955, particularly and repeatedly drew attention to the remarkable degree of self-control over aggression exerted by the citizens of Respectable Britain, particularly when one considers their violent past (and, it might be added in 1982, their violent present). Indeed, it seemed to him to be the "central problem for the understanding of the English character":

> . . . in public life today, the English are certainly among the most peaceful, gentle, courteous and orderly populations that the civilised world has ever seen. But from

the psychological point of view this is still the same problem; the control of aggression when it has gone to such remarkable lengths that you hardly ever see a fight in a bar (a not uncommon spectacle in most of the rest of Europe or the USA) when football crowds are as orderly as church meetings . . . this orderliness and gentleness, this absence of overt aggression calls for an explanation if the dynamics of English character are to be effectively described.

What is amazing today in an England disturbed by riots and the growth of violent crime, a country whose football crowds are known throughout Europe for their aggressive hooliganism, is that there could have been such a peaceful interlude in Britain's history. The British no longer, like Professor Gorer, ask of their distant past: "What has happened to all this aggression, this violence, this combativeness and mockery?" They know that much of it is gradually seeping back.

Respectable Britain Declines

The decline of Respectable Britain, the eclipse of the era of the law-abiding British, can ultimately be traced to the ever-increasing bureaucratic centralization of British society in the twentieth century and the linked, but independent, rise of a corrosive ethic of socialist egalitarianism. Both these changes undermined the moral fabric of Respectable Britain and eroded its central belief in individual personal responsibility. The bureaucratization of both private and public institutions in Britain has slowly resulted in a change in the moral outlook of the British elite from one of moralism to one of what I have termed causalism. Whereas the aim of the moralist is always to distribute benefits and penalties according to the moral deserts of the people involved in a situation, causalists seek rather to minimize the overall harm and suffering experienced by the various parties regardless of their moral status or past behavior. The moralist seeks justice while the causalist seeks welfare. Causalists are essentially then short-term negative utilitarians who seek always to minimize immediate harm, distress, or suffering in the particular, observable situations with which they are confronted. They tend to consider only the short-term consequences of their decisions and to assume that people's moral attitudes remain unaffected by these decisions.

In some ways the view that I have termed causalism emerges naturally in an increasingly bureaucratic society. Indeed, the causalist mode of tackling moral questions is one that developed originally because it was the most convenient way of governing the relationship between large bureaucratic organizations. Business corporations, government departments, and labor unions are not people; the relationships between them tend to be viewed increasingly as questions of cause and effect and of accountability and liability rather than praise and blame, reward and punishment. The legal relationships between such institutions are almost necessarily causalist in nature. The growth of Lord Devlin's category of quasi-criminal laws is a good example of this:

> The distinguishing mark between the criminal and the quasi-criminal lies not in the use of a statutory provision but in the presence or absence of moral content in the statutory provision containing the offence . . . The first distinguishing mark of the quasi-criminal law is that a breach of it does not mean that the offender has done anything morally wrong. The second distinguishing mark is that the law frequently does not care whether it catches the actual offender or not. Owners of goods are frequently made absolutely liable for what happens to the goods while they are under their control even if they are in no way responsible for the interferences; an example is when food is contaminated or adulterated. Likewise, they may be made liable for the acts of their agents even if they have expressly forbidden the acts which caused the offence. This sort of measure can be justified by the argument that it induces persons in charge of an organization to take steps to see that the law is enforced in respect of things under their control.

An essentially similar moral can be drawn from Devlin's description of the law of tort which is clearly based on causalist rather than moralist principles:

> But that is not the way in which the law of tort has grown up nor is it the function it now performs. Normally the relevant question in this branch of the law is not 'Who is to blame?' but 'Who is to pay if things go wrong?'; and the judgement is expressed as a sum fined not as a punishment for blameworthiness but as compensation for damage done. I do not think that a branch of the law whose object is to provide compensation for damage can be used directly to serve a moral purpose. The reason put shortly is that while liability can be made to depend on moral guilt, full compensation for injury done cannot be made to depend on the degree of moral guilt; guilt depends upon a state of mind but damage done does not.

As this branch of the law has become increasingly important, and as criminal law has come to constitute a shrinking proportion of our total laws, so questions of guilt and innocence have moved to the periphery of our legal and moral thinking.

These tendencies in British law reach back far into the nineteenth century and beyond, but in recent years they have become far more dominant as large impersonal institutions have become more important, and their relationships have become more complex. Members of the rule-making British elite are more and more involved in making, operating, and manipulating rules of this kind to govern and regulate large bureaucratic institutions. In consequence, their thinking on social and economic issues of *all* kinds tends to become less concerned with the moral guilt of individuals and seeing that each man gets his deserts and to move with the causalist regulation of great corporations so as to avoid harm and provide compensation for damage regardless of blameworthiness. Eventually, as I have shown elsewhere, men who spend their time arguing about corporations and bureaucracies in this way come to regard the moral behavior of individuals in similar terms. Causalism comes to involve the application of the ethos of the law regulating bureaucracies to questions of individual morality and moral responsibility.

Moral Rules Neutralized

An elite, whose moral thinking is predominantly causalist rather than moralist, is less able to make confident moral demands on the ordinary citizen. A society that no longer sees the world predominantly in terms of individual responsibility or of reward and blame is less likely to be able to insist on the moral guilt of its delinquents. The delinquent and potentially delinquent members of a society are rarely completely amoral persons; rather they are individuals who accept the moral demands of their society—for example, that violence or theft or vandalism is wrong—but who find reasons to excuse their own failure to live up to these demands. They live in a precariously balanced moral world in which their adherence to moral rules tends to be neutralized by various forms of subjective evasion of personal responsibility: what they have done or are tempted to do is not "really their own fault," is "not really as wrong as it looks," is "no worse than what goes on elsewhere." In a causalist society, such excuses and forms of self-deception are more plausible and more widely accepted, because they echo the moral uncertainties of the elite itself. The enhanced, illicit self-justifications and moral evasions of the delinquent are but a reflection of the doubts about moral responsibility that grow and fester in the minds of those who manage an increasingly bureaucratic society.

The link between bureaucratization, causalism, and delinquency that I have suggested is one that will tend to exist in most industrial societies and probably underlies the current widespread rise in crime, deviance, and delinquency in those societies. However, it does not follow that such a rise is inevitable. Some societies in the free world, notably Japan and Switzerland, have been able to absorb, adapt, and resist bureaucratization in such a way as to avoid the erosion of their moral order. In Japan the incidence of illegitimacy has fallen dramatically in the twentieth century from 8.8 percent of all live births in 1900 to 0.9 percent in 1968. Furthermore "the rate of non-traffic penal code offences known to the (Japanese) police per 100,000 population decreased from 1,756 in 1950 to 1,476 in 1960 to 1,232 in 1970 and to 1,159 in 1980." The case of Switzerland is particularly instructive for in contrast to the rapidly rising incidence of crime and illegitimacy that has characterized Britain and Sweden in the middle years of the twentieth century, the Swiss have, until very recently, not experienced any change in the rates of either of these two indices of social disorganization. The proportion of live births that were illegitimate remained low and practically constant (it varied between 3.2 and 4.8 percents) in Switzerland between 1876 and 1968. This is in marked contrast to the U-curve pattern to be found in the British Isles and Scandinavia. Even more remarkable is Switzerland's freedom from crime: recorded crime rates are very low and show little increase over time. Thus, "as measured by convictions the total Swiss rates for violations of the Swiss criminal code remained almost constant from 1960 to 1971 as [did] offences against property rates. . . . Conviction trend data in five European countries (Switzerland, Belgium, Denmark, Norway, England, and Wales) have shown that Switzerland was the only country with general stability in the conviction rates and even some decreasing." Studies of victimization of the records of insurance companies and of the untroubled-by-crime daily behavior and experience of the ordinary Swiss citizen prove that the Swiss official statistics on crime are, in fact, a reasonably true reflection of a genuinely crime-free society. The key question is: how has respectable Switzerland managed to maintain the kind of crime-free society which the British only achieved for a brief and transient period in their history? The reasons for the success of the Swiss in avoiding crime are similar to those for the earlier success of the British. They are the obverse of the reasons for the current failure of the British (or the Swedes) to deal with crime effectively.

Switzerland, like the respectable Britain of a past era, owes its freedom from crime to the highly developed sense of individual responsibility of its citizens. The Swiss have been able to preserve this vital first line of defense against crime, because they have avoided the worst aspects of twentieth-century bureaucracy—bureaucratic centralization and bureaucratic egalitarianism. The Swiss sense of personal responsibility is rooted in the high degree of general responsibility that the Swiss citizen has in political and economic affairs. Swiss society is characterized by "Political decentralization of the government . . . particularly at the cantonal and communal levels. At these levels the individual citizen plays an important role in the government, assuming greater responsibility for social and crime control measures. In Sweden (it could equally well be Britain), a Prime Minister can state that "a society has to an increasing extent taken the responsibility of individuals. Social reforms have required that more and more people must communicate with authorities." Following a different road the Swiss have largely given only a limited role to the government. As a result, centralized welfare programs and government controls are more limited in Switzerland and more reliance has been placed on the individual citizen and the work goal orientation among Swiss youth. "The Swiss still believe

that except for state and vocational group insurance each person should try to save with the incentive to build up some capital or to have voluntary insurance. Such an approach which emphasizes a strong work ethic and the need for future goals is still being instilled in the Swiss youth."

The Swiss Model

The contrast between the centralized Swedish welfare state and Swiss welfare arrangements also expresses and exaggerates another vital difference between these two societies—their view of equality. The Swiss ideal of equality is essentially one of equality of responsibility, of equality between government and people, something that is remarkably lacking in egalitarian Sweden.

> In Switzerland social security is treated as insurance provided by a company, the citizen seeing himself as a customer and hence the master patronising a service. In Sweden the position is reversed. The citizen has been taught or chosen to believe that he is the servant, humbly suing for favours from his master, the State. It is a kind of serf mentality, constantly imprinted and not only in the sphere of social welfare.

The modern Swede, or the modern Briton, is robbed of his sense of individual responsibility by the over-centralized, over-bureaucratized society in which he lives, a society whose very nature owes much to an egalitarian ideology very different from that of the Swiss. This ideology seeks to use the bureaucratic machinery of the state to compel individuals to be equal to one another—equal not in responsibility but in fortune, attainment, and worthiness. Both the aims of such a socialistic ideology and the means which its proponents have been forced to use are *necessarily* destructive of the ordinary citizen's sense of personal moral responsibility. It is easy to see why the means used have this effect—the equalization of faculties between different geographical areas for its own sake, or for the benefit of particular social classes or ethnic groups who often live in specific relatively homogeneous areas, necessarily involves greater centralization. Attempts to produce greater equality of educational attainment also tend to produce larger schools and larger catchment areas, which simultaneously impair the school's ability to act as a training ground for personal responsibility *and* the local community's sense of responsibility for the school. Moreover, the very idea of achieving equality through social and political regulation is in itself incompatible with the ideal of personal responsibility. Egalitarianism compounds the problem inherent in what I have termed causalism, for ultimately the egalitarian is forced to argue that people should be treated equally regardless of their individual behavior and deserts.

Indeed, within the framework of an ideology of distributive justice, individuals rapidly cease to have deserts or personal responsibility at all. For the egalitarian ideologue of this type, a person's position in life is essentially arbitrary and can be subject to egalitarian regulation at will. Ultimately, not merely are the rich and the poor, the lucky and the unlucky, the intelligent and the stupid to be made equal, but also the virtuous and the wicked.

Societies with low levels of crime, such as Switzerland or once Respectable Britain, are, or were, characterized by a strong and widespread sense of personal responsibility which grew out of their highly decentralized political and welfare systems. Therefore, "Communities or cities that wish to prevent crime should encourage greater political decentralization by developing small government units and encouraging citizen responsibility for obedience to the law and crime control." In such societies, effective police forces can be organized which not only deter criminals but also act as a crucial moral influence in the local community.

Since inequality is not a cause of crime, crime rates cannot be reduced by the political pursuit of social equality. Indeed, policies that have aimed at producing equality through political and bureaucratic intervention have been the underlying cause of the rise in crime in Britain and Sweden in recent years. Any society that wishes to reduce crime would be well advised to abandon policies based on bureaucratic egalitarianism, which are ultimately destructive of society's first line of defense against crime—the ordinary citizen's sense of personal moral responsibility.

What does this mean in relation to America's crime problem and possible solutions? This study suggests that past policies for dealing with crime in America may have failed because they too have been formulated within a framework of egalitarian and bureaucratic thinking. What is needed is a set of policies drawn up outside that framework of thinking which address the problem of how to create a widespread sense of personal responsibility in America. The Swiss experience suggests that this is not an entirely impossible task.

Coping with Justice

In 1922, Roscoe Pound and Felix Frankfurter urged that the criminal justice system be judged not "by the occasional dramatic case but by its normal humdrum operations."

The American public has generally ignored this advice.

In their choice of television shows, tabloid newpapers, popular fiction, and political rhetoric, Americans are drawn to the most fanciful, gruesome, bizarre, or self-serving portrayals of criminal justice. Public attention goes to the Juan Coronas, the Gary Gilmores, the Patricia Hearsts. Parole becomes the subject of a TV network news item, it seems, only when someone like Charles Manson comes up for it. It took an attempted presidential assassination to get the "insanity defense" into the headlines. President Reagan himself appears to be partial to "horror stories." Complaining that felons too often escape punishment as a result of legal technicalities, he recently cited a bizarre Florida case where a drug conviction was thrown out because the search warrant authorizing police to inspect a couple's home did not extend to the baby's diapers, where the illicit cache was found.

Thus, the dramatic regularly elbows aside the routine. What actually happens between the time a typical criminal suspect is arrested by police and the time he or she enters prison or returns to the streets remains widely misunderstood. Justice can be as unpleasant in its gritty details as it is ennobling in its virtuous

abstraction. But Americans avert their eyes from the criminal justice system at their own peril. If crime deserves punishment, if the public deserves protection, and if all citizens deserve due process, then what happens from arrest to incarceration (or release) deserves close attention.

"You have the right to remain silent." So begins the Miranda warning, read by arresting officers to criminal suspects. First required by Chief Justice Earl Warren's Supreme Court in 1966, the warning has become second nature to a generation of police officers. Contrary to what some critics of the Warren Court claim, the Miranda warning does nothing to protect criminals unduly. Ernesto Miranda himself, an Arizona drifter convicted of rape and kidnapping, won only the right to a new trial after the court ruled that police officers had failed to inform him of his rights. He did not go free. He was re-tried, convicted, and returned to jail.

For both law enforcement officials and the accused, bail is a major concern soon after arrest. Originating in England more than a thousand years ago, the bail system attempted to guarantee appearance at trial by requiring a money deposit for release from jail until judgment had been handed down. Then, as now, bail also served as a means to keep crime-prone suspects in custody before trial. Under the current system, however, many of those who are jailed before trial should not be and many of those who are not, should be.

To the suspect, posting bail means freedom. Most of those arrested do manage to find the cash amount set by the court. The bail bondsman, a fixture in poor urban neighborhoods, will post bail quickly for suspects. His fee is a flat, nonrefundable 10 percent of the bail amount. (In New York City in 1973, 40 percent of defendants were required to post more than $1,000.) Contrary to public opinion, this system works, at least in getting suspects to appear for court proceedings. A 1976 survey of courts in 20 U.S. cities conducted by criminologist Wayne Thomas found that only five percent of the accused failed to show.

This essay has been adapted from chapters of Crime and Public Policy *written by Steven R. Schlesinger, Acting Director of the U.S. Bureau of Justice Statistics (criminal procedure), Brian Forst of INSLAW, Inc. (prosecution and sentencing), Daniel Glaser of the University of Southern California (the supervision of offenders outside of prison), Alfred Blumstein, J. Erik Jonsson Professor of Urban Systems and Operations Research at Carnegie-Mellon University (prison populations and capacity), and Peter W. Greenwood of the Rand Corporation (the effects of incapacitation).*

Two Reforms

Those suspects, however, who cannot post bail remain in custody regardless of the seriousness of their offenses. The U.S. Justice Department estimated in 1978 that 60,000 people—nearly 40 percent of all prisoners in local detention facilities—were simply awaiting trial. Studies show that these defendants face a triple disadvantage: more convictions, more prison terms, and longer prison terms than those who make bail. Confined in prison, they are not, as Steven R. Schlesinger, Acting Director of the U.S. Bureau of Justice Statistics, explains, "completely free to aid in the preparation of their own defense, to locate evidence, assist their attorneys, and hold a job (both to earn money to pay counsel and to prove reliability at their trials)." Bail, in short, discriminates against the poor.

As a crime *prevention* measure, moreover, bail is in large measure ineffective. One suspect in six out on bail, according to a recent study, returns, not to face trial, but to face new charges (and one-third of these are re-arrested more than once). The alternative is no more acceptable: Detaining all likely repeat offenders would jam already-crowded jails. And in all probability, many suspects who would *not* commit another crime if released, and who *would* show up for trial, would be penalized.

Whatever its defects, the original U.S. bail system remained largely unchanged from 1789, when the Judiciary Act created the federal bail system, until the passage of the Bail Reform Act of 1966. The 1966 Act established and encouraged nonfinancial conditions for release such as release on recognizance (ROR). It also assumed that pretrial release decisions would be based on the likelihood of an individual's appearance at trial rather than on the danger presented by his freedom. In 1970, however, Congress empowered the Washington, D.C., Superior Court to detain without bail any suspect whose alleged crime and prior record indicated that he was dangerous to the community. As is usually the case in law enforcement, state and local law, under which the vast majority of offenders are processed, has gradually followed the lead of the federal government. Public debate in the last 15 years has centered on the use of ROR programs and preventive detention.

Screening Suspects

ROR programs rely on actuarial tables based on factors such as the suspect's community and family ties, his prior record, and his employment history to estimate the chance of his returning for trial. Prisoners judged as low risks are released. Having proven as effective as traditional bail programs—Manhattan served as the first laboratory—ROR has been adopted by 120 cities. Among its advantages: It is less expensive than jailing suspects; it operates more quickly than the bail system; and it does not discriminate against the poor.

Preventive detention is more controversial, since it amounts to imprisonment before conviction. (Contrary to popular belief, the right of a defendant to be "presumed innocent" applies only to the trial; were it otherwise, no arrests would be made in the first place.) Nine states now permit their courts to consider a potential threat to community safety in decisions to grant bail. In 1981, the Reagan administration proposed that preventive detention be allowed in federal cases. What makes preventive detention attractive is that it would keep the most dangerous recidivists off the streets while perhaps helping to reduce the fear of crime in the local community. In 1982, Arizona voters approved a referendum that would deny bail to any suspect "found to pose a danger to society." In its major legal test so far, *U.S.* v. *Edwards,* preventive detention was ruled constitutional in 1981 by the D.C. Court of Appeals, a decision the U.S. Supreme Court declined to review.

While defendants are worrying about posting bail, prosecutors are deciding which cases they want to pursue. Each attorney in a typical big-city prosecutor's office must decide how to dispose of about 100 felony cases per year. Obviously, a prosecutor cannot give Watergate-level attention to every third-rate burglary. Even the toughest prosecutor will free more suspected criminals than the most lenient judge. As Brian Forst of INSLAW, Inc. (formerly the Institute for Law and Social Research) has written, "about 40 percent of [adult] felony cases are either rejected outright at the initial screening stage or dropped by the prosecutor soon afterward." Prosecutors say that most often it is lack of evidence—weapons, stolen goods, eyewitnesses accounts—that forces them to abandon cases. This lack of evidence results more from poor police work than from a criminal's skills. In seven U.S. cities during 1977-78, 22 percent of the local police officers who made arrests made not a single arrest that led to a conviction. A mere 12 percent of the policemen were responsible for *one-half* of all criminal convictions. Not surprisingly, the most "productive" officers turned out to be especially persistent about finding witnesses and more conscientious about follow-up investigation. They worked harder and smarter.

The second most common reason prosecutors dismiss charges is that the offense is not worth the bother. Prosecutors will sometimes divert less serious offenders into programs of counseling, restitution, or community service. In most instances, "trivial offense" cases are dropped outright.

Search and Seizure

The "exclusionary rule," which forbids the use of illegally obtained evidence in court, is said by its critics, including the President, to hamper prosecution greatly. Although the controversy is growing, the issue is not new. The Supreme Court imposed the rule on federal

AFTER THE ARREST: DISPOSING OF CASES

Out of every 100 felony arrests

65 are brought to district attorney → 25 are rejected or dismissed by prosecutor

40 are accepted for prosecution

35 are sent to juvenile courts

34 plead guilty or go to trial

9 are imprisoned (more than 1 year)

6 are dismissed by judge or fail to appear after pretrial release

11 are jailed (less than 1 year)

12 get probation

32 are convicted (5 in trial)

20 are incarcerated

2 are acquitted in trial

Source: INSLAW, Inc.; U.S. Department of Justice.

Not shown above: recidivism. A study conducted in Oregon reveals that, of every 100 persons arrested in a given year, 35 will be arrested again at least once within three years, 17 at least twice.

courts in 1886 and on state courts for many crimes in 1961. Its chief purpose is to deter police misconduct, but most of the evidence suggests that it fails to achieve this goal. For one thing, the impact of the rule falls more directly on prosecutors than on individual police officers (whose performance is usually judged by the number of arrests they make, not by the convictions that follow). Meanwhile, the exclusionary rule impedes the truth-finding function of the courts, fails to distinguish between flagrant and "good faith" errors by a police officer, benefits only the guilty, and undermines public respect for the judicial system.

Supporters of the exclusionary rule note that, in the nation as a whole, prosecutors drop only about one percent of all felony and serious misdemeanor cases a year because of the Fourth Amendment "search and seizure" procedural requirements. Yet, as Schlesinger points out that one percent still amounts to 55,000-60,000 cases.* He adds that "if the exclusionary rule is misguided, then the release of even one convictable

person is one release too many." The Supreme Court in late 1982 agreed to reconsider the exclusionary rule in its 1983 term, even as new proposals were being floated by Schlesinger and others to curb police misbehavior by making officers *as individuals* subject to disciplinary proceedings and liable for damages.

Copping a Plea

Courtroom drama rarely interrupts the peristaltic advance of a case through the criminal justice system. The television triumphs of Perry Mason notwithstanding, only about seven percent of all felony suspects have their guilt or innocence established by the clash of opposing lawyers and the judgment of a jury or judge.

When prosecutors decide that the nature of the evidence and the offense *does* warrant pressing on, nine out of 10 times they win a conviction by plea bargaining. So routine are these negotiations that they may take no more than five to 10 minutes to complete in a prosecutor's office or a judge's chambers. The form of the bargain is always the same: In return for relaxed prosecution, the defendant does not contest the charges. The substance of these agreements varies widely. As one Assistant U.S. Attorney told sociologists John Hagan and Ilene Bernstein, "We'll let [the felony suspect] plead to a misdemeanor and won't prosecute . . . all the way . . . to charging him with exactly what he did and saying nice things about him at sentencing."

Like most other aspects of the criminal justice system, plea bargaining has drawn intense criticism in recent years. Defense lawyer Seymour Wishman has

*For a good overview of the subject, see *The Effects of the Exclusionary Rule: A Study in California,* U.S. Department of Justice, 1982. Regardless of the number of cases actually dropped, the suppression hearings and appellate litigation made necessary by the rule are a major drain on the courts' time. A 1979 General Accounting Office study of 42 of the 95 U.S. Attorneys' offices in the country found that "thirty-three percent of the defendants who went to trial filed Fourth Amendment suppression motions." According to the report, the exclusionary rule was the single most important issue arising most frequently in federal criminal trials. At the appellate level in 1979-81, more than 22 percent of the criminal cases reaching the U.S. Court of Appeals of the District of Columbia required a decision as to whether evidence should be excluded.

Police: The Thin Blue Line

Television's police dramas typically feature at least one arrest per episode. In real life, the average cop in a large (250,000+ people) American city makes only about 25 "collars" per *year.* Of these, only six are for major (or "index") crimes. Fewer than one out of five index crimes is "solved" by an arrest. Why is the figure so low?

One reason is that relatively few police officers are actively engaged at any time in combating crime. New York City boasts a police force of 28,000, but thanks to court appearances, administrative duties, and the burden of paperwork, only 6,600 are out on the streets during any 24-hour period, and this force is divided into three eight-hour shifts. According to a study by the Police Foundation, officers on patrol spend about half their time writing traffic tickets, investigating traffic accidents, waiting for tow trucks, arresting drunks, and traveling to and from the police station, the police garage, the courthouse, and their "beats." Another one-fourth of duty time is spent relieving boredom and tension—eating, resting, talking on the radio, girl-watching.

In the time remaining, the police cruise the streets and respond to calls. Seventy-five percent of all crimes are discovered well after the fact, and the perpetrators are unlikely to be apprehended. The police try to focus their attention instead on the other 25 percent ("involvement crimes"), where the victim has been in direct contact with the criminal. Reports coming in on the "911" or other emergency numbers, however, are often poorly screened at headquarters; patrol officers, as a result, must often deal with trivial complaints that could be handled by phone.

Victims are also slow in calling, if they call at all. (An estimated 47 percent of violent crimes and 26 percent of property crimes go unreported.) To judge from a survey of Jacksonville, Peoria, Rochester, and San Diego, 73 percent of all calls come after the critical first minute and 46 percent come after *five* minutes. Arrest statistics suggest that waiting five minutes is as bad as waiting 60. When police arrive, witnesses may be unavailable, unable to speak English, or so traumatized by the incident that their accounts are unreliable. All of which suggests that a rapid "response time" by police officers, something the public clamors for, is in fact a negligible contribution in the fight against crime. Luck seems more important.

---

charged that plea bargaining "often hides the incompetence or unlawful behavior of law enforcement officials or conceals the preferential treatment of defendants." The National Advisory Commission on Criminal Justice Standards and Goals recommended in 1973 that plea bargaining be abolished. Alaska, El Paso, Philadelphia, and other jurisdictions have experimented with doing just that. Yet few deny that plea bargaining will persist.

There are several reasons for its durability. It is time honored if not venerable. During the 1920s, political scientist Raymond Moley, later an adviser to President Franklin Roosevelt, studied the American criminal justice system and found plea bargaining already both pervasive and entrenched. And plea bargaining is quick and cheap. California's Judicial Council found in 1974 that a jury trial in the state consumed an average of 24 hours of court time at a cost of more than $3,000; a guilty plea took 15 minutes and cost about $215.

In New York City, 90 percent of all defendants, unable to afford a lawyer even for a brief trial, must rely on court-assigned attorneys or public defenders. Such counsel spends an average of only 30 minutes with each client before adjudication. Under such circumstances, a jury trial may well appear to the accused as an invitation to disaster. A plea bargain becomes a more attractive alternative. Prosecutors also like to avoid trials because of their unpredictability.

Moreover, doing away with plea bargaining has its drawbacks. Two years after banning it, El Paso found city courts hopelessly backlogged. Authorities had to relent and permit some kinds of negotiations. Philadelphia discovered that its prosecutors simply switched to "trial bargaining," making deals on whether a defendant would receive a full jury trial or a so-called bench trial. Because bench trials last only a few minutes, the new bargaining differed little in results from the old. For better or worse, plea bargaining endures.

Judges and Sentencing

During the past 10 years, prosecutors have increasingly tried to target their best efforts at the "career criminal." As in ROR programs, the aim is to distinguish between the typical suspect whose run-in with the law is an unusual event and the hard-core minority who have criminal lifestyles. Bolstered by studies documenting the existence of a small but very active group of chronic criminals, the criminal justice system has mobilized to put them out of business. The Washington, D.C., and New York City police departments have formed career criminal task forces. San Diego, New Orleans, Kalamazoo, and 95 other cities have established career criminal prosecution teams. These teams resist plea bargaining and seek tough sentences. Their record, however, is mixed. A statewide effort in California boosted the conviction rate on the most serious charges (rape, murder, armed robbery, and so on) from 60 to 85 percent and won sentences that were a year longer than those awarded in similar cases not specially prosecuted. A 1981 Justice Department survey, however, revealed that the four big-city career criminal prosecution teams it studied won neither more convictions nor severer sentences. Still, the popularity of targeting career criminals continues to grow.

Sentencing practices vary widely. Depending on the location and the crime, judges, juries, prosecutors, or elected officials—or all four—may decide how the guilty are punished. In Texas and a dozen other states, the jury votes on the sentence; most states require jury sentencing in capital cases. In many jurisdictions, prosecutors and defense attorneys can settle on penalties in "sentence-bargaining" sessions and have the presiding judge rubber-stamp the agreed-upon punishment.

Judges have the single greatest influence on the sentence. Criminologist Brian Forst notes that sentences are determined primarily on the basis of who the sentencing judge is rather than on the basis of the seriousness of the crime, the criminal's prior record, and the criminal's plea, all put together. Judges are nonetheless generally tougher on the repeat offender than on the first-time criminal, more lenient on those who admit their guilt than on those who deny it and are convicted. Charles Silberman found that, in New York City, judges were three times more likely to imprison the robber who had victimized a stranger than the one who robbed an acquaintance. They tended to treat women more leniently than men for the same offense.

Most judges apparently do not discriminate against blacks. "Blacks are overrepresented in prison populations primarily because of their overrepresentation in arrests for the more serious crime types," a 1982 National Science Foundation panel concluded.

Actions by state legislatures have taken away some judicial discretion. By 1978, six states had instituted "determinate sentencing" laws. Under these laws, judges retain the right to grant probation to low-risk offenders but must adhere to legislatively set sentences when putting an offender in jail. Six other states have removed the judges' sentencing power altogether in certain cases with mandatory sentencing laws that require prison terms, usually for armed, violent, or drug-related crimes. Many jurisdictions make use of nonbinding guidelines. Thus, in Maryland, judges are advised to give consecutive rather than concurrent life sentences in murder cases if the defendants have also been convicted of abduction or rape. The new legislation reflects a dramatic change that has occurred since 1970 in the commonly accepted rationale for putting people behind bars.

The Demise of Rehabilitation

Of American penitentiaries, Alexis de Tocqueville wrote in 1833: "It is not yet known to what degree the wicked may be regenerated, and by what means this regeneration may be obtained." Yet, from the Progressive era through the 1960s, the assumption that prisons could and should transform thieves, hoodlums, and murderers into law-abiding citizens dominated the criminal justice system. The rehabilitative ideal influenced a vast array of penal developments in the 20th century. Prisons became "correctional institutions." Rehabilitation was the reason for the indeterminate sentence (not to mention for the creation of the first American juvenile court in 1899). When prison officials decided that a convict had been successfully "rehabilitated," they would recommend his release. Despite many examples of excessive leniency—one thinks of the Norman Mailer-induced parole in 1981 of Jack Henry Abbott, a convicted killer who went on to kill again after 45 days of freedom—the fact remains that those who make parole decisions usually believe in what they are doing.

And yet, ever since World War II, researchers have been compiling evidence that *no* rehabilitative program seems to work, at least in the aggregate. One-third of "rehabilitated" convicts, it turns out, commit crimes after release, about the same number as "unrehabilitated" ex-convicts. The late criminologist Robert Martinson of the City College of New York wrote the epitaph for the rehabilitative ideal in 1974. Summarizing 231 research studies, he concluded: "With few and isolated exceptions, the rehabilitative efforts that have been reported so far have had little appreciable effect on recidivism." Plastic surgery didn't help, counseling didn't help, job training didn't help. Judging by one Danish study, even castration proved insufficient to bring the recidivism rate of male sex offenders down to zero.

The debate about what criminal punishment could and could not achieve had actually come to a head well before Martinson published his findings. Frightened by rising crime rates, the American public during the late 1960s demanded, in effect, that "retribution" replace rehabilitation as the purpose of incarceration. Alabama Governor George Wallace made a surprisingly strong showing in the 1968 presidential race with promises to "stop pussyfooting around" and to imprison lawbreakers "and throw away the key." New York's passage in 1971 of tough legislation providing mandatory sentences for drug law violations reflected the same impulse.

By the mid-1970s, the idea of "just deserts" was enjoying a certain vogue. Punishment, the argument went, should fit the crime and be based on no other criteria. Only so would it increase respect for the law and thus deter crime. Many elected officials used these claims in promoting mandatory sentencing laws. In any event, more people began going to jail more often. Between 1974 and 1979, the number of men in jail as a percentage of the adult male population jumped 40 percent.

Cost-Effective Justice

By the end of the decade, the most observable effect of tougher imprisonment policies was overcrowded prisons. Courts in 31 states had decided that wretched prison living conditions required judicial intervention.* In a typical action in 1976, Alabama Judge Frank Johnson ordered state prison authorities to provide at least 60 square feet of space per inmate. State legislators soon counted up the costs of toughness—$50,000 to $70,000 for one new prison cell, $10,000 to $15,000 a year to keep a prisoner in it. During 1980-81, voters in Michigan and New York turned down prison-building referendums. In New Mexico, the legislature approved a $107 million prison construction bill only after the worst prison riot in U.S. history left 43 dead in the state penitentiary south of Santa Fe in February 1980.

The lesson of the 1970s seems to be that retribution as a crime-fighting philosophy has its limitations, too. While the crime rate seems of late to have steadied, population trends rather than tougher sentences are probably the reason. Meanwhile, because mandatory sentencing laws suffer from rigidity, the trend toward their adoption has slowed. New York has modified its drug laws to allow lesser offenders to plea bargain. The reason: Juries often refused to convict lesser offenders if conviction required harsh punishment. Among public officials, a consensus arose that the *certainty,* not the *severity,* of punishment best deterred crime.

Increasingly, criminal punishment today emphasizes cost-effectiveness above all other goals. "Incapacitation" is the by-word of this new approach. The least expensive and most lenient treatment goes to criminals least likely to commit serious crimes again, regardless of the seriousness of their offense. The most expensive, that is to say, the harshest punishment goes to those who, in the words of Carnegie-Mellon University's Alfred Blumstein, "represent the greatest crime threat if they were outside, either because the crimes they will be committing are the most serious, because they will be committing them at the highest rate, or they can be expected to continue committing them for the longest time into the future." Legal attention in the 1980s focuses on the removal of the most dangerous at the least cost.

This philosophy may seem to be nothing more than common sense, but considering how many long-ac-

cepted criminal justice goals it contradicts, it represents a significant development. The advocates of cost-effective justice take little interest in reforming the wrongdoer. They downplay the importance of "just deserts," an eye for an eye. They ignore the goal of putting away larger numbers of criminals. And they rely heavily on the unpopular sanctions of probation and parole.

Assessing 'Client Risk'

Thus, the average convicted criminal is now more likely to find himself spending more time out on the streets: 1.5 million of the 2.3 million U.S. convicts in 1980 were under court-ordered "supervised release." Another 270,000 were on parole, the supervised release that follows incarceration. The number of convicts on probation or parole increased 24 percent between 1976 and 1981.

The probationer or parolee also submits to more sophisticated supervision than in the past. In Wisconsin, all convicts on release formerly met with staff supervisors once a month. No more. Frequency of contact now ranges from once every 14 to once every 90 days, with the figure determined by an "Assessment of Client Risk Scale" similar to ones used in ROR programs. (Taken into account are such things as number of times the "client" has changed his address in the last 12 months of freedom, percentage of this time employed, alcohol problems, and so on.) The test, variations of which are used elsewhere, has reduced violations by the most closely watched while not affecting violation rates among the least supervised.

Authorities are also making heavier use of halfway houses. As criminologist Daniel Glaser notes, "halfway houses and work release are usually justified primarily as ways of helping prisoners become accustomed to community life before they are more completely free, but these residences also impose considerable control on offenders." Parolees must sleep at the halfway house. They must account for their whereabouts at work or with friends. They must take tests for alcohol and drug use—a once-cumbersome procedure now made easy by development of portable electronic urinalysis equipment. ("Open an attache case, perform a few simple steps. . . ." begins a full-page Syva Company advertisement in the latest American Correctional Association directory.) Halfway houses cost half as much as prisons and are growing more common. To ease prison overcrowding during 1981-82, California tripled the number of inmates assigned to halfway houses in major metropolitan areas. By using actuarial risk tables to select the people released, the state brought the halfway house escape rate to a 20-year low.

Worth a Try?

Glaser reports that some judges have begun sentencing criminals to halfway houses with no initial stay in

---

*Four out of five convicted felons find themselves confined in a medium- or maximum-security facility. One out of two such facilities in America is more than 80 years old. A prisoner is likely to share with another inmate a cell designed for a single occupant, accommodations that the Supreme Court held (in *Bell* v. *Wolfish,* 1979) did not necessarily constitute cruel and unusual punishment. Prisoners are guarded by officers whose education is, on the average, only slightly better than their own and whose salaries average $15,000 per year. If California's prison system is typical, prisoners face a four percent chance of serious injury in any given year. They are likely to suffer homosexual rape, especially if they are young and white. Slightly more than half of them will be released within one year.

THE INCIDENCE OF CRIME: COMPARATIVE INDICATORS
(Percent of U.S. households touched in any year)

While serious crime is widespread, so are other calamities that Americans fear less (right). Nor does fear of crime correspond to its actual incidence (below right), and studies show that city folk feel safer in their own neighborhood, even if it is unsafe, than in other neighborhoods, even if much safer. Crime rates vary not only with age and race (above right) but also with the season (below); oddly, scholars have found no sure relationship between crime and unemployment.

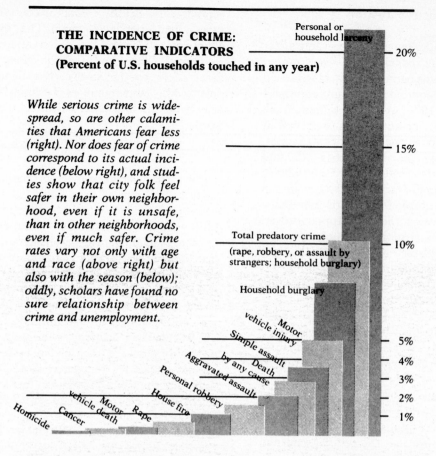

Personal or household larceny — 20%

— 15%

Total predatory crime (rape, robbery, or assault by strangers; household burglary) — 10%

Household burglary

Motor vehicle injury

Simple assault — 5%

Death by any cause — 4%

Aggravated assault — 3%

Personal robbery — 2%

House fire — 1%

Homicide Cancer Motor vehicle death Rape

CRIME AND THE SEASON: Fluctuations in rate relative to yearly average

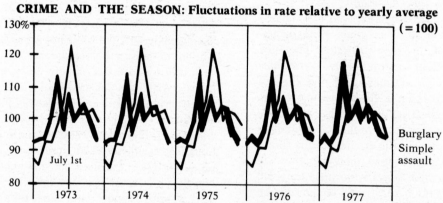

(= 100)

130%
120
110
100
90
80

July 1st

1973 1974 1975 1976 1977

Burglary
Simple assault

prison. Rather than halfway *out* of prison, he notes, these inmates are halfway *in*. With prison congestion unlikely to ease until the 1990s, when, demographers say, the U.S. population of crime-prone young males will have greatly shrunk, the trend toward a "community-based" correctional system is likely to continue. In Massachusetts, halfway houses have entirely replaced reformatories for juveniles. However, the placement of halfway houses has ignited scores of "not-in-my-neighborhood" protests in places ranging from Prince George's County, Maryland, to Long Beach, California. Local opposition could retard the spread of such facilities in coming years, no matter how cost-effective they are.

While many low-risk lawbreakers may be safely placed back in the community, believers in incapacitation demand that high-risk offenders be incarcerated.

Recent figures show this is happening. Between 1974 and 1979, the proportion of inmates serving time for violent crimes rose from 52 to 57 percent of all inmates.

As a sentencing practice, this "put-'em-away" approach naturally complements the career criminal control efforts of police forces and prosecutors. Judges and parole boards identify high-risk criminals with yet another variation on the actuarial table. The Federal Parole Board guidelines, for example, allow offenders to be graded on a zero-to-11 scale based on various factors and recommend fixed prison terms for each grade of offender in seven categories of crime. Thus, a heroin addict with two prior convictions and two stints in the state pen, who was under 18 when first incarcerated, who had violated parole at least once, and who had spent less than six months at work or in school in the two

ARRESTS IN 1981 BY RACE, AGE, AND OFFENSE (FBI Index Crimes)

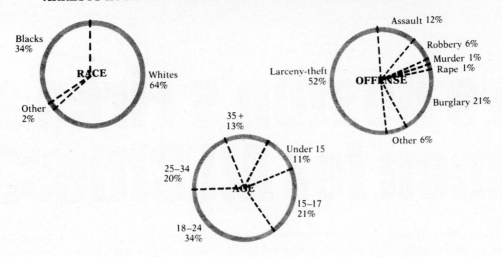

FEDERAL AND STATE PRISON POPULATION, 1925–1980

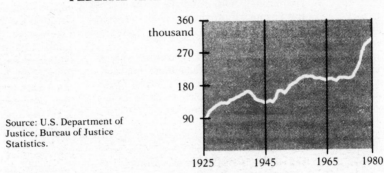

Source: U.S. Department of Justice, Bureau of Justice Statistics.

VICTIMIZATION AND THE FEAR OF CRIME

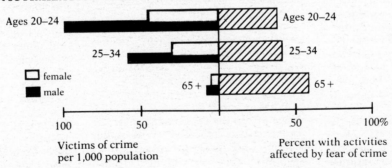

years prior to his latest arrest would have a total of two points—marking him as a poor risk. If convicted of arson, he would get a prison sentence of at least 78 months.

Whether an incapacitation policy can help lower the crime rate by locking up the most active criminals will not be known for certain for years. Rand Corporation researcher Peter Greenwood asserts that because murder, rape, and assault are so rare for any one offender, the incidence of these crimes will not be affected by incapacitation. Nor, he believes, will incapacitation inhibit those convicted of larceny, fraud, and auto theft. Because these offenders now go to jail infrequently, imprisoning more of them would put an intolerable burden on the prison system.

"The crimes for which selective incapacitation principles appear most appropriate are burglary and robbery," Greenwood concludes. "They are the high volume predatory offenses of which the public is most fearful. They are also the offenses in which career criminals predominate, and they are the crimes for which a substantial number of convicted defendants are currently incarcerated."

The logic of incapacitation appears sound and its goal seems attainable. It offers, as other methods controlling crime once seemed to, a strategy for reducing crime without exceeding the country's capabilities. If not the most draconian solution to the problem, it is at least the best practical solution in a turbulent society where the financial cost of justice may soon rival the financial cost of crime.

Are Boston's Fires an Omen for All Cities?

Experts think unusual motives may be at work in the surge of arson that afflicts one metropolis, threatens others.

BOSTON

Hailed just a few years ago as a model in the fight against arson, this historic city is beset by a wave of fire setting that authorities seem powerless to halt.

Officials worry that the 1982 total of more than 1,400 blazes classed as deliberate or suspicious—most of them ignited since June—may signal a return to the level reached during the mid-1970s, the high point in an earlier surge of arson. So severe is the epidemic that Mayor Kevin White is preparing emergency steps to deal with it.

As bad as Boston's problem is, it is far from unique. The National Fire Protection Association reports that after rising for two years the number of deliberately set fires in the United States fell slightly in 1981. But suspicious fires, many of which are presumed to be arson, jumped 23 percent.

"Virtually every major city—whether it's New York, Detroit or Cleveland—is suffering as badly as Boston," declares Robert May of the International Association of Arson Investigators.

The motives for arson include insurance fraud, revenge and vandalism—all traditional causes. But there is increasing worry that a relatively new motive may now be at work: The torching of decaying structures occupied by the poor to clear the way for expensive housing for the well-to-do.

"When the land becomes worth more than the building, the building burns," declares Ernest Garneau of Urban Educational Systems, a Boston-based firm specializing in arson prevention.

Nowhere is this process more vividly seen here than in Highland Park, which is an area of ramshackle office buildings, row houses and tenements in the Roxbury section—a 15-minute drive from downtown Boston and such national treasures as Faneuil Hall and the Old State House.

Fires occur so often in Highland Park that its residents—mostly poor and black—are routinely roused at night by the wail of fire engines. Firefighters sometimes find themselves battling several multiple-alarm blazes at once.

Almost every block bears the scars of fire: Rubble-strewn vacant lots, boarded-up buildings, scavengers picking bricks out of partially toppled walls or prying copper pipes from the charred shell of a row house.

Authorities anticipating more flames have posted signs that proclaim in large red letters: "Hazardous building. Use caution during fire-fighting operations."

The fires are "crazy and dangerous," laments the Rev. Thomas Payne of Roxbury's 352-year-old First Church, a wooden relic that has been menaced when nearby buildings have burned. "Arson is destabilizing the neighborhood," he says, "and may force out all but the urban pioneers who decide to hang on."

What is most disturbing to Bostonians is that the crisis comes after the problem had appeared to be under control. Community groups and public officials, aided by federal funds, launched an anti-arson drive in the mid-1970s. An arson-for-profit ring—31 persons in all—was broken up and the surge of fires leveled off.

That arson is swelling again is blamed partly on cuts in anti-arson efforts. It is also being attributed by some to a suspected outbreak of "urban-renewal arson" or "instant land clearance."

Many experts believe that the owners of aging structures, facing horrendous maintenance bills and even higher costs to restore or demolish property, are taking the easy way out: Setting fires to clear their land for developers.

"It's a pattern," says Ben Haith of the Roxbury Highland's Neighborhood Association. "An absentee landlord puts less and less money into his property, taxes become delinquent and all of a sudden the house is on fire." Haith notes that plans are under way for a subway extension down what is known as the "Southwest Corridor," a swath through the city once assembled for an expressway project later abandoned. Land adjoining the route, including Highland Park, is a tempting target for developers because white-collar workers suffer from a shortage of housing near downtown.

Yet no one has been charged in an urban-renewal arson plot, and city officials contend that the theory remains unproved.

Comments Martha Goldsmith, housing adviser to Mayor White: "Big tracts have been sitting in some of those areas for years going begging. I don't see why someone would want to burn more property." Still, Goldsmith is "uncomfortable that we can't explain these fires."

"Crazy motives." Some officials say the main culprits are vandals and a few landowners who burn deteriorating property to reap insurance proceeds. Fire Commissioner George H. Paul, who blames "thrill seekers" for many of the fires, says: "People have all kinds of crazy motives. Some just set fires after they see reports in the media of other fires."

Others disagree, contending that the most recent fires were not the work of bored teenagers or pyromaniacs.

"With the high price of gasoline these days, most vandals don't go to the trouble of dragging 25 gallons up several flights of stairs day after day," asserts Lawrence Curran of First Security Services Corporation, which checks into suspicious fires for insurers.

City officials and private experts agree on at least this much: The dwindling resources available to fight arson spell deepening disaster for many

Fight Against Arson On the Back Burner

Though the national rate of deliberately set fires began leveling off two years ago, the respite could be short-lived.

Federal aid to help localities fight arson—after reaching about 17 million dollars a year in the 1970s—has been trimmed to just over 5 million dollars annually in the squeeze on the federal budget. At the same time, hard-pressed state and local governments have slashed arson investigations markedly.

The insurance industry is attempting to blunt the impact of these reductions. "With everyone else pulling out, companies are getting more active," says Doss Sauerteig of the Insurance Committee for Arson Control. Increasingly, firms are setting up special anti-arson units, backing legislation to stiffen arson penalties and refusing to pay suspicious claims. To prevent fraud, firms are pooling data on those who seek fire-loss payments. Most states now protect insurers against lawsuits inspired by their anti-arson efforts.

The insurance industry, the Ford Foundation and other private organizations have started bankrolling some of the activities previously funded by Uncle Sam—such as neighborhood anti-arson patrols and projects that seek to identify arson suspects by analyzing city and insurance-company records.

Experts agree, however, that these steps are taking up only part of the slack in the anti-arson drive.

neighborhoods. The Boston Fire Department, which has primary investigative responsibility, has seen its budget shrink 20 percent in two years under a state referendum that held down taxes.

Meanwhile, an arson "early-warning system" devised by officials and neighborhood groups in the mid-1970s has all but collapsed for lack of money. Under the system, researchers studied records of vulnerable buildings, looking for signs that owners were avoiding tax payments, increasing insurance or severely cutting back maintenance.

In some cases, the state attorney general's office notified property owners that they were under scrutiny. While major fires increased in number in the city as a whole, they dropped in the areas where the housing studies were done.

"When owners know they're being looked at, it has a chilling effect," reports one investigator.

Though volunteers in a half-dozen neighborhoods still use the technique sporadically, federal support has ended. Similarly, U.S. funding for an arson unit in the attorney general's office expired in October, and no new money is in sight. "It's ironic that this happened at a time when our expertise is needed more than ever," says Assistant Atty. Gen. John Donohue.

Massachusetts lawmakers voted $100,000 in each of the last two years for arson prevention, but the money remains unspent. Why? Community groups and the state fire marshal are arguing in court over whether the funds should go to the fire marshal to hire more investigators or to private anti-arson efforts.

Mayor White, whose administration is being buffeted by a federal corruption investigation, has come under increasing attack from citizens fed up with the slippage in anti-arson efforts. In one of the few actions taken so far, Fire Commissioner Paul has installed computers that he says will enable his squad to study fire patterns in an effort to outwit arsonists.

Federal cases pending. Meanwhile, the U.S. Bureau of Alcohol, Tobacco and Firearms is devoting more manpower to arson probes. Daniel Hartnett of the agency's Boston office says his unit has several promising cases pending before grand juries.

A better deterrent, say some community leaders, would be a drive to convert Boston's more than 1,000 abandoned buildings from arson targets into livable housing. A little of this has already been done. One example: In the Dorchester section, a six-unit apartment house virtually abandoned by its owner was refurbished with a $75,000 loan from a new state land bank and labor by local residents.

Declares City Councilman Bruce Bolling: "We can't depend on massive federal doles. The mayor should be assembling a public-private partnership to find the money for rehabilitating these areas." Mayor White said recently he would form such an organization.

While advocates of more enforcement and better arson prevention squabble over which approach should be stressed, houses in Highland Park and nearby areas continue to go up in flames.

Observes insurance investigator Curran: "Unless we take action soon or get some good luck, eventually there will be nothing of interest left here for arsonists to burn."

By TED GEST

Families and Crime

Travis Hirschi

Travis Hirschi, 47, is a professor of public policy at the University of Arizona, Tucson. Born in Rockville, Utah, he received a B.A. from the University of Utah (1957) and a Ph.D. from the University of California, Berkeley (1968). His books include Understanding Crime, *with Michael Gottfredson (1980),* Causes of Delinquency *(1969), and* Delinquency Research, *with Hanan C. Selvin (1967).*

Since the early 1970s, the Oregon Social Learning Center in Eugene, Oregon, has treated hundreds of families with "problem" children, children who bite, kick, scratch, whine, lie, cheat, and steal. As might be expected nowadays, this group of psychologists began with the assumption that the proper way to train difficult children is to reward their good deeds and ignore their bad ones.

The idea was, of course, that eventually the children would be so wrapped up in doing good that they would no longer consider evil. But after much struggling, the scholarly practitioners in Oregon came to the conclusion that children must be *punished* for their misdeeds if they are to learn to live without them.*

This conclusion may come as no surprise to millions of American parents who have spent years talking to their children, yelling at them, spanking them, cutting off their allowances, and in general doing whatever they could think of to try to get them to behave.

But the importance of parental discipline has been a rare notion among social scientists, especially those who deal with crime and delinquency. Criminologists tend to become interested in people only after they are capable of criminal acts. Not only is it then too late to do

*See "Children Who Steal," by G.R. Patterson in *Understanding Crime* (Sage, 1980), edited by Travis Hirschi and Michael Gottfredson.

anything about their family situation; it is also too late to learn much about what their home life was like during the "child-rearing" years. As a result, we have many explanations of crime that implicate broad socioeconomic or narrow psychological factors but few that look to the family itself.

Thus, the Oregon group is swimming against the current, doing what few students of crime have had the time or inclination to do. They are actually going into the homes of families with potentially delinquent children and watching them in operation. And they are coming up with some not-so-revolutionary ideas.

In fact, the Oregon researchers start pretty much with the basics. They tell us that, in order for a parent to teach a child not to use force and fraud, the parent must (a) monitor the child's behavior, (b) recognize deviant behavior when it occurs, and (c) punish such behavior. This seems obvious enough. The parent who cares for the child will watch his behavior, see him doing things he should not do, and correct him. Presto! A socialized, decent human being.

Where might this simple system go wrong? It can go wrong in any one of four ways. Parents may not care for their child (in which case, none of the other conditions would be met); parents, even if they care, may not have the time or energy to monitor their child's behavior; the parents, even if they care *and* monitor, may not see anything wrong with their youngster's actions; and finally, even if everything else is in place, the parents may not have the inclination or the means to impose punishment.

I am impressed by the simplicity of this model. I believe it organizes most of what we know about the families of delinquents. I also believe that, when we consider the potential impact of any proposed governmental action on crime and delinquency, we should specifically consider its impact on the ability of parents to monitor, recognize, and punish the misbehavior of their children. A classic example is "full-employment policy."

If one asks professors of criminology why the youth crime rate is so high, or if one asks students in criminology courses why a particular group has an unusually high rate of crime, they will almost invariably mention "unemployment" or "underemployment." If one points out that homicide, rape, and assault do not typically produce much in the way of income, undergraduates can quickly figure out how to get to these crimes from joblessness by way of something like frustration or rage.

Thus, armed with the notion that people "turn to crime" only when nothing better is available, we ignore family considerations and, as best we can, try to provide good jobs for young people. What do we expect to happen? Employment of an adolescent would presumably not much affect his parents' ability to monitor his behavior. Teenagers are outside the home a good deal anyway, and the employer would to some extent act as a surrogate monitor. The parents' affection for their offspring may, if anything, be improved by his willingness to reduce the burden on his family, and work is certainly not going to affect the parents' ability to recognize deviant behavior. The only element we have left in our model of child-rearing is *punishment*. How, if at all, does the employment of a youth affect the family's ability to punish his deviant behavior?

A Minor Paradox

The power of the family in this situation will depend on the resources available to it relative to the resources available to the child. It will also depend on the child's aspirations. If the youngster wants to go to college at his parents' expense and to continue to drive the family Buick on weekends, and if he is really only picking up pocket money on the job, the damage to parental control is presumably minimal.

But if the child does not want to go to college, if his family does not own a car, and if the money he earns provides him a level of living which is equal or superior to that of his family, he is by definition no longer dependent on them. Affection and monitoring had better have done the job already, because the "child-rearing" days are over.

An outstanding feature of recent times has been the growing independence of adolescents from the family, made possible by expansion and differentiation of the labor market. This has resulted in an increased dependence of the teenager on other adolescents. But peers do not take the place of parents as socializing agents: They have little or no investment in the outcome, are less likely to recognize deviant behavior, and, most important, do not possess the authority necessary to inflict punishment.

Moreover, research that looks directly at juvenile delinquents offers no support of the notion that they are economically deprived when compared to other adolescents in their immediate area. On the contrary, young delinquents are more likely to be employed, more likely to be well paid for the work they do, and more likely to enjoy the fruits of independence: sex, drugs, gambling, drinking, and job-quitting.

By looking directly at the family, we are thus able to resolve one of the minor paradoxes of our time, the fact that crime is caused by affluence *and* by poverty. General affluence to some extent weakens the control of all families. It especially weakens the control of those families in which the adolescent is able to realize a disposable income equal to that of his low-income parents (or parent) almost from the day he finds a job. Unfortunately, life for him does not freeze at this point. His earnings do not keep up with the demands on them. Most offenders eventually show up on the lower end of the financial spectrum, thanks to the very factors that explain their criminality. Individuals who have not been taught to get along with others, to delay the pursuit of pleasure, or to abstain from violence and fraud simply do not do very well in the labor market.

Back to the Protestant Ethic

They do not do very well as parents, either. A 1977 study (*The Delinquent Way of Life,* by D.J. West and D.P. Farrington) concluded: "The fact that delinquency is transmitted from one generation to the next is indisputable." The authors found that fewer than five percent of the families they surveyed accounted for almost half of the criminal convictions in the entire sample.

Why should the children of offenders be unusually vulnerable to temptation? If we had the complete answer to this question, we would be much further down the road to understanding crime than we are. But we do have important clues. Recall that the model advanced above assumes that bad behavior is not something that parents have to work at *cultivating* but rather something that requires hard effort to *weed out*. Research shows that parents with criminal records do not encourage criminality in their children and are in fact as "censorious" of their illicit activities as are parents with no record of criminal involvement. But not "wanting" criminal behavior in one's children and being "upset" when it occurs, do not necessarily mean that great energy has been expended to prevent it. Criminal activity revolves around payoffs in the short run. There is thus little reason to expect offenders to be much interested in child-rearing, where gratification, as often as not, is delayed.

And indeed, according to research, supervision of offspring in families where one or both parents has a criminal background is often "lax" or "inadequate" or "poor." Punishment tends to be "cheap": that is, short term (yelling and screaming, slapping and hitting) with little or no follow-up.

The Best Offense . . .

In *The Death and Life of the American City* (1961), Jane Jacobs cited the anonymity of modern urban life as one of the chief causes of neighborhood crime. Not only had once tightly knit communities become unraveled, but people had left their stoops and gone indoors—lured by air conditioning and tele-

Insignia of the countrywide Neighborhood Watch program.

vision, perhaps, or pushed by pollution, high-rise buildings, traffic congestion . . . and crime. No one was watching the streets. Ten years later, drawing on the ideas of Jacobs, Robert Ardrey, and others, Oscar Newman argued in *Defensible Space* (1972) that "people will defend themselves given the right physical framework"—an environment that provided a sense of "territoriality" and therefore enhanced "informal social control."

During the 1970s, experiments in both "watching" and "defensible space" were conducted throughout the United States. The results, to judge from surveys by political scientist Charles Murray and the Police Foundation's Lawrence Sherman, have not been a clear success.

The defensible-space strategy—brighter streetlights; windows in housing projects arranged to put more "eyes on the street"; local streets narrowed, routed, or blocked to discourage cruising "outsiders"; symbolic barriers (e.g., tree planters) to create semiprivate spaces that would generate possessive, protective community attitudes—appealed to city officials because it promised to reduce crime regardless of other factors (such as poverty or broken families). Housing projects or residential areas designed on defensible-space principles, like Clason Point and Markham Gardens in New York City and Asylum Hill in Hartford, come into fashion. Soon, defensible-space concepts were being applied to schools, commercial strips, and subway stations.

The demonstration projects, however, did not live up to expectations. At Clason Point, for example, crime did indeed decrease between 5 p.m. and 9 p.m. but it increased between midnight and 5 a.m. At Asylum Hill, robberies and burglaries decreased initially but then returned to "normal" levels. One

problem, apparently, was that offenders, rather than steering clear, quickly learned to adjust to the new environment. Many of them, moreover, turned out to be not outsiders but insiders—community residents. Ironically, though, the *fear* of crime in Clason Point and Asylum Hill seemed to have lessened considerably, and researchers found optimistic signs of more "neighboring."

In the end, Charles Murray concludes, the crime-reducing effects of defensible-space projects "depend crucially on the pre-existing social environment"—on the proportion of welfare families, the teen/adult ratio, whether or not residents own their apartments, length of residence, ethnic mix. Where crime is worst, he writes, defensible-space policies will have the least effect.

Experiments in "watching" have had a slightly better record. The Fairfax County, Virginia, police, for example, credit Neighborhood Watch with a 30 percent decrease in burglaries in the past year. The same pattern has been observed elsewhere. (Some five million Americans are involved in such efforts.) A study in Seattle revealed, however, that after an initial surge of enthusiasm, citizens tend to lose interest—and crime rates climb back up.

Another application of "watching" is preventive patrol. As Lawrence Sherman notes, most police officers cruise in squad cars: "What the patrol car officer sees is familiar buildings with unfamiliar people. What the public sees is a familiar police car with an unfamiliar officer in it." Patrol car officers are waiting to respond (the "dial-a-cop" strategy), rather than watching to prevent. In experiments in Newark and Kansas City, selected neighborhoods were provided with stepped-up *foot* patrols. While the patrols had no effect on serious crime, local residents told researchers that the patrolmen had reduced the incidence of lesser infractions—broken windows, drunkenness, panhandling—that tend to advertise the lack of "social control" in a neighborhood and thus to breed more serious crime. Since disorder has been shown by many studies to increase fear of crime, it appears that foot-patrol officers reduced fear by reducing disorder. And, because fear of crime is an important factor in the flight of businesses and families from central cities, reducing public fear is an important achievement in itself, one that might deter crime in the long run.

The foot-patrol experiments had another positive outcome: Foot-patrol officers were more satisfied with their jobs than those confined to automobiles.

I suspect that a more subtle element of child-rearing is also involved. This is the matter of recognition of deviant behavior. According to research at the Oregon Social Learning Center, many parents in "problem families" do not even *recognize* criminal behavior in their children. These parents may discount or ignore reports that their son or daughter steals on the grounds that they are unproved and should not be used to justify punishment.

As it happens, those parents, regardless of income, who succeed in crime prevention seem inclined to err in the direction of over-control, to see seeds of trouble in laziness, unreliability, disrespect for adults, and lack of concern for property. A catalogue of their attitudes could probably be entitled "The Protestant Ethic" or "Middle-Class Values."

Helping Parents Cope

Yet even a parent who knows what to do and has the will to do it may be hampered for other reasons. The percentage of the population divorced, the percentage of the homes headed by women only, and the percentage of unattached individuals in a community are among the most powerful predictors of crime rates. In most, but not all, studies that directly compare children living with both biological parents and children living in a "broken" or reconstituted home, the youngsters from intact families have lower rates of crime.*

Some reasons for this seem clear. For one thing, a single parent (usually a woman) must devote a good deal of time to support and maintenance activities, which often include holding down a job, that are to some extent shared in the two-parent family. She must do so in the absence of psychological and social support. And she is less free to devote time to monitoring and

*See, for example, "The Broken Home and Delinquent Behavior," by Karen Wilkinson in *Understanding Crime* (Sage, 1980), edited by Travis Hirschi and Michael Gottfredson.

punishment. As early as 1950, a study by Sheldon and Eleanor Glueck showed that mothers who worked, whether regularly or occasionally, were more likely to raise delinquent children than were women who did not work. This same report also revealed that the effect on delinquency of a mother working was *completely* accounted for by the quality of supervision she provided. When a mother was able to provide supervision for her children, her employment had no effect on the likelihood of delinquency.

The decline of the family is real enough. The extended household that was so effective in controlling everyone's behavior remains only in vestigial form; the nuclear family that replaced it does not have the stability and continuity it once had. One response, especially common among crime analysts, is to take note of these facts but to conclude that nothing can be done about them. Such neglect is reinforced by "modern" theories of crime, which assume that people are good by nature and that individuals would be law-abiding were it not for the flaws in the society around them.

This kind of stance toward the family is one I think we should avoid.

If nothing else, research on crime and the family may help prevent us from making a bad situation worse—for example, by adopting policies that, perhaps unwittingly, make the parents' job harder. And who knows what we may learn? It would be presumptuous to conclude in advance that studies of the family will have no useful application. The technique of child-rearing is not that complex, and someone may yet discover simple measures for improving the efficacy of parents in America as crime control agents. Since parents number in the millions, work for nothing, are stuck with the job, and usually prefer law-abiding children, they are a potential resource we cannot afford to ignore. Even modest bolstering of their role could result in large savings of time and money now devoted to correcting their mistakes.

19 MILLION SINGLES

Their Joys and Frustrations

Later marriages and more divorces are fast swelling the ranks of Americans living alone—an experience that is liberating for many and depressing for others.

Evette Everett, a 25-year-old Atlanta graphic artist, thrives on the freedom and flexibility that comes from striking out on her own.

Richard Tallant, a 39-year-old unemployed machinist from Lakewood, Ohio, is struggling to rebuild his life after a divorce that ended his marriage of 13 years.

Mary Lou Condon, 53, has left the grief of widowhood behind and is busy meeting the challenges of her job as assistant nursing director of a Hartford, Conn., hospital.

Despite the differences in their lives, Everett, Tallant and Condon share a common bond as members of one of the fastest-growing groups in America—people who live alone.

The figures tell a dramatic tale: Between 1970 and 1982, their ranks swelled from 10.9 million to 19.4 million—a 78 percent jump. "This is unprecedented in U.S. history," says psychologist Phillip Shaver of the University of Denver. "People are opting for increased independence."

As their numbers grow, the live-alones—most of whom reside in or near big cities—are altering the nation's housing and leisure markets. They also are inspiring scores of new services and products ranging from video dating to specially packaged foods.

Fueling the singles boom are a high divorce rate and a trend toward marrying later in life. The relative affluence of the nation, even in a time of recession, means that more young people can move into apartments of their own instead of staying with parents or having roommates. Observes psychologist Anne Peplau of the University of California at Los Angeles: "Affluence makes living alone possible. Whether it is desirable depends on the individual."

Quest for Independence

Almost a third of those living alone have never been married. Their ranks rose from 2.8 million to almost 6 million between 1970 and 1981, in large measure because of an increase in the young-adult population.

Typical is George Drapeau III, a 30-year-old marketing consultant who lives in a two-bedroom cooperative apartment in Mamaroneck, N.Y. Being on his own, he has time to build his business as well as take frequent weekend ski trips, buy a new car every few years and vacation in Europe. "You don't need an extra car or an extra room in the house, and you don't have an extra mouth to feed," says Drapeau.

Today's young adults, many of them products of the "me" generation, grew up at a time when "do your own thing" was the prevailing philosophy. They enjoy the freedom and flexibility that single living offers, says sociologist Peter Stein of William Paterson College in Wayne, N.J.

Two decades ago, people often married right after leaving high school or college, but today many people want to build a career before stepping into marriage. The median age at first marriage has increased two full years since 1960—from 22.8 to 24.8 years for men and from 20.3 to 22.3 for women.

Economics and employment shifts are big reasons for going solo. Says sociologist Stein: "If a career opportunity opens elsewhere, a single person can pick up and move without worrying about family considerations, and single people are able to spend money as they want rather than within the confines of family decision making."

Shifting societal attitudes ease the way for singles. In the past, sociologists observe, the unmarried were viewed as unusual, but that is no longer the case in a country tolerant of diverse lifestyles. Helping to revamp old views is the changing role of women. Says UCLA's Peplau: "The women's movement makes it acceptable for women to live on their own before they get married, and more want to have the opportunity to do that."

"I am selfish about my time . . ." Graphic artist Everett is among those taking advantage of the freedom gained by women. "There's nobody to take care of me but myself, and I like it that way," she says. But Everett, who lives in a duplex apartment, does worry about crime. In choosing an apartment, safety is her primary concern. "I can't live where I have to worry about getting out of a car at night," she says. Eventually, Everett would like a close relationship with a man, but acknowledges that "it will take time to break out of the single lifestyle and switch to a companion lifestyle. I am selfish about my time and what I do with it."

Although young adults make up the largest proportion of never married people living by themselves, sociologists say that a growing number of career women in their late 30s and early 40s are also putting off marrying. As they get older, they find the supply of eligible males dwindling. "Professional women want a certain kind of guy, and it is not easy to find that person," reports the University of Denver's Shaver.

Margaret A. Kilgore, director of communications for the western region of Ernst & Whinney, a major accounting firm, is in her 40s and lives alone in a 16th-floor apartment overlooking the beach in Santa Monica, Calif. "I have always traveled a lot and worked odd hours, and that has made maintaining a personal life difficult," she explains. Friends who constantly drop in and her work leave little time entirely free, but in idle moments she likes to "close the door and settle down with a good book." Adds Kilgore: "I don't think the joys of solitude can be underestimated— if it doesn't last too long."

After Divorce: Picking Up the Pieces

For another group of people—those who have suffered through divorces—the solitude of single life may be anything but welcome. And as the rate of split-ups soared between 1970 and 1981, the number of divorced people living by themselves grew by 150 percent, from 1.5 million to 3.7 million.

Psychologists say that most divorced people endure an initial period of trauma but usually recover as time passes.

Five years after her divorce, Ruth Relyea, a 37-year-old federal employe, finds that she relishes single living. She shares her home in Fairfax County, Va., a suburb of Washington, D.C., with a dog and two cats and spends spare time doing yard work and attending concerts. "I can do what I want, when I want, as I want," she says. "The only constraints are those I impose on myself."

Less enthusiastic is unemployed Ohio machinist Tallant, who still lives in the house that he had shared with his wife and three children. "Living alone still gets to me sometimes, but I try not to let it bother me," he says some three years after his divorce. The recent loss of his job compounded his problem. "There are times when I really get down," he says. But a woman friend and involvement in Parents Without Partners, an organization for single parents, keep him from getting too low.

Experts say that of all those who live alone, divorced men are most likely to have troubles. Studies show that many such men are more vulnerable to heart attacks and other health problems.

By contrast, psychologist Shaver in his book *In Search of Intimacy* writes that "women...seem better able to find helpful social support after a marriage fails. They are also better equipped to live alone, having mastered more of the required skills—shopping, cooking, cleaning and daily planning."

Studies by Leonard Cargan, a sociologist at Wright State University in Dayton, Ohio, found that divorced people are almost twice as likely as those who have never married to say that they have no one with whom to discuss problems.

Though they generally have many more sexual relationships than those who never married, the divorced are less likely to be happy with their sex lives. Says Cargan: "Immediately after divorce, they may go through a lot of partners to prove to themselves that they are still attractive and loved. But they probably compare these relationships to what they used to have in marriage and find that they are not as satisfied."

Nonetheless, the ranks of divorced people living by themselves are likely to keep expanding, given the rate at which marriages are coming unraveled. What's more, an increasing number are thinking twice before taking a new spouse. "Divorced people generally want to remarry, but they don't want to get into a bad marriage again," says sociologist Stein. "So living alone may not be a bad way for them to lead their lives."

A Lifestyle of Their Own

To help the millions of divorced and never married people find the companionship they so often crave, a diverse network of enterprises has sprung up—dating agencies, magazines, singles bars, travel bureaus and a host of others.

"Everyone wants to meet someone special," observes Joan Hendrickson, owner of the Georgetown Connection, a video dating service in Washington that reports it has more than 400 clients, most of them professional people. For annual membership fees of $450, or $350 for six months, people are helped to introduce themselves to one another through individual video recordings and written profiles.

Such arrangements, their backers argue, are a more discreet route to companionship than the singles scene. Joe O'Connell, president of People Resources in New York City, which operates a video dating business and holds

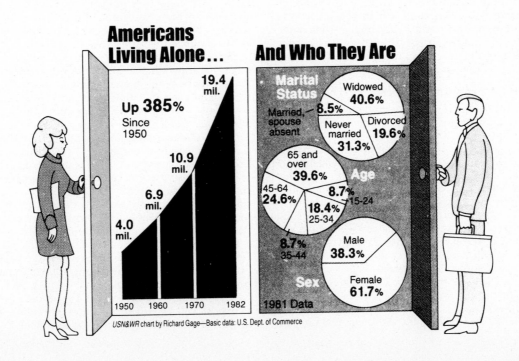

Americans Living Alone...

Up **385%** Since 1950

4.0 mil. — 1950
6.9 mil. — 1960
10.9 mil. — 1970
19.4 mil. — 1982

And Who They Are

Marital Status:
Widowed 40.6%
Married, spouse absent 8.5%
Never married 31.3%
Divorced 19.6%

Age:
65 and over 39.6%
45-64 24.6%
15-24 8.7%
25-34 18.4%
35-44 8.7%

Sex:
Male 38.3%
Female 61.7%

1981 Data

USN&WR chart by Richard Gage—Basic data: U.S. Dept. of Commerce workshops and seminars for singles, says that bars and discos have lost their allure, especially for those over 35. "The older crowd can't stand the bar scene," he says.

People who deal with them regularly say that singles today are more straight-laced than they were several years ago. Says Hendrickson: "People tried sexual freedom and found that it was not so great. They have swung around to more traditional values, and with herpes on the scene people are really concerned."

In addition to trying video dating, singles are joining health clubs, signing up for special weekends at resorts and taking courses at universities—all avenues for meeting people in relatively relaxed settings.

Sydelle Baskind, who runs a travel agency in West Hartford, Conn., caters to people who live alone. Her singles travel as a group, get acquainted at cocktail parties in airport lounges and even hold discussions on the singles lifestyle.

Windjammer Barefoot Cruises, with sailings from Miami to the Bahamas and the Caribbean, includes two trips especially for singles in its annual schedule. Chuck Werner, marketing director of the firm, says that a lot of people over 40 go on the cruises. "In the past, they regarded themselves as widows, divorced or old maids," he says. "Now, they consider themselves singles."

The personals. More singles also are trying an approach that they once scorned—personal advertisements in local and national magazines. The *Washingtonian* in the nation's capital has several pages of these ads in every issue. Magazines and newspapers for singles are sprouting in such cities as Milwaukee and Cincinnati. A national magazine, *Intro*, carries an array of articles about everything from cooking for one to office romances, plus about 40 pages of classified ads. Example: "Nordic blonde, tall, long-legged, successful doctor seeks sensitive, aware, dynamic, intelligent, financially independent male."

Other singles prefer to meet people via more conventional channels, such as through friends or co-workers. Many churches also are reaching out to singles. The singles ministry of Hyde Park Community United Methodist Church in Cincinnati has tripled its membership in the past two years and currently has 3,000 on its mailing list.

In Washington, Adas Israel Congregation holds a monthly Friday-night service for singles that began with a few dozen people and now draws 1,300 from as far away as Wilmington, Del. Associate Rabbi Stephen Listfield says Judaism is traditionally family oriented and many singles "felt completely alienated or indifferent because there was hardly any way for them to be involved in the community." Now, says Listfield, the synagogue is making them feel welcome.

For Business: An Expanding Market

Besides services catering to the emotional and social needs of singles, all sorts of businesses have cropped up to fill their basic wants.

In Coconut Grove, Fla., a condominium complex being built for the single professional has units for $90,000 to $135,000. Nikki Rutenberg, marketing director, says the place is for those who "want to go out the front door and jog, play tennis, run by the marina and eat in the restaurants."

Somerset Park Apartments in Troy, Mich., a Detroit suburb, features amenities that draw singles—who make up about 25 percent of the 6,000 tenants. Among the attractions: A nine-hole golf course, five swimming pools, eight tennis courts, a park and picnic grounds.

For those who want the privacy of living alone but also some help in managing housing costs, developer Oskar Brecher of Edgewater, N.J., offers "mingles" condominiums. Costing $142,500 to $236,000, the units contain two

bedrooms with separate bathrooms and closets and a common living room. "Each person has a precinct of privacy," says Brecher.

Singles account for a high proportion of housing sales throughout the U.S., and their preference for smaller, detached homes and for condominiums is helping to shape the market. A recent survey by the National Association of Realtors found that singles constitute 25 percent of all first-time home buyers and also a high proportion of second and third-time purchasers. "Singles now feel they don't have to wait to acquire trappings that were once associated with the married state," observes Ann Clurman, vice president of the market-research firm of Yankelovich, Skelly & White.

On New York's Madison Avenue, advertising agencies are coming to view singles as a burgeoning new market with substantial discretionary income. A study by Young & Rubicam, a New York ad agency, concludes that singles, especially those between 18 and 34, are above-average consumers of such commodities as liquor, stereo equipment, books, foreign cars, most sporting goods and casual apparel. They also are more likely to shop in gourmet and health-food stores and to dine out. "There is going to have to be more concentration on this market," says Adrienne Darling, an executive at Young & Rubicam.

Already, some advertisers are targeting singles. Cathy Pullis, a research analyst at the J. Walter Thompson advertising agency, says that more commercials for such products as salad dressing, coffee and detergent are aimed at the single male. Campbell Soup zeroes in on people who live alone by marketing Soup for One, and many other firms are thinking about new packaging aimed at singles. Even so, a considerable number of businesses continue to neglect the singles market. Bob Foeppel, program director of a national singles conference planned for next year in Washington, complains that "you go into a supermarket and you find big roasts, lamb chops packed four to a package. Everything is geared to the family."

The Bitter and the Sweet

As successful as many people are in adjusting to a singles lifestyle, the question remains: Is it the best way to live?

Some experts say that growth of the singles industry is testimony to the emotional starvation of many who live alone. "The loneliness industry would not be as broad and successful if there were not lots and lots of lonely people," says Stephen Goldston, director of the office of prevention at the National Institute of Mental Health.

Even many who say they are happy living alone acknowledge that they miss having someone around with whom to share experiences. "Some days I go home very tired and think how good it is that I don't have to cook dinner for someone else and be charming and witty," says Rozanne Weissman, public-affairs director of the Communications Workers of America in Washington. "But there are other days when I want to come home and share sorrows, frustrations and happiness, and there is not anyone there."

Psychologists have found that, of all people living alone, those who have recently experienced the rupturing of a relationship—typically through divorce or death—are the most likely to be lonely. But people who have a network of friends and live alone by choice are usually content.

How long will the boom in single living last? Sociologist Cargan of Wright State University says the trend is largely a product of growth in the young-adult population. He expects a tapering off when that growth is reversed. The Census Bureau estimates that the number of people between 21 and 29 will shrink from 39 million in 1985 to 36 million in 1990, then drop below 33 million in 1995.

Still, as long as the divorce rate remains high and people put off marriage to get a better foothold in their careers, singles will constitute a large segment of the population. The swelling in the ranks of the elderly also means additions to the numbers living on their own.

All this points to a big demand for new systems of emotional support for people who love the independence of solo living yet thirst for companionship and friendship in good times and bad. Observes psychologist Shaver of the University of Denver: "People will acknowledge that they want more social support and contact and will figure out ways to get it."

By ALVIN P. SANOFF with the magazine's domestic bureaus

Millions Who Are Old and Alone

Young singles and their lifestyle may grab most of the attention, but widows and widowers make up the biggest segment of Americans living alone.

Among these 7.7 million older people who are on their own, women age 65 and above are in the vast majority—outnumbering their male counterparts by almost 6 to 1. Reasons for the gender gap: Women generally outlive their spouses and are less likely to remarry than men.

While young live-alones often spend time searching for potential marriage partners, older people typically seek companionship among friends and family. Studies show that about 80 percent of senior citizens have children living within an hour's drive from them. Tora Bikson, a Rand Corporation psychologist, says that though "a lot of the elderly want to be within easy access of their families, they prefer to live by themselves. They don't like the idea of being put in someone's guest room and being in a situation where they don't know what their role is."

Like many, Chloe Jarrett, 74, treasures her independence. After her husband died four years ago, she remained in her small, two-bedroom home in Cartersville, Ga. Though she gets lonely, Jarrett does not feel isolated because she has sisters and sisters-in-law living in the same town and a daughter, only 90 minutes away, who visits often. "I don't know how it would be without relatives who care for me," she says.

Psychologists have found that older people living by themselves generally endure loneliness better than their young counterparts. After a nationwide survey, psychologist Phillip Shaver of the University of Denver concluded that loneliness declines with age. Explains Leo Baldwin, housing-program coordinator of the American Association of Retired Persons: "Older people recognize that many of them will spend years living alone. With that resignation and a determination to make the best of it, a great share of them do quite well."

Senior citizens on their own don't attract as much attention from business as younger live-alones, but firms in the travel, housing and health-insurance industries see them as a key part of the expanding market that older people in general represent. Grand Circle Travel in New York City finds that serving that market pays handsomely. The agency puts together trips for the elderly to every part of the world including China, the Middle East and India, and in the last decade has enjoyed a tenfold increase in business.

Housing market. The federal government and private developers are kept busy providing shelter for older people. The government has built more than 1 million units for senior citizens, most living by themselves. Private-housing complexes, such as those built by Rossmoor Leisure World, contain a high proportion of older people on their own. Sixty-three percent of the residents of Leisure World in Silver Spring, Md., for instance, are widows and widowers.

For many of the elderly, being on their own is proof of physical and mental vigor. "They think it is an accomplishment. Symbolically, it is very important to them," says psychologist Anne Peplau of the University of California at Los Angeles.

How Drugs Sap The Nation's Strength

To a degree never seen before, the U.S. has a monkey on its back—a drug problem reaching into every region, every age group, every social class.

THE SCOURGE OF DRUGS, which for years has afflicted America's youth, is now so widespread among adults that it threatens to sap the nation's strength at a critical juncture in its history.

Millions of Americans—from children in schoolyards to computer analysts in California's Silicon Valley and stockbrokers on Wall Street—are turning on to all kinds of pot, pills and powders, giving the United States the highest rate of drug abuse of any developed country on the globe.

The U.S. is carrying this burden as it struggles to hold its own against unprecedented scientific, technological and economic challenges not only from the Soviet Union, but also from Japan and American allies in Western Europe.

Industry is losing as much as 25 billion dollars a year as a result of employes who snort, swallow, inhale or inject illicit substances. The toll takes the form of slowed productivity, absenteeism, lateness and irrational decisions.

At the same time, the academic achievement of American youngsters, though up a bit in recent months, has slipped sharply over the last 15 years, and some experts believe drugs and alcohol helped cause the decline.

Crime and accidents, which bring untold loss and grief to families and individuals, are increasingly linked to drugs.

But law enforcement is powerless to stem the traffic in marijuana, cocaine and other drugs. Authorities are seizing and destroying record amounts. Yet the overall supply keeps swelling. Finding pot or coke is now no more difficult in many places than buying a six-pack of beer after the bars close.

The epidemic is so extensive that gains in one segment of the population tend to be offset by reversals in another. Example: Even though drug use by teenagers is declining, dope is more pervasive than ever among middle-class adults—the people on whom an industrial society depends for leadership and creative energy.

Carlton Turner, White House drug-abuse adviser, sums up the problem: "It's spread all through society. There's no way it's under control."

In 1962, only 4 percent of adults age 18 to 25 had ever smoked marijuana, or pot. By last year, that figure had risen to 64 percent. Among the 182.5 million Americans age 12 or older, more than 57 million—31.3 percent—had tried marijuana. With cocaine, the picture is similar. Two decades ago, only a small fraction of the populace had encountered it, let alone used it. By last year, some 22 million people had done so.

Among adults 26 and older, about 8.4 million have smoked pot and 1.5 million have taken cocaine in the last month, according to the latest government figures.

Correspondents for *U.S. News & World Report* found drug abuse to be greatest on the Eastern Seaboard and on the West Coast, as well as in Colorado, where the ski resorts of the affluent have spawned a thriving cocaine trade.

From Los Angeles: "It's rampant," says Allan Rosenthal, program coordinator at the Beverly Glen Hospital.

From New York: "There's an explosion of substances being used," reports Kevin E. McEneaney, senior vice president at Phoenix House Foundation, Inc., a national anti-drug organization. In some New York social circles, it is fashionable to offer coke or a bright array of pep pills as hors d'oeuvres at cocktail parties.

The magazine's correspondents found drug abuse rising in every region, however, including some of the most conservative areas. Methamphetamines, called "speed," abound in Dallas. In Mississippi's Gulfport area, a study last fall found that about a fifth of school-age marijuana smokers started when they were between 10 and 12 years old. No social class is immune. A New York State study showed drug use highest in families earning $50,000 or more a year.

Doped Up at the Workplace

No one has measured how all this pill popping, injecting and inhaling has affected the national output. Yet the growth of U.S. productivity has been lagging behind that of other major industrial nations, none of which has a drug problem as serious. Between 1967 and 1981, America's manufacturing output advanced 39 percent. In the same period, Japan's leaped 209 percent, France's climbed 98 percent, West Germany's, 90 percent, and Britain's, 57 percent.

Though drug abuse is far from the only problem afflicting U.S. industry, it plainly is throwing sand in the nation's industrial engine. Marvin Leonard, vice president of the New Orleans-based Pendleton Detectives, Inc., estimates that 30 percent of the U.S. work force uses drugs. "Almost any field we go into, we can find a problem," he reports.

An official of the U.S. Health and Human Services Department says HHS's 25-billion-dollar estimate of annual industrial losses is conservative. Dale Masi, head of HHS's employe-counseling services, explains: "The estimate doesn't include hidden costs such as disability pay, workers' compensation and loss of co-workers' and supervisors' time."

Drug abuse is "a problem American industry cannot afford to ignore," warns Peter Bensinger, former head of the Drug Enforcement Administration (DEA) and now a consultant to firms seeking to cope with drug and alcohol difficulties.

Bensinger cites a small Chicago-area tool-manufacturing firm where the bookkeeper was taking Quaaludes, a sleep-promoting drug. "Checks were getting lost," Bensinger recalls. "Funds were not getting allocated. Inventory wasn't accounted for. The company nearly went bankrupt."

In Houston, a division of the National Supply Company was hit a year ago with a decline in output and a rise in absenteeism, stealing and discipline problems. Drugs were the cause. After a six-month probe, police and company officials raided a drug deal in progress on the company parking lot with sirens blaring and lights flashing. Twenty-one employes were fired. Drug use plummeted. Within a week, minor injuries were cut in half, and efficiency rates jumped 20 points. Pilferage and absenteeism also declined.

The bigger the company, the bigger the potential problem. Roger Smith, chairman of General Motors, has said that absenteeism, much of it due to drug and alcohol abuse, costs the corporation a billion dollars a year. Among other problems GM has found: Mike Dinsmore, a hoist operator, admitted being so stoned that he dropped cars he was lifting from one point on the production line to another. The cars had to be scrapped, and thousands of dollars were lost.

Even the nuclear industry has been affected. In California, a group of former workers disclosed two years ago that after smoking pot they and others did shoddy repairs on the steam generator of a San Onofre nuclear reactor. A Nuclear Regulatory Commission spokesman said their work was corrected and no permanent damage done. Even so, he admitted that "no doubt there is a cost."

In many fields where creativity is at a premium—from the high-tech computer world to the Hollywood film-and-music realm—cocaine is the drug of choice. "People get the feeling that 'I can do anything better on coke,'" says Marian Fischman of the University of Chicago.

Tests show just the opposite. "Cocaine produces real impairment"—rapid heart rate, raised blood pressure and, if used regularly, symptoms similar to schizophrenia, Fischman adds.

In Hollywood, a press agent for several well-known entertainers discounts stories about films being ruined because stars are spaced out on drugs. But he says: "Sometimes actors come to work coked out, and that halts production. They are sent home. The film is shot around them, and they do their part later."

The Schools: A "Heinz 57" Variety of Drugs

Among the best measures of teenage academic performance are the Scholastic Aptitude Tests taken by college-bound high-school seniors. From 1967 to 1982—the years in which high-school drug use soared—SAT verbal scores skidded 40 points and math totals fell 25.

"Chronic marijuana users have short-term memory problems and are often so lethargic they can't cope with academic demands," reports Alexander Astin of the University of California at Los Angeles, who has surveyed college freshmen across the nation for the last 17 years. Other reasons for the academic decline are weakened curricula, permissiveness and excessive TV viewing. But, says Astin, "we shouldn't discount drug abuse as a factor."

The sharp rise in teenagers' smoking marijuana has abated in the last four years. Yet their numbers are still huge. About 6.4 million have tried it; 2.6 million have smoked it in the last month. Moreover, the average age of youngsters using pot for the first time is falling. Experimenters under age 10 turn up more and more, federal officials say.

William Pollin, director of the National Institute on Drug Abuse, notes that 29 percent of high-school seniors say they have used marijuana in the last month, down from 37 percent in 1979. "We're beginning to see some good news, but we're still left with a dreadful situation," he adds, "because the 29 percent figure represents a thirtyfold increase in the last 20 years."

Lloyd Johnston, program director of the Institute for Social Research at the University of Michigan, has surveyed U.S. high-school seniors and studied reports from other nations. His findings: "I don't know of any other country where nearly two thirds of the seniors have tried illicit drugs before they finish high school. And more than a third of them have illicitly used drugs other than marijuana."

Stimulants of all kinds are now "the big thing in the schools," laments Lee Rush of the Chicago-based Central States Institute of Addiction. "Marijuana has leveled off, and alcohol is up. There's a lot of combining—mainly stimulants and alcohol. Kids used to take marijuana alone, but now it's Heinz 57," he says, referring to the variety of drugs youngsters try at any one time.

No one knows how many people die each year of drug abuse—mainly overdoses and suicides with drugs. Such victims surely number in the thousands, according to government experts. Additional thousands of people—a third more last year than in 1981—are landing in hospitals from heroin and cocaine overdoses. Marijuana alone rarely sends anyone to an emergency room, but it can have that result when used heavily and combined with other drugs. Chronic marijuana smoking can also impair the heart and lungs, decrease sperm count, interfere with ovulation and hinder the body's immune system, says U.S. Surgeon General C. Everett Koop.

Even more alarming is the growing number of serious accidents and crimes blamed on drugs. Federal traffic-safety officials say nearly 10,000 young people die in auto wrecks each year, primarily because of alcohol or drugs. One result: Teenagers are the only age group whose life expectancy is not increasing.

A recent federal study of 18 train accidents involving drugs or alcohol put the toll at 25 rail workers killed, 13 injured and 25 million dollars' worth of property damaged.

Crime is an even bigger problem. A Justice Department survey of state-prison inmates shows more than half took illegal drugs during the month before they committed their crimes. Almost a third were under the influence of an illicit drug at the time they committed the offenses.

New York police estimate that nearly a quarter of the city's homicides are drug related. In San Francisco, dope is believed to be an element in 7 of every 10 crimes. Hard drugs, such as heroin, are so expensive—more than $2,000 a gram—that addicts often must commit robberies or burglaries regularly to support their habits.

Atty. Gen. William French Smith worries about drug money corrupting public officials: "When a sheriff accepts $50,000 to look the other way while traffickers make a single landing at a makeshift airport, as happened last year, the drug problem becomes an assault on the very foundations of law and law enforcement."

Other officials point out the enormous sums that the drug culture siphons off from the economy. Trafficking is an 80-to-90-billion-dollar-a-year business—all of it untaxed.

5. VICTIMS

Putting Users on the Couch

Why the relentless surge in drug abuse? The answers offered by the experts range from the pressures of a competitive society to boredom, affluence and the self-indulgence of the "me" generation. Says Rush of the Central States Institute of Addiction: "Look who's the middle class now—the flower kids of the '60s. The middle class has always been involved in drugs. Once it was alcohol. Then it was tranquilizers prescribed by doctors. The difference now is that the middle class is using illicit drugs and what once were considered 'hard' drugs."

Fred W. Garcia of the Colorado Department of Health explains: "The message is out: It's O.K. to do drugs. If you have a headache, take a pill. If you want to relax, have a drink. If you want to feel different, do a chemical."

Then, too, when blame is passed around, the media get a share. "Cocaine has been glamorized," asserts James Burke of the Drug Enforcement Administration's Denver office. "People read about athletes, entertainers and those in the professions being involved with cocaine. It has acquired the connotation of a status symbol."

Francis Mullen, Jr., acting DEA administrator in Washington, believes "the entertainment industry to a large degree has let us down" by all too often depicting drug use as "normal." That impression is also conveyed by other means. "Opium" is the name of a well-known perfume. T-shirts are widely sold with such slogans as "A Friend With Weed Is a Friend Indeed."

In some circles, it has become socially acceptable for upper-middle-class people—including doctors, lawyers and stockbrokers—not only to use dope but to sell it. Such trafficking "is a lot more lucrative than buying a Holiday Inn," says a Justice Department official. "It provides a much quicker turnaround on investment."

Drugs are becoming an investment of another kind. In New York, an electronic-equipment manufacturer found his sales force was providing cocaine to customers rather than taking them out for drinks. Similar practices are reported in Hollywood and Texas. A Houston consultant marvels: "I see cocaine becoming a negotiable instrument."

"Digging a Hole in the Ocean"

Mullen of the Drug Enforcement Administration concedes that authorities are falling far short of choking off the influx of illegal drugs from abroad. "We seized about twice as much heroin, three times as much cocaine and 40 percent more marijuana in 1982 than we did in 1981," he says. "Yet all these drugs remain easily available."

The General Accounting Office (GAO), the investigative arm of Congress, estimates that the 2.8 million pounds of marijuana seized at the nation's borders last year was only 16 percent of the supply, the 608 pounds of heroin confiscated was just 10 percent of the total and the 12,500 pounds of cocaine intercepted was only 11 percent of the amount on the street.

About 75 percent of the marijuana and cocaine coming into the U.S. is funneled through Colombia. The Bogotá regime refuses to cooperate in suppressing the trade. U.S. officials also charge that Cuba is abetting the Caribbean drug traffic.

The frustrations involved in trying to interdict drugs smuggled from abroad can be seen in the record of the South Florida Task Force, organized in March, 1982, under the aegis of Vice President Bush. Drug seizures and arrests jumped markedly, and the area's crime rate fell dramatically. But the GAO warns that "it is doubtful whether the task force can have any substantial long-term impact on drug availability." Indeed, many law-enforcement officials in neighboring states complain that heroin and cocaine now flood into the country through their jurisdictions.

For U.S.—a Dubious Distinction

Americans may flinch when they hear the United States described as a drug-happy society, but the facts are indisputable: Illicit-drug use per capita in the U.S. exceeds that of any other industrial nation.

Among European nations, West Germany has the most serious heroin problem. Still, the situation is worse in America, which has 450,000 to 500,000 addicts.

The Soviet Union has negligible drug problems, although it suffers heavily from alcoholism.

Japan, America's keenest economic competitor, fought off amphetamine and heroin epidemics after World War II with stringent laws. It took the same approach with marijuana. Foreigners caught with pot are arrested and deported. Japan now has the lowest illegal-drug consumption of any developed nation.

Dr. Gabriel Nahas of Columbia University, an expert on drug use here and abroad, says the U.S. in 1980 became "the world's largest consumer of marijuana, ahead of countries where it has been used for centuries—India, Pakistan, Afghanistan, Iran and Egypt."

Nahas notes that Egypt, a nation long dominated by hashish—the Arabic word for marijuana—imposed harsh penalties to reduce drug use in the 1950s and 1960s. At that time, its per capita consumption of hashish was only one tenth that of the U.S.

The United States does not lead the world in heroin addiction. That distinction belongs to Iran, with up to 1 million heroin and opium junkies. At least two other Third World countries—Pakistan and Malaysia—also have higher heroin-use rates than the U.S., experts say.

Complicating matters further, an expanding share of the pot market is supplied by domestic sources. Officials once thought 2.6 million pounds of marijuana was grown in the U.S.—about 7 percent of the national supply. But last year the DEA destroyed more than 3.6 million pounds. "Now we think that as much as 20 percent of the nation's marijuana is grown domestically," says Mullen.

Senator Joseph Biden (D-Del.), describing the government's efforts as hampered by interagency turf wars and backbiting, is sponsoring a bill to concentrate antidrug authority in one cabinet-level official.

DEA officials and White House drug adviser Turner oppose the "drug czar" proposal, which President Reagan vetoed last year, arguing that it would only create more tensions among government officials. DEA officials insist that the U.S., with an extra 1,200 people, 12 new federal antidrug task forces and an additional 127.5 million dollars in enforcement funds this year, will make more headway in the future. But that new effort has been slow getting started.

Other officials are skeptical anyway that law enforcement alone can reduce the supply of illicit drugs very much. "It's like digging a hole in the ocean," says Sterling Johnson, special assistant district attorney in New York City.

Calling "Cocaine Anonymous"

Funds for federal drug-education and treatment programs have been sliced in half—from 458 million dollars in 1980 to 206 million dollars this year. Yet private programs are sprouting around the country.

One innovative approach is being tried by Addiction Research and Treatment Services clinics in Colorado. Cocaine patients have the option of signing "contingency

When the Navy Decreed "Zero Tolerance" of Drugs

As bleak as the drug picture is nationally, in the U.S. armed forces the news is upbeat. Results of an extensive survey, to be announced soon, are expected to show big declines in drug use in the military since 1980.

That was the year the Pentagon discovered that nearly half of its junior enlisted personnel had smoked pot in the previous 12 months and more than a third had lit up in the previous month.

Penalties were stiffened, and new programs were devised to strip drugs of their glamour. The Navy tried extra hard. Not only had it found 48 percent of its sailors were smoking pot at two major bases in 1980, but in May, 1981, it suffered a second blow.

During a training exercise, a jet crashed into the U.S.S. *Nimitz*, killing 14 and injuring 42. Drugs did not cause the crash, the Pentagon ruled later. But six of the dead flight-deck crewmen had traces of marijuana in their bodies. That showed drug use aboard ship, and it raised questions of whether those crewmen might have lived had they abstained.

Adm. Thomas B. Hayward, then chief of naval operations, ordered "zero tolerance" of drug abuse. His words, which reverberated throughout the Navy: "Not on my watch, not in my division, not in my Navy."

Now, says a Navy spokesman, "We're using all the tools we can"—mandatory urinalyses, drug-detecting dogs, warrant officers with antidrug training and expanded remedial-education programs for drug users. As a result, pot smoking has been cut in half.

contracts." These documents subject them to immediate adverse consequences should they return to drugs.

For example, an accountant gave the clinic a signed confession to be sent to the State Board of Accountancy admitting his habit and surrendering his certification if he resumes cocaine use. Another patient, a staunch Republican, gave a $1,000 check for Senator Edward Kennedy (D-Mass.), to be mailed if the patient goes back on the drug.

"Cocaine Anonymous" groups have been started in various places. The Motion Picture and Television Fund has begun weekly meetings for cocaine users, and the American Federation of Television and Radio Artists has established a 24-hour hot line to help members with drug or alcohol problems.

There are an estimated 5,000 employe-assistance programs in industry, and many are showing signs of success. One example is the Lockheed Corporation's drug-and-alcohol program in Marietta, Ga. Of 1,200 employes enrolled, 43 percent have markedly reduced their absenteeism, and the company's medical payments have dropped 21 percent.

Schools are attacking drug abuse in a variety of ways. Los Angeles schools allow young police officers to pose as students to ferret out dope dealers. In Lewisville, Tex., the high school and its parent-teacher-student association offer rewards to students who provide tips leading to the arrests and convictions of other students using or selling drugs.

Some experts say the best way to reduce drug abuse permanently is to educate people, especially the young, about its dangers. Some 3,000 parent groups around the country are trying to do just that. First Lady Nancy Reagan has made a number of speeches championing their efforts.

Keith Schuchard, research director of the Parent Resources Institute on Drug Education in Atlanta, says the approach is starting to work. Youngsters around the country are particularly worried about scientific reports that marijuana can interfere with sex and growth hormones, she says, adding: "The kids know they're vulnerable, and they're also worried about reproduction."

Still, though drug use has fallen among students, the trend could easily reverse. Dr. Robert DuPont, Jr., former head of the National Institute on Drug Abuse, says the percentage of high-school seniors who perceive marijuana as harmful is rising. "But more than half of them still don't think it's dangerous," he cautions. "So we've got a long way to go."

By SUSANNA McBEE with SARAH PETERSON in Houston and the magazine's other domestic bureaus

Hunting for the Hidden Killers

Disease detectives face a never ending quest

They could not afford to jump to conclusions—any conclusions. Their only hope was to be grindingly, interminably thorough. Otherwise, they could pursue a course of investigation for hours or days, only to find it ended nowhere.
—*The Andromeda Strain* by Michael Crichton

 The enemy is always time—an agonizing reminder of the suffering that can result from staying one step behind an elusive killer. At the outset of each new inquiry, they may not even know the description of their quarry, but its power is often all too evident. Along with old-fashioned legwork and intuitive insights, the specialists use the latest in scientific technology to compile and compare clues about nature's threatening puzzles. Such is the work, such is the mission, such are the stakes for America's disease detectives, whose special calling it is to track invisible killers, to identify mysterious illnesses that erupt from nowhere to menace life and health. Today an elite cadre of these experts—pathologists and epidemiologists, assisted by a larger army of lab technicians and doctors—are coordinating their skills in an effort to conquer a new threat: Acquired Immune Deficiency Syndrome, the confounding killer known as AIDS.

As of last week, there were 1,641 victims of AIDS, including 644 deaths, since it was first identified as a disease in the U.S. two years ago. Each month an average of 165 new cases is reported. The largest concentration of victims is in New York City (732 cases, 284 deaths). San Francisco has the next largest outbreak (160 cases, 54 deaths), followed by Los Angeles (100 cases, 40 deaths). AIDS is spreading, albeit slowly, to other nations; 122 cases have been reported in 17 countries.

AIDS attacks its victims by knocking out the immune system, thus leaving them defenseless against a host of "opportunistic" infections. A rare form of cancer or pneumonia becomes a deadly invader, but so does a fungus or a common virus. Thus far, there is no cure for AIDS and its source remains unknown. "We've looked at a lot of suspects," says Dr. Anthony Fauci of the National Institutes of Health (NIH), "but we have not come up with enough grounds for an indictment."

Asking questions. Hunting for clues. Testing theories. Hitting blind alleys. Asking more questions. The assault on the mystery of AIDS is a prime example of how disease detection works. The foundation has been laid by epidemiologists who have carefully analyzed the spread of the disease. So far, 75.9% of the victims in the U.S. have been active homosexual men, 16% intravenous drug users, 5% immigrants from Haiti, and 1% hemophiliacs. Only 96 victims so far are not known to be members of one of these risk groups. More than 90% of the victims are males between the ages of 20 and 49; young people account for just 1.3%. One cause for concern is that the incubation period of AIDS may be anywhere from six months to three years, and many people may have the disease without knowing it.

T he outbreak of an epidemic* can provoke a primal panic by raising the specter of a rampant "Andromeda strain." Indeed, perhaps the most severe side effect of AIDS has been the largely unwarranted hysteria that has accompanied the syndrome (*see following story*). In order to allay fears that

---

*The classic definition of an epidemic is an outbreak of disease affecting 1% of the population. But most doctors now agree on a newer criterion and declare an epidemic whenever the incidence of a disease rises above its normal "background level," or rate of natural occurrence.

AIDS is widely contagious, Secretary of Health and Human Services Margaret Heckler last week visited the Warren Magnuson Clinical Center in Bethesda, Md., where she shook hands with AIDS victims and sat at their bedsides. Said Heckler: "What's just as bad as the disease is the fear of the disease. The fear has become irrational." Explains Dr. James Curran, head of the AIDS task force at Atlanta's Centers for Disease Control (CDC): "For a person not in a known risk group, the risk is not only minimal but likely to remain minimal. It apparently is not spread through routine contact or through respiration, like the flu." Indeed, none of the hundreds of health-care workers who have treated patients have been infected by AIDS.

Nevertheless, Heckler stressed to the patients that "AIDS is our No. 1 health concern and the epidemic is our No. 1 priority." Her department, which includes CDC and NIH, is spending $14 million on AIDS research this year and requesting $12 million more. Some gay activists have charged that the Reagan Administration is neglecting AIDS because it primarily affects homosexuals. (In fact, the money allocated to AIDS research so far is greater than the $20 million spent over eight years on toxic shock syndrome and Legionnaire's disease.) Heckler's department also publishes a biweekly bulletin reporting the findings of researchers; next week it will start operating a toll-free hotline (800-342-AIDS) to answer questions about the syndrome.

American health officials once dreamed of eliminating infectious diseases, at least in the U.S. That Faustian ambition has been foiled by the mobility of American society, the influx of tourists and immigrants (illegal as well as legal), changes in technology that create new, inviting environments for organisms and, most notably, by casual intimacies encouraged by the sexual revolution. As many as 20 million Americans may now suffer from genital herpes, an incurable but nonfatal disease. In addition, an estimated 1 million new cases of gonorrhea and 100,000 of syphillis are reported each year. "What may be different these days is the number of persons who can be exposed in a short period," says Dr. William Foege, 47, director of the CDC. "The average AIDS victim has had 60 different sexual partners in the past twelve months."

The struggle to conquer such epidemics, and the fear they spread, is the work of a special breed. They are spiritual descendants of Dr. John Snow (1813-58), who tracked the incidence of cholera during the London epidemic of 1831 and stemmed further devastation by shutting down one of the city's water pumps. In the past few decades, his followers have significantly improved the quality of life. In much of the world they have virtually eliminated the threat of such onetime plagues as polio, smallpox, cholera and diphtheria.

Those medical-mystery solvers include general practitioners and specialists who become involved in a particular case because it affects their patients. Others can be found among the nation's state and local public health officers. Researchers at the NIH supply scientific support. Coordinating this network, and indeed serving as the FBI of disease detection and the Interpol for medical sleuths around the globe, are the 4,030 workers at the CDC. The vanguard of this organization is the center's Epidemic Intelligence Service (EIS), which sends out its corps of 120 young, bright and determined investigators around the U.S. and the world. "We see the CDC people as our sort of big brother," says Nevada Health Official Dr. Otto Ravenholt.

The CDC complex near Atlanta belies its importance. Its headquarters are located in a squat suburban brick building, graced in front by a bust of Hygeia, the Greek goddess of health. Some sections are housed in wooden barracks around a former Army hospital. The agency, then known as Malaria Control in War Areas (MCWA), was created in 1942 to find ways to protect U.S. soldiers against malaria. The organization has since taken part in the successful campaign against polio (by pioneering the use of the Salk vaccine), and lessened the threat of rabies (by showing it could be carried by bats). The CDC also conducted nationwide childhood immunization programs for measles, mumps and rubella. Says Director Foege: "Today 5,000 children are running around who would be in their graves if it weren't for these programs."

For all its successes, the CDC has had to fight for funds—including money to set up EIS in 1951—by stressing the national security benefits of the center. In 1981, the White House considered cutting the CDC budget by 23%; Richard Schweiker, who was then HHS Secretary, successfully fought to protect its funds. With the current concern about AIDS, the CDC seems secure for the present; its 1983 budget is $261 million, less than 1% of the amount spent for Medicare and Medicaid.

Each year the CDC accepts 60 or so people involved in health care for a two-year tour of duty with the EIS. "We look for the bright, somewhat aggressive independent thinker," says Dr. Lyle Conrad, head of the division's field service officers. About half are based in Atlanta; the rest are assigned to public health departments around the country, with which the CDC works closely. All are on call 24 hours a day, ready to go wherever a disease breaks out, be it food poisoning or a case of primary pneumonic plague that appeared in 1980 in California (all 185 people who were exposed to the victim were inoculated six hours after the disease was confirmed). After completing their two years, EIS graduates are given a prized emblem of their craft: a key chain with a tiny metal keg of Watney's Red Barrel Beer, served at the John Snow Pub on the site of the infamous water pump in London.

In addition to the 1,000 requests for help that come from state and local agencies each year, the CDC undertakes about 50 projects overseas. Recent examples: tackling a polio epidemic in Indonesia, meningitis in Upper Volta, malaria in Zanzibar, toxic reaction to polluted cooking oil in Spain and observing an immunization program against childhood diseases in China. Dr. Bess Miller, 35, was exhausted from working on the AIDS epidemic last year when the phone at home rang one evening. "My first thought was that they wanted to send me somewhere," she recalls. They did. Soon she was in the Israeli-occupied West Bank investigating a mysterious malady afflicting young Palestinian schoolgirls. Miller and Israeli health officials concluded that the problem was caused by a wave of hysteria; it soon disappeared.

CDC's most sophisticated facility is its Maximum Containment Laboratory, which handles highly lethal diseases that have no known antidotes. Workers, all of whom are volunteers, must punch in a code to open the outer shell of the lab; after a trip through a chemical-shower chamber, they must provide another personal number to gain access to the pressurized inner sanctum. There the scientists wear seamless blue space suits, equipped with their own air filtration systems, to work with some of the world's most lethal microbes, including those that cause Lassa fever and Ebola virus, two maladies that produce severe internal bleeding and are native to Africa. There have been no fatalities in the lab. When a worker is exposed to a disease, he is flown to the Army's Medical Research Institute of Infectious Diseases in Frederick, Md.

Other CDC experts work with Immigration and Naturalization Service officials to prevent exotic diseases from entering the country. Laboratory Director Joseph McCormick, who studied Lassa fever in Sierra Leone, sped to the Atlanta airport in a four-wheel-drive vehicle during a snowstorm last January to pick up a mysteriously ailing passenger from Nigeria. The man was placed in an isolation room until it was certain he was not suffering from one of the deadly viruses.

The case that made the CDC known to the public at large remains a classic in the annals of medical detective work. In July 1976, Pennsylvania chapters of the American Legion held a rollicking convention at Philadelphia's Bellevue Stratford Hotel. In the next few days, eleven Pennsylvanians died, apparently of pneumonia; a Legion officer alerted health authorities that the victims all had attended the convention. A phone call was made to Atlanta for help. Late that night, Dr. Theodore Tsai, an EIS officer, arrived in the state health office, carrying a cooler, to collect blood samples and respiratory secretions. He was the first of 32 CDC officials who worked on the case.

With a malady of unknown cause, the first step is to decide how to define it. "We wanted the definition to be broad enough to include most cases, but not so broad that it would include everybody with a cold," Tsai recalls. Six EIS agents fanned out across the state, questioning other suspected victims. Where did they eat and drink? Were the windows open in their hotel rooms? What events did they attend? A more detailed survey went out to all 4,400 Legionnaires who had attended the convention, and 3,500 were returned within three days. Other agents followed up stray leads, like a call from a magician who admitted lighting a sparkler at the hotel. Back in Atlanta, clinicians noticed the high white blood cell counts in specimens from the victims, and began to search for bacteria under their microscopes.

At first CDC experts suspected an attack of swine flu, which health officials had been fearing that year. But the evidence did not support that hypothesis. Some who had merely walked past the hotel contracted the disease. Yet it was noncontagious: no one caught it from the original 182 victims, 29 of whom died. Nor were any bacteria found. "The picture slowly evolved that we didn't know what we were dealing with," Tsai remembers.

The outbreak vanished as quickly as it began, but researchers at CDC, including Microbiologist Joseph McCade, 43, continued to examine the specimens taken from the victims. Five months after the convention, he took another look at some red sausage-shaped bacteria and concluded that they were the culprits. They had festered in the water of the hotel's cooling tower and had been carried through the air as the water evap-

Sleuthing Is the Fun

He has about him the air of restless energy and dedication that is characteristic of the breed, but his interest was slow to blossom. Son of a chemist from Canton, Mass., Scott Holmberg, 33, majored in English at Harvard. Then he joined the Peace Corps in 1971 and found himself working alone in the desolate villages of Ethiopia, struggling to learn Amharic, the country's language. It was there that the power of science changed his life. He vaccinated tens of thousands of people against smallpox as part of a team that effectively stopped the disease in the area. Many villagers, who believed he was a doctor, came to him with their afflictions, but he could do little to help. Recalls Holmberg: "I was frustrated by not knowing what was going on."

Holmberg sent for his old college biology book (he had received a gentleman's C in the course) and pored over it at night. By the time he returned to the U.S. in 1973, he had decided to become a doctor. In a year of dedicated slogging, he took the necessary preliminary courses and then graduated from Columbia University's medical school. He was determined to join the CDC, much to the amusement and disdain of more success-oriented classmates. "I was called a Goody Two-Shoes," he remembers.

Holmberg became an Epidemic Intelligence Service officer in July 1982. His salary: $38,000. "There is no place in the world to study epidemiology like the CDC," he says. "You can go as far as your curiosity will take you."

That can be pretty far. A month after joining the CDC, Holmberg was on the Pacific island of Truk fighting an outbreak of cholera. For two months he was virtually isolated from his superiors, talking weekly on a short-wave radio to a CDC doctor in Hawaii to report progress and get advice. He and the health officials on Truk discovered that cholera, previously thought to be transmitted only in water, apparently was also being spread by infected people handling food in the victims' homes. Says Holmberg: "Knowing it is a food-borne disease may make quite a difference in how we handle future outbreaks."

Last February the CDC sent Holmberg to Minnesota to help local authorities cope with an outbreak of intestinal disease caused by *Salmonella newport*. Groping for a lead, Holmberg visited several of the victims in their homes. "I stuck my head in their refrigerators. I asked things you would never ask your friends, as nicely as possible, about diarrhea, bowel habits, food preparation, how often they washed their hands, drug use." Working with local health authorities, Holmberg eventually traced the probable cause of the disease to a herd of cows in a muddy field in South Dakota.

Holmberg, who married Maureen Shields, a pediatric nurse, in 1981, has been in the field for three of his eleven months so far with CDC. In Atlanta he spends much of his time analyzing the data he has collected. Holmberg frets occasionally about becoming a workaholic, but clearly loves his job. "The medical sleuthing—that's the most fun. The clues start to fall into place step by step as you go through it." The disease detective's zeal is admired by his superiors. "His is the old hard-work ethic," says Dr. Mitchell Cohen, Holmberg's supervisor. "What we constantly do is pose questions. If one question doesn't pan out, he'll take another approach."

Holmberg has just signed on for another year at CDC. "I'll probably stay in public health one way or another," he says. "I'm going to spend a significant portion of my career in backwoods, dirty places trying to stop diseases that I don't like. That includes all of them."

orated. The antibiotic Erythromycin proved effective in treating the disease, and many similar cooling towers across the country are now chlorinated to guard against another outbreak.

Another famed mystery was solved primarily by the epidemiologists rather than the lab scientists. In January 1980, doctors in Wisconsin and Minnesota noticed that an unusual number of young women were suddenly developing high temperatures and low blood pressure, with potentially fatal results; out of the 55 patients in the CDC's initial study, seven had died by the end of May. Dr. Kathryn Shands of EIS led the CDC investigation, developing a clear definition for what soon became known as toxic shock syndrome and recording in detail all the cases.

A staphylococcus bacterium was clearly the cause of the outbreak, but the medical question was "Why?" Through further epidemiological studies, the medical sleuths found that most of the new cases under investigation involved menstruating women who had been using tampons. A majority had used Procter & Gamble's Rely tampons, a new superabsorbent brand, which may have provided an environment that encouraged bacterial growth. After the product was removed from the market, the number of reported toxic shock cases dropped sharply.

One of the few blemishes on the CDC's record involves an epidemic that never happened. In 1976, swine flu broke out at Fort Dix, N.J., killing one soldier. Health officials worried about the similarity of the virus to one that had caused the deadly 1918 influenza pandemic that killed more than 500,000 Americans. At President Gerald Ford's urging, a $100 million program was rushed into being to immunize people across the country. Not only did no epidemic break out, but 100 or so people came down with a syndrome, apparently connected to the vaccines, that caused partial paralysis. Ninety million unused doses were left over. Officials say that the swine flu debacle was one reason why the Carter Administration decided not to reappoint Dr. David Sencer, who was then the CDC director and is now Commissioner of the New York City Board of Health. Sencer was replaced by Foege, an articulate career public health official from Washington who led the worldwide crusade to eliminate smallpox.

Sometimes serendipity plays a role in discovering a new approach to a familiar disease. Last summer a 42-year-old drug addict, unable to talk, bent over and hardly able to move, was brought to the Santa Clara Valley Medical Center. His symptoms were similiar to those of patients afflicted with Parkinson's disease, which usually affects the elderly. Dr. William Langston speculated that the cause might be something in the heroin that the victim used. The doctor and his team were able to track down others who had used the same batch of the drug and found similar reactions. Through a chance conversation with another doctor, help from police, and tips resulting from a newspaper story, Langston uncovered other cases and obtained samples of the bad drug.

Several months later Langston read an article in a medical journal about a chemist who had killed himself after contracting Parkinson's-like symptoms from a dose of artificial heroin. From a report analyzing the dead chemist's brain, Langston found that the heroin involved contained an additive similar to the one in the bad batch of heroin he had been studying. The mysterious ingredient, a chemical known as MPTP, had moved from the blood into the brain and damaged the same area affected by Parkinson's disease. No other substance is known to do that. Last April Dr. Irwin Kopin of the National Institute of Mental Health, co-author of the journal article, announced that he had used MPTP to induce Parkinsonism in rhesus monkeys. The work of these two men suggests that the previously unexplained symptoms of Parkinson's might result from exposure to MPTP, and thus that the disease itself may be caused by environmental factors.

Nothing in the history of disease detection compares in size or intensity with the chase now under way to solve the mystery of AIDS. It began in early 1981, when Dr. Michael Gottlieb of U.C.L.A. told Los Angeles health officials that he had five patients, all of them active homosexuals, who were suffering from an unusual and deadly form of pneumonia, *pneumocystis carinii*. More alarming still, their immune systems seemed to have broken down. Gottlieb and an EIS agent based in Los Angeles reported the grim news in CDC's weekly publication. Almost simultaneously, Dr. Alvin Friedman-Kien of New York University noted that several of his homosexual patients had the same weakened immune systems and were suffering from Kaposi's sarcoma, a rare cancer of the skin usually seen only in older men. Later that summer Dr. Harold Jaffe of CDC, while attending a conference in California, was told of an additional case of a young homosexual suffering from Kaposi's.

"We were struck by how strange this was," recalls Jaffe. A group of medical detectives at the CDC was organized into an AIDS task force under the direction of Dr. Curran, a venereal disease specialist. They quickly uncovered 50 cases around the country that fit the definition of what the CDC officially dubbed AIDS. Initially it seemed that the culprit might be amyl nitrate or butyl nitrate, often known as "Rush" or "poppers," which are inhalants that provide a short-lasting high. But a study comparing homosexuals with AIDS to disease-free gays showed little correlation with use of the drug. The 20-page questionnaire disclosed, however, that AIDS victims tended to be sexually promiscuous. In addition, some were the passive partners in anal intercourse.

Then came another clue: reports of drug abusers, most of them heterosexual, coming down with AIDS. This added credence to the theory that a virus or some other infectious agent, transmitted by dirty needles as well as by sexual contact, might be the cause. This conjecture was supported by evidence that sexual partners of drug users, and even a few children of those with the disease, had contracted what seemed to be AIDS. So had a few hemophiliacs and blood-transfusion recipients. One baby in San Francisco with symptoms of AIDS, it was discovered, had been given blood from a donor who turned out to have the disease.

The strongest evidence that an infectious agent was on the loose came from what has been called the Los Angeles cluster. Interviewing victims, investigators began compiling the names of their sex partners. Three different men, none of whom knew each other, each mentioned the same man in New York City; he turned out to be an AIDS victim. Since then, 40 cases in ten cities have been linked to one another by sexual relationships.

The next clue was confusing. Immigrants from Haiti turned up with AIDS. Not only was this puzzling—many claimed they were neither homosexuals nor drug users—but the discovery raised special problems for the epidemiologists. Homosexuality is scorned in Haiti, and the victims were reluctant to talk about their sexual habits. The language barrier also played a role; it was hard for investigators to describe in Creole—the everyday patois of Haiti—the homosexual acts in question, particularly since the same word applies to both homosexuality and transvestism. Many of the immigrants were in the U.S. illegally, and thus understandably reluctant to talk to Government agents about anything.

The Haitian connection is still puzzling. The disease apparently broke out on the impoverished Caribbean isle in 1981, at about the same time as it did in the U.S. Some experts suspect that AIDS is caused by a newly introduced viral agent from Africa, where Kaposi's is common, and may have been transmitted by Haitians who once worked in Zaïre. Port-au-Prince has many popular gay bars, and the disease could have been brought back to the U.S. by visiting Americans—or taken to Haiti by Americans in the first place. Recent investigations suggest that the disease is probably transmitted in Haiti, much as it is in the U.S., by homosexual activity or by dirty needles, and that Haitians have no more propensity for the disease than victims in the U.S.

As the search and speculation went on, researchers in U.S. labs added their own clues: the blood of AIDS victims has an imbalance among the cells that help govern the production of antibodies. A normal immune system has twice as many helper T-cells, which stimulate the making of antibodies, as it does suppressor T-cells, which keep antibody production under control. In an AIDS victim, the ratio may be reversed. Often there are fewer cells of both types.

Based on what is known so far, two theories have emerged. One is that AIDS is caused by a specific agent, most probably a virus. "The infectious-agent hypothesis is much stronger than it was months ago," says Curran, reflecting the prevailing opinion at CDC. NIH Researcher Fauci, who staunchly believes that the culprit is a virus, has been collecting helper T-cells from AIDS victims to look for bits of viruses within their genetic codes. So far, however, this and other complex methods of detecting viruses have yielded nothing conclusive. Suspicion focuses on two viruses: one is a member of the herpes family called CMV; the other, called human T-cell leukemia virus, or HTLV, is linked to leukemia and lymphoma.

The other theory is that the immune system of AIDS victims is simply overpowered by the assault of a variety of infections. Both drug users and active homosexuals are continually bombarded by a gallery of illnesses. Repeated exposure to the herpes virus, or to sperm entering the blood after anal intercourse, can lead to elevated levels of suppressor T-cells. The immune system eventually is so badly altered that, as one researcher puts it, "the whole thing explodes." Other experts combine the two theories, speculating that a new virus may indeed be involved, but that it only takes hold when a combination of factors affects the potential victim, such as an imbalanced immune system or certain genetic characteristics.

Whatever theory may prove to be correct, the research has provided inspiration for fresh studies by epidemiologists. The levels of T-cells, the presence of HTLV and CMV viruses, and the swelling of lymph glands are regarded as possible "markers" that indicate the early stages of AIDS. At the New York Blood Center, Dr. Cladd Stevens and Friedman-Kien are examining the blood of homosexuals who do not have AIDS to see what factor might be unique to those who do develop the syndrome. By chance they have thousands of samples of blood, 1,500 of them from homosexuals now being studied, which were collected in 1979 for an unrelated hepatitis-B project. To date, 18 men in the survey have developed AIDS.

No cure is in sight. But the research already has benefited some patients. New knowledge about the immune system has inspired doctors to be more careful when treating Kaposi's to use therapies that do not lead to further suppression of the immune system. Fauci of NIH has conducted a bone marrow transplant that bolsters a patient's immune system. Along with many other researchers, he is testing the effects on AIDS patients of new forms of interferon, a component of the human immune system that can now be reproduced by genetic engineering.

Despite the concern about the death and suffering of its victims, and despite the lack of any solution so far, health officials are optimistic that science will eventually conquer AIDS. "We've beaten other diseases, and we're determined to beat this one too," says HHS Secretary Heckler.

Heckler's opinion, which is shared by many medical detectives, is rooted in a century of victories over diseases whose ravages once shaped the course of history. Only a few decades ago, fear of a polio outbreak could empty schools; victims in iron lungs would be put on exhibit in small towns to raise money for the March of Dimes. All that is history now.

Optimism about AIDS is bolstered by new weapons being added to the medical arsenal. Interferon holds the promise of retarding the growth of cancerous cells. Potentially as powerful is a process that creates new cells called hybridomas. Cells that build antibodies against specific diseases are fused with tumor cells to make hybrids, which have the durability of tumors and the power to create antibodies. These cells may eventually be used to develop vaccines that will protect humans against new diseases and can help the body fight certain cancers.

Nevertheless, optimism is tempered by knowledge that the struggle against disease never ends. Of the deadly African Ebola virus, Foege says: "What keeps it from spreading here? I don't know." Thus research work on Ebola at Atlanta's Maximum Containment Lab goes on. Another potential threat is a subviral particle that combines with the hepatitis-B virus to cause more severe infections and liver cancer. Discovered in 1977, this so-called Delta agent is starting to show up in high-risk groups, including some of the same ones who develop AIDS. Even the victory over smallpox permits no complacency. In its place, a disease called monkeypox has erupted in Africa. "It's probably a disease that's been around a long time but has been masked by smallpox," Foege says. "Once you get rid of one disease, a new one becomes visible."

Then there are the scourges that have always been with us, the Legionnaire's bacteria that suddenly find an environment in which to flourish anew momentarily, or the influenza virus that undergoes minor mutations to spring forth with renewed vigor. Indeed, of all the potential disease agents looming on the horizon, it is the familiar flu virus that worries Foege the most. "I fully anticipate that possibly in our lifetime we will see another flu strain that is as deadly as 1918. We have not figured out good ways to counter that." The same holds for the most common of bacteria and viruses, like the staphylococcus, which are adept at evolving into new forms.

"Just a few years ago, in an excess of *hubris,* I predicted we were nearly finished with the problem of infection," Dr. Lewis Thomas, noted biologist and prizewinning author (*The Lives of a Cell*), observed recently. "I take it back." Through the heroic struggle of medical sleuths, most diseases faced today can be controlled, as some day AIDS will be. But microbes, which have existed on this planet far longer than man, show no signs of being unconditionally conquered. Amid the billions that exist harmoniously around us, there will always be some that become unexpectedly disruptive, mysteriously virulent. Said Thomas: "There is a lot more research to be done, not just about AIDS but into infectious diseases in general. We have not run out of adversaries, nor is it likely we will do so for a long time to come." Thus the disease detectives must keep pounding the pavement, peering through microscopes, asking their questions. —*By Walter Isaacson. Reported by Joseph N. Boyce/Atlanta and Peter Stoler/-Washington, with other bureaus*

The Real Epidemic: Fear and Despair

AIDS isolates many of its victims and is changing the gay life-style

In Manhattan last week a WABC-TV crew refused to enter the Gay Men's Health Crisis office to cover a story on AIDS. Two back-up crews also balked at going in. Said one of the technicians: "Look, nobody knows anything about AIDS. What makes them so cocksure I'm not going to get it from a sweaty palm?" One of the homosexuals in the office had a question of his own: "Do you understand now that we're treated like lepers?"

As the deaths from AIDS-related diseases continue to rise, so does hysteria about possible contagion. AIDS victims and members of high-risk groups—male homosexuals, Haitians, hemophiliacs and intravenous drug users—are being shunned by their communities, their fellow workers, and sometimes their friends and families. Three nurses at a hospital in San Jose, Calif., quit rather than deal with AIDS cases; some staff members at San Francisco General Hospital refused to carry trays to such patients.

About half of the dentists in San Francisco, which has had 160 known AIDS cases, now wear some protective covering, usually rubber gloves, while treating "high-risk" patients. "It's awkward," admits Dr. Gerald Fraser, "but there's no way around it." According to the American Dental Association, gloves are not enough: its council on dental therapeutics recommends that dentists and their assistants wear masks and eye coverings as well while treating their patients.

As more and more homosexuals contract AIDS, gay men in general are encountering a new strain of prejudice. One family, dining in a San Bernardino restaurant, demanded that an effeminate waiter be fired on the spot. Several conservatives, including Columnist Pat Buchanan, have raised the question of whether homosexuals should be barred from all food-handling jobs, and diners in several cities boycotted restaurants rumored to have gay chefs. A New York City prison official conceded that there is no evidence linking AIDS to food handling; nonetheless, to calm other prisoners, he barred "overt homosexuals" from food lines. One AIDS victim, having dinner at the home of a homosexual friend in Los Angeles, noticed that he was the only guest whose food was served on a paper plate.

A Worcester, Mass., woman wondered if she should banish her gay son from her home, just on the chance he might have AIDS. Half of the chorus at the San Francisco opera, which used to share supplies of base makeup, now bring their own from home. One Atlanta woman is careful to take her own soap and towels on each visit to her health club. In San Francisco, one man with AIDS was induced to leave a jury by those chosen to serve with him. Two other AIDS victims scheduled to appear on a local TV show were instead relegated to the makeup room where they had to field questions by telephone. The purpose of the show: to ease anxiety over AIDS.

Haitians are especially feeling the pressure. One Miami shoe store refused to let a Haitian customer try on shoes unless he bought them. Employers and landlords in several cities have asked officials for permission to fire or evict Haitians, some of whom have learned to reassure employers and associates by claiming they are from French-speaking Martinique. Montreal's 34,000-member Haitian community, which represents the largest group of blacks in town, fears that AIDS will touch off a serious wave of race hatred. Local cab companies, which employ about 800 Haitian drivers, say that many customers specify *pas de noirs* (no blacks) as drivers.

Undertakers are wary of handling AIDS victims, arguing that contact with blood is inevitable during embalming. The New York State Funeral Directors Association urges members not to take AIDS cases until the government steps in with guidelines. New York's Governor Mario Cuomo responded by proposing a bill that could terminate the license of any funeral director who refuses AIDS victims. "People don't even want to bury us when we're dead," says William Runyon, who lost his job at a Minneapolis blood-products laboratory when he got AIDS. "It makes you feel real useless."

Hospitals and blood banks still lack a consistent policy on homosexual blood donors. Several communities discourage such donations. The New York Blood Center asks homosexuals who have had multiple sex partners not to give blood, and the American Red Cross, which collects about half of the 12 million units of blood given each year, now excludes "all sexually active homosexuals." Dr. Alvin Friedman-Kien of New York University, who studies blood transmission data, points out that of 10 million transfusions in the past three years, only ten have been linked, even tenuously, to AIDS cases. Jo-hanna Pyndyck of the New York Blood Center insists, "We don't have to worry about the nation's blood supply being contaminated." Still, some doctors are privately advising patients and friends to make a list of acquaintances with the same blood type, just in case an emergency transfusion is needed.

The Red Cross last week reported a 16.1% slump in blood collections and cited a variety of reasons including "misinformation about AIDS." "Some people are scared of donating for reasons that are not apparent," says Dr. Alfred Katz, executive director of blood services. "There is absolutely no association between AIDS and donating blood. We can't say that loudly enough." Last week the Red Cross put out a call for healthy donors.

Male homosexuals, the group at greatest risk, have been devastated by the AIDS attacks. In New York and California, centers of the outbreak, every gay man seems to have known someone who has died. Philip Lanzaratta, 41, of New York City knows 27 men who have succumbed to AIDS, and now Lanzaratta may be dying of AIDS himself. He continues to work. A woman who is aware of his condition hired him for her travel agency. Says Lanzaratta's longtime lover, John Lunning: "If it weren't for his strength, I'd jump out the window."

In homosexual communities, groups have sprung up to help AIDS victims. Says New York Psychologist Harold Kooden: "For many, this has been their first non-sexualized way of relating to other gay men." One such group is Seattle's Chicken Soup Brigade, which cooks and runs errands for AIDS patients and other gays who are unable to care for themselves. "We've got to make life easier for these people. They don't have much time left," says D.M. Joshua. "I'm concerned with my gay brethren, dammit!"

Because of the long incubation period, no sexually active homosexual can be sure he does not already have the disease. Says Jim Fishman of Boston, a psychiatric social worker whose case load is 70% homosexual: "Nine out of ten calls I get are related to AIDS, and anything will set these men off—a lingering cough, a blotch on the skin, you name it. Talk of suicide is not unusual at all. The common response is, 'If I get AIDS, I'll kill myself.'" Paul Di Angelo, a Boston pastry chef who has AIDS, is depressed by the possibility that his lover may have it too.

"It's frightening," he says. "I need him now, to love and support me. Both of us being sick at the same time is a devastating thought."

Some AIDS victims face a second trauma: having to tell their parents that they are gay as well as suffering from the disease. The mother of Charles Barden learned he was a homosexual from a front-page story in the Atlanta *Journal and Constitution.* "My phone rang and Mom was in tears," says Barden. "I didn't want to tell them. I didn't want to hurt them."

AIDS has clearly changed the rules of the sexual game for homosexuals. Anonymous and casual sex can be fatal. Says Mel Rosen of the Gay Men's Health Crisis: "People are saying, 'If I only want to go to bed with someone once, then I won't go to bed with them at all.'" Says Craig Rowland, 34, of Manhattan: "You're always looking at a potential partner and thinking, Is this the one who will kill me?" Rowland screens out men who look rundown, or who have suspicious strawberry marks associated with some forms of AIDS. "Then I get his health history. I say, I'm concerned about my health and I'd like to know about yours."

Some gays are attempting to remain celibate or turning their attention to older partners, on the theory that AIDS is likely to strike younger, more sexually active men. Others have set up sexual collectives, usually groups of three to twelve men, who promise to have sex only within the group. All twelve men in a Fort Lauderdale group, aged 23 to 63, see the same gay doctor every other month to test for venereal disease and hepatitis.

On the coasts, where most of the AIDS cases have occurred, business at gay bars reportedly is down 10% to 20%, and attendance at bathhouses is off 10% to 50%. The Club Bath Chain, which operates in 43 cities, says that New York and San Francisco are "a disaster," down more than 50%, with Boston and Baltimore off 20% and Houston 15%. San Francisco recommends that bath owners display signs warning about the danger of AIDS, and even some gays have proposed that the baths be closed as a health hazard. "It's suicidal to go to the baths—they're dark and filthy," says Arthur Bell, a gay columnist for New York City's trendy, leftist *Village Voice.*

Gay groups are promoting the use of condoms, even though their effectiveness in protecting against AIDS has not been established. At Walgreen's drug store in the heart of gay San Francisco, Pharmacist Steve Margules says his business shows the change in homosexual behavior: prescriptions for venereal disease are down, but sales of prophylactics are way up. "I

sell through orders as fast as I can get them in," he says.

Some footloose gays are turning to monogamy. Peter Schiffman, 30, a Manhattan ad salesman, says he was encouraged to fidelity by his terrified boyfriend, who is "totally freaked out by AIDS." For many homosexuals accustomed to having many partners, staying faithful to one lover is not an option. New York Psychiatrist Norman Levy says he sees more gay patients in therapy these days because "they have become aware that they had become addicted to anonymous sex as a way of coping with stress and tension." For some, the allure of the unknown stranger is too strong, or the idea of social life without instant sex is unthinkable. Says Atlanta Gay Activist Frank Scheuren: "The tradition in the gay community is that you have sex first, then talk."

Still, Scheuren sees a trend toward calmer and more cautious sex lives. "There is even an effort to start courtships again," he says. At gay bars and parties, there is far more hand holding and the sort of coy romance usually associated with heterosexuality. Says Los Angeles Gay Activist Steve Schulte: "The sex object will become a love object; gays will find new ways to be affectionate with one another, and new ways to be erotic."

The AIDS reaction has its dark side. The gay culture is awash with rumors of unnamed victims who are purposely trying to infect as many others as possible. And some homosexuals have become increasingly reckless in response to the crisis. Three San Francisco therapists distributed questionnaires to 1,000 gays last March. While 30% of the 600 respondents had become more cautious in their sex lives, 10% said they had increased high-risk sexual behavior since learning of AIDS. One of the therapists, Psychologist William Horstman, calls the group "fatalistic risk enhancers," who offer such explanations as "I'm already exposed, so it doesn't matter any more." "I don't think the gay world is as concerned as the straight world," says Steve McPartland, 29, who has AIDS and writes a Q. & A. column on the subject for *Gay Community News,* a Boston weekly. "I go to the bars and nothing has changed. Most gay men, it seems to me, are not altering their lifestyles . . . I don't understand it."

Some of the recklessness, says Psychologist Rhonda Linde of the Boston AIDS Action Committee, is a way of coping with fear and also defying the medical establishment, which is urging the homosexual to change his life. "Such a man," she says, "may step up the frequency with which he has anonymous sex." Homosexuals are now under heavy

psychological pressure, she says, because "AIDS can kill you, and when you start equating sex with death, you're treading on emotionally sensitive ground."

Though Europe has only occasional scattered cases of AIDS, many members of gay communities now regard warily American homosexuals or nationals who have recently been to the U.S. Homosexuals at Cambridge University complain of cool treatment from their friends after returning from study at American universities. Says one: "No one is panicking, but there seems to be the feeling, 'Why take the risk?'" West Germany has 20 AIDS cases, and an American homosexual in Berlin says, "Guys from the United States are unpopular. Pulling trade in Berlin has become quite difficult of late." Some U.S. experts believe that Berlin, a center for homosexuals, will be the center for the first major outbreak of AIDS on the Continent.

For homosexuals, the AIDS scare is also a political setback: after a decade of social gains and increasing tolerance, gays are suddenly pariahs again. "What we're seeing here is the re-diseasing of homosexuality," says Rick Crane, program director at San Francisco's AIDS/Kaposi's Sarcoma Research and Education Foundation. "We get everything from fundamentalist crap about AIDS being a moral scourge to pseudo concern for gays," says Los Angeles' Schulte. "There's this soft, ugly underside that gets fed by the AIDS scare. It's scarier than the disease, because that kind of stigmatizing will outlast the disease."

Last week the Rev. Greg Dixon of the Moral Majority wrote: "If homosexuals are not stopped, they will in time infect the entire nation, and America will be destroyed." Some gays are beginning to feel a moral responsibility for AIDS. Says the Rev. Jay Deacon, a homosexual minister in Chicago: "There's a lot of 'This is God's judgment on wicked sinners—the Sodomites are being judged.' Intellectually people don't buy that, but in their guts there's a lot of guilt." The threat of AIDS can awaken old doubts about the homosexual life, or sexual activity in general. Says Fishman of Boston's AIDS Action Committee: "Many men have internalized social and moral judgments that being gay, and/or being sexually active, is sinful."

Unquestionably AIDS is reshaping homosexual communities and pushing many toward mainstream mores, just as the herpes epidemic has restricted the sexual adventuring of many straights. The sexual revolution clearly is not over, but the '80s are proving to be a dangerous decade both for gays and straights who like casual sex and plenty of it. —*By John Leo. Reported by Elizabeth Taylor/New York and Dick Thompson/San Francisco, with other bureaus*

A Key to Unlock the Asylum?

Jean Bethke Elshtain

Jean Bethke Elshtain teaches political theory at the University of Massachusetts at Amherst and is a frequent contributor to The Nation.

The rights of mentally retarded people to decent and effective care have never received much support from an indifferent society and budget-conscious legislatures. Last month the U.S. Supreme Court tossed out as unconstitutionally vague a patients' "bill of rights" section in the Federal Developmentally Disabled Assistance and Bill of Rights Act of 1975, which provides Federal aid to state mental institutions. Upon pain of losing Federal funding under the act, the State of Pennsylvania had been ordered by a lower court to transfer patient from the Pennhurst State School, where conditions were found to be "abominable," to community-care facilities.

The callousness of the Supreme Court's ruling aside [see editorial, "Retarded Rights," *The Nation,* May 9], the case itself reflected the growing popularity of community-based therapy as an alternative to confinement in large, centralized facilities.

Deinstitutionalization has been called by its supporters a "social revolution" whose aim is to empty state hospitals for the mentally ill, the retarded, the "deviant." All such institutions will be closed down, and their patients reintegrated into the broader community. Institutionalization, once seen as a humane solution to problems of the mentally handicapped, has itself become a problem, they argue. Rather than providing therapy and care that aims at sending a well-equipped individual back into the world, institutions destroy social skills and reinforce the most destructive patterns of behavior. One advocate of deinstitutionalization, Benedict Alper, claims that "the institution as a means of coping with the problems of specific sectors of our population seems at this point to have run its course. Whether one is aged, below par intellectually or emotionally, delinquent, alcoholic, or drug-addicted, the source—and the remedy—of the problem lies in the communities where such people come from." Alper, and those who share his views, offer an alternative vision of therapeutic communities, with diverse social support facilities and halfway homes, training institutions and rehabilitative residences, that would reach out to embrace the once shunned, excluded, shut-away and ostracized.

Critics of community care argue that it is absurd to see institutions, per se, as evil, though many were and still are. Many "clients," they say, require sophisticated care available only in a total, structured setting. They insist, moreover, that deinstitutionalization programs have so far been half-baked and careless. The elderly, the mentally ill or the incompetent, juvenile offenders— all have been "dumped" into communities that are suspicious, hostile and completely unprepared for them. The result, they say, has been chaos, as the following news items attest:

> Federal mental health planners envisioned the flowering of a network of support services to care for deinstitutionalized patients at the community level through the stimulus of Federal seed money. But 1,300 of the 2,000 community health centers projected for 1980 have failed to materialize and many that did have failed to service this chronically ill population. Deinstitutionalization, an ostensibly humane treatment program, has degenerated into a tragic crisis. Public scrutiny of the situation needs to begin now
> —*The New York Times*, January 26, 1980

> Increasing numbers of patients discharged from mental institutions are entering nursing homes, an ironic result of the restructuring of health care financing and legislation to encourage the removal of patients from mental institutions and to promote a continuum of health care services on the community level. . . . An NIMH (National Institute of Mental Health) workgroup report analyzes the problems that beset the delivery of mental health services in certified nursing homes and raises serious questions about the adequacy of care received by mentally ill patients, particularly the mentally ill elderly.
> —*National Health Standards Clearinghouse Information Bulletin*, August 1980

> De-institutionalized mental patients have so overwhelmed the new facilities at Boston's famous Pine Street Inn that admission of guests will be limited to homeless men and women with no other options. . . . While the problem is not new . . . the number of patients seeking shelter has increased so much . . . that "they are driving out the people we were established to serve." Testifying at a State House hearing last

year, Kip Tiernan, founder of Rosie's Place, a 10-bed survival home for women . . . said that women mental patients were being discharged from state hospitals with "no more than a piece of paper in their hands giving out our address."
—*Boston Globe,* August 21, 1980

A brief history of how we have arrived at the current impasse is instructive. By the late eighteenth century the market relations of early capitalist society had already exerted a corrosive effect on traditional social relations, including kinship ties and communities. The reciprocal ties of the old feudal and land-based system, which dictated both dependence and aid between dominant and subordinate classes, had broken down. No longer could society rely upon this network to make provision, however inadequate, for those individuals within the community who were chronically ill, mentally incompetent, or infirm. As the numbers of dependent and "maladjusted" grew, the now fragmented traditional community could no longer cope. Social reformers hoped to solve the problem by creating institutions—workhouses, asylums, hospitals, reformatories and so on—to treat, succor, rehabilitate and punish. David Rothman, in his book *The Discovery of the Asylum,* has documented the headlong rush toward institutionalization in the America of the 1840s and 1850s. According to Rothman, "One can properly label the Jacksonian years the 'age of the asylum.' " He continues: "The asylum was to fulfill a dual purpose for its innovators. It would rehabilitate inmates and then, by virtue of its success, set an example of right action for the larger society. There was a utopian flavor to this first venture, one that looked to reform the deviant and dependent and to serve as a model for others. The well-ordered asylum would exemplify the proper principles of social organization and thus . . . insure the safety of the republic.''

What went wrong? The supporters of deinstitutionalization attempt to answer that question by insisting that institutionalization per se is suspect, regardless of the quality of care, the staff-client ratio and all the rest. It is suspect, in their minds, because of its denial of individual freedom. This acute focus on "the individual," which was a prime concern of the 1960s counterculture, helped to spur widespread investigations and exposés of the abuses of total institutions. The image of the asylum as a place of refuge gave way to the image of the coercive institution that stripped individuals of their civil rights and forced them to undergo what the sociologist Erving Goffman called "rituals of degradation." They were drugged into passivity, the better to "manage" them. Some critics went so far as to deny altogether that humanitarian impulses created asylums in the first place.

Anything, these critics urged, would be better than "this." And patients, for the most part, agreed. Almost to a person, patients on the outside—those who are willing and able to convey their experiences—say that despite all the "hassles" and inadequate facilities on the "outside," they prefer this "least restrictive environment" to that most restrictive of all, the total institution. And, of course, one

must agree that these patients' civil rights and liberties must have top priority in any evaluation of deinstitutionalization.

The problem with many "freedom of the patient" advocates, however, is their exclusive preoccupation with freedom *from* total control. They neglect any consideration of what freedom is *for*—what should be done to guarantee patients employment, housing, education, therapy and decent lives. Despite this inadequate appreciation of what freedom means, there is no doubt that a genuine concern with civil and social rights has been, and remains an essential part of, the deinstitutionalization effort. Like the original advocates of institutionalization, supporters of community care also see themselves as humanitarians.

Unfortunately, the authentic humanitarian impulse behind deinstitutionalization was soon tainted by a concern with reducing expenditures for the care and support of clients. State and local governments faced with severe fiscal crises were tempted to clear out the wards of state institutions. Their already enormous labor expenditures had burgeoned with the unionization of state employees, which "virtually doubled unit costs," according to sociologist P. R. Dingman. Court decisions that forbade the use of unpaid patient labor and set minimal standards for treatment necessitated additional expenditures. Dingman claims: "Rising costs more than any other factor have made it obvious that support of state hospitals is politically unfeasible . . . that is the principal factor behind the present push to get rid of state hospitals.''

Humanitarian arguments for deinstitutionalization are caricatured if they are seen as mere cover for economizing. Nonetheless, advocates of care in the community—at least in the state bureaucracies working toward dismantling institutional systems—have been forced by economic logic into a compromise position that threatens to overshadow humane considerations. Fiscal logic won the day in California's big push to deinstitutionalize while Ronald Reagan was governor, as it did during New York's disastrous early experiences under Nelson Rockefeller. The Massachusetts effort has been more complex. The state has made a serious, though wholly inadequate, attempt to create actual community support facilities. But that fiscal logic has begun to seem inexorable; as it gains wider adherence, the movement toward deinstitutionalization gains a blind momentum, like a locomotive out of control. The idea is irresistible: "Be a good guy and save money!" Recently the Massachusetts chief of Human Services, Charles Mahoney, inadvertently expressed the duality of motives behind deinstitutionalization when he commented that the alternative treatment "saves money and allows some otherwise 'hopeless' patients to make progress.''

Given the current condition of the American political economy, and the proliferation of taxpayer revolts, saving money becomes the overriding preoccupation, and the deinstitutionalized individual fades into the murky shadows of social concern. In the words of Andrew Scull, author of *Decarceration:*

The promise of . . . cost savings largely explains the

curious political alliance which has fostered and supported decarceration. Social policies which allegedly benefit the poorest and most desperate segments of the community do not ordinarily arouse particular enthusiasm among the so-called fiscal conservatives. The goal of returning mental patients to the community is clearly an exception, for in addition to the liberal adherents one might expect, it has attracted prominent, sometimes decisive support from their ranks.

And so the original critics of deinstitutionalization have been joined by those who have observed its effects—the plight of former clients and the pressures on communities where the deinstitutionalized have been "dumped" in large numbers. These critics claim that the result has been to "warehouse" people in smaller, less centralized institutions, rather than to free them. They stress the inadequacy of current community care and point out that the communities into which former patients are supposedly integrated are themselves deteriorating.

Finally, the current critics claim the massive effort to deinstitutionalize has put enormous pressure on the poorest urban neighborhoods and on lower-income sections in smaller towns and cities. Some neighborhoods, according to a report issued by the Health Planning Council for Greater Boston, dated September 18, 1980, have become "saturated with a disproportionate number of residences while wealthier and more politically astute communities have resisted the burgeoning of such services in their areas. Resentment seems rampant in both types of communities."

To be sure, much of this resentment is sheer prejudice and fear of the unknown. But the point here is that the less well off are once again paying the social costs of liberal reform. Deinstitutionalized clients are being ghettoized in poor neighborhoods while residents in middle- and upper-middle-income communities enact restrictive zoning ordinances in order to avoid assuming their share of the social burden. Social critics Julian and Eileen Wolpert have noted that "the growing ghettoization of the returning ex-patients along with other dependent groups in the population; the growing succession of inner-city land use to institutions providing services to the dependent and needy; . . . the forced immobility of the chronically disabled within deteriorated urban neighborhoods" have all been exacerbated by deinstitutionalization.

What, then, is to be done? Despite all the possible abuses and difficulties, by any reckoning of human rights and social good, adequate community care is the preferable route for most if not all in need of special treatment and attention. But this social logic must not be undermined by market imperatives. For the truth of the matter is that if deinstitutionalization is to work as it ought, we would need a complex system of social support services that would cost *more* than the present massive institutions, with their drugged-out populations.

For deinstitutionalization to work, the following social services, minimally, on all levels and in all communities, are necessary: day care, day treatment, education of the mentally retarded and other developmentally disabled individuals, family service programs providing parent counseling, housing for family visitations, transportation allowances, health education, medical and dental rehabilitation, psychiatric and psychological services, remedial schooling, vocational training, adoption services for hard-to-place children, after-care programs, aggressive preventive medicine, community-based group homes, community liaison workers, community residences, jobs for all—juveniles through the elderly—and so on. This sort of comprehensive system, because it would rely on the therapeutic power of human compassion, would represent a complex social challenge and a great social achievement.

It is clear that current deinstitutionalization efforts, even the best, come nowhere close to this vision. If it is true that one can judge a society by how it treats its most ill, vulnerable and dependent members, our society, and the political economy that spawned it, must be judged very harshly indeed by even minimal standards of decency and justice.

Future

What does the future hold? World peace? Economic prosperity? Healthy children? Decent housing? Equal and ample education? A government effective in handling social problems? All those issues formed the basis of the American dream a generation ago, but not all were realized. The future will most likely bring new social problems that will continue to confound society's efforts for success.

One approach to the future is to trace the prospective paths of social movements which exist today. The opening selections show how society might look in the future. The article on divorce and families fifty years from now describes how today's problems might become tomorrow's socially accepted behavior.

Members of society in the future may look back on the present differently than the way we look back on the past. While we blame social problems on prejudices, racism, and class distinctions, the future may blame us for physical problems: toxic waste, poisoned water, and radiation. Some members of society regard the past as a period that was uneducated and unscientific. Society in the future may condemn our abuses of education and technology for leaving behind so much pollution and so little resources. In short, the twenty-first century may look back and see present times as the unwise and wasteful period of the industrial labor society.

Several selections about the government, energy, the economy, and foreign affairs examine current problems and urge you to form your own conclusions about the future. The article on Japan is useful for developing a different perspective on how another industrial society is beginning to doubt its progress. Another article questions the assumptions used in the development of our foreign policy and stresses that business must *not* continue as usual.

Looking Ahead: Challenge Questions

What is a realistic method for predicting the future?

How might today's crises become tomorrow's typical behavior?

How might today's achievements become tomorrow's problems?

How must our society change its current attitudes in order to succeed in the future?

Japan and the United States are trading partners. How will changes in Japan affect the United States in the future?

What problems might a retired person have to face in the future?

In the future, will society be able to clean up the environment? Or will our wastefulness be a fact of their lives?

Inheriting the Earth

Joseph P. Martino

Joseph Martino, a member of the Technology Forecasting Group at the University of Dayton Research Institute, has degrees in physics, electrical engineering, and mathematics. He is an associate editor of Technological Forecasting and Social Change.

How are the interests of future generations to be protected? How are we to keep our grandchildren from inheriting a polluted environment and exhausted natural resources?

The prevailing answer among futurists might be summarized as follows:

"It's not the case that if people are free to make their own decisions things will work out okay. People are short-sighted. They discount the future very heavily. No matter how concerned in the abstract with the world their grandchildren will inherit, people are willing to take a profit now without regard to the costs if those costs can be postponed long enough.

"Nor is it just a matter of a few selfish individuals. If it benefited all of us now living, we might be willing to use up some irreplaceable resource, thus denying it to our grandchildren. Or we might dump some toxic waste that they will have to clean up.

"Someone has to speak up for the future! We cannot depend upon short-sighted people, each looking out for his own interests, to take care of the future. We must limit freedom to the extent necessary to assure that we don't benefit ourselves at the expense of the future."

This is the solution proposed by most futurists. Since the future can't vote now, our descendants must be given a vote through the political process. In particular, some of our welfare must be sacrificed to increase the welfare of future generations. And this sacrifice must be imposed by the far-sighted on the short-sighted if future generations are to come into a decent world.

Futurists thus tend to arrive at the conclusion that only governmental intervention can protect the interests of the long-term future. Writes futurist Daniel Bell, in his book *The Cultural Contradictions of Capitalism*: "The decisive social change taking place in our time—because of the interdependence of men and the aggregative character of economic actions, the rise of externalities and social costs, and the need to control the effects of technical change—is the subordination of the economic function to the political order." In the same book he also says, "Ours is a world that will require more authority and more regulation."

Likewise Abraham Sirkin, writing in the *Futurist*, says: "Because of potential shortages, higher costs, environmental dangers, growing congestion, and increased safeguards against crime and terrorism, we will have to accept some unaccustomed restraints on our freedom of movement, action and ownership."

We thus end up with the unappealing idea of reducing the liberty of the present inhabitants of the earth in order to enhance the material well-being of future inhabitants. But is this really required? Consider two concrete examples involving the interests of people who will live in the future: helium conservation, and the disposal of toxic wastes.

The Helium Dilemma

HELIUM is an inert gas that has a variety of commercial uses. Perhaps its best-known use is for inflating lighter-than-air craft such as dirigibles and blimps. It is actually more widely used, however, for inert-gas welding, as a constituent of anaesthetic and breathing mixtures for medical purposes, as an inert carrier gas in chemical processes, and as a coolant or heat-transfer agent in energy production.

Helium occurs as a trace constituent of the atmosphere and, more important, mixed with natural gas in some gas fields. Formed as a harmless decay product of uranium and thorium, it tends to collect in the same types of rock formations as natural gas does. Thus, helium is currently produced commercially by extracting it from natural gas before the gas is burned. If the gas were simply burned, the helium would be dissipated into the atmosphere.

Now we confront a dilemma. The amount of helium that could be extracted from the natural gas being consumed today is far greater than the current market can consume. It is expected that after the year 2000, though, helium consumption will grow to several times today's level as a result of increasing use in energy production. Unfortunately, it is expected that the helium-bearing natural gas fields will be exhausted about the year 2000. So, just at the time when demand is expected to increase, the existing supplies could disappear.

People in the future could obtain helium directly from the atmosphere, at an estimated cost of about 50 times what it costs to extract it from natural gas. Helium could also be obtained in the production of liquid oxygen, at a cost of about 5 times what it costs to extract it from natural gas. (In effect, removing oxygen, nitrogen, and other gases from a tank of air increases the concentration of helium in the remainder, thus making it cheaper to extract than if it were extracted from ordinary air.) But the projected demand for oxygen and other atmospheric gases would provide only enough helium to meet one-fifth of the expected demand.

So it appears to be simply common sense to conserve helium now, when it is readily available at low cost, so it will be available in the future when it will be both costly to produce and in great demand. And for many years the federal government has in fact maintained a helium conservation program. The helium is extracted from natural gas and pumped back underground into exhausted natural gas fields, to be extracted again in the future when needed. The taxpayers are paying the costs of extraction and storage.

There has been considerable discussion of this helium conservation program, all in terms of how much people today should be willing to sacrifice for the benefit of people in the future. Clearly, it is a sacrifice: tax monies are being expended now so that in the future helium will be available at much lower cost than it would have been otherwise. Clearly, also, it is an exercise in coercion: it represents a lessening of people's freedom to use the wealth they have produced as they choose; instead, their wealth is used to benefit their descendants.

Resource Speculation

LET'S DIGRESS for a moment from the helium conservation issue to the more general issue of exhaustible resources. How does the owner of an exhaustible resource behave if he is looking out for his own interests? In the view of some futurists, that owner will want to get his profit as rapidly as possible. He will therefore exhaust that resource as quickly as he can, with no thought for the future. So at some later date, even though people will need that resource, it will have been used up.

But consider: If a particular resource will be more valuable in the future than it is today, it is in the interest of the owner to conserve that resource so that he can sell it at the higher price that will prevail in the future. The only real question facing the owner of the resource is how rapidly the price will increase. Will he garner more income by extracting the resource now and investing the returns in some other activity or by preserving the resource for later sale? If the rate of increase of the price of that resource is greater than the productivity of money invested in some other activity (say the interest rate paid on a money market fund), then it makes sense for the owner to conserve the resource.

Does that conservation involve any sacrifice on the part of the owner? No. He does not need to raise the question of whether he prefers the good of other people in the future to his present good and, if so, how much. If the price of an exhaustible resource is increasing rapidly enough, it is to the owner's best interest to conserve that resource for future sale.

Suppose, though, that the price of the resource is not increasing rapidly enough in the present, but it will become much more valuable 20 to 30 years hence (as is the expected case for helium). The owner might well be dead by then, so how would it benefit him at all to conserve the resource? If the waiting time is quite long, doesn't the owner really have no choice but to exhaust the resource now? Doesn't the finite lifetime of the owner force him to take a short-sighted view?

This argument overlooks the fact that an exhaustible resource has a sale value. For instance, the owner of a mine can remove the ore and sell it, or he can sell the mine itself to someone else who will remove the ore. The sale price of any resource is based on expected future income from that resource. The sale price of a mine, for instance, is based on the amount of ore believed to be in it and the expected future sale price of that ore. Partial exploitation of an exhaustible resource lowers the selling price, since it reduces the potential future income. So the owner of an exhaustible resource always faces a trade-off between current income from the resource and the sale value of that resource, and it is in his self-interest to consume (exploit) the resource at a rate that maximizes his *total* wealth: current income from exploiting part of the resource plus the sale value of the remainder.

Consider a specific example. Savings and loan institutions have no hesitation in making 30-year mortgages even though many of their depositors will have died or will have withdrawn their money before then. That is, they lend money for a 30-year period even though the owners of that money may not be around in 30 years. They do this because the resulting mortgages have a market value. They can be sold to other banks at a price based on their expected future income (this amounts to the unpaid balance discounted at the interest rate available for current investments). Because of this possibility of resale, it makes sense for the depositors to invest their money in resources that have a 30-year pay-off period.

The same holds true for railroad and utility bonds. These are often issued with maturity dates 30 or 40 years in the future. Why do people buy them when they probably cannot expect to live to cash them in? Simply because there is a ready market for them. A given bond may change hands several times between issuance and maturity. It gives each successive owner the opportunity to increase his wealth by receiving interest, as well as holding a claim on the return of principal.

Thus, it is quite possible to take the needs of the future into account by permitting the establishment of markets in which assets with future values can be bought and sold. It may be objected that the people of the future cannot bid in such a market. While true, that is irrelevant. If some resource is likely to be valuable in the future, it pays someone who is alive now to invest in that resource and hold it for later sale. The fact that the waiting period may be longer than any single individual can wait is also irrelevant. As long as a resource is expected to have a higher value at some future date, people will buy it as an investment, and the price at which it can be sold will rise as the future date approaches.

Of course, there can be no certainty that a given resource will increase in value. For instance, people now expect that there will be a big demand for helium after the year 2000. But in the 1920s it was also expected there would be a big future demand for helium for lighter-than-air craft. That demand did not materialize. Anyone who stored helium in anticipation of a large market for helium for inflating dirigibles would have lost money.

Someone who holds a resource in anticipation that it will increase in value is known as a speculator. While the term is often used pejoratively, in actuality the speculator performs an important function. The purpose of any market in assets with a future pay-off is to transfer risk from people who do not want to bear it to people who are willing to bear it for a price. The speculator, then, is someone who believes an asset will increase in value but who is willing to assume the risk that it will not. He will demand a premium for assuming that risk, and the greater the risk, the greater the premium he will demand. The function of the speculator can be more easily performed if there is a market in which people can readily buy and sell assets with future pay-offs.

Such a market would actively foster conservation of resources. While speculators are interested in profit rather than in conservation per se, speculation in resources with an expected large future demand automatically results in conservation. The people of the present cannot exploit a resource unless they first outbid the people of the future, as represented by the speculator. Thus the interests of the people who will live in the future are actively protected even though they cannot bid in the market.

Government Muddling

WITH THIS UNDERstanding, let us now return to the problem of helium conservation. We can see that if helium is going to be in great demand in the future as compared with the present, there is money to be made in storing it for future sale. So conserving helium does not require sacrifices in the present for the good of people living in the future. Instead, it requires postponement of current consumption by those who invest in storing helium. But this is no different from any other investment. In each case, the postponement of current consumption is rewarded if the investment pays off. At most, it represents only a temporary sacrifice, a sacrifice that is compensated for if the investor has made a sound investment.

In fact, it appears that storing helium is a profitable enterprise. Several analyses indicate that if the expected future demand actually develops, the government will get back not only its investment in helium but interest on the money tied up in the enterprise. There is no guarantee, however, that the expected demand will actually develop.

The result, then, is that the government helium storage program has turned us all into involuntary speculators. Our tax money is being used to speculate in helium ownership. We are all being asked to bear the risk that helium will actually be in great demand in the future.

But there is more to it than that. If the expected demand actually develops, the government will sell helium at a profit, and presumably the taxes of people in the future will be slightly lower than they otherwise would have been. That is, people in the future will have helium available at a lower price than without the storage program, and they will also pay lower taxes. Meanwhile, we in the present are paying higher taxes than we would without the storage program. This amounts to a direct transfer of wealth to the people of the future—who, if the economy continues to grow, will be wealthier than we are. Hence we are not only being forced to speculate; we stand no chance of gaining even if the speculation pays off. We are being asked to make a sacrifice for the benefit of people who are likely to be wealthier than we are.

This whole arrangement is hardly fair from any standpoint. The people now living lose, no matter what happens to the demand for helium. The people of the future cannot lose, no matter what happens.

All in all, it would be better if the risks of helium storage were borne voluntarily by speculators who believe the demand for helium is going to grow. They would risk their own money, not anyone else's. By being able to sell out whenever they choose, they could obtain some portion of the gain during their lifetimes. And if the demand failed to develop, the speculators, not taxpayers, would stand the whole loss.

So we have to ask, why hasn't a private market in helium storage developed, since it has a high likelihood of being profitable? Why do people buy 40-year railroad bonds but not shares in ownership of stored helium?

The problem goes back to 1917, when it appeared that helium would be needed for military dirigibles. To assure adequate supplies, the government established a monopoly over extraction and sale of helium. Even though the large-scale military uses never developed, this government monopoly continued until 1961.

During the late 1950s, a shortage of helium actually developed, since the Bureau of Mines did not have the manufacturing capacity to meet total demand. Rather than simply expand capacity, a new program was established. The Bureau of Mines would buy helium for both sale and storage. Private companies were permitted to extract helium from natural gas and to sell it to the bureau or to nongovernment users. The bureau retained a monopoly on sales to government users and to government contractors. The price set for helium by the Bureau of Mines was intended to recover all costs of the operation, including interest.

The scheme went awry right from the start. The private companies were able to undercut the Bureau of Mines' selling price for helium, taking away the nongovernment market. Thus the long-term purchase contracts the bureau had entered into resulted in more helium going into storage than originally planned. More helium was being conserved than had originally been intended. From the standpoint of the original purpose of the program, this would not matter. The government would still get its money back, but at a later date than originally anticipated. But if private companies could profitably engage in helium sale, why did they not also go into the business of helium storage?

Perhaps the most immediate reason there is no private investment in helium storage is everyone's assumption that this is the government's job. But over the longer term, the existing government-owned stockpile of helium presents a serious threat. It represents an enormous market overhang that the government could dump at any time for purely political reasons. For instance, if the price went up, the government might sell helium to "stabilize prices" or to "avoid market dislocations that would accompany a precipitous rise in prices." Since the officials making the decisions do not have their own money invested in storing helium, they might well sell it in order to depress prices, for the benefit of small but politically influential groups of helium users. It would not be the first time government officials betrayed the taxpayer for the benefit of influential constituents.

This constant threat of government dumping of helium, any time it appears that the owners of privately stored helium might make a profit, is sufficient to discourage private storage. By its own actions, then, the government has driven private speculators out of the helium storage market, has converted all American taxpayers into speculators in helium, and has guaranteed that the present generation loses while a future generation that is likely to be richer stands to win a great deal.

Valuing the Future

THIS CONCRETE example of helium conservation illustrates several general points about the conservation of exhaustible resources. These apply to all situations of exhaustible resources that are of value both in the present and in the future.

First, the argument that the future cannot vote today, nor can it bid in today's markets, is true but irrelevant. If a resource is going to be needed in the future, then its owners will have an interest in conserving some of it for future use. The more valuable the resource will be in the future, the more of it they will conserve as opposed to exploiting now. This remains true even if the time when the resource is greatly valued will be after the death of the present owners—so long as a market exists in which the resources can be bought and sold.

Second, the frame of reference in which futurists typically discuss the problem of exhaustible resources—of sacrificing welfare in the present to increase welfare in the future—misapprehends the true issue. If people are willing to speculate on a higher value for the resource by holding it as an investment (and thereby conserving it), they are not making any sacrifice. They expect to be rewarded by the investment paying off. And if it doesn't—if the resource is not more valuable in the future—the speculators' loss still does not represent a sacrifice of their welfare for the benefit of someone else; it represents the penalty for making a bad investment.

Third, the conservation of exhaustible resources that will be needed in the future can be greatly aided by better forecasts of future demand. George Stigler, the University of Chicago economist, has listed as one of the classic instances of market failure the failure to anticipate the future properly. An individual may not perceive his own best interests if he fails to anticipate the future. In particular, the owner of an exhaustible resource may decide to exploit it now because it will have no value later. If he is wrong about that, he will suffer a loss or will gain less than he could have by conserving the resource. That is, a mistaken belief about the future value of a resource harms the present owner as well as would-be future users. Better forecasts, which made clear the likely level of future demand for a resource, would benefit both the present owner and would-be future users.

Fourth, futurists can greatly assist the functioning of markets in resources with future value by providing good forecasts of future demand for those resources. In this role, they can do much more good than they can by urging governments to require sacrifices in the present generation for the welfare of future generations. Such coercion may benefit no one at all, or it might benefit a wealthier future at the expense of the present. It may even harm the future by causing malinvestment in the present.

With regard to exhaustible resources, then, we can conclude that freedom in the present does more good for both the present and the future than does coercion, no matter how well-intentioned that coercion may be.

The Waste Dilemma

TOXIC WASTES are the direct opposite of exhaustible resources: they are actually worth less than nothing, because it costs resources to dispose of them. Hence they can be a problem for both the present and the future.

Our concern here will be the long-term storage of toxic wastes. This differs from the problem of pollution that is emitted as soon as it is produced. Pollution exists as an environmental externality only because people have been denied property rights in the environment. Recognizing these rights would allow us to treat pollution as trespass. The victim could take the polluter to court or sell the right to pollute, at a price acceptable to both him and the would-be polluter. With toxic wastes, however, we are concerned with the problem of "pollutants" that are intended to be kept out of the environment by storing them.

Consider some toxic chemical that has no economic value and must be kept segregated from the environment "forever." (Note that radioactive wastes eventually decay, even if it takes millions of years for some of them to do so. Some toxic chemicals, especially heavy metals, never decay. Their "half life" is infinite. Hence they may pose a more severe problem than do radioactive wastes.) Suppose someone stores a large quantity of such a chemical in containers that might reasonably be expected to corrode or leak in, say, 50 years, and the stored wastes will then become a significant environmental hazard. But what can the people who will be faced with that hazard do? The company that stored the chemicals might have gone out of business. The company officers who made the storage decision have probably all died. Who can be sued? Who can be held responsible for solving the problem?

This example illustrates the nature of the dilemma. It appears possible for people in the present to leave behind a mess for the future to clean up. It appears that people in the present can escape responsibility completely if they can postpone the day of reckoning long enough. Moreover, it appears that there is no possible "marketplace" solution, as there is with exhaustible resources. There is no one who will speculate by buying toxic wastes, since clearly they are not expected to increase in value. They represent a dead loss, since it will cost resources to store them safely.

Under such circumstances, it appears necessary to have someone in the present "vote" on behalf of the future. It appears necessary to exercise coercion to prevent people from irresponsibly dumping their wastes in such a manner as to create problems for future generations.

But appearances are often deceiving. They are in this case. Not only can the interests of the future be protected by a free society with a free economy, but this protection can be accomplished without coercing anyone.

Short-sighted Disposal?

LET'S START with a simple case. Assume an individual has some toxic wastes that he wishes to dispose of. Assume he has a plot of ground on which to do so. Assume further he intends to use a disposal method that will ensure that the waste will never leak across the property boundaries. However, the plot of ground on which he disposes of the waste will be contaminated and useless for any purposes ever after.

To many futurists, this is precisely the kind of situation that should be avoided. Contaminating the land in that fashion means it can never be used for anything else. People in the future would be denied the use of that land unless they went to the expense, often inordinate, of decontaminating it.

Consider, however, why an individual would contaminate a piece of land in that fashion: only if that method of waste disposal were less costly than any alternative method. The land has alternative uses, and it therefore has a price that represents the stream of income from the most valuable of those alternative uses. So disposal of waste by contaminating a plot of ground is not "free." The person disposing of the waste is out the selling price of the land. But since he is willing to accept that cost, it must be presumed that any alternative disposal method costs even more.

But here, the futurist might respond, is precisely the problem. By his short-sighted focus on costs, the "disposer" has denied the use of a piece of land to all future generations. But let's look at this "short-sighted focus on costs."

There are methods for disposing of

toxic wastes other than land disposal. For instance, they can be neutralized chemically or subjected to high-temperature combustion in special burners. These other methods of waste disposal also consume resources, however. In particular, other methods may require human labor, energy, and chemicals obtained from exhaustible resources.

In a free economy, the cost of any resource is an accurate reflection of the value society places on that resource—and that includes an estimate of the future value of the resource, just as the selling price of land includes an estimate of future income from the land. Thus the fact that other waste-disposal alternatives cost more than does contaminating a piece of land means that society places a greater present-and-future value on the resources consumed by those alternatives than it places on the piece of land.

If the owner of the toxic wastes and the land were prevented from contaminating the land, the people alive in the future would have it for use. But they would *not* have for use any of the exhaustible resources consumed by an alternative disposal method. Moreover, they would not have the results of using renewable resources in their most-valued use instead of in disposal of the waste. Put another way, if the waste is disposed of by some alternative means, the people alive in the future would inherit an additional usable piece of land but would also inherit a smaller capital stock, a poorer economy, and a more depleted supply of exhaustible resources.

Which of the two outcomes would the people of the future prefer: the additional land and a poorer economy, or a richer economy but not the particular piece of land? In actuality, it is impossible to know; any claim one way or the other must be recognized as being possibly in error. The important point is that basing the decision on relative costs is *not being short-sighted*. Instead, it represents a decision based on society's current best estimate of the present *and future* value of the sets of resources required for each of the alternative disposal methods.

The futurist may respond that this view leads to absurd results. Suppose each generation contaminates a certain amount of land, arguing that the people in successive generations would prefer a richer economy to the land. Eventually every bit of land on the earth's surface would be contaminated. An attitude that leads to such an absurd outcome cannot be correct.

But this argument is wrong, because it attempts to hold values constant, while in fact people are constantly responding to the changing scarcity of resources. The first plots of ground selected for waste storage will be those that have the lowest value. That is, the plots selected will be those whose alternative uses are valued least by society. But once the least-valued plots are used, additional waste disposal will have to be done on land with more and more valuable alternative uses. Eventually the value of the land for alternative uses, as reflected by its price, will exceed the cost of alternative methods of disposal. (This is already happening to landfill sites for trash disposal near large cities.) At that point, people will switch from disposing of waste by contaminating land to disposing of waste by some alternative means. Again, the cost of various means of toxic waste disposal will reflect present *and future* values of the alternative uses for the resources consumed by waste disposal.

The point is simply that in a free economy, the means selected for toxic waste disposal will utilize those resources (land, labor, energy, capital equipment, materials) whose alternative uses, both present and future, have the least value. Just as with the case of exhaustible resources, futurists can play an important role in helping society make decisions about toxic waste disposal. This role does not consist in attempting to "speak for the future" by insisting on one or another specific approach to waste disposal. Instead, it involves providing better estimates of what the future value of various resources will be. These estimates will affect current prices for the resources, as speculators attempt to profit from projected shortages. Accurate estimates of future demand for particular resources will help the market satisfy the demands of the future, despite the truism that the future cannot bid in the market.

Dumping on the Present

BUT WE'RE NOT finished with the problems of waste disposal. Suppose someone contaminates a plot of ground by disposing of toxic waste on it and then tries to sell that plot. The selling price should be based on expected future income from the plot, less the cost of decontaminating it. But this will be true only if the buyer knows the land has been used for disposal of toxic waste. What if the "disposer" passes off the land to an unsuspecting buyer? This is a clear-cut case of fraud and deception.

One of the classic roles of government in a free society is protecting people against fraud and deception. The precise nature of the laws required may be subject to debate, but at a minimum they should require disclosure to the buyer that land has been used for toxic waste disposal. Perhaps even public registration of the fact of disposal should be required. Failure to disclose or register should be punishable as an attempt at fraud or deception. Moreover, the buyer should be able to obtain redress. Freedom to contaminate one's own land by using it for toxic waste disposal does not include "freedom" to defraud or deceive others about the uses to which the land has been put.

There is yet more to the problem. We have so far assumed that the disposal method restricts the wastes to a particular plot of ground, which is owned by the disposer. What about disposal methods that threaten leakage across boundary lines?

Immediate leakage is no different from any other type of pollution; it should be treated as trespass. Private property rights in the environment provide adequate protection against this problem. It is delayed leakage that concerns the futurist.

Suppose someone stores steel drums of toxic waste on his own property. It is reasonable to predict that eventually the drums will corrode, and the toxic waste will leak out. Its spread then may be unlimited. Diffusion through the soil, leaching by rainwater, etc., may carry the waste to a neighbor's property. And so, asks the futurist, what then? The wastes have been stored for perhaps 50 years. The owner of the land is dead. He made no attempt to sell the land, and it has probably passed into the possession of the state for failure to pay back taxes. Now who is responsible for the cleanup? The taxpayers? Hasn't the market allowed the disposer to escape the consequences of his actions? Doesn't that mean that some kind of coercion is justified to prevent people from acting in such an irresponsible fashion?

We must again note that the value of any resource is based on expected future income. In particular, this includes the value of the land adjacent to that on which the waste was stored. Wastes whose leakage can reasonably be predicted reduce the expected future value of the adjacent land. Even a slight risk of leakage will reduce to some degree the future value of the land. This reduction is reflected in a reduction in current value. Thus, storage of wastes in a manner that has some possibility of leakage represents an immediate and direct reduction in the value of adjacent land. The owners of that land have a legitimate grievance *in the present*. It is not necessary to await the future, and the possible catastrophe, to object to "impermanent" storage methods. The fact of a future problem is reflected in the present, in a diminution of the value of potentially affected property.

Once it is recognized that a possible future threat produces a legitimate grievance in the present, the inability of the future to vote today, or to bid in today's markets, becomes irrelevant. The people living in the present already have adequate reason for protecting the interests of the future. The interests of the future are reflected in present-day interests. In particular, disposal of toxic waste in a manner that poses a future threat is in fact a violation of rights of people alive now.

One need not get tangled up in issues of how much welfare the people of today ought to be willing to sacrifice to assure greater welfare for people in the future. A threat that may exist in the future results in a reduction in the welfare of specific, identifiable people living now. The proper role of the state should be to provide protection and redress for those people whose present welfare is being reduced. Coercion of the present, on behalf of the future, is unnecessary.

The Future of Freedom

THUS THE FREQUENT call by futurists for coercion of the present to assure the welfare of the future arises from three misunderstandings about the nature of freedom.

The first is that freedom means "doing just as you please." Freedom is in fact limited by the rights of others and is conditioned by the expected consequences of actions. The rights of others are defendable under the law. The coercive power of the state is properly deployed to protect those rights and presents a definite limit on doing as one pleases. Expected consequences of actions also place limits on doing as one pleases. People who take actions that result in unpleasant consequences for themselves either learn better or lose the power to act. In a free society, these limits and constraints mean that the interests of others, both present and future, are taken into account in people's actions.

The second misunderstanding is that since the people of the future cannot vote in present elections, and cannot bid in present markets, they are ignored in present-day decisions that will affect them. As we have seen for the cases of both exhaustible resources and toxic wastes, the interests of people of the future are reflected in the interests of specific, identifiable people of today. When those now living protect their present interests, they are also protecting the interests of the future.

The third misunderstanding is that if the future is taken care of by people in the present acting in their own interests, then there is no need for "futuring" by futurists. Yet a free society, in which people seek their best interests within the limits set by the rights of others, very definitely needs good "futuring." How else can people know what their best interests are if they do not know what future conditions will be like? How can they know which resources to use now if they do not know which will be in greatest demand in the future and which will therefore "bring more" if held off the market? How can they know that certain actions should be prevented if they do not know those actions will injure them, now or later? Obviously they cannot.

Futurists should cease calling for sacrifice in the present on behalf of the future, for more coercion in the present, and for government intervention in the interests of the future. Rather than seeking a world in which coercion is used to achieve the particular future they desire, futurists should seek a world of freedom, because in such a world it will be in people's self-interest to take their advice.

The Information Society:
THE PATH TO POST-INDUSTRIAL GROWTH

Graham T. T. Molitor

Graham T. T. Molitor is president of Public Policy Forecasting, Inc., 9208 Wooden Bridge Road, Potomac, Maryland 20854. He served as chairman of the World Future Society's Second General Assembly (1975), served on the White House Advisory Committee on Social Indicators, and was research director, White House Conference on the Industrial World Ahead.

Runaway inflation, slowed economic growth, lagging productivity, and the depression of traditionally strong industries are now focusing much-needed attention on America's economic plight. But such immediate concerns distract people from the underlying transformation of the American economy that has given rise to these dislocating effects.

Simply stated, agriculture and manufacturing no longer constitute the foundation of the economy. A new economic order has emerged—one based not on material goods but on information.

The much-heralded post-industrial society has been with us since the mid-1950s. As modern technologies and innovations restructure the economy, they bring with them a host of new issues that demand response.

A new universe of policy questions now confronts society. Choices must be made about how best to invest scarce time and resources to encourage economic progress, and about the pervasive influence of computers and electronic data processing on such issues as individual privacy. These choices will help determine America's future economic and social health.

Many people still believe that America remains in the grip of the Industrial Revolution. Such a notion is far out of date. The high point of American work force employment in manufacturing, commerce, and industry came not during World War II, as most people might guess, but in 1920, when 53% of the work force was so employed. In that year, 28% of the workers were engaged in agriculture and extractive industries, and 19% were employed in information, knowledge, education, and other service enterprises.

The distribution of the work force in contemporary America is far different. By 1976, only 4% were engaged in agriculture, 29% were in manufacturing, 50%—fully one-half—were in information, and 17% were in other service occupations.

Economically, politically, and socially, the importance of manufacturing is fading fast. By the year 2000, a mere 2% of the American work force will work in agriculture, 22% will be in manufacturing, and 66%—two-thirds—will be allied with information. An additional 10% will provide other services.

This is a basic profile of post-industrial society. As it takes shape, America will continue to suffer from the structural dislocations of an economy adjusting to new economic underpinnings.

Pre-industrial society—America before World War I—depended on labor in drawing resources from nature's bounty.

In industrial society—America in the middle of the century—man-machine combinations used energy from the natural environment to transform nature into a technical environment. This form of economic activity depended heavily on energy.

The Knowledge Revolution

But now, in post-industrial society, the major resource is knowledge. Intangibles have replaced tangible material goods as the dominant factor in commercial enterprise, the central assets, and the primary source of wealth and power. A new set of "knowledge industries" are on the rise. They include a vast range of endeavors:

• All aspects of the printing and publishing trades.

• The communications and telecommunications industries—broadcasting, periodicals, journals, libraries, accounting, teleprocessing, word processing, and so forth.

• Communications and knowledge professionals, including

From *The Futurist*, April 1981, published by the World Future Society, 4916 St. Elmo Avenue, Washington, D.C. 20014.

journalists, research scientists, engineers, social scientists, and educators on all levels from pre-school to postgraduate and from trade school to on-the-job training. Also included are policy researchers, think-tank workers, and swelling numbers of professionals whose primary contributions are their brains, not their brawn.

• Last, and crucially important, are the companies engaged in the research, manufacture, and distribution of communications equipment—such firms as AT&T, Xerox, IBM, Control Data, RCA, Texas Instruments, and even Exxon (fast becoming a major factor in communications high technology).

Information processing equipment, supplies, and services expenditures alone are likely to reach $62 billion during 1981. The annual growth rate of 12-15% makes it a standout amidst other faltering sectors.

The companies involved are blue chips in more than one sense of the term. They are destined to be the business giants of the future, eventually eclipsing the older industrial giants, such as General Motors, that dominated a bygone age.

The production, understanding, and control of knowledge have become essential, especially in the advanced nations. Knowledge and information industries are fast be-

coming the decisive factors in the growth of the productive forces of nations.

The knowledge revolution already has invaded other areas of the economy. Livestock are fed by computer from computer-controlled diets. The most productive automobile factories in existence, in Japan, are also the most highly automated. Robotics is taking over.

Drastic Changes for Society

A wide range of new and emerging information technologies will reshape many facets of society. Some of these innovations will mean drastic changes for the trans-

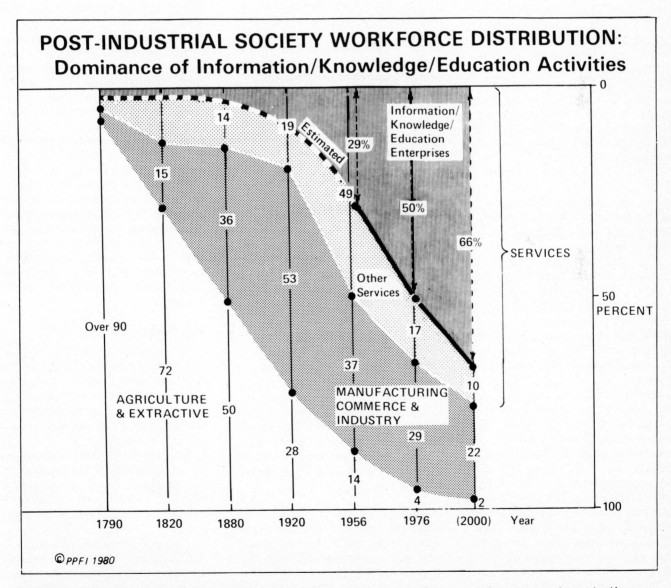

POST-INDUSTRIAL SOCIETY WORKFORCE DISTRIBUTION: Dominance of Information/Knowledge/Education Activities

© PPFI 1980

The distribution of workers in different sectors of the American economy changed dramatically over the last century, as society evolved from agricultural to post-industrial. Some important turning points were 1880, when 50% of the workers were in agriculture; 1920, when about 50% were in manufacturing; and 1976, when more than half were in information industries.

6. FUTURE

portation industry. Americans are not far away from the time when people will conduct many of their transactions—banking, shopping, and even jobs—electronically. People will no longer have to commute to work, but will communicate instead. High energy costs will encourage the rapid introduction of elaborate electronic home entertainment systems.

The desperate need for more efficient use of resources will also accelerate such trends. In no small part, these developments will eventually reduce energy requirements.

In the past, technology has always solved problems of limited resources. For example, futurist Buckminster Fuller reminded us in his 1969 book *Utopia or Oblivion* that a one-quarter-ton communications satellite outperformed 150,000 tons of transoceanic cable. Since then, the cost and efficiency of commercial communications satellites has improved drastically and further advances already on the horizon assure continued remarkable improvement. The Federal Communications Commission's approval last December of launching 20 to 26 domestic communications satellites will add substantially to the eight satellites presently in orbit.

The information revolution promises a vast new range of potential home information services—electronic fund transfer systems, electronic shopping, electronic mail terminals, interactive TV, pay cable TV, teleconferencing, video recorders, and home computers.

Bringing electronic data processing within the reach of mass marketing grows ever closer as costs decline. During 1980, microprocessor costs declined at an annual rate of 22%, information storage costs fell by a 40% rate, and communications equipment dropped at an 11% clip. As costs dropped, sales grew. The work horse, personal home computers, grew at an astounding rate of 60% in 1980.

These telecommunications services are destined to become the dominant source of information re-

ceived by U.S. citizens, eventually displacing the current dominance of the ubiquitous TV set, telephone, radio, phonograph, and tape recorder.

New Technologies Evolve

Historically, newer, more efficient and convenient communications media have supplanted established ones. At first, the more advanced medium supplements the earlier one; then the earlier mode wanes as the new technology becomes the dominant source or conduit of information.

This pattern has held true from the time language replaced guttural communication and gesticulation as the primary means of communication to the present day, the most recent dramatic example being when television replaced radio and the printed word as the primary source of information.

Television is without a doubt the dominant communications medium today. The average person spends more time watching TV than following any other single leisure-time pursuit. The number of daily household viewing hours increased from 4.6 hours in 1950 to 6.2 hours in 1977.

Most households have more than one TV set (an average of 1.67 per household in 1979), and nearly every household has at least one— an estimated 98% of American households did in 1978.

The tremendous decline in the cost of TV sets has made them increasingly available to the masses. Initially, sets cost $500; current prices run under $100.

Within any communications medium, improved versions regularly supplant the old. Years ago, large-screen black-and-white televisions succeeded smaller-screen models. In turn, color TV replaced black-and-white TV.

Innovations in the works promise an exciting future for television. The number of TV channels available will greatly expand with the growth of cable TV, satellite broadcast TV signals, and microwave and other exotic transmission modes.

Video recordings and two-way (interactive) cable TV will provide still another means for expanding the versatility and richness of the information and entertainment available from TV. Flat-screen, full-wall projection television and even holographic (3-D) projection systems show technological promise.

While current activity focuses on television, the stage already is set for the emerging communications modes to dominate and supersede it. Telecommunications—and particularly the advent of computers as a main element in information handling—is already creating waves.

Electronic data processing (EDP) will become the next step in a long line of innovations in communications.

EDP is probably not the last step in this process. The coming years may see some startling developments in areas exploiting potential powers of extrasensory perception (ESP) and parapsychological phenomena. One can only imagine the effects of technologies that provide information in advance of the actual occurrence of events.

But for the foreseeable future, computers will provide the largest changes. The information revolution is upon us. What steel, petroleum, and the induction motor were to the industrial revolution, computers and semiconductors will be to the post-industrial society.

The Information Business

At this point, America is by far the world leader in information industries. Information equipment sales for 1980 are estimated at $30.5 billion in the U.S., contrasted with $8.6 billion in the second-ranked nation, Japan.

America leads all other countries by large margins in the production of computers. Value of production in U.S.: $13.3 billion; in second-ranked Japan: $2.9 billion (1979 figures).

As market dominance in the new information growth sector steadily grows in importance, new rivalries loom on the horizon, particularly for the United States, Japan, and West Germany. World economic and political leadership will increasingly depend on competitive advantage in the new growth sectors.

Although the U.S. now leads, some indicators suggest that the country's competitors are rapidly catching up. In a knowledge-based economy, research and development are especially important and can be indicators of coming innovations and future economic progress. In the U.S., the funds spent on research and development have declined in the last few years. West Germany increased R&D expenditure as a percentage of gross national product by approximately 50% from 1964 to 1978. During the same period, Japan's increased by 30%. The U.S. underwent a 23% *decline.*

The U.S. has been making relatively lesser commitments in other areas of investment with long lead times, such as the numbers of graduates in science and high-technology disciplines and investments in new plants and equipment.

Patents, whether applied for or granted, indicate advances in applied science and engineering and are another crude indicator of technological progress. They provide tangible evidence of successful research and development and represent an important step toward commercial application.

While simple quantitative counts of patents do not reflect the potential of the inventions, they do give a rough guide to the number of innovations one can expect in the next few years. In this era of the information-based economy, such innovations are important to economic progress.

More patents are granted annually in the United States than in any other country in the world. In recent years, the gap has been closing. In 1965, the U.S. granted more patents than Japan and West Germany combined. But by 1977, the number of patents granted in Japan alone was fast approaching the number of U.S. patents granted.

Patent applications tell another story of recent Japanese growth. In 1965, Japan and West Germany together accounted for about 50% more patent applications than the United States. By 1970, Japan and West Germany accounted for almost twice the number of patents applied for in the U.S. Japan alone had 50% more patent applications than the U.S. in 1977.

These factors imply that America's leadership position could de-

COMMUNICATIONS — INNOVATION AND DOMINANCE

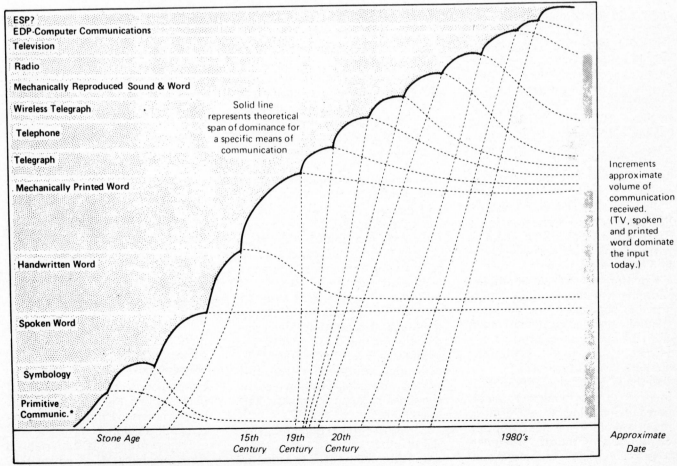

Solid line represents theoretical span of dominance for a specific means of communication

Increments approximate volume of communication received. (TV, spoken and printed word dominate the input today.)

*Primitive guttural communication and gesticulation

As new communications technologies are introduced, older, more traditional ones wane in importance. And as these supplementary media take hold, people are exposed to ever-increasing amounts of information.

6. FUTURE

cline over the next few years. While U.S. industries lead in many categories, their lead could be lost. Japan is playing "catch-up ball." Japan's long-term game plan, with active government support and active encouragement of huge Japanese vertical and horizontal combines (with antitrust immunity), accounts for the fact that an increasing number of Japanese firms are to be counted among the world's largest electronics manufacturers. "Japan, Inc." is a formidable competitor.

Japan openly avows the goal of seeking world domination of global telecommunications. America needs a similar government resolve to spearhead global market penetration, superiority, and dominance in critical information industries. Japan and its far-flung affiliates already control production in many telecommunications categories, both electronic and optical.

The World Marketplace

America might do well to reassess its antitrust policy. World economics has radically altered in the post-World War II period.

The Communist countries centralize all trade with non-Communist countries in just a few state trading companies. No more than 10 or 15 companies in Russia or China trade with the rest of the world.

Open cartel registries in Western European countries encourage industrial combinations to attain a parity of scale for effective competition in world markets.

Government-assisted multiple-industry collaborators in Japan strive to penetrate world markets. Centrally planned economies other than Communist nations (e.g., France) also focus economic strength in world markets.

Perhaps the most significant factor of all is the growing importance of regional trading blocs. The most important of these is the European Economic Community. Member country integration of internal and external trade relations makes their impact in certain sectors, such as agriculture, extremely effective.

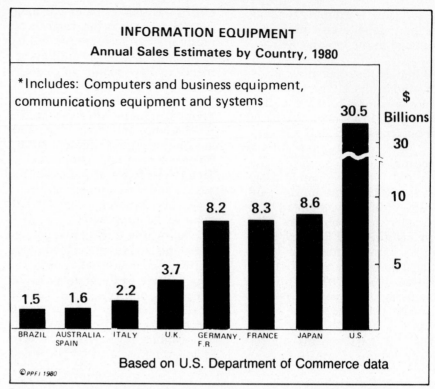

INFORMATION EQUIPMENT
Annual Sales Estimates by Country, 1980

*Includes: Computers and business equipment, communications equipment and systems

$ Billions

BRAZIL	AUSTRALIA. SPAIN	ITALY	U.K.	GERMANY F.R.	FRANCE	JAPAN	U.S.
1.5	1.6	2.2	3.7	8.2	8.3	8.6	30.5

©PPFI 1980

Based on U.S. Department of Commerce data

The United States is in the vanguard of the movement toward the post-industrial, information-based economy. It leads the world in the sale of information equipment, but the author contends that the U.S. could easily lose its lead if it makes the wrong policy decisions.

Not to be overlooked is the growing significance of commodity-oriented trading authorities. The most notable is the Organization of Petroleum Exporting Countries (OPEC), but it is not the only one.

These realities of competition in a changed world market call for economic power on a scale larger than ever. New legal guidelines that encourage rather than hobble and hamper large-scale economic units are indicated if the U.S. is to remain a meaningful and major economic world power. Parity of scale among economic competitors is crucially important.

The success of current antitrust suits aimed at breaking up America's biggest communication companies—notably AT&T and IBM—would surely adversely affect U.S. economic competitiveness and advance the global position of giant combines in Japan, Germany, and elsewhere.

Governmental regulatory tethers of other sorts also may hamstring the ability of U.S. firms to compete against other huge organizations that presently dominate world markets.

At the same time, the government should continue efforts to encourage competition *within* the communications industry. Emergent communications technologies, such as cable TV and satellite transmission, although still in infancy, are certain to grow by leaps and bounds. Federal policies should encourage competition between these new media as well as with the old. Fostering inter-industry competition should promote better service, a variety of choices, and lower prices.

Regulating Communications Media

Without a doubt, the government will be involved with the communications industry in many ways. In the past, as new communications technologies and products reached the market, abuses by promoters eventually led to government regulation.

This century has experienced three major cycles in which new communications technologies came to the fore:

• Low-cost, mass-circulation

"penny press" at the turn of the century.

- Radio during the early 1900s.
- Television in the mid-1900s.

In each case, over-zealous promotion and advertising led to excesses and abuses. Self-regulatory efforts eventually gave way to government-mandated standards.

TV content and advertising, for instance, have been under seige in recent years by consumer critics. During the 1970s, American advertisers responded by undertaking self-regulation. The National Advertising Review Board, an industry supreme court of advertising review, was created. Better Business Bureau budgets and responsibilities increased. The National Association of Broadcasters TV code was updated. Numerous business association and private company codes of broadcasting ethics were revamped. Federal regulatory and legislative solutions are moving toward mandating action should serious shortcomings in these efforts become evident.

Regulating Electronic Data Processing

This same pattern will undoubtedly hold for this century's fourth emerging communications technology, as electronic data processing (EDP) becomes more widespread. Information technologies, like most innovations, entail both positive and negative effects.

Society will have to sort through many of these developments to decide how to deal with them. The far-reaching consequences of EDP will result in an overwhelming number of public policy issues. In fact, Public Policy Forecasting, Inc., has identified an astounding number of these issues—nearly 2,000—and studied the directions many are likely to take.

For example, the integration of information systems steadily centralizes data, as well as the power implicit in the control of knowledge. At the same time, other developments, such as interactive, two-way telecommunications, push society toward decentralization. A free democracy depends in no small measure on maintaining

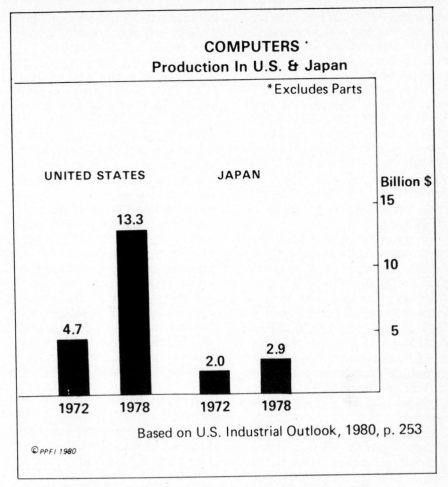

The United States produces more computers than any other nation, far more than second-ranked Japan. "Japan, Inc.," however, is an awesome competitor, and there are indicators that America's lead could be slipping.

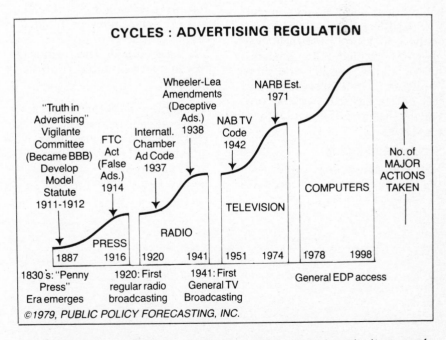

Each time a new communications technology gains widespread use, abuses lead to a wave of consumerism and advertising regulation. This pattern has held true for the penny press, radio, and television so far in this century. The author foresees a new wave of regulation dealing with electronic data processing and computers as they become more common in the next 20 years.

189

an appropriate balance between the centralization and decentralization of information and knowledge. This is one area of upcoming public debate.

The amassing of large and detailed personnel dossiers of various kinds that EDP allows will draw increasing concern. The consolidation of this information through central computer banks will draw particular criticism. Citizens increasingly will need to be protected from unreasonable invasions of privacy.

The growing bodies of financial and economic data about bank customers and credit card users will prompt legislation to protect them from unwarranted invasions of privacy. More safeguards, particularly those restricting unauthorized use and third-party access, will be established. Tighter rules governing unauthorized access to or burgeoning dissemination of personal medical records will be imposed.

Employee privileges to inspect personnel records will be vastly expanded, including rights to: examine, hold, and copy their files; be consulted concerning the release of records or use of them for purposes other than those originally intended; correct, update, or submit their point of view on controversial matters; and restrict the scope and kinds of information allowed to be filed. Stiffer penalties for violations, simpler and more convenient civil processes, and judicial safeguards will be provided to assure fulfillment of these provisions.

Stricter Safeguards

Stricter safeguards governing the release of criminal records will be imposed. More laws expunging "blots" in criminal records for one-time follies will be enacted.

A continuing lightning rod for public policy concern involves America's headlong plunge toward the checkless-cashless society. The arbitrary power of "gatekeepers" controlling access to credit approval and ratings will be constrained so as not to unreasonably deny citizens access to financial exchange systems.

The more widespread the use of computers becomes, the greater will be the opportunity for fraud, embezzlement, trespass, and other criminal abuse. New computer crime control laws are coming.

Private sector eavesdropping and covert surveillance in all its myriad forms will be restricted. Concurrently, the use of these measures by law enforcement officials will be facilitated, especially in cases involving organized crime, narcotics offenses, and national security.

Polygraph and personality testing—either as a precondition of hiring or of continuous employment—will be discouraged. However, laws allowing their use at the subject's option (and free of coercion) will grow in number.

Computer-dialed telephone solicitations, so-called "junk calls," already have been prohibited in certain jurisdictions—Great Britain, for example. The further diffusion of reasonable controls is likely.

Freedom of information laws, sunshine legislation, and the like, still riding high, may fade with adverse experiences of openness and as memories of Watergate wane. The pendulum will swing back toward government secrecy. Too much openness will be seen as frustrating forthright action; the need to safeguard personal information will be given keener attention; and Cold War dictates will impose national security restrictions. Arrogant and wanton secrecy in government, however, will not be tolerated.

Royal commissions, White House task forces, and investigatory committees of all kinds already have begun to address these and other issues. Further government interest and action are coming.

The information revolution is causing fundamental economic, political, and social changes, both domestically and around the world. The changes raise new issues society has never before had to consider. As computers come to pervade all areas of life, the next 20 years should see some lively debate over these public policy issues, as people must decide how much the privacy of the individual must be protected, how much openness in government and business is necessary, whether or not large communications companies should be broken up or allowed to grow to a scale competitive with those of other countries, what portion of its resources the U.S. needs to devote to research and development, and how to support information technologies to advance economic growth.

With the number, magnitude, and complexity of the issues to be resolved, one thing is certain: despite the current anti-regulatory mood, further government involvement in the information sector is inevitable.

BEYOND DUMPING:

The Surprising Solution To The Love Canal Problem

Bruce Piasecki

Bruce Piasecki teaches at Clarkson College of Technology in Potsdam, New York, and is now editing a book on toxic waste controls.

A familiar advertisement by Monsanto proclaims, "without chemicals, life itself would be impossible." Without toxic wastes, life would still be possible, but it certainly would be bleaker.

This isn't an apology for the 77 billion pounds of these wastes that are produced each year in the United States, but a realization that they have become an integral part of our daily life. Sulfuric acid and mercury are inevitable by-products of the pulp and paper industry. The manufacture of life-saving drugs produces zinc and other heavy metals. The textile industry generates toxic dyes and organic chlorine. Even the common doorknob requires electroplating, which generates large volumes of rinse waters and sludges laced with cyanide. For America's major industries, toxic wastes are as ubiquitous and inevitable as the garbage trucks that prowl through America's neighborhoods each morning to cart away old newspapers, broken egg shells, and other assorted trash.

Just because we generate toxic wastes doesn't mean they have to kill us. But as Love Canal and a host of other examples demonstrate, they're doing just that, though that should come as no surprise when you consider what we do with our lead, mercury, chlorinated hydrocarbons, PCBs benzene, cyanides, and various other poisons. For the most part we simply dump them—into landfills, abandoned wells, holding ponds, open fields, and even old Titan missile silos. And then we cross our fingers and hope for the best.

This dump-and-hope approach has prompted people like former California Congressman John Moss to call the problem of toxic wastes "the sleeping giant of the decade" and has led to widespread calls for better dumps. Dumps that are properly identified and policed 24 hours a day—and monitored for generations. Dumps that confine waste in corrosion-resistant containers. Dumps with impermeable liners to prevent groundwater contamination. Dumps that aren't right next door to housing developments, drinking water supplies, and children's playgrounds.

But dumps nevertheless. Yet as the toxic waste cognoscenti know, the search for the perfect dump is about as fruitful as trying to build a perpetual motion machine. Containers corrode and leak. Rainwater seeps into underground storage areas. Aquifers supplying drinking water eventually become contaminated. In one case in Texas, for example, wastes supposedly pumped into a 9,000-foot-deep well came back to haunt nearby residents in their kitchen sinks. A report by Princeton University's Hazardous Waste Research Program last summer graphically illustrated the problem: among state-of-the-art landfills that far exceeded current federal standards, some were leaking large amounts of contaminants after only two years of use.

The lesson in all this is obvious but usually

overlooked. The last thing we should do with our toxic wastes is figure out the best way to dump them. Instead, we should do something safer and far more sensible: turn them into harmless chemicals and make some money selling what's left over.

Before dismissing this as a modern day version of the alchemist's lead-into-gold fantasy, consider one thing: detoxification of hazardous waste happens to be standard operating procedure in much of the rest of the industrial world. In the Netherlands, the Chemical Waste Act of 1976 explicitly prohibited the dumping of a wide range of toxic wastes, a ban that has since spawned a thriving waste detoxification business. In Denmark, the Kommunekemi plant handles every toxic waste in the country. And if it can't destroy or recycle a particular waste, the Danes don't dump it—they put it in storage until they can find a way to treat it.

Holland and Denmark are not exactly world-class industrial powers—like West Germany, for example. But those who doubt that detoxification is both effective and economical need only visit any of that country's 15 waste treatment facilities, which are operated as part of a coordinated national program. The West Germans detoxify 85 percent of all their hazardous wastes. To them, detoxification has virtues beyond merely protecting their citizens. For example, through a process known as "chlorinolysis" the Farbwerke Hoechst company converts chlorinated hydrocarbons (a group of chemicals that includes PCBs, a known carcinogen; DDT-related pesticides; and kepone) and other toxic residues from organic chemical production into useful substances such as carbon tetrachloride, a valuable solvent used as a degreaser for machine parts and in other industrial processes. The company detoxifies about 8,000 tons of waste each year through chlorinolysis, but it has even grander ambitions. Hoechst recently began construction of a new plant that can handle 50,000 tons per year—allowing it to start *importing* wastes from other European producers.

West Germany's example hasn't gone unnoticed in at least one corner of the United States. In 1981 California Governor Jerry Brown appointed a special Toxic Waste Group to examine alternatives for the 1.3 million tons of hazardous wastes disposed annually in the state's landfills. Prepared in cooperation with representatives from Dow Chemical, Friends of the Earth, and various academic institutions, the report concluded that 75 percent of California's toxic wastes could economically be recycled, treated, or detoxified. Brown since has established a low-interest loan program for building detoxification facilities; to discourage dumping he has instituted new dumping rules and increased the state's landfill tax by 600 percent. Hit with additional charges of $4 million, Chevron and Getty are now dumping far less waste. "We don't like to refer to these regulations as *banning* dumping," explains Gary Davis, a waste management specialist for the state. "But that is what they are meant to do eventually for California."

Before you assume California's anti-dumping crusade will cause many beleaguered manufacturers to throw in the towel, consider the numbers. California industry now spends about $17 million to dispose of its high-priority wastes in landfills, and that will increase in the next two years to about $30 million. Using alternative treatment technology for this high-priority waste will cost only about $50 million a year, the state estimates. The additional $20-30 million annual cost will be spread among almost 4,000 California businesses with gross sales exceeding $30 billion. The two biggest waste generators—the chemical and petroleum industries—also have the highest profit margins of all other manufacturers. "There are no good reasons why the entire nation shouldn't rectify its toxic predicament by the end of this decade," Governor Brown says. "The knowledge is there. The tools have been developed. All that is required now is the political will."

Toxic-change Operations

California still dumps most of its toxic wastes, but compared to the rest of the United States, it's a pioneer. After producing three times as much toxic waste per citizen as West Germany, American industry proceeds to dump 80 percent of it into unlined surface impoundments (pits, ponds and lagoons) and unsecured landfills. Less than 20 percent is treated in any way, and the most common method—incineration—is often conducted under uncontrolled conditions that transfer the toxics into the atmosphere.

For a country that prides itself on its technological sophistication, this enthusiasm for dumping is not only appalling, but downright mystifying. It's especially so when one considers how relatively simple, inexpensive, and elegant some of the best detoxification techniques are.

For example, until recently waste water and sludges contaminated with heavy metals such as lead, nickel, and mercury could be detoxified only at exorbitant cost. These wastes were usually dumped in holding ponds and landfills, but because of their persistence often worked their way into water supplies and the food chain.

In 1978 L.J. Bailin of Lockheed Missiles and Space Company, Inc. developed a technique called microwave plasma detoxification that treats heavy metals with the same ease that microwave ovens handle baked potatoes. A neutral gas, usually pure oxygen, is irradiated with microwaves. This transforms the gas molecules into a highly reactive state, causing them to combine with the heavy metals, which break into harmless compounds and marketable grades of scarce metals. The MWP process can also be applied to deadly wastes such as kepone, DDT-related pesticides, and dioxin, and recent research endorses this process for the detoxification of cancer-causing nitrosamines and nerve poisons from the military.

The real beauty of MWP is both its ease and its relatively low cost. The process produces no troublesome emissions and eliminates unnecessary transportation of wastes; prototype trucks have been developed that can detoxify 50-100 pounds of these wastes per hour at the dump site. At a cost of about $400 per wet metric ton, MWP at first might seem uncompetitive with landfill costs of about $40 a ton. But the $400/ton figure is for a very early prototype; a recent EPA report estimated the widespread use of MWP and the resulting improvements in design could decrease costs "by a factor of 10." The cost of dumping will move in the opposite direction as regulations get tougher and existing landfills reach capacity.

Other wastes can be treated biologically. This approach has been of limited value until recently because most biological agents have been appropriate only for very dilute wastes. But new mutant bacteria—known as "superbugs"—can now handle several thousand times the toxic concentration of their precursors. One new culture can remove cyanide wastes from coking operations at steel mills for only two cents per thousand gallons of waste water. A mixture of several other microbes feeds on 2,4,5-T, the toxic component of the defoliant Agent Orange. Yet another superbug eats benzene, the ubiquitous carcinogen once used as a chemical feedstock to produce PCBs, pesticides, linoleum, and varnishes.

Unfortunately, these new superbugs are doing little while the wastes they could render harmless remain a hazard. The Air Force spends more than $100,000 a year monitoring 2.3 million gallons of stockpiled Agent Orange; each day an estimated fifteen 55-gallon drums develop new leaks. Massive stockpiles of benzene are now being dumped into landfills, even though the chemical quickly vaporizes and, when exposed to sunlight, produces a toxic smog.

Dumping Über Alles

So where are all the MWP trucks, the chlorinolysis plants, the new superbugs? For the most part, they're stuck on the drawing boards or in the laboratory while hazardous waste dumping continues to increase at a distinctly unhealthy clip. This would be dismaying enough were it not for another thing: the very federal agency ostensibly responsible for doing something to solve the hazardous waste problem is working to make sure things stay that way.

The particular agency is the Environmental Protection Agency which, in all fairness, had almost nothing to do with hazardous wastes until 1978. Before then, dumping was largely the responsibility of individual states, some of which regulated toxic waste dumping and some of which made it clear to dumpers that as long as their enforcers didn't see anything, no one would make any trouble.

But by 1978, shamed by disclosures about Love Canal, Congress had ordered the EPA to set up uniform federal standards governing toxic waste dumping. The purpose of the law went beyond cleaning up old, contaminated dumps and making new ones more secure. Congress hoped stricter regulations, by forcing toxic waste producers to pay higher dumping costs, would spur detoxification efforts.

Congress was thus addressing the major reason detoxification has been virtually ignored by American producers while the Europeans have been busy building integrated treatment centers. Dumping is too cheap and too easy. A good example of the problem is found in the textile industry, which annually produces nearly 200,000 wet metric tons of hazardous waste laced with toxic dyes, organic chlorine, and heavy metals. A recent analysis of the textile industry by Booz-Allen and Hamilton, EPA's major consulting firm, estimated that these wastes could be reduced nearly 80 percent while adding less than one percent to total production costs. Yet textile companies have done almost nothing; as the report subtly suggests, a company would have to be foolish to add this burden in the absence of any EPA regulations restricting dumping.

For the same reason, no commercial-scale chlorinolysis plant exists in America, despite the process's proven track record in Europe. Chlorinolysis detoxifies chlorinated hydrocarbons (a family of chemicals that are usually used in agriculture) by subjecting them to high pressure and low temperatures. The EPA estimates the process would add less than one percent to manufacturing costs. Yet while these wastes pose one of the greatest hazards in landfills—and some, like Agent Orange, are considered *too* toxic for existing landfills—in the absence of stiffer federal regulations there is little economic incentive for a company to use this technique.

The Carter EPA began to change these incentives through stricter dumping regulations that have caused landfill charges to at least double at most sites. Carter also moved to tighten something known as the "small generator provision," which, pound for pound, is the most serious loophole in current toxic waste regulations. Of the 760,000 toxic waste producers in America, 695,000 are still exempt from most regulations because they generate less than 2,200 pounds (1,000 kilograms) of hazardous wastes per month. According to the Office of Technology Assessment, more than 6.5 billion pounds of toxics a year are thus exempt from all federal regulations. In May 1980 the EPA announced it intended to reduce the threshold to just 220 pounds within two years.

These were only tentative steps toward detoxification, and hardly in the same league as California's virtual declaration of war against dumping. (California, for example, has no small generator exemption.) But at least they were steps in the right direction. Encouraged by signs from Washington, many businesses began to develop detoxification technology to capture a part of what they predicted would be a fast-growing market.

With All Deliberate Speed

Many criticisms—some deserved, some not—have been leveled against the Environmental Protection Agency since Anne Gorsuch took its helm. But when it comes to toxic waste disposal, there's no room for equivocation: the agency's record has been inexcusable. Within only a few months Gorsuch made it clear that she thought her job was not to encourage detoxification but to make dumping as easy—and therefore as cheap—as she could.

Gorsuch took one step toward this end in the case of liquid waste dumping. In the years after Love Canal many states prohibited the dumping of liquid wastes in landfills. The reason was simple. Liquids contaminate much faster than solids; moreover, when they leak from storage, the drums that once contained them often crush under the weight of the overlying earth. This in turn breaks the seal of dirt and metal designed to restrict water from entering the landfill. The water then mixes with the toxic chemicals and contaminates adjoining groundwater supplies.

By 1981, 11 states, including New York and Michigan, had banned liquid dumping in their major commercial landfills. This forced thousands of companies to treat their wastes by transforming them into easier-to-handle solids or by detoxifying them all together. But in February 1982 Gorsuch suddenly overruled these bans, creating an open season on liquid dumping. The ensuing public outrage forced Gorsuch to reinstitute the ban just 27 days later, but she has since indicated she may lift it again in some modified version.

The liquid dumping episode pales next to the decision to overrule the Carter administration's plans to reduce the small generator loophole. Last June EPA official Rita Lavelle—a former official for Aerojet General Corporation, which has been charged with illegally dumping hazardous waste in California—told a Senate subcommittee that tightening the loophole was just the kind of onerous federal regulation the administration wanted to shift from the backs of small entrepreneurs. Lavelle also claimed the change would triple EPA enforcement costs and prove an "administrative inconvenience."

The EPA's subsequent decision to keep the loophole intact not only revealed its attitude about dumping, but bespoke a profound ignorance of how regulation works. It's not an army of EPA inspectors snooping around the backlots of service stations that will force most small generators to comply with the law. Rather, it's the mere threat of a penalty. More important, a toxic is a toxic, whether it's dumped by Dow Chemical or a small electroplating shop. That point was made quite graphically by the National Solid Waste Man-

agement Association, the primary trade group representing the firms that run America's landfills. The association vigorously opposed the EPA decision, citing hundreds of cases of garbage shipments exploding because of hazardous wastes and numerous garbagemen injured from handling them. Indeed, of the first 115 contaminated dumping sites identified by Congress for emergency cleanup, 65 were standard solid-waste facilities and municipal dumps that had been accepting untreated toxic wastes from small producers.

Along with these decisions, the EPA has repeatedly delayed implementation of proposed regulations that would make dumping safer but more expensive. The approach seems to have a certain free market logic that goes as far as forcing detoxification firms out of business. Within two weeks of the EPA's lifting of the liquid-waste ban, the IT Corporation announced it was discontinuing building high-technology detoxification systems. As New Jersey Representative James Florio notes, "Unless the administration issues meaningful dumping regulations, the same free market forces that brought us Love Canal will stifle detoxification efforts."

That's putting it mildly; Gorsuch's policies are helping ensure that the detoxification industry will be stillborn, if indeed it ever sees the light of day. That's why some of the most vociferous critics of EPA's foot dragging and backsliding are the large chemical waste handlers who also run large dumps. Many began investing in detoxification techniques during the Carter administration—only to see Gorsuch's actions since then undermine potential markets. This February a group calling itself the Hazardous Waste Treatment Council formed and immediately began filing suits against the EPA to force it to tighten dumping regulations. Although Marvin B. Durning, the council's senior attorney, declined to provide a list of his clients, other reliable sources confirm that its membership includes ENSCO, SCA Services, and Rollins—three of the nation's largest hazardous waste handlers.

With detoxification efforts stunted, those states who want to detoxify wastes don't have many options. New York's Hazardous Waste Disposal Advisory Committee recently looked into the matter and discovered that nearly 30 percent of the state's total annual volume of waste—about 800 million pounds—could not be treated with even the most rudimentary of techniques simply because there was an acute shortage of facilities. Dumping was the only choice.

Last January, U.S. District Court Judge Gerhard A. Gesell finally lost patience with EPA's repeated requests to delay stiffer regulations on dumping. He minced few words. "What Congress directed to be done is now almost four years overdue and the EPA contemplates at least two more years of indecision and procrastination," he declared. "The agency, moreover, has ignored the court's deadline orders, offering excuse after excuse for avoiding its responsibility . . . and demonstrated that it has neither the ability nor the will to do what Congress and the court have repeatedly ordered."

It's always dismaying when a court is forced to order a government agency to obey the law. But in the case of toxic wastes, there are additional reasons for dismay. The obstacle to detoxification is not a lack of technology, nor is it cost. Over the long run detoxification is actually cheaper than watching landfills for decades and trying to clean up after the inevitable leaks and spills. Nor are EPA's professionals ignorant of the alternatives to dumping. Scientists usually avoid politics, but occasionally they show a remarkable frankness in their comments, which was certainly the case when William Sanjour, chief of the EPA's Hazardous Waste Implementation Branch, wrote to congratulate Jerry Brown on California's program. "We have known for a decade that hazardous wastes can be managed properly . . . yet we have had to watch the unfolding of one horror story after another while solutions are sought in every direction but the right one," he wrote.

But having defied the laws of Congress, the EPA now appears willing to take on the laws of nature. The United States has less than 18 years of landfill capacity left; if nothing were done at all, the increasing shortage of dumping space would ultimately give detoxification a future. But EPA feels compelled to do something about this shortage, as was revealed in a notice in the October 18, 1982 issue of *Inside EPA,* an internal agency newsletter. The notice revealed that EPA officials are considering changing existing regulations to permit toxic waste dumping in 100-year flood plains if dikes are built around the dumpsites—or if the waste handler files an emergency removal plan with the EPA. It's a terrifying vision: as the flood waters slowly rise, one can imagine the bulldozers frantically trying to remove the corroded drums of PCBs and cyanides—no doubt so they can then be dumped somewhere else.

Radioactivity For the Oceans

David E. Kaplan and Ida Landauer

David E. Kaplan and Ida Landauer write for the Center for Investigative Reporting in Oakland, California. This article was sponsored by the center's Nuclear Navy Project.

The aging hulks of two Polaris nuclear submarines are rusting in their berths at Seattle's Navy shipyard. The subs are still "hot" from years of nuclear propulsion even though the highly radioactive spent fuel has been removed. These two vessels, the U.S.S. Abraham Lincoln and the U.S.S. Theodore Roosevelt, are only part of a growing mass of nuclear waste the Navy has generated over the years, a problem it may soon solve by ending a twelve-year moratorium on ocean dumping of radioactive waste. A recent Navy plan calls for dumping more than 100 nuclear submarines, with their reactors intact, off the coasts of the United States.

The submarines and their reactors are reminders that the Navy has amassed one of the country's most formidable nuclear complexes. Few Americans realize that most of the nation's nuclear power plants are operated by the Navy, not by utility companies. The Navy maintains 151 propulsion reactors aboard its subs, cruisers and aircraft carriers, and another nine at training centers in Connecticut, Idaho and New York. By contrast, there are only seventy-three commercial reactors in the nation.

Under the Navy's plan, the decommissioned, defueled submarines would be towed out to sea at a rate of three or four a year over the next thirty years and be dumped in waters of 14,000 feet or more at locations approved by the Environmental Protection Agency. More than 100 sites are being considered, but the Navy gives top priority to two potential graveyards just within U.S. territorial waters: one 160 miles southwest of Cape Mendocino off the California coast, and the other 200 miles southeast of Cape Hatteras off the coast of North Carolina.

"The Navy is moving as fast as the law allows—or faster—toward disposing of its worn-out nuclear submarines by scuttling them," says California State Senator Barry Keene, a vocal critic of the Navy's plan. Keene, whose coastal district borders a proposed dump site, believes the dumping could begin within a year, although a Navy spokesman says it may not start for five years.

Keene is leading a broad-based antidumping coalition on the West Coast similar to the one that has opposed the Reagan Administration's plans for offshore oil drilling. The alliance includes Governor Jerry Brown and other prominent state officials, sport and commercial fishermen, coastal residents and members of environmental groups. The coalition was aided last August when the California legislature passed a resolution urging a halt to further ocean dumping until its environmental impact is better understood. Residents of North Carolina and their representatives in Congress have also expressed opposition, as have the governors of Guam and Hawaii.

The House of Representatives joined the fray in mid-September by passing, on a voice vote, a two-year moratorium on the ocean dumping of low-level nuclear waste. The bill requires close Congressional scrutiny of any dumping after the moratorium. A similar bill in the Senate, sponsored by Republican John Chafee, is gaining support despite opposition from the Reagan Administration. A vote on the Senate bill may come as early as November.

As an alternative to ocean dumping, the Navy is considering a plan to dispose of the submarines on land. This would entail cutting out the ships' reactor compartments and transporting them to a Federal dump site at Savannah River, Georgia, or Hanford, Washington. Some Navy officials, however, prefer sea disposal because of the ease of towing the subs offshore and flooding them until they sink. Land disposal would be costlier, they say, and would expose shipyard personnel to much greater amounts of the radioactive elements still present in the defueled subs.

"The driving factor here is that the Navy must find a permanent disposal site for its nuclear subs," says Navy spokesman Lieut. Bob Schmermund. "The subs have a useful lifetime of about twenty to thirty years, so it's better we start looking now for a solution before they begin to pile up at our shipyards." Schmermund says there are already

"Radioactivity for the Oceans," David E. Kaplan and Ida Landauer, *The Nation,* October 9, 1983. Reprinted by permission.

four decommissioned subs awaiting disposal, a fifth—the U.S.S. Nautilus—will be used as a museum after it is decontaminated.

The Navy is also under pressure to retire many of the subs because of U.S. obligations under the SALT treaty of 1972. The agreement with the Soviet Union expired in 1977, but protocols that freeze at 710 the number of ballistic-missile launchers American subs may carry were extended. With the impending commissioning of seven huge Trident subs, each with twenty-four launchers, the Navy is eager to decommission its aging fleet of ten Polaris subs, which are fitted with only sixteen launchers each.

The Navy is expected to present a draft environmental impact statement in November on its submarine-disposal plan. There will be sixty days for public comment, and a final statement should be ready within six months. Barry Keene and other critics charge that the Navy's plan is timed to coincide with the proposal of new regulations by the E.P.A. allowing ocean dumping of nuclear waste. The regulations will reportedly be published this year.

Opponents of the E.P.A.'s proposed regulations were shocked last May when Glen Sjoblom was appointed director of the agency's Office of Radiation Programs. Sjoblom was formerly the Navy's assistant director of naval reactors, and he helped develop its plan for scuttling the old subs. As head of the E.P.A. office, he will oversee the evaluation of the Navy plan, and his report will be the principal guide for E.P.A. Administrator Anne Gorsuch.

Keene blasted the appointment, calling Sjoblom "one of the Navy's leading advocates of ocean dumping of radioactive waste." The E.P.A. responded that Sjoblom is "a highly qualified radiation protection professional [whose] expertise will be of benefit to the agency in ensuring a thorough technical review" of the Navy's plans.

Part of Sjoblom's new job will be to predict the hazards posed by the Navy's dumping of its irradiated subs. In an official statement on the disposal plan, the Navy asserted that the defueled subs are "considered low-level radioactive waste" and fall well within E.P.A. guidelines. But critics of the proposal, including the Union of Concerned Scientists, believe the Navy is underestimating the amount of radioactivity in the subs. Marvin Resnikoff, a physicist at the Council on Economic Priorities, points to the presence of such isotopes as nickel 59, with a radioactive half-life of 80,000 years, and niobium 94, with a half-life of more than 20,000 years. These elements, he says, indicate the subs should be considered far more dangerous than "low-level" waste.

Keene charges that the E.P.A. is planning to change its definition of low-level waste to accommodate the Navy. E.P.A. officials deny the charge, but sources at the agency confirm that discussions about a change are indeed under way. Moreover, the amounts the Navy proposes to dump are so large that they will greatly expand the scope of ocean dumping. According to a 1980 article in *Science* magazine, a single nuclear submarine contains up to 50,000 curies of radioactivity. To put this in some perspective, there is estimated to be a total of 94,000 curies in the oceans now

from *all* the waste dumped there by the United States over more than twenty years.

Three Navy reactors already lie at the bottom of the Atlantic Ocean. Two of the submarines sank accidentally. The U.S.S. Thresher collapsed off the New England coast in 1963, and the U.S.S. Scorpion sank off the Azores in 1968. The Navy has monitored the locations in which the subs went down, and it reports finding only small amounts of cobalt 60, a radioactive isotope with a half-life of almost five and a half years. These ships are cited by the Navy as evidence that dumping would not create a health hazard.

The Navy has a tougher time proving no hazards were created by the third reactor's sinking. In 1959, Adm. Hyman Rickover, the "father" of the nuclear Navy, decided to abandon the sodium-cooled reactor developed for the U.S.S. Seawolf, the world's second nuclear-powered vessel. The Seawolf's reactor, plagued by leaks and corrosion, was replaced with one cooled by pressurized water, the system used by its predecessor, the U.S.S. Nautilus, and by most other reactors. On April 18, 1959, without public announcement, the Navy towed the Seawolf's defective sodium reactor about 120 miles off the Delaware-Maryland coast and dumped it 9,000 feet down. In 1980, a *Boston Globe* investigation revealed that the Navy, despite an apparently lengthy search, has since been unable to locate the reactor.

The Navy has thrown other radioactive refuse into the ocean over the years. From 1946 to 1970, more than 89,000 barrels of radioactive waste, much of it from Navy shipyards and radiation labs, were dumped in fifty locations off the nation's coastlines. The exact number is not known because record-keeping at the time was notoriously poor. A check by the E.P.A. found that one quarter of the barrels at the Farallon Islands dump thirty miles west of San Francisco were ruptured and leaking. Despite government claims that only low-level waste was dumped, evidence in recently unearthed documents from the Atomic Energy Commission indicates that more than 1,000 barrels of high-level waste, most of it from the Navy's Bettis Laboratory in Pittsburgh, were disposed.

A debate still rages in scientific and policy circles over the safety of nuclear dump sites. The United States has spent only $250,000 since 1974 to study existing dumps, little of which has gone to study health hazards. Meanwhile, the government has spent $30 million to find ways to bury high-level waste beneath the ocean floor.

At Congressional hearings in 1980, the E.P.A. pledged to monitor the dump sites in heavily fished areas, but the agency—citing "changing program priorities"—recently admitted it is now monitoring only fish catches. Although the E.P.A. has pronounced the dump sites safe, at hearings on ocean dumping on August 7 in California, Director of Health Beverlee Myers pointed to the findings of state scientists and others of significant levels of plutonium, strontium and cesium in fish taken from waters near the Farallons.

The issue may come to a head next February at a meeting of the signatories of the London Dumping Convention, the international treaty that regulates ocean dumping of radioactive waste. Some fifty member nations will consider an amendment offered by two small Pacific island nations to ban all ocean dumping. The proposal is supported by the Scandinavian countries but faces bitter opposition from the United States, Japan and several countries in Europe.

The Pacific islanders are fighting a Japanese plan to dump as much as 100,000 curies annually into the ocean north of Micronesia. Opposition from Pacific island nations and trust territories grew so intense last year that the Japanese government delayed its program in order to launch a public-relations campaign and explore "interim" measures to handle the waste.

Jackson Davis, a marine biologist at the University of California at Santa Cruz, is a scientific adviser to many of the Pacific nations fighting the Japanese proposal. Davis, one of the first scientists to call attention to the health hazards of U.S. coastal dumps, is worried that large-scale operations like those being considered by the U.S. Navy and Japan will open the oceans to massive dumping of high-level as well as low-level waste. "The United States is using the Japanese program as a trial balloon," he says. "It's the same area of the Pacific that the United States is studying for high-level waste disposal.

"And the Navy's program—here we have a precedent being set to start dumping power reactors. In the United States we have as many as seventy power reactors which will need decommissioning within fifteen years. It's opening the door to an activity that could be disastrous. The British have already made it clear they wish to follow the lead of the United States in dumping their reactors into the ocean."

Davis believes the long-range effects of this policy can already be seen in Western Europe, where a handful of countries—Belgium, Switzerland and England—continue to dump low-level waste into the North Atlantic. He cites a recent report by two English government scientists that indicates that people who eat seafood contaminated from dumps near the Windscale reprocessing plant in England receive the equivalent of at least 300 X-rays in a lifetime. The radiation of two nuclear submarines, adds Davis, equals all the "radwaste" dumped into English waters annually.

With the realization that radioactive wastes are creeping up the marine food chain, European opponents of ocean dumping are intensifying their fight. During the last several weeks, members of Greenpeace have repeatedly attempted to block dumping operations by positioning their boats beneath the docks of ships dumping nuclear cargo and, in two cases, chaining themselves to the ships' unloading cranes. Although the actions received little attention in the United States, they generated widespread press coverage in Western Europe, including a cover story in *Der Spiegel*, the West German newsweekly. And, accompanied by growing public opposition, they have had at least one substantial effect: in mid-September the Dutch government announced an end to fifteen years of dumping nuclear wastes into the Atlantic.

Greenpeace U.S.A. has hinted that it might physically block renewed attempts at ocean dumping by the United States. Other environmental groups are stepping up their own campaigns. Opponents here believe, as Keene put it, that it will take increasing "political clamor" to stop U.S. plans to drop new loads of radioactive waste into the world's oceans.

When the economy rebounds
WILL 'SMOKESTACK AMERICA'?

MICHAEL K. EVANS

Dr. Evans is president of Evans Economics Inc., Washington; chief economist for McMahan, Brafman, Morgan & Co.; and an IW contributing editor.

The upcoming economic recovery, regardless of its exact starting date, will be an upturn unlike any other in our history. The industrial sector will share in it far less than has previously been the case.

There are two basic reasons for the stunted growth. First, both the domestic and international recoveries will be much more moderate—or anemic—than has been the case in the last 35 years. And second, to put it bluntly, America has lost the ability to compete on a worldwide basis.

As a result, only about 1 million of the 2.9 million U.S. manufacturing jobs lost in the last three and a half years will ever reappear.

The inability to compete has many causes. For some sectors the list begins and ends with overpriced labor. Steelworkers' total labor costs averaged $23 an hour in this country last year. Such an elevated figure sabotages any efforts of domestic steel producers to compete with Japanese labor at $8 an hour and South Korean labor at $2 to $3 an hour. But U.S. labor has always been much higher-priced than labor in foreign countries; indeed, the percentage gap is actually smaller now than it was a few decades ago. During the last two decades the average cost of labor in the U.S. manufacturing sector has increased fourfold; in West Germany, however, it has

increased by a factor of 13, and in Japan by a factor of 24!

If we could compete in the 1950s, why not now?

The overvalued dollar is one reason. The dollar has, indeed, increased 40% from its lows in 1979 and 1980. And, while it fell slightly late last year, most of this decline was reversed early this year. Yet the dollar is still lower than it was in the late 1960s and substantially below the levels of the late 1950s.

In addition to the recent spurt in the dollar, the U.S. government often treats exporters as if they had leprosy. Virtually every other country in the world subsidizes exports through favorable credit terms; and most countries exclude exports from their value-added tax. Thus, U.S. exporters face a triple whammy—the overvalued dollar, less-favorable financing terms, and higher tax rates.

High-cost capital is another reason for the lack of American competitiveness. When the Fed pushed interest rates up to 21½% early in 1981, no other industrialized nation followed its lead. The beneficial aspects of the 1981 tax-reduction legislation were completely swamped by high interest rates. Whereas the tax cuts would have stimulated an additional $10 billion in investment per year, the marginal effect of higher interest rates was to *reduce* investment by $25 billion per year.

Government regulations are also expensive, especially those dealing with pollution control—a burden not borne by manufacturing facilities in Third World nations. Plants for producing steel and smelting aluminum and copper are welcomed much more

warmly in countries where the jobs may mean the difference between eating and not eating than they are in the U.S.

Yet, despite all these disadvantages which American heavy industry faces, the problems lie much deeper. Indeed, they cannot be fixed even by more moderate wage increases, a more moderately priced dollar, lower interest rates, or less regulation.

Poor analogy. Some sectors of the economy will post impressive gains during the forthcoming recovery. However, they will be the high-technology, information and business services, and leisure-time segments, just as has been the case for the last several years. Which raises the important question: How can the United States economy prosper if all of America is selling fried chicken or operating video arcades?

This dilemma does not bother some optimists, who draw an analogy between the manufacturing and agriculture sectors. One hundred years ago one person produced enough food for 4.4 others. Nowadays one person can produce enough food for 77 others. The increase in agricultural productivity freed labor for manufacturing, trade, and service jobs, thus enriching productivity and wealth. Perhaps, it is suggested, the manufacturing needs of the economy can be met with a very small proportion of the labor force, releasing the rest for more esoteric occupations.

To a certain extent, such a shift has been underway for years. In 1947, production workers in manufacturing represented 30% of all U. S. employees. The proportion declined to less than 14% by 1982.

WHERE HAVE ALL THE JOBS GONE?
(JOB FIGURES ARE IN THOUSANDS)

	MID-1979	DEC. 1982	JOBS LOST	PERCENT DECREASE	ESTIMATED JOB GAIN IN NEXT FIVE YEARS
U. S. MANUFACTURING INDUSTRIES WITH GREATER THAN 20% EMPLOYMENT LOSS					
Iron & steel	836	466	370	44.3	70
Nonferrous metals	448	339	109	24.3	30
Fabricated metals	1,742	1,373	369	21.1	150
Engines & turbines	150	104	46	30.7	10
Farm machinery	189	117	72	38.1	15
Construction machinery	398	277	121	30.4	30
Machine tools	370	292	78	21.1	20
Spec. & gen'l. ind. machinery	534	425	109	20.4	40
Heavy elec. machinery	385	297	88	22.9	30
Autos	1,047	649	398	38.0	100
Building materials	1,523	1,160	363	23.8	150
OTHER INDUSTRIES					
Textiles and apparel	2,217	1,842	375	16.9	150
Food	1,736	1,620	116	6.7	70
Paper	715	650	65	9.1	40
Chemicals	1,114	1,052	62	5.6	14
ALL OTHER MFG.	7,653	7,498	155	2.0	126
TOTAL U. S. MANUFACTURING	**21,057**	**18,161**	**2,896**	**13.8**	**1,045**

Source: Evans Economics Inc.

But there is a fundamental difference between agriculture and manufacturing. We are still the world's *low-cost* producer of agricultural products. However, we are close to being the world's *high-cost* producer in many basic manufacturing industries, notably steel. While we don't have as many farmers left, because we are good at it, we don't have as many manufacturing jobs left, because we are bad at it. The structure of the U. S. economy cannot survive in its present form if it has to import most of its manufactured products because it is so inefficient.

Over the last three and a half years almost 3 million jobs have been lost in the manufactuirng sector. The table above shows where the largest declines have occurred—more than 2 million jobs disappeared in metals, machinery, transportation equipment, and building materials. Although some of these losses are due to the recession, most of the jobs will never be replaced. Only about 1 million will be replaced in the next five years or so. The rest have been lost—to overseas competitors and to a changing world.

Thinking 'fewer.' Besides the U. S.'s competitive disadvantages in world markets, however, there has been a fundamental shift in demand. Not only do most American consumers no longer favor big cars and big houses; they are also buying fewer smaller cars and houses.

From the introduction of the automobile until 1979 the ratio of cars/person had steadily increased. During the 1970s the increase in this ratio accounted for about 3 million car sales per year; the remaining sales were due to increases in the car-buying-age population and the replacement market. In 1979, however, this saturation curve leveled off and the cars/person ratio has declined slightly over the last four years.

Although part of this decline could be attributed to the recession, the causes are much more fundamental. The number of people aged 16 to 24 will drop by 6 million during the 1980s; and though teen-agers generally buy used—rather than new—cars, the "trickle up" effect nonetheless used to translate into an increase in new-car sales. In addition, the sharp increase in the real price of operating a car—mainly gasoline—has dimmed the luster of owning a second or third car for many families.

The housing industry is the other major disappointment. Three years ago demographers claimed that the country needed a minimum of 1.8 million housing starts a year just to meet the demand created by new families and the demolition of decrepit and substandard units. Yet, housing starts during the last two years have declined to 1.1 million per year. It would thus follow that we should now have a severe housing shortage of about 1.4 million units. But anyone who follows housing markets knows that most areas of the country are currently suffering from a glut, not a shortage.

What happened? The economics overwhelmed the demographics. It turns out that, during the 1970s, many people were buying far more living space than they needed, in terms of square feet and the number of houses purchased. When the crunch came, people simply reduced their housing requirements. This trend was abetted by the fact that housing was no longer such a superb investment—one which easily outperformed the rate of inflation.

Even though interest rates have fallen significantly in the last six months and the stock market has rallied mightily, housing prices continue to stagnate or decline. As a result, the investment allure of housing has vanished completely. Therefore, housing starts are unlikely to average more than 1.6 million per year for the next five years. This is clearly an improvement over the miserable performance of the last two years, but it is far below the levels reached in the last decade. Starts averaged 1.93 million per year in the 1977-79 period and 2.17 million per year in the 1971-73 period.

Given the dramatic downsizing of autos coupled with generally weak demand, the sluggish demand for housing and thus for appliances, and the capital-goods malaise caused by high real-interest rates and low profit margins and utilization rates, the outlook for steel is bleak, indeed. Domestic steel production probably will not be much above 70 million tons this year. Even in the more advanced stages of the recovery it is unlikely that steel production will exceed 80 million tons per year, compared with an average of 93 million tons during the 1970s and the peak of 111 million tons in 1973.

What 'safety valve'? The picture we have painted of recovery is not a very cheerful one for "Smokestack America": A steel industry reduced to two-thirds its former size, a car market of no more than 10 million per year—including imports—and a housing industry which will be lucky to average 1.6 million units per year.

Moreover, there has been a continued decline in the percent of GNP invested in rebuilding our aging industrial plant. Which raises another question: With all the shutdowns and the lack of reinvestment, what productive facilities will remain to manufacture the goods we will need when the recovery does gather momentum?

Of course, companies have always chosen to shut down their oldest and least efficient plants in every recession; layoffs inevitably follow, and the unemployment rate rises by 3 or 4 percentage points. However, once the boom begins, the process traditionally has been reversed. During the first phase of the upturn the economy continues to operate with only its most efficient capital. However, as demand increases, the older, less efficient plant and equipment are pressed back into service. This does not occur unless prices rise sufficiently to cover the higher costs—which, indeed, does happen. Eventually, the increase in inflation and the decline in productivity translate into a reduction in corporate profits, a lack of savings, higher interest rates, and the next recession.

Our point is not to rehash business-cycle theory, but rather to demonstrate that the system will not work this way anymore, for most of the outmoded capital stock has been set aside on a permanent, rather than a temporary, basis. Those steel mills built in 1907 will never reopen again. The auto plant designed to build big-size V-8 engines is as irrelevant as a factory to build vacuum tubes.

Back-up capacity, in many cases, no longer exists—which is the flip side of saying that all those jobs have disappeared for good. This leads to somewhat of a paradox, however. If the back-up capacity is not there—if businesses have permanently downsized in response to reduced demand—and existing plant and equipment continue to get older and less efficient, then perhaps we will have more inflation rather than less. The "safety valve" will be gone; and when the economy reaches the point at which demand exceeds available

supply, prices will rise faster than usual.

That certainly would happen if the United States still functioned essentially as a closed society—i.e., if foreign trade were insignificant. Even with an open economy it would occur if bottlenecks and shortages were to develop simultaneously at home and abroad, as occurred in 1973. However, a repeat of the 1973 crunch is very unlikely in the next boom. In the last four years the United States economy was not the only one to slow drastically. The economic miracle has come to an end in West Germany; real GNP there has grown a total of only 0.2% over the last three years. Even in Japan the growth rate has slowed remarkably, from a 10.4% annual average during the 1960-73 period to a 3.2% rate over the last three years.

It could be argued that the same cyclical phenomena which have combined to diminish capital spending in this country also apply elsewhere. But, whereas the U. S. has chosen to cure the recession by reducing saving and investment through higher interest rates, other countries have not fallen into the same trap.

Furthermore, production facilities are being started and expanded all the time in Third World countries, using government-subsidized capital and the latest technology.

A losing battle? Thus, the "safety valve" that will open when U. S. demand starts to push against the limits of sharply reduced capacity will turn out to be another flood of imports. As a result, imports will grow at least twice as fast as exports over the next five years, with heavy emphasis on machinery as well as basic materials and consumer goods.

Is there anything we can do about this?

In the case of steel, no. We cannot compete against $3/hour labor—accompanied by modern and efficient plants, deepwater ports, low-cost capital, and export subsidies.

In the case of autos, maybe. The car of the future will be almost completely international—engines built in one country, tires in another, radios in a third, fan belts in a fourth,

window glass in a fifth, and so on. The GM-Toyota and GM-Isuzu agreements clearly presage this trend, as do the Chrysler K-cars with Mitsubishi engines. If the U. S. can produce quality parts and market American cars that are domestic in name only, the industry could survive. But it will be a struggle which will involve every aspect of cost-cutting.

In the case of housing, foreign competition is obviously not a threat, but demand for housing will continue to be sluggish. This will reduce demand for building materials and appliances—and appliance makers are already being battered by foreign competition, particularly the consumer-electronics segment.

In the case of machinery, however, the U. S. has a great opportunity: to combine the industrial experience already imbedded in the manufacturing process with the new technologies such as robotics, CAD/CAM, and laser-beam technology. The machinery sector thus represents the brightest spot in the heavy industry picture—but its potential won't be realized unless these new technologies are supported by generous infusions of both financial and human capital.

The U. S. will be hard pressed to keep its lead in computer technology as the Japanese make new thrusts, and will require technological breakthroughs on a much more rapid scale than ever before. However, with the renaissance of the venture-capital industry, it should be possible to accomplish that goal.

Thus, the forthcoming upturn will differ from its predecessors in that Smokestack America will not recover at a fast pace. If we insist on erecting such protectionist barriers as local-content bills, and on intensifying subsidies to the most inefficient producers, the U. S. will become a second-rate economic power. However, a redirection of both financial and human capital—toward coupling basic industrial know-how with the latest emerging technologies—will eventually provide an industrial base that could reestablish the primacy of the U. S. in the world economy.

Polluting the Most Vulnerable

Tracy Freedman and David Weir

Tracy Freedman and David Weir are staff writers at the Center for Investigative Reporting in San Francisco. This story was sponsored by the center's Project on Children and Environmental Regulations. The authors wish to thank the Children's Defense Fund for its invaluable assistance.

A great deal of press attention has been paid to Environmental Protection Agency appointees' dismantling of environmental laws, but the harmful consequences of their policies have drawn little notice. In particular, signs of the growing health crisis for children, who are substantially more sensitive than adults to the toxic effects of many pollutants, have been all but ignored by reporters and regulators alike.

Formerly rare, more than 6,000 new cases of cancer in children are reported each year. Cancer is now the second leading cause of childhood death, after accidents, and much of it is thought to be environmental in origin. An apparent explosion of learning disabilities and a rise in national demand for "special education" is linked by many experts to children's exposures to chemical neurotoxins. Despite years of preventive government programs, one in twenty-five children—and one in four inner-city black children—suffer from low-level lead poisoning, which causes irreversible brain damage and behavioral problems.

For many children, the growing burden of environmental contaminants and Reagan's environmental policies have proved a disaster which could promise a lifetime of reduced potential and debilitating disease.

Regulations that did not adequately protect children when they *were* enforced are no longer being enforced. Funding for research on the effects of environmental pollutants on the young, which was begun by the Carter Administration, has been discontinued. In its 1982 and 1983 budgets, this Administration cut E.P.A. research and development funds by nearly 24 percent, including a 69 percent cut in water-quality research, eliminating studies of toxic matter in drinking water (which many scientists think is a major source of cancer); a 42 percent cut in pesticide research; a 94 percent cut in radiation research; and an 87 percent cut in pollutant studies. And last December, the Office of Management and Budget floated a proposal to cut the E.P.A.'s 1984 research budget by an additional 23 percent, which would mean a more than 50 percent decline in funding since Reagan took office.

The President and his appointees have also fought the banning of certain suspected cancer-causing substances. Two that are particularly dangerous to children are formaldehyde and DEHP (di [2-ethylhexyl] Phthalate), both of which have been proved to cause cancer in laboratory animals. Formaldehyde is used in many common items—wall paneling, pressed-wood furniture, permanent press clothing—and thousands of tons of it are produced every year. DEHP, which is added to plastic to make it soft and pliable, is present in an alarming number of baby products—bottles, toys and pacifiers, for example. It also can leach from plastic tubes used in electric milking machines, contaminating the milk. Both formaldehyde and DEHP were targeted for regulation by the E.P.A. during the Carter Administration, partly because they posed a cancer risk to infants.

Last spring, however, attempts to regulate both chemicals were abandoned. John Hernandez, then the E.P.A.'s Deputy Administrator, held a series of closed-door "science courts" with chemical and other industry representatives, to which only two scientists not employed by the industry were invited. Upon the completion of those "hearings," Assistant Administrator John Todhunter ruled that neither DEHP nor formaldehyde was enough of a cancer risk to warrant regulation. Todhunter made his decision despite the opposition of the American Cancer Society, the World Health Organization and researchers from seven Federal agencies. The E.P.A.'s carcinogen assessment chief, Dr. Roy Albert, subsequently resigned because of his disagreement with Todhunter's decision and other agency rulings.

"The sensible part of the scientific community considers formaldehyde a likely human carcinogen, and I do too," Dr. Albert said in a telephone interview. "If you start giving credence to P.R. men and the formaldehyde industry, you're losing your grip on reality.''

Jackie Warren, senior staff attorney for the Natural Resources Defense Council, an environmental group now suing the E.P.A. over the formaldehyde decision, said, "This Administration wants to redefine the principle for assessing cancer risk to a point so high that nothing will ever qualify. At this rate, nothing's going to be done about formaldehyde, or any other chemical, until there are dead bodies stacked up in the streets.''

Reagan's E.P.A. has also abdicated its responsibility for seeing that toxic substances found in areas where children play are cleaned up. Last October, Assistant Administrator Rita Lavelle rejected the State of Arkansas' request for funds to remove oil-laden dirt contaminated by PCBs, which have been linked to liver and blood diseases and cancer, from a public alley in Fort Smith, despite concentrations reaching an astonishing 133,000 parts per million parts of soil, or 13 percent by weight. In rejecting Arkansas' request for $8,000 to erect a temporary fence around the site, Lavelle argued that "in order for a child to consume the *acute lethal dose* of PCBs, the child would have to eat about 150 grams of oil-laden dirt, the equivalent of about three large candy bars." (Emphasis added.) Lavelle ignored the effects of far lower concentrations of PCBs on test animals; her only concern was whether a child might bolt down a fatal amount of the contaminated soil.

Confronted by the extensive contamination at Times Beach and other sites throughout Missouri, the agency attempted to relax the standard for "safe" levels of the most toxic form of dioxin, a chemical so lethal that one forty-thousandth of a gram can kill a two-pound animal. In deciding whether to clean up fifty dioxin-contaminated sites, the agency proposed setting the "safe" level at more than 10,000 times that found at Love Canal, in Niagara Falls, New York, after the cleanup. E.P.A. internal documents, which were leaked to the Environmental Defense Fund, estimate that some children playing in the dioxin-laden dirt in Missouri have as high as a seven-in-ten chance of developing cancer—and are, according to one agency attorney, human "guinea pigs."

But the action that would have been most harmful to children was the Administration's attempt to nullify the regulations on leaded gasoline. That crusade was carried out by Vice President Bush's Task Force on Regulatory Relief, in response to complaints from oil and gas refiners. The task force recommended "reforms" that would have doubled the permissible level of lead in the air. Lead in the air has been linked to lead poisoning, which causes brain damage and behavioral problems in children, and the move would have reversed nearly a century's efforts to protect the young from overexposure to a substance whose harmful effects have been incontrovertibly established.

Even before Reagan came to office, the E.P.A.'s record on lead was compromised. From 1972 to 1976, while regulations reducing lead in gasoline were delayed by industry, an estimated 20 million children were exposed to dangerous lead concentrations. At least half a million of those children, by the most conservative estimates, incurred low-level lead poisoning. During this time the E.P.A. also buckled under to industry and for years delayed a generic standard for lead in the air. Clarence Ditlow of the Center for Auto Safety called this delay "one of the most tragic oversights this country has gone through." And David Schoenbrod, who as an attorney for the Natural Resources Defense Council took the E.P.A. to court over lead standards on numerous occasions, in a 1980 book called the government's tactics "a prostitution of science and a rip-off of the taxpayers."

Despite the 1976 gasoline standard, lead is still a health hazard. Indeed, if a healthy environment for children were really a political priority, the current exposure levels would be considered a national emergency.

§ Thirteen years after the passage of the Clean Air Act, 600,000 tons of lead are released into the environment every year, and only half the states have set air-quality standards.

§ Canned foods, especially juices and condensed milk products consumed by infants, carry high levels of lead, but they are unregulated by the Food and Drug Administration.

§ As many as 50 million housing units built before 1960 (when the paint industry began lowering lead levels in its products) may contain paint dangerously high in lead, despite the millions of dollars the Department of Housing and Urban Development has directed toward removing the problem. In only a small number of these units have lead levels been reduced.

There are few substances more cumulatively harmful to children than lead. If an adult ate a lead paint chip the size of a postage stamp every day over a period of a few months, he or she might develop headaches; the identical portion consumed daily by a child for the same period of time could cause permanent brain damage or death. Lead in the air, in the soil and in household dust is absorbed by thousands of youngsters every year. Most of that lead is emitted by cars burning leaded gasoline.

Despite the evidence that children continue to be exposed to dangerous amounts of lead, Reagan slashed funds for lead screening and poisoning prevention programs by 25 percent in his fiscal 1982 budget and shifted part of the burden for enforcing the present standards to the states, where other children's programs are competing for limited funds.

As a result, cities with the most serious lead poisoning problems will receive from a third to a half less than they did in 1981. According to a study conducted by the Center for Science in the Public Interest, Jersey City, projects a 47 percent cut in funding for lead poisoning programs in the next fiscal year and a 75 percent reduction in the number of children screened; Cleveland expects a 46 percent cut, with 19 percent fewer children screened.

Nevertheless, former E.P.A. Administrator Anne Burford insisted last summer that relaxing the lead standard would not harm children. Burford made her statement despite an internal report by Joel Schwartz of the E.P.A.'s energy economics branch, which found that doubling the permissible level of lead emissions in the atmosphere per year would increase the incidence of lead poisoning among black 2- and 3-year-olds in inner-city areas by an average of 2 to 4 percent. Schwartz estimated that in Chicago, cases of lead poisoning among 6- and 7-year-olds would rise by 9 percent; in New York City, by 14 percent; and in Louisville, Kentucky, by 44 percent. In 1983, relaxing the standard would save industry at most $100 million, while the cost to society—in hospitalization, special education, mental health care and reduced adult earning power for the poisoned children—could reach as high as $1.4 billion.

In contrast, between 1976 and 1980 the lead content of gasoline was reduced by 32 percent, resulting in an average drop of 37 percent in the levels of lead in the blood of children tested by the Centers for Disease Control in Atlanta.

Fortunately, the task force proposals were not adopted. Determined lobbying by a coalition of environmentalists, state and Federal officials, pediatricians and children's advocates forced the Administration to back down. An editorial in *The Wall Street Journal* complained that environmentalists had manipulated an "emotional issue" in order to "derail Reaganite deregulatory efforts," but in truth, it was a small but important victory for children in a battle that should never have been waged.

While the scientific proof of lead's harmfulness is overwhelming, there is no similar mass of evidence on the special dangers to children that newer chemicals and pollutants might pose. Many scientists believe some of them are hazardous (and the E.P.A. sponsored a conference in 1981 on children's vulnerability to pollutants), but the data needed for proof are lacking. The little that is known about children's sensitivity to pollutants gives cause for concern.

Even infants in the womb are exposed to dangerous chemicals—some natural, some synthetic, many of them suspected of causing cancer or birth defects. A blizzard of chemicals penetrates the placenta and affects the fetus when it is acutely vulnerable. And a baby's first nourishment—mother's milk, in many cases—may be laced with toxic pesticides that are in the food chain.

Toddlers ingest lead, mercury and other metals that are mixed with the dirt in parks and playgrounds, which are often located on former industrial sites. Because their bodies cannot break down these substances, up to 40 percent of the poison may be absorbed, twice what older people might absorb under similar circumstances. Wooden playground equipment is often saturated with arsenic or some other toxic chemical as a preservative. Because the skin of infants and young children is highly permeable, they may absorb these substances by brushing against a slide or swing. Hundreds of thousands of children between the ages of 3 and 6 ingest lead by nibbling on chips of sweet-tasting paint, which they find flaking off the walls of houses in which they live or play.

By the time they are 8 years old, most children's organs filter toxins more efficiently than their parents' do, but for younger children the process takes much longer. An infant's liver, for example, takes seven times as long as an adult's to detoxify certain drugs and chemicals. The brain, nervous system, immune system and liver of an infant are especially susceptible to environmental pollutants. A child's brain grows in spurts, and its sensitivity to pollutants may fluctuate daily.

"There is tremendous concern today by toxicologists that the brain may be the most vulnerable organ to environmental assault," says Dr. Bambi Young of the Center for Science in the Public Interest. "It is becoming clear to the health community that even modest exposures are compromising the child's ability to learn and function in the classroom."

Studies of the effects of hazardous-waste spills show that pollutants are more damaging to children than to adults. In San Jose, California, fifteen children who lived near the Fairchild Camera and Instrument Corporation's plant—where 60,000 gallons of industrial solvents (including TCE, trichloroethylene, which has caused cancer in laboratory animals) had leaked from underground storage tanks, contaminating drinking water—were born with what state officials describe as a "cluster" of congenital heart defects. A group of their parents sued Fairchild, claiming that the chemicals had caused birth defects, miscarriages and infant deaths, though health officials are doubtful that a causal link between the accident and the increased incidence of heart defects can be established.

Children who played in the streams and landfill near Love Canal suffered a disproportionately high rate of minimal brain dysfunction, while their parents did not. Dr. Beverly Paigen, an environmental health researcher who recently concluded a study of those children, believes the dozens of neurotoxins buried at Love Canal caused many children to have learning problems. U.S. government tests have shown that chemical levels in the air were well within the Occupational Safety and Health Administration's limits for adult workers.

Children who receive poor medical care or suffer from vitamin deficiencies or malnutrition are especially vulnerable to the effects of pollution. Even before the Administration began making cuts in the food stamp program and in programs specifically designed to improve children's nutritional intake, nearly one in two black children between the ages of 6 and 11 suffered from Vitamin A deficiency. Sixty-five percent of all 2- and 3-year-olds did not have enough calcium in their diets, and well over 90 percent of them did not get enough iron. Children with vitamin and mineral deficiencies have lowered resistance to the effects of cancer-causing pesticides like DDT, harmful metals like lead and cadmium, and persistent toxins like PCBs. Children whose diets do not provide sufficient iron, for example, can suffer irreversible brain damage from toxic materials.

Children who have been robbed of their natural curiosity and vitality by environmental poisons seem dull and apathetic to their teachers. "We all respond to kids in terms of how well they behave," points out Nancy Amidei, director of the Food Research and Action Center. "We don't stimulate listless kids, and we spend very little time with incorrigible or difficult kids.''

Dr. Frank Oski, chairman of the department of pediatrics at the State University of New York's Upstate Medical Center, believes ''90 percent of the difference in performance in aptitude and achievement between black and white kids is dietary and environmental in nature.'' He calls the current epidemic of low-level lead poisoning ''an example of how the environment can produce a whole generation of intellectually disadvantaged people.'' Such young people, says Kenneth Keniston, former chairman and director of the now disbanded Carnegie Council on Children, ''are systematically trained for failure.''

The young serve as a kind of early warning system for environmental contamination, like the green and white spider plants residents of Harrisburg, Pennsylvania, placed on their windowsills in the belief that the leaves would change color when radioactivity levels rose. Unfortunately, the Federal government has not used the ample data it has on children's vulnerability to pollutants to devise standards that are relevant to them. Rather, the government regards children as though they had adult tolerances.

For example, the E.P.A. sets pesticide-residue standards for more than 500 chemicals found in food. It does this by juggling information about people's eating habits and information about what levels of these chemicals are ''safe.'' But the system discriminates against the young. First, the E.P.A. uses the average diet of a 132-pound male teen-ager to compute the acceptable pesticide exposures for infants, despite the fact that their lower body weight and limited diet make them more vulnerable. Second, although the E.P.A. makes adjustments for infants' high milk intake, its regulations are based on adult levels of consumption. Acceptable levels for children are arrived at by arbitrarily multiplying the presumed safe adult concentrations by a factor of 10 or 100. Third, unlike the F.D.A., which encourages pharmaceutical companies to test their products on young animals, the E.P.A. uses only grown animals in testing pesticides.

A mass experiment beginning in 1981, in which Hawaiian infants and pregnant women were the involuntary subjects, may yield more definitive evidence on the effects of pesticide-tainted foods. For periods of as long as seventeen months in some cases, residents of Oahu unwittingly drank milk that was heavily contaminated with heptachlor, a carcinogenic pesticide. Although the E.P.A. banned the substance years ago, Hawaii's politically influential pineapple growers, principally Del Monte and Castle & Cooke, were allowed to phase out its use gradually. Oahu dairy cows had been fed pineapple tops that were contaminated with the pesticide, and last summer laboratory tests of their milk found that it contained more than seven times the acceptable level of heptachlor; samples of human breast milk contained dosages that were three times the E.P.A.'s ''safe'' level. Sales of the contaminated milk were not halted until virtually the entire population of Oahu had been exposed.

Worse, although the E.P.A. had known for ten years that the heptachlor standard for milk was obsolete, only last September did the agency suggest that the F.D.A. revise it. The F.D.A. did so, cutting it to one third of its previous level, but a former pesticide expert for Dow Chemical, Ted Norton, maintains that the new standard is inadequate to protect infants less than seven months old.

The government's air pollution regulations, like its pesticide-residue standards, offer only minimal protection to the young. Although the Reagan Administration and its allies in industry have attacked the Clean Air Act of 1970 as an example of ''overregulation,'' it in fact underregulates most of the pollutants especially dangerous to children.

E.P.A. regulations fail to take into account the differences in size, exposure and rate of absorption between adults and children. If they did, everything from the placement of air monitors to the choice of which air pollutants to regulate would have to be changed drastically.

Under the Clean Air Act, the E.P.A. has established ''safe'' levels of exposure for seven ''criteria pollutants''— all of them well-known byproducts of smokestack industries. In setting those standards, the agency relied on tests performed on healthy college students. From this data it then extrapolated the standards for infants, the elderly, asthmatics and people with heart conditions. To obtain a 100-fold ''margin of safety,'' for example, the ''safe'' level for adults was reduced by a factor of ten. There are several major flaws in this approach.

For one thing, the agency considers ''adverse effects'' to be skin rashes, burning eyes and the like. A pollutant that does not cause such problems, even if it might cause chronic diseases or cancers years after exposure, would not be regulated.

Also, the E.P.A.'s ''hazardous pollutant standards,'' established to control newer and more complex substances in the air, fail to do just that. Only four such standards have been promulgated to date, none of them during the present Administration. Scores of other toxins that have been developed in recent years, such as TCE, may be even more dangerous, but remain unregulated as well. None of the approximately 1,000 new chemicals that flood the marketplace each year are tested for their effects on young animals because there is no law requiring such testing. Considering the plethora of exotic new chemical mutagens, teratogens, carcinogens and poisons, that amounts to playing Russian roulette with children's lives—and those of generations to come.

Even if designated E.P.A. Administrator William Ruckelshaus is confirmed and purges all of the agency's pro-business Reagan appointees, the regulations that ignore children will still be on the books. Even assuming that the new Administrator and his staff are fully committed to protecting the environment, the question remains: Who at the E.P.A. will revamp the existing rules to protect society's most vulnerable members?

As a first step, the E.P.A. and the F.D.A. should test the

effects of all new chemicals on young animals to determine the long-term threats they pose to those with the longest life expectancy—children. Second, all environmental and health laws should be amended with the special vulnerability of the young in mind. Two good places to begin are the Clean Air and Clean Water Acts, both of which come before Congress for renewal this year.

Protecting the environment should not be a partisan issue, but protecting children seems to be nobody's issue. Neither the Democrats nor the Republicans have expressed interest in programs to safeguard them. However, a potentially effective forum for discussing issues that affect children, including environmental health protection, is the new Select Committee on Children, Youth, and Families, founded and chaired by Democratic Representative George Miller, a strong advocate for the young.

But while the politicians on Capitol Hill debate dollars and statistics and abstract threats, the human cost mounts. To fully grasp that cost, we must turn, finally, to the children who bear it every day of their lives—children like Eric Grant. By the time dangerously high levels of lead were discovered in his blood in 1976, Eric was 5 years old, and the damage to his central nervous system was irreversible. Today he has trouble concentrating on his schoolwork. He is fidgety and nervous, and the slightest noise distracts him. Being black and poor, Eric Grant had two strikes against him; lead poisoning is likely to be strike three. Meanwhile, the Alameda County, California, Lead Screening Project, which found Eric and treated him before his problem got worse, was disbanded because of cuts in Federal funding. Other children growing up in Eric's neighborhood are doomed to repeat the same vicious cycle.

UNTYING THE ENERGY KNOT

Benjamin Zycher

BENJAMIN ZYCHER is a senior staff economist on the Council of Economic Advisers. The views expressed in this article do not necessarily represent those of the Council of Economic Advisers.

What is PEPIG? What is it is trying to do to us or, in its view, "for" us?

Why, PEPIG is Washington's Permanent Energy Policy Interest Group. Composed of bureaucrats, consultants, researchers, academics, staffers, and others (including—don't tell anyone—this author), it grew along with the energy policy regulatory labyrinth of the 1970s. Some of its members have long experience stemming from previous regulatory exercises, such as the Mandatory Oil Import Quota Program, 1959–73. But today, threatened by the success of the market, PEPIG finds its interest to lie in a renewed expansion of the scope and pervasiveness of government activity and policy in the energy area.

With decontrol of oil and the end of the energy "crisis," PEPIG has had far less to do recently. Longing for the halcyon days of the federal thermostat police, PEPIG now has put forth a flood of proposals for new policies, interventions, subsidies, and taxes, each of which would have the unsurprising effect of increasing the influence and authority of PEPIG.

Of particular interest here are three general policy proposals: synthetic fuels subsidies, oil import tariffs, and oil price and allocation controls in the event of supply disruptions. The basic rationale presented for these proposals is summarized nicely in the following paragraph by Robert Bowie of the Brookings Institution in the *Christian Science Monitor* of March 25, 1983. Truly a masterpiece, this paragraph is suitable for framing because almost every sentence contains a basic error:

Lower prices and uncertainty about the energy outlook could seriously impede many of the measures needed for secure energy supply for the coming decades. The current decline in [OPEC] oil exports is due in part to the economic recession as well as to the drawing down of inventories by oil firms in place of purchases. But it is also the result of energy conservation, recovery of more costly oil, and substitution of other fuels. All these changes, which have been promoted by the higher cost of oil, could be discouraged by a sharp fall in oil prices. Thus, with economic revival and depletion of oil inventories, the consequence could be another sharp rise in oil prices in the next year or so, made more severe by "panic" buying as in past crises.

In other words, we all should be terribly concerned that oil prices today aren't as high as they used to be. The reassertion of market forces in oil pricing has brought about this frightening situation, depriving us of "certainty," not to mention the government's capacity to impose regulations, taxes, and controls to force us into "appropriate" patterns of energy use. In short, says Bowie, markets do not work.

But Bowie is wrong; all the evidence shows that markets do work very well indeed. The arguments set forth below for various forms of government control over energy (all representing variations on the theme enunciated in the above passage) are refuted by an examination of the realities of the energy market.

Subsidies for Alternative Energy

Government subsidies to develop such alternative energy sources as synthetic fuels are necessary because the private sector lacks sufficient incentives to make the necessary investments on its own. This is both because the full future value of the fuels cannot be received in the form of prices, and because the investments themselves are extremely risky.

This statement implicitly recognizes the fact that lower oil prices have made some alternative energy development investments, like synthetic fuels, uneconomic. But it is precisely the role of markets to allocate and reallocate resources efficiently in response to changing prices. Society may get less deep drilling or synthetic fuels, but it will get more of other things— things that will be more valuable than what has been forgone, assuming that prices are more credible measures of value than are the solemn pronouncements of government officials.

In fact, the full future value of synthetic fuels would be completely recoverable simply because technologies in this area are fully patentable. If patent lives are too short, then they should be extended—but this problem hardly justifies government subsidies.

The "risk" argument doesn't hold up, because government subsidies don't *reduce* risk, which exists because the future is difficult to predict either by entrepreneurs or bureaucrats. Instead, government subsidies only *reallocate* risk, from the private sector onto the taxpayers. Risk is a cost, and thus must be borne by individual human beings; projects themselves don't bear risk. A given investor can reduce his risk by avoiding "risky" projects and by diversifying his portfolio. The market, then, promotes specialization by allocating risk to those most willing to bear it. The market constantly undertakes a variety of projects that have long lead times, long economic lives, and uncertain futures; many of these are energy-related. Synthetic fuels subsidies are no more justified on "risk" grounds than are subsidies to other classes of investment.

6. FUTURE

National Security Vulnerability

Our vulnerability to the effects of an oil supply disruption is determined directly by the degree to which we are dependent on insecure sources of foreign oil. To the extent we can reduce our dependence by producing more fuel domestically, we will reduce our national vulnerability to overseas oil supply disruptions.

This argument has been repeated so often and for so long by pundits, politicians, and bureaucrats that it has acquired the status of an Eleventh Commandment. That it is largely false does not prevent its use as a rationale for all manner of proposals for greater government intervention in the energy market.

The seeming simplicity and self-evident nature of the argument begin to unravel when we seek to define what "vulnerability" means. (Bowie falls into the same trap in the passage cited above when he uses the term "secure energy supply" without defining what it is to be secure from.) Our "vulnerability" must be vulnerability to the economic effects of significant oil price increases, of which there are first-order effects and second-order effects. The first-order effects are felt in an increase in the price of all energy domestically, accompanied by other short-term economic dislocations caused by the relative change in prices (people buying less energy and more of other things). But the key point is that if international oil prices rise, these effects would occur *regardless of whether we imported all of our oil or none of it.* A nation totally self-sufficient faces the same crude oil prices as a nation totally dependent on foreign sources because the price of oil in any given country is determined by the world market price.

Even a so-called "targeted" embargo—as when a major oil-producing nation refuses to sell its oil to a particular importing nation—is not a serious threat, because oil can be reallocated with ease; a nontargeted nation can merely increase its purchases of oil and sell the excess to the targeted nation. Therefore, neither energy price increases nor short-term dislocations due to price changes, nor supply reallocations, are linked to the degree of "dependence" on foreign oil. Regulations and programs that seek to encourage self-sufficiency, then, simply have no relevance to reducing "vulnerability" to, or enhancing "security" from, these effects.

The degree to which we are dependent does affect the second-order effects of a foreign-oil price increase: an increase in the amount of U.S. wealth transferred overseas, and a fluctuation in exchange rates and thus in the prices of imported goods. But a significant reduction of the size of wealth transfers overseas would require either massive subsidies to businesses or other costly government programs. In any case, wealth transfers are private costs, so it is unclear why government should try to prevent them at all. As far as the exchange rate is concerned, propping up the dollar is a time-honored but nonetheless inappropriate activity of the government. It is also usually a financial loser, since government has proved itself particularly inept at predicting exchange-rate movements; our helpful government, as it were, usually loses our shirts.

Fighting Complacency with a Tariff

We cannot afford to become complacent. Low oil prices encourage consumption and so will lead to high prices in the future; in the meantime, they discourage conservation and development of alternative fuels. A tariff on imported oil would counter the negative effects of low oil prices, while at the same time help to reduce the federal deficit and provide a way to transfer some of OPEC's wealth back into the domestic economy.

"Complacency" here seems to signify that if there is no "crisis" there must be something wrong. Beyond that, however, many of the ingredients in this argument are simply incorrect. The statement that present low oil prices will lead to future high oil prices (which echoes Robert Bowie's conjecture quoted earlier) ignores the fact that reduced aggregate oil demand has led to a lower price and a new stable market at that price. We may be consuming more at the lower price than we would be at the higher price, but it does not follow that prices will therefore be forced up. If the market expected prices to rise tomorrow, then it would have strong incentives to bid them up today. That it does not do so implies strongly that the market does not expect prices to rise tomorrow, again because lower aggregate demand has pushed prices down.

To bemoan a reduction in conservation or the development of alternative energy sources is likewise to ignore the fact that these programs themselves are not free. The market properly and efficiently determines the degree of conservation, the allocation of resources among different fuels, and the output of alternatives; all of these tend to increase when oil prices rise, and decrease when they fall. There is no reason for consumers to bear, through a tariff, higher-cost conservation and alternative energy when lower-priced energy is available to them.

As far as "reducing the deficit" is concerned, this has become a rationale for every conceivable kind of tax measure. But it should be remembered that benefits to the U.S. Treasury are not the same as benefits to the U.S. economy. In other words, there is no reason to believe that, at any given level of federal spending, oil tariffs are a better tax instrument than debt finance.

A unilateral U.S. tariff would not even be particularly effective in terms of reducing the world price of oil. It might reduce the demand in the United States for OPEC oil, but a multilateral tariff imposed by many oil-importing nations simultaneously would be required to affect world demand substantially and thus world prices. The prospects of reaching a joint tariff agreement are indeed remote. Furthermore, to say that the tariff would transfer wealth back to the "domestic economy" obscures the likely outcome that the public sector would be better off, while the private sector would be worse off.

Why is it that a few years ago predictions of rising oil prices were used to justify oil import tariff proposals, while today predictions of falling oil prices are used to justify a tariff? It is difficult to avoid the suspicion that the real motivation for tariff proposals is increased government revenue along with more work, authority, and influence for groups like PEPIG. In fact, a tariff would be a bureaucratic godsend, for special interests from all over the country would be lining up to press for exemptions and credits. Petrochemical producers would argue that the tariff makes it impossible for them to compete; home heating oil consumers in the Northeast would petition for tax credits; small oil refiners would plead for special considerations; loopholes would be created, and then would have to be monitored to ensure that they didn't become too big. Foreign-policy considerations would add to the administrative burden and complexity. For example, during the Mandatory Oil Import Quota Program, Canadian and Mexican oil were exempt from quotas under the overland exemption. This did not please the Venezuelans, so the Brownsville U-turn was instituted: Venezuelan crude oil was shipped by tanker to Brownsville, Texas, where it was landed in bond and loaded onto trucks that then drove across the bridge into Mexico, made a U-turn, and returned into the United States, thus qualifying the Venezuelan oil for the "overland" exemption. If a tariff is imposed, watch out for similar schemes.

The Market Doesn't Work

Markets work well for small disruptions or minor changes in the external economic environment, but large problems require centralized planning and control.

This argument, of course, is the principal premise lurking behind all of the other arguments, and it continues to be made despite the ludicrous results of government energy policy during past disruptions, which were in fact relatively minor. When these results are pointed out, PEPIG's rejoinder is that there are economies of scale in regulation: For the government to regulate anything, it must regulate everything. In other words, past government policies failed not because they tried to do too much, but because they were permitted to do too little!

In fact, markets, when left alone, have worked quite well during the many oil supply disruptions of the past thirty years; gasoline lines and chaos accompanied only those disruptions that took place under the regulatory regimes. A forty-four-month disruption stemming from the nationalization of the Iranian oilfields began in early 1951; the size of the oil production decrease was equal to 15 percent of the production of the then ten major noncommunist foreign producers. The 1956 Suez war resulted in a production drop of more than twice this magnitude for about four months. In late 1966 a small disruption resulted from a dispute between Syria and Iraq over fees on the Iraqi pipelines crossing Syria. In mid-1967, the Six Day War disrupted about 12 percent of the major noncommunist production. A small disruption resulted from the Nigerian civil war in 1967–68. In 1970 a 5 percent disruption accompanied the Libyan price controversy and some damage to a pipeline in Syria. In 1971 the Algerian nationalization of the oil companies resulted in a small supply cutback for about five months. A small disruption accompanied political turmoil in Lebanon in 1973. The Middle East war of October 1973 resulted in production cuts and a closing of the Suez Canal. The Lebanese civil war produced a small disruption in mid-1976. About a year later, a small disruption was caused by fires at the Abqaiq field in Saudi Arabia. The Iranian revolution in late 1978 resulted in a substantial supply cut during late 1978 and much of 1979. Finally, the current Iran-Iraq hostilities have reduced Persian Gulf production substantially for an extended period.

These disruptions differ greatly in magnitude, duration, and other characteristics. Different government policies and responses accompanied them. Nonetheless, one single salient observation stands out: The market adjusted smoothly in every episode where government controls were absent. The two major disruptions resulting in queues, chaos, and confusion were the very ones with price and allocation control labyrinths in place: in late 1973, and again in 1978-79.

This record is not surprising. The very advantage of markets is that they facilitate and reward smooth adjustment to changes in the external environment. Bureaucracies do not, and inherently are incapable of rapid change. Bureaucracies have no choice but to use historical patterns as benchmarks; but constant, dynamic changes in the private economy mean that historical patterns often have little or no relationship to future situations.

When disruptions occur, our policy should be to minimize the harm. Energy supply disruptions mean that less energy is available; price and allocation controls cannot produce more energy. Instead, we should ensure that the fuels that remain available are used most productively, and that incentives remain to produce substitute fuels. Only markets can achieve these objectives.

In fact, elaborate government schemes and controls discourage the private sector from preparing adequately for disruptions. Both those who expect to see their oil confiscated through price and allocation controls, and those who expect the government to bail them out through the very same controls, will have little incentive to prepare if controls are expected.

Finally, only free markets are consistent with personal freedom and the circumscription of government power. A necessary consequence of government intervention is that only those willing to submit to the government and possessing the greatest political clout will benefit from controls. Opponents of regulatory schemes, unless they have other horses to trade, are unlikely to get special allocations of fuel during a disruption.

A rational energy policy relying on market forces would start with abolition of the Department of Energy. This case has nothing to do with budget savings, which would be relatively trivial. Abolition of the DOE is a worthy goal because, good intentions notwithstanding, the energy bureaucracy is an important interest group that will benefit greatly if we return to the regulatory policies of the recent past. The DOE also provides a focus for the appeals of all the other concentrated interest groups who find the regulatory apparatus advantageous to them. In short, abolition of the DOE would remove a powerful voice within the government, however muted during the Reagan administration, calling for a return to the perverse policies of the past.

It should be remembered that while it is difficult to cheat an honest man, it is impossible to cheat a cynic. Beware, then, of PEPIG and the beguiling arguments of would-be energy regulators, whose policies, if permitted once again to take hold, will lead us into yet another great energy "crisis."

Photovoltaics

A Solar Technology for Powering Tomorrow

Photovoltaics is the technology by which the world's most abundant resource—sunlight—is converted directly into electricity. Solar photovoltaic systems can be installed in remote villages—where electricity is unknown—as well as on suburban rooftops, providing reliable, inflation-proof power to millions. But the widespread use of solar cells hinges on one major challenge: cost reduction.

Christopher Flavin

Christopher Flavin is a senior researcher with the Worldwatch Institute (1776 Massachusetts Avenue, N.W., Washington, D.C. 20036). He is coauthor of *Renewable Energy: The Power to Choose* (W.W. Norton, 1983).

Solar photovoltaic cells have been called the ultimate energy technology. Environmentally benign and without moving parts, solar cells convert sunlight, the world's most abundant and widespread renewable energy source, into electricity, one of the most versatile and valuable energy forms.

Solar photovoltaics may become one of the most rapidly expanding energy sources—and one of the biggest growth industries—of the late twentieth century. Photovoltaics production has increased at a rate of more than 50% annually for the last five years, and a steady stream of companies is entering the solar electricity business. Many governments have dramatically boosted their support of photovoltaics, and international competition is growing. In contrast to recent declines in the use of oil, abandonment of synthetic fuel projects, and financial troubles in the nuclear power industry, photovoltaics is a healthy "sunrise" industry.

The current market for solar cells is limited, focusing on specialized applications in areas not yet reached by utility lines. These remote-site uses are surprisingly numerous and diverse, however, spread throughout the developing and industrial worlds.

And sales are growing rapidly. Portable solar-cell modules, for example, are popular on boats and train cabooses. Remote mountain cabins and scientific research stations are beginning to rely on photovoltaics rather than diesel generators. A market for photovoltaics to power microwave repeaters and other communications installations is growing rapidly.

Additional future uses for photovoltaics will be found at remote military installations—amounting to 100 megawatts of new solar cells each year in the United States alone, according to one study. In these and many other uses, solar-electric systems are now more economical and reliable than alternatives.

Solar-Powering the Third World

During the next decade, small stand-alone uses for photovoltaics will almost certainly predominate. There are still millions of houses in remote areas of Australia, Europe, North America, and the Soviet Union that are not connected to power lines. And in developing countries, most villages and rural areas still lack access to a steady supply of electricity. The dream of extending central grids into the "heart of darkness" has faded in the face of mounting Third World debts and the rising cost of power plants and electric lines. If millions of peasants and villagers are to have electricity in their lifetimes, most will have to rely on small, decentralized energy systems.

Small-scale uses that are already economical include refrigerators for perishable food and medicines, communications systems, television sets, lights, and mills. Water pumping is a particularly good use for solar electricity since sunlight is usually available when water is most needed. In the Third World, just a few hundred watts of power—minuscule by an industrial nation's standards—can have an enormous effect on village life, providing basic amenities for the first time.

If solar cell prices fall 50% or more as expected in the next five years, solar power will become economical for virtually all electricity applications in Third World villages.

Interest in photovoltaics has been particularly strong in the Philippines and Thailand, whose governments encourage the use of photovoltaics imported from Europe and the United States for communications, water pumping, and other applications. A half dozen developing countries will soon have indigenous photovoltaics industries. India and Mexico are developing government-owned photovoltaics industries and installing solar-electric systems in the countryside. The Pakistani government plans to introduce solar electricity in 14 villages by 1984.

The foreign-aid programs of industrial nations have also begun to include photovoltaics. France has had major programs under way since the mid-1970s to install solar-powered pumps and television sets in West Africa. The television sets, modified to require as little as 20 watts of power, bring educational programs to people in remote areas at a reasonable cost. The U.S. Agency for International Development installed eight specially designed solar-powered vaccine refrigerators at rural health centers in 1982 and has another dozen small-scale photovoltaics projects under way, mainly in Africa. In Somalia, relief groups have brought in more than a hundred photovoltaic water-pumping systems to be used at refugee camps.

Solar Development Progressing Slowly

Studies and demonstration projects sponsored by the United Nations Development Programme (UNDP), the World Health Organization, and the World Bank show that no established and reliable market yet exists for photovoltaic systems in most developing countries and that the quality of the equipment sold is uneven. In many areas, protecting arrays of solar panels from dust storms and keeping them clean is also a problem.

Development specialists, however, are generally confident that such obstacles can be overcome and that photovoltaics will gradually gain broad appeal for small-scale Third World uses. They are particularly interested in the potential of solar-powered pumping systems, since drinking water and adequate irrigation are two of the most urgent needs in many rural areas.

One of the more ambitious plans for photovoltaics is to provide electricity for villages. The first experimental village system was installed in the Schuchuli village on the Papago Indian Reservation in Arizona in 1978. Since then, its 3.5 kilowatts of cells have powered water pumps, lights, refrigerators, and communal washing and sewing machines for the village's 95 residents, who previously had no electricity. A much larger 25-kilowatt system installed early this year in a Tunisian village pumps water and performs other agricultural tasks, as well as meeting household needs.

Several other experimental village systems have been set up and carefully monitored, and all confirm the enormous potential of this concept. For many of the world's poor who are still without electricity, photovoltaics may soon be a reliable power source. First, however, governments and international aid agencies must arrange innovative financing. Today, only the wealthier developing countries are purchasing photovoltaics, while many African nations and others that most need a new source of electricity cannot afford it.

Solar Power in the Modern World

Decentralized solar-electricity systems are likely to play an important role in industrial regions as well. Solar cells can be placed on rooftops, turning buildings of all kinds into electricity generators. Photovoltaics thus has the potential to give ordinary people a measure of energy independence unprecedented in the modern world.

With solar-electric systems on their rooftops, people will no longer be vulnerable to fuel price increases. With battery storage, power will stay on even if a storm knocks down local electrical lines. All of this brings psychological satisfaction as well as practical benefits.

Together with wind turbines, geothermal energy, co-generation, and small-scale hydropower, photovoltaics could gradually decentralize existing power systems. Utilities would not only produce power but would also become energy brokers, distributing electricity generated by tens of thousands of small producers.

If these new energy relationships are to evolve, rooftop solar-power systems must be connected with the utility grids that are the main source of power in most industrial countries.

The main reason for making the utility connection is economic: electrical battery storage can as much as double the total cost of solar power, but batteries are not needed if a utility provides backup electricity. A utility hookup requires an electricity inverter, an inexpensive device that converts the direct current a solar cell produces into alternating current compatible with the electricity in utility lines. Special controls regulate the electricity going in and out of a building, and two meters are installed—one measuring the electricity sold by the utility to the household and the other measuring the power going from the house to the utility. Another possibility is a single meter running backward as well as forward.

A 1981 study by the U.S. Solar Energy Research Institute shows that in most parts of the United States a moderately sized solar-electric system on an energy-efficient house can provide *more* electricity than the house uses. However, since much of this power would be generated when it is not needed by the homeowner (and would be sold to the utility), the household would depend on the utility for electricity when the sun is not shining. In some months, the utility would actually send the customer a check rather than a bill!

Designing the Solar Building

Architects and engineers in the United States and Japan have already begun designing solar-electric buildings. Like solar water heaters, photovoltaic systems require an unshaded southern exposure and durable materials. Lightweight photovoltaic panels need little additional structural support, but they do require more roof space than thermal collectors do—30 to 50 square meters for a typical household-size system in a sunny region.

In the United States, approximately one-third of existing residential buildings could use photovoltaics—a total of 20 million houses. However, taking maximum advantage of photovoltaic electricity will require

Investing in the Sun

The solar-cell industry has expanded rapidly in recent years, attracting ever larger investments. But each year the amount of investment needed to attain a competitive position in the industry grows. To make photovoltaic technologies profitable, production costs must be lowered by using large-scale manufacturing processes that require sizable initial investments.

A cause of concern for some is that the largest source of new capital in photovoltaics in recent years has been the oil industry. By 1981, eight oil companies in the United States and two in France had invested in photovoltaics, together bringing close to $100 million to the industry each year. Petroleum firms have purchased controlling interests in some solar-cell companies, and they own minority shares in others. Three solar-cell firms that are wholly or partly owned by oil companies—all from the United States—had an estimated 80% of the worldwide market for photovoltaics in 1981, according to the Center for Renewable Resources, a U.S. public-interest group. Others hold a dominant position in developing new technologies not yet commercialized.

The rush to invest in photovoltaics occurred simultaneously with the withdrawal by some oil companies from the solar water-heater market. One explanation is that the solar-collector industry depends largely on plumbing skills and the success of small retail outlets, areas in which the oil industry has little experience. Although they also lack expertise in photovoltaics and other semiconductor devices, oil firms do have experience with long-term, high-payoff R&D programs.

Because of generally tight capital markets and high interest rates, few other companies can invest tens of millions of dollars in a speculative industry where large payoffs are at least 5 or 10 years away. Oil company executives see photovoltaics as an emerging industry in which they can use their financial muscle productively. Oil industry strategists also see investment in photovoltaics as an important step in the creation of diversified energy companies that will outlast the petroleum era.

These developments have raised a red flag for many solar-energy advocates. They fear that oil companies, with large holdings in natural gas, coal, and uranium, are now getting a lock on sunshine as well. In his 1980 book *The Sun Betrayed*, Ray Reece alleges that oil firms intend to slow down the development of photovoltaics until oil wells run dry, when they can then monopolize the solar-cell industry.

Karl Frieden of the National Center for Economic Alternatives echoes these fears: "The oil companies will hold solar power hostage, while maximizing their profits from more limited conventional fuel supplies." A study of the photovoltaics industry by Barrett Stambler of the Center for Renewable Resources, though more restrained, concludes that the solar-cell industry already lacks competitiveness and suggests that at least one company practices predatory pricing—selling photovoltaics below cost in order to drive other firms out of business.

Most solar industry executives and many independent analysts reject these charges. George Tenet of the Solar Energy Industries Association, which has several oil company members, claims, "The number of competitors has consistently increased and the selling price has consistently decreased . . . . There's no attempt to stifle competition or suppress new technology."

Tenet and others point out that oil and photovoltaics compete in separate markets and that too many companies are currently involved for any one firm to contain photovoltaics until the world runs out of oil. Industry analysts note that patent protection in photovoltaic technology is inherently weak and not likely to block the entry of new firms. And Morris Adelman, an economist at the Massachusetts Institute of Technology, concludes: "The notion that the energy giants, controlling the biggest part of the manufacturing capacity in photovoltaics, could set the price artificially high to protect their other investments is unrealistic."

The truth in this controversy probably lies somewhere between the two extremes. Oil company investments have, in fact, spurred the photovoltaics industry, and so far the companies with support from the oil industry appear to have innovative, aggressive development programs.

There is, nonetheless, cause for concern. Large corporations tend to be relatively hidebound and unimaginative, whereas smaller companies have made a disproportionate share of the world's industrial breakthroughs. In photovoltaics, the pioneering small companies have been bought out at an earlier stage in their development than was the case in semiconductors and most other technologies.

Oil companies bring abundant capital to the solar-cell industry. But they have no experience in this field, and their record of innovation is unlikely to match that of smaller companies.

that electricity be used more efficiently and that new houses be designed with this technology in mind.

The world's first specially designed photovoltaic residence was built in Phoenix, Arizona, in 1980 with the help of funding by the U.S. Department of Energy. Since then, approximately a dozen solar-electric buildings have been built, most of them experimental houses in the United States. At least one architectural firm has begun designing solar-electric homes commercially, and others are considering entering the field. These houses have been an important proving ground, allowing architects to experiment with different designs, improving their aesthetics and ruggedness.

Because rooftop solar systems are exposed to the elements and falling debris, they must be exceptionally durable. Recent innovative designs integrate solar cells into the roofs themselves, and solar cells may one day become a major roofing material. One design mounts photovoltaic panels on tracks, allowing them to slide easily on or off the roof. Another company has developed a photovoltaic shingle that provides power and also protects the roof.

In all cases, ease of installation and repair is essential. Some solar-electric systems can be added to a properly designed house in just a few hours. Architects have already demonstrated that solar-electric buildings can be attractive. While some are brashly modern—dominated by their photovoltaic systems—others have a variety of traditional styles that make the solar systems barely noticeable.

Toward an Economical Solar System

A bona fide market for solar-electric houses should emerge when the cost of a photovoltaic module falls to $2 to $3 per watt—approximately one-fourth of the current level. This should happen by the early 1990s at the latest. At this price range, a 3-kilowatt system providing 50% of a household's electricity needs could be installed for between $12,000 and $18,000.

At first the market will be dominated by wealthier homeowners, but as prices fall below $2 per watt, solar-electric homes will be generating electricity at a price competitive with utility-generated power. With tax credits such as those already in place in some countries, solar-electric houses would clearly be economical.

Some people look at rooftop photovoltaics as an energy panacea that will soon price utilities right out of the electricity business. Such views are fanciful and could be self-defeating. Solar electricity is not going to become cheap anytime in the foreseeable future. Rather, photovoltaics will gradually reach price competitiveness with conventional generating technologies and then only slowly undercut them, probably around the turn of the century.

Communities in all but the most overcast climates should eventually be able to obtain at least one-fourth of their electricity from rooftop photovoltaics. But these photovoltaic systems will never stand alone if the goal is economical, uninterrupted power. The sun often shines brightly only a few hours a day, but electricity is needed continuously. It makes sense, therefore, to link solar-electric systems with other generating technologies, including the many other renewable energy sources now being developed. Careful planning can produce a diverse but still economical and reliable power system.

Goals for Solar Power

The big news in the photovoltaics industry in the early 1980s is that it is prospering—despite a worldwide recession in which many more-established industries are on the brink of insolvency. Production of solar cells has expanded fivefold during a three-year period in which the world economy grew at a meager 1% annual rate. Based on manufacturing plants now under construction and unprecedented marketing efforts on the part of several large companies, prolific growth of about 50% per year is virtually guaranteed for the next three to five years. By 1986, the photovoltaics industry worldwide will probably be producing five times as many solar cells as it did in 1982.

Much more difficult to answer is the question of how widely photovoltaics will be used in the more distant future. Since the early 1970s, many predictions have been made about photovoltaics, but most are based on dubious assumptions about the potential for cost reduction, future economic conditions, and the rate of growth in electricity demand. As the estimates and assumptions are amassed, uncertainty multiplies.

The goal of the U.S. photovoltaics program, as formulated by Congress in 1978, is to double the manufacture of solar cells each year in order to reach an annual output of 2,000 megawatts of cells by 1988 (250 times the 1982 total). The U.S. Department of Energy subsequently established a target of obtaining one quad (quadrillion Btu's) of energy from photovoltaics by the year 2000. This would require an installed capacity of more than 50,000 megawatts, or about half as much power as nuclear plants provide today.

The United States has already fallen short of the production trends required to meet these goals, and there is now general agreement that they will be reached much later than planned. The Reagan administration's cutbacks in the photovoltaics budget and its abandonment of commercialization programs have dealt U.S. photovoltaics goals an additional crippling blow.

What went wrong? Does the slippage of these targets mean the United States should reduce efforts to harness photovoltaic electricity?

In truth, the main problem is not with solar-cell technology but with the goals themselves, which call for unrealistically rapid progress. Photovoltaics continues to follow a remarkable cost curve, with prices falling by an average of more than 50% every five years. But because of the large investment needed in automated manufacturing processes, progress gets tougher the further prices fall.

Laboratory achievements have been impressive, but time and money are needed to get from the lab to the factory, an inevitable truth that solar-cell forecasters tried to sidestep. Their goals called for solar electricity to become widespread much faster than has nuclear power, although only a small fraction of the funds that have been

6. FUTURE

committed to nuclear-power development is being spent on solar-technology development.

Reduced Demand for Electricity?

Predictions about photovoltaics also often assume that the world has an insatiable appetite for electricity. Many analysts echo the unrealistic forecasts of the utility industry, which still sees electricity use in industrial countries growing by two-thirds in the next 18 years.

The unspoken assumption in these forecasts is that, despite rapidly rising electricity prices, the world will continue to substitute electricity for all other forms of energy. Some boost their forecasts even higher by assuming that the electric car will be commonplace within the next decade.

Such analyses are well out of line with current energy trends. Energy conservation and modest economic growth are now the driving forces in the energy marketplace—something that no realistic photovoltaics forecast can ignore. Data from several major industrial countries show 1% to 2% yearly growth in electricity use, in some cases slower than the growth rate of the economy as a whole. Credible forecasters now project very slow or even no growth in electricity use during the next two decades.

Interestingly, this low growth rate has been partly caused by the very trends that boost the prospects for photovoltaics—soaring costs for coal and nuclear power plants. Electricity prices will almost certainly continue to rise during the next decade, since coal and nuclear energy are by far the largest new power sources coming on line during this period, and many power plants are suffering massive cost overruns that have yet to be financed. Assuming rapid electricity growth during this period is a kind of wishful analysis reminiscent of the early days of nuclear power.

Because of slower growth in electricity use, the absolute size of the market for photovoltaics during the next two decades will be smaller than was assumed a few years ago. In the major industrial countries, which already have considerable utility overcapacity, few new power plants are needed.

New electricity generation, however, will be needed in developing countries and in industrial nations, as older power plants are replaced. These will be sizable markets for photovoltaics, though not as large as was once thought.

As a result, photovoltaics will likely be introduced gradually over the next 20 years. This is actually an asset, because if solar-electric systems are introduced slowly, they can be linked effectively to existing power sources and employed in the most efficient manner. Nuclear power provides a good example of what can go wrong if a technology is too quickly forced on an unprepared world.

In an energy-conserving era, solar electricity has a major role to play. Photovoltaic technologies and energy-conservation technologies have a naturally synergistic relationship. The lower the power requirements of a particular device, the more practical solar-electric systems become. One improvement helps encourage another. French and Japanese companies, for instance, have worked hard to reduce the electricity needs of television sets and calculators so that they can be powered with solar cells.

A large American "all-electric" house would be hard to power with photovoltaics, but the "low-energy" houses now popular in Scandinavia would be quite adaptable. The more that electricity requirements can be reduced in households and industries throughout the world, the closer we will be to widespread, practical use of photovoltaics. This, in turn, will spur the increased efficiency of motors and buildings.

The Future of Photovoltaics

A few predictions are now possible. Based on the most recent cost trends, photovoltaics should begin replacing most diesel generators and become the largest new source of electricity for villages in many developing countries within a few years. Third World governments and international aid agencies, however, must help introduce solar-electric systems if they are to be widely used.

Most important are financing mechanisms for poorer areas of the Third World. By the late 1980s, centralized photovoltaic power stations should become conventional generating technologies in many regions, and utilities will lead the way in introducing solar electricity. By the early 1990s, rooftop solar-electric systems should begin to catch on around the world.

Worldwide annual production of photovoltaics will probably rise to between 200 and 300 megawatts of capacity by 1990 and to more than 1,000 megawatts by the end of the century. This will make the photovoltaics business a billion-dollar industry by the late 1980s and push it close to the $10 billion mark by the year 2000.

Total installed solar-electric capacity will probably be between 5,000 and 10,000 megawatts by century's end. Although this will be enough capacity to supply only a fraction of the world's electricity, it will set the stage for the rapid introduction of solar electricity in the following years. By the middle of the next century, photovoltaics may provide between 20% and 30% of the world's electricity and serve as a cornerstone of a sustainable global power system.

The exact pace of photovoltaics development and the installed capacity in particular years will depend mainly on how fast large-scale, low-cost manufacturing processes are introduced. Today, the largest photovoltaics plants being built produce between 2 and 3 megawatts of solar cells a year. Building more advanced plants that annually produce solar cells capable of generating 20 or 30 megawatts could lead to module costs of less than one-fourth of the current cost. The catch, of course, is that such plants will be expensive and companies will not build them until the market grows substantially.

The most important step that governments can take is to help stimulate the market for solar-electric systems by providing special grants and loans and by purchasing photovoltaics directly for use on government buildings and military facilities and for the poor. Demonstration projects and educational

Centralized Solar Power

As an alternative to stand-alone photovoltaic systems in remote villages and independent systems on urban rooftops, the concept of electricity generation from large, centralized photovoltaic power systems has long fascinated some scientists and planners. As early as the 1960s, University of Arizona researchers proposed using massive solar arrays in deserts to supply much of the world's power.

Large solar-electric systems do have some modest economies of scale, and, at least until recently, they seemed to match most closely the popular conception of how a modern power system should be structured. Utilities have a growing interest in photovoltaics, and centralized solar power, they feel, ensures that they will get a piece of the action.

The most controversial plan for harnessing solar electricity is the solar-power satellite. Several researchers in the United States have proposed placing large arrays of solar cells—about the area of Manhattan—in stationary orbit around the earth, using microwave transmitters to convey the power to land-based receivers. The idea has come under fire for a variety of economic and environmental reasons. And it will be decades at least before the vast quantity of materials needed to build an orbital power station can be boosted into space—or mined from the moon.

Other centralized photovoltaic designs show more promise. Government and private researchers in the last few years have begun designing large, earth-based photovoltaic power systems. The effort, however, has been overshadowed by much larger programs in Europe and the United States to develop solar thermal power plants using concentrated sunlight to boil water and turn a turbine and generator. Although these more conventional solar systems have a large potential in some sunny regions, photovoltaics likely will be more economical and more flexible as well. And, since 1980, government funding of solar thermal power systems has declined while funding of photovoltaics has risen in most countries.

Only a few large photovoltaic projects have been built so far. A 240-kilowatt solar-power project using concentrators was completed in Arizona in 1982. It provides electricity for the Sky Harbor Airport near Phoenix and was largely financed by the U.S. Department of Energy.

A similar system, funded jointly by the Saudi Arabian and U.S. governments, was installed in Saudi Arabia in 1982. It generates 350 kilowatts of solar power with diesel back-up for three Saudi villages.

Meanwhile, utilities in California lead in integrating solar-power systems into their electricity grids. The Sacramento Municipal Utility District (SMUD) has begun work on a 100-megawatt (100,000 kilowatt) photovoltaic power plant scheduled for completion by 1994 at a total cost of more than $250 million.

The first phase of the project, funded partly by the federal and state governments, will place 1 megawatt (1,000 kilowatts) in operation by 1984. The project will use flat-plate arrays on 1,100 acres of now-vacant land adjacent to the Rancho Seco nuclear power plant, and generate one-tenth as much power as the nuclear plant does.

The first privately funded photovoltaic power plant is under way in southern California. Financed and built by the ARCO Solar photovoltaics company, the project will feed 1 megawatt of power from flat-plate solar arrays mounted on computer-controlled tracking devices into the lines of the Southern California Edison Company beginning in 1983. In Italy, a 1-megawatt government-funded photovoltaic plant called the Delphos project is also scheduled for completion in 1983.

These utility projects are harbingers of things to come. As many as 10 similar projects will likely be announced in the next few years, mostly in the western United States and southern Europe, where ample sunlight can help utilities phase out their existing oil-fired power plants.

Utility planners point out that land availability will not be a problem for the foreseeable future, particularly since there is much unused land adjacent to existing power plants and along power-line rights of way.

Beyond boosting electricity supplies, these projects create a large new market for the photovoltaics industry, helping to bring down costs and improving the economic feasibility of all photovoltaic installations. The Sacramento project alone could, by the mid-1980s, add more solar cells each year than are currently produced worldwide.

No other energy technology has the versatility of photovoltaics. David Morris of the Institute for Local Self-Reliance in the United States observes: "Using the same energy source—sunlight—and the same technology, we could have the most decentralized or the most centralized form of electricity generation in history."

The question of which uses for solar electricity will prove economical and popular has already caused controversy. Advocates of centralized solar power cite the economic advantages of large photovoltaic systems, since one set of power lines and control devices can serve a large installation.

On the other hand, the partisans of decentralized solar electricity counter that if solar-electric systems are placed on rooftops and fully integrated into industries and households, they could one day be cheaper than centrally generated power and permit energy independence as well.

No clear resolution to this argument is in sight, and different uses of solar power are likely to emerge simultaneously.

6. FUTURE

programs such as those of the European Economic Commission can also encourage production. Equally critical is the success of the photovoltaics industry in raising needed capital. Careful planning and close relationships between photovoltaics companies and the investment community are essential.

The benefits of solar electricity cannot be measured simply in kilowatts or percentage points alone. Photovoltaic systems cause fewer environmental problems than any other means of generating electricity. They are a particularly striking contrast to coal and nuclear power, the most rapidly growing electricity sources today. Each of these poses environmental risks on an unprecedented global scale. Photovoltaics, on the other hand, is a major step toward an ecological and sustainable energy system.

Photovoltaics also has a strategic value that other energy sources lack. It will make small amounts of power available in virtually any corner of the globe, allowing developing countries to leapfrog the now prohibitively expensive process of extending electricity grids to all areas. Rarely do the world's poorest have a chance to benefit from one of the world's most advanced technologies. Photovoltaics not only can help remove some of the drudgery of village life, but by powering communications systems it can help educate people and bind together emerging nations.

The potential contribution of photovoltaics is perhaps most visible in the happiness of an African nomad who experiences running water for the first time. It is also clear in the improved health of an Indian villager who uses solar electricity to refrigerate food and medicine. Thanks to the advances being made in this seemingly exotic new technology, the living standards of hundreds of millions of people can be significantly raised in the next few decades.

Economic Strategies for a Narcissistic Society

Murray L. Weidenbaum

Murray L. Weidenbaum is Mallinckrodt Distinguished University Professor and director of the Center for the Study of American Business at Washington University, St. Louis. He served during 1981-82 as President Reagan's first chairman of the Council of Economic Advisers. His most recent books are Business, Government, and the Public *and* The Future of Business Regulation.

This is a fascinating time to evaluate the American economy. To twist an old phrase, economists rush in where angels fear to tread. I acknowledge at the outset that my crystal ball is especially foggy. To those who do not share my sense of uncertainty, I can only say that if your crystal ball is not equally foggy, something is wrong.

The U.S. economy is in the early stages of important long-term change. These changes are not variations on a constant theme; rather, crosscurrents characterize economic policy and economic performance. Let me provide a few examples. The 1980s—in contrast to the 1970s, which witnessed a rise in the share of the national income taken by federal taxation—will be characterized by declining federal tax burdens. This is a result of the 1981 tax cuts, including the indexing of personal income taxes to begin in 1985.

Unless existing law is reversed, the Treasury's share of the national income will be declining, from 21 percent in 1981 to about 19 percent in 1985. Two percent may not sound like much, but consider that 2 percent of a $4 trillion economy means an extra $80 billion in the annual pool of private savings. That should provide an important stimulus to investment and future growth.

But the failure to trim government spending on a magnitude anywhere near that of the tax cuts has contributed to a substantial increase in budget deficits. The annual flow of red ink is rising from $62 billion in fiscal year 1981 to $110 billion in fiscal year 1982. The deficit is heading into the neighborhood of $200 billion—a very rough neighborhood—not only for fiscal year 1983 but for 1984 and 1985, as well. Surely, large portions of current deficits are a result of the recession, but the estimates for future years assume significant economic recovery. The financing of such large deficits during a period of expansion will mean competition with private investment for the limited supply of savings. This might be called an example of the Feds giveth and the Feds taketh away. With respect to their influence on private capital formation, tax reductions and rising deficits represent contradictory governmental forces.

One economic lesson from the past two years is clear: the notion that the way to cut government spending is to cut taxes constitutes wishful thinking. In its most extreme form, this idea was expressed as, "The only way to reduce spending is to reduce revenues." As many had suspected (and as recent experience has confirmed) the most effective way to cut government spending is a more conventional way, to reduce appropriations. Easier said than done.

Every business group enthusiastically supports cuts in welfare programs, but maritime or textile or steel subsidies are looked at differently. Such subsidies, it is said, are essential for economic growth and national prosperity. Nor will anyone be surprised that farm groups are unswervingly enthusiastic about cutting urban programs. Farm price supports, of course, are a very different matter. Likewise, labor groups are quite willing to cut farm programs as well as business subsidies, but only so long as the social programs are spared. On occasion, these groups may unite.

Try closing any obsolete government installation. I can predict with 99.9 percent accuracy the local reaction. A phalanx of labor people, city government officials, and the chamber of commerce will bitterly oppose this blow to the local economy. They will discover a new unity in pointing out how important that Navy yard or that Army base is. We are all for economy in government, they will say, but why pick on us? It is ironic that the overwhelming majorities in favor of balancing the budget—as shown in virtually every public opinion poll—are far larger than the numbers supporting any individual budget cut. Pogo was right. The enemy, they is us.

Recent years have also witnessed an important change with respect to regulation. In striking contrast to the 1960s and the 1970s, the federal government has not embarked upon a single significant new regulatory activity over the past two years. The current emphasis is on carrying out existing regulatory mandates at a lower cost. Fiscal year 1982 was the first in many years that the federal government's expenditures for regulation declined in real terms. The number of employees in federal regulatory agencies actually fell, from a high of more than 90,000 in 1980 down to 79,000 in 1982. A further decline, to 76,000, is projected for 1983.

Simultaneously, however, another form of government involvement in business is on the rise—protectionism. Around the world, regulation of foreign trade is expanding rampantly. Though there is no shortage of foreign protectionist practices that one could properly protest, America's own hands are hardly clean. Recent U.S. government intervention in foreign trade has included boycotting grain sales to the Soviet Union, prohibiting participation in the Siberian natural gas pipeline, forcing West European nations to set up quotas on their steel exports to us, establishing quotas on our imports of sugar, and coaxing the Japanese into limiting their exports of automobiles to the United States. Applications for further protection come from almost every segment of the economy—mushrooms, ceramic tableware, casein, and others. Casein, by the way, is a vegetable substitute that is not even made in the United States. But last year the nonexistent casein industry called for protection. The list goes on—edible seaweeds, mechanics' shop towels, and even manhole covers.

Any but the most partisan observer must be struck by the lack of balance and the self-serving nature of the current debate on foreign trade. Everyone advocates open markets and free trade overseas. All want to eliminate "their" barriers to our exports. Our barriers to their exports, however, are a different matter and do not generate much interest over here.

Let me explain this by way of an uncomplicated example. Country A is on one side of the ocean, and Country B is on the other. Country B has a large export surplus with Country A, and Country A experiences great difficulty getting its exports into Country B. Sound familiar? Country B, of course, is Japan (big trade surplus), and Country A is the United States (big trade deficit). One finds, too, that Country B is the United States, and Country A is Western Europe. Over the past decade, America has had a large trade surplus with the European Community—almost as large as our deficit with Japan—and we have erected an array of obstacles before European exports to the United States. Although many Americans are agitated over U.S. trade deficits

with Japan, how many are even aware of our large trade surpluses with Western Europe? It is not surprising that, given this disparity in awareness, protectionist pressures are on the rise.

To combat protectionism, the basic reason for its popularity must be understood. Protectionism is an effective means by which small, but well-organized, groups use a nation's political process to their advantage. The costs are borne by the mass of consumers, who are not even aware of the burdens imposed on them in the form of higher prices. Thus, protectionism can be thought of as a hidden tax on the consumer. I cannot unambiguously state that the federal government will be intervening less in the American economy in the 1980s than it did in the 1970s. At best, I can describe shifts in the composition of government intervention in the economy.

During the past two years, substantial progress has been made in reducing inflation. Cutting the inflation rate by more than half has involved many adjustments, which in turn have caused serious strains. There have been losers as well as winners.

The benefits of reduced inflation have been substantial. The bulk of the American public, for the first time in many years, have achieved increases in real disposable income and, even during recession, have seen their real income remain historically high. This improvement did not result from some sudden spurt in nominal income. Rather, it was brought about by a reduction in the inflation and tax wedges between nominal and real income. The transition to a less inflationary economy has not been easy, though, and losers have been more vocal than the winners. The losses in this environment of lower inflation come in many forms. Ill-conceived company investments and expense commitments are no longer automatically bailed out by inflation. Long-term commitments for wage increases are more difficult to pass on in the form of higher prices. Art, gold, and postage stamps are no longer attractive investments in a continually rising price level; they are once again seen as consumables.

Although many consumers are enjoying improved living standards, an enhanced sense of well-being has not yet surfaced. Fear of unemployment still dominates. Also, the typical business firm's experience in the new economic environment has thus far been negative: namely, declining real sales volumes and reduced profitability. Yet, the adjustments to lower inflation include many productivity-enhancing changes. These range from lower overhead costs to greater factory efficiency. Such changes are likely to enhance the productivity and competitiveness of the American economy, but only over an extended period of time. As is the case in so many policy areas, the costs are felt earlier than the benefits. This makes for nasty politics but is the essence of the investment process and of economic growth.

Another set of crosscurrents is the dual effort to expand, in the long run, private investment in capital goods and, in the short run, to increase outlays for government durable goods—weapon systems. My intention is not to debate the merits of either expansion. The United States lives in a dangerous world, and a compelling case can be made for some strengthening of the military establishment. Surely, too, rising private investment is the key to economic growth and higher living standards.

In the short run, though, the recession has caused such substantial amounts of excess capacity that, for the next few years, capacity will be adequate to meet both military and civilian needs. Rapid growth in both areas could well occur by the middle of the decade. The Pentagon's estimates of military-procurement outlays imply production rates more rapid than those at the peak of the Vietnam War. Moreover, the present expansion is occurring after a decade of steady reduction in the defense industrial base. Thus, some potential bottlenecks can already be discerned.

Over the next six years, the United States can expect double-digit increases in real output year after year for many defense-related industries, ranging from metal stamping and aluminum to semiconductors and computers. In some sectors, the availability of plant capacity is in doubt. For example, the Commerce Department projects requirements for lead smelting and refining to rise by 12 percent from 1979 to 1985, but expects economically efficient capacity to decline by 4 percent. Brass and copper foundries' output will rise by 32 percent, but capacity will increase only 25 percent.

Some of our basic metal-processing industries will likely increase their dependence on foreign sources of supply. Such imports will leap from 27 percent to 45 percent in the strategic electrometallurgical products industry, for instance, and from 33 percent to 45 percent in the case of zinc. The matter-of-fact way in which the Commerce Department reports such increased foreign dependence is ironic. On many other occasions, the hoary national security argument is trotted out to justify a host of protectionist subsidies for sectors of the economy far less closely related to national defense output.

Military and civilian investment outlays compete for similar, often identical, resources. As the Council of Economic Advisers pointed out in its 1982 annual report, some crowding out of private investment may occur during the peak period of America's military buildup. A substantial transfer of resources from civilian to defense production can be expected to increase prices in many of the affected industries. Both the Pentagon and the private purchaser will have to pay more for the goods produced by these industries. This premium will increase with the size of the defense budget.

How will competing military and civilian demands for capital goods be reconciled? The answer will be seen either in another round of budget cuts or in the working of the marketplace. In the latter case, Americans probably will find that the price system operates with a vengeance. That means renewed inflationary pressures!

It is always difficult to forecast with any confidence what will come of diverse and contradictory trends. I foresee undramatic but essentially positive economic conditions in the years ahead. The odds now favor modest economic growth over the next several years, accompanied by moderate inflation. This happy turn of events is not written in the stars. It will not come about automatically, and its continuance during the second half of the 1980s will likely require another set of adjustments in economic policy, in order to deal with the new problems that will probably arise. The political process is not going to keep economic policy on automatic pilot for any length of time.

The positive economic outcome I describe is more likely to occur if we are willing to make some difficult decisions. First, labor and management in each industry must confront the competitive problems that challenge them, rather than seek government bailouts. Although discussions of economic policy will inevitably focus on public-sector actions, ours is a system in which most economic decisions are made in the private sector. So many of the difficulties facing the automobile and steel industries, for instance, are the result of stupid decisions by the companies and the unions themselves. These decisions have pushed labor costs far beyond those of other American manufacturing industries. Until recently, these prodigal industries have emphasized high unit profit in stagnant market areas. The easy answer to today's difficulties—which often unites management and labor—is to appeal to Washington for credit, import restraints, or some other subsidy. The bill, of course, is paid by consumers and taxpayers. The easy way out should be opposed, for it gives the wrong signals for future economic behavior.

Second, government decisionmakers must face up to the fact that the 1981 tax cuts have not been matched by expenditure reductions. In a very real sense, those tax cuts have not yet been earned. They can be earned, however, by reducing the rapid growth of federal outlays. Three major areas of the budget are promising candidates for further pruning:

■ The first and largest is the area of entitlements. Fundamental changes will not be made until the public recognizes the large extent to which the "social insurance" programs include large components of subsidy or welfare. Thus, the average monthly social security check is far larger than it would be if benefits were based solely on employee/employer contributions plus earnings on those contributions. Yet, the typical beneficiary is certain that he or she is getting only what was paid for. This pervasive myth constitutes a major challenge to economic education and policymaking.

■ Another area of potential cuts is defense. Official projections of military spending, in real terms, have risen during the past two years from 5 percent to 9 percent annually. I see very little evidence that this sharp upward movement is either needed or economically feasible. I see no reason to act on the odd presumption that our military posture has deteriorated in the past twenty-five months. An intensive analysis, adopting the tough-minded attitude taken toward many civilian spending activities, should be given to the military budget.

- Still more budget cuts can be made in imbedded subsidies. Advocates of smaller federal budgets typically focus on entitlements and defense spending. I have discovered a third category of the budget: "all other." Contrary to widespread belief, not all the items in this area of the budget are social programs, nor have they already been cut to the bone. Generously funded programs such as subsidies to dairy, tobacco, and sugar producers as well as to shipbuilders and ship operators are good—or bad—examples. These and many other special benefits to specific sectors of society are in the budget simply because of the political muscle of the producer or of the special-interest groups that support them. Given the outlook for substantial deficit spending, more of those sacred cows in the federal budget should be taken out of the feedlot and led to slaughter.

Finally, to face the real economic problems of today, America must focus more on its own shortcomings, rather than blame all its economic difficulties on foreign devils. We should begin by acknowledging the obstacles that we have put in the way of our own exports. For example, the Trans-Alaskan Pipeline Act prohibits the export of oil from North Slope fields. A rider to an Interior Department appropriations act bans timber exports from federal lands west of the 100th meridian. The Export Administration Act establishes controls on the export of goods and technology that would be detrimental to our national security. That sounds both serious and prudent. But, in practice, the act covers grain, domestically produced crude oil, unprocessed red cedar, and horses exported by sea. Export restraints, moreover, do not generate short-run results alone. Thus, the main impact of the U.S. embargo of soybean exports in 1974 was to induce Japan to invest in alternative sources, notably in Brazil. As a result, U.S. agriculture lost, perhaps permanently, an important world market.

Rather than close world trade—as so many advocates of protection would have us do, on a so-called reciprocal basis—America should start the process of opening up trade. As a beginning, we can reduce many domestic barriers that inhibit our own exports. Then we could "reciprocate" by reducing some U.S. barriers to exports from other nations. Rather than precipitate a return to the "beggar they neighbor" policy of the 1930s, such an enlightened policy could spur a more positive response by other nations and improve our own domestic economic position.

Time and Decisionmaking

If anything has been learned in the field of economic policy during the past few years, it is that one should be wary of simple solutions. Many vexing problems face us. Though the choices are hard, those problems must be faced. The alternative is to embrace yet another set of economic nostrums. The mounting pressure for a return to the gold standard shows that the panacea approach is alive and well. At the other end of the political spectrum, a burst of interest in "industrial policy" or reindustrialization provides another example.

Given the momentum of many of the trends I have described, any delay in making the necessary decisions will cause the choices to become less attractive. Once government spending programs get under way, it is not only politically difficult to restrain them, but it also becomes harder to justify reductions in them on the basis of economic analysis. For at that point, the practical argument becomes compelling—What is the value of half a bridge? Even if a project would, in the aggregate, never pass a reasonable benefit/cost test, once considerable outlays have been made, the benefits may equal or even exceed the additional costs. Thus, time becomes a crucial variable in governmental decisionmaking. Shakespeare said it more elegantly, though in a rather different connection: "If it were done when 'tis done, then 'twere well it were done quickly."

JAPAN:
All the Hazards and Threats of Success

After their miracle, the Japanese fear "advanced nations' disease"

The two characters above, evoking the island nation's mythic origins from the sun, represent Nihon, Japan

Outside the Ryoanji temple, the newest Japanese surfaces shine. The taxi drivers bustle, sweeping huge feather dusters over their cars, flicking specks from the bright metal. The ritual, a writer once remarked, makes them look like chambermaids in the first act of a French farce. But it is utterly Japanese, a set piece: the drivers handle their dusters like samurai. The scene is a sort of cartoon of the busy, fastidious superego that is supposed to preside in the Japanese psyche. The drivers even wear white gloves. There is probably not a dirty taxicab in Japan.

These taxis in the old capital city of Kyoto wait outside the doors of the ineffable, of another Japan entirely. The Ryoanji temple's Zen rock garden—five austerely abstract boulder mounds set in a sea of curried sand pebbles—is a celebrated spiritual masterpiece. The garden is absolutely still, and yet tense with an obscurely bullying profundity. A guide whispers the sermons in the stones, the allegories: the rocks are, maybe, tigers swimming across the sea. Or they are whales rocking in the deep. Or perhaps they are these mysterious islands themselves: Japan. The abbot of Ryoanji, in a perfect eloquence of abnegation, wrote that the place should be called simply the "Garden of Nothingness."

The Zen silence is shattered. A swarm of schoolchildren in black uniforms enters, frisking and chattering. They horse around obliviously in the timelessness. Their teacher bellows at them through a battery-powered megaphone: "All right, now: Meditate!"

A Westerner fidgets whenever he is asked to be impressed by nothingness. A Japanese is a good deal more at home with the native mysteries. But Japan almost always involves a certain intellectual wind shear. What one sees when contemplating those islands often depends upon the culture of the beholder.

Somehow that will have to change. The rest of the world must begin to perceive what the Japanese perceive. And the Japanese must reciprocate. The global economy cannot run on so many cultural subjectivities. Japan has become too powerful and too crucially interconnected in the world to be so little understood, or so little understanding. Akio Morita, the cofounder of Sony, likes to tell his employees that the company is a "fate-sharing vessel." They are all in the same boat. The Japanese for most of their history have thought of their islands as

the fate-sharing vessel. The definition of the boat must now be expanded. It must learn to make accommodations for the world at large.

This will be difficult. Japan's culture, always kinetic, is now veering into territory where it has never been before. The Japanese postwar economic miracle is cresting. Japan is a fascinating success, as a business and as a society. It is prosperous and famously homogeneous, safe and civil, bound together by a social contract that is startlingly effective. Yet, paradoxically, Japan's very success has grown threatening, its future shadowed and complicated. The Japanese face new problems, inside, among their densely close-woven tribe, and outside, with the rest of the world.

The Japanese have been known in the past for being able to turn their civilization on a dime. After 215 years of deliberate feudal isolation during the Tokugawa period, Japan threw itself open in 1854. It was, wrote Arthur Koestler, like breaking the window of a pressurized cabin: the Japanese crashed out into the world devouring everything that had been done or thought in the rest of the planet during their long encapsulation (the late Renaissance, the Enlightenment, the Industrial Revolution). Rarely has there been an ingestion of foreign influence so smoothly accomplished. The Japanese did something of the same thing after World War II. Military fascism did not work. The entire people switched over with amazing cultural equilibrium to democracy under a constitution partly devised by a group of young lawyers on Douglas MacArthur's staff.

According to the stereotype, the Japanese are merely clever copiers of other people's inventions. Now the Japanese find that they are on the verge of joining the leaders of the world. They do so almost reluctantly; the role makes them uncomfortable. Now they must do the inventing. Says Prime Minister Yasuhiro Nakasone: "We must formulate a society for which there is no precedent in any other country."

The new international troubles of the Japanese arise from their doing almost too well at their economic ventures. After 1945, Japan's industrial plant was in ashes. MacArthur said that he hoped eventually to rebuild the country to the point where it would become "the Switzerland of Asia." Today, Japan is the second most powerful economy in the free world. Its trillion-dollar-a-year industrial machine accounts for 10% of the world's output. By 1990, the Japanese may achieve a per capita gross national product that surpasses that of the U.S. As a 19th century French tourist said of another island people, the English: *"Mon Dieu, comme ils travaillent!"*

Japan's best friends in the world are still the Americans, a fact that should give the Japanese pause. For even Americans view the Japanese with suspicion and ambivalence, with fascination and admiration and resentment intermingled. A poll by the Los Angeles *Times* last spring found that 68% of Americans favor trade restrictions to protect American industries and jobs. The American trade deficit with Japan could well reach a menacing $21 billion this year. It results partly from superior Japanese competitiveness and products, partly from unfair Japanese barriers to trade, and partly from an overvalued dollar and undervalued yen. Most Democratic presidential candidates, including Walter Mondale, have courted the labor vote by urging new kinds of protectionism. A former Japanese ambassador to the U.S., Nobuhiko Ushiba, said in April that he had "never seen the mood on Capitol Hill as ugly as it is now toward the Japanese." Unemployed Americans focus their anger upon the Japanese, at least when they are not blaming Ronald Reagan. In West Virginia, a charity raised money by selling sledgehammer hits on a Toyota. A recession bumper sticker read: WHEN YOU BOUGHT YOUR JAPANESE CAR, 10 AMERICANS LOST THEIR JOBS.

Other peoples tend to be even more critical. If the protectionist noises in America amount to a sort of restive snarling here and there across the countryside, such sounds abroad are full screams that sometimes translate into government policy. The French last October began funneling Japanese videotape-recorder imports through a tiny customs station at Poitiers. Some 200,000 items were blocked by delays for inspection and other red tape until the ban was lifted in April this year. As other economies around the world feel increasingly threatened, their fears could set off waves of protectionism that might cripple the world economy.

The world looks at Japan through one lens, the Japanese see themselves through another. Japan is a global force with an insular mentality, a superior organism that still harbors the soul of a small, isolated land. Living on their archipelago in the "Pacific Ring of Fire," vulnerable as always to earthquakes and typhoons, virtually unarmed, without any significant natural resources, dependent on the outside world for oil and food, the Japanese have a hard time seeing themselves as any kind of threat. "In our history of 2,000 years," says Taro Aso, a member of the Japanese parliament, "this is the first time that the Japanese have not had to worry about poverty. We are *nouveau riche,* a nation of farmers a short time ago. It is difficult to accept international responsibilities when you have an inferiority complex."

The Japanese also argue, correctly in part, that the Americans use them as scapegoats, blaming them for the failures—managerial, cultural—of American business and labor. Says Brookings Institution Economist Lawrence Krause: "The damage that the Japanese do to the U.S. is trivial compared to what we do to ourselves—through bad management and bad planning."

The Japanese approach to other nations has grown far more sophisticated recently. Japanese businessmen have led the way. They have traveled the world and studied its languages. They have worked its trade routes with single-minded energy and curiosity, selling their wares, studying everything, plundering the remotest cultures and factories for information. They are Oriental Vikings armed with cameras and a samurai's resistance to jet lag. Prime Minister Nakasone has displayed a newly extraverted international style for a Japanese leader. He has, among other things, awakened what is for the Japanese the painful subject of their rearming, or at any rate contributing a greater share to the defense of the non-Communist world.

Japanese problems at home are also the complicating side effects of stress. Many Japanese fear that they are beginning to suffer from what they call "advanced nations' disease," though the attack is not yet acute. In a recent poll, 89% of Japanese described themselves as happy with their lives. The present undoubtedly looks handsome compared with the bleak aftermath of the war. Many of the men who are now in the middle management of Mitsui and Mitsubishi were babies being fed a grain of rice at a time in 1946. Morita and Masaru Ibuka founded Sony that year by scrounging around in the fire-bombed ruins of Tokyo for parts with which to build broadcasting equipment.

But if the Japanese are happy, why does Japan hurt so much in so many different ways? It is as if the Japanese have been single-mindedly intent, since the catastrophic end of the war, upon survival and then success. Now, in the fulfillment of so many of their ambitions, they have raised their eyes and looked about them, and seen that success has a price.

Everywhere in Japan, one senses an intricate serenity that comes to a people who know precisely what to expect from each other. But one also senses—occasionally, distantly—a disconcerted, vaguely frantic emotional vibration, a feeling of dislocation and alienation and incipient loss. The Japanese are almost obsessively aware of their problems; it is possible that they exaggerate them in order to execute a subtle kind of psychological evasion—the domestic concerns relieving them, implicitly, of larger international responsibilities.

Yet the difficulties are real enough. It is a myth much advertised in the West, for example, that the vast majority of Japanese workers enjoy lifetime employment, a fondly cooperative relationship with management and a mutual delight in the company song. True, there is less than 3% unemployment. But, in fact, Japan has a schizophrenic business system, a dual economy. The myth applies to 30% of it, in the high-tech and highly productive companies. But the other 70% of Japanese workers labor in smaller, considerably less efficient industries. There, they receive low wages and few financial benefits, if any. Such workers bounce from job to job within that traditional economy; last year there were 17,000 bankruptcies in Japan.

The Japanese, in their pursuit of commercial success, have neglected a thousand social and civic details. They need the parks and playgrounds and sidewalks that they never got around to building. Their lives are often almost unbearably constricted. They commute two, three or four hours a day to work from claustrophobia-inducing apartments out in suburban regions that look like an interminable Bridgeport smudging into the outskirts of Albuquerque. Some 75% of the population lives in the narrow Pacific corridor from Tokyo to Hiroshima. Land prices are impossibly high (more than $100 per sq. ft. in suburban Tokyo). Newly married couples despair of ever owning a house (a typical two-room Tokyo apartment measuring 400 sq. ft. costs more than $83,000). The clutter of Japanese life is not only difficult, it is sometimes noxious. Lakes and swamps are polluted. For a people with an exquisite and even rhapsodic appreciation of nature, the Japanese are capable of casually littering and ravaging it.

Even though much of the Japanese gene pool originally derives from Korea, the 669,800 Koreans who live in Japan, some of whose families have been in the country for generations, are subjected to systematic discrimination. They rarely advance to the better jobs in Japanese corporations. The situation of those privately referred to as eta is worse. They are the Japanese Untouchables. Even though they are physically indistinguishable from other Japanese, the 2 million to 3 million eta are frequently relegated to ghettos and menial work. Few marry outside their caste (Japan has a class of private detectives who specialize in checking into these matters), and most are destined to spend their lives in a strange shadow. The reasons for this degradation are obscure. It may be because they are descendants of people who, centuries ago, performed what was regarded as unclean work, slaughtering animals for leather, tending graves. Eta means much filth; the word has been officially struck from the language. The polite term these days for the eta is *Burakumin,* hamlet people.

One major, if more subtle, Japanese problem is simply actuarial. Japan is getting very old, very fast. In the next 35 years, the country will undergo a stunning demographic transformation. By 2000, 16% of the population will be 65 years old or older, up from 9% in 1980. It will increase to 21.8% by 2020. By comparison, 11% of the U.S. population will be 65 or older in 2000, 15% in 2020.

A Confucian society traditionally reveres its aged. The elderly in Japan are still treated with far greater respect than they are in most Western countries. But the burden of providing for them in the future may shake the Japanese conscience. The centuries-long custom whereby sons give their parents a home and care for them in old age is difficult to maintain in a country where housing is so crowded. The Japanese household is getting smaller, embracing two generations, or only one, instead of three. Wives are discovering the pleasures and independence of life without a mother-in-law's demanding, authoritarian presence. A loneliness and isolation, more typical of the West than of Japan, has settled in upon many of the aged. Groups of old people have staged repeated marches on the Ministry of Health and Welfare in Tokyo, demanding more services.

The middle-aged too are feeling afflicted, though somewhat less despairingly. One Japanese writer, Hitoshi Kato, recently quoted a middle-aged steel company executive who sounded rather like the American *Man in the Gray Flannel Suit* of a generation ago: "We work hard, but even we don't know what we work for. Those of the war generation experienced hunger, and that spurred them to work with a passion . . . But look at us. The corporate framework is already established, and growth has its limits. The prospects for promotion are limited too. We just work to support our wives and children and meet our mortgage payments."

Some Japanese still choose a traditional form of release: the violence done to oneself. Japan's suicide rate, about 15 per 100,000, is higher than that of the U.S., though lower than those of most North or East European countries. Suicide in Japan was long surrounded by a romantic and aesthetic aura that arose from the samurai tradition. Now it seems an especially unhappy and unheroic spectacle. A group called the Japan Association for the Prevention of Parent-Child Suicide has been established to try to discourage such tragedies. Some 400 occur every year. In recent weeks a man threw himself and his two children into a river, a family of four drove into a river, a mother strangled her child and then took her own life. There is a pattern: the parents cannot pay back loans or cannot endure the financial pressures of their lives. One psychiatrist observes, "Japanese kill themselves for more or less altruistic reasons, not out of egoism or self-pity." And they kill the children to spare them the pain of growing up without their parents. Lately police have found dozens of bodies in the forests around Mount Fuji. People travel from all over Japan to commit suicide there. The place has been named "Suicide Forest." The police have posted blunt notices there that killing oneself is not romantic, that bodies are eaten by animals or decay and can be smelled 50 meters away.

It is their young who most trouble the Japanese. They are a remarkably law-abiding people. Yet at graduation time this spring, more than 10% of the nation's junior high schools were guarded by the police. A group of teen-agers in Yokohama not long ago beat several street bums to death. Gangs of motorcycle riders taunt the police on Saturday nights; they blast past the stations and dare police to chase them through the maze of traffic. Juvenile delinquency, historically always low, has increased 80% since 1972. A White Paper issued by the Prime Minister's office concluded of today's youth: "They are devoid of perseverance, dependent upon others and self-centered."

Everyone in Japan talks about the violence in the junior high schools. Students threaten their teachers, even pull knives on them. The Japanese discuss such incidents, curiously enough, without much anger, without the punitive tone one might expect. But they worry. Of course, the violence done in all the schools in Japan in a year probably cannot match what the students in New York City schools commit in a month. Still, the Japanese seem to sense in the rebelliousness of the junior high school students a glimpse of the future, and it frightens them. A country that has lived so long and so successfully on the disciplines of obedience and respect for elders and scholars is shocked and mystified by children who rise up from their chairs and threaten their teachers.

Many Japanese fear that in part the educational system itself is to blame. It has produced marvels of mass literacy (nearly 100%), but also of mass conformity. It rewards dogged rote learning, but not the kind of daring involved in making creative and unorthodox intellectual connections. "Every Japanese child," says one writer, "has a kind of invisible wire rack inserted into its body and mind," like flowers in an arrangement, like a bonsai tree. The Japanese examination system subjects the young to purgatories of cramming. It is one more symptom of a densely determined and obligated life, and some of the young these days are escaping into a sort of minor league anarchy.

At Tokyo's Yoyogi Park every Sunday, groups of momentarily rebellious adolescents come to perform a strange exhibition. They grease their hair into ducktails and put on black pegged pants and leather jackets, or else polka-dot crinoline skirts, and they group around tape-deck machines and dance to rock 'n' roll: boys with boys, girls with girls. In Japan it is always the group, even in rebellion. The spectacle is strangely sweet and sad.

The fascination of the young for things American is wistful and sometimes weirdly askew. But it reflects a larger cross-cultural longing. In some ways, America and Japan are interesting commentaries on each other. The Japanese affinity for Americans represents in part the simple attraction of opposites. The Japanese live an intricate and compact life—119 million of them crowded onto islands the size of Montana. No new blood, or little, has entered the Japanese gene pool for 1,200 years. Americans are a sprawlingly expansive people whose chromosomes are a genetic brawl, an ingathering from all the tribes of the world. America is an intellectual dream, a reverie of the Enlightenment. The American civic principle is freedom and equality. The Japanese civic logic is mutual obligation, hierarchy, and the overriding primacy of the group. Japan is governed by *on*, by an almost infinitely complicated network of responsibility and debt and reciprocity: what each Japanese owes every other, and what each owes the entire group. America built a society around the idea that all fates are almost indefinitely reversible, around the idea of moving on, of clearing new land, changing jobs, changing roles, changing identities. The Japanese did not have new frontiers to run to; fates and roles have always seemed more settled there.

The Japanese think of Americans as far-ranging hunters, individualists, carnivores. They think of themselves as wet-rice farmers, rooted for many centuries in the same corner of the same prefecture. Perhaps each culture is wistful for the virtues and attractions of the other. Japan has, in any case, none of that American sense of immense, liberating, heartbreaking distances; Japan is put together like a watchwork, with cunning economy. The small, busy factories hum along flush against the rice fields, with apartment buildings jammed up against the other side. Japan is a very intimate country, with all of the rules and dangers of intimacy. It has been said that the Japanese have cultivated their silences and intuitive communication because they are a people with small rooms and paper walls.

The Japanese are not only intimate with themselves, but with their gods. They have no transcendent God of the Judaeo-Christian kind. The divine presents no forbidding immensities, no snow fields of abstraction, no terrible threats. The ancient Shinto deities, ancestors really, are essentially earthbound; they share the islands with the Japanese, and they can be summoned at a shrine by merely clapping one's hands. It is a friendly religion. But because of Shinto, the very earth and air and trees and mountains of Japan are numinous, filled with preternatural life. One secret of Japanese commercial success may have something to do with Shintoism, with the way that the tribe, and everything it does, achieves mythic importance. A French business executive, Antoine Riboud, remarked, "What struck me first was the degree of seriousness with which the Japanese consider economic activity as such. They conceive of it as a civic matter, way above the mere quest for profit."

6. FUTURE

Shintoism has a sort of ethical partner in the Japanese soul. The American commercial itch went to church with the Calvinists. The Japanese conscience has been shaped by Confucianism, a system of social ethics based on five relationships: father and son, older brother and younger brother, ruler and subject, friend and friend, husband and wife. But Confucianism has a Calvinist spine. It is the moral architecture of Japan, of the Japanese group and the hierarchical systems of address and deference. The Japanese find it easier to deal with one another as unequals than as equals. They must know whether the person addressed is superior or inferior to them in status. The up-or-down vectors of all relationships are crucial. They always exchange business cards on meeting, in order to tune their language to one another's relative status. All this makes for close-woven judgments and the most delicate calculations when the Japanese meet socially.

The language also makes for a certain elaborate vagueness. In Japanese, the verb comes at the end of the sentence, rather than in the middle. It is thus possible to state the subject and object of the sentence, all the while watching the reaction, and then adjust the verb (which states the relation between subject and object), softening it, for example, if the sentence begins to seem too strong, or displeasing. The speaker may even change his mind and insert a negative at the end, thereby reversing the entire meaning of the sentence, but preserving the human relationship. The Japanese approach to things is essentially one of indirection.

The Japanese have married feudalism to high capitalism, and that union has brought forth a formidable machine. The hierarchical feudal virtues—the emphasis on authority and loyalty and deference—remain in place despite much individual mobility. They legitimize the entire enterprise. Japan is a private club—almost a private race. It is possible to overstate the idea that everything in Japan is done by consensus, the idea that the entire country is a committee. Still, being Japanese is the most important reality in the life of any Japanese. Japan may be the first society to combine the sensibility of the modern mass with the house rules of a small tribe.

A certain quality of the American '50s clings to Japan now, the '50s refracted through the Japanese glass. Terms like conformity recur. The problems of youth violence recall the American *Blackboard Jungle*. But some of the behavior seems essentially innocent. If Japan is afflicted by its new worries, it remains an extraordinarily successful society by almost every measure. The social muscle tone is firm, the civic climate earnest and naive. If it is true that the Japanese are somehow spiritually located now in the American '50s, are they doomed to endure the sequel, the cultural turmoil that arrived in the American '60s? The Japanese are conscious of the possibility. When they look at what America and Western Europe have done with their economic maturity, they see as much to avoid as to emulate. They see considerable failure: economic, social and moral.

What both maddens and fascinates Americans about the Japanese success is the mystique of it. A shelf of dopesters' literature has been published to explain the Japanese phenomenon. Some is quite discerning, more of it is nonsense. The latter treats Japanese success as a sort of mystical trick, a performance of managerial jujitsu. A concealed racist premise of these analyses is that—what's this—a colony of ants has taught itself to waltz. The wonder is not that they do it well, but that they do it at all.

Yet the Japanese are not entirely unhappy about this myth-mongering. It keeps the world at a necessary psychological distance. It also permits a subtle form of cultural intimidation. Mystique has the effect of allowing Japanese business negotiators, for example, to play by Japanese rules, on the turf of Japanese psychology. The Japanese do not like to be understood too easily. It is possible that they do not like to be understood at all. Perhaps they have been studying Stonewall Jackson, who once instructed: "Always mystify, mislead and surprise the enemy, if possible."

Foreigners contemplating the Japanese tend to fall into two schools of perception: there are the elaborationists and the simplists. The elaborationists see an infinitely subtle and refined and complex people whose minds and customs are deeply rooted, reaching back centuries through a thousand laminations in time. Most Japanese are elaborationists about Japan. It is part of their cultural self-defense.

The simplists see Japan as a society that is vivid, vibrant and depthless. The Japanese, say the simplists, are a skitteringly nervous, suggestible and insecure people, quick (too quick) to change, given to adopting fads from abroad and Japanizing them. A facile people, living in the present and the immediate future, a sharp trading race. The truth, almost surely, is an amalgamation of the two perceptions. That is only fitting. Japan is a masterpiece of contradictions, of East and West, of exquisite politesse and oafish rudeness, of a certain lacquered arrogance combined with a strange insecurity in the presence of things foreign.

One of the most painful intricacies of the Japanese undertaking is this: Japan, by becoming such an economic phenomenon, has incurred new responsibilities. Yet those responsibilities cannot be fulfilled if the Japanese remain true to some of the characteristics that made them so successful in the first place. The Japanese are both distinguished and confined by their own culture. Their culture is their charm, their force, their secret and their gravest limitation. It gives them both method and identity and an enveloping inhibition. The Japanese attach such total meaning to themselves that for them, few intellectual excursions outside that circle can be significant.

Japan has become an economic superpower, but not yet a cultural or a political or a moral superpower. The deepest questions of the Japanese future revolve around Japan's capacity to transcend the limitations of its identity. Both the U.S. and the Soviet Union attempt to export ideals: for better and for worse, they stand for something in the world. What does Japan represent? Does Japan have a universal meaning? Or is its meaning, unlike its products, destined to remain confined to the home islands? Do superior products embody ideals?

The Japanese have set a breathless commercial pace for themselves and for the world. Can they maintain it? The old values are eroding now. In the next decades, the Japanese will be thrown back more upon their cultural reflexes and improvisational gifts. Those talents will determine whether Japan will be remembered as a great civilization, or merely a minutely distinctive one, full of brilliant energy.   —*By Lance Morrow.*

Reported by Edwin M. Reingold/Tokyo

A GENERATION AT RISK

When the baby boomers reach Golden Pond

Robert N. Butler

Robert N. Butler is chairman of the Ritter Department of Geriatrics and Adult Development at The Mount Sinai School of Medicine in New York City. He is the former director of the National Institute on Aging and author of the influential book, Why Survive? Being Old in America *(Harper & Row, 1975).*

The time is now to build into our personal and corporate behavior the realities of a long life ending not in the 60s and 70s but in the 80s and 90s. More and more of us are reaching these years. This is where some revolutionary trends of modern life are taking us as predecessors, successors and members of the baby-boom generation.

We are relatively unprepared. Yes, we do worry about pensions and Social Security income and the costs of Medicare. Only beginning to sting are long-term care expenses and associated taxes affecting corporate, government, individual and family budgets. These costs are harbingers of a complex future that we must begin to plan for systematically, starting now.

The 20th century has seen average life expectancy in this country move from under 50 to over 70. Our society has become incredibly efficient at bringing children into maturity. Today's infant has a 50–50 chance of living more than the biblical three score and 10.

Converging with this expansion of average life expectancy is a second great trend: the aging of that enormous cohort of 76.4 million persons born in the 1946–1964 period. This baby-boom cohort will continue to stress our institutions: the schools were among the first to feel their impact, then the job market; next will be pension plans, Social Security, medical and social care, and other institutions concerned with later life.

The baby boomers constitute a generation at risk. The critical years of their retirement will start about 2010. By 2030, there will be over 50 million retirees, twice today's 65-and-over population. Where 1 in 9 Americans are elderly today, the ratio a half century hence may be 1 in 5, assuming that fertility stays at about the replacement level.

If baby boomers have fewer children per family than their predecessors, this expectation will have profound socioeconomic consequences. The ratio of Americans of typical working age to Americans 65-and-over will reach 2 to 1 as baby-boom retirements increase, considerably under today's 3 to 1. However, the total number of dependents—under 18 and over 65—per 100 working-age Americans will actually be fewer in 2030 than in 1970 or 1960. (See table on page 42.) Presumably, workers will spend less on children and will have more for the elderly.

I disagree with warnings that generational conflict will occur when younger workers are forced to support ever growing numbers of elderly. Not only does this line of argument ignore the decline projected in children per household, which will reduce the overall dependency costs of the baby boomers, it overlooks as well the income transfers that go on from elders to the young.

According to A.J. Jaffe in *The New York Statistician* for November–December 1982, the total dependency ratio in today's population is about 1 to 1, and in 2050 "about half of the total population will still be supporting the other half. . . . The change in the dependency burden is the shift from more younger to more older persons." Jaffe believes that the cost of raising and educating the child population about equals total retirement benefits. "It is evading the issue, if not outright misuse of statistics, only to compare the working force and the over 65," he says.

6. FUTURE

One of the most divisive measures for meeting costs of dependency would be government-enforced "filial responsibility"—that is, requiring children to help support their elderly parents. The Reagan Administration has announced a regulatory change in the Medicaid program to allow states to recover, when possible, nursing-home expenses from the children of poor patients. Experience with such policies has shown that they are administrative nightmares. Even when effective, they may result in family disruption, as resources are withdrawn from support of younger members of a family and given to older members. We have no need for coercive and disruptive measures in a society that can meet old-age needs humanely and efficiently with private or social insurance. Moreover, "filial responsibility" cannot help the 1 in 4 nursing-home patients who have no family.

On a scale no other birth cohort has confronted, the baby boomers will confront a double challenge. First, as they approach and enter retirement, they will have to balance their own needs with those of parents and even grandparents. This is illustrated by the 68-year-old daughter who oversees the care, at home or in an institution, of an 87-year-old mother while dealing with her own need for chronic care and that of her 72-year-old husband on a slender retirement income.

Second, as the baby boomers reach the oldest ages, they will have fewer family members to turn to for the same kind of help they gave in earlier years. Not only are more people living to the ages of highest sickness rates but family structure is changing: fewer children, more divorce, and more social isolation, especially because of widowhood. Given the continued emphasis on mobility and living independently, the elders of tomorrow may have to turn to strangers, particularly paid employees of social-service and health-care organizations.

This double challenge will grow rapidly as the population of the most frail elders increases: now one third of all elders, they will comprise 40 percent in only 10 years. The challenge will spread faster among older women, blacks, and Hispanics, since these groups of elderly are growing faster than the total 65-and-over population. For older women, the challenge will be particularly intense; they outlive men and typically are the mainstays of long-term care within the family.

The age distribution of the U.S. population seems to me to be far less a matter for concern than is the future of the economy. Whatever economic complications the baby boom causes for itself through low fertility could be compensated for by a more productive economy, one that utilizes the able elderly. Excluding them from roles in wealth production would represent an immense failure of heart and imagination. The longevity revolution will test our economy's capacity to use the added labor potential.

To minimize dependency and maximize productivity, our society will have to spur institutional change.

Age discrimination (as I wrote in these pages in November 1980) serves to maximize dependency and minimize productivity among the elderly. In our personal and corporate lives, we must continue to break down barriers of myth and prejudice.

We will need organized approaches through government and the private sector to improve income maintenance and support systems. This means well-directed investment in biomedical, sociobehavioral and productivity-related gerontological research. We must originate, refine, and routinize programs to help preserve (and recover) health and productivity at any phase of the adult life cycle. Surely this is one of the best ways to reduce the dependency costs of the generation at risk.

Extending the Work Span

How shall we finance the added years of life? Assuming a life span of 85 years, we can imagine the working portion as about half, counting 20 years for retirement and 25 for maturation and education. A 40-year work span could easily accommodate two or more careers.

We could add to savings by extending the work span—by delaying retirement, by taking less leisure time during the working years, and banking the income, and by investing more in public and private pension programs. A delayed-retirement strategy implies a full-employment economy. Will our society have jobs for everyone as the baby boomers move toward old age? If we are evolving into a society that needs fewer people in the conventional work force, how will individuals build up reserves for retirement? Will automation drastically alter the education-work-retirement proportions of the life span?

These questions must be answered if we are serious about reducing risks for the baby-boom generation and its children. Likewise, we must ask hard questions about the solidity and efficiency of retirement-income programs, including Social Security, private pensions, and individual retirement accounts. Major evaluations should be made of the use of tax breaks to encourage people to plan for their own retirement. Should the goal be to encourage those who can to save more, allowing income to escape Federal taxation? Or should the goal be to assure an adequate basic income in retirement for all (for example, through higher Social Security benefits based on higher taxes and more income transferring)? Do we need a better balance between these goals than now exists?

Unfortunately, planning for population aging tends to occur in relatively narrow contexts, in response to perceived institutional crises. The recent deliberations of the National Commission on Social Security Reform extended gingerly into some of the issues of health and productivity. But the approach was to shore up the Social Security financing, and this necessarily limited the explorations. Nonetheless, the Commission's recommendations offer an entrée into some of the practical issues of planning for population aging.

The bipartisan panel dealt with short- and long-range problems. A deficit of somewhere between $150 billion and $200 billion in Social Security revenue was projected for the 1983–89 period. The panel recommended that this could be made up by a combination of taxes and benefit cuts. Some of these proposed actions would also reduce deficits expected after 2020, when the baby-boom retirees would reach a peak. However, an unresolved issue was how to meet fully the long-range gap.

Republican appointees on the Commission endorsed a gradual rise in the age of full entitlement, or indexing of that age to improvements in average life expectancy. They argued that postponing the age to 68 would be sufficient to keep the program sound through the mid-21st century.

Democratic appointees called the proposed age change a benefit cut for young workers confronting higher taxes over the proposed longer period until retirement. Such a step was unnecessary now, they argued, since the long-range deficit might well be made up through economic growth or additional tax increases.

The consensus recommendation of the Commission, however, omitted any call for an age change and instead advocated a policy of encouraging retirement at age 66, 67, or 68 by raising benefits by 8 percent for each year of delay. Congress was divided on the issue, and in the end prescribed a gradual rise to age 67 by the early 21st century. This provision is in the law signed by President Reagan.

Neither the Commission nor Congress directly raised the question of whether the United States spends enough on its Social Security program. Other advanced countries—with proportions of elderly the U.S. has yet to experience—seem able to manage a greater investment. Some devote twice the proportion of gross national product to benefits comparable to those offered under our Social Security system.

A major intent of proposals to raise the full benefits age is clear: each year of delay means the individual will put more money into the system and will take less out of it. Attempts to assure the system's soundness are praiseworthy, but we must consider some implications. Will jobs be available? Will they be open to older workers? Will employers or the government be willing to retrain them? Will they be healthy enough and willing to work? Or will they see delayed retirement as an unprofitable trade of healthy years for sick years?

Corporations in various fields have demonstrated ways of keeping older workers on the job, encouraging their re-entry into the work force, and developing part-time arrangements to meet retirees' needs for supplementary cash, as well as their own needs for their skills and for flexible scheduling. *Young Programs for Older Workers*, published by Work in America Institute in 1980, provides case studies of such programs.

Wm. Wrigley Jr. Company has a long-standing practice of phased retirement for employees at age 65: The first year the employee takes a month off without pay, the second year, two months, and the third year, three months. For each year he works from age 65 to 70, the employee adds 8 percent to his base pension; $100 of pension income at age 65 thus becomes $147 at age 70. The term phased retirement, or flexible

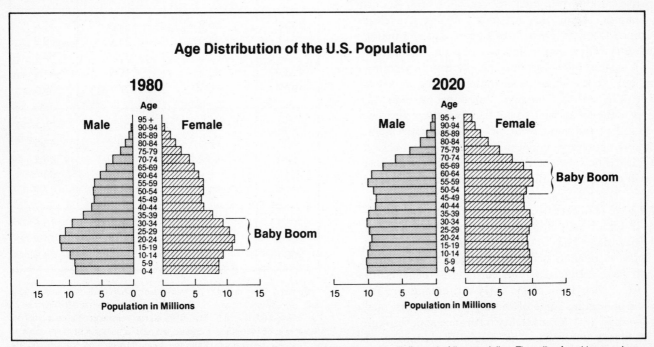

The size of the baby-boom generation in 1980, and the projected size in 2020, compared with the rest of the population. The ratio of working-age Americans to those 65+ will decline to 2:1 as baby-boom retirements increase, considerably under today's 3:1. (Source: The Social Security Administration)

retirement, describes any program that allows the employee to gradually change the proportion of leisure time to work time, whether in the form of shorter days, shorter weeks, or months off.

There are various other arrangements to accommodate older workers. IBM fosters second careers to help individuals adjust to technologic and business changes and, when retirement is imminent, to develop new interests and skills. Tektronix Inc. employs a medical placement specialist to redesign jobs for better efficiency and improved job satisfaction on the part of workers who have physical limitations. A carpenter with a back injury can still saw and use the lathe but can't bend to trim moldings; that part of his job is eliminated, and instead he is given part of another job, say, driving a truck and delivering supplies. The Toro Company has a program that uses part-timers in two ways: some do regular part-time work and others are on call for overload periods.

Surveys show that many retirees want to work, that many workers in their 50s intend to extend their working careers, and that business recognition of older-worker productivity is increasing. Employment agencies for older workers have developed to serve these parties. In Los Angeles, a Second Careers Program—a nonprofit organization administered by the Los Angeles Voluntary Action Center—has been assisting companies since 1975 to begin or enlarge pre-retirement and retirement programs and to identify opportunities for volunteer and paid second-career jobs. Mature Temps, formed by the Colonial Penn Group, provides jobs for people over age 50 through 14 offices around the country.

A lot more has to be done to provide options in employment and retirement for older workers. Robert W. Feagles, senior vice president of The Travelers Insurance Company, which two years ago eliminated mandatory retirement, points out that our society has built a system allowing more people to enjoy retirement but, at the same time, limits choices for older people. "In reality," he says, "most people over 65, whatever they may wish to do, face two stark alternatives: either full-time work or full-time retirement, with few options in between." Most private pension systems define retirement so strictly that even a short interval of paid work threatens loss of benefits. Social Security is a prime example of the earnings test.

We have to differentiate the expectations and conditions of tomorrow's older workers from those of today and yesterday. The fact is that two thirds of Social Security retirements occur before age 65. These individuals have actuarially reduced monthly benefits for the rest of their lives. Some early retirements are for reasons of health. Some of these persons are disabled but do not qualify for disability insurance and, through it, Medicare coverage. The disability definition of Social Security has been criticized as unduly severe: an individual must be unable to perform in any job no matter where it is in the nation; older workers cannot be expected to move thousands of miles just to find a job they are able to do. (The commissioners who proposed a change in the full benefits age also suggested provisions to assist sick early retirees, this group confronts reduced benefits at a time of above-average sickness costs—and no eligibility for Medicare until age 65.)

The One-Hoss-Shay Issue

The Commission also considered the notion that people should be able to have longer work lives because improvements in longevity have been accompanied by improvements in health. In June 1982, as director of the National Institute on Aging, I discussed the point at the panel's request, along with Dr. Jacob Feldman of the National Center for Health Statistics.

The Commission wanted comments on a hypothesis set forth by Dr. James Fries of Stanford University that the natural limit of the human life span is about 85 years. Fries's policy-relevant point is that the period of morbidity in later life is shortening; people are likely to stay healthy longer, deteriorating much like the "one hoss shay" in the poem, almost all at once. If true, the trend might provide support for raising the Social Security full-benefit age beyond 65. In addition, the hypothesis offers the comforting prospect of mod-

Younger and Older Dependents			
Year	Number under 18 per 100 aged 18–64	Number 65+ per 100 aged 18–64	Total
1930	58.9	9.1	68.0
1940	48.9	11.0	59.9
1950	51.0	13.4	64.4
1960	65.1	16.8	81.9
1970	61.4	17.7	79.1
1980	47.2	18.6	65.8
1990	43.5	20.0	63.5
2000	43.2	19.9	63.1
2010	39.2	20.2	59.4
2020	41.2	26.0	67.2
2030	42.0	31.8	73.8
2040	41.2	30.6	71.8
2050	41.7	30.2	71.9

Projections of the numbers of "dependents" in the U.S. population, young and old (derived from U.S. Census figures by Herman B. Brotman, a consulting gerontologist). The table shows that while the proportion of those over 65 will steadily increase, the relative numbers of those under 18 is generally decreasing. Thus, the total "burden" on the working-age population of both young and old would not be unreasonable. In fact, the proportion of dependents may have been higher in 1960 and 1970.

eration in the spiraling costs of Medicare and Medicaid as sickness diminishes in late life.

Trend data from the National Health Interview Survey do not support the Fries hypothesis. Sickness and disability rates by age bracket appear to have held steady over the last decade. Conceivably, this could change. However, applying current rates to the growing elderly population, we project a heavier load of sickness and disability in the 21st century.

Policymakers cannot reasonably ignore this projection, even though some anecdotal evidence suggests that the elders of today are in better health than their forebears. Some surely are. But some reach old age already sick, their lives preserved by medical care. Some live to the oldest ages despite great handicaps. And some maintain good health almost to the very end of life. How this mixed picture relates to ability to work is not precisely clear, since we lack objective criteria for assessing various physical and psychological factors in relation to different kinds of work.

This issue was made most clear to me when the National Institute on Aging, at Congressional behest, reviewed the Federal requirement for mandatory retirement of commercial airline pilots at age 60. Was it medically justified? This was hard to say, since there were no conclusive data on whether pilots were more or less like the general population, in which cardiovascular and other morbidity and mortality rates rise sharply in the 60s. Modern airliners are better staffed and powered than those of 1959 when the rule was imposed. But no one could say definitely that a fine record of passenger safety would be maintained. Undoubtedly, some pilots are mandatorily retired with unnecessary loss of their productivity.

The pilot issue is a special case. But it illustrates the shortcomings of our knowledge of aging and disease processes in relation to practical decisions important in population aging. Based on trends, our best guess is that the proportions of the population with disabilities will stay about the same. For the age bracket 65 to 74, which includes the years relevant to the benefits-age issue, the proportion with a limitation on activity due to a chronic illness or disability is projected to be about the same in 2020 as in 1980: about 35 percent. However, the number will double in that period to 10.7 million, reflecting the baby boom.

The activity limitations—joint stiffness, visual and hearing impairment, cardiovascular problems, and other handicaps—need not be so serious as to prevent employment. Policies could be adopted to promote employment of such people. The working day or week could be adjusted. Work environments and tasks might be modified. For instance, in regard to pilots, a report prepared for the National Institute on Aging notes: "Research on human factor engineering suggests that alterations in cockpit and equipment design can be made that will take into account decrements in performance, so that small changes in physical capability will not significantly affect a pilot's ability to fly safely."

Ways of making such changes for all kinds of jobs are being, and surely will be, researched and tested. The willingness of public and private sectors to pay their fair share for the accommodations would be an important issue. We are already seeing controversy between government and corporate interests over the recent law requiring job-based health insurance to supplant Medicare as the primary coverage for older workers. The companies oppose the law since private insurance costs more for older workers than for younger workers.

But we must also plan for persons with serious functional limitations who require considerable social support, including medical, hospital, nursing home, and at-home services. We must keep in mind that this group constitutes a sizable minority, but a minority nonetheless, of the elderly population. At any one time, only 1 person in 20 of the general elderly population is in a nursing home; the proportion after age 80 is 1 in 5. This is an important point in considering needs for both institutional and community-based services. According to some estimates, a population double the 1.3 million nursing-home residents is in need of long-term care services in the community. If true, the market for major long-term care services is probably about 4 million of the nation's 26 million elderly.

Because mortality and sickness rates accelerate markedly after age 75, the size of this population has implications for the development of health and social services. It is growing fast — over 9 million today, probably 14 million by 2000. The fastest growing segment of the entire U.S. population is the group aged 85 and older. In 1980, there were 2.6 million, or 1.1 percent of the U.S. population at this age. In 2020, there will be 7.6 million, or 2.5 percent.

Between 1980 and 2020, the 75-and-over population with activity limitations due to chronic conditions will increase 2.5 times, to 10.7 million. The number of short-stay hospitalizations will rise to 104.6 million days from 45.8 million. Instead of 1.1 million in nursing homes, there will be 2.7 million. The number of physician visits will double. Personal expenditure for health care will more than double for the aged, while it rises by 50 percent for the entire U.S. population. Nursing-home expenditures will be in the forefront.

The Geriatrics Gap

Geriatric researchers seek ways to prevent a slow decline in various body systems and to help the patient adjust to changed conditions. They also study a variety of special problems of the elderly. The reactions of the older person to drugs, infection, pain, heart attacks, and other conditions may be different from the reactions of younger adults. For example, mental confusion, not chest pain, may be symptomatic of a heart attack in the older person. So-called senility, or senile dementia, may be reversible once the cause of confusion and memory loss is traced to a treatable cause, such as infection, malnutrition, alcoholism, drug abuse, or depression. Geriatric practice must be concerned with educating patients and families on the true nature of illness in old age, lest misconceptions like "it's just old age" delay treatment beyond the time when it can be most effective.

Unfortunately, the field of geriatrics is underdeveloped in this country. Scientific research into the processes of aging did not expand until recently, and some new conclusions are beginning to appear. Several studies have been done that show far less deterioration in information-processing and problem-solving abilities than investigators in the 1930s had thought.

Some of the most significant conclusions from recent gerontologic research are cautionary. First, what sometimes looks like psychological deterioration due to aging may in fact be more the result of a poor socioeconomic background or little education. For example, a 60-year-old born in 1910 may have greater ability than a 60-year-old born in 1880 simply because he has had a better education.

The enactment of Medicare in 1965 was not accompanied by major investments in research, manpower for service and for research, or by the organization and funding of geriatric services. Medicare was, and is, a benefit package based on what young adults need. It emphasizes short-term or acute care.

The Medicare nursing-home benefit, called "extended care" at first, was basically for convalescence after hospitalization. Because costs could not be forecast reliably, Congress omitted long-term care from the Medicare law. Administrative definitions of reimbursable illness costs exclude coverage of what is disparagingly called "custodial services," some of which are essential to the survival or functioning of patients who are not likely to get "better." For want of home care and other mundane assistance, sound geriatric principles cannot be applied, and some patients become expensive institutional cases.

The only large-scale program of long-term care benefits is found in Medicaid, the Federally aided program of state benefits for the poor. Medicaid money accounts for about half the annual $22 billion spent on nursing-home care. (The other half comes directly from patients or families.) The program's growth is threatening many state treasuries. Unless costs can be moderated, taxes will increase and the increases will cut into profits and wages. This is one reason why some forward-looking business groups are examining long-term care issues and their responsibilities for assisting in resolving them.

Private insurance has eschewed coverage of nursing-home and homemaker services. Reimbursement arrangements under conventional health insurance policies are ill suited to geriatric practice. Only grudgingly do they recognize time spent hearing out, examining, and counseling a patient, or the use of experts in medicine, nursing, and social work as a diagnostic and treatment team. The team approach, a cornerstone of geriatrics, disintegrates at the billing office and dies at the bank. A breakthrough in insurance coverage, through private or public approaches, or a combination of them, is sorely needed.

In addition, we will have to somehow meet the demand for more geriatric physicians—a prospect that now seems unlikely since only a small number of the nation's 127 medical schools have professors of geriatrics or required courses in geriatrics.

Organizing for Productive Aging

How may we organize our thinking for action in the interests of today's elderly and the generation at risk? Plans under way at the Mount Sinai Medical Center in New York City may provide one model.

In 1982, the Medical Center established the nation's first medical school department of geriatrics. The Gerald and May Ellen Ritter Foundation funded the department and the Brookdale Foundation supported the chair in geriatrics that I occupy. The department has six faculty members and eight postgraduate fellows. Wholehearted support by the trustees and administration assured substantial room for mandatory instruction in geriatrics in a crowded medical curriculum. A biomedical research program was authorized. Plans for inpatient and outpatient services for geriatric patients and their families were completed. In addition to providing the community with home care and a wellness clinic, the department is creating a geriatric assessment and referral unit to assist physicians, patients, and families in defining and carrying out programs of care. Special clinics will be devoted to patients with senile dementia, menopausal problems, incontinence, and mobility limitations.

Students and medical residents will be exposed to the well and ill elderly in the community at the hospital and at the Jewish Home and Hospital for Aged. The latter, a nationally recognized long-term care institution, will become a teaching nursing home—a counterpart of the teaching hospital.

To conduct policy-related research and analysis and to raise public and professional awareness of population aging, the department is creating an Institute for Studies of Health and Aging. Applying a broad conception of health, the Institute plans to organize these divisions as funds become available:

☐ The Center for Productive Aging, to study and offer consultation services on issues involved in enhancing the contributions of the older population to the economy and to family and civic life. The center will advise on such topics as: personnel policies and programs for long-term health and productivity; objective criteria for personal and corporate decisions on work and retirement, and adaptation of the elderly to work tasks and environments.

☐ The Center for Long-Term Care Systems, to focus particularly on long-term care insurance. The center will provide advice and information to corporations, labor unions, health-care organizations, senior citizen groups, and others concerned about long-term care and geriatrics.

☐ The Leadership Forum on Population Aging, to air the issues of population aging in seminars and other formats of practical use to public and private decision-makers. An Aging Information Service will serve the public and mass media as well as private clients.

☐ The Center for International Aging Studies, to bring policy specialists and social and health-care professionals together to examine population-aging issues of international significance. A program of regular exchange between U.S. and foreign teachers and practitioners is contemplated to accelerate the diffusion of geriatric knowledge and skills.

☐ The National Reference Center on Geriatric Education, to promote the development of geriatric training by collecting and disseminating innovative curricula and teaching materials and by advising schools on how to get started.

With well-conceived policies, later life will be a time of options. Even if impaired in some way, we will have opportunities to be productive; we will maintain our vigor for as long as possible, and we will not easily lose our personal autonomy. Supportive programs will exist, staffed by perceptive and humane practitioners, paid for by some contributory method that protects us against impoverishment and affirms our dignity. We will be proud of these accomplishments and leave them to our children. They will say we knew how to age well.

FOREIGN POLICY
OUTMODED ASSUMPTIONS

Henry Steele Commager

Henry Steele Commager, noted historian and educator, has taught at many universities here and abroad. He is now at work on a fifty-volume work, The Rise of the American Nation.

"*WHEN SOCIETY REQUIRES to be rebuilt, there is no use in attempting to rebuild it on the old plan.*"

" *No great improvements in the lot of mankind are possible, until a great change takes place in the fundamental constitution of their modes of thought.*"

John Stuart Mill's admonitions are still valid. Since the Truman Doctrine of 1947—perhaps since Hiroshima and Nagasaki—the United States has been locked into a Cold War whose temperature has fluctuated over the years, and now threatens to become incandescent. The origins of that war have fascinated a generation of historians whose disagreements are by now irremediable, perhaps because the explanations are not to be found so much in unraveling the tangled skein of history as in probing the philosophical and psychological assumptions that were uncritically adopted at the beginning of hostilities, and that have not yet been subjected to serious re-examination by those in power.

How are we to explain our obsession with communism, our paranoid hostility to the Soviet Union, our preoccupation with the Cold War, our reliance on military rather than political or diplomatic solutions, and our new readiness to entertain as a possibility what was long regarded as unthinkable—atomic warfare?

Can we avoid the "unthinkable" and rebuild a world of peace and order without a change in the "fundamental constitution of [our] modes of thought"—modes of thought themselves largely re-sponsible for the crisis that glares upon us with relentless insistence from every quarter of the horizon?

Some of those assumptions have long enjoyed the dignity of official endorsement; some have been eroded in principle but linger on in official ideology—and are held together by passionate emotional harmony; some are sustained by interests so deeply entrenched that they seem invulnerable to criticism. As a body, the catechism of assumptions resembles in many respects that of the Moral Majority: it is rooted in emotion rather than in reason; it is negative rather than positive in its objectives; it is inspired by fear rather than by confidence; it is inconsistent and even contradictory in logic.

Consider some of those assumptions that have proved most tenacious.

First is the assumption that the world is divided between two great ideological and power groups, one dedicated to freedom, the other to slavery. History appointed the United States to represent and defend the first. The Soviet Union, whether by appointment or not is unclear, represents the second. These two worlds have been, for thirty years, locked in fateful combat.

This simplistic picture has, over the years, been badly distorted by developments that do not fit its logic: the conflict between China and Russia; our own almost nonchalant rapprochement with China; the emergence of a new power bloc in the Middle East; and the growing reluctance of many members of the "free-world" coalition to respect either the freedom or the morality to whose defense we are committed. None of these developments has as yet persuaded many Americans to modify their original conviction that communism is the inveterate enemy.

A second assumption is implicit in the first: that communism, especially the Soviet variety, is not only dedicated to the enslavement of men but is godless and deeply immoral. Therefore the Soviet Union can never be relied upon to keep its word; it is engaged in ceaseless aggrandizement; it makes a mockery of international law and human dignity, and trusts only force. From all this it follows that for us to substitute diplomatic negotiations for military power would be to fall into a trap from which we could not extricate ourselves.

This assumption, to be sure, has deep roots in our history and our psychology. Though perhaps no other nation of modern times has had such spectacular success at the diplomatic table as the United States, Americans have long deluded themselves with the notion that their diplomats—invariably virtuous and innocent—have been consistently seduced and betrayed by wily Old World diplomats. This is, needless to say, fantasy. The Treaty of Paris of 1783 represented a spectacular triumph of American diplomats over both the British and the French, and the new nation found itself not thirteen independent states hugging the Atlantic but a vast empire. Twenty years later Jefferson intended to secure no more than New Orleans, but found that, thanks to Napoleon's impatience, the Treaty of 1803 doubled the territory of the United States without war and almost without cost. No one really won the War of 1812, but American diplomats won the negotiations at Ghent, and after that treaty, and the Battle of New Orleans, Europe left America alone. In 1871, the United States collected substantial awards from Great Britain for her violations of neutrality during the Civil War—violations of international law that were tame compared with those we now commit as a matter of course. In

1898, we dictated our own terms to Spain; and if in 1919 Wilson was not able to get all the Fourteen Points into the Treaty of Versailles, he did get his associates to set up a League of Nations, which we subsequently scuttled. Certainly we were in command in 1945, dictating terms not only to Germany and Japan but to our allies as well—terms characterized on the whole by magnanimity. Yalta, which most Americans have been led to believe a diplomatic defeat, was no such thing: in the military circumstances of February, 1945 (when American forces had not yet crossed the Rhine), it constituted an American success.

As for violation of international law, treaties, and agreements, and of the territorial integrity of weaker nations, the record of the Soviet Union is indeed deplorable. Whether it differs greatly from the American record depends, no doubt, upon the point of view. Little need to rehearse that record: suffice it to say that the CIA has at least tried to be as subversive as the KGB in many parts of the globe, that intervention in Cuba, the Dominican Republic, and Guatemala was no less in violation of law than the Soviet invasions of Hungary and Czechoslovakia, and that a ten-year undeclared war in Vietnam, with casualties of some two million, both military and civilian, and bombardment with three times the tonnage dropped on Germany and Japan in World War II contrasts unfavorably with the much-condemned Soviet invasion of Afghanistan.

Nothing surprising about all this except that a people brought up, for the most part, on the New Testament should so readily ignore the question raised by Matthew: "Why beholdest thou the mote that is in thy brother's eye, but considerest not the beam that is in thine own eye?"

A third assumption is rooted in the second: that the Soviet Union is the mortal enemy of the United States and that her animosity is implacable. This assumption, implicit in innumerable statements by President Reagan and Secretary of Defense Caspar Weinberger, dictates most of our current political and military programs. The term "dictates" is appropriate, for we no longer appear to be masters of our own destiny or even in control of our policies, but react with almost Pavlovian response to the real or imagined policies of the Soviet Union. Clearly, our reaction to the Polish crisis is animated more by hostility to the So-

viet Union than by compassion for Poland.

In all this we rarely ask ourselves what the Soviet Union has to gain by destroying the United States. In the past neither czarist nor Communist Russia has been an "enemy" of the United States, and in the twentieth century Russia was allied with or associated with the United States in two major wars. Nor do many Americans pause to acknowledge that the Communists have more ground for fearing the United States than we have for fearing them: after all, American military forces invaded the Soviet Union at Archangel and Vladivostok to prevent the Bolshevik takeover and remained on Russian soil for well over two years: had Communist forces invaded the United States in, let us say, Alaska or Florida, we would not be quite so forgetful.

That the ideological conflict between the Soviet Union and the United States is deep and perhaps irremediable cannot be denied. It is sobering to recall that during the early years of the nineteenth century—and, indeed, again during our Civil War—much of Europe looked upon the United States as we now look upon the Soviet Union, and with more justification. The new American republic did indeed threaten the peace and security of Old World nations. Republicanism, democracy, constitutionalism, and social equality challenged all Old World monarchies and class societies. That challenge was practical—millions of Europeans found refuge in America—and it was philosophical, as well. Listen to Prince Metternich, the greatest and most powerful European statesman of his generation, excoriate the United States for proclaiming the Monroe Doctrine:

These United States . . . have suddenly left a sphere too narrow for their ambition, and have astonished Europe by a new act of revolt, more unprovoked, fully as audacious, and no less dangerous than the former [against Britain]. They have distinctly and exactly announced their intention to set not only power against power, but, to express it more exactly, altar against altar. In their indecent declarations they have cast blame and scorn on the institutions of Europe most worthy of respect. . . . In permitting themselves these unprovoked attacks, in fostering revolutions wherever they show themselves, in regretting those which have failed, in extend-

ing a helping hand to those which seem to prosper, they lend new strength to the apostles of sedition, and re-animate the courage of every conspirator. If this flood of evil doctrines and pernicious examples should extend over the whole of America, what would become of our religious and political institutions, of the moral forces of our governments, and of the conservative system which has saved Europe from complete dissolution?

Nor was this paranoia confined to spokesmen of autocratic countries. Here is what the leading British journal of its day—*Blackwood's Edinburgh Magazine*—had to say of Lincoln's Emancipation Proclamation:

Monstrous, reckless, devilish. . . . It proves . . . [that] rather than lose their trade and custom, the North would league itself with Beelzebub and seek to make a hell of half a continent. In return this atrocious act justifies the South in hoisting the black flag . . . And thus . . . we are called upon to contemplate a war more full of horrors and wickedness than any which stands recorded in the world's history.

The exacerbation of anti-Russian paranoia by this administration is not in fact in the mainstream of American experience. We have had less excuse for it than any other major nation, for since 1815 we have never been threatened by external aggression by any nation except Japan nor, except for the Civil War, by serious ideological conflicts.

Our current crisis dramatizes the wisdom of President Washington's warning, in his Farewell Address:

. . . nothing is more essential than that permanent, inveterate antipathies against particular nations . . . be excluded; and that in place of them just and amicable feelings towards all should be cultivated. The nation which indulges towards another an habitual hatred or an habitual fondness is in some degree a slave. It is a slave to its animosity or to its affection . . . Antipathy in one nation against another disposes each more readily to offer insult and injury . . .

IT IS PERHAPS THIS enslavement to our own animosity that explains a fourth major assumption—one we might call the Dr. Strangelove syndrome: that we could fight and "win" an atomic war, that the loss of 50 million to 100 million lives would be "acceptable," that the Republic could survive and flourish after such a victory. An atomic war is no longer "unthinkable"; perhaps it never was: after all, we are the only nation ever to use the atomic weapon against an enemy. Now spokesmen of both our parties have declared that in an "emergency" we would not hesitate to use it again. In all this we are reminded of the moral of slavery: when a "necessary evil" becomes necessary enough, it ceases to be an evil.

This philosophy is a product, or a by-product, of a fifth assumption: that the most effective way, and perhaps the only way, to counter the threat of communism is neither political, economic, nor moral but quite simply military, and that the mere threat of overwhelming military might will persuade all rivals to abandon the field.

This is, to be sure, a familiar maxim: it was Voltaire who observed that God is always for the big battalions. But there is an older wisdom. More than three centuries ago Francis Bacon wrote, "Walled towers, stored arsenals, and armories, goodly races of horse, chariots of war, elephants, ordnance, artillery and the like—all this is but a sheep in lion's skin, except the breed and disposition of the people be stout . . ."

That is still true, though we must rephrase it to comport with modern weaponry. The futility of reliance on superiority in nuclear arms should have been clear as early as 1949, when the Russians astonished most of the "experts" by detonating their own atomic bomb a decade earlier than had been expected. Certainly it should be clear by now that the Russians can produce anything that we can produce, and that the notion of "winning" an arms race is fantasy. The hope—perhaps the only hope—of avoiding a nuclear war lies not in adding another $1,500 billion to the $2,000 billion we have already spent on the military since the close of World War II but in mutual abandonment of that race, and a cooperative program of systematic reduction of existing nuclear arms.

As for security, that is indeed to be found in the "stoutness" and the disposition of the people—in their courage, intelligence, and resourcefulness, and in the preservation and nurture of that common wealth with which Nature has endowed them. The most serious threat to national security is in the wastage of human and the exhaustion of natural resources. It is in permitting our industrial and technological enterprises, our transportation system, our financial health, to deteriorate, our cities to decay into slums, our schools to fail of their primary functions of education, our society to be ravaged by poverty, lawlessness, racial strife, class hostilities, and injustice. It is in a leadership that lacks prudence, wisdom, and vision. It is in a society whose leaders no longer invoke, and whose people no longer take seriously, those concepts of public virtue, of the pursuit of happiness, and of the fiduciary obligation to posterity that were the all-but-universal precepts of the generation that founded the Republic.

A sixth assumption is a by-product of the fifth: that the security of the United States is bound up with and dependent on whatever regimes throughout the globe are ostentatiously anti-Communist. Our record here is a dismal one, yet instead of repudiating that record, the present administration seems determined to outstrip it. We persist in regarding South Korea and Taiwan as not only friends but allies; we practically forced Pakistan to accept billions of dollars for arms; we have abandoned all pretense of holding aloof from the tyrannical regimes of Chile and Argentina; we even conjure up a distinction between "authoritarian" and "totalitarian" regimes, whose only real distinction is whether they are authoritarian on our side or not. The vocabulary of this administration, as of Nixon's, inevitably conjures up what Thucydides said of the corruption of language in the Athens of his day: "What used to be described as a thoughtless act of aggression, was now regarded as the courage one would expect to find in a party member . . . fanatical enthusiasm was the mark of a real man . . . anyone who held violent opinions could always be trusted . . . and to plot successfully was a sign of intelligence."

To many of the peoples of the Third World, and even of the European world, the United States appears to be what the Holy Alliance was in the early nineteenth century. The analogy does not favor the United States, for while the Holy Alliance, for all its interventions in Spain and Italy and Greece, had the good sense to keep out of distant continents, the United States does not. What our interventions throughout the globe—Vietnam, Cambodia, Angola, Nicaragua, El Salvador, and Iran—have in common with those of the Holy Alliance is their failure.

MUCH OF OUR NEW "imperialism" is rooted in a seventh assumption: that the United States is not only a Western but an African and an Asian power.

That the United States is a world power is incontestable. Clearly, too, it is by virtue of geography an Atlantic power and a Pacific power, and it is by virtue of history something of a European power—a fact convincingly vindicated by participation in two world wars. But the United States is no more an Asian power than China or Japan is an American power. We have never permitted an Asian power to establish a military presence in the American continents. We bought Alaska from Russia, and the 1912 Lodge Corollary to the Monroe Doctrine extended that doctrine to "any Government, not American." It was the illusion that we could control the internal politics of China that distracted us from a recognition of reality for a quarter-century: certainly the greatest blunder in the history of American diplomacy. Even now, notwithstanding the commonsense reversal of that misguided policy by Nixon and Kissinger, we have not yet wholly rid ourselves of the purblind notion that we can, and should, "play the China card"—a notion that in its arrogance and in its vulgarity must represent the low-water mark of American foreign policy.

Another corollary of our reliance on the military for security is dramatized by an eighth assumption: that to achieve security it is proper for government to conscript science and scholarship for the purposes of war, cold or not; that, in short, the scientific, philosophical, and cultural community should be an instrument of the State for secular purposes.

This principle was not embraced by those who founded the Republic nor, for that matter, by the philosophers of the Enlightenment in the Old World. During the American Revolution, Benjamin Franklin joined with the French minister of finance, Jacques Necker, to decree immunity for Captain Cook because he was "engaged in pursuits beneficial to mankind." In the midst of the Napoleonic Wars, the French Institute conferred its gold medal on the great British scientist Humphrey Davy, and while the war was still raging, Sir Humphrey crossed the Channel to accept that honor. "If two countries are at war," he said, "the men of science are not." Napoleon himself shared this view: during his victorious campaign in Germany, he spared the university city of Göttingen from bombardment because it was the home of the greatest of classical scholars, Christian Heyne. And it was Napoleon, too, who, at the request of Joseph Banks of the Royal Society, freed the great geologist Dolomieu from the dungeons of Naples. Edward Jenner, the discoverer of the smallpox vaccine, put it for his whole generation: "The sciences are never at war. Peace must always preside in the bosoms of those whose object is the augmentation of human happiness."

It was Thomas Jefferson who stated this principle most clearly and most eloquently, and this at a time when he himself had abandoned his study and his laboratory to serve in the Virginia legislature. In 1778, he addressed a letter to the scientist David Rittenhouse, then serving as treasurer to the Commonwealth of Pennsylvania:

> Your time for two years past has . . . been principally employed in the civil government of your country. Tho' I have been aware of the authority our cause would acquire with the world from its being known that yourself and Doctr. Franklin were zealous friends to it, and am myself duly impressed with a sense of arduousness of government, and the obligation those are under who are able to conduct it, yet I am also satisfied there is an order of geniuses above that obligation, and therefore exempted from it. No body can conceive that nature ever intended to throw away a Newton upon the occupations of a crown. It would have been a prodigality for which even the conduct of providence might have been ar-

raigned, had he been by birth annexed to what was so far below him.

A NINTH ASSUMPTION, PERHAPS the most intractable of all, is that any of the fundamental problems that confront us—and other nations of the globe—can be resolved within the framework of the nation-state system. The inescapable fact, dramatized by the energy crisis, the population crisis, the armaments race, and so forth, is that nationalism as we have known it in the nineteenth and much of the twentieth century is as much of an anachronism today as was States Rights when Calhoun preached it and Jefferson Davis fought for it. Just as we know, or should know, that none of our domestic problems can be solved within the artificial boundaries of the states, so none of our global problems can be solved within the largely artificial boundaries of nations—artificial not so much in the eyes of history as in the eyes of Nature. Nature, as the dispenser of all resources, knows no boundaries between North and South Dakota or Kansas and Nebraska, no boundaries, for that matter, between Canada, the United States, and Mexico, and very few between the two Americas, Europe, Asia, and Africa. Every major problem that confronts us is global—energy, pollution, the destruction of the oceans and the seas, the erosion of agricultural and forest lands, the control of epidemics and of plant and animal diseases, famine in large parts of Asia and Africa and a population increase that promises to aggravate famine, inflation, international terrorism, nuclear pollution, and nuclear-arms control. Not one of these can be

solved within the limits of a single nation.

Even to mitigate these problems requires the cooperation of statesmen, scientists, and moral philosophers in every country. Americans should find it easier to achieve such cooperation than did the peoples of Old World nations, for they are the heirs and the beneficiaries of a philosophy that proclaimed that *all* men were created equal and endowed with unalienable rights to life, liberty, and the pursuit of happiness.

Of all the assumptions I have discussed, that which takes nationalism for granted is perhaps the most deeply rooted and the most tenacious. Yet when we reflect that assumptions, even certainties, no less tenacious in the past—about the very nature of the cosmic system, about the superiority of one race to all others, about the naturalness of women's subordination to men, about the providential order of a class society, about the absolute necessity of a state church or religion—have all given way to the implacable pressure of science and of reality, we may conclude that what Tocqueville wrote well over a century ago is still valid:

> The world that is rising into existence is still half encumbered by the remains of the world that is waning into decay; and amid the vast perplexity of human affairs none can say how much of ancient institutions and former customs will remain or how much will completely disappear.

If some of our ancient institutions do not disappear, there is little likelihood that we shall remain.

A NEW LOOK AT THE POPULATION PROBLEM

**Jean van der Tak,
Carl Haub, and Elaine Murphy**

High population growth
in developing nations
is putting tremendous
pressures on the earth's
resources, environment,
and social fabric. Here is
an up-to-date report
on what may be the most
critical problem of the
late twentieth century.

The human population of the
earth probably passed the 4.3 billion
point in 1979, increasing by some 74
million each year. We say "probably" because population data are
still scanty and unreliable for parts
of Asia and Africa although demographers are becoming adept at
making plausible estimates from de-
ficient data. At its current 1.7% rate
of increase, every three years the
world population grows by nearly
as many people as the 220 million
living in the U.S. in 1979. Every five
days we add another million people
to our human population.

This population explosion seems
all the more awesome when seen in
the perspective of humanity's development as a species. During the
hundreds of thousands of years of
the Old Stone Age when *Homo
sapiens* was a hunter and food gath-
erer, for example, the world population probably never exceeded 10
million.

The world reached its first *billion*
around 1800—some two to five million years after the appearance of
the first humanlike creatures. Adding the second billion took about
130 years to 1930. The third billion
was reached after only 30 years, in
1960, and the fourth after 15 years,
in 1975. About 1965, the world's
rate of population growth climbed
to 2%—a rate at which numbers
double in 35 years.

The explosive buildup of world
population is putting tremendous
pressures on the earth's resources,
environment, and social fabric. The
pressures are currently felt most
acutely in less developed countries
(LDCs) where hundreds of millions
already live in abject poverty and
hunger. But the pressures are compounded by the developed countries' high per capita consumption of
resources and output of pollution.
The population predicament is
shared by all humanity.

Historical Population Changes

A look at the changes in birth and
death rates in developed countries
over the last two centuries, in fact,
gives a partial indication of how the
population explosion came about.
We use Sweden as an example, but
the historical pattern of Sweden's
birth and death rates is typical of
other Western European countries.
Until the late eighteenth century,
both rates fluctuated at a relatively
high level. Then as the Industrial
Revolution accelerated in the early
nineteenth century, the death rate
began to fall gradually, followed
some 50 to 70 years later by the
birthrate. By the 1930s, both were at
low levels. Today, following a brief

post-World War II rise in the birthrate, Sweden's annual births and
deaths are in balance and the population has stopped growing from natural increase. This pattern applies
generally to the now developed
countries, although there are exceptions.

Since the 1930s, demographers
have sought to explain how and
why this evolution from high to low
birth and death rates came about in
today's developed countries. The
best known explanation, based
mainly on what was thought to be
the experience in Western Europe, is
known as the demographic transition theory. In its "classic" form,
this theory describes three stages:

• The initial stage of potentially
high population growth evolves
from a backdrop of high death rates
reflecting harsh living conditions
and high birthrates needed to com-
pensate for high infant mortality.
With improved living conditions
and control over disease brought
about by "modernization," death
rates begin to fall. At first, birthrates remain high, causing a rise in
population growth.

• During the subsequent transitional stage, the rate of population
growth is still relatively high, but a
decline in birthrates becomes well
established. The small-family ideal
arises first among "upwardly mobile" couples, particularly in cities,
who come to see too many children
as a hindrance to taking advantage
of the opportunities offered by the
expanding industrial economy. The
preference for few children gradually diffuses throughout the country,
aided by declining rates of infant
mortality.

From *The Futurist*, April 1980. THE FUTURIST, published by the World Future Society, 4916 St. Elmo Avenue, Washington,
D.C. 20014.

• The stage of very low or zero population growth is reached when mortality is low and fertility hovers around replacement level. Fertility could stabilize below replacement level, leading, in the absence of net immigration, to an eventual decline in the absolute size of a country's population.

Birth and Death Rates in Transition

Most of today's growth is taking place among the some three-quarters of the world's population living in the less developed regions—Latin America, Africa, and Asia (minus Japan). Here, previously high death rates fell rapidly after World War II and by about 1977 were at the comparatively low level of 12 deaths per 1,000 population per year. Birthrates are still at an average 33 per 1,000 population annually. As a result, the developing regions are growing at a rapid 2.1% each year. By contrast, among the other quar- ter of the globe's population in de- veloped regions (the U.S. and Can- ada, Europe, the U.S.S.R., Japan, Australia, and New Zealand), the annual rate of growth now stands at a much lower 0.7%—reflecting an average birthrate of 16 per 1,000 and a death rate of 9.

Although reliable data to verify trends are lacking for many less de- veloped countries, most demogra- phers are now convinced that fertil- ity has begun to decline in develop- ing countries as a whole, and in some LDCs the decline is much more rapid than it was in Europe. At the same time, the precipitous decline in LDC death rates that marked the 1950s and early 1960s appears to have slowed.

Parker Mauldin and the late Ber- nard Berelson, former Population Council researchers, estimated that in the decade from 1965 to 1975 the birthrate of 94 LDCs with 98% of the developing world's population declined on average about 13%, from about 41 to 35.5 births per 1,000 population. In 28 developing countries containing over two- thirds of the world's population, the decline ranged from 10 to 40%. The decline was most marked in Asia and Latin America. Sub-Saharan Africa showed virtually no fertility decline and, with death rates contin- uing to fall, population growth in Africa had climbed to 2.9% about 1977, the highest of any region.

The slowdown in declining death rates, which economist Davidson Gwatkin calls "the end of an era," seems related to the rise of dysen- tery, diarrhea, and pneumonia as leading causes of death, particularly among infants and children. These diseases, often precipitated by mal- nutrition, are harder to control with modern medicine and physician- and clinic-based health services. Eradicating them takes improved living conditions, especially more and better food and education. For most developing countries, rapid

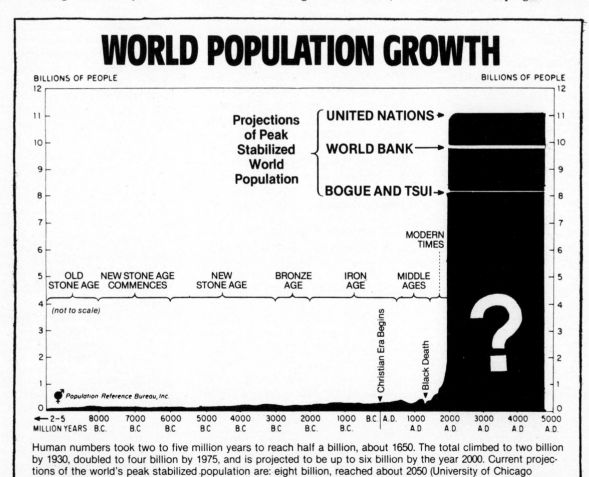

Human numbers took two to five million years to reach half a billion, about 1650. The total climbed to two billion by 1930, doubled to four billion by 1975, and is projected to be up to six billion by the year 2000. Current projec- tions of the world's peak stabilized population are: eight billion, reached about 2050 (University of Chicago demographers Donald Bogue and Amy Ong Tsui); about ten billion, around 2090 (World Bank); or eleven billion about 2125 (United Nations).

James O'Brien for the Population Reference Bureau, Inc.

6. FUTURE

population growth has frustrated this possibility.

The beginnings of fertility decline in many LDCs and the slowdown in mortality decline have combined to stop the steady rise in the world's rate of population growth. The peak was probably passed somewhere in the mid-1960s—a time that some experts have called a "demographic watershed." The world's birthrate fell below 30 for the first time on record around 1975 and by 1977 was at an unprecedented 28 per 1,000 population.

Though encouraging, these trends still add up to huge numbers. The current 1.7% world growth rate is adding some 74 million a year to today's global total of about 4.3 billion. By 2000, 20 years hence, the United Nations projects a total world population of 6.2 billion, with the lowered growth rate of 1.5% translating into an annual net increase of about 93 million people. Some 90% of the 2 billion increase in the next two decades will take place in the developing world.

Consequences of Rapid Population Growth

The consequences of rapid population growth are evident across the spectrum of human, animal, and plant life. In the less developed world, despite the recent slight slowdown, population is still growing in some countries at rates that could double the numbers of people in just over 20 years. These countries are already hard pressed to supply their current populations with decent living conditions. In countries like the U.S. that have undergone the demographic transition, the problem seems to be of a different order of magnitude. A growth rate of under 1%, which would take a century or more to double a country's population, seems less threatening. Yet when put in the context of other global challenges, including continuation of economic progress, balancing world supplies of food, energy, and natural resources, and preservation of the global environment, the growth of the industrialized countries appears nearly as critical.

Economic Development

Besides exporting the medical and public health revolution to the rest of the world, the Western industrialized nations have also tried, since World War II, to speed economic development and hence raise levels of living in the developing world. Improving living conditions requires that economic growth significantly outpace population growth. From 1960 to 1976, overall economic growth in low-income developing countries nearly matched that of the industrialized countries, and economic growth in middle-income LDCs was spectacular. But because of much more rapid population growth, the developing world's gain in income *per capita*, and thus levels of living, was much less. Rapid population growth diverts resources that might otherwise be available for investment in development.

The discouraging cycle of development handicapped by excessive population growth, and of rapid population growth continuing because the majority of families perceive little chance for economic progress, can be overcome only through a variety of carefully formulated, vigorously pursued measures adapted to each country's needs. But one of the principal requirements in most less developed countries is clearly the earliest possible reduction of high fertility rates.

Unemployment and Urbanization

In the two remaining decades of this century, the disheartening effects of past and future population growth in developing countries may be most evident in their exploding labor forces and cities.

The International Labour Office (ILO) estimates that in 1975 there were around 283 million people unemployed or underemployed in the non-Communist developing world —40% of the workforce of some 700 million outside China and other Communist countries.

According to the ILO, the high and in some cases rising population growth rates of the late 1960s and early 1970s will translate into an increase in the developing world's labor force from 1.13 billion in 1975 to 1.91 billion in 2000. With these 780 million new workers added to the 283 million currently unemployed or underemployed (outside China), this quarter century will see the need for more than a billion new jobs in the developing world, where job-creating development is proceeding all too slowly. Particularly worrisome is the high projected labor force growth—and hence probably also unemployment— among urban youth aged 15 to 24, politically and socially the most volatile of all age groups.

To make matters worse, by the year 2000, over half the world's population is likely to be living in towns and cities, up from 39% in 1975.

Enormous numbers of people are involved. Between 1950 and 1975, the urban population of developing countries grew by some 400 million people. Between 1975 and 2000, the increase will be close to one billion.

The problem is aggravated by the concentration of urban dwellers in very large cities. In 1950, only one city of the developing world (Greater Buenos Aires) had a population over 5 million, compared to five such cities in the industrialized countries. By the year 2000, according to World Bank projections, the developing world will have about 40 cities this size and the developed world 12. Eighteen cities in developing countries are expected to have more than 10 million inhabitants, and one at least—Mexico City— may well have three times that number.

Housing, both urban and rural, is another critical problem. In Asia, the backlog of needed housing units in urban areas increased from 22 million dwellings in 1960 to 72 million in 1975; in Asia's rural areas, the need for housing units went from 125 to 219 million in the same 15 years.

Health facilities are on a similar treadmill. Inability to keep up with the demand from growing populations is part of the explanation for the recent slowdown in mortality declines in less developed countries. The World Health Organization estimates that 80 to 90% of rural populations in developing countries have no access to health care. The urban poor are scarcely better off. In Sao Paulo, for example, infant mortality has recently risen, malaria and bubonic plague have reappeared, and meningitis reached epidemic proportions in 1974.

Food

Since World War II, food production worldwide has increased at a slightly faster rate than population. But most of the improvement in food supply *per person* has been in the already well-fed industrialized countries.

From 1961 through 1976, developing countries as a whole improved food production at a faster rate than developed countries, but because of rampant population growth, their per capita food output grew at a much slower pace. The gain in per capita food production averaged a steady 1.4% in industrialized countries during this period. In developing countries, by contrast, annual per capita gains were already below 1% in the 1960s and nearly vanished in the early 1970s when droughts slashed yields across Asia and Africa. With better weather, expanded irrigation, and other investments, agricultural production has since improved in the developing world, particularly in Asia, but the situation remains precarious. In India, for example, the 20 million tons of grain reserves collected during four years of good harvests are expected to be drawn down heavily following 1979's late and erratic monsoon rains and poor harvest.

Environment

A last critical issue for future generations is the growing pressure of population on the global environment.

In recent decades, the earth's vegetation cover (croplands, forests, and grasslands), fisheries, water sources, and atmosphere have undergone a sharply increased rate of depletion and pollution.

A large part of this is again due to high production and consumption life-styles, coupled with still-growing populations, in industrialized countries. Environmental degradation has also resulted from the desperate efforts of rapidly growing im-

poverished populations in developing nations to survive. Vast areas of Africa, South and Southeast Asia, the Middle East, and Latin America have been crippled by slash-and-burn agriculture, overcropping, overgrazing, and consequent wind and water erosion.

This environmental loss and damage is occurring in a world of 4 billion people. In 20 years, the number of human consumers and polluters is expected to be around 6 billion and still growing.

World Response to the Problem

Over the past 10 to 15 years, there has been an encouraging increase in world awareness of population problems. Many developing countries have seen the need for urgent action to reduce rapid population growth if their development efforts are not to be greatly impaired or totally frustrated. In 1960, of *all* countries in the world, only India and Pakistan supported organized family planning programs, both for the avowed purpose of reducing birthrates. By 1978, 35 less developed countries—with 77% of the developing world's population—had official policies to reduce population growth. Another 30, with 15% of LDC population, supported family planning programs for other than demographic reasons. Only 7% of the developing world's people lived in the 66 nations that have no family planning activities.

Family Planning "Versus" Development

Family planning programs in less developed countries vary widely in quality and effectiveness. As former Population Council researchers Mauldin and Berelson put it, these programs "range from vigorous and continuous efforts under skilled management to weak and spotty performance under indifferent administration, on down to no effort at all." How much of the recent fertility decline in LDCs can be attributed to these organized programs? Would birthrates have come down anyway as social and economic development increased couples' motivation to reduce family size, in line with the classical demographic transition theory? These questions have

been hotly debated in recent years as the world seeks ways to speed fertility decline in an effort to ward off potentially disastrous overcrowding, deprivation, and disorder.

These same questions were addressed at the 1974 World Population Conference in Bucharest, and it was recognized that the broad economic and social development thought to be necessary before most couples will opt for small families would be a long time in coming for many less developed countries. But research and experience seemed to show that particular elements of development are especially effective in bringing down birthrates. These include the following:

• **Reduction of infant and child mortality.** When parents can be assured that more of their children will survive to adulthood, they generally have fewer "insurance" births.

• **Expansion of basic education, especially for girls.** Studies in Latin America reveal that women who have completed primary school average about two fewer children than those who have not. For both men and women, education broadens views of life's opportunities and potentialities and reduces resistance to social change, including family planning.

• **Enhancing the status of women.** In addition to increasing women's opportunities for education, most observers agree that enhancing the general status of women socially, economically, and politically could contribute more than any other measure to reduced fertility.

• **More equitable distribution of the benefits of economic growth.** Experience in Taiwan, South Korea, Sri Lanka, and the state of Kerala in India indicates that economic growth is likely to have the most beneficial effects on fertility where the masses share equitably in that growth through increased income, employment, and access to land and health and education facilities.

• **Raising the age of marriage.** Mauldin and Berelson estimated that 35 to 40% of the 1965-75 birthrate decline in the developing countries they studied was accounted for by rising age at marriage, especially of women. This appears to be in-

6. FUTURE

fluenced by more education and employment for women and the "drive to improve socioeconomic status," as in Sri Lanka where the average age at marriage is among the highest in the developing world—28 for men and 24 for women.

Recent Family Planning Success Stories

At the time of the 1974 Bucharest population conference, family planning in the developing world could boast of successes only in the special city-states of Singapore and Hong Kong, or in such countries as Taiwan and South Korea where fertility had started downward before government programs began and where there was considerable socioeconomic development. It was not clear that family planning programs could trigger the transition from high to low birthrates in other countries that did not enjoy similar economic progress. But since then, several family planning program success stories have demonstrated that much can be achieved in circumstances that appear far from ripe ground, as judged by classical demographic transition theory. If these successes can be repeated elsewhere, the prospects for accelerated fertility decline in the coming decades could be much improved.

Chief among these successes is China, with a per capita income of about $410 and a huge agrarian population only 30 years removed from age-old traditions of large families. With over a fifth of the world's population at some 960 million at the end of 1978, what happens in China has enormous bearing on the future size and growth rate of the world's population. According to recent government statistics, China's birthrate at the end of 1978 was down to 20; its death rate was 8; and the rate of natural increase was thus 12 per 1,000, or 1.2%. This was equal to the U.S. rate of natural increase in 1964.

The elements of China's success include community-based, free provision of all birth control methods, including sterilization and abortion, by teams of trained, local "barefoot doctors," one of which is always a woman; locally planned and implemented birth quotas; and attempts to integrate women fully into all aspects of society.

On June 18, 1979, Premier Hua Kuofeng declared to the National People's Congress that the government now aims for a natural increase rate of 1% in 1979; 0.5% by 1985; zero growth by 2000; and, over the long run, a negative growth rate that will reduce the absolute size of the total population. In pursuit of this ambitious goal, a "birth planning law" is now being shaped to encourage the one-child family. Under discussion are proposals to reward one-child couples with substantial child-care subsidies until the child reaches 14, priorities in housing and the child's schooling, and—most important—a generous monthly pension upon the parents' retirement, even for rural peasants who now receive no such benefit.

Another success story is found in the densely packed, overwhelmingly rural and poor island of Bali, Indonesia, where two thirds of the women are unschooled. Here, the birthrate fell from 44 per 1,000 at the end of the 1960s to 28 in 1976 when more than half of eligible couples were using modern contraception—up from virtually no use five years earlier before the government family planning program began. Trained village people distribute pills; IUD insertions are readily available; and household heads themselves, through the traditional *banjar* (hamlet) councils, monitor contraceptive use.

In rural, tradition-bound Thailand, the Community-Based Family Planning Services, working side-by-side with an increasingly strong government program, in four-and-a-half years brought low-cost, efficient pill and condom services, manned by part-time local distributors, to villages containing over 16 million people. In some villages, as many as 80% of eligible couples now use modern contraception and the national total fertility rate was down to four-and-a-half children per woman in 1977—two children less than in the mid-1960s.

Unmet Needs for Family Planning

Despite specific successes, recent surveys show that family planning still has far to go in the developing world if a massive global population is to be avoided in the future. The International Planned Parenthood Federation (IPPF), in its 1976 Survey of Unmet Needs in Family Planning, found that contraceptive use in over 200 countries taken together had increased only 1% a year in the five years since its first such survey in 1971, to reach 35% of eligible couples. Contraceptive use was at or below 20% in most of the developing world compared to 65% and over in developed regions. Moreover, in these five years, the *number* of fecund women worldwide *not* practicing contraception rose from 342 to 361 million, a result of the large numbers of young women entering the childbearing ages. Only half of the world's couples of reproductive age were estimated to have sufficient knowledge of contraception to plan their families. The IPPF report indicated that contraceptive knowledge and practice would have to increase at a much faster pace if the world is to reach even the average family size of just under four children that would be required by 2000 in order to achieve replacement-level fertility about 2045 and a stabilized world population of 15 billion by the year 2100.

The Outlook

What lies ahead? All are agreed that the world's present growth rate of 1.7%, which would double human numbers in just 41 years, cannot continue indefinitely. It is also clear, however, that—barring a nuclear holocaust or massive famine—a much larger population lies ahead for the developing countries and the world as a whole. With close to half of the developing world's population now under age 15, the relentless arithmetic of population momentum will carry waves of population growth into the twenty-first century even if replacement-level fertility—essentially, an average family of two children—were miraculously to be achieved everywhere tomorrow. Just when the earth's population will stop growing and how large it then will be depends crucially on when that worldwide replacement-level fertility is reached.

Current "medium" projections for world population in the year 2000, just around the corner, range from a low of 5.9 billion to a high of 6.4 billion—a difference of "only" half a billion. For further into the future, demographers' opinions vary much more widely. Demographers Donald J. Bogue and Amy Ong Tsui predict a rapid slowdown to zero growth and a peak global total population of about 8.1 billion by 2050, provided that family planning programs are pursued vigorously in the developing world and steady gains in social and economic development continue. The most recently published long-range projections of the United Nations put the peak at about 11 billion about a century and a half from now. World Bank estimates fall in between. "If current trends continue," the Bank projects replacement-level fertility for the world as a whole about 2020 and a stabilized population of 9.8 billion some 70 years later.

Worldwatch Institute President Lester Brown doubts that global population as high as 12 billion (an earlier projection of the United Nations) will ever be reached. He sees crucial biological systems—fisheries, forests, grasslands, and croplands—and oil resources already showing unsupportable strains at the current 4.3 billion. He predicts that further mounting pressures on vital resources, translated into unemployment, lowered per capita income, and inflation, will force restricted childbearing on individual couples and stabilized population policies on governments that do not now have them. To ward off collapse of the earth's major biological systems, Brown urges a "concerted global effort to slam on the demographic brakes" with the aim of halting population growth just short of 6 billion about 2015.

Brown admits that this "exceedingly ambitious" target would be extremely difficult for African countries in particular, where birthrates are now between 40 and 50. But the alternative could be the return of the famines that claimed hundreds of thousands of lives across the southern fringe of the Sahara in the early 1970s. And in achieving the target, Brown observes that "no country would have to reduce its birthrate any more rapidly than Barbados,

China, Costa Rica, Indonesia, and Singapore already have."

To Speed Fertility Decline

Efforts heroic enough to meet Brown's timetable are probably unimaginable in the two decades remaining to the twentieth century. But clearly birthrate declines must be accelerated now in most LDCs if the world is to avoid an eventual population so massive that the future of humanity and its ecological support system would be jeopardized. The approaches currently being pursued or proposed to speed these declines include both efforts to improve family planning services and "beyond family planning" measures to enhance motivation for smaller families. They can be summed up as follows:

• **More and improved family planning services.** Surveys and experience in Asia and Latin America show that readily available, well-advertised services can, in many cases, boost contraceptive practice rates dramatically, even in illiterate, rural, poor populations.

• **Information and education.** Over the long run, population education can change family-size attitudes. In the short run, information about contraception, an integral part of most family planning programs, helps spur contraceptive acceptance.

• **Restructured development.** This is the "message of Bucharest," that is, to push those elements of development that appear to be most directly related to lowered fertility: reductions in infant mortality, improvements in women's status, better education and nutrition, and generally more equitable distribution of the benefits of development.

• **Incentives/disincentives.** Singapore, a pioneer in this approach, with housing, tax, and maternity policies designed to discourage more than two children per family, has now reduced its fertility to replacement level.

• **Pressures and sanctions.** Some observers feel that voluntary family planning, even coupled with measurable gains in levels of living, cannot be expected to reduce LDC birthrates rapidly in the near future because most couples in developing countries, they claim, still *want*

large families. People concerned about the apparent gap in developing countries between desired family size and replacement-level fertility argue that closing the gap may take politically organized peer pressure, as in China.

Although the emphasis may vary with individual country situations, all of these approaches are and will doubtless be necessary if fertility is to decline rapidly to replacement level in the coming two or three decades. The only other alternative to staving off an intolerable ultimate global population size is higher death rates and that choice is unacceptable. Migration to industrial countries has eased population pressure for some small and medium-size developing countries—Algeria, Mexico, Morocco, Tunisia, and Turkey, for example. But international migration on the scale that would be required to make a significant difference for countries the size of India and Pakistan is now impossible. India alone adds 13 million to the world's population every year—the same number currently estimated for the refugees that are now straining the entire free world's absorptive capacities.

The world is already overcrowded at 4.3 billion—in both developed and developing countries—and is destined to become much more crowded. We can no longer avoid a world of at least 6 billion and then, probably, some decades later, 8 billion. But the actions we take now could—and must—avert the even greater stresses, poverty, and hunger that would prevail in a world of 10, 11, or more billions.

About the Authors

Jean van der Tak is Director of Publications at the Population Reference Bureau in Washington, D.C., Carl Haub is Staff Demographer, and Elaine Murphy is Director of Population Education. Their address is: Population Reference Bureau, Inc., 1337 Connecticut Avenue, N.W., Washington, D.C. 20036.

Founded in 1929 by Guy Burch, who is credited with coining the expression "the population explosion," the Population Reference Bureau is a private, nonprofit educational organization that disseminates information on the facts and implications of national and world population trends. This article is taken from the authors' recent Population Reference Bureau Bulletin, "Our Population Predicament: A New Look."

INDEX

absenteeism, of workers and drug abuse, 162, 163
Acquired Immune Deficiency Syndrome (AIDS): and Center for Disease Control, 166, 167; effect of, on gay lifestyle, 171-172; theories on causes of, 169
advertising: and children, 126; and single people, 160
affirmative action, 92, 100
aging: of America, 226-231; of Japan, 223
agriculture, and America's farm problem, 44-49
AIDS, see Acquired Immune Deficiency Syndrome
Air Force, see Army Air Force
Alaskan natural gas pipeline, pre-billing of consumers for cost of, 28
American dream, disillusionment with, 4-7
Andarko Basin, deep gas reserves in, 58
antitrust policy, effect of U.S., on competition in world market, 188
Argentina, foreign debt of, 51
Army Air Force vs. Navy, in nuclear arms race, 33-38
arson, 152, 153
Asians, 98-99
asylums, see institutions

baby boom cohort, aging of, 225-231
bail, 144, 145
balanced-budget amendment, 32
Bank for International Settlements, 51, 52
banking system, collapse of international, 50-54
Basel Concordat of 1975, 51, 52
behaviorism, use of, for better world, 12-14
"black labor," 69
blacks: earnings differentials of whites vs., 100-102; education for, 91-94; history of legal decisions concerning, 99-100; poverty statistics of, compared to whites, 79-82; effects of unemployment on, 83-84; sentencing practices of judges toward, 148
bonuses, for company managers, 72, 73
Boston, problem of arson in, 152-153
Brazil, foreign debt of, 51, 54
bridges, cost of repair, in U.S., 9
Britain, see England
Brown's Ferry nuclear power plant, fire at, 39
burglary: and Neighborhood Watch, 156; and selective incapacitation, 151

campaign funds: congressional misuse of, 24-25; need for public financing of, 28
career criminals: and selective incapacitation, 130, 131, 148, 150, 151; stiffer sentences for, 130, 131, 147, 148
Carter Administration: civil-service reform of, 20-22; gas price controls under, 57; Russian grain embargo under, 46; efforts to tax excessive executive compensation, 75
Center for Disease Control (CDC), 166-168
central banks, as lenders of last resort, 52-53

"Chicano," 103-104
chief executive officers (CEO's), salaries and fringe benefits of, 72-75
child abuse, 126
children: as dependent consumers, 125, 126, 127; and drug abuse, 163; effects of environmental pollutants on, 202-206; and parents of delinquent, 154-157; status of, in American family, 124, 125
chlorinolysis, 192
cities: condition of American, 5, 15-16; destruction of, vs. military targets, 34-38
civil service: Carter's reform of, 20-22; history of protective legislation for employees in, 20-21; Reagan's reform of, 23
cocaine, 162-165
commercials, T.V. and children, 126, 127
commodity loan, for farmers, 47
communications industries, 184-190
community care vs. state hospitals, for mentally ill or retarded, 173-175
computers, 190
compulsory schooling, effect of, on crime rate in England, 139, 140
Congress: misuse of campaign funds by members of, 24-25; special interest group, pressures on, 26-28
Congressional Budget and Impoundment Control Act of 1974, 29
consumerism, and children, 124-127
contingencies of reinforcement, 12
corporations: excessive compensation to executives of, 72-75; vs. individual taxpayers, 76-78; overseas investments by, 77-78; tax write-offs of, as cause of federal deficit, 76-78
counterforce/no cities targeting, 34, 35, 38
crime: and arson, 152-153; breakdown of individual personal responsibility as cause of, 141, 142; career criminals, 130-132, 147, 148; pessimism of combating, 137; criminal justice system, 144-151; decline in rate of, 130; and families with delinquents, 154-157; and drug abuse, 163, 164; in England, causes of increase, 137-143; and effectiveness of foot patrol officers, 156; neighborhood, 156; and selective incapacitation, 130-132; 148, 150, 151; in Sweden, 138; theory concerning causes of in United States, 133-136
crime and punishment, breakdown of community of as cause of crime in U.S., 133-136
criminal justice system, 144-151

decontrol, impact of, on natural gas, 56, 58, 59, 60
deep gas, United States discoveries of, 57-58
defensible-space strategy, and neighborhood crime, 156
deferred compensation, for company managers, 73
deficiency payment, for farmers, 47

deinstitutionalization, of mentally ill and retarded, 173-175
delinquents, see juvenile delinquents
demographic transition theory, 236-237
determinate sentencing, 148
detoxification, vs. dumping of toxic waste, 191-195
developing countries: foreign debt of, 50; consequences of reduced financial aid to, 53
deviant behavior: and families with juvenile delinquents, 154-157; historical patterns of, in England, 137-143
disease detectives, 166-170
"displaced homemakers," 80
divorce: effect of, on people living alone, 158, 159; statistics on, in U.S., 5
drug abuse, 130, 138, 162-165
drug-education, 164, 165
due process, 144-151
dumping: vs. detoxification of toxic wastes, 191-195; of radioactive waste in oceans, 196-198

education: 13; for blacks, 91-94; federal budget cuts in, 93; need to reform financing of, 93
elderly: of Japan, 223; and living alone, 161; poverty among, 5, 80; effect of unemployment on, 84-85
electronic data processing (EDP): 186; regulation of, 189-190
employment, effect of, on juvenile delinquency, 155
England, crime rate in, 137-143
Enrico Fermi II reactor, accident at, 40
environmental pollutants, effects of, on children, 202-206
Environmental Protection Agency (EPA), lead standard of, 203-204; pesticide-residue standards of, 205; ocean dumping of radioactive waste, 197-198; under Reagan Administration, 202-206; on dumping of toxic waste, 193-195
Epidemic Intelligence Service, 167
Equal Rights Amendment (ERA), 107, 108
Eurocredits, 51
European Economic Community (EEC), 188
exclusionary rule, 145, 146
executive compensation, excessive 72-75

family, 124-127, 157
farms, trouble with American, 44-49
federal agencies, off-budget, 29-30
federal budget: additional areas for cutting, 219-220; cuts in education, 93; deficit, 10, 76-78, 217; off-budget spending to mask deficit in, 29-32
Federal Communications Commission (FCC), 126, 127
Federal Election Commission (FEC), 24
Federal Financing Bank (FFB), 30
federal government: agricultural price supports of, 45, 47-49; role of, in civil rights, 94; civil-service reforms under Carter, 20-22; in energy market, 207-209; arguments against intervention by, 178-183; role of, in natural re-

Credits/Acknowledgments

Cover design by Charles Vitelli

1. Perspectives
Facing overview—Courtesy HUD, Washington, D.C.
2. Politics
Facing overview—The Capitol Building.
3. Economy and Employment
Facing overview—USDA-Soil Conservation Service.

4. Inequality
Facing overview—Dover *Pictorial Archive* Series, Dover Publications, Inc.
5. Victims
Facing overview—UNICEF photo.
6. Future
Facing overview—EPA Documerica.

WE WANT YOUR ADVICE

ANNUAL EDITIONS: SOCIAL PROBLEMS 84/85

Article Rating Form

Here is an opportunity for you to have direct input into the next revision of this reader. We would like you to rate each of the 50 articles listed below, using the following scale:

1. **Excellent: should definitely be retained**
2. **Above average: should probably be retained**
3. **Below average: should probably be deleted**
4. **Poor: should definitely be deleted**

Your ratings will play a vital part in the next revision. So please mail this prepaid form to us just as soon as you complete it.
Thanks for your help!

Rating	Article	Rating	Article
	1. What Has Happened to the American Dream?		26. Kids as Consumers and Commodities
	2. An America in Need of Repair		27. Why Crime's Rapid Rise May Be Over
	3. Utopia or Disaster: Interview with B.F. Skinner		28. Crime and Punishment
	4. In Search of American Optimism		29. Some Causes of Crime: Crime, Bureaucracy, and Equality
	5. Bureaucrats 2, Presidents 0		30. Coping with Justice
	6. How Lawmakers Misuse Your Campaign Donations		31. Are Boston's Fires an Omen for All Cities?
	7. PAC's Americana: The Threat of Political Action Committees		32. Families and Crime
	8. Off the Books: Uncle Sam's Creative Accounting		33. 19 Million Singles
	9. Bureaucracy and the Bomb: The Hidden Factor Behind Nuclear Madness		34. How Drugs Sap the Nation's Strength
	10. At N.R.C. It's Safety Last		35. Hunting for the Hidden Killers
	11. America's Real Farm Problem: It Can Be Solved		36. The Real Epidemic: Fear and Despair
	12. Big Oil vs. Cheap Gas		37. A Key to Unlock the Asylum?
	13. Rescuing the Banking System		38. Inheriting the Earth
	14. The Potential Impacts of Robotics		39. The Information Society: The Path to Post-Industrial Growth
	15. The End of the "Labor Society"		40. Beyond Dumping: The Surprising Solution to the Love Canal Problem
	16. Richer Than All Their Tribe		41. Radioactivity for the Oceans
	17. The Secret History of the Deficit		42. When the Economy Rebounds Will "Smoke Stack America"?
	18. New Faces of Poverty		43. Polluting the Most Vulnerable
	19. Economic Cold Spell Freezes "Outsiders"		44. Untying the Energy Knot
	20. Carla: "It's Very Hard to Say I'm Poor"		45. Photovoltaics: A Solar Technology for Powering Tomorrow
	21. The State of Education for Black Americans		46. Economic Strategies for a Narcissistic Society
	22. Hyphenated Americans—Economic Aspects		47. Japan: All the Hazards and Threats of Success
	23. How Long Till Equality		48. A Generation at Risk: When the Baby Boomers Reach Golden Pond
	24. Coming into Your Own in a Man's World		49. Foreign Policy: Outmoded Assumptions
	25. The Social Security Fix		50. A New Look at the Population Problem

(continued on back)

ABOUT YOU

Name _____ Date _____

Are you a teacher? ☐ Or student? ☐

Your School Name _____

Department _____

Address _____

City _____ State _____ Zip _____

School Telephone # _____

YOUR COMMENTS ARE IMPORTANT TO US!

Please fill in the following information:

For which course did you use this book? _____

Did you use a text with this Annual Edition?   ☐ yes ☐ no

The title of the text: _____

What are your general reactions to the Annual Editions concept?

Have you read any particular articles recently that you think should be included in the next edition?

Are there any articles you feel should be replaced in the next edition? Why?

Are there other areas that you feel would utilize an Annual Edition?

May we contact you for editorial input?

May we quote you from above?

No Postage
Necessary
if Mailed
in the
United States

SOCIAL PROBLEMS 84/85

BUSINESS REPLY MAIL
First Class   Permit No. 84   Guilford, CT

Postage will be paid by addressee

The Dushkin Publishing Group, Inc.
Sluice Dock
Guilford, Connecticut 06437